The Science and Passion of Communism

Historical Materialism Book Series

The Historical Materialism Book Series is a major publishing initiative of the radical left. The capitalist crisis of the twenty-first century has been met by a resurgence of interest in critical Marxist theory. At the same time, the publishing institutions committed to Marxism have contracted markedly since the high point of the 1970s. The Historical Materialism Book Series is dedicated to addressing this situation by making available important works of Marxist theory. The aim of the series is to publish important theoretical contributions as the basis for vigorous intellectual debate and exchange on the left.

The peer-reviewed series publishes original monographs, translated texts, and reprints of classics across the bounds of academic disciplinary agendas and across the divisions of the left. The series is particularly concerned to encourage the internationalization of Marxist debate and aims to translate significant studies from beyond the English-speaking world.

For a full list of titles in the Historical Materialism Book Series available in paperback from Haymarket Books, visit:
https://www.haymarketbooks.org/series_collections/1-historical-materialism

The Science and Passion of Communism

Selected Writings of Amadeo Bordiga
(1912–1965)

Amadeo Bordiga

Edited by
Pietro Basso

Translated by
Giacomo Donis and Patrick Camiller

Haymarket Books
Chicago, IL

First published in 2020 by Brill Academic Publishers, The Netherlands
© 2020 Koninklijke Brill NV, Leiden, The Netherlands

Published in paperback in 2021 by
Haymarket Books
P.O. Box 180165
Chicago, IL 60618
773-583-7884
www.haymarketbooks.org

ISBN: 978-1-64259-347-1

Distributed to the trade in the US through Consortium Book Sales and Distribution (www.cbsd.com) and internationally through Ingram Publisher Services International (www.ingramcontent.com).

This book was published with the generous support of Lannan Foundation and Wallace Action Fund.

Special discounts are available for bulk purchases by organizations and institutions. Please call 773-583-7884 or email info@haymarketbooks.org for more information.

Cover design and art by David Mabb. Cover art is a detail of *Long Live the New! no. 41*. Kazimir Malevich drawing on Morris & Co. design, paint and wallpaper on canvas (2016).

Printed in the United States.

10 9 8 7 6 5 4 3 2 1

Library of Congress Cataloging-in-Publication data is available.

Bordiga's pass at the VI Enlarged Executive Committee of the Communist International, Moscow, 1926, at which he made his famous speech against Stalin and the perspective of socialism in one country.

Contents

SECTION 2
The Critique of Triumphant Capitalism

SECTION 3
On the 'Gigantic Movement of Emancipation' of the Coloured Peoples

SECTION 4
On the Revolutionary Prospects of Communism

SECTION 5
On the Party

Bordiga's pass at the VI Enlarged Executive Committee of the Communist International, Moscow, 1926, at which he made his famous speech against Stalin and the perspective of socialism in one country.

I dedicate this anthology to the memory of Paolo Turco, a valiant, internationalist militant and a close friend for a long period of my life, who guided me in discovering the revolutionary thought of the eagle-eyed Amadeo Bordiga, without concealing his weak points. I much regret that I will be unable to present him with a copy of this book, which, strictly speaking, he was more entitled than me to compile, because of his greater proficiency in the subject.

∴

Acknowledgements

The completion of this work took me much more time and study than I had imagined. My gratitude is due above all to the Bordiga Foundation, in the persons of Michele Fatica and Maria Scattola, and to the editors of the Historical Materialism Book Series, primarily Sebastian Budgen, for the great patience with which they awaited the preparation of the anthology for publication.

Friendly thanks also to Lucia Pradella, who some years ago proposed the project to me, and to Charles-André Udry, who, with his generosity and breadth of vision, contributed to its fulfilment.

The writings of Amadeo Bordiga, especially from the period after the Second World War, are as interesting as they are tough to translate because of their highly personal style. To preserve their energy, acumen and ardour, Giacomo Donis had to lavish all his competence and passion in rendering them into English. It has been instructive, even exciting, for me to work shoulder to shoulder with him on the task.

Sincere thanks also to Patrick Camiller, who excellently translated the introduction and some of Bordiga's texts,[1] and to David Broder, an attentive reader of all the material.

The manuscript of the introduction was read by Roberto Taddeo, Alessandro Mantovani and Paola Tonello: their encouragement, prompt advice and critical points, which I hope to have taken to heart, were invaluable in the production of the final text.

---

1 Most of Bordiga's texts have been translated by Giacomo Donis. The only texts translated by Patrick Camiller are the following: 1) Against the War as Long as It Lasts, 2) Nothing to correct, 3) Against Abstentionism, 4) Report on Fascism to the Fifth Congress of the Communist International, 5) The Trotsky Question, 6) Letter to Korsch and 7) Forty Years of Organically Analysing Russia Events within the Drama of World History and Social Development.

Figures

All illustrations can be found in the separate Illustration Section following the Index.

Yesterday's Battles and Today's World

1 Amadeo Bordiga: Who Was He?

Amadeo Bordiga was one of the greatest figures of the Third International. Not by chance did Trotsky, a man rather stinting with praise, characterize his revolutionary thought as 'living, muscular and full-blooded'.[1] Yet Bordiga's theoretical and political battles remain virtually unknown, particularly outside Italy. Or else they are largely, if not entirely, travestied – above all in Italy itself, because of the violent hatred that Togliatti's PCI directed against him.[2]

Bordiga's name makes only rare appearances in histories of the international workers' movement, usually in connection with his dispute with Lenin at the Second Congress of the Communist International over participation in elections and bourgeois parliaments, or, less often, with reference to the 'powerful, though solitary, assault' (as E.H. Carr put it[3]) that he dared to launch in 1926 against the triumphant Stalinist leadership of the Russian Communist Party and the Comintern. On that occasion, as a real lone voice at the Sixth Enlarged Executive Committee of the International, he forcefully argued that, since developments in Russia were crucial for the course of the world revolution, they should be discussed and decided upon not only by the Russian party but by the whole 'general staff' of the world revolution. It was a fundamental question of principle, and one with exceptional practical significance.

But even when forced to recall Bordiga's presence and the positions he took at such crucial junctures, historians have nearly always assigned to him no more

---

1 Trotsky 1975, p. 410. In this letter to the Bordigist group around the journal *Prometeo*, written in Constantinople on 25 September 1929, Trotsky further described Bordiga's thought as the 'diametric opposite' of Togliatti's, which in his view was 'always directed in the last analysis to the defence of opportunism'.

2 In the Stalin period, no calumny was spared Bordiga and the Italian Communist Left: he was branded a thug or mobster and even – the height of infamy – a 'mask of the Gestapo'. Typical in this respect are Togliatti's directives for the editing of a special 'notebook' on the thirtieth anniversary of the founding of the PCI: 'Naturally refrain from presenting objectively the notorious Bordigist doctrines. Do it only in a critical and destructive mode' (*Rinascita* 48, 4 December 1970). It was no different from the treatment meted out to Trotsky and other later critics of Stalinism.

3 Carr 1978, Vol. 3, p. 502. The German delegate Arthur Rosenberg similarly called it a 'great speech in principle'.

than a vague location within the European communist left, losing sight of the *specificity* of his battle and of the Communist Party of Italy for the Communist International. There are very few exceptions to this rule: the ones in English are the well-documented research of J. Chiaradia, a penetrating text by L. Gold ner, a mention in passing by P. Anderson, a hasty, but perspicuous, recollection by M. van der Linden in his collection *Western Marxism and the Soviet Union.* Period.[4]

Even less known is the wealth of theoretical analyses produced by Bordiga after the Second World War with the help of a small group of comrades. We owe to him an unsurpassed analysis of the socio-economic structure of Stalin's Russia, of its 'mixture of state capitalism and private capitalism in which the dose of the former [was] diminishing'[5] and particularly the evolution of its agriculture, as well as a caustic critique of the false Stalinist equation between a statised and a socialist economy. But the range of Bordiga's work between 1945 and 1965 was considerably broader. In an unequal battle, both against the minstrels of a hegemonic Yankee super-capitalism and a Stalinism at the height of its influence, he and his comrades presented an original Marxist critique of capitalism on a world scale, engaging in constant, all-round polemic with the latest developments in its US epicentre and basing themselves on a deep understanding of what was for Marx the foundation of capitalist social relations. This too was the bedrock on which Bordiga reformulated the programme of social transformations for the revolution to come.

Although his labours were certainly not philological, Bordiga also left behind the first (almost unknown) commentaries on the *Grundrisse* and the 'Unpublished Chapter Six' of *Capital,* as well as a magnificent exposition of the *Economic and Philosophical Manuscripts.*[6] The writings in the second part of the present anthology are only a few fragments from this vast output, which also grappled with the fetishisation of science and technology and the revolution-

---

4   Chiaradia 1972 and 2001; Goldner 1995; Anderson 1976, pp. 52 ff. (which argues that it was not Gramsci but Bordiga who 'formulated the true nature of the distinction between East and West' and underlined the difference between the preconditions of revolution in Russia and the West); the special issue of *Revolutionary History,* 5, No. 4, spring 1995, entitled *Through Fascism, War and Revolution: Trotskyism and Left Communism in Italy,* with essays by P. Casciola, A. Peregalli and P. Broué; Van der Linden 2007, pp. 122–6; Buick 1987; Drake 2003 (chapter 6, on Bordiga, contains quite a few banalities and stupidities); Ciferri 2009; Broder 2013. It should be noted, however, that thanks to the work of John Riddell, we now have the records of the Fourth Congress of the Communist International, where Bordiga and the 'Italian question' played an important role; see Riddell (ed.) 2012.
5   Bordiga 1976a, p. 653.
6   Bordiga 1976b, pp. 178 ff. and Bordiga 1972.

ary theory of knowledge, giving birth to the idea that it is necessary to 'overturn the [bourgeois] cognitive pyramid'. A reading of these texts should serve as a stimulus to further studies, which in my view will be full of real surprises. Just one example is how Bordiga already understood in the 1950s that Marx's and Marxist critique of political economy was from the beginning an ecological critique: that is, it radically questioned not only the relation between capital and labour, but also the capital-nature and capital-species relationships; not only did it not separate these off, still less oppose them to the capital-labour relation, but it treated them as two sides of the same coin. Bordiga's particular attention to the 'agrarian question', almost unique in the panorama of 'Western communism', has its roots in this total vision of the capitalist mode of production and the succession of modes of production in history.

Amadeo Bordiga: great figure of the twentieth-century international communist movement, great unknown. Particularly for the non-Italian-speaking public.

Of course, there have been attempts to render his writings into more widely spoken languages, ranging from English to French, Russian to Arabic. But these translations[7] have had a dreadfully limited circulation – usually no more than the cluster of small groups disputing Bordiga's legacy, which have helped to dissipate and sterilise his thought, often by emphasising its most frail and questionable aspects and constructing around it a counterproductive mythology. As a result, without wishing it, they have tended to reinforce the liquidationist view of Bordiga circulated by intellectuals and social-democratic historians, for whom there is nothing to learn from him and his battles except an abstract, more moral than political, attachment to Marxism reduced to arid metaphysical principles.

The real picture is very different, in every sense. Beyond the one-sidedness, forced arguments and downright errors with which many have wanted, or felt obliged, to reproach him, both in the interwar period and since the Second World War, Amadeo Bordiga has bequeathed to us *a lesson of great relevance for the present day and for a fast-approaching future* filled with threats and promises. Despite the inevitable limits of any selection of his writings, from a corpus of dozens of books and hundreds of essays and articles, this anthology has sought to encourage readers and activists, especially from the younger genera-

---

7   The English translations, in particular, are by no means faultless. One reason for this is the objective difficulty of doing justice to Bordiga's prose – sometimes rough, always lively and personal, and studded with neologisms, aphorisms and dialect expressions that have made some compare him to the great Italian writer Carlo Emilio Gadda. Alfred Rosmer speaks of the 'extraordinary volubility [of Bordiga's language], which in congresses brought shorthand writers to despair'; Rosmer 2016, p. 22.

tion, to get to know Amadeo Bordiga for the man he really was – and to discover for themselves how topical his essential battles remain to this day.

2   The Formation of the Workers' Movement in Italy

In the history of the communist movement, Bordiga's name is linked to the emergence of a genuine Left in Italy in the years immediately prior to the First World War; this came out of a prolonged struggle against the reformism of the PSI (Italian Socialist Party), the violent eruption of antagonisms within world capitalism that eventually led to world war, the unravelling of the Second International and the birth of a new International. Let us look briefly at what came before, beginning with a few points on Italy in the late nineteenth and early twentieth centuries.

With its communes and famous cities such as Venice and Florence, Italy was for centuries a hothouse in which some of the first seeds of the capitalist mode of production germinated. Its chronic disunity, however, meant that the development of large industry came later than in other European countries, another reason being that it could not compete with Britain, France or the Netherlands in overseas colonial ventures. Thus, at the time of unification (1861), the Italian economy still had a poorly organised industry made up of small to medium-sized firms lacking capital and machinery and reliant on traditional working methods, in a country also badly off in terms of raw materials. The working class consisted more of artisans than industrial workers. In 1881, firms in the silk industry – the most important export sector – had an average of 20.2 employees, half of them women and children, while the figure for tanneries was even lower at 8.8. This, too, explains why the experience of the First International left no deep socialist traces here. The traces it did leave behind were saturated with Mazzini's theory of interclass cooperation, so hostile to the development of class antagonisms that it branded strikes as a form of violence, or with the Bakuninist anarchism that was very active in Italy between 1864 and 1872. In any case, there were no significant traces of Marx's thought.[8]

---

8   See Nettlau 1928. It should not be forgotten that one of the first great propagators of Marx's economic thought in Italy was the anarchist Carlo Cafiero, whose compendium from Volume One of *Capital* dates from 1879.
    The modest influence of the International in Italy (750 members in 1871) was considerably boosted by the Paris Commune, which Marx, Bakunin and Garibaldi all defended and exalted in their different ways. Mazzini, on the other hand, immediately and openly opposed it: see Popa (ed.) 1972, pp. 177–227. It was widely held in Italy at the time that the Commune was

The decades after unification did, however, witness the birth and country-wide spread, especially in the Centre and North, of the first workers' associations, mutual societies, circles, leagues and cooperatives, which formed the social and organisational backdrop to Italian socialism and the arrival of Marx's and Engels's positions in the early 1870s.[9] It has been said that socialism had a premature birth in Italy; ideas from countries with an already constituted capitalism reached the peninsula before machinery and capital.[10] But what kind of socialism was it? It was a socialist *movement* with highly vague and eclectic ideological characteristics, and with a social base often consisting more of peasants and day labourers than industrial workers, more popular than proletarian. Not until 1892, after a number of vain attempts, did an organisation with a certain solidity take shape: the Italian Socialist Party (PSI).[11] For the next thirty years, until the foundation of the Communist Party of Italy in January 1921, it would be the party of the working-class vanguard. As the ideas of Mazzini entered into crisis with the rise of class struggles, and as the Bakuninist nuclei broke up following the failure of improvised insurrections, the way was clear for a socialist *organisation* with the modern features of a mass party, an organisation, in fact, whose composition was the same as that of the movement out of which it was born. Its ideology was a mixture of 'souped-up republicanism, adjusted corporatism, diluted anarchism, and a lively but rather woolly faith in the socialist destiny of humanity. [...] And such faith was the moral and ideological bond capable of holding together the new team and forging it into a single body.'[12] The actual reality of this 'body' was a federation of socially, politically and geographically heterogeneous components.

In writing a history of the PSI, which was his own party for a decade, Bordiga pointed to some genuine expressions of revolutionary spirit, such as Andrea Costa's anti-colonialist call 'Out of Africa!' (1894) and his firm opposition to the

------

the child of the International; an exiled communard, Benoît Malon, was active during this period, helping in the publication of the socialist *La Plebe* in Lodi, the only paper close to the positions of Marx and Engels.

9   See Marx and Engels 1972.

10   Manacorda 1971, p. 44.

11   In fact, the party did not take this name until the Parma Congress in 1895. German Social Democracy had come into being in 1875, the French Workers' Party in 1880, and the Second International in 1889.

12   Arfé 1977, pp. 15–16. This hybrid, the author notes, was reminiscent of a plaster figure of Marx circulating in Italian socialist milieux at the time, which Engels thought very similar to ... Garibaldi. There was probably a copy of it in Bordiga's house in Naples, when it was raided and turned upside down by the Fascist militia in late 1926. On that occasion, the head of the squad ordered that the bust should not be touched, on the grounds that it was a representation of none other than Garibaldi.

China expedition (1900). But he rightly commented that the first tendency to emerge clearly from this magma was the *reformist* tendency.[13] The Rome congress in September 1900, at the height of the Bernstein debate, saw this happen in a very special way. The leading exponent of the reformist current, Filippo Turati, did not subscribe to Bernstein's theses: he continued to appeal in principle to Marxism and stressed that the final aim of the PSI's activity, albeit in an indefinite future, was socialism. But his perspective was essentially similar to the one outlined by the father of German and European revisionism. The workers' movement could, indeed should, advance toward socialism in a peaceful manner, within the framework of Italy's national economic development and parliamentary democratic institutions. It could do this through struggles (Turati never formally renounced the class struggle), elections, pivotal parliamentary action and the gradual transformation of bourgeois institutions, engaging in alliances or convergences with left-wing bourgeois forces but always maintaining its organisational autonomy.[14] This fully defines, in a gradualist and reformist key, the relationship between democracy and socialism, reducing socialism to the process of *indefinite expansion of democracy.* Turati's approach, which encountered no robust opposition inside the party, would guide the PSI's parliamentary activity in the first decade of the twentieth century, as well as its work in the union movement and public administration. Local branches were given the greatest autonomy in applying the line. And this autonomy, operating from small towns to large cities, gave rise to uninhibited electoral blocs with 'progressive' or 'popular' anti-clerical forces, often masonic in character and completely alien to the working class and the perspective of socialism. Such municipalism was a hallmark of Turati's PSI, which glorified its 'red islands' as if they were anticipations of socialist society.

On the eve of the twentieth century, therefore, reformist socialism took on a definite shape in Italy. Two developments in society encouraged this: the sharpening of class antagonisms in town and country in the 1890s, and the victory of the 'industrialist party' in the bourgeois camp.

In the first twenty years after unification, the development of the Italian economy was truly unremarkable, with the sole exception of the year 1873 that

---

13   [Bordiga] 1972 [1964], pp. 18 ff. The work is anonymous, but the author's identity is beyond doubt.

14   As a young man, Turati already clearly defined his conception of socialism in a letter of 12 March 1878 to Achille Loria: 'My socialism, more tendency and movement than system, is essentially practical, historical and gradual; it will avail itself of all honest and effective means both socialist and non-socialist, without arbitrarily excluding anything a priori [...]; a socialism that will triumph through evolution or revolution according to the times and the circumstances'; Turati 1982, p. 2.

marked the highpoint of expansion in Europe. The years from 1887 to 1894 were truly dire, when the irruption of American agricultural produce in Europe and the onset of commercial hostilities with France led to a full-scale farming crisis. This triggered a great movement in Sicily involving more than 70,000 day labourers and small farmers (both men and women), shepherds, mineworkers, artisans, and unemployed or underemployed urban proletarians. Their uprising to demand higher day wages and the abolition of taxes and duties on consumption goods, and to wrest less suffocating contracts from landowners and sub-letters, was drowned in blood by the Crispi government and the private forces of landowners and Mafia bosses. More than a hundred demonstrators were murdered. The king decreed a state of siege, with emergency laws and military courts, which resulted in the arrest and internment of thousands. Four years later, in May 1898, this scene of violent social clashes was repeated in Milan, the capital of an industrialising northern Italy, spreading out from the Pirelli factory. Here discontent over low wages and unemployment fused with anger against the Pelloux government over the rising price of bread. Alarmed by the outbreak of similar protests in Romagna, Puglia, Naples and Florence, the government sent in the army and police against tens of thousands of workers who had taken to the streets and set up barricades. At least one hundred proletarians were killed in Milan and thousands more, including a number of socialist deputies, were arrested and immediately given punitive sentences. Two years later, on 29 July 1900, the anarchist Gaetano Bresci assassinated King Umberto I at Monza to avenge the dead of Sicily and Milan. All these events explosively intertwined workers' and farmers' struggles (more than a thousand strikes took place in the countryside, mainly in the Po valley, between 1900 and 1904), both for material demands and against the government. Together with the growing prestige of the Socialist Party, this induced the bourgeoisie to lower its mailed fist and to operate a 'liberal turn'. So began the Giolitti decade (1903–14), which brought the intensive economic and political modernisation of Italy. Under the astute and watchful eye of the young king Vittorio Emanuele III, the liberal state enlarged its social and electoral base with the aim of making the established order more stable.

The 'turn' registered the change in the relationship of forces between the property-owning and working classes. But it was also the result of the victory of the 'industrialist party' over the 'landowning party' among the propertied classes. For many years, following the example of Germany and the economic nationalism of Friedrich List and the academic *Kathedersozialisten*,[15] the most

---

15   See Castronovo 1975, pp. 83 ff.

dynamic components of Italy's rising industry pushed hard for the state to play an active role in protecting national interests and promoting economic take-off. A group of former Garibaldians took the lead in this, supporting the new government economic policy with patriotic themes in a perspective of social reconciliation. The protectionist and industrialist policies looked like a squaring of the circle. Besides, similar tendencies were operating elsewhere in Europe. If Italian capitalists did not wish to resign themselves to a rearguard role, they had to compete in a vastly expanding world market. Whether they liked it or not, Northern landowners and their more or less absenteeist counterparts in the South understood and accepted the challenge: there were no alternatives. The force of the American whirlwind made such a change of course all the more urgent, and within a few years the Italian productive landscape was quite different. The steel, electrical, chemical and automobile industries became the commanding heights of the national economy. New forms of organisation appeared in the factories, now equipped with modern machinery and capable foreign technicians. Investment surged forward, and the first major concentrations of industrial and financial capital took shape. Italy did not cease to be a battlefield for (declining) French and (rising) German interests, but it began to stand – and wanted to stand – on its own feet. Arms production grew significantly. Colonial impulses had more and more scope to develop in Africa and the Balkans. Whether or not the Giolitti decade saw the take-off of Italian industry – some think this did not happen until the First World War – the favourable international conjuncture meant that it was able to achieve a veritable qualitative leap. And the political and cultural dynamics of Italian society became much closer to those of the most developed European countries.

This also applied to the workers' movement. Benefiting from an economic and political climate that left more room for social conflicts, and from a sharp rise in the numbers of industrial workers, the labour movement expanded rapidly, so that by 1913 it embraced 1,700,000 workers in various leagues, regional associations and trade federations. In 1901 Federterra – the Federation of Land Workers, organising farmhands and small farmers – came into being. In 1906 the General Confederation of Labour was constituted. Meanwhile the Socialist Party extended recruitment to the whole of the country, passing from 19,121 members in 1896 to 45,800 in 1904, and remaining above 43,000 until 1908. It had a lively youth federation, in which Bordiga served his apprenticeship from 1910. The PSI also created a number of press organs and took control of many local councils, especially in Emilia and Tuscany. It also expanded its network of flanking institutions – mutual societies, consumption and production cooperatives (the National League, firmly in reformist hands, comprised some two thousand cooperatives in 1910), *case del popolo* ventures, libraries and people's universities. The parliamentary party sponsored new social legislation to protect female and youth labour in factories, to introduce insurance schemes, and to enshrine guarantees relating to employment and rights at work (above all, the right to strike) for industrial workers and public employees. The PSI also played an active role in the creation and operation of organisms such as the Higher Labour Council, the People's Institutes and the public housing projects, which had the task of mediating between the interests of capital and labour.

As in other countries, most notably Germany with its model party of the Second International, this imposing array of activities gave an effective leading role not so much to the PSI's leadership bodies as to its parliamentary group and the heads of the trade union movement. Rosa Luxemburg's analysis of the German situation contained much that fitted Italy too. The strong growth of the union movement, she noted, automatically produced a high degree of autonomy from the party and gave rise to a layer of functionaries whose short-sighted bureaucratic mentality was characteristic of a period of peaceful economic struggles. Such figures were the mouthpieces of an 'uncritical trade-union optimism', which went hand in hand with an 'uncritical parliamentary optimism' regarding the unlimited improvement of working and living conditions within the established social order.[16] This 'uncritical optimism' – ultimately about the fate of capitalism – ran contrary to the 'social-democratic' perspective, to the revolutionary perspective of socialism. The only difference between Germany and Italy was that the PSI leadership itself, over and above that of the unions and the parliamentary group, was in the best of cases totally confused about the crucial relationship between immediate struggles and final goals. Until 1910, as the liberal growth era persisted and the purchasing power of wages grew faster than the national product, the primacy of the reformist current in the party remained firm at the level of ideology and legislative action; there was no lack of conflict, but the left remained weak and marginal. This reformist education of the organised working masses by the union bosses (Buozzi, Rigola, D'Aragona, and so on) and parliamentary leaders of the PSI had lasting anti-revolutionary effects, which made themselves felt at the tumultuous, decisive highpoint of class antagonisms in Italy: the *biennio rosso* of 1919–20. The birth of the Communist Party of Italy in January 1921, the final outcome of a decade of fierce battles waged by the nascent communist left within the PSI, the labour movement and Italian society at large, was not enough to off-

---

16   See Luxemburg 1970.

set these effects of an earlier period of protracted economic growth. A leading figure in those battles had been the young Amadeo Bordiga.[17]

3   A Decade of Struggle against Reformism (1911–21)

The main fronts on which the left fought these battles were: opposition to the war in Libya (1911) and defeatist activity over Italy's involvement in the First World War (1915–18); opposition to electoralism or any kind of political bloc with bourgeois forces; proletarian union organisation along class lines; and positions on the revolution in Russia and the founding of the new International. I speak of battles in the plural, but in reality they formed a single, unitary battle to endow the Italian proletariat with a solid communist party rooted in Marxist theory and firmly incorporated into the international communist movement and the socialist revolution. There were weaknesses here and there, and we shall speak of them later, but if we look back today without prejudices we cannot fail to be amazed and filled with admiration at the energy and coherence and the results achieved. Of course, the battle first against reformism and second against maximalism was not led by a solitary hero or a handful of heroes fallen from the sky. What fuelled it, and drew thousands of young workers to its ranks – in August 1921 the Communist Party of Italy (PCd'I) had 32,000 members, 95 percent of them urban or agricultural workers – was an imposing chain of struggles of the Italian proletariat. This confirmed Marx's thesis that it is always the class itself that organises itself into a political party, and that this party becomes in turn the organiser of the class at a level quantitatively and qualitatively higher than the one at which it started. The battle of the left received oxygen, strength and clear guidelines for action from the extraordinary situation that developed out of the crisis of the Second International and saw the birth of Lenin's and Trotsky's Communist International amid the explosive crisis of international capitalism. But Bordiga, an internationalist like few others, made a point of underlining that the PCd'I was 'no import'.[18] And it was true.

---

17   Born in Portici (Naples) on 13 June 1889, Amadeo Bordiga joined the PSI in 1910 at the age of 21, when he was still an engineering student. His father Oreste, originally from Piedmont, was a professor of agrarian science. His mother, Zaira degli Amadei, came from an aristocratic Florentine family that had been active on the side of the Risorgimento. On the social-political context in Naples in the early twentieth century, see the fundamental work: Fatica 1971.

18   See 'Il bolscevismo, pianta d'ogni clima', in *Il Soviet* 10, 23 February 1919: 'Bolshevism is alive in Italy, and not as an import, since socialism lives and struggles wherever there are exploited people who aim at their emancipation. This has made its first great breakt-

It all began with the aggressive war against the population of Tripolitania and Cyrenaica, two regions later given the ancient Roman name Libya, when the Italian state intervened to snatch them from the disintegrating Ottoman empire, in competition with other European colonial powers. The war shook the Liberal-Socialist idyll of the early years of the century. The Socialist parliamentary group supported the Liberal Giolitti government in a vote of confidence, earning itself the mocking remark from the prime minister: 'Karl Marx has been stored away in the attic.' Then, at the end of September 1911, with parliament closed for the holidays, the government sent a large expedition of 80,000 men to fight the Turks in North Africa. The decision split the Socialists: one group of MPs (Bissolati and his friends) and some of the union bosses weighed in behind the war, while the national party and the General Confederation of Labour declared a general strike against it. This was only partly successful, since most workers were influenced or dazed by nationalist propaganda that presented Libya as a 'second America'. Still, the very fact of the strike marked the beginning of a radicalisation process within the PSI, in which an 'intransigent' wing, at the congresses of Modena (15 October 1911) and Reggio Emilia (7–10 July 1912), acquired the features of an ever more distinct tendency. It was during this process, both inside and outside the youth federation, that Bordiga's anti-militarism was forged and sharpened.

This had its origins in a kind of humanitarian rejection of the war in principle, on the grounds that it 'enshrine[d] the principles of violence and collective arrogance as wellsprings of progress and civilisation, idealising brute force, seeking to destroy our vision of a society based on harmony and fraternity'. Very soon, however, Bordiga moved on to denounce the *class aims* of the war, which he saw as serving the ruling classes, certainly not the ruled. He delivered a withering critique of patriotism and nationalism as weapons of bourgeois class domination over the proletariat. He roundly dismissed the blackmail of: 'Now that war has broken out, how can we be against it?' Since the interests pursued by the nation at war did not coincide at all with the interests of the working class, he had no hesitation or scruple in breaking the national unity. The Balkan wars and the approach of the world war gave further arguments for Bordiga's ceaseless anti-war propaganda. In his numerous writings on the subject, he rebutted the misleading 'nationality principle' – which in the new historical context had become the right of the strongest to subjugate other nations – and the equally false category of 'defensive war', behind which lurked the economic

hrough in Russia, and we, who find our whole programme in the formidable events of the Russian revolution, have headed these columns with the magical Slav word "Soviet", now become the symbol of the international revolution'.

foundations and imperialist appetites of the world's strongest powers. But this too generalizing and somewhat abstract approach to the national question led to a certain one-sidedness, which he would correct after the Second World War by differentiating between historical events peculiar to Europe and those of 'the East' (about which he would recognise the acuteness of Lenin's position at the Second Congress of the Communist International).[19]

At the outbreak of the First World War, the PSI settled on the ambiguous *neutralist* formulation coined by Lazzari: 'Neither join the war nor sabotage it.' Bordiga did not formally repudiate this, but he thought it too narrow since it could be confused with the murky neutralism of the Italian bourgeoisie. In fact, the Italian state did remain 'neutral' at first, simply in order to maximise its advantages and to minimise its losses. The main problem with Lazzari's formula, in Bordiga's eyes, was that it envisaged a mere spectator's role for the proletariat, in a situation that deeply concerned it and indeed struck at its heart. In Bordiga's own, somewhat forced, version, neutrality meant something different: 'intensified socialist fervour in the struggle against the bourgeois state, accentuation of class antagonism, the true source of any revolutionary tendency', the only force able to keep the monarchic-bourgeois state out of the war 'under the pressure of the proletarian masses'.[20] Even before 24 May 1915, when the Italian ruling class ended its prevarication and entered the war on the side of the Triple Entente (Britain, France and Russia), Bordiga criticised the old socialist anti-militarism that had merely outlined initiatives to prevent war but had not been prepared to act against war once it had broken out. The tragic spectacle of so many European socialists 'converted to war' then led him to propose a new anti-militarism that would not be an end in itself and have no illusion that war between states could be abolished as long as capitalism endured – a militarism that would indissolubly link the struggle against war with the anti-capitalist struggle for socialism. Once war broke out, such a new *socialist anti-militarism* would not refrain from action of its own or let itself be shackled by patriotic chains; it would show itself able and willing to continue the class struggle during the war, reaching out to and confidently addressing the working classes of the other belligerent countries. This is why, at the moment when Italy entered the war, the Neapolitan revolutionary greeted with relief the death of 'neutralism': 'this infelicitous word that brought us so much slander'. And he urged the PSI to show by its deeds that 'anti-militarism and internationalism [were] not empty concepts', because they contained a clear commitment to fight 'against the war, for anti-militarist international socialism'.

---

19   Bordiga 1976c, pp. 169–74.
20   'Per farci intendere', in *Il Socialista*, 3 December 1914, reprinted in Bordiga 1998, pp. 154–6.

The striking aspect of Bordiga's analysis is not so much his highlighting of the capitalism-militarism nexus, which he shared with other Marxists of the early twentieth century, as *the close linkage of militarism and democracy*, which would become most evident in and after the Second World War. Among early twentieth-century socialists, and even more among Stalinised Communists of the 1930s and 1940s, there was a widespread, if not hegemonic, belief that militarism was a specific attribute of the Central Powers and later of Nazi Germany, resulting from the prevalence in them of backward or anti-democratic forms. Bordiga, however, already in 1917, formulated this most lucid of historical judgements: 'Modern war is based on such coefficients and has such characteristics that the militarily most modern state is the one in which industrial, commercial, administrative and financial resources are the greatest, and in which political forms have evolved to the point of "democracy". This is true for the correlation – that is, the contemporaneous development – of all these activities, and it is true also because only a liberal or even social-reformist policy approach can achieve for the state that "national concord" which is the prerequisite of success in the war. Hence there is not an antithesis but a historical convergence between militarism and democracy.'[21]

It has been said that Bordiga's position, which he developed autonomously with few international contacts, did not go as far as Lenin's call to 'convert the imperialist war into civil war'.[22] Such was the case for Rosa Luxemburg and Karl Liebknecht, too. In both Italy and Germany, however, we need to take into account the considerable differences with the situation in Russia, where the social contradictions were at a more explosive level, partly because of the mountain of ordinary soldiers killed in the Tsarist army. In principle, Bordiga's

---

21 'La rivoluzione russa nella interpretazione socialista', in *L'Avanguardia* 509, 21 October 1917, reprinted in Bordiga 1998, p. 345. And again: 'Militarism is not a [...] remnant from other times but the product of new times; it is the child of capitalism and its characteristic political form, democracy' (Bordiga 1998, p. 305). After the Second World War he would write: 'More democracy means not less war but more militarism: a thesis we have upheld for half a century' (Bordiga 1972 [1964], Vol. 1, p. 233). It is a commonplace today, for those with eyes to see, that for more than seventy years – and for who knows how much longer to come – the maximum of militarism has been expressed precisely by the world's most powerful democracy.

22 See De Clementi 1971, pp. 45 ff. De Clementi writes: 'This critical period in the history of international socialism had an attentive observer in Bordiga. Far from expressing themselves in a dogmatic approach, his firmness of principles enabled him to acquire an awareness equal to that of European vanguards engaged in the quest for new strategic solutions' (1971, p. 37). It should be borne in mind that Bordiga enthusiastically welcomed the manifesto against the looming 'European war' issued by the extraordinary Basle Congress of the Second International: see Bordiga 1996, Vol. 1, pp. 142–4.

position featured *all* the basic elements of revolutionary defeatism: it was clear
to him as early as February 1917 that the 'socialist goal after the war would not
have a peaceful shape but take the form of class revolution'.[23] This internationalist class stamp of his battle during the First World War would be one of the
hallmarks of the PCd'I, placing it among the most active protagonists in the
early years of the Communist International. Nor was Bordiga's activity confined
to propaganda. We find him engaged in anti-war agitation right from the beginning of his militancy; in the 'formidable red week' of June 1914, whose social and
political movement had clearly anti-militarist overtones; in the polemic against
Mussolini's sudden volte-face, which he was one of the very first to understand
and condemn;[24] and in the attempt (not as successful as hoped) to organise a
mass protest in Naples against Italy's entry into the war. Was it possible to do
more or better?

---

23   [Bordiga] 1972 [1964], Vol. 1, p. 106.
24   Benito Mussolini, then editor of the PSI daily *Avanti*, published his key text 'From Abso-
      lute Neutrality to Active, Functional Neutrality' on 18 October 1914. Bordiga immediately
      wrote a response, 'For Active, Functional Antimilitarism' (*Il Socialista* 22, 22 October 1914),
      in which he once more set out his distinctive version of neutralism. 'We neutralists? Soon
      we will be accused of pacifism. But while holding that the state should remain neutral, we
      remain its open enemies, *active and operative*. We have many accounts to settle with the
      Salandra government. Let us agitate for the political victims. Let us continue the antibour-
      geois, anti-militarist propaganda and activity. Let us concede no truces or suspensions, let
      us close the way to the mirage of national unity that has dazzled the French and Ger-
      man comrades'. In his history of the communist left, Bordiga recalls: 'So we antibourgeois
      Italian socialists, opposed to the war and to the state, were not neutralists with regard to
      the state but interventionists in the class struggle and tomorrow in the civil war that alone
      could have prevented the war'; [Bordiga] 1972 [1964], Vol. 1, p. 94. In the same work (p. 227),
      he admits that the reaction of the 'young left' to Mussolini's ever more interventionist pos-
      itions 'came late', and he considers this 'one of the many harmful effects of admiration for
      great personalities'.
          The young Antonio Gramsci, by contrast, initially sympathised with Mussolini's pos-
      ition, which was clearly a prelude to intervention on the side of the Triple Entente. His
      reason for this, set out in an article in *Il Grido del Popolo* on 31 October 1914, was a strong
      appeal to the *national* character and function of the Socialist Party: 'The Socialist Party to
      which we dedicate our energies is the *Italian* Socialist Party, which is to say that section
      of the Socialist International which has taken on the task of winning the Italian nation
      for the International. This immediate task, this day-to-day task, gives the Party particu-
      lar, national characteristics, which commit it to assuming a specific function, a particular
      responsibility in Italian life. The Party is a State in potential, which is gradually matur-
      ing: a rival to the bourgeois State, which is seeking, through its daily struggle with this
      enemy, and through the development of its own internal dialectic, to create the organs
      it needs to overcome and absorb its opponent. And, in carrying out this function, the
      Party is autonomous. It depends on the International only for its ultimate aim, and for
      the essential nature of its struggle, as a struggle between classes'. 'An Active and Func-

If limitations and weak points can be identified in this battle, then they concern Bordiga's continuing confidence in the long-term possibility of reorienting virtually the whole of the maximalist tendency of the PSI, and the scant consideration he showed for the popular resistance in Tripoli and Cyrenaica to Italian aggression. In his writings against the war in Libya, the rare references to local peoples mention them only as the 'famished' or 'impoverished' Arab population, as victims but never as possible subjects of history. This attitude is linked to the fact that during those years Bordiga did not yet grasp the existence of a national question, a *national oppression*, in the colonies and semicolonies – as we can see from the reservations (similar to those of the maximalist Serrati) that he expressed about the theses on the national question adopted at the Second Congress of the Communist International. Only after the Second World War would he return to the theme of the powerful 'awakening of the coloured peoples', situating himself much closer to the positions about which he had expressed puzzlement or partial disagreement in 1920.[25]

The second front in the struggle against reformism and for a consistently revolutionary position that Bordiga led inside the PSI and the working class centred on electoralism and any kind of political bloc between socialists and bourgeois forces. In his history of the communist left, Bordiga himself states that its birth in Naples, his native city, was closely bound up with the 'long and violent battle against hypermanifestations of electoralist ignominy, which has an infamous history everywhere and always, but which reached a peak of pathological infection in Naples in the early twentieth century.'[26] In that city, by far the most important in southern Italy and then the largest in the whole country, the limited forces of the PSI were marked by the threefold corrupting influence of freemasonry, localism and a tendency to form electoral blocs with organised forces or single individuals displaying a democratic, radical, anticlerical, republican or even liberal orientation. In the resulting hotchpotch, there was even room for positions overtly or covertly favourable to the war in Libya, and later to Mussolinism, as well as for syndicalist currents that spoke of bar-

---

tional Neutrality', in Gramsci 1979, pp. 3–4. Gramsci went on to reproach Angelo Tasca for a misinterpretation of Mussolini's position. But just two weeks later, on 15 November 1914, the recently expelled Mussolini brought out a new paper in favour of intervention in the war: *Il Popolo d'Italia*. Gramsci's thesis regarding the essential *national* function of the proletariat and the Communist Party would recur insistently in the *Prison Notebooks*.

25   See the third section of Part Two of this anthology.

26   [Bordiga] 1972 [1964], Vol. 1, p. 71.

ricades but were subreformist in their actual practice. Nothing was missing –
some actually wanted to develop a 'southern socialism' in opposition to 'northern socialism'.[27]

Bordiga and other comrades acted decisively in the face of this mood, which
was an affront to the honour of anyone who really believed in the ideals of
socialism. They cut their ties with the Naples branch of the Party and, on 2 April
1912, founded the 'Karl Marx' revolutionary socialist circle;[28] its aim was to give
Neapolitan socialism a class profile, to study the works of Marx, to do intensive
propaganda activity among the workers, including against the war with Turkey
in Libya, and in its way to compete in the electoral arena. In contrast to the
'exultant electoral orgies', where workers were called upon to back the *arriv-
iste*, and sometimes business-oriented, ambitions of the few', the circle insisted
that for Marxist socialism elections were only a *means* to make its own perspective, principles and programme better known, not an end in itself with the
objective, or mania, of electoral success. It rejected the idea that, because of the
insufficiently developed capitalist economy, the tactics pursued in the South
should be different from those in the North. There were obviously differences
between the two parts of the country, but the very fact that the workers' movement was only beginning to take shape in the South meant that intransigent
tactics should be adopted there with particular rigour, in order to distinguish
the Socialist Party from all parties defending the established order by hook or
by crook. Moral or legal arguments counted for nothing against this demand
for autonomy and identity: an alliance among all honest people from every
class and party would certainly not solve the 'moral question', except by showing that today's honest bourgeois become tomorrow's dishonest bourgeois; the
solution to this 'dreary question' lay, on the contrary, in differentiation between
classes and class interests, and between the respective political parties. As to
the camorras running local authorities in the Mezzogiorno, they were nothing but the tentacles of the 'grand camorra of the business world, personified
by the landowners of the South and the steel bosses and sugar barons of the
North'. This grand camorra, constituted by the national capitalist system, could
be effectively combated only through 'a unitary tactic for the North and the
South, [...] a systematic tactic of antibourgeois struggle'.

---

27   'Ai Socialisti d'Italia. Il "Carlo Marx" per il socialismo meridionale e contro le degene-
     razioni dell'Unione Socialista Napoletana' e 'Il socialismo napoletano e le sue morbose
     degenerazioni', in Bordiga 1996, Vol. 1, pp. 375 ff., 467 ff.
28   Apart from Bordiga, its founding members were Mario and Ida Bianchi, Gustavo Savarese,
     Adele Giannuzzi, Enrichetta Giannelli, Ortensia De Meo (later Bordiga's wife) and Ertulio
     Esposito. Subsequently, Ruggiero Grieco and Oreste Lizzadri also joined the group.

In this framework, local council elections were a terrain of class struggle, and any victory there should convert socialist communes into weapons directed against 'the bourgeois capitalist that exploits us'.[29] Therefore, the Socialist Party should enter into no popular or democratic bloc against the clerical cabals or undisguised business elites; it should openly struggle against these, but also against the demagogic opposition of the democratic parties, often under the control of masonic circles closely tied to Giolitti's policies and everywhere hostile to the workers' interests. To give Neapolitan socialism a class profile, intransigent, consistently revolutionary and above the prevailing confusion, was thus a task that the whole of the Socialist Party should give itself. It finally did this at the Ancona congress in April 1914, the last before the world war and the first at which the Marxist left around Bordiga made itself known nationally in all its combativity and theoretical preparedness.[30] The congress affirmed the incompatibility of socialism and freemasonry, dissolving the Naples federation. Although the decision was not as clear-cut as the founders of the Karl Marx circle had hoped, it impelled them to re-enter the Naples branch of the party. Here they soon became the nucleus of its leadership, thanks to the intense agitation of the Settimana Rossa that brought to the fore 'seasoned and resolute proletarian vanguards' among the tram, railway and metallurgical workers, the best social material to cleanse and reforge the party in Naples.[31]

In the 1912–14 period of fierce struggle against electoralism, ideas began to take shape in Bordiga – above all, a complete opposition between democracy and socialism – that would lead him to become a convinced supporter of abstentionism. Whereas, for Turati, Treves and other reformist deputies, socialism was the distant goal to be approached in a series of gradual steps, in a long march through the state and its institutions, Bordiga saw things very differently. There had been a historical period when newly born sections of the proletariat had fought alongside the bourgeoisie against the decrepit feudal landed aristo-

---

29   Bordiga 1972 [1964], Vol. 1, pp. 413–17: these expressions are taken from Bordiga's speech at the Fourteenth National Congress of the PSI, held at Ancona from 26 to 29 April 1914.

30   This refers to the PSI as a whole, since Bordiga and his comrades in the Marx circle had already stood out at the FGSI youth congress in Bologna (September 1912) and in their heated polemic against the 'culturalists' in the following months. In contrast to the traditional sequence of 'study, profession of socialist views and political activity', they emphasised the sequence that 'actually corresponded to determinist materialism: economic class inferiority, instinctive rebellion, violent action, socialist feelings and belief – and, within the party that groups together individuals, the conscious doctrine of revolution. These were the theses that Lenin, then unknown to us, had presented in 1903'. Bordiga 1972 [1964], Vol. 1, p. 63; see also L. Gerosa's introduction to Bordiga 1972 [1964], Vol. 1, pp. xlff. and the relevant texts in that volume.

31   See Fatica 1971, p. 226.

cracy, but that period was well and truly over. As the bourgeoisie ceased to be a revolutionary class and 'became conservative by force of circumstance', the 'proletariat understood that it could not rest content with the ostensible political equality conceded by bourgeois democracy and prepared itself for other conquests'. It did this through its trade organisations, and through a focus on its class programme of expropriation and socialisation of the means of production and exchange. From that point on, socialism projected itself not only as the overcoming of bourgeois democracy but as its antithesis, its 'complete negation'. Bourgeois democracy was meant to achieve harmony between the classes; but the socialist proletariat sought the further development of class struggle, because only that, rather than education and reforms, could shake off the yoke of capital. Bourgeois democracy, Bordiga wrote, 'is profoundly colonialist and therefore militarist', because it expresses the capitalist requirement of a constant quest for and conquest of new markets; 'the proletariat is by definition internationalist and anti-militarist'. The evolutionary line of bourgeois democracy is not 'a continual ascent towards equality and justice, but a parabola that reaches its peak and then comes back down towards a final crisis' (a far-sighted vision of the inevitable historical decline of democracy). And again:

> Democracy sees the representative system as the means to solve any problem of collective interest; we see it as the mask of a social oligarchy that uses the lure of political equality to keep the workers oppressed. Democracy seeks the statisation and centralisation of social activities and functions; socialism sees the bourgeois state as its real enemy; socialism is for the maximum of local administrative autonomy. Democracy seeks state education; we see this as no less of a danger than religious control of education. Democracy sees dogma only beneath the priest's cassock; we see it also beneath the army officer's cloak, beneath dynastic and national insignias, beneath all the present-day institutions, and above all in the principle of *private property*.[32]

In principle, this opposition between bourgeois democracy and socialism makes perfect sense, but it also misses *something important*: the distinction between the struggle in defence of bourgeois democracy and the struggle to defend the freedoms that the proletariat enjoyed after decades of struggle to

---

32   'Democrazia e socialismo', in Bordiga 1972 [1964], Vol. 1, p. 455. According to Alessandro Mantovani, Bordiga's viewpoint is 'antidemocraticism on principle' – closer to Libertarianism than Marxism as expressed in Lenin or Luxemburg's thought (Mantovani 2019, pp. 54–7).

gain them. In those years, as the reader will see, Bordiga wrote against anarchist and syndicalist abstentionism, rejecting its apolitical approach and any form of neutrality or indifference on major social and political issues. Such attitudes lulled the workers to sleep, instead of awakening them to an awareness of social relations and an understanding of their own interests. Social revolution, he argued, was 'a political matter' and should be properly prepared 'on the political terrain'. In contrast to the great majority of the PSI, however, he did not understand this as primarily the terrain of elections or parliament. He emphasised that the workers should 'learn always to engage in politics *directly*', assuming this task in the first person, not oscillating 'like a herd of sheep between one party and another, storing up only betrayals and disillusionment'.[33]

This theme of *direct political action* on the workers' part would be the leitmotif of Bordiga's later rejection of participation in elections. He and the comrades of the 'abstentionist faction' engaged in work to detoxify the party and the most active section of the Italian proletariat from the electoralist, institutionalist, democratic drug, essentially from *reformism*, and to promote revolutionary re-education particularly among new working-class layers turning to the PSI in a combative spirit but without adequate training. This activity was fundamental in laying the ground for the Communist Party of Italy. And it is quite legitimate to compare it to the turn in German social democracy executed by Rosa Luxemburg and her like-minded comrades, although even in the white-hot situation of December 1918 she declared herself in favour of participation in elections. One can discuss a contradiction in Bordiga between definitions of electoral involvement as a merely secondary, tactical issue and theoretical-propagandistic formulations that treat it in general, even abstract, terms as a question of principle. We shall return to this later. But it remains beyond dispute that in the spring and summer of 1919, at the highpoint of the class struggles in Italy (and internationally), a real choice was posed between preparation for elections and preparation for revolution. At that decisive juncture, the 'grand saturnalian ballot' staged by the bourgeoisie and endorsed by the reformists (with a Pyrrhic victory of 156 parliamentary seats) actually served to *rein in and deflect* the insurrectional movement, the political general strike and even the workers' material gains. It was not the 'doctrinaire' Amadeo Bordiga but the 'concrete' historical circumstances that presented this alternative:

> The resource then offered by history, which the party [PSI] let escape precisely because of its deplorable lack of Marxist theoretical maturity, was to block the way to the enemy's manoeuvres – an enemy who knew

---

33   'Perché siamo intransigenti', in Bordiga 1972 [1964], Vol. 1, p. 277.

that the flow to the ballot box would head off the impact of the revolutionary torrent. If the proletariat, shaking off democratic illusions, had burned the parliamentary ship behind it, the struggle would have ended very differently. It was the duty of the revolutionary party to try to achieve this magnificent outcome, by acting to thwart the other alternative. But revolutionary is what the party was not.[34]

Already at the important meeting of the intransigent revolutionary faction,[35] held illegally in Florence on 18 November 1917 a few days after Italy's military defeat at Caporetto, Bordiga had warned: 'We must act. The industrial proletariat is tired. But it is armed. We must act.' But his words had not produced effective results, even in the whole of the faction. The *intransigenti* had averted the danger that the PSI would get sucked into the swamp of patriotism and national unity – no mean feat, given the tragic experiences that were shaking the parties in France and Germany around that time. But although the PSI continued to behave as 'one of the best parties of the Second International' in relation to the war, it lacked the revolutionary determination and strategic and tactical clarity that the situation demanded. And no one can say that parliamentarism, electoralism and legalism had nothing to do with it!

The third front in the struggle of Bordiga and the nascent Left against reformism involved the relationship between party and unions. As they saw it, this relationship was turned upside down, in the sense that the PSI leadership and the party as a whole were *subordinate* to the parliamentary group and the leadership of the General Confederation of Labour, and not vice versa. Hence, for the entire decade before the birth of the PCd'I, there was a ceaseless theoretical, political and organisational contest between reformists and revolutionaries – not only in Naples, since the positions of the Karl Marx circle found a growing echo elsewhere, especially in Turin, Milan and other industrialised parts of

---

34   Bordiga 1972 [1964], Vol. 1, p. 175; Bordiga 1973 [1960], p. 103. Cf. Bordiga's speech of 5 October 1919 at the Bologna congress: 'Here we are today in the course of making communism a reality, in the field where the revolutionary process is imminent. Today, participation in the elections means collaboration with the bourgeoisie ... Therefore, comrades, we maintain that the present situation of the international proletariat and the present political situation in Italy are of such a nature that to participate in the elections and parliamentary life means betraying the class struggle' (Bordiga 2010, Vol. 3, pp. 401–2). In the years between 1914 and 1919, however, Bordiga showed a number of times that he was ready to give up the 'prior insistence on abstention', as long as the PSI majority broke with the reformists.

35   A first nucleus of this faction, mainly consisting of comrades from Milan, Turin, Florence and Naples, was formed between late July and early August 1917.

the country. From the beginning, they were characterised by the attention they gave to the industrial proletariat and to involvement in its struggles.[36] Beginning with the Settimana Rossa of June 1914, they stepped up their activity 'to distance the proletariat from its reformist leaders and to confer an unequivocably revolutionary direction on the political line' of the Naples organisation.[37] This intense union activity with a rigorous class orientation would be a constant feature of the anti-reformist struggle waged by Bordiga and the Left (later Communist Left) within the PSI. It is therefore foolish to think that his position can be dismissed as that of a doctrinaire remote from the conditions of the working class and indifferent to their immediate struggles.

What is true is that here too Bordiga's position differed sharply from the generic maximalist one,[38] and that it was opposed to both the practice and the theoretical-political coordinates of union and political reformism. In his eyes, the party should not be subordinate to the leading group in the unions, because the party was more revolutionary and closer than the unions to the class as a whole; it was the only organ that consistently represented the historical aspirations of the working class. The party, not the unions, was the true organ of the dictatorship of the proletariat. Thus, there was nothing at all alien about trade union activity – on the contrary, it was the 'first duty' of the party. Members were expected to participate actively in strikes, introducing political themes and the ultimate goals of the party (the seizure of power, class dictatorship, etc.). The aim of this was not to split the unions, but to penetrate them and

---

36   In the Settimana Rossa, Bordiga was the only state railways functionary to join the protest strike against the killings of demonstrators in Ancona – and for this he was dismissed from his job. As Fatica notes, 'it was the only sacking that took place in silence, since the employee in question did not wish there to be any outcry over his personal circumstances' (1971, p. 184). Another of the railwaymen dismissed on political grounds was Francesco Misiano.

37   Fatica 1971, p. 226. Cf. L. Gerosa's introduction to Vol. 1 of Bordiga 1996, pp. xlff. In Naples, a provincial structure of the metalworkers' union (FIOM) was formed in September 1916, and an overarching CGL Camera del Lavoro (Chamber of Labour) in August 1918; in both cases, the group around Bordiga made an important contribution and provided strong support. See De Clementi 1971, pp. 47–8, 59–75, who writes: 'The most innovative aspect of Bordiga's strategy, which has tended to be undervalued or ignored, was its respect for and constant encouragement of the workers' own control of their struggles. The guarantees of this were daily sectoral meetings empowered to make decisions, which limited the role of workers' delegates in negotiations to one of channels of communication' (De Clementi 1971, pp. 68–9). For documentary evidence of this activity, see De Benedetti 1974.

38   However, as late as October 1919, Bordiga was still using the terms revolutionary, bolshevik and maximalist as synonyms, which did not correspond to the reality (see Bordiga 2010, Vol. 3, p. 394). Lenin was closer to the mark, when he defined maximalism in terms of a gap between words and deeds. After the Second World War, Bordiga would describe his earlier use of the term maximalist as 'infelicitous'.

win them over. A split in political reformism was necessary and beneficial; but a split in the union movement would be negative, because the unions should contain and organise the mass of workers. As to the union structures, Bordiga thought the branch and trade levels higher than individual factories, since they grouped together and coordinated different situations. This does not mean that he was hostile to factory councils, as it has sometimes been wrongly claimed. He simply considered them more *limited* than sectoral and regional bodies, and thought them of a qualitatively different order from soviets. In any case, all union bodies could play the role of carrying the revolutionary movement forward (rather than holding it back), provided only that they were led by the party:

> Sovietism is not a hotchpoth of unions. In the revolutionary period, and in the communist order, the labour union has a part to play that is anything but pre-eminent; but the character of the organism is political. [...] As it develops, the revolution [...] discards the viewpoints of both reformist workerism and syndicalism. And revolutionary practice places its trust in the political action of the working class.[39]

At this point (April 1919), Bordiga directed his polemic both against the 'antirevolutionary decisions' of the Confederation of Labour bosses, with their electoralist gradualism and their perspective of a constituent assembly of occupational groups rather than soviet power, and against the anarcho-syndicalist spokesmen of the Unione sindacale (USI), with their 'antithesis between political movement and union movement' and their dangerous rejection of centralism.[40] But he also distanced himself from the passive, wavering and conciliatory attitude of the PSI's maximalist leadership, which, though aware of the growing divergence between the reformist union bosses and the party's declared course, never resolved to level a serious accusation against them. Embryonically, and more and more explicitly in the following period, Bordiga's approach contained a critique of Gramsci's *Ordine Novo* perspective, which took over in its way some of the basic themes of workerism and syndicalism.

In the end – though this is certainly not the end of the story – Bordiga's antireformist battle within the PSI, the working class and Italian society developed around the 'interpretation' of the Russian Revolution and the founding of the

---

39   'La confederazione del Lavoro contro il "Soviet"', in Bordiga 2010, Vol. 3, pp. 161–2. But see the entire section from pp. 159–226.
40   See Bordiga 1972 [1964], Vol. 1, pp. 110, 125 ff.; and Bordiga 2010, Vol. 3, p. 161.

new International. Though not fully informed about events in Russia, Bordiga immediately grasped that the revolution there, together with the exit from the war and denunciations of its imperialist character, broke up the fratricidal orgy and, above all in Germany, opened a new historical period of revolutionary uprisings under the aegis of 'true internationalism'. Unlike Gramsci, who described the October Revolution as a refutation of Marxism,[41] he saw in the Russia of 1917 'the technological-economic conditions of the Germany of 1848'. In line with the theses of the *Communist Manifesto*, he therefore argued: 'What did not happen in Germany, for complex reasons, has happened in Russia in 1917. It is therefore not right to say that the beginning of the socialist revolution is anti-Marxist, precisely in the country where the bourgeois revolution has not yet been accomplished.'[42]

The conquest of power by the proletariat, a necessarily authoritarian, extralegal process lasting a relatively short time, did not, however, coincide with the real transformation of 'social institutions'. Particularly in a country like Russia, this was possible only through 'a long period of class dictatorship', which would 'violently' remove 'the counter-revolutionary obstacles as it had violently broken down the defences of the old regime'. After the Second World War, Bordiga would develop exhaustively and at great length this theme of the asynchronicity of political and social revolution, of the *dual revolution*, which in 1917–18 he outlined summarily, without a specific analysis of the social-economic situation in Russia.

In the full claims that he made for them, the Russian events demolished a twofold illusion: the bourgeois illusion that Marxism and social revolution had been definitively laid to rest; and the reformist illusion that a 'peaceful democratic revolution' was possible. They also gave the lie to the simplistic view of anarchists and syndicalists – that once the state was overthrown, a new non-capitalist economy could be established all at once. For, given the scale of the social and economic transformations to be accomplished, a number of generations might be required for the advent of socialist society. Nevertheless, the Russian October opened *a new history on a world scale* and placed the 'International Social Revolution' on the order of the day.

Few European communists grasped as powerfully as Bordiga this *directly global* significance of the Russian Revolution – although he would later be critical of attempts to apply the Bolsheviks' tactics mechanically in Western Europe. What he took from the Bolsheviks and imitated was their 'utter intransigence' toward the bourgeois parties and other socialist formations, their con-

41   Gramsci, 'The Revolution Against *Capital*', in Gramsci 1979, pp. 39–42.
42   'Gli insegnamenti della nuova storia', in Bordiga 1998, Vol. 2, pp. 418–19.

sistent adherence to the maximum programme (hence Bordiga's talk of the 'Russian maximalists'), which allowed them to win the trust and allegiance of the great majority of Russian workers. The Bolsheviks, then, were the *symmetrical opposite* of the Italian reformists and of all who sought to hang out with them and never make a break. Not by chance, in December 1918, did Bordiga and his comrades in the communist abstentionist faction decide to call their weekly paper *Il Soviet*. And they gave a correct framework for understanding the soviet, as the political organ of class power representing the 'collective interests of the working class', which took upon itself alone the task of directing the entire life of society. This contrasted sharply with the vision of the *L'Ordine Nuovo* group and the weight it attached to factory councils. Bordiga did recognise the tasks of these in the socialisation and management of single enterprises, but he was adamant that 'the organ of proletarian liberation is the working-class political party', for only the party was capable of expressing the general, historical interest of the class and unifying the forces of the proletariat.[43]

Equally lucid is Bordiga's understanding of the need for a new International. The question was posed for Lenin and Trotsky as early as the end of 1914. Just a few months later, on 23 May 1915, in an article for *Avanti* included in this anthology, Bordiga stated: 'Either inside or outside the national preconception and its patriotic scruples. Either towards a nationalistic pseudo-socialism or towards a new International.' The war, the catastrophe of 'socialist' patriotism, and the Russian Revolution made this alternative *categorical*; it could no longer be postponed. The swamp-like PSI, however, tried to avoid the choice with all manner of expedients. Serrati's 'unitary' position was the best (or worst) representative of its fatal hesitation. In March 1919 the party leadership refused to get involved in the reconstitution of the Second International and, under pressure from working-class supporters of the Russian Revolution, adhered to the Third International. But the decision was purely symbolic. 'Advocates of national defence, opponents of violent means and proletarian dictatorship, and even proponents of ministerial collaboration with the progressive bourgeoisie'[44] remained inside the PSI, free to contradict in words and deeds the formal decisions of the party. In short, a horde of anti-internationalists.

In the course of 1919, under the impact of the social and political radicalisation in Italy and Europe (Germany, Austria, Hungary), the battle waged by Bordiga and the Communist Faction became more intense. This is how Bordiga later recalled the setting for the great postwar proletarian upsurge:

---

43   See Bordiga's speech on the constitution of soviets at the PSI National Council of 18–
      22 April 1920 in Milan, in Bordiga 2011, Vol. 4, pp. 159 ff.
44   Gerosa, 'Introduzione' to Bordiga 2011, Vol. 4, p. lxii.

The trade-union economic struggle, in which the Italian proletariat drew on powerful traditions, flared up again everywhere without delay. But the brightness of the explosion would be inexplicable had it not been for the lively political opposition of the whole proletariat to the war, more energetic than that of the party, whose doubts and hesitations we have highlighted [...]. [...] The masses found themselves on the terrain onto which, among countless difficulties, the most decisive wing of its political organisation had known how to move. Their revolt was spontaneous, in tune from one end of the country to the other, from the cities to the countryside, and all levels of the bourgeoisie trembled before the advances that the proletariat was beginning to make.[45]

The 'red year' 1919 saw the conquest of an eight-hour day for 500,000 metalworkers, struggles against the rising cost of living, a general strike in protest at the ransacking of the PSI daily *Avanti*'s offices, a movement involving more than a million workers in struggle, and the birth of the factory councils. The fiery year 1920 then followed with the April strike movement in Turin, unrest among a million farm labourers and peasants, a wave of factory occupations and a huge rise in union membership. The same period witnessed the foundation of the International and revolutionary upheavals in other European countries. But why then did the 'sectarian' and 'intransigent' Bordiga – among the first to consider a split in the PSI necessary – not overcome his hesitations and act without further ado, as some comrades in the faction (O. Damen, for instance) wanted?

There were several reasons for this. First, almost until the end, he thought it might be possible to win the whole of the maximalist current to revolutionary positions. Second, the development of class antagonisms in Italy still seemed insufficient, and he therefore 'waited' (in active mode) for the most combative section of the working class, on the basis of its own experience, to reject more sharply the hesitations, conciliatory spirit and legalism of the PSI leadership. Third, his aim was to found a communist party with sufficient strength to influence the course of events, with the capacity to guide the imposing postwar proletarian and social struggles toward an insurrectionary, soviet-type outcome. And fourth, he had confidence in the help of the International. In the end, the inevitable split did not take with it the majority of the socialist proletariat; in Bordiga's view, it came too late. The 'so favourable objective situation' was wasted. But the Communist Party of Italy was anything but a phantasm.

---

45   Bordiga 1972 [1964], Vol. 1, pp. 125–6; cf. Maione 1975, which is unsympathetic to Bordiga.

4   The PCd'I and the Struggle against Fascism

The Partito Comunista d'Italia (PCd'I), the Italian section of the Communist
International, was born on 21 January 1921 in Leghorn, through a split from the
PSI. The tempestuous postwar situation in Italy and internationally had long
put a severe strain on relations with the incorrigible reformists who led the
parliamentary group and the Confederation of Labour, and events in Russia
and the founding of the Third International had made the supporters of the
revolutionary communist perspective even more determined than before. Bordiga and his closest comrades had argued as early as 1917 that the reformists
should be expelled from the party, and the following year, becoming more and
more convinced that a split was inevitable, they formed the abstentionist communist faction. At the Bologna congress in 1919, they tabled for discussion a new
party programme that would authorise a full 'return to classical Marxist socialism', the founding of a communist party, affiliation to the Third International
and acceptance of its rules and disciplinary norms. They also pushed for the
expulsion of all who 'claim that the emancipation of the proletariat is possible
in a democratic system and who reject the method of armed struggle against
the bourgeoisie to install the proletarian dictatorship'. They remained isolated,
however, because the appeal for party unity prevailed in other left tendencies.
But in a few feverish months, the powerful workers' struggles of 1920 and the
Communist International Second Congress severe reproving of PSI's representative Serrati brought about a new scenario. The call of the abstentionist communists for an agreement among revolutionary elements within the party was
now endorsed by the pro-election maximalists from Milan (led by Fortichiari
and Repossi) and by the group in Turin (including Gramsci, Tasca, Terracini
and Togliatti) that had begun publishing *L'Ordine Nuovo* in May 1919. So came
into being the Communist Fraction, which in October 1920 issued a programmatic manifesto to party comrades and branches: the abstentionists, for their
part, dropped their preconditions and accepted participation in national and
local elections in order to 'develop revolutionary propaganda and agitation,
and to hasten the break-up of the bourgeois organs of representative democracy'.[46]
    At the Livorno congress of the PSI the Communist Fraction, and Bordiga
above all, argued that the 'final crisis of the capitalist system' faced the proletariat in Italy too with an *obligatory way forward*: to overthrow the power of

---

46   Bordiga 2011, Vol. 4, p. 318. The manifesto was signed by N. Bombacci, A. Bordiga, B. Forti-
      chiari, A. Gramsci, F. Misiano, L. Polano, L. Repossi and U. Terracini.

the bourgeoisie and to establish the dictatorship of the proletariat. The catastrophic war, followed by the two 'red years', had been pushing the workers in
this direction. In contrast to what the reformists maintained, the 'Italian revolution' was a possibility. It was not true that it would be condemned in advance
to isolation and defeat, since it would 'insert itself into the world revolution,
becoming the point at which it passed from east to west, and perhaps com-
plementing its emergence throughout Central Europe. For if there had been
something distinctive about the situation of the Russian revolution, it was the
geographical conditions that allowed it to be confined for three years behind an
insurmountable barrier that today proves powerless to contain it.' This was why
it was necessary to prepare the masses for the inevitability of revolution, for the
'exigencies of the revolutionary process', and to end the hesitations and uncertainties that produced only disillusionment and loss of confidence among the
workers. It was therefore necessary to separate at once from the reformists, who
systematically sabotaged the preparation of the revolution and the achievement of a revolutionary outcome. In the present situation, Bordiga insisted, 'the
revolutionary problem [had] reached full maturity and appeared as a *problem
of action*, as leadership of a veritable war between the working class and bourgeois power'. In the wake of bolshevism, the new International had traced the
way forward, pointed to soviet power as the new revolutionary form of the state
apparatus, set out the tasks of the communist party, and established 21 conditions for affiliation that debarred opportunists. There was no room for further
postponements. Now was the moment to found the communist party, to move
'towards the final struggle, towards the Soviet Republic in Italy'.[47] The records
note 'enthusiastic applause' from the communists.

The communist motion received 58,783 votes at the congress (more than a
third, but perhaps less than expected), against 14,695 for the reformist motion
and 98,028 for the centrist one championed by Serrati. Delegates representing
more than 47,000 members (out of a total of 216,337 in late 1920, 55,313 belonging to the youth federation) did not express a vote. Many of these members
must not have joined the PSI before 1919–20, since at the end of 1918 the PSI
had issued just 24,359 party cards. However, the PCd'I communists were a solid
force, rooted in the main industrial areas and cities (Turin, Alessandria, Novara,
Milan, Mantua, Pavia, Trieste, Genoa, Florence, Pisa, Ancona, Bari, Naples). The
maximalist input was considerable in Emilia-Romagna, where many union officials and deputies joined the new party, while in other regions, especially in the
South, people with an anarcho-syndicalist background were strongly represen-

---

47   Bordiga 2014, Vol. 5, pp. 11–84.

ted in it. There was also a large communist presence in the most important
union, the CGL, which in late 1920 organised 2,150,000 workers (435,000 in
the Camere del lavoro, the rest through trade federations). In a contested ballot at the congress in February 1921, the communists won 432,564 votes (and
claimed another 150,000), with a particular strength in the Camere del lavoro;
the socialists, who had always led the CGL with their most moderate figures,
obtained 1,435,873.[48] At the end of 1921 the PCd'I had more than 42,000 members and a sizeable publishing and propaganda apparatus: three daily newspapers, two fortnightly magazines (one political, the other geared to the trade
unions), and twenty or so local papers (one in Slovenian). At the general elections in May 1921, it won approximately 290,000 votes and ended up with 15
deputies.

Largely made up of workers, with a modest number of peasants, the PCd'I
had a young membership and leadership.[49] Although Bordiga's authority was
uncontested in the first three years, it was not a homogeneous party. Three
different components – abstentionists, *L'Ordine Nuovo* people, and maximalists[50] – had come together and 'fused' under the impact of the advancing proletarian movement in Italy and Europe, and under the massive influence of
October and Russian Bolshevism, while all expecting a revolutionary dénoue-
ment to come soon. But when the movement suddenly began to ebb and difficulties piled up, the diversity of origins and traditions forcefully reasserted
itself, and the unity, discipline and unanimity of the early period gave way to a
series of ever sharper internal disputes. Bordiga was aware of this lack of homo-
geneity – indeed, he openly referred to it in his speech at Leghorn.[51] This was

---

48   Martinelli 1977, pp. 140–52, 166–72. The communists were also present in the USI (the
     anarcho-syndicalist Unione Sindacale Italiana, whose base welcomed the birth of the
     PCd'I) and the SFI (the railwaymen's union), the other two union organisations that gave
     birth in February 1922 to the Alleanza del lavoro. The PCd'I had only 400 female members,
     but it published a women's paper, *La compagna*, with an initial print-run of 15,000.

49   The first executive committee consisted of Bordiga, the undisputed head of the party,
     who was not yet 32 at the Leghorn congress, while Grieco was 28, Terracini 26, and Forti-
     chiari and Repossi (the 'oldies') 39. According to Bordiga, they were 'interchangeable' and
     'ensured a day-to-day continuity in the party's work': only Bordiga and Grieco came out of
     the abstentionist faction. There was not yet a post of general secretary: one was eventually
     created in 1924 for Gramsci.

50   Among these, the historian Cortesi notes, there was also 'a theorist of political oppor-
     tunism who had always been critical of Marxism': Antonio Graziadei.

51   Having claimed that the doctrine, method and tactics of the new party were those of 'the
     Moscow theses', he admitted that there might be differences or disagreements on 'one or
     another of these points'; for example, 'Gramsci might be on a false track or be following
     a wrong thesis when I am on the right one, but we are all fighting for the same result, all

one reason for his strenuous activity to make the PCd'I a cohesive, centralised organisation finally rid of the localism and provincialism that had character-ised the PSI, alien to personal or group manoeuvres, and capable of defending itself against Fascist aggression. These energetic organisational efforts on Bor-diga's part would eventually be of benefit to those who, from 1923 on, set about radically altering, and then abandoning, the party's original course.

Whatever limitations one may see in this activity, the factor that under-mined it more than any other was the *late birth* of the PCd'I: late in the sense that the class struggle in Italy had peaked,[52] the revolutionary process in Ger-many, Russia and Central Europe was on the ebb,[53] and the capitalist liberal-democratic and Fascist counteroffensive was in danger of overwhelming it. At the moment of the Party's birth, its leading group (unlike Zinoviev) had no illu-sion that insurrection was in the offing, but it felt sure that the *period* was still one in which a great revolutionary assault could be mounted in Italy and inter-nationally, and made preparations accordingly. The harsh facts saw to it that this certainty was belied.

Scarcely had the factory occupation movement exhausted itself when the bosses hit out at the working class with a series of mass sackings (thousands at Fiat in Turin, including numerous communists and union activists, the 'insub-ordinates'), contract cancellations, and wage cuts averaging 20–25 percent and rising as high as 70 percent. In the space of a few months, the leap in infla-tion and unemployment (up fourfold between December 1920 and September 1921) led to impoverishment and mass hunger. Union membership plummeted. The main employers' bodies, the General Confederation of Industry and the Federation of Agrarian Landowners, profited from the grave economic crisis to force the unconditional surrender of workers and day labourers in a number of places, to trample on the recent eight-hour day agreements, to tighten fact-

---

making the effort that constitutes a programme or method'. And he trusted that every-one would adhere to the 'international discipline' to which they were alive (Bordiga 2014, Vol. 5, p. 84).

52   'The split came late at Leghorn. Later still, after the March on Rome, was the hope of dig-ging up the Socialist Party again with Serrati' (Bordiga 1973 [1960], p. 105). He took some of the blame himself for this lateness: 'We may have committed some mistakes: for example, that of having oriented too late, and initially with insufficient determination, to the break' with the PSI (*Rassegna comunista* 13, 15 November 1921). In Lenin's opinion, the split should have taken place back in 1919, at the Bologna congress.

53   In his *Storia della sinistra comunista* (1972 [1964], Vol. 1, p. 70), Bordiga spoke of 1919 as the 'year of the greatest revolutionary vitality up to this day'. In that year itself, he wrote that the 'bourgeois organism' was 'in a condition of crisis and decomposition' (Bordiga 2010, Vol. 3, p. 401).

ory discipline, and to speed up work rhythms. In parallel, from late 1920, Fascist squads staged a series of attacks on *camere del lavoro*, Socialist Party offices, cooperatives, 'red' local councils and individual militants, which by the following spring had become unrelenting.[54] It was a complete turnaround from the *biennio rosso* and the great postwar advances of the workers' movement. Things became even more complex and dramatic in 1922, when the Fascist movement, now calling itself the National Fascist Party, began to hold major street demonstrations capable of organising – even at a military level and according to a precise strategy of action – petty-bourgeois social layers declassed by the war and the crisis, and desperate crowds of people without work and began to approach the industrial centres of the North having conquered the agricultural regions of the Po valley. The state apparatuses, whether at the top (governments) or at the base (prefectures, police detachments), lent support to this onslaught, which caused thousands of deaths and injuries among the workers.

Amid the irresistible decomposition of the old liberal institutions, in which six increasingly unstable governments followed one another in three years, the ruling class and the monarchy gradually placed their trust in the newcomer Mussolini. His 'March on Rome', to take the reins of power in October 1922, enjoyed all possible complicity from the established institutions, and his first government, which included the Catholic Partito Popolare of Luigi Sturzo, the Liberals, the Italian Social Democrats and the Nationalists, was initially supported by both Giolitti and De Gasperi. Only the veto of the old Right kept out the Socialist Baldesi, one of the heads of the CGL, who had made himself available for this squalid service.

As soon as it came into being, therefore, the PCd'I found itself having to confront 'one of the most complex class struggles in the classical European area'[55] and the new political phenomenon of Fascism.[56] At the same time it also had to define itself clearly in relation to reformism and maximalism, so as to contend with them for influence over the working masses, and to educate in revolu-

---

54   See Natoli 1982; Tasca 1972. These two works contain useful information and sharp analysis in matters of detail, but my own viewpoint on the rise of Fascism is far from theirs, especially from Tasca's.

55   Cortesi, 'Amadeo Bordiga: per un profilo storico', in Cortesi (ed.) 1999, p. 18.

56   In 1931, Trotsky wrote: 'The Italian Communist Party [...] did not take account of the full sweep of the Fascist danger'; it did not understand its 'particular traits', or the anti-proletarian mobilisation of the petty bourgeoisie; it excluded ('with the sole exception of Gramsci') 'the possibility of the Fascists' seizing power'. And he concluded: 'One must not let out of sight the fact that Italian Fascism was then a new phenomenon, and only in the process of formation; it wouldn't have been an easy task even for a more experienced party to distinguish its specific traits' ('What Next?', in Trotsky 1971, pp. 248–9).

tionary perspectives and discipline a membership that had come to politics in a context of sharp social struggles but great ideological confusion. It might be said that, in its handling of tactics, the Bordiga-led PCd'I proved immature and inadequate to this *awesome struggle on two fronts* – and such was indeed the case. But one should beware of arguing this on the basis of facile formulations, including the 'Separate from Turati and ally with him' slogan proposed by Lenin, the master of revolutionary tactics. It is enough to glance at how the PSI led by Serrati's maximalists positioned itself in the face of the bloody Fascist onslaught: a policy of passivity, resignation and 'non-resistance'; in any case, never leave the confines of legality, have the 'courage of cowardice', as Turati put it. The PSI thought that Fascism was almost certainly an ephemeral phenomenon, and instead of an organised militant response, it sought a truce with the Fascists and a 'return to normality'. This led to the shameful 'pacification agreement' that the PSI and CGL signed with Mussolini's deputies on 3 August 1921, under the auspices of Prime Minister Ivanoe Bonomi (a former Socialist) and the speaker of the Chamber of Deputies, Enrico De Nicola. It was a pact with a clearly anti-communist and anti-proletarian content, which demonstrated the complicity of both reformist and maximalist Socialists with the democratic and 'subversive' political components of the ruling class.

It might be said – and again it would be true – that Bordiga underestimated the rising strength of Italian Fascism, in the belief that the bourgeoisie would prefer to play the social-democratic card and back figures like Noske in Germany. Nor, to be sure, was it a mistake of no importance. Nevertheless, if we stick to the facts, the PCd'I under Bordiga's leadership was the only organised force in the Italian workers' movement that *really* fought against Fascism and Fascist violence. And it began the fight immediately. On 2 March 1921, little over a month after its foundation, before the anti-Fascist Arditi del popolo appeared like a meteor in the skies, the Communist Party issued the following appeal:

> The blows of bourgeois violence are showing the masses that it is necessary to abandon the dangerous illusions of reformism and to get rid of the weak-kneed preachers of a social peace that lies outside what is historically possible. The watchword of the Communist Party is to accept the struggle on the terrain to which the bourgeoisie has descended, irresistibly drawn there by the mortal crisis that is tearing it apart; to answer preparation with preparation, organisation with organisation, framework with framework, discipline with discipline, force with force, arms with arms.[57]

---

57 *Manifesti e altri documenti politici* 1922, pp. 34–5.

The PCd'I was also the only body in the workers' movement that knew how to equip itself with an underground structure (although weak) and its own military action units, in which it also accepted anarchists and syndicalists 'so long as they undertook not to be bound by other disciplinary ties in their operations'.[58] It may be – though I am not sure – that the PCd'I leadership was too rigid in its attitude to the Arditi del popolo, at least in certain cities. But it should be borne in mind that: (1) the promoters of that movement were nearly all ex-officers and maverick soldiers inspired by D'Annunzio, with a 'combat' mentality similar to that of nationalist and Fascist *arditismo*; (2) its leading lights proved to be dubious figures, here today and gone tomorrow; (3) its political programme was to restore order and democratic normality; and (4) the International was not correct in defining it as a 'popular movement with a proletarian base', since it had that characteristic in only a few places. The PCd'I did not have a closed mind to the Arditi in principle, nor did it 'repudiate' them. There were cases of joint work in some cities, involving a 'technical' division of labour. But it refused to place its members under the command of an alien organisation with an ideology and aims different from its own, and instructed those who joined the Arditi to return to the Party's military bodies. It would be superficial to leave out of account the fact that, in the situation at that time, the PCI was engaged in the difficult task of educating its members and sympathisers in a rigorous sense of discipline and military activity completely unknown in the old hyperlegalist Socialist Party. This was the main purpose in keeping comrades within the Party's own military structures.[59] However the question is still open.[60]

---

58   The difficulty of this should not be underestimated. As Tasca observed, 'the Italian people has neither revolutionary traditions nor a passion for arms. [...] The working-class militant places himself outside the law, and *feels* outside the law, as soon as he takes a pistol out of his pocket' (1972, Vol. 1, p. 192).

59   The PCI established an (illegal) Office 1 under Bruno Fortichiari in Milan. Its report to the Executive Committee of the Communist International on 14 December 1921 stated: 'It must always be borne in mind that people in our party still prefer to be revolutionary in a loud, turbulent manner and adapt with difficulty to patient and tenacious underground work'. See *Storia della sinistra comunista. Dal luglio 1921 al maggio 1922* 1997, Vol. 4, p. 165. See also Gerosa, 'Introduzione' to Bordiga 2015, Vol. 6, pp. xlviiiff., 486 ff.; Erba 2008.

60   In his relevant recent work, Alessandro Mantovani recognizes both CPI's important role and commitment in the armed struggle against Fascism, while sharply criticizing its attitude towards the Arditi del popolo, which he regards as stemming from "counterproductive doctrinarism". Indeed, revolutions cannot be politically pure, since they have always revealed new unpredictable facets. A "spontaneous proletarian response to the shortcomings of the proletarian parties in the physical fight against Fascism", the Arditi del popolo were in fact one of them. According to Mantovani, the Party's inadequate attitude towards the Arditi del popolo descended from Bordiga's somehow apolitical conception of politics (Mantovani 2019, pp. 53–79).

Another accusation made against Bordiga and the PCd'I is that they were too wary of the Alleanza del Lavoro, an inter-union alliance promoted in February 1922 by the railwaymen's union (FSI) and strictly controlled by the CGL reformists. A few points need to be considered in assessing this reproach. Months earlier, in August 1921, the PCd'I had directed to the CGL, USI and FSI a proposal for joint action of the entire working class against the bosses' offensive, around defensive goals that were far from extreme (the eight-hour day, respect for industrial and farm agreements, protection of the value of wages, guarantees of an average workers' pay for laid-off workers, and full rights of union organisation). The proposal was immediately torpedoed by the CGL, rejected by the USI, and left unanswered by the FSI. The Communists then relaunched it at an important meeting of the CGL in Verona, in November of the same year, giving voice to a growing sense of unity among the workers.

In some respects, then, but *on a different basis*, the constitution of the Alleanza del Lavoro revived the proposal for united action made by the Communists' trade-union committee – indeed, Bordiga described it as 'the first result of the intense campaign that the Communist Party has been developing since the summer of last year in favour of the united front'.[61] In this regard, the PCd'I proposed to work towards a nationwide general strike, around a set of demands both economic (defence of wage levels and work agreements) and political (resistance to the 'terrorist intervention of Fascist bands and to bullying or harassment by the state authorities');[62] and to work towards it by emphasising direct action by the working masses and the formation *from below* of unitary committees representing the different unions. For months, driven on by the Profintern in Moscow, the Communists argued for the merger of the USI and SFI with the CGL, insisting on the need to meet the employers' and Fascists' offensive with a general strike of the whole Italian proletariat and on a turn away from the Trade Union International in Amsterdam to the rival one promoted by Moscow – which the CGL refused to countenance. The reformist 'law-abiding strike' of 1–3 August, to use Turati's formulation, was seen as a means to secure a democratic coalition government, but it was called off at the very moment when it was going from strength to strength: the government

---

61   Bordiga 2015, Vol. 6, pp. 497–8.
62   See Spriano 1976, p. 196. This historian too, though hypercritical of Bordiga, has to recognise that the disastrous failure of the attempted general strikes, on 18–19 July in Piedmont and Lombardy and on 1–3 August, was entirely the fault of the reformist trade-union bureaucracies and the chronic indecision of the maximalists. 'Defeated, suffocated and repressed', Spriano writes, 'the strike of 1–3 August was the last glow of the resistance to Fascism' (1976, p. 212). And even in that action the Communists had been in the front rank.

did fall, then everyone was told to go home! If this disaster opened the gates
wide for the final advance to Fascism, there can be no doubt that the blame lay
entirely with the reformists.[63]

'At the most difficult moment', Bordiga claimed with pride, 'there was only
the Communist Party on the stage of proletarian political activity'; the PCd'I
was the sole force with a proletarian base that waged a serious fight against
Fascism.[64] Proof of this was that, a few months after its installation, the demo-
Fascist government headed by Mussolini decided to unleash its 'great blow
against communism'. On 3 February 1923, Amadeo Bordiga was arrested together with 5,000 other comrades, the most prominent among them being Communist regional secretaries and union cadres. It was a veritable manhunt, perfectly coordinated by the police and the Fascist squads. Terracini wrote to the
PCd'I organisation in the United States:

> Our party is not bending or giving way. A quarter of its number have
> been arrested, the links of its organisation broken, the voice of its press
> smothered, its branches dissolved, its leader, Comrade Bordiga, removed,
> its members threatened with death and torture. Yet the Communist Party
> of Italy has already resumed its functions and started work again.[65]

Nevertheless, it was a sudden and terrible blow. To escape arrest and persecu-
tion, more than 100,000 working-class Communists and sympathisers took the
road of emigration. And although, at the end of the year, after a brilliant self-
defence that further enhanced his prestige,[66] Bordiga was released along with
other PCd'I leaders by a judiciary not yet enthralled to the Fascists, the active Party membership was down to no more than 9,000 and its organisational
structure severely mangled.[67]

---

63   It should be noted, however, that in an article written in the heat of the moment Bordiga
     maintained that the strike had not been a failure: it had been badly prepared and 'broken
     off by those in the leadership of it'; and 'despite the Fascist bravado (the order to put an
     end to the strike) and the Socialist cowardice, the proletariat is standing on its feet: the
     proletariat is not beaten'. See Bordiga 2017, Vol. 7, pp. 214–16.
64   Bordiga 2017, Vol. 7, p. 550. Bordiga's proud claim is understandable, but we should not
     forget that groups of anarchists and some rank-and-file Socialist Party militants were also
     in the forefront of some important clashes with Fascist forces.
65   Spriano 1976, p. 260. Terracini's letter was published in the North-American newspaper
     'Alba nuova', March 17, 1923.
66   The details can be read in: *Il processo ai comunisti italiani* 1924, Rome: Libreria editrice del
     PCI.
67   A second proof of our thesis is that, out of 4,671 sentenced by the special courts of the
     Fascist regime, 4,030 (nearly 90 percent) would be Communist activists, largely below the
     age of 30.

As to interpretations of Fascism, the one that Bordiga progressively refined continued to be the most solid in Italy and internationally, and it is no accident that it was he who gave the main report on the phenomenon at both the fourth and fifth congresses of the Communist International. Whereas for Gramsci Fascism was an expression of the agrarian bourgeoisie[68] (in conflict with the industrial bourgeoisie) and was attributable to Italy's backwardness, Bordiga argued: 'It is not an organisation of agrarian interests opposed to those of industrial capitalism [...]. Fascism is a large and unified movement of the ruling class', capable of taking advantage of 'all particular and local interests of different groups of agricultural and industrial employers'. Whereas Gramsci highlighted its anti-democratic character, and in 1924, after the assassination of Matteotti, proposed a united front of all democratic anti-Fascist forces (the so-called Aventine opposition, which proved bankrupt), Bordiga insisted that Fascism lay on a continuum with bourgeois democracy and was helped to power in every way by bourgeois-democratic forces and liberal-democratic state apparatuses. Whereas for Radek, 'the Fascists represented the petty bourgeoisie', which had come to power with bourgeois support and would 'now be required to carry out the programme not of the petty bourgeoisie, but of capitalism', rendering Fascism 'the weakest of Europe's counter-revolutionary powers';[69] for Bordiga, it was the expression of the 'big bourgeoisie [...], big capitalists of industry, the banks, commerce, and big landowners', and its mass base comprised large numbers of 'discontented' from small to middle bourgeois strata, especially intellectual bourgeois youth; and the fact that the Fascists were 'excellently organised and firm in their views' and had a leader of 'great political dexterity' meant that it could 'be foreseen that the Fascist government w[ould] be far from unstable.' Whereas for Gramsci the key for reading Fascism was essentially Italian, for Bordiga it was an integral part of the international offensive of the bourgeoisie, and it was not excluded that it would gain a foothold in various ways in other countries. It is true that Bordiga exaggerated, and *made a mistake*, in predicting that Fascism would be 'liberal and democratic'; but he neither exaggerated nor made a mistake in writing off the democratic opposition to Fascism as inconsistent and hypocritical, and in arguing that 'for the struggle against Fascism we can count only on the proletarian revolutionary

---

68   See Togliatti 1969a, p. 102. One even finds in Gramsci this astounding idea: 'A movement like Fascism, *which has no roots in the economy*, which is the result of social decomposition, asserts itself only through individual violence and systematic terror' (Gramsci 1971, p. 163, emphases added). For Gramsci's theoretical oscillations on the phenomenon of Fascism, see De Felice 1972, pp. 176 ff.; and Salvadori 1973, pp. 330 ff.

69   Riddell (ed.) 2012, p. 389. Zinoviev, too, defined Fascism as 'truly a petty-bourgeois phenomenon' (Riddell (ed.) 2012, p. 1051).

International'. Perhaps Bordiga exaggerated in denying that there was anything
new about Fascism at an intellectual level. But in his report to the Fifth Congress of the International (2 July 1924), he described with considerable acumen
its novelty at a political-organisational level, highlighting its modernity and its
complex political and social manoeuvring. Let us hear what he said:

> Fascism [...] deploys a new factor that the old parties completely lacked,
> a *powerful fighting apparatus* – powerful both as a political organisation
> and as a military organisation. This shows that in the present grave crisis
> of capitalism the state apparatus is *no longer sufficient* to defend the bour-
> geoisie; it must be complemented with a well organised party that works
> throughout the country, endeavouring to find points of support among
> the middle layers and perhaps even to draw closer to certain layers of the
> working class. During this crisis, the bourgeoisie can confront the loom-
> ing revolution only through *the mobilisation of non-bourgeois classes*.
>   What is the relationship between Fascism and the proletariat? Fas-
> cism is by its nature an anti-socialist and therefore anti-proletarian move-
> ment. [...] But it would be wrong to identify it mechanically with tradi-
> tional right-wing reaction: with the state of siege, its regime of terror, its
> emergency laws, its banning of revolutionary organisations. Fascism goes
> farther than that. It is a more *modern*, more sophisticated, movement,
> which seeks at the same time to gain influence among the proletarian
> masses. For that purpose, it unhesitatingly takes over the principles of
> trade-union organisation. It tries to establish economic workers' organ-
> isations. [...]
>   Of course, the Fascist union movement differs from the true union
> movement on a very characteristic point: it recruits not only among the
> ranks of the working class but in those of all classes, since in reality it is a
> profession-based form of organisation. It aims to create parallel organisa-
> tions of the workers and the employers, on the basis of class collaboration.
>   So, we have reached a point at which Fascism and democracy meet up.
> Fascism essentially repeats the old game of the left-bourgeois parties and
> social democracy: that is, it calls the proletariat to a *civil truce*.[70]

---

70   *Quaderni internazionalisti* 1992, pp. 244–5 (emphases added). Elsewhere Bordiga speaks
     of Fascism as 'a synthesis of the two methods of bourgeois rule'. If there is a recurrent lim-
     itation in all of Bordiga's analyses of Fascism, it is his scant attention to the disorganising
     impact of Fascist terrorist violence on the working classes. It would be childish to reduce
     Fascism to the violence of its bands, but – though understandable for propagandistic and
     psychological reasons – there is no need to exaggerate in the opposite direction.

5   The PCd'I and the International

On 2 July 1924, when Bordiga gave his important report on Fascism to the Fifth Congress of the Communist International, it was already a year since the Moscow Executive had divested him of his position of authority in the PCd'I leadership at the time when he was languishing in prison. This paradox says much about Bordiga's high profile during the key years of the International, in whose life he participated intensely, in the conviction that the revolutionary struggle of the Italian Communists and the international revolution had a common destiny.

Lenin himself saw to it that Bordiga took part in the Second Congress, reserving for him a 'warm, affectionate welcome'.[71] Bordiga was only a guest, but he intervened several times in the debates to express his radical, general disagreement with the Italian reformists, who had been received in Moscow with quite undeserved honours. He was responsible for one of the 21 conditions of affiliation to the International – the only one not proposed by the Bolsheviks – which was designed to make it as difficult as possible for disguised reformists to join its ranks. Bordiga participated openly and actively in the second, fourth and fifth congresses, spurning any kind of tactical subterfuge when differences emerged with the authoritative leadership of the International. Out of discipline, he agreed to yield to more than one decision he did not share, earning from Zinoviev the title 'soldier of the revolution'. And he continued to do so until he saw a danger of complete deviation from the founding principles of Marxist communism. The Russian Revolution, Bolshevism and the International had been decisive in the formation of Bordiga and the Communist Left in Italy. This would again be apparent after the Second World War. But if we consider the history of the International and the revolutionary cycle from 1917 to 1923 as a totality, the reverse is also true: Bordiga, the PCd'I and the Italian workers' movement were a living part of the gigantic effort of millions of exploited and hundreds of thousands of Communist militants to open the way to a new era – to the revolutionisation of capitalist political, economic and social relations.

Although the Second Congress marked the highpoint of Bordiga's convergence with the positions of the Comintern Executive, even there he had a dispute with Lenin over the question of revolutionary parliamentarism or antiparliamentarism. This gave rise to a legend that the ever sharper divergence between Bordiga and the PCd'I with the Comintern leadership centred on the

---

71   See Pannunzio 1921, pp. 13–14.

issue of participation in elections versus abstention in principle. Togliatti and his associates constructed and fuelled this legend in order to caricature the theoretical and political battle against the superstition, illusions and deception of democratic elections, which was integral to the preparatory work for the foundation of the PCd'I. But the reality was different.

It might be said that Bordiga contributed to the legend with some of his attitudes, some of his writings that presented matters in absolute, general tones as a question of principle, and his own insistence on abstentionism as a distinctive characteristic of his group. Bordiga himself recognised as much after the Second World War.[72] Nevertheless, whenever he was forced to choose between his abstentionist convictions and the party discipline involved in electoral participation – first in the PSI, then in the Communist Party – he had no hesitation: 'Centralisation is the cornerstone of our theoretical and practical method; I am a centralist first, an abstentionist second.'[73] That was the case in 1919, when he was head of the Communist Abstentionist Fraction in the PSI; the next year, at the Second Congress in Moscow; in 1921 in the leadership of the PCd'I, when he held that it was right to participate in elections in a period of political reaction; and in 1924, when he was in the opposition in the PCd'I and, apart from supporting participation in the general elections (which he described as a 'most felicitous political act'), he forced through the return of Communist deputies to parliament against the 'ridiculous period of withdrawal' (the Aventine) decided by the new centrist leadership.[74] After the Second World War, too, Bordiga agreed to work with the International Communist Party, a majority of which thought it appropriate to stand in the elections of June 1946 and April 1948, albeit with thoroughly meagre results. If we wish to be objective, therefore,

---

72   In his 'Introduzione' to Bordiga 2011, Vol. 4 (Note 40), Gerosa quotes a passage that Bordiga wrote in 1953: 'The over-general posing of the question made things difficult, and all Italian Communists fell back on the decision of the Second Congress in Moscow (June 1920), where the solution was clear: in principle, everyone against parliamentarism; in tactics, we should settle neither on participation always and everywhere, nor on a boycott always and everywhere'. His speech 'on the question of parliamentarism' at the Second Congress of the Communist International did indeed have the defect of posing things 'too generally', although Lenin's reply was hardly one of his most memorable.

73   Bordiga 2014, Vol. 5, p. 205.

74   Not by chance was the speech marking the return to parliament entrusted to the Bordigist Luigi Repossi, and it was a tough speech that resulted in an attempted Fascist assault on him. Looking back on those years in December 1951, in his 'Tesi caratteristiche del Partito', Bordiga wrote: 'The opposition within the Communist Party of Italy was based not on the theses of abstentionism but on other fundamental questions': quoted in Saggioro 2010, p. 363.

it has to be accepted that *in his actions* – which sometimes openly contradict strained polemical formulations that suggest the opposite – Amadeo Bordiga remained consistent with the position he expressed in Moscow in 1920: participation or non-participation in elections was a *secondary* issue, which should not 'give rise to a split in the communist movement'. The abstentionism of Bordiga and the Italian Communist Left was motivated with arguments that had to do with the Party's tactics and effectiveness of action; they did not see it as the matter of principle that the Dutch *Tribune* group, the council communists and much of the KPD in Germany, the IWW in the United States, and the Shop Stewards movement in Britain claimed it to be.[75] It would not acquire this status of principle until the early 1950s. Later, in the mid-1960s, Bordiga drew the following balance sheet:

A great effort was made to show him [the 'colossal Marxist' Lenin] the historical potency of bourgeois parliamentarism: he had all the elements of the picture before his eyes, but he held that our subversive power would have been greater. Trotsky too had lived in the West, but he did not see the question well either. We went into parliaments to knock them down. They are still standing, and the people we sent there reason like [...] classical social democrats. Of all the vigour that Lenin restored to Marxism, nothing has remained firm. To attribute blame has no importance in Marxist terms; but Lenin, too, has his share of the responsibility.[76]

So, what were the *fundamental* questions on which the differences that Bordiga and his closest comrades had with the International took shape, matured and finally exploded? A first, immediate answer is: the conception of the united front, the workers' government, and unification of the PCd'I and PSI. We need to explore a deeper layer, however, which in my view concerns *the relationship*

---

75   In a hitherto unpublished text, Mantovani recalls an episode at the Second Congress when Bordiga, aware of the diversity of viewpoints, asked the delegates from 'western left parties' *not* to vote for the theses on parliamentarism presented by the Italian Communist Fraction. Mantovani considers Bordiga to have been the 'furthest to the right' of the 'western leftists', insofar as he was the most committed to reconciling the western left and bolshevism. *Intorno alla storia del Partito comunista internazionalista di D. Erba. È tutta un'altra storia ... o forse no*, November 2012, p. 9. I share this judgement.

76   Bordiga 1972 [1964], p. 85. See also Gerosa's 'Introduzione' to Bordiga 2011, Vol. 4, pp. 25 ff., where it is noted that at the Second Congress even Bukharin – usually the most polemical against Bordiga – recognised that he was nine-tenths in agreement with him on the subject.

between party and class, perhaps also *the conception of the revolutionary process itself*, the leftward material and ideological shift of the masses (and not only the workers) at that historical juncture, and how the process should have been encouraged and 'guided'.

It is well known that at the Third Congress (June–July 1921) the Comintern leadership addressed the growing difficulties of the revolutionary movement in Europe, with the defeats in Hungary, Germany (the *Märzaktion*), Italy (the ending of the factory occupations for reasons of exhaustion) and other countries (France, Yugoslavia, Czechoslovakia). Trotsky's main report and final speech contain some highly expressive sentences:

> The revolution is not so docile, nor so domesticated as to be led on a leash, as we once imagined. The revolution has its own fluctuations, its own crises and its own favourable conjunctures. [...] Now we see and feel that we are not so immediately near to the goal, to the conquest of power, to the world revolution. Back in 1919 we said to ourselves: 'It is a question of months.' Now we can say: 'It is perhaps a question of years.'[77]

It should be noted that the art of bourgeois counter-revolution reached its height at the point when the capitalist social order faced its greatest peril. The Communist parties had to grapple with the first signs of a capitalist economic recovery, with the 'great capacity for resistance' of the capitalist system, and with the emergence of new and more aggressive reactionary forces, including the militarised Freikorps in Germany and the Fascist squads in Italy. They also had to reckon with the continuing vitality of the reformist parties, which still commanded the allegiance of the great majority of workers in Britain, the United States, Belgium, the Netherlands, Denmark and Sweden, and retained considerable influence in Germany, Italy and Austria, despite their open complicity with the anti-proletarian policies of the capitalist class and its repressive apparatuses, and their primary responsibility for them in a number of cases, as in Germany where 20,000 workers were killed between 1919 and 1921 under social-democratic governments. The situation in Europe, as well as the 'absolute necessity' for Russia to take measures in favour of the peasantry after the end of the terrible civil war, to 'stimulate the recovery of its productive forces' by means of the New Economic Policy (NEP), led the leadership of the International to conceive a 'new tactic', the tactic of the united front.

---

77   Trotsky 1973, p. 284.

Lenin, as usual, did not gild the pill. On the NEP he said: 'So long as there is no revolution in other countries, only agreement with the peasantry can save the socialist revolution in Russia.'[78] As to the united front, he presented it as a *provisional retreat*, to prepare a new offensive when the right conditions had been created. Given the skilful, tenacious resistance of the bourgeoisie internationally and in individual countries, and given the limited proletarian forces directly organised and influenced by the communists, the obligatory next step was 'to win over the majority of the proletariat, the exploited and the rural workers'. 'To the masses!', 'A workers' united front!': these were the slogans of the Third Congress. The efforts of the Communist parties, especially where they were supported by only a small minority of the proletariat, were to be concentrated in this direction, since otherwise there could be no victorious offensive. This meant fighting the reformists and semi-reformists for influence over the broad masses, not on the terrain of 'theoretical discussions about democracy and dictatorship' but through full participation in struggles for intermediate or partial objectives, for 'the question of bread, of wages, of clothes and homes for the workers'.[79]

The directives of the Third Congress were mandatory and modelled themselves on the open letter sent by the Communist VKPD in Germany to the Social Democrats of the SPD and the centrists of the USPD. For the 'new tactic', though aimed at the mass of the proletariat, whether organised or not in the reformist parties, involved a different relationship with those parties as such, and hence with their leaderships: one of inviting/challenging them to unity of action, to a workers' united front and anti-bourgeois initiatives. At the top of the International, however, interpretations of the united front were by no means unanimous, either in 1921 or in later years. For Bukharin, it was a tactic that could be changed in 24 hours, to be inserted into the 'theory of the offensive', whereas for Radek it was a long-term programme that served defensive needs. Zinoviev, elastic as ever, let it be understood that it could be a directive for a long period, or even for a whole epoch. And in the writings of Lenin and Trotsky the terms tactic and strategy seem interchangeable with reference to it. Equally uncertain is the meaning of the 'workers' government' (or 'workers' and peasants' government') that was supposed to concretise the 'new tactic'. Hence the casuistic discussion at the Fourth Congress: it could be a social-democratic or left-liberal government (to be voted for, if necessary); it could be

---

78   'Report on the Substitution of a Tax in Kind for the Surplus-Grain Appropriation System', in Lenin 1965, p. 215.

79   See 'Extracts from a Manifesto of the ECCI on the Conclusion of the Third Comintern Congress' (17 July 1921), in Degras (ed.) 1956, pp. 282–3.

a social-democratic/communist coalition government, imposed by struggle or by parliamentary agreements; and it could be a cautiously worded equivalent of the dictatorship of the proletariat. In fact, after the collapse of the coalition governments in Saxony and Thuringia in October 1923, that is what it was: 'for the Comintern, the watchword of a workers' and farmers' government is the watchword of the dictatorship of the proletariat'. Thus, in little more than two years from the Third Congress, the united front tactic was reconfigured, or downgraded, into a simple 'method of agitation or revolutionary mass mobilisation', to be used *from below* against the leaders of counter-revolutionary social democracy, who in some texts are already described as 'the left wing of Fascism'.[80] I recall this contradictory picture because, in historical reconstructions of those crucial years, there is often a tendency to simplify by placing the International on one side, as a single correct pole of thought and action, and the infantile extremist Bordiga on the other side, embodying the path of error and conflated with all other left critics of the united front policy. Things were more complicated.

Bordiga and the PCd'I during the period of his leadership did not oppose the slogan 'To the masses!' or the tactic of the united front. Indeed, *they called for both*. Only they had specific interpretations of their own, differing both from KPD rejectionists and from critics in the French Communist Party with a syndicalist background. Terracini spoke at the Third Congress on behalf of the PCd'I, with an exaggerated insistence on final goals, a naïve objection to any emphasis on the majority of the working class, an advocacy of small parties almost over larger ones, an even more dubious opposition between general struggles (peculiar to communists) and partial actions (left to reformists), and an abstract reference to the 'theory of the offensive'. All these positions fell to pieces under the axe of Lenin's reply. On the other hand, the Rome Theses – drafted by Bordiga personally the following year – were a serious effort to present to the whole International a way of reading the question of tactics that was different, if only in part, from that of the Third Congress. For this reason, they dealt only in code with the Italian situation, and there was certainly something anomalous about them since the Rome Congress in March 1922 was the first real PCd'I congress, and the Party and the Italian working class were then facing the (underestimated) danger of a Fascist takeover. The anomaly is explained by the fact that the declared aim of the Theses was to help establish on clearly defined tracks 'complex fundamental

---

80   Hajek 1972; Hajek, 'La discussione sul fronte unico e la rivoluzione mancata in Germania', in Hajek 1980, pp. 441–63.

problems of concern to the whole of the international communist movement'. Bordiga would later say that he had conceived them in this way as 'a measure against the triumphant return of the democratic cretinism that we [had] detected'.[81]

The Rome Theses and the Draft Theses for the Fourth Congress of the Communist International were presented as *general* theses, in the sense that they referred neither to a particular country nor to a particular political period. Bordiga took on board the aim of winning the majority of the working class, although he restricted this to 'the majority of organised workers'. Similarly, he recognised that in order to win influence over the masses, proselytism and propaganda for the party's ideas were insufficient; 'the party', he emphasised, 'must participate in every action to which the proletariat is driven by its economic condition'. Indeed, he took this as the key terrain for the 'perspective of the united front': whether other proletarian organisations (labour unions) rejected the communist appeal for united action, or whether they accepted it and, in the course of the action, demonstrated their inconsistencies or cowardice. For in either case the communist party would increase its influence over the masses, showing itself to be the proletarian force most dedicated to class struggle and unity and 'the best prepared to lead the proletarian cause to victory' – all the more so if 'the communist party has previously waged a campaign on the basis of precise proposals that guarantee the success of the struggle', and if it has been 'in the front ranks of the common action'. It should be noted that, in accepting and proposing with conviction the labour united front, Bordiga corrected his own previous stand in 1919 against unification of the existing union federations in Italy.[82] And as we saw earlier with regard to the Alleanza del Lavoro, the united front of labour unions necessarily involved *political* tasks as well, both direct (the defence of workers) and indirect (pressure on the government). Also consistent with the formulations of the International was Bordiga's point that polemics in the union movement and the political arena should always make a distinction between leaders and the masses to which they referred. Besides, it was fairly obvious that the basic framework of the Rome Theses and the Draft Theses was not a theory of 'the offensive at all costs' à la Terracini. Bordiga, it is good to recall, defended from beginning to end the adoption of NEP and the reasons that Lenin gave for it, and he was less optimistic than various members of the ECCI about the prospects in Italy and internationally.

---

81   This expression comes from a letter of 1961 to B. Bibbi: see Saggioro 2014, p. 102.
82   See Bordiga's article 'L'errore dell'unità proletaria', in Bordiga 2010, Vol. 3, pp. 208–11.

Up to this point, then, the differences between the two formulations were
a matter of shades rather than substance. With regard to the workers' government, however, the Rome Theses – and Bordiga's statements in later years –
were more outright in their rejection, and it may be that Bordiga's formula
tion 'a united front in the unions but not politically' was inadequate, since
it left scope for a rejection of the political terrain altogether. But that is not
what Bordiga was proposing, in either theory or practice. What he opposed was
any political bloc or alliance with reformists or centrists – and his rejection of
that became all the more radical in the events leading up to the planned, but
abortive, fusion of the PSI and PCd'I. Let us look at this for a moment, before
returning to the Rome Theses.

The Comintern leadership, beginning with Lenin, paid great attention to
developments in Italy, considering that the situation there was close to the
decisive struggle for power. Both before and after the birth of the PCd'I, it nurtured the project of attracting the bulk of the PSI into its own ranks[83] – a project
that ended in disappointment even after the PSI, already abandoned by the
Communists at Leghorn, suffered another split in October 1922, and the break-
away Unitary Socialist Party (PSU), under the leadership of Turati, Treves and
Matteotti, came out openly and unequivocally against communism. This new
split happened because, on the eve of Mussolini's power grab, the reformists
cultivated the fantasy that they could bar his path through an alliance with the
'liberal' bourgeoisie, the very ones who for years had been preparing the ground
for him. In Moscow, Zinoviev, Radek, Bukharin and even Trotsky felt sure that,
with the hardened reformists out of the way, a fusion between the PCd'I and
the PSI was now a real possibility.

The great majority of the PCd'I, however, was of the view that in late 1922 Serrati's PSI was further to the right than two years earlier; that its basic instincts
were anti-communist; that its prestige among the workers was in steep decline
(Gramsci, too, noted this with sarcasm);[84] that its policy was one of do-nothing

83   Širinja 1970, pp. 107–29. Perhaps too much credit was given to Serrati generally in Moscow,
     although Lenin did not mince his words and described him as belonging to 'the camp of
     the international capitalists, the camp that is against us': see 'Notes of a Publicist', in Lenin
     1973, Vol. 33, p. 211.
84   'To fuse the two parties is like wanting to marry Gianduia [a figure from the *commedia
     d'arte* strongly associated with the city of Turin] to the king of Peru, which does not have a
     king, nor therefore a king's daughter', Gramsci said on 15 November 1922 at the Fourth Con-
     gress, at a meeting between the PCd'I delegation and the Comintern commission dealing
     with the Italian question. A remark the previous year about the PSI was no less biting:
     'Today the communists realize that through their energetic action they are being saved
     from the grave, released from the embrace of a corpse'. *L'Ordine Nuovo*, 1/82, 23 March 1921.

passivity in the face of attacks by bourgeois reaction; that its only difference with the reformists was over the parliamentary tactic to follow; and that any fusion with it would therefore cause grave damage to the PCd'I, introducing friendships, relations, methods and ties between members and party organs and the 'social-democrats and opportunists'. If the aim was to win over workers still under the influence of the PSI – and Bordiga was in complete agreement with that – then it would be better to provide for Socialists to join the PCd'I on an individual basis, while working to eliminate the PSI, rather than to give it undeserved credit through a fusion with the PCd'I. The prestige of the Communists in the working class was anyway growing, even though the scope of their political action was very limited and the advent of Fascism marked a defeat for the whole working-class movement.[85]

These were the terms in which 'the Italian question' was posed and amply discussed at the Fourth Congress of the International, held in Moscow between 5 November and 5 December 1922. The Comintern Executive would not budge, however, insisting that it was necessary to work for a fusion between the two parties and to constitute the Unified Communist Party of Italy by March of the following year. Bordiga and the PCd'I yielded: they thought it right that the Executive should prevail over the national sections. But Bordiga did not agree to conduct the talks with the PSI himself. In the end, the long-awaited fusion process broke down – not only, or perhaps mainly, because of passive resistance by the PCd'I leadership, but because a will to defend the Socialists' 'identity' and autonomy, together with a refusal to burn the bridges to the reformists, proved more powerful in the PSI, beginning with its parliamentary group.[86] Zinoviev and the Comintern Executive had dreamed of netting 15–20,000 Socialists, but in the end only 2,000 joined the PCd'I in 1924, and most of those were from the peasantry rather than the proletariat. It may be that in Moscow they underestimated either the stubborn anti-communism of most of the maximalists or the disorientation and demoralisation among the working class, which was certainly not pushing to join the PCd'I *en masse* (that had failed to materialise once before, in much more favourable circumstances, at Leghorn).

So, Bordiga and the PCd'I (excluding the Tasca-Graziadei tendency) spurned not only fusion but an alliance with the PSI ('social democracy'). Their reasons were twofold: it would undermine the *total independence* of the Communist Party, which was the strongest guarantee for the key moments of the revolutionary confrontation, and whose membership selection had reached

---

85   Bordiga 2017, Vol. 7, pp. 543 ff.
86   See Spriano 1976, ch. XVII.

a 'wonderful degree of perfection' that should in no way be compromised; and it would hinder, rather than favour, the formation of a left-wing or social-democratic government because of the radical aversion of the bourgeoisie to the communists. Any such agreement with the PSI, Bordiga argued, would demoralise the most combative section of the proletariat, since an alliance with it in government would mean renouncing a large part of the Party's own programme. The dispute provisionally ended in a compromise. In the middle of 1922, the PCd'I agreed to propagandise for a 'workers' government' as a 'pseudonym for the dictatorship of the proletariat' (a formulation allowed by Zinoviev); and the Comintern Executive agreed that local committees of the Alleanza del Lavoro should be considered as if they were organs of the 'united workers' front against Fascism' called for by the International – which was not the case. It is true, however, partly in conflict with the official position that sharply distinguished between a trade-union front and a political front, the PCd'I representatives maintained contact with the representatives of other political forces. This happened systematically at meetings of the Alleanza del Lavoro, as it did in a series of clashes (especially those of a mass character, in Parma and Ancona, for example) with the Fascists; it happened in the preparation of the unitary committee in Rome, on 6 July 1921, where for the first time the Arditi del Popolo paraded in an initiative against Fascism called by the Camera del Lavoro that Lenin considered of great importance as an example of 'conquest of majority' by the communists; it happened at other moments of intense party activity not related to the unions; and it even happened that Gramsci – not unknown to everyone, I think – tried unsuccessfully to make contact with D'Annunzio![87]

All this involved only a temporary compromise, however, for a combination of opposite reasons. Bordiga and the various European leftists could point to the 'open letter' and the Berlin conference of the three Internationals in April 1922 – which had been unsuccessful despite the concessions made by the Moscow delegation – as well as to the considerable difficulties in putting together a trade-union united front with results favourable to the working class and the communists. The Comintern Executive, for its part, had set its sights on

---

87   See the long 'Relazione del Partito comunista d'Italia al IV congresso dell'Internazionale comunista, ottobre 1922', in Bordiga 2017, Vol. 7, pp. 373–448, complete with 24 attachments; Lenin 1971c, pp. 386, 388, 392; Caprioglio 1962, pp. 263–74. On 23 July 1922, Bordiga wrote to Zinoviev (with a copy to Gramsci): 'Our party has everywhere taken the initiative in the anti-Fascist struggle, pushing into action the Alleanza del Lavoro committees which, in quite a lot of towns, have been enlarged with representatives of organisations of every political tendency' (Bordiga 2017, Vol. 7, p. 187).

a political front and on fusion between the PCd'I and PSI, fearing that the series of major and minor defeats might lead to isolation of the communists from a proletariat which, though on the defensive, was still highly combative and capable of being won to a revolutionary perspective.

The Fascist breakthrough sharpened these concerns and fuelled a torrent of accusations against Bordiga and the PCd'I at the Fourth Congress: maximalism, sectarianism, sterile radicalism, absurd division between economics and politics, syndicalism, infantilism, even an openness to putschist and terrorist ideas. Among all the exaggerated criticisms, some of them truly malevolent, three would actually seem to identify weak points in Bordiga's approach. First, according to Bukharin, 'he does not look for the living logic but wants to establish the unknown. He wants to list all the hypotheses and to draw up all kinds of cautious measures so as not to make a mistake'. Second, Radek: 'he has the illusion that the party is totally independent of historical situations'. Third – more moderate – Zinoviev, who accused Bordiga and the Italian party of being 'a little doctrinaire'. What is common to these criticisms, then, is the notion that Bordiga was increasingly focused on the party's role in developing the revolutionary process; some passages in the Rome Theses (especially Theses 24 and 25) even cast it as a *demiurge*, suggesting that it should do everything to anticipate the process and to control it rationally in accordance with a predefined set of tactical schemes. In this account, the analysis of actual 'situations' – that is, of the development of class conflicts – is no longer the basis for the party's action and the decisions it takes on the ground in line with its principles, programme and strategy; rather, it is downgraded to a merely 'integrative' (that is, subsidiary) element in the solution of tactical problems, a mere means of *verifying* 'the correctness of the programmatic approach' and of the party's predictions.

Furthermore, immediately after the foundation of the PCd'I, Bordiga had begun to outline a conception of the party as *organ of the class*, not simply a part or vanguard of it. This differed from what we might call the classical vision of the party – beginning with Marx's formulation, 'the workers who organise themselves into a class, and hence into a political party' – and suggested more and more emphatically that the party was *constitutive* of the class. This was a different, though not counterposed, way of regarding the party. For although there was nothing new in Bordiga's rejection of a static, statistical-sociological conception of class, or his insistence that the founding of the party was an indispensable moment in the passage from class in itself to class for itself, he introduced a new emphasis that 'the class *presupposes* the party', that the revolutionary action of the class 'lies in the *delegation* of its leadership to the party', that 'the class lives, struggles, advances and triumphs, thanks to the work

of the forces it has clarified within the travails of history', that 'it is not possible
to speak of real class action [...] where it is not in the presence of the party'.[88]
This set of emphases already configured a vision of the party-class relationship
in which the first term of the inseparable binomial dominates the second – or
(after the Second World War) comes to *absorb* it, or even to *cancel* it as a fundamental revolutionary factor. The party, Bordiga stated a number of times, is
at once the *product* of class conflict and a *factor* in it, but in a series of steps
the factor-element comes to tower over the product-element. This explains a
formulation in the theses on tactics about the primary need to preserve the
party from risks and dangers, as if, by occupying a rigorously protected, aseptic
space, it can ignore the development of class initiatives as a whole, the party-
class relationship, and the overall state of the conflict between the classes. It
also explains a certain abstractness in Bordiga's thinking about what the party
ought to be, in the sense that it is more doctrinal than historically determinate,
as we can see from many of his writings on tactics during that period. It certainly cannot be said that the dangers he saw on the horizon were imaginary –
quite the contrary! Some passages sound truly prophetic,[89] and some judgements – on the PSI, for example – are factually indisputable. But his view of
the revolutionary process remains conditioned, *limited*, as if he were surveying
an extensive battlefield through the slit of a castle rampart and seeing only part
of the rival armies from too great a distance. Bordiga himself outlined, and only
outlined, this limitation forty years later:

> The total revolutionary bankruptcy in the western capitalist countries is
> demonstrating how the use made of Lenin's slogan of 'flexibility' degen-
> erated into an abuse analogous to what Lenin imputed at the time to
> Kautsky & Co. We have seen the historical reasons why Lenin thought
> it more urgent *in that turn* to fight against the dangers of *rigidity* rather
> those of excessive *flexibility*. We who dared to overestimate the dangers of
> flexibility, and of excessive concessions to it, were concerned for the sal-
> vation of the *party*; Lenin was attending to the salvation of the *European*

---

88   Bordiga 2014, Vol. 5, pp. 207–14, 356–69.
89   To quote but one: 'We foresee that, if this method of limitless tactical oscillations and
      ad hoc convergences between opposed political parties were to continue, the results of
      bloody experiences of class struggle would be gradually demolished, and the outcome
      would not be brilliant successes but dissipation of the revolutionary energies of the pro-
      letariat, with the danger that opportunism once more celebrates its saturnalia over the
      defeat of the revolution, painting its forces as uncertain and hesitant on the road to Dam-
      ascus' (Bordiga 2015, Vol. 6, p. 506).

revolution, without which the Russian revolution was lost. We can say that his vision was great, but those who blabber about a revolutionary Russia today cannot dare to do so.[90]

Here is the point – 'we face graver questions than the struggle against the centrists' – which opposes Lenin to Terracini. His eyes are fixed on the salvation of the European, Russian and international revolution, as the affairs of the peoples of the East increasingly occupy his attention; we must 'learn to prepare the revolution', by studying things from the beginning. The gaze of Lenin and the best of bolshevism is directed at the *totality* of the revolutionary process. It is within that process, not above or outside it, that the salvation or ruin of the party will be decided. And in recognising the greatness of this vision, Bordiga seems to admit its superiority over his concern to highlight the mere 'salvation of the party', almost as an independent entity. This limitation also explains the discrepancy we have noted between Bordiga's deep attachment to the principles of Marxism and his insufficient capacity to link up guiding principles, programme, strategy and tactics in a *party initiative* fully corresponding to the tumultuous, indeed unpredictable, developments in the class struggle. Party action is conceived and implemented with a certain imbalance towards propaganda, and conversely with perhaps an overemphasis on the trade-union side of the class struggle. 'Concrete analysis of the concrete situation' once again proves lacking, at least in part. But this inadequacy in relation to 'the immense tasks facing us' was due also to the limitations of the 'general development of the communist movement internationally', and could certainly not be overcome by returning to the situation before the birth of the PCd'I.[91]

Two other sources of friction with some of the Bolshevik leaders of the Comintern were less conspicuous in the Twenties: the role of the middle layers and the anticolonial struggle. As we shall see, both re-emerged with great force after the Second World War. Let us simply note here that at the fourth Congress of the Comintern there was truth in the Turkish delegate Orhan's polemical point that PCd'I policies, like those of other western parties, did not set out the tasks of communists in the colonies.[92] One need only look at the page on the colonial question in its Action Programme of October 1922: although the peoples of Libya had been resisting Italian colonialism for years, it merely stated that since the proletariat and capitalism were absent in the

90   Bordiga 1973 [1960], p. 97.
91   See 'Amadeo Bordiga a dieci anni dalla sua scomparsa', *Il lavoratore comunista*, January–February 1981.
92   See Riddell (ed.) 2012, p. 723.

African colonies 'class struggle, or anyway social struggle, [was] an impossibility' there. It was a rather surprising assertion,[93] which would be corrected in
the period after 1945.

6   1926: In Lyons against Gramsci, in Moscow against Stalin

The year 1923 was a critical, and terrible, one for the workers' movement, for
the Communist International, for the PCd'I, and for Bordiga. In Germany and
much of Eastern Europe, the revolutionary upsurge of the masses continued
under the whip of material deprivation, even gaining fresh vigour. However,
the European bourgeoisies put up tenacious resistance and resorted to openly
terrorist methods. Exploiting opposed nationalisms and the reactionary mobilisation of sizeable middle layers, they also profited from social and political
divisions within the proletariat to force it to yield. The decisive battle took place
in Germany, ending in the dramatic failure of the 'workers' government' in
Saxony and Thuringia and an equally unsuccessful attempt to organise a coun-
trywide workers' uprising.[94] In November, the KPD – which had meanwhile
tilted dangerously toward 'national bolshevism' – was declared an illegal organisation. Heavy defeats were also suffered in Bulgaria and Poland, at the hands
of the Zankov and Dmowski-Korfanty governments respectively. In the same
time period (October–November), the split in the Norwegian Labour Party
played itself out. And – as if that were not enough – on 15 December, after two
months of working-class unrest and the outbreak of the 'scissors crisis', Stalin
and Zinoviev gave the green light for the pernicious campaign against Trotsky
and 'Trotskyism',[95] the formal beginning of the break-up of the Bolshevik leading group.
    In Italy things were certainly no better. As we have seen, 1923 was the year
of the first Mussolini government's 'anti-communist round-up', which severely
hit the party's activity, and also the year in which the International (in June)
used its authority to rejig the PCd'I executive committee. Bordiga, still in prison,

---

93   Bordiga 2017, Vol. 7, pp. 484–5. To be frank, it is not the only such statement. In the Report
       on Fascism to the Fifth Comintern Congress, for example, we read: 'As the necessary his-
       torical and social preconditions are lacking today, we cannot speak seriously today of
       Italian imperialism' (Quaderni internazionalisti 1992, p. 260). This is all the more aston-
       ishing if we compare it with the notion of a 'Serb imperialism' (Bordiga 2015, Vol. 6,
       p. 139).
94   See Broué 2005, Ch. 41.
95   See Carr 1954, Ch. 13.

was removed from the body, together with Terracini, Grieco and Repossi, on the grounds that they had thwarted the fusion with the PSI. Tasca and Volta, from the right minority of the party, joined the committee instead, presenting themselves as the wing of the PCd'I that correctly interpreted and 'sincerely' applied the decisions of the International. It was the first time that the leaders of a national section had been directly appointed by Moscow. Bordiga's leadership was even held partly responsible for the advent of Fascism, and the attacks on it were so bitter that they undermined the unity of the leading group that had emerged from the Leghorn congress.

Bordiga, who had actually resigned from the executive in March, responded with a manifesto-like document that fully defended the line followed in Italy. The PCd'I could not be blamed for the success of the bourgeois and Fascist offensive, he argued, because it was only a minority force within the proletariat and did not have the capacity to launch a revolutionary offensive. Under the circumstances, it could only 'ensure the greatest possible defensive unity of the proletariat' – and it did this with its own forces alone not in a sectarian spirit but out of necessity. In fact, it offered 'to struggle together with workers from any political party'. An understanding with the maximalists was impossible because of how they had behaved since Leghorn, which had been in keeping with the whole of their past history. Still less had a fusion been on the cards. An attempt to force this through at any price, against the reality on the ground, would have meant *liquidating* the party 'as it had arisen at Leghorn and fought not without honour for more than two years'; it would have meant pushing 'the Italian proletariat back into the dull, lifeless maximalist "centrism" with all its contemptible chatter'. Bordiga did not stop at that. He feared that the International's reckless new tactical moves might lead it to alter the programme, principles and organisational criteria on which the international communist party had come into being in 1919–20. With a lucid eye, he sensed that the danger – of which there were as yet only signs – might before long become more serious and eventually give rise to a full-blown crisis in the international arena. For this reason, he proposed that the Italian party should hold a deep discussion on the differences with the International, providing adequate information to a membership that had hitherto been little apprised of developments. And he asked the International to examine more carefully the results of the Party's activity and to 'draw a complete balance-sheet of it'.[96]

---

96 Il 'Manifesto' di Bordiga. A tutti i compagni del Partito comunista d'Italia (written in prison in Summer 1923), http://www.quinterna.org/archivio/1921_1923/manifesto_bordiga.htm.

Gramsci categorically refused to endorse the document drafted by Bordiga. In contrast to other members of the PCd'I majority, who did no more than suggest minor modifications, he declared his disagreement with the substance of the manifesto, claiming that he had 'a different conception of the party, of its function, and of the relations it should establish with the masses who did not belong to any party and with the population in general'. Little by little, he spelled out a whole series of criticisms of Bordiga, the most radical being that he theorised the party outside 'the dialectical process in which the spontaneous movement of the revolutionary masses and the centre's will to organize and lead converged with each other'. Unlike Togliatti, Terracini, Fortichiari, Scoccimarro, Leonetti and Tresso, he thought no compromise was possible because of Bordiga's 'deep conviction that he was right'. In the end, according to Gramsci, he aimed to make the PCd'I 'the potential centre for all the left forces that might develop internationally', whereas the course of the International in tactical matters was valid and should replace the existing direction of the CP: 'Amadeo takes the viewpoint of an international minority. We should take the viewpoint of a national majority.'

In a deft, intense campaign that he waged without scruple between Spring 1923 and Spring 1924, Gramsci managed to isolate Bordiga from nearly all the components of the Party's initial leadership group and to prevent the publication of his manifesto. He did this by playing on the major difficulties facing the party, and on the doubts that these difficulties and the tensions with the International had generated about the correctness of the line that Bordiga had been pursuing. More: he suggested to the Moscow Executive a reorganisation of the party from abroad, with new elements chosen on the authority of the International, since 'in the present conditions [...] Amadeo would not have much difficulty in polarising the great majority of the party around himself'. So, the task of winning the party to make of it 'a great mass party', rather than 'a sickly minority movement', had to be initiated from above by its Central Committee.[97] He was not wrong. At the first open clash between the two increasingly opposed positions, which took place at the clandestine national conference in Como on 18 May 1924, a clear majority of the branch delegates (35 branch secretaries out of 45, and four interregional secretaries out of five) sided with Bordiga. Scarcely four percent of the branch delegates expressed agreement with the centre, but Gramsci refused to give up and warned that Bordiga's attitude was similar to that of Trotsky. Trotsky was creating disquiet in the ranks of the Russian party and the international workers' movement, and threatened to 'put in danger the

---

97   Togliatti 1969a, pp. 150–7, 175, 190–7, 266, 273.

very conquests of the revolution'.[98] Similarly, he claimed that Bordiga's behaviour – for example, in refusing to stand in the 1924 general elections (while fully agreeing that the PCd'I should participate in them) – threatened to have a demoralising effect on a membership already suffering the blows of Fascist repression.

The offensive conducted by the tightly knit group around Gramsci, who took over as general secretary in August 1924, became increasingly aggressive in the run-up to the third clandestine congress of the PCd'I, held in Lyons, France from 20 to 26 January 1926. Thanks in part to heavy irregularities that the Left noted and denounced,[99] the centre bloc in the party obtained an overwhelming majority of votes (90.8 percent) for its theses. The party's *new general line*, impelled decisively by Gramsci, had been formulated in the period between Como and Lyons. Of course, it showed traces of the 'revolutionary ebb-tide that had begun at the end of 1923, that is, after the defeat of the revolutionary movement in Germany', an ebb that assumed international proportions in the following years.[100] Objectively, it may be regarded as a line of retreat, in a context that the International, too, defined as a relative stabilisation of the world capitalist system. But Gramsci, convinced that a crisis of Italian Fascism was imminent and that the stabilisation itself was highly superficial, launched the party's new line with a famous voluntarist rallying-cry against the 'pessimism' that was 'oppressing even the most experienced and responsible militants' and

---

98   'Lo stato operaio': 'Gramsci's Intervention at the Como Conference', 29 May 1924, in Gramsci 1978, p. 350. The first of Gramsci's and Togliatti's explicit attacks on Trotsky date from May 1924. On 6 February 1925, Gramsci further claimed that the division in the Communist Party was 'splitting the [Russian] state' and 'producing a counter-revolutionary movement', although he added that 'this does not mean that Trotsky is a counter-revolutionary' ('Report to the Central Committee: 6 February 1925', in Gramsci 1978, p. 392). At the international level, a false idea has spread that Gramsci was somehow sympathetic to Trotsky, but in reality he always stood shoulder to shoulder with the anti-Trotsky bloc, merely expressing a hope – at the point when Trotsky's defeat was certain – that the bloc would not 'win a crushing victory' and would 'avoid excessive measures' (Gramsci 1978, p. 583). Even so, this timid reservation led to a break in personal relations with Togliatti. Subsequently, Togliatti himself attributed to Gramsci an extremely violent expression in relation to Trotsky: 'he is the whore of Fascism' (Togliatti 1971, p. 36). We do not know whether he really said that, but it is certain that in October 1926 Gramsci showed complete solidarity with the Stalinised majority of the Comintern leadership and the policy of 'bolshevisation' of parties belonging to the International.

99   The most spectacular was the automatic attribution of the votes of absent delegates to the motion proposed by the centre. A total of 60–70 comrades took part in the Lyon Congress, almost the same as the number present at the Como Conference.

100   Trotsky 1970, p. 679.

represented 'a great danger – perhaps the gravest at the present moment'.[101] He
would later bitterly recognise how much his reading of the Italian and international situation had been detached from reality.

What are the main points in Gramsci's analysis underpinning the turn at
the Lyons Congress? First, he emphasised the weak, backward and incomplete
character of the development of capitalism in Italy, as well as the fact that
agriculture in the south had largely remained stuck in a feudal, or anyway
pre-capitalist, stage. He further systematically highlighted the contradictions
within the Italian bourgeoisie and the frictions with Fascism, which he still saw
as a mainly agrarian phenomenon with a mass base in the urban petty bourgeoisie. Gramsci also paid great attention to what differentiated democratic
forces in Italy from the most aggressively reactionary. The historical-political
framework that he gradually theorised in a series of contributions was that
of an *unfinished bourgeois revolution*, which the proletariat and the Communist Party had both a national and class task of bringing to completion. The
growing importance he attached to the questions of the peasantry and the
Mezzogiorno – which eventually became paramount in his thinking – may be
explained in terms of this context.

It is therefore not surprising that the PCd'I conducted itself in the way that
it did in the first major test of the new line and the new leadership: that is, the
'Aventine secession' of June 1924–January 1925, when democratic and liberal
forces boycotted parliament in protest at the murder of the reformist Socialist
Party secretary, Giacomo Matteotti. In contrast to the position of Bordiga, who
was hostile to any opening to bourgeois political forces on the grounds that
it would compromise the political autonomy of the proletariat, the Communist Party tagged along behind the initiative.[102] It eventually withdrew from it
only when the danger increased that – given the immobility and nullity of the
Aventine bloc – the Maximalists would steal a march on the Communists by
quitting it first. It was no accident that the vigorous speech marking the return
to parliament was entrusted to Luigi Repossi, a worker associated with Bordiga's positions, who braved physical threats from Fascist deputies and accused
the Mussolini government of being a bunch of killers.

Despite continual zig-zags, the sharp change of line illustrated by the Aventine episode was evident. Complying with Comintern tactical directives, and in
some degree nudging them *to the right*, the political activity of the PCd'I now

---

101   Gramsci, 'Against Pessimism', 15 March 1924, in Gramsci 1978, p. 298.
102   Gramsci characterised the Aventine bloc as 'a representative and executive body of all
       anti-Fascist currents, which appeals for direct action by the Italian people': see 'L'Anti-
       parlamento', *L'Unità*, 11 November 1924.

seemed geared to the establishment of stable relations with all the democratic forces in Italian society, not only with those that took the workers' movement as their point of reference. In a series of ever quickening steps, the final goal was resituated at the end of a *gradual, stage-by-stage evolution from democracy to socialism*, in which the party's essential task was 'winning the majority of workers and *transforming in molecular fashion the bases of the democratic state*'.[103] Gramsci underlined the importance of 'intermediate solutions of general political problems', considering them a 'bridge towards the party's slogans' for agitation among the mass base of counter-revolutionary parties and forces, a means of winning ever larger non-proletarian strata to the cause of socialism. There is not yet an explicit renunciation of socialist revolution and revolutionary insurrection; that would come after the Second World War, when the PCI was redefined under Togliatti's leadership as 'a party of a new type'. But already the central role of politics as ad hoc manoeuvring, with the theme of hegemony to the fore, paves the way for the idea of a gradual conquest of power through the growing influence of the Communist Party in the proletariat, and over the peasantry, broad layers of intellectuals, and society as a whole. According to the theses put forward by Gramsci and Togliatti and adopted at the Lyons Congress, such an evolution was possible because 'the proletariat appears as the only element which by its nature has a unificatory function, capable of coordinating the whole of society', and whose programme is alone capable of guaranteeing the unity of the state.[104] In several respects, the Theses maintained so many areas of ambiguity that they could subsequently be interpreted in almost opposite ways. It is beyond doubt, however, that in the name of loyalty to the International and its strategic and tactical line, they marked a *first, decisive step towards nationalisation of the communist proletarian movement in Italy and the triumph of reformism in its ranks*. This was true in two senses. The Lyons Theses projected the international economic-political framework and the international vicissitudes of the communist movement onto an ever more distant horizon; and, conversely, they emphasised the national-democratic responsibilities of the working class to the nation as a whole, by assigning it the task to complete the bourgeois revolution in accord with the forces of democracy.

---

103 These assertions are contained in Gramsci's report of August 1924 to the Central Committee, in which he maintained that 'the Fascist regime is *dying* [...] because it has actually helped to accelerate the crisis of the middle classes initiated after the War' (Gramsci 1978, pp. 367, 353). Cf. Spriano 1976, pp. 398–9.

104 'The Italian Situation and the Tasks of the PCI', in Gramsci 1978, p. 471. In his semi-official autobiography, Togliatti claims to have actually drafted the theses himself: see Togliatti 1953, p. 152.

In Lyons, the forces of the Left around Bordiga, much depleted by a number of defections, found themselves in great difficulty after a harsh defeat at the political-organisational level. In July 1925 the Left had been forced to disband the Comitato d'Intesa (Liaison Commitee),[105] the body that some of its members had created to oppose in an organised manner the party's drift into opportunism. It was at this juncture that the centrist leadership introduced into the Party's internal life the inquisitorial tones typical of Stalinism. Members of the Left were singled out and branded as 'worthless', 'morally corrupt' or 'guilty of political degeneration and moral bankruptcy'; it was suggested that they were 'agents provocateurs' or had a 'counter-revolutionary potential'. A second problem was the fact that the new levy of party members in 1924–25, following the disintegration of Socialist Party forces, had a low level of training and political maturity (as Togliatti himself admitted) and often belonged to non-proletarian social layers such as tenant-farmers and artisans;[106] clearly this was not the best audience for the theses of the Left. A final likely handicap was Bordiga's refusal to take on any position in the party, despite his having been its most prestigious leader.[107] The centrists were able to present this conduct as a kind of sabotage of the Party's activity.

Nevertheless, in Lyons, in a seven-hour speech that he gave without a single sheet of notes, Bordiga forcefully replied to Gramsci's equally long and demanding report. We do not have a written record of what he said, but there is reason to believe that he did not deviate from the statements contained in full in this anthology. What differentiates the theses of the Left from those of Gramsci and Togliatti is above all their framing of Italian events in the international context: 'The political and organisational situation within our party cannot be definitively resolved within a national framework, because the solution depends on the development of the internal situation and policy of the entire

---

105   Quaderni internazionalisti 1996. The creation of the Committee was an initiative of O. Damen, B. Fortichiari, F. Gullo, O. Perrone, L. Repossi and C. Venegoni. Bordiga initially refused to join it, but later entered it only to help bring about its dissolution.

106   See Spriano 1976, p. 489, which estimates the PCI card-carrying membership in late 1925 at 27–28,000. For contrasting interpretations of the Lyons Congress and the two previous years, see also Peregalli and Saggioro 1998, Ch. 1; De Clementi 1971, Ch. 8; Cortesi (ed.) 1999, pp. 155 ff.; Galli 1976, pp. 121 ff.; Martinelli 1977, Ch. 6; and Basile and Leni 2014, Ch. 30. The only available official account of the congress is the one that Gramsci gave to R. Ravagnan, published in *L'Unità*, 24 February 1926, and now in Gramsci, 1972, pp. 651–71.

107   As late as 22 March 1925, protected by a large force of stewards against Fascist disturbances, Bordiga spoke on the role of the middle classes to a cheering audience of at least three thousand at the Sforza Castle in Milan. Bruno Fortichiari, who had invited him to speak, was removed from his post as Milan party secretary as a result.

International.' This was a constant in Bordiga's positions: he closely linked the fortunes of communism in Italy with those of the international communist movement – indeed, he considered the latter to be the 'priority'.[108] The theses of the Left started from basic questions for an essentially political reason: Bordiga and his close comrades were (rightly) convinced that the danger of *unprincipled opportunism* hung over both the International and the PCd'I. That is why they dwelled so much on certain core principles, beginning with the nature of the party and its activity and tactics. The Left had already expressed itself on the Comintern's tactical directives at the Fourth and Fifth Congresses in Moscow, rejecting the perspective of a 'workers' government' and a political united front with the reformist organisations, while favouring a united front of labour unions. The document contains nothing particularly new concerning the positions of the Italian Left. I would, however, like to impress on the reader what the theses say about the 'Russian questions', because it may be compared with the themes that Bordiga would develop a few days later in Moscow at two encounters with Stalin, and with the solidly historical-materialist and internationalist method of their formulation:

The Russian question must be placed before the International for a full study. The elements of the question are as follows: according to Lenin, in the present Russian economy there is a mixture of pre-bourgeois and bourgeois elements, state capitalism and socialism. State-controlled large-scale industry is socialist to the extent that it obeys the productive imperatives of the state, which is a politically proletarian state. The distribution of its products is nonetheless accomplished in a capitalist manner; that is, through the mechanism of the competitive free market.

In principle it cannot be excluded that this system not only keep (as it in fact does) the workers in a less than flourishing economic condition that they accept out of the revolutionary consciousness they have acquired, but that it evolve in the direction of an increased extraction of surplus value through the price paid by the workers for foodstuffs and the price paid by the state and the conditions it obtains in its purchases, in concessions, in trade, and in all its relations with foreign capitalism. This is the way to pose the question of whether the socialist elements of the Russian economy are progressing or retreating, a question that also includes the technical performance and sound organisation of state industry.

---

108   At this level, notes Cortesi, 'the greatness of Bordiga is imposing' (1999, p. 31).

The construction of full socialism, extended to both production and distribution, industry and agriculture, is impossible in a single country. A progressive development of the socialist elements in the Russian economy, assuming the failure of counter-revolutionary plans based on internal factors (rich peasants, new bourgeoisie and petty-bourgeoisie) and external factors (imperialist powers), is nonetheless still possible. Whether these plans take the form of internal or external aggression or of a progressive sabotage and deflection of Russian social life and the life of the Russian state, which will lead them on a slow involution ending in a complete loss of their proletarian features – if these plans are to be thwarted, the close collaboration and contribution of all the parties of the International will be absolutely essential.

Above all it is necessary to ensure proletarian Russia and the Russian Communist Party the active and energetic support of the proletarian vanguard, particularly in the imperialist countries. Not only must any aggression be thwarted and pressure brought to bear on the bourgeois states as regards their relations with Russia, but it is necessary above all that the Russian party be assisted by its sister parties in resolving its problems. It is true that these parties have no direct experience in the problems of government, but in spite of this they will contribute to the solution of such problems by adding a revolutionary class coefficient deriving directly from the real class struggle as it unfolds in their respective countries.

As we have shown, the present relations within the Communist International are not equal to these tasks. Changes are urgently needed, above all to counter the organisational, tactical and political excesses of so-called 'bolshevisation'.

But in Lyons, the Left's polemic against centrism focused mainly on conceptions of the party, and on its tactics (in relation to the analysis of national capitalism and political developments) and its internal life.

The conception of the party developed by Gramsci and *L'Ordine Nuovo* was criticised as being at once labourist/workerist and voluntarist-elitist. On the one hand, it embedded the party in the working class as it is, 'in an economic, statistical sense', making it part of the class and requiring it – even at moments of depression and weak autonomy among the class itself – to be a mass party, in accordance with the axiom that a real communist party must in all circumstances be a mass party. On the other hand, the Gramscian conception had the voluntarist or idealist[109] features of 'an elite distinct from, and superior to, the

---

109   In Lyons, the accusations of idealism were reciprocal. For Gramsci, the Rome Theses were

other social elements making up the working class', a kind of demiurge that, by virtue of its moral and intellectual superiority, was capable of shaping the class and the whole of society. The Left rejected both these versions, seeing the communist party instead as a repository of the historical programme of the working class, a 'class organ [that] expresses the full extent of its will and initiative in the entire field of its action'. In unfavourable historical circumstances, the party may be quite limited in numbers – indeed, that is actually to be preferred, so that it keeps itself as free as possible from outside elements that corrode its revolutionary nature. Because of its selective character, it is certainly tougher and less pliable than the class, more autonomous with regard to the pressure of the class enemy. But it should never think of itself as an organism endowed with infallibility. In contrast to what Stalin was arguing in those years,[110] it was possible for the communist party to degenerate since it was not only an active force but also a *product* of historical development. And it really would degenerate if it did not give precise tactical norms for action, or *a fortiori* if it adopted 'the ghastly opportunist formula that a communist party is free to adopt any and all means and any and all methods'. To safeguard it, neither principles nor organisational measures were sufficient. Once again Bordiga insisted on the special importance of tactics: 'It is not (only) the good party that makes good tactics, but good tactics that make the good party.' And tactics can, and must, be broadly outlined in advance – a theme on which Bordiga dwelled in the Rome Theses, in a line of argument that is not altogether convincing.

The divergence with the centrist theses is clearer in the analysis of national capitalism and, in particular, its political evolution. In Bordiga's view, it is a mistake to insist on the 'insufficient development of industrial capitalism', because, despite the quantitative limits of capitalist development in Italy, political power there has for some time been solidly and entirely in the hands of the capitalist bourgeoisie. That class has had the time and means to develop 'a rich and complex tradition of government', learning to make use of both the liberal-democratic and the reactionary-Fascist method of government. Hence it would be quite wrong to imagine that there is a fundamental dualism between liberal-democratic and reactionary-Fascist forces in Italy. The former, the theses

---

'essentially inspired by the philosophy of [Benedetto] Croce', and the method of analysis peculiar to Bordiga was not the materialist method but 'the old method of conceptual dialectics peculiar to pre-Marxist and even pre-Hegelian philosophy'. On the idealist roots of Gramsci's thought, the most penetrating study is Riechers 1970.

110   In his report to the Fourteenth Congress of the Communist Party (B), held in December 1925, Stalin declared in his axiomatic style: 'Our Party does not and will not degenerate, because it is constructed in such a way that it cannot degenerate'. Bukharin, too, was captivated by the idea of the party's 'incorruptibility'.

of the Left rightly argue, have been 'protagonists of a phase of the counter-revolutionary struggle dialectically connected with the Fascist phase and decisive for the defeat of the proletariat'. It is therefore delusory, and contrary to communist principles, to conjure up an anti-parliament in the way that the centrists do; such an institution could have had no other character than that of an alliance between communists and liberal-democratic bourgeois parties, even if the aim had been to base it on workers' and farmers' committees.[111]

The clash between Left and Centre also concerned party action and discipline. Gramsci and his group attacked the Party's conduct in the early years because of its sectarianism and even 'corporatism', arguing that it had been jointly responsible for the defeat at the hands of Fascism. Bordiga fully defended it, on the grounds that, despite the party's efforts to protect its own existence and to organise a united class front, 'the defeat of the proletariat was inevitable' because of the defeatist policies of other worker-based parties and the union leaderships associated with them.

The Left regarded the centrists' overestimation of factory councils and dismissal of labour unions for the revolution as another deviation of principle, and also criticised their tactical openness to (in its view reactionary) regional autonomy. At the same time, it issued a harsh and prescient judgement on 'bolshevisation', seeing it as 'indicative of a pedestrian and inadequate application of the Russian experience. In many countries an apparatus whose selection and functioning are based on criteria that are largely artificial already tends to cause a – perhaps involuntary – paralysis of spontaneous initiatives and proletarian and class energies.' As to the formation of factions, Bordiga held that it could be neither prevented nor impeded by organisational measures, but only through a 'felicitous approach to the problems of doctrine and political action' that the class struggle placed on the agenda. If such an approach was lacking, it was both inevitable and salutary that factions should come into being to attempt to preserve the class nature of the party.

It may be the case – we have no definite evidence – that after the heavy defeat in Lyons Amadeo Bordiga pinned some hopes on the Sixth Enlarged Executive Committee meeting of the Communist International, which began

---

111   That this was not a polemical inference on Bordiga's part is shown by the fact that, after the Lyons Congress, Gramsci wrote that 'we have sought and will in all probability continue to seek a relationship of alliance' with the so-called Republican Concentration: 'We and the Republican Concentration', in Gramsci 1978, p. 572. The next year (1927), Togliatti already launched the strategy of attention to national-popular forces – a distant precursor of the 'Salerno turn' of 1944, involving national unity even with monarchists in order to 'crush Hitlerite Germany' in a war alongside the Anglo-American imperialists: see Togliatti 1969b, and Cortesi 1975, pp. 1–44.

work in Moscow on 17 February. His previous trips to Moscow for the Second, Fourth[112] and Fifth Congresses of the International had certainly not been unproductive, since they had allowed him to set out his positions at the most important gathering of all: the world assizes of the communist movement. Besides, he had become familiar with the violent attacks on Trotsky, and found it useful to establish direct contact with him and with the Russian Opposition. Zinoviev, still in office as president of the International, had been repeating for years his intention to have Bordiga in Moscow as one of the Comintern vice-presidents,[113] and Bordiga sensed that, were it not for his temporary pos-

---

112   In 1922 Bordiga travelled to Russia twice: first in June, together with the representative of the Right, Antonio Graziadei, in response to Zinoviev's request that they clear up 'misunderstandings' about differences between the PCd'I and the Comintern leadership; and again in November for the Fourth Congress. So in fact he made five trips to Moscow between 1920 (as an invitee rather than delegate to the Second Congress) and 1926. Over those years, he had important tasks such as representing the International at the congress of the French Communist Party in 1921, participating in the Comintern delegation to the conference of the Three Internationals in Berlin (in April 1922), and reporting on Fascism at both the Fourth and the Fifth Congress of the Communist International.

113   Gramsci, too, thought such a solution might be desirable. Despite his sharp clash with Bordiga, he favoured a policy of 'rehabilitating' him and getting him involved, and at the Lyons Congress he insisted that Bordiga should be on the new Central Committee. Although most reluctant, Bordiga eventually agreed to enter it along with Venegoni as representative of the Left. But he resisted Gramsci's pressure for him to join the secretariat. In the subsequent months, Gramsci drew up a proposal to send Bordiga to Moscow to regain his position on the Comintern Executive. Bordiga did not dismiss the idea, taking his time and showing some interest, but in the end, perhaps mainly because of Togliatti's opposition, nothing came of the planned transfer to Moscow (see Peregalli and Saggioro 1998, pp. 129–45). What is certain – and embarrassing for Gramsci's admirers – is the profound esteem he felt for Bordiga, a man of such value that he doubted whether even a team of three comrades could effectively replace him (Togliatti 1969a, pp. 228–9). Equally certain, and embarrassing for most of Bordiga's followers, is his great esteem for Gramsci – a 'remarkable man' (Bordiga 1972 [1964], p. 115), 'who assuredly merited all my admiration' – and the friendly feelings he had towards him until the end. Camilla Ravera testifies that the first message Bordiga sent from Ustica was the following: 'Must get Gramsci out of the hands of the Fascists, must get Gramsci out of Ustica' (in *La frazione comunista al convegno di Imola* 1971, p. 32). A strange coincidence made them meet again at Formia, where Bordiga had withdrawn to live in the house of his wife Ortensia De Meo, and where Gramsci was interned, between December 1933 and August 1935, in the clinic of Dr. Cusumano, a friend of the Bordiga family (Peregalli and Saggioro 1998, pp. 211–13). Gramsci the theorist, however, always remained for Bordiga an idealist alien to Marxism, less 'orthodox' even than Turati, 'and it's always bad when this fact is passed over in silence'. As late as 1960–61, Bordiga claimed to have used 'the most flexible acceptance of party discipline even with regard to parliamentary participation', in a 'loyal' attempt to 'draw to the Marxist camp' the Gramscian current under the spell of immediatism (Bordiga 1973 [1960], pp. 86–7). A complicated relationship, then.

ition in the Troika, he would have ended up on the same side as Trotsky. So, there was some reason to hope that the trip might prove useful. Although the Comintern presidium did not uphold his complaint against irregularities on the centrists' part in the run up to Lyons, Bordiga had the temperament and authority to secure a meeting with Stalin for the Italian delegates. Stalin had recently emerged triumphant from the Fourteenth Congress of the CPSU(B), and his involvement was almost certainly the work of Togliatti, who was worried over his own inability to counter Bordiga's arguments adequately. Bordiga, for his part, had a very long discussion with Trotsky.

The meeting between the Italian delegation and Stalin, on 22 February, centred on the 'Russian question', which just a few days earlier the CPSU(B) had asked *not* to be brought before the International. Bordiga posed the fundamental question of principle, fraught with practical implications, which he had already raised in 1921: who should discuss and decide on the prospects of socialism in Russia, the Russian party alone or the whole International? His cut and thrust at the meeting with Stalin is memorable, as is his extensive speech at the plenum of the Comintern Executive. His questions to Stalin addressed a number of very awkward issues: the Workers' Opposition in Leningrad; the concessions granted to middle peasants; the campaign against Trotsky; the disagreements that Stalin had had with Lenin on key matters such as the insurrection and the continuation of the war; what would happen in Russia if the revolution did not develop in Europe for some time longer. In a context already marked by intimidation and oppressive conformism, he was not afraid to argue that Russian questions were not 'essentially Russian' but concerned the entire international communist movement, and that the International as a whole should therefore discuss and deliberate on them.

This theme was at the heart of Bordiga's speech at the plenum on 23 February, when his challenge extended to the whole policy of the International and to the role that the Russian party played in it. 'The magnificent experience of the Russian party is precious, but *beyond that* we need something more': namely, thorough knowledge of the conditions needed to overthrow the modern parliamentary-liberal capitalist state in the countries of advanced capitalism, whose defensive capacities are superior to those of the autocratic states, and which has rather greater means to push the workers' movement in an opportunist direction. To beat such a strong and experienced adversary as the European bourgeois democracies, it was not enough for communist parties to exist: they also had to gather broad masses around them. So, Bordiga agreed with the theses adopted at the Third Congress of the International, but not with the subsequent tactical applications, which had impaired the distinctive character of the communist party and therefore its capacity to win the working masses to its cause. The responsibilities for the disaster in Germany also had to be laid at the door of the erroneous general tactical directives of the International. With regard to Russia itself, Bordiga pointed to the growing weight, and political intrusion, of the middle peasantry and NEPmen, and forcefully proposed that debate on the future of the Russian revolution should involve all national sections of the International, given also the ceaseless pressure exerted by world capitalism. He attacked bolshevisation and its mechanical claim to be spreading the 'Russian model' everywhere. He criticised the idea that organisational formulas, especially ones based on single workplaces such as factory cells, could solve the problem of revolution, since revolution was never simply a question of organisational forms. He argued that the emergence of factions and breaches of discipline should be considered not as the cause but as the symptom of a grave crisis facing the Comintern. He foresaw that the 'regime of terror' and humiliation then being established in the International – which was certainly not a revolutionary development – would aggravate the situation. His speech ended with this prescient judgement: 'The spectacle of this plenary session opens up gloomy prospects for the changes to come in the International. I shall therefore vote against the draft resolution before us'.[114]

Bordiga's intervention dominated the meeting of the Enlarged Executive. Zinoviev, Bukharin, Thälmann, Manuilsky and others could not forgo replying to him. But he did not retreat and again underlined the profound difference between the Russian state apparatus overthrown by the revolution and the apparatuses of the Western bourgeois democracies, which had been stabilised much earlier and were much stronger and more capable of steering and diverting the mobilisation of the working masses. One of the main targets of his criticism was the method of blaming particular individuals for defeats suffered by national parties, instead of assuming collective responsibility for them and attributing them to aspects of a mistaken or inadequate course of action. He also repeated the demand for a new congress of the International, to consider 'precisely the relationship between the revolutionary struggle of the world proletariat and the policies of the Russian state and the Communist Party of the Soviet Union, it being clear that the discussion of these problems should be properly prepared in all sections of the International'.[115] He did not find any allies, however. His was the only vote against. His hope of international support for his oppositional struggle came to nothing, although for some time he continued to think that a reorientation of the International was possible. Not

---

114   Peregalli and Saggioro 1998, Ch. 2.
115   Ibid., p. 125.

by chance, towards the end of his reply, he expressed a hope that 'a left-wing resistance would appear against this rightist danger': 'I do not say a faction', he clarified, 'but a resistance by forces of the left on an international scale. However, I declare frankly that such a healthy, useful and necessary reaction cannot and must not take the form of a manoeuvre or intrigue.'[116]

The grandeur of this 'powerful, though solitary, assault' on the triumphant Stalinist leadership of the Russian party and the International has been recognised by E.H. Carr and other historians. Luigi Cortesi, for example, wrote:

> The clash between Bordiga and Stalin at the Sixth Enlarged Executive of the Communist International has an impressive grandeur; it was one of the moments when a great historical problem of the present and future was identified and finally condensed with critical intelligence in a few terse lines. There are pages in the history of the movement that do not 'make politics' but construct and defend its morality. Amadeo's indomitable conduct in the dense argument with Stalin was one such page, and it was perhaps the most elevated in the history of Italian communism. It is clear that beyond this episode lies a whole process of political consciousness that most leaders of the Italian party remained outside, with disastrous consequences. I do not wish to linger over this point, but only to say that Bordiga's resistance to the tactical turns that began immediately after Leghorn should be re-examined in terms not only of engineering schemas but also of the analytic and prognostic capacities of the political leader and thinker. In this respect, a whole new reading of Bordiga remains to be done, and it may be easier after the epochal fault that has opened up between that historical period and our own.[117]

I doubt whether the term 'morality' is the most appropriate. But I am sure that if, at that terrible juncture, Bordiga managed to sustain the class critique of 'socialism in one country' and Russification of the International, it was due to a thoroughly solid attachment to the principles and cornerstones of Marxist theory that has too often been branded as doctrinaire. It may be argued – and rightly so – that Bordiga and the Italian Communist Left did not succeed in providing a 'complete organic answer' to the key questions: *where is Russia going?* and *where is the international communist movement going?* But they have the great merit that they posed such questions and provided 'the key to

---

116   Ibid., p. 124.
117   Cortesi (ed.) 1999, p. 32.

the enigma', by calling attention – beyond economic statistics on the degree of capitalist expansion – to class relations and class struggle and the ways in which these were reflected in the party.[118]

It may be argued that, however lucid their analyses and vision, Bordiga and the Italian Communist Left, like the whole of left-wing anti-Stalinism, were incapable of 'providing new strategic directions and gathering the necessary forces' to sustain them[119] – one reason for this being their schematism and tactical rigidity, or even their lack of understanding of the function of tactics. That's a fair point. But let us be clear that in 1926–27, with the defeat of the general strike in Britain and the bloody suppression of the insurrections in Shanghai and Canton,[120] a historical period was coming to an end. And let us be clear that the defeat of Bordiga was part of this general failure of the first great storming of the heavens by the international proletariat. Besides, the formation of the Italian Communist Party itself can only be understood as part of the cycle of revolution that began with the Russian October. The victors of 1926 in Lyons and Moscow were the liquidators, not the continuators, of that cycle; it is of little or no matter whether they wished it or not, whether they were aware of it or not. The stubborn resistance and counter-offensive of the capitalist system had left their mark within the communist movement.

7   The 'Dark Years' (1926–45) and the Return to the Arena

The year 1926 was a watershed: not only for the Italian Left, but also for the Bolshevik Party itself, 'violently tossed by its constitutive base'. It was 'a genuine catastrophe for the whole of the world communist movement, which faded with the same prodigious speed in decline that had marked its rise, on the wave of the Russian October, to full Marxist positions.'[121] Bordiga never attributed the catastrophe to the limitations of the Russian revolution – he always considered it an epoch-making event of exceptional historical breadth – but rather to the lack of support from the West European proletariat and the failure of the proletarian revolution to develop in the West. The depth of the catastrophe was demonstrated by the whole later course of the proletarian movement.

---

118   Quaderni del Programma comunista 1980, pp. 29–30.
119   Cortesi (ed.) 1999, p. 19.
120   On the responsibilities of the International in these two events, see Perrone 1976, pp. 41–5; Trotsky, Vujovic and Zinoviev 1977; and Isaacs 1961.
121   See [Turco] 1981, p. 17.

Against the expectations of both Bordiga and Trotsky, unfavourable external circumstances made it impossible to recapture the International, or 'bits' of it.

In Italy, agony (as Gramsci believed), Fascism dealt the knock-out blow to the Communist Party, which, following the round-ups of 1923, had already been deprived of potential working-class recruits forced into emigration. Using the pretext of an attempt on Mussolini's life by the young Anteo Zamboni, on 31 October 1926 in Bologna, the regime operated a final turn of the screw by dissolving all parties and associations opposed to it and establishing a Special Court for the Defence of the State. Thousands of arrests and detentions, targeted assassinations, bloody beatings, and attacks involving the burning and destruction of political offices, disrupted the activity of the PCd'I. At the end of the year, a third of the Party's active members were in jail, although some of them would be released within a few weeks. Gramsci, his parliamentary immunity notwithstanding, was arrested at his home in Rome together with other central leaders. Bordiga kept on the run, but was arrested on 20 November after his house in Naples was taken apart. He was confined in Ustica with several dozen senior party members, including Gramsci himself. In October 1927 he was transferred for ten months to Palermo prison, accused of attempting to escape and reconstituting the Communist Party. Eventually acquitted, he was then rearrested and detained, this time in Ponza, until 21 November 1929. In March 1930 he learned from the newspapers that he had been expelled from the party, on charges of factionalism and having 'supported, defended and adopted the positions of the Trotskyist opposition'. Despite his expulsion and isolation, he was followed everywhere by two policemen until June 1934 and even afterwards kept under surveillance.[122]

After 1926, a number of militants (mostly young workers) remained active in Italy[123] and above all Belgium and France; they gave rise to the Left Fraction of the PCd'I (in 1928), then the Communist Left Fraction (1935–45), and had

---

122   Togliatti, for his part, wrote of him in unforgettable prose: 'Bordiga today lives in Italy as a Trotskyist scoundrel, protected by the police and Fascists, hated by the workers as a traitor should be hated' (Togliatti 1971, p. 29). In reality, Bordiga had been struck off the professional register of engineers, prevented from having his own office, placed under police surveillance, and subjected to a number of Fascist provocations. From 1929 until the 1960s, he lived modestly from his profession as an engineer, the social-political dimensions of which are well documented in Gerosa and Fatica 2006.

123   In the North, Onorato Damen (one of the internationalist militants most persecuted by the Fascists), Luigi Repossi and Bruno Fortichiari were active trying to link up comrades in prison or internal exile with others at liberty but operating underground.

contacts also in Russia, the United States and Mexico. Their main press organs were *Prometeo* (1928–38), *Bilan* (1933–38) and again *Prometeo* (1943–45). There is not a straight line between the positions and activity of this group, or groups, and the experience of the PCd'I and the opposition struggle of the Italian Communist Left in the International. Nor is possible to speak of the Left current as a unitary whole, as we can see from the 'rifts, dispersion and weakness within it', its relations with other formations of the anti-Stalinist opposition, its analysis of the Spanish Civil War and practical attitude to events there, or its analysis of the Second World War and relations with the partisan and anti-Fascist movements. Further proof of this is the postwar experience, when different realities – 'Bordiga, the external fraction or fractions, the centre inside northern Italy, the internal fractions in southern Italy' – flowed into the Internationalist Communist Party 'without merging in unity'.[124] Still, there remains the heroic effort to express a militant, internationalist class position, at tragic junctures when communists, who a few years earlier had thought the beginning of the world revolution to be unstoppable, were compelled to work out a completely new orientation.[125]

Unlike these groups of comrades, Bordiga remained silent until 1944, in effect holding himself apart from their unstinting attempts to maintain a theoretical, programmatic and organisational continuity with the early PCd'I. His last public act before the long silence was a letter he wrote to Karl Korsch on 28 October 1926. At the Enlarged Executive meeting in February, Bordiga had hoped to see the birth of an international Left. But the exchange with Korsch soon brought out important areas of disagreement. For Bordiga, it was completely mistaken to write off the Russian revolution as a 'bourgeois revolution', and simplistic to argue that capitalism was expanding in Russia; rather, he saw 'new, historically unprecedented forms of class struggle' there, which needed to be analysed without schematism. Stalin's policy toward the middle classes had to be criticised and totally rejected, but it was wrong to argue that it was the only possible policy. It was also wrong to attack the Russian Opposition because it

---

124 See [Turco] 1983, p. 16. This abortive fusion reminds one of the birth of the Left and the early years of the PCd'I, when different opinions were held inside the Left on the split with the PSI, whether electoral abstention was a tactic or a principle, the national and colonial questions, and the constitution of the Liaison Committee (see Mantovani, *È tutta un'altra storia … o forse no …*, cit., p. 5).

125 See 'Bilan' 1979; *La guerra di Spagna* 2000; Corrente comunista internazionale 1984, *La sinistra comunista italiana 1927–1952*, Naples; Bourrinet 2016; *Prometeo, organo del Partito comunista internazionalista, 1943–1945* 1995. Trotsky polemicised against these groups of comrades, referring to their sectarian character and their 'passive expectancy under a cover of idealist messianism': see Trotsky 1979, p. 533.

had had to make a momentary act of submission. A true and solid international Left could arise only through complete ideological and political clarification and an adequate balance-sheet of the Comintern experience, without recourse to short-term expedients or manoeuvres. For want of such a possibility, it was as well for each opposition group to proceed in parallel with others, while remaining inside the International. There should be no concession to the developing rightist deviation in the International, but it was not the moment for splits. It was necessary to be patient and to bear injustices stoically: 'It is still possible to wait. New external events will come, and anyway I reckon that the *state of emergency* system will end in exhaustion before it has obliged us to take up provocations.'

In this conviction, which the facts would soon belie, Bordiga did not take part in the laborious effort of his old comrades-in-arms, nor did he ever refer to it subsequently. At first, perhaps, he thought it the result of impatience. But once he realised the depth of the defeat in Italy and the International, he considered it a pointless enterprise probably afflicted with extremism (which is what it was). Similarly, he saw no point in trying to put together a network of international contacts. Trotsky offered to organise his expatriation from Italy, but he rejected the idea, apparently replying that it was 'impossible to straighten the legs' of crabs.[126] As far as we know, he had no steady contact with comrades abroad and only continued to meet some comrades in Naples, including his close friend Ludovico Tarsia.

This complete detachment from the 'formal party' – insofar as there could be one in a counter-revolutionary period – and from the workers' struggles of the time points at least to a peculiar vision of the relationship between theory, programme, intervention and organisation.

A rather schematic way of relating to the tasks of the revolutionary leader hindered a link-up between the Bordiga legacy and the Fraction's legacy, as well as their harmonious involvement in the struggles of the Thirties (which were as vital as those of the period of ascent). In this partial 'fall' we see the legacy of the way in which a robust Left took shape in Italy; it objectively lacked the elements of a long 'run-in' period of preparation, such as existed in the case of the Bolshevik Party. And let us remember that that run-in was not enough for the Russian party to pass

---

126   Trotsky, A. Rosmer and M. Rosmer 1982, p. 29; Peregalli and Saggioro 1998, pp. 194–7. On
       the relationship between Bordiga/Italian Communist Left and Trotsky and Trotskyism, see
       'Partito e classe', November 1978 (with some documents unpublished in Italy).

unscathed through the counter-revolutionary cycle (the depth of which should be properly gauged before launching into retroactive miracle-obsessed reviews).[127]

Despite Bordiga's waiting posture, his spectre still hovered over the Italian party in 1937–38, provoking a series of self-criticisms on the part of its leaders that they had not combated Bordigism and Trotskyism to the end, as well as a decision by the Comintern to dissolve the whole Central Committee and replace it with a trusted Organizing Centre of its choice.[128] Even when Togliatti landed in Naples in March 1944, one of his first questions was: 'And Bordiga? What is Bordiga doing?' And when he heard the reassuring answer that he was doing nothing, he replied: 'That's impossible, try to figure it out.'[129] Bordiga was in Formia at the time, then with his sick wife in Rome facing great financial difficulties. He rejected every offer of assistance and every proposal for him to affiliate politically, until finally, towards the end of 1944, his old comrades in the Left persuaded him to return to the arena by drafting the Party's political platform and to take part in the constitution of the Internationalist Communist Party (ICP) in June–July 1945 (and the later split that issued in the Internationalist Communist Party/Programma comunista in 1952).

And so we come to the second period (1945–65) of Amadeo Bordiga's activity. It was obviously linked to the first period, but the radically different social-historical context decisively influenced the character of his activity. The years 1912–26 witnessed the incubation and then explosion of the greatest revolutionary cycle in modern history, with the Russian and European industrial proletariat and the poor peasant masses of Russia as its main protagonists. For revolutionary communists, the objective was to advance the world proletarian revolution and to ensure its victory. During those years, amid the cataclysm produced by a brigandish war for the division of the world, the Second International foundered (though only partially) and a new International, 'communist, really proletarian, really internationalist and really revolutionary' (Lenin), came into being, the international party 'of the final struggles and the final victory' (Trotsky). The Russian revolution and the Bolshevik Party were the driving

---

127   [Turco] 1981. It should be said that none of the leading exponents of the left opposition to Stalinism in the Third International, not even Trotsky, succeeded in the titanic enterprise of maintaining complete continuity with the highest precepts of the Third International. And if we are to be objective about the Italian situation, we should recall that, with much larger forces, the PCI under Togliatti's leadership withdrew substantially from the struggle in Italy (see Volumes 2 and 3 of Spriano 1976; and Red Link 2006, p. 54).

128   See Spriano 1976, Vol. 3, Ch. 13.

129   Peregalli and Saggioro 1998, p. 237.

force and guiding centre of this process, which was by no means limited to Russia. In Italy, spurred on by paroxysms of class struggle, a communist party consisting of a few tens of thousands of members took shape. For at least three years Bordiga was the undisputed political leader of this party, charis- matic, well known and held in high esteem in the whole International. Scarcely had the PCd'I seen the light of day when it faced a gruelling test: on the one hand, frontal attacks from the Fascist squads; on the other, growing disagree- ment with the leadership of the International, not least over the most suitable policy to confront the Fascists. Bordiga the political leader came out of that period heavily defeated. The extreme harshness of the defeat suffered by Bor- diga and the Italian Communist Left should be seen mainly in relation to the depth of the counter-revolutionary cycle that began in the first half of the 1920s, and which reflected the overwhelming material and ideological strength of international capitalism directed by the democratic states. While the vic- torious revolution in Russia remained isolated in the most unfavourable social environment, the construction of national sections of the Communist Interna- tional, amid difficulties in confronting the bourgeois counteroffensive, showed a fragile character due in turn to the previous cycle of development of the work- ers' movement. It is true that the revolution expanded in the East, but the gap between the proletariat of Western Europe and the oppressed masses of the colonial and semicolonial countries remained impossible to bridge in the short term. This said on the overpowering strength of the enemy forces of capital- ist international counter-revolution, we have to add that the specific form and depth of the defeat suffered by Bordiga was caused also by reason of his own errors of evaluation and his schematic vision of the revolutionary process and the role of the party within it. Defeated, amid the widespread defeat of the revolutionary movement, but with his head held high.

The second period of Bordiga's activity coincided with the period of 'myth- ical' capitalist prosperity in the West, known as the 'thirty glorious years' of postwar reconstruction and marked by high growth rates and the emergence in Europe too of the consumer society. This long period was utterly unfavour- able for the organised political activity of communists. In Italy, there was only a brief interval – March 1943 to June 1947 – when the fall of Fascism and an ensu- ing surge of agitation among workers, day-labourers and farmers in the North and South enabled the most diehard revolutionary internationalists from the PCd'I to carry out effective political work in direct contact with the masses.[130]

---

130   See Erba 2012; Saggioro 2010; and the penetrating reviews of these two books in Mantovani, *È tutta un'altra storia ... o forse no ...*, cit.; and idem, *Note a margine di "Nè con Truman
né con Stalin"*, March 2012.

Amadeo Bordiga did not share the expectations of many comrades that the new postwar period would see a revolutionary upsurge. He was also struck by their major confusion on key questions such as the historical-political conjuncture, the nature of the USSR, or the position they should have on the existing unions and their initiatives. For these reasons, he was not fully convinced that it was a good idea to resume political activity, and he never formally joined either of the organisations that emerged during those years. Indeed, as late as 1948 he reproached some comrades for wanting to constitute the party 'in advance'. In his view, preliminary work was still necessary: to straighten out 'the theory of class struggle with regard to determinants, agencies and relationships of forces'.[131] This was the essential task he set himself over the next 20 years, in a huge body of very valuable theoretical and political work that we should know and study (and encourage others to know and study). During those decades, we shall no longer find Bordiga the political leader of the 1912–26 period, but rather Bordiga the top-level Marxist theorist. Was he just a tireless riveter working on old material, as he liked to present himself with exaggerated modesty? No, he was the author of an original, not always 'orthodox', reconstruction of Marxist theory geared to the latest developments of capital, which was then engaged in completing the passage from formal domination to capital's real domination of labour and the whole of social reproduction.

In my opinion, the weakest and most ephemeral segment of this great work is the one that most of his followers consider decisive: his conception of the party and of the relationship between party and class. In this respect, his long period of complete detachment from the workers' movement could not but have been a handicap, as was the sparsity of postwar organisational experiences in which he was involved.[132] These displayed a much more pronounced distance between theory/programme and intervention/organisation than at the highpoints of the 1914–23 period and did not enable him to interact with the revival of working-class and student struggles in the 1960s. Thus, in some of Bordiga's postwar writings, the party is always considered too abstractly and in the end swallows up the class by making it disappear as the fundamental factor of the revolutionary process. Here is one typical formulation: 'What remains is the party as the actual organ that defines the class, fights for the class, governs for the class in its time, and paves the way for the end of governments and

---

131   Peregalli and Saggioro 1998, p. 252.
132   I am referring to the Internationalist Communist Party (from 1944 to 1952) and the Internationalist Communist Party/Programma comunista, later International Communist Party (from 1952 to 1966), after which his relations with comrades became less frequent also for health reasons.

classes.'[133] Similarly infertile, and in sharp contradiction to his belief that the revolution is not a question of organisational form, is his attempt to preserve the party organisation in a historically unfavourable situation, by means of new organisational recipes such as 'organic centralism' (an elusive, rather mysteri ous formula), de facto elimination of any organisational rules, anonymity, or emphasis on the faith of party members more than their capacity to understand. Equally open to criticism are his swallowing of Jacques Camatte's idealist thesis on the party as 'anticipation of the future *Gemeinwesen*', and certain polemical exaggerations regarding the total cancellation of the role of individuals in the life of society.

These weaknesses, contradictions or ingenuous contrivances do not affect the extraordinary value of the theoretical and analytic work in Bordiga's second postwar period, which he performed together with a small group of Italian and French comrades.[134] The pivotal character of this work lies in its revival of Marx's critique of political economy, as applied to the latest developments of capitalism on a world scale, and above all to the two pillars of the new world order: the 'socialist' USSR and Yankee 'super-capitalism'. It also lies in Bordiga's focus on the distinctive features of socialism and communism disfigured by anti-Marxist 'state Marxism'. It was no mean achievement to have done this in the midst of the great upswing in capitalist accumulation and the consolidation of the capitalist order sealed by the Yalta accords. This is why it is superficial, indeed unacceptable, to write off the second period (1945–65) of the life of the thinker and revolutionary militant Amadeo Bordiga, or to snub his representation of the programme of communism as if it were simply a repetition of things already said and accounted for. That is not what it is.

8   The 'Russian Question'

I cannot, of course, deal here with all the themes in Amadeo Bordiga's 20-plus volumes of writings, which, apart from repeatedly focusing in depth on the history of the workers' movement and revolutions, range from history to anthro-

---

133   'L'invarianza storica del marxismo, falsa risorsa dell'attivismo', *Sul filo del tempo*, 1953. In this vision, the working-class party almost (or without almost!) comes to be the demiurge of the history of the class and the revolution. I also find puzzling, to say the least, his idea of a 'monoclass and monoparty' revolution in the West – that is, a somehow 'pure' revolution, which takes it for granted that in the future revolutionary conjuncture there will be the proletariat on one side and the whole gamut of non-proletarian strata on the other.

134   B. Maffi, G. Bianchini, O. Perrone, S. Voute, and in the final years J. Camatte and R. Dangeville.

pology, economics to physics, the agrarian question to ecology and militarism, and the remote past of 'primitive' societies (one of the passions and interests he had in common with Marx) to the communist future. As in the selection of texts for this anthology, I shall concentrate on a few areas where Bordiga's contribution as a communist theorist was and is fundamental and in advance of his times. From this point on, postwar social developments will therefore remain somewhat in the background, since in no respect was Bordiga's experience as a political leader in the 1912–26 period repeated in the years after the Second World War. For the same reason, I will say little about Italy. Although the small group of (mostly Italian) comrades active around Bordiga after 1951–52 included some working-class nuclei, they were in effect a working group – a research community, we might say – engaged in the production and, to a limited extent, dissemination of *Programma comunista* but lacking a real field of political intervention. Their function in practice was to accompany and support the titanic effort of theoretical analysis and updating of the foundations of Marxism that was carried out almost exclusively by Bordiga – although, as we shall see, they did not always absorb the results of his labours.[135]

It is inevitable that we should begin with the complex and highly controversial 'Russian question'. Marcel van der Linden, in his broad survey of Western Marxist analyses of developments in Soviet Russia, finds that Bordiga's position stands out in three respects: his 'striving to obtain a detailed empirical insight', his understanding of it not as a post-capitalist society but as a society on the road to capitalism, and his reference to an 'idiosyncratic type of capitalism'.[136] The quantity of often detailed factual material in Bordiga's writings on Russia

---

135   In this sense, the claim of these comrades was well founded: 'Amadeo Bordiga, revolutionary militant, not solitary thinker' (supplement to *Programma comunista*, 5/1996). But I think Saggioro was also right when he wrote: 'Bordiga was loved and worshipped by most of the comrades, but he was not understood because of the great distance that lay in many respects between himself and the others. Politically, too, the aptitude for understanding and growing is strengthened through exercise of the critical spirit, but this was not favoured in Programma comunista. We have seen that it is not forcing things to say that in it there was a "ban on thinking with one's own head"' (2010, p. 221). Turco underlines a no less important aspect of Programma comunista that caused a series of organisational rifts between the 1960s and 1982: 'its inability to pass non-traumatically from the sphere of guiding principles to the practice of intervention in accordance with those principles' (1983) – essentially, that is, a pronounced weakness in politics (cf. Mantovani 2016, 'Insegna qualcosa la disgregazione del bordighismo? Commento a Benjamin Lalbat, Les bordiguistes sans Bordiga', July). Evidently, Bordiga had some responsibility for all this – and we should not forget the enormous weight that social isolation always has in structuring relations inside small militant groups and their external activity.

136   Van der Linden 2007, pp. 123–5.

is indeed impressive. They serve to support his thesis of a Russia in transition *to* capitalism, not *from* capitalism to socialism, in the context of state industrialism and a declining compromise with the peasantry paid for by the industrial proletariat.[137] This approach was methodologically bound to contest in some form, though from a position of terrible isolation, the current apologetics for the 'fatherland of socialism', a veritable myth oriented to the most combative part of the proletariat internationally, not only the workers organised in Togliatti's PCI. How can myths be debunked except by opposing the harsh reality to them? To wage such a battle, today undoubtedly won at a theoretical level but then so much against the current that it seemed quixotic, it was essential to focus rigorously – taking Marx's thought as the basis – on the distinctive characteristics of the capitalist mode of production and distribution. This was what Linden called (rightly) an 'idiosyncratic conception' of capitalism. It was also essential to explain again clearly, in the face of the monstrous mystifications of 'actual socialism', what socialism and communism really were. Liliana Grilli has faithfully and perspicaciously summarised this indefatigable effort on Bordiga's part, and I will follow her step by step. The starting point – that the Russian revolution did not take place 'against *Capital*', as Gramsci claimed, but in accordance with *Capital* – is based on a complete reconstruction of Lenin's internationalist strategy, which saw the Russian revolution as the first step in the world proletarian revolution, rather than assigning it the impossible task of immediately transforming the social-economic relations of Russia in 1917 in a socialist direction. According to Bordiga, Lenin operated in a continuum going back to Marx and Engels: he was fully aware that the revolution in Russia had a *dual character*, 'socialist in politics, capitalist in economics'. At the level of economics, all it could realistically aim to achieve was the modernisation of the Russian economy, by moving it forward from parcelised petty-commodity production in the countryside (with patriarchal residues) towards state capitalism. Despite the existence of the Soviet regime, the development of state industry should not be misleadingly dressed up as socialist (here the criticism of Trotsky is both implicit and explicit). To be sure, it was a step towards socialism, in the sense that the economy might be transformed in the future in a socialist direction, but nothing more. Grilli rightly argues that Bordiga presented, and shared, Lenin's strategy as *centred* on the promotion of socialist revolution elsewhere in the world; he felicitously combined 'great audacity in the political domain' with an 'extreme, realistic moderation in the economic domain'.

---

137   Bordiga's chief writings on the subject are contained in the following volumes: Bordiga
         1976a; Bordiga 1990; Bordiga 1975; and Bordiga 1977. Nearly all of these texts date from the
         years between 1952 and 1959.

This would be enough to clearly differentiate Bordiga's analysis and position from those of most of the Western communist left, which saw NEP as formal confirmation of the straightforwardly bourgeois nature of the Russian revolution.[138] For Bordiga defended NEP after both world wars.[139] More generally, he embraced the concept of 'slow, gradual development of the relations of production in Russia', admitting that it might pause on capitalist forms and even take 'steps back' to kindle them. What decided things positively or negatively was the course of the proletarian struggle worldwide, and in particular the victory (or retreat) of the proletarian revolution in Western Europe, where capitalism was already widely established and had laid the basis for socialist transformations in the economy. The key point in the Bolshevik internationalist strategy was the expectation of proletarian revolution in Europe. Thus, what happened in Russia is only really explicable by reference to the international context. The tension or acute contradiction in Russia between proletarian power in the hands of the Communist Party and an incipiently capitalist economic structure was sustainable for a relatively long period (Lenin speculated 10 to 20 years), but only on condition that the social revolution did not beat a retreat outside Russia – and that the Russian Communist Party was not sucked in and *nationalised* by the Russian state. This is the reason why Bordiga insisted so much in 1925–26 on 'overturning the pyramid', so that the primacy of the International over the Russian party, and of the Russian party over the Russian state, was established or re-established. That overturning did not happen. The strength of the *world* bourgeois counter-revolution was such that it forced the International into, first, a number of tactical concessions, and then into a reversal-abandonment of its original revolutionary strategy through the adoption of the theory and politics of 'socialism in one country' – a theoretical nonsense covering up a political defeat, and then a political crime. Isolated from the Western proletariat, its natural ally, the Russian proletariat was trapped by economic and social forces that the development of the Russian economy in a capitalist direction constantly fuelled, and deprived of any political autonomy

---

138   See Bongiovanni (ed.) 1975, pp. 103–72.

139   Bordiga 2015, pp. 284–7. It should be noted that he maintained this defence at the congress of the French Communist Party in Marseille in December 1921 (ibid., pp. 309 ff.), where he was officially representing the Comintern. After the Second World War, he wrote: 'It is one thing to criticise the reformism of the bourgeois state, another to fall prey to sentimental fancies and fail to see that the great forms of economy replace each other not in fits and starts but by passing through long transitional periods that it is pointless to deny or deprecate, as – in the present case – "vile commerce" was despised by the "patriarchal, old-Russian, half-aristocratic, half-peasant" spirit. The socialist task then was to introduce bourgeois commerce, calling it aloud by both its first and family names' (1976a, p. 455).

through the crushing of the Left Opposition in the Bolshevik Party. As Stalinism became the hegemonic force in the International, it managed to give a
counter-revolutionary direction to the entire workers' movement, by means
of a series of moves that began in 1926 and ended in active participation in
the second great imperialist slaughter. 'It all went together [...] with a series
of "ideological renunciations of class-antithetical positions on social, administrative, political, judicial, philosophical and religious issues", which conspired
to make of Stalinism an "open and deadly sworn enemy of the working class and
its historical path to communism".[140] Stalinism was revolutionary in performing the task of capitalist development in Russia; it was counter-revolutionary
in its adulteration of Marxist theory, its reversal of the revolutionary strategy of
the Comintern, its liquidation of genuine communists, and its donning of the
'mask of victorious socialism' to cover up its betrayal.[141]

But what actually happened to the social-economic structure of Russia
under Stalinist rule? The first part of Bordiga's answer refers to the persistence of the typical categories of a capitalist society: commodity, market, money,
profit, wage, firm. Where these are alive and kicking, there cannot be socialism.
And it is precisely with regard to these categories, particularly the firm or enterprise, that Bordiga's reconstruction is most illuminating. As he sees it, the key
aspect is not the juridical one of state or private *ownership* of the enterprise and
the means of production, but the fact that, also in self-styled socialist Russia, all
the activity of producing goods and services takes place through a multiplicity
of enterprises, that is, distinct economic units with 'proper accounting' geared
to *profitability*. Crucially, there is extraction of surplus-value, and this appropriation takes place with the aim of (capital) accumulation. State ownership
or planning changes nothing in the capitalist framework of this economy: first
of all, because the economically active state has been around for a long time
in capitalist economies, so that statised economy = socialist economy is a false
equation. Moreover, there is rather less of a really statised, fully nationalised
economy in Russia than its rulers flaunt. Much of the activity of large-scale state
industry is contracted out to small and medium-sized firms that have not been
expropriated ('that would be a crime', Stalin said). And the picture in the coun-

---

140   Grilli, 'Oltre il "mito Urss": il capitale come "forza sociale" e l'abolizione del valore', in
       Cortesi (ed.) 1999, pp. 316–17. I have been drawing on this excellent article, itself a com-
       pendium and updating of the invaluable: Grilli 1982. In these studies, Grilli notes that the
       works of Carr, Dobb, Bettelheim and (I would add) Lewin contain many useful elements
       confirming Bordiga's analysis, despite the diversity of ideological and political orienta-
       tions.
141   Bordiga 1976a, p. 47.

tryside, which Bordiga subjects to a highly accurate investigation, points even more in the same direction. There the state-run economy (*sovkhozy*) is definitely a minority phenomenon, overshadowed by cooperative management (*kolkhozy*) and small family plots (of which there are tens of millions); and none of these three forms of organising food production is socialist. The *kolkhoz* is neither fish nor fowl, comprising four social figures in one: small landowners running their own farms; wage labourers; enterprise stakeholders who receive a share of its profits; and collective landowners. Again, none of these relates to socialism. What we see, rather, is a 'sub-bourgeois' solution of the agrarian question, with a very large space for peasant individualism, especially after the campaign against the kulaks.[142]

Similarly, 'socialist planning' – the other great 'anti-capitalist' boast of Stalinist propaganda – is certainly not planning of production *ex ante*, based on physical data and geared to 'enlargement of the producers' lives' and reduction of effort. The reality is simply *ex post* registration of what has already occurred through the 'spontaneous' initiative of separate individual economic actors (enterprises), plus a mere forecasting instrument for the future based on that registration process and oriented to higher production for the sake of production. Just as little can one regard as a sign of socialism the long-sustained growth of industrial output or the rise in labour productivity due to reductions in the size of the workforce. Indeed, once again refuting official propaganda, Bordiga identifies in Russia the same historical tendency to a slowdown in output growth that can be seen in the advanced capitalist countries. The economy of the 'fatherland of socialism' also follows the typical trajectory of a young capitalism that starts out with feverish growth rates, at the expense of an 'underpaid' proletariat, and then slows down because of the general laws of capital accumulation laid bare by Marx (rising organic composition of capital, tendency of the rate of profit to fall, etc.).

In Stalin's Russia, then, there is no trace of a socialist economy that has replaced production based on value with 'anti-commodity, anti-wage and anti-enterprise' production, or is at least heading in that direction. Nor does it make any sense to speak of a 'socialist market', which is a contradiction in terms.

---

142   Bordiga observes: 'The abolition of private land-ownership is only apparent (and more so, as we shall see, in the case of housing and other property), since the state may grant concessions to cooperative entities and private families'. The only thing missing is 'alienability for money', but, if 'usufruct is perpetual and irrevocable by the state' (it suffices to pay a tax) and can 'even be passed on as an inheritance', what we have is 'the full transformation of state ownership into cooperative ownership (large kolkhoz enterprise) and private ownership (family plots and houses)'. Marx would say that 'with like relations of production, there is like form of ownership' (ibid., p. 620).

But, it may be asked, if this is a full-blown capitalist economy, where are the capitalists? Is what we see a capitalism without capitalists? Far from focusing on the state bureaucracy – which he regards as a false track – Bordiga's answer directs our attention to the enterprise. All regimes of class divided societies have had a bureaucracy. This cannot be a class that stands on its own two feet; it simply serves the dominant class in a given social-economic formation.[143] Therefore, it is necessary to look at the economic substructure, at the enterprises. It is there, in the *interest networks* thrown up by each enterprise in the radius of its own activity, that we can identify in Russia the agents of the impersonal power of capital – not only Russian but world capital, moreover, since 'Soviet' Russia is not an island entire unto itself. In Russia, the bourgeoisie in its classical form – the totality of individual private owners of enterprises – was destroyed by the revolution. But since the mechanism of enterprise commodity production was not destroyed, and since wage labour was not abolished, capital is present there in new forms[144] as the *social force that commands and exploits labour* and *appropriates labour products for the purpose of its own self-valorisation*. Although state ownership of the means of production (labelled 'socialist', no less) in large-scale industry has mystified the web of enterprise interests marked by typically capitalist 'social vampirism', that web will sooner or later come to 'admit' that it is capitalist, and to demand less complicated institutional forms so that it can function more efficiently and expeditiously. Then the confessed functionaries of capital, too, will become a more evident physical presence. The Twentieth Congress of the cpsu – Bordiga notes – was a 'huge leap' in this direction. The rest will come, including a dash by enterprises to shake off the already rather loose central controls. Well, what else happened with the advent of Gorbachev's perestroika? Where did tens of thousands appear from in a flash, eager to apply the new shibboleths of enterprise 'autonomy, self-sufficiency, self-finance and

---

143   It should be noted that Bordiga engaged in correspondence with Bruno Rizzi, author of *The Bureaucratization of the World*: see Saggioro 2014, pp. 374–84.

144   In a letter of 9 July 1951, Bordiga wrote to Onorato Damen that one should proceed 'circumspectly' with regard to 'present-day Russian society', since we are facing 'something historically new', the first case of a revolution that 'curls up on itself and disappears' (see Damen 2011, p. 56). Bordiga rejects Damen's idea that the ussr of the early Fifties is a fully developed state capitalism, 'the most organic, clearly defined and complete manifestation' of the tendency of the most advanced industrial countries toward 'ever greater state intervention', a kind of historical vanguard along that road (p. 53). For Bordiga, Russia is simply *tending* towards (full) capitalism, not the last word in capitalist development! That is why he thinks the formulation 'state industrialism', or large-scale state industrialism, is the most appropriate way to describe it.

self-management'? Which long-term processes generated the Yeltsin-era sharks of wild privatisation and sell-outs to the West, if not the 'interest networks' consolidated in decades of false socialism and perceptively identified by Bordiga?[145]

9   The Critique of Triumphant Capitalism

Bordiga's critique of 'the latest capitalism' – not Stalinist Russia, to be sure, but the triumphant capitalism of the West and its undisputed, star-spangled champion – is no less acute. As in the case of the 'Russian question', the weapons of this critique are those forged by Marx, Engels and the Marxist school. However, the uses to which Bordiga puts them are certainly original and throw open a window on the capitalism of the twenty-first century.

Bordiga's starting point, already in the late 1940s, is an investigation of the relationship between ownership and capital.[146] In those years, the revisionist vulgate was all the rage and basing itself on two pillars: a counterposition between private ownership and state ownership of the means of production, and a presentation of capital in the shape of individual capitalists (with an irresistible tendency to find goodies and baddies, enlightened progressives and diehard reactionaries). Amadeo Bordiga aimed his blows precisely at these two pillars, until they finally snapped (at a theoretical level). He began by pointing out that capital, far from being characterised by private ownership of the means of production, had abolished on a large scale private ownership rights over the instruments of production, by separating the direct producers (peasantry, artisans) from the conditions of social production. More: recent developments were involving a *divorce between ownership and capital*. More and more capital was being freed up, with the result that some capitalist firms no longer 'owned any real estate, in some cases not even a fixed headquarters or an appreciable quantity of machinery'. Conversely, Bordiga wrote, property was being 'diluted and dissimulated' or presented as the property of collective entities. The space for concessions and subcontractors was growing, as was the importance of

---

145   [Turco] 1992, which updates to December 1991 Bordiga's analysis of Russia and complements it with some general considerations on the political position of the proletariat in this 'catastrophic' process. Indeed, if there is one area that remains obscure, or insufficiently illuminated, in Bordiga's investigation, it is the evolution of the relationship between state, party and proletarian masses in Russia after the revolution, and more generally how this relationship fitted into the post-revolutionary state.

146   Bordiga 1980.

management relations in comparison with the holding of rights and capital assets. And this process clearly demonstrated that capital was more and more a *social force*, an *impersonal social power*, to which corresponded *social property* absolute possession-ownership of the social product, but not necessarily (individual) rights over the means of production. Bordiga concluded from this that capitalists, too, would increasingly have impersonal, abstract, mobile features, associated more with a generic activity of producing profits (if only future profits) than with a specific entrepreneurial activity.

The second step in Bordiga's investigation concerned the shifting centre of gravity in the capitalist class as a whole 'from productive techniques to speculative manoeuvres'. The thesis, already formulated by Lenin, that 'capitalism is becoming increasingly parasitic' should not be understood in the sense that power lies more in the hands of financial than industrial capitalists, since the separation between these figures of capital is more apparent than substantive. There is in reality a growing symbiosis of the two, which means that the largest trusts control a large number of small to medium-sized firms and eventually swallow them up, in both the national and international arenas. Lenin's thesis should be understood as follows: the tendency to parasitism implies that the maximum profit margin and maximum degree of social control move ever further from the hands of entrepreneurs producing socially useful (or at least potentially useful) innovations and more and more into the hands of speculators and speculative banditry. Insurance companies are a perfect example of financial institutions that net colossal sums of (other people's) money, which can then be invested profitably without any ties; they are a prototype of the ultimate figure of the capitalist, 'the capitalist without capital', rather as 'dialectically, modern capital is *capital without a boss*, headless'. Bordiga was speaking of the INA (Italian National Insurance Institute), but he considered its turnover child's play in comparison with the manoeuvres and institutions of the US business world. If such colossi go into the red, there nothing to fear: the loss is promptly passed on to the community by the state (do you remember the case of AIG, the American International Group, in 2008?). Decades before hedge funds and powerful tax haven circuits acquired a fundamental role in the world economy, Bordiga saw in the proliferation of what were already called 'shell companies' the expression of a basic tendency of contemporary capitalism, and looked closely at the 'network of deep international links' maintained by these 'beneficiaries from speculative corporate plans'.[147]

---

147   Bordiga 1982, pp. 67–9.

As to the welfare state and welfare economy – fashionable in Fifties America before becoming so in Europe, too – Bordiga situated the phenomenon by referring to the Malthusian theory of the 'necessity for continually rising unproductive consumption'. The increasingly parasitic character of capitalism was spilling over to its consumers, he argued, through the creation of a mass of *proletarian customers*. For now it was a question not so much of luxury consumption for the few as of a single 'indistinct mass of national consumers', forced 'to consume like imbeciles: little food, lots of supplies for fictitious needs'. The proletariat, too, was now being pushed to buy commodities that answered artificially created, useless and harmful needs, placed under the dictatorship of 'standardised consumption'. The consumerist orgy under way, peddled as the entry of the whole society into the welfare era, seemed to him to express 'the malaise of a society in disintegration'. A 'demented economy' offered the answer to this malaise by doping it with commodities, nine-tenths of which did not serve 'healthy living of the human species'. This was how the late-capitalist economy legitimised itself, by producing more and more to calm its insatiable hunger for surplus labour, and any increase in the already high productivity of labour served – instead of slashing the working day – to yank up production still further.[148] Nor was the spiral self-limiting: 'Not being able to stop the infernal pace of accumulation, this humanity, parasite of itself, burns and destroys surplus profits and surplus values in a circle of madness, and makes its conditions of existence ever more straitened and senseless.'[149]

The unstoppable spread of parasitism visible in the most recent trends was making capitalism an economy of waste. And, of course, the prime form of waste is the 'vast annihilation of efforts of human labour'. In a series of bitingly sarcastic articles on supposed natural disasters, Bordiga depicted the capitalist economy as a 'disaster economy' that structurally needed its commodity-products 'to last for as little time as possible', especially in the construction industry. It had a growing structural need for *destruction*:

The *hunger for surplus labour* not only leads to extortion from the living of so much labour-power that it shortens their existence but also turns the destruction of dead labour into a good deal, replacing still useful products

---

148   Bordiga 1976b, pp. 127–34, 154–6. At the same time, however, given that ground rent is beyond the grasp of capital, the equation: 'capitalism = high cost of bread' has not ceased to be true: see Bordiga 1979, p. 183.

149   Bordiga 1976b, p. 155. This is evident today as the explosion of wage-earners' family debt becomes a general phenomenon in the wealthiest countries.

with other living labour. Like Maramaldo,[150] capitalism, oppressor of the living, is the murderer also of the dead.[151]

The burning hunger for surplus-value, depicted by Marx in *Capital*, becomes a 'fierce hunger for disasters and destruction'. In its development, capitalism has become 'unsuited to the social function of passing on the labour of the present generation to future ones and of using the labour of past [generations] for that purpose'. Hence it loses interest in maintenance and stakes everything on gigantic construction projects. Its biggest business, the 'deal of the century', is the postwar reconstruction, and its 'superproductive weapon' is the atom bomb. Here is how Bordiga put it in 1951, when he set out a social-economic law concerning the relationship between capital and the natural environment. In some respects, he was in advance of the literature that is today all the rage:

> The most modern *high capitalism* shows serious points of recoil in the defensive struggle against the attacks of natural forces on the human species. The reasons for this are closely bound up with social class, and it is enough to reverse the advantage that comes from the progress of theoretical and applied science. But we shall seek to indict it for the fact that its atomic aims have aggravated the intensity of meteor showers and will tomorrow so provoke nature as to make the earth and its atmosphere inhabitable, and even to break its very skeleton by triggering 'chain reactions' of all the elements in the nuclear complexes. For now we shall establish an economic and social law of parallelism between the greatest efficiency in the exploitation of labour and human life, and ever less efficient rational defence against the natural environment, in the broadest sense of the term.[152]

---

150   The Italian condottiere Fabrizio Maramaldo, a ruthless mercenary and ravager, has a bad name in Italian history and popular memory for the way he murdered Francesco Ferrucci, captain of the Florentine army and his old enemy, grievously wounded and a prisoner, in 1530, violating all principles of chivalrous action in wartime.

151   Bordiga 1978, p. 37. On the declining use rate of commodities as a characteristic of late capitalism, see Mészáros 1995, although in his work the author makes no reference to Bordiga.

152   Bordiga 1978, p. 21. Today's ecological literature, however, almost never grasps the fundamental causes of the effects that it identifies and denounces; it lacks an adequate understanding of the capitalist mode of production and its evolution, and, if it deals at all with the capital-nature relationship, it almost never links it to the capital-labour and capital-human species relationships with which that is inseparably bound up.

None of this entails any kind of glorification of nature and 'the natural', nor, in my view, any concessions to anti-technologism; it simply underlines that science and technology are more and more subjugated to business speculation and the interests of the most powerful states – a clear example of this being the craze for verticalism in construction: 'capitalism is verticalist, communism will be horizontalist'.[153]

What part does the state have in this growing parasitism of the capitalist system? Above all, Bordiga insists, its function in producing welfare should not be exaggerated. For if welfare is in 'arithmetic progression', the state is in 'geometric progression'. The fact is that the state as 'cop state', 'a simpler defender of bourgeois privilege', is turning ever more 'into the coffer state', whose monetary assets 'serve to increase the accumulated wealth of the bourgeoisie, while its liabilities crush the shoulders of the proletariat. With national loans the economic servitude of the working class is reasserted. Then, if the workers actually accede to the state's senseless appeal and buy their exploiters' government bonds, their servitude is asserted for the third time over!'[154]

Fundamental, therefore, is the role of the fiscal system, state finances and public debt which is – as Marx put it – the only 'part of the so-called national wealth that actually passes into the collective ownership of modern nations'. While the public debt serves to create an asset for the capitalists and a liability for the propertyless masses, the fiscal system strikes at the working class and is an instrument for the expropriation of small producers. These are certainly not new features of capitalism. What is new, according to Bordiga, is that state debt in Italy, as in USA and Stalin's Russia, has become permanent and 'in formidable progression', with a correspondingly greater subjugation of the state to the 'high-capitalist minority' (the 20 families in large-scale Italian industry, for example). New, too, is the less and less liberal, more and more bureaucratic-totalitarian character of the democratic states. In late capitalism, there is a hypertrophy of the state, and the development of 'a militarism that outclasses those of the thousands of years of our history'. This does not mean, however, that the state swallows up capital. The opposite is true: the driving force always remains capital as a *global* social power, since 'world capital has for a century constituted a single monopolistic group'. The state, the capitalist states, are simply the machines that operate it. Hence, when they have business dealings with large companies, they systematically play the part of 'suckers'. As a rule, public utility is private big business, and private utility a public rip-off.[155]

---

153   Ibid., p. 112.
154   [Bordiga] 1992, p. 20.
155   See Bordiga 1982, *passim*.

Nor does Bordiga make any concession to the Zeitgeist in respect of a 'one class society' – that is, a gradual levelling of social conditions until everyone ends up middle class. On the basis of vast empirical research into the course of world capitalism, with particular reference to the United States, he argues that, although it is possible for capital to raise the level of average existence on a world scale, it is impossible for it to 'reduce income inequality between metropolises and colonial and vassal states, between advanced industrial areas and backward agrarian areas or areas of primordial agriculture, and above all between social classes of the same country, including the one where the prince of imperial capitalism raises its slave-dealing banner'.[156]

The best incarnation of high capitalism was obviously the 'record-breakers of America', who were in a position to advance – or even donate – to Italy and the other defeated European countries the capital they needed to restart accumulation and banish starvation: 'It isn't war, but it's still playing on death.' The billions of dollars involved in the Marshall Plan and its canned food shipments enabled the American capitalists – who kept 'our proletarian comrades of the United States' under an iron heel – to become the exploiters of the 'enslaved European masses'. If they had been self-aware, and not subdued by the defeats or stunned by the wartime slaughter, the European workers would have rejected the Marshall Plan; that would have been the only response consistent with the interests of the working classes. But that did not happen, and it was now possible to see that, with a simple time lag, the postwar reconstruction and capitalist relaunch were following the same path as the one mapped out by the super-bosses across the ocean – a path based on hypertrophied financial speculation, consumerism, debt creation, militarism, and oppression of coloured peoples. At a time when Stalin and his followers insistently talked of a 'dual market', Bordiga foresaw that the power of the single world market would inevitably make itself felt behind the 'Iron Curtain'. No long-term equilibrium was possible with the global capitalist market but only emulation and, in the end, a fight for supremacy. Again war was appearing as the keyword in the 'civilisation' of capital, particularly 'democratic super-capitalism'. 'Korea is the whole world', Bordiga wrote; 'Koreans are the proletarians of all countries', designated victims of this declining civilisation, until with the return of revolution they once more become protagonists of a new era that must make capital and its laws disappear – and with them the proletariat itself.

---

156 [Bordiga] 1992, p. 58. The studies conducted over the years by Bordiga and his comrades are collected in *Il corso del capitalismo mondiale nell'esperienza storica e nella dottrina di Marx 1750–1990* (1991).

In 1999 Liliana Grilli noted that, with his distinctive 'theory of capitalism' fully derived from Marxian political economy, Bordiga appeared more topical than he had half a century earlier. She found confirmation of this in the economic literature, where the concepts of 'denationalisation' and 'deterritorialisation' of capital, 'globalisation' of the economy, and 'networks' of supranational interests had acquired a central position.[157] The reader should judge, however, not from the (often superficial) economic literature but from the reality of world economics and politics.

10   The Revolutionary Perspective of Communism

The critique of Stalinist 'socialism' and the parallel critique of its apparent antagonist, Yankee super-capitalism, led in Bordiga to the same conclusion: *capitalism* – when it claims to be welfarist, popular, social or social-democratic, self-managing, human or even socialist – is still always governed by unchangeable laws that make it a system of exploitation and oppression of labour by the tandem of capital and the capitalist state. Contrary to what many believed in the golden age of sharply rising output and labour productivity, the historical trajectory of capitalist development did not tend to alleviate the crushing of labour, or to produce greater social equality and a broadening of democracy. Indeed, it pointed in the *opposite* direction: toward the maximum concentration and centralisation of capital, the most intense and 'rational' exploitation of labour, the greatest social polarisation, and the growing despotism of the state in so far as it was ever more subject to capital. And although regimes on both sides of the 'Iron Curtain' harped on about planning or state intervention to correct market imbalances (it was the heyday of Keynesianism), the structural contrast between productive forces and forms of production could not fail to reassert itself and would inevitably result in the explosion of large-scale crises.

---

157   Grilli 1982, pp. 340–1. Jacques Camatte argues that, in studying the present stage of capitalism and 'defining the specificity of the epoch in which rule of capital was more and more asserting itself' in the form of real domination, Bordiga deliberately held back and 'did not wish at all to innovate'; 'he sought only to be a commentator, to prove that everything had already been made explicit', and in this lay 'the tragic character of his existence' ('Bordiga e la passione del comunismo', in Bordiga 1972, pp. 3–4). Camatte puts his finger on a real contradiction, but although Bordiga was conditioned by this constant demand for invariance in revolutionary Marxism, he made his own particular use of the categories of Marx's critique of political economy in grappling with the latest new developments of capitalism and, more generally, in proposing a key for an 'anti-productivist' reading of Marx's theory.

Of course, Bordiga recognised that the revolution had undergone a tragic defeat. The counter-revolution in both East and West was celebrating its Saturnalia. Yet 'a historical cause is not lost because it is postponed to a later hearing'[158] The recovery of working class organisational strength was not just close, Bordiga warned, and there should be no illusions that revenge for the defeats was immediately on the cards. A huge earthquake had shattered the communist movement. It was necessary to begin again from the basics. Following in the wake of Marx and Engels, the aim should be to redeploy their sharp critique of political economy and to reconstruct the authentic programme of communism. Bordiga devoted powerful writings to this task, brightly illuminating what distinguished communism from capitalism and from the self-styled socialisms of yesterday and today (Russian, Chinese, Yugoslav, Vietnamese, Cuban, Venezuelan and so forth).[159]

In one of these texts, which I have selected for the anthology,[160] it is no accident that Bordiga starts from the agrarian question. Unlike the majority of 'Western Marxists', he occupied himself with it from the early 1920s on,[161] taking on board the relevant Theses of the Second Congress of the Communist International. He well knew that both collective food provision and the supply of products for industry and public services depended on the state of the agrarian economy. He also realised that in the countryside the transition to socialism involved highly complicated problems of social-economic rela-

---

158   [Bordiga] 1976a, p. 241.

159   These are the most appealing texts for authors such as Camatte and Dauvé, who like to counterpose a good Marxian Bordiga to a misguided Leninist Bordiga. See, for example, Dauvé's *Notes on Trotsky, Pannekoek, Bordiga* (2009), at www.libcom.org, which states: 'Bordiga wrote several studies on some of Marx's most important texts. In 1960 he said that the whole of Marx's work was a description of communism. This is undoubtedly the most profound comment made about Marx'. Camatte writes in similar vein: 'The whole of his work is determined by the vision of communism' (Camatte 1978, p. 169). I agree on this point, but not on the existence of two Bordigas. These authors completely disregard the epochal class confrontation necessary to arrive at socialism and communism, and the inevitably complex and tortuous social-historical road that separates capitalism from communism – or else they have a simplistic and idealised notion of that road. To describe the future communist society is not the same as to reach it, unless you imagine it is possible to get there by riding on the back of your own thought.

160   *Il programma rivoluzionario della società comunista elimina ogni forma di proprietà del suolo, degli impianti di produzione e dei prodotti del lavoro*, pp. 426–460.

161   Bordiga, 'La questione agraria (elementi marxisti del problema)', in Bordiga 2014, pp. 393–451; idem, 'Dall'economia capitalistica al comunismo', in Bordiga 2015, pp. 12–32. Loren Goldner is one of the few researchers to have underlined the central importance of the agrarian question in Bordiga's thought. 'Bordiga's idea that capitalism equals the agrarian revolution is perhaps the key to the 20th century' – see Goldner 1995, p. 83.

tions, which Stalinist revisionism addressed in Russia in a way that was upside down from the point of view of class politics. A commentary on Engels's text of 1894 allowed Bordiga to establish some solid points of reference.[162] First: peasants are an important factor in the population and in production and political power, particularly in the colonial countries. Second: landowners and bourgeois have continually sought to pit the peasantry against the proletariat, by accusing workers and communists of wishing to eliminate private property. Third: in reality, small peasant property is doomed by the very development of capitalism; its disappearance should not be regretted, because it is a form of servitude rather than liberty for the peasantry, and is less productive than large-scale capitalist agriculture and less useful to society. Fourth: understandably attracted by the mirage of owning the land they work, peasants have often opposed the workers, but nothing says that this must necessarily happen. Fifth: the proletarian perspective is not the defence of small landholdings advocated by reformist peasant parties around the world; it is the nationalisation of the land. Depending on the situation that the proletarian power inherits, the farming of nationalised land will initially take place in small family units, in collective (cooperative) forms, or in modern state enterprises. Then, a long process of technological and organisational changes will tend toward the *social management* of the land, operated by, and in the interests of, the agricultural and industrial workers as a whole – indeed, of *society* as a whole, including those who for various reasons other than privilege are unable to work. Of course, this will be a society organised on a new basis, which will no longer be that of the production of commodities and value.

To delineate the communist programme still more clearly, and not only in agriculture, Bordiga used an unpublished text by Marx on the nationalisation of the land. He drew out of it a key point: the negation of *any* form of land ownership, whether by a single individual, by associated individuals-cultivators (cooperatives, the famous Russian kolkhozes), by the state or nation, or even by society. For any form of property is in one way or another *private*, in the sense that it allocates to particular individuals, associated individuals or a particular class (and therefore to a *part* of society) the power to manage common land *for themselves*, for private interests of their own. Instead, reflecting on Marx's category of 'transfer' and then on his explicit statements in Chapter 46 of Volume Three of *Capital*, Bordiga emphasises that communism envisages not so much the abolition as the *disappearance* of any form of land ownership, even the social form of ownership by the whole society. In the theory of commun-

---

162   Engels 1990, pp. 481–502.

ism, society should become the simple *usufructuary* of the land, thoughtfully *administering* it so as to improve it and pass it on to future generations:

> Management of the land, the keystone of the entire social problem, must be directed towards the best future development of the earth's population. The *society* of living human beings can be seen to be above the limitations of states, of nations and, when it will be transformed into a 'higher organisation', of classes as well (we will not only be beyond the somewhat pedestrian opposition of 'idle classes' and 'productive classes' but also that between urban and rural, manual and intellectual productive classes, as Marx teaches). And yet this society that will present itself as an aggregation of several billion people will, in its temporal limit, represent an ever smaller portion of the 'human species', even as it grows larger due to the longer life expectancy of its members.
>
> For the first time in history, this society will voluntarily and scientifically subordinate itself to the *species*; which is to say, will organise itself in forms that best respond to the ends of future humanity.

This is the *maximum* programme of communism, which envisages that, together with the death of property, the death of capital and the end of (even collective) property-owning individualism,[163] the life of the species will have primacy over individual generations. Communism is a *life plan for the species*. Communist society will for the first time formulate such a unified plan of production and consumption based on social needs, by bringing to bear the vast body of sci-

---

163   The radical Marxist critique of bourgeois individualism (with some polemical exaggerations due perhaps to the taste for paradox for which Damen reproached Bordiga) is expressed in 'Contenuto originale del programma comunista è l'annullamento della persona singola come soggetto economico, titolare di diritti ed attore della storia', in Bordiga 1972, pp. 73–110. Equally rich in fertile suggestions is a text written in 1959, 'Commentarii dei manoscritti del 1844. Cardini del programma comunista' (ibid., pp. 111–63; the title is Camatte's, instead of the 'Programma comunista' under which it was originally published). Here Bordiga finds in the *Economic-Philosophical Manuscripts of 1844* the first complete formulation of the full communist programme regarding economic, interpersonal, sexual and moral relations, an affirmation of Marx's 'no less secular and original' social theses – 'neither God nor the State nor the family (very different from the bourgeois [conceptions] that seem to eavesdrop on them)' – and a corrosive critique of the various forms of 'crude communism'. Gerosa has rightly pointed out that Bordiga 'firmly opposed the counterposition between an early humanistic and philosophical Marx and a mature Marx the economist and sociologist of capitalism'. See *Archivio della Fondazione Amadeo Bordiga. La biblioteca, la corrispondenza, le carte di argomento politico ed urbanistico di Amadeo Bordiga* 2013, p. 88.

entific and social knowledge accumulated through human labour across space and time.[164] The communist movement, therefore, cannot but oppose any form of communalism, syndicalism or statism – since communist society will have neither classes nor state but base itself on social administration of the products of associated labour. We are talking here not only of land but of the factories and all the products of human labour, where the dead labour/living labour and fixed capital/circulating capital antitheses correspond to the property/usufruct antithesis. Bordiga foresees, however, that it will be necessary to overturn language: instead of amortisation, the constant mad renewal of plant as rapidly as possible at the expense of the proletariat, there will be *renewal* in which the primacy goes to living labour. Machinery will serve to lighten the burden for workers: it will reduce labour to the minimum necessary and make the workers' lives painless and many-sided, ceasing to be a means of profit maximisation for those who own it and leech off the labour and lives of others. The primacy will then lie with use value rather than exchange value. And there will be a *decline* of the law of value, not its perpetuation under socialism, as Joseph Stalin foresaw on the eve of his death.[165]

So, what will become of the machinery, the fixed industrial capital, 'the science and technology elaborated and deposited in the social brain', which His Majesty Capital today holds tight in its clutches? In the international communist society, this too will enter the usufruct of 'society organised in a higher form', and will be employed for the safety of the species 'against the physical necessity of nature, which will be its only adversary'. Here is Bordiga's magnificent conclusion:

> Our aim here is to draw another, no less genuine, conclusion from genuine sources that are far more valid and clear today than in the epoch of their origin. When the proletarian revolution puts an end to the squandering of science, a work of the social brain; when labour time is reduced to a minimum and becomes human joy; when the Monster of fixed capital – *CAPITAL*, this transient historical product – is raised to a human form, which does not mean *conquered* for man and for society but *abolished* –

---

164 Today this 'primacy' exists only in a private, commodified caricature – the often demented (and damaging) total dedication of mothers and fathers to *their own* children – or in the grotesque, demagogic declarations by the greatest polluters and destroyers of the soil that they have seen the light and intend to respect the land and the environment – but starting many decades from now and without any really binding commitment.

165 See Stalin 1972. Bordiga's withering reply is in Bordiga 1975.

THEN industry will behave *like the land*, once instruments such as the soil have been liberated from *any form of ownership*.

At this point, the first commentary (in Italian) on the *Grundrisse* suddenly appears.[166] Bursting headlong into the contemporary debate,[167] Bordiga pokes fun at those who suppose that Marxists are afraid of automation. We afraid? As if we expected anything else! Automation heralds the end of the capitalist law of value and surplus-value. Automated machinery today instils fear, or even terror, because it rules despotically over the labour time and lives of a humanity enslaved through the wages system and compelled to sell its labour power. This impersonal monster dominates those who have created it, being nothing other than a gigantic accumulation of 'dead' human labour, expropriated and given a metallic form. By enabling production processes to reach hitherto unknown levels of speed and continuity, it understandably appears to the working class as a destroyer of jobs, sucking up their vital energies and crushing their need for happiness. *But* the proletarian revolution can transform it into a 'redeemer',[168] snatching the 'cold monster' from the grip of capital that has made it a serial killer, and giving it 'a new human soul'. In this way, the revolution 'revives grieving generations trampled down by class systems, breaks the curse left by Science and social oppression, and tightens the bond between species knowledge gained in an awesome series of struggles and the secure well-being of *social man*, the human species, freed of misery'.[169]

Bordiga takes over Marx's category of the 'social brain' to clinch a rivet that is dear to him: technology, science, knowledge and know-how are products of social man, of the social individual (understood as a 'social body'), and are the results of the life and activity of the human species. After the long historical cycle of their private, exclusivist, class appropriation, which has never been as monopolistic as under the rule of capital, these powers of the social hand and brain operating on the forces of nature must return to the 'Immortal Social Body', that is, to the species. Their roaring development, materialised in automation, has made obsolete and absurdly parsimonious the measuring of immediate labour time, since immediate labour is no longer the principal

---

166   See 'Who's Afraid of Automation?', in this anthology, pp. 461–475.
167   It should be noted that the first small print run of Friedrich Pollock's classic *Automation.*
       Materialen zur Beurteilung der ökonomischen und sozialen Folgen, Frankfurt/Main: Euro-
       päische Verlagsanstalt, dates from 1956, and that Bordiga published his text in 1957.
168   For a number of commentators on Marx's famous fragment on machinery, however, cap-
       italism itself carries things to the point where (in Bordiga's reading) only the social revolu-
       tion can depose it: see Negri 1991.
169   Bordiga 1976b, p. 198.

agent of production. For capital, however – and this is the contradiction – such measurement remains a matter of its own life and death. Carried to an extreme, this contradiction cannot but explode. And the explosion will blow up the law of value and, in drastically reducing the working day, generate an unlimited expansion of 'time available for the species – for its material and mental development, and its harmony of delights'. For Bordiga, this text of Marx's contains 'the last judgement on market society'; for Rosdolsky it is one of 'the boldest visions attained by the human imagination';[170] and for both, the essential requirement for the judgement and the vision to become a reality is the revolutionary overthrow of the rule of capital. This will lay the ground to reduce the working day, to cut production by billions of labour hours, to disinvest capital, to raise production costs, to eradicate that pathological habit of consuming useless and harmful goods which is another aspect of the workers' social oppression, and thus to attain a level of 'underproduction', or 'drastic reduction in the output', of capital goods. Marx's Department II (production of means of consumption, particularly food) will finally gain primacy over Department I (production of means of production): 'The present-day orchestra has already cut our eardrums.'[171]

Poetry? Utopia? No, for Bordiga and his comrades in 'Programma comunista', it was a prediction and scientific description of the future communist society to which Marx devoted his whole life. And to recover that vision was the main political priority, because without revolutionary theory and the revolutionary programme any future movement would be doomed to failure. At the same time, this recovery would serve to demystify all the forms of adulterated socialism that prevailed in the 1950s in the existing international workers' movement. The road to full communism, by definition international, would be a long and arduous road: Bordiga never tired of repeating this. But the fixation on com-

---

170   Rosdolsky 1977, p. 425.
171   Bordiga 1975, p. 69. In this connection, Loren Goldner has spoken of Bordiga's 'viable, non-developmentalist Marxism', and noted that he alone in the anti-Stalinist revolutionary Left regarded the development of the productive forces in Russia as proof that the USSR was *in no way* a workers' state: see Goldner 1995, p. 80. Adam Buick, on the other hand, identifies what he considers a scientistic conception of the direction of socialism on Bordiga's part, in his faith in a 'central administration which would be the direct successor of the vanguard party' (1987). The role envisaged for the mass of the proletariat after the revolution does indeed remain a weak point in Bordiga's 'construction'. Lenin clearly expressed the necessity that the entire working population should be actively involved 'in all *state* affairs and in all the complex problems of abolishing capitalism' (Lenin 1966, p. 25). Similarly, Rosa Luxemburg maintained that there could be socialism only on the basis of the broadest organised activity of the mass of the proletariat.

munism also served to delineate the programme of immediate revolutionary changes in the postwar countries of mature capitalism, with a view to a new attack on the capitalist order driven by a great crisis that was sure to come 'by 1975'.[172] Bordiga saw himself as merely hammering home old formulas, renewing and updating the programme of the Manifesto of 1848 that reflected a context of 'dual revolution' decidedly outdated in Italy, Europe and the West in the 1950s. The reader can judge from the following how much the new programme (drafted in May 1953) was *in advance* of the times, and how it aimed to untie knots that would become ever more tangled in later decades and would have to be cut all the more decisively as the years went by.

Here is a list of such demands:

a)   'Disinvestment of capital', namely, destination of a far smaller part of the product to instrumental rather than consumer goods.

b)   'Raising the costs of production' to be able to give higher pay for less labour-time, as long as wage-market-money continue to exist.

c)   'Drastic reduction of the working day', at least to half the current hours, absorbing unemployment and antisocial activities.

d)   Once the volume of production has been reduced with a plan of 'underproduction' that concentrates production in the most necessary areas, 'authoritarian control of consumption', combating the fashionable advertising of useless-damaging-luxury goods, and forcefully abolishing activities devoted to reactionary psychological propaganda.

e)   Rapid 'breaking of the limits of enterprise', with the transferral of authority not of the personnel but of the materials of labour, moving towards a new plan of consumption.

f)   'Rapid abolition of social security of a mercantile type', to replace it with the social alimentation of non-workers, up to an initial minimum.

g)   'Stopping the construction' of houses and workplaces around the large, and also the small, cities, as a first step towards the population's uniform

---

172   See the letter to Umberto Terracini of 4 March 1969, quoted in Saggioro 2014, pp. 205–6. The first significant crisis of the postwar years did indeed break out in 1974, but it did not have the cataclysmic character predicted by Bordiga. From the point of view of Marxist method, his claim to foresee the precise moment of a general crisis of capitalism is rather curious, as is the schema mapping the subsequent revolutionary upsurge on the basis of the previous revolutionary cycle (albeit with Continental Europe now as the driving force, and Stalin's industrialised Russia as part of a second wave). The latter is particularly curious if we consider Bordiga's attention to the entry of newly independent countries onto the world market, both as fields for the development of young capitalisms and as arenas for the class struggle of the exploited masses.

distribution in the countryside. Prohibition of useless traffic to reduce traffic jams, speed and volume.

h)   'Resolute struggle against professional specialisation' and the social division of labour, with the abolition of careers and titles.

i)   Obvious immediate measures, closer to the political ones, to make schools, the press, all the means of the diffusion of information, and the network of shows and entertainment subject to the communist state.

The Russian question or 'socialism in one country'; critique of the hyper-developed and ultra-militarist democratic imperialism of the United States, Britain and their allies (including Italy's 'narrow-gauge' imperialism, against which he ceaselessly railed); reconstruction of the full programme of Marxist communism: Bordiga's vast postwar labours did not end there. Overcoming the reservations he expressed in the Twenties about the positions of Lenin and the Second Comintern Congress, and making up for his obvious delays in addressing the theme after the Second World War too, Bordiga began to focus in the early 1950s on the incandescent awakening of the coloured peoples.[173] While the proletarian revolution had suffered defeats in Europe and shrivelled almost to vanishing point in Russia, it was drawing in huge new forces in the East. It would therefore have been an absurdity, indeed a form of desertion, to ignore the formidable waves of anti-feudal civil wars that were sweeping away decrepit institutions of oppression, or the national independence wars that were giving US-European imperialism a hard time. What was happening in the countries dominated and controlled by the old and new imperialism was a 'genuine social revolution', albeit one limited to the establishment of bourgeois social relations. This national agrarian revolution was bringing closer the emancipation of the proletariat and the exploited through the formation of a modern industrial system, through their involvement in revolutionary movements that in many cases marked their entry into world history as active players, and through the blows inflicted on the world capitalist order. Bordiga rejected the dressing up of these movements as socialist or communist, but he held that the battle should be unreservedly supported:

The revolution is under way and it is our revolution: that was the message that Amadeo sent out to the thin lines of militants who had remained

---

173   In 'La Piattaforma Politica del Partito' (1945), there is still only a hasty and dismissive reference to the question in Point 21, where it is subsumed under the 'partial and contingent survival of demands for national liberation' and the 'liquidation of islands of feudalism and other such wreckage of history' (*Per l'organica sistemazione dei principi comunisti*, cit., p. 123). A definitely erroneous position.

in the breach against the current of the times; it was not a consolatory message, but the accurate reading of a historical course in which Marxists should firmly anchor themselves, for the battles of the present and the future. Hardly one number of Amadeo's paper of the time, first *Battaglia comunista* (until 1952), then *Programma comunista*, does not follow this path with the 'devouring passion' of the militant who does not need to 'imagine' the revolution to come, because the revolution *is alive and is methodically at work*.[174]

On this question, too, Bordiga did not have much luck: after his death, and even before, most of the militants involved in *Programma comunista* adopted an orientation that was fundamentally indifferentist. His interventions on the national and colonial question did, however, put forward important theses on the inadequacy or falseness of the wooden dichotomy between bourgeoisie and proletariat. In the contest between capitalism and socialism, he argued, other social classes are also in the field: the 'non-proletarian lower classes' in the metropolitan countries, and coloured 'races' and peoples in the rest of the planet. And the relentless march of these 'yellow and black brothers' might allow the lagging 'white' proletarians to make up for lost time, by rekindling the class struggle in the metropolitan centres.[175] In the 1950s, the link-up that the Second Comintern Congress in Moscow and the Congress of the Peoples of the East in Baku had projected between the workers of the world and the oppressed peoples was a long way off; the fuzzy, self-interested 'brotherliness' of all the national socialisms toward one another, customarily involving unequal relations, double-crossing and, if necessary, open warfare, was only a tawdry mystification. Nevertheless, Bordiga pointed to the extraordinary emancipatory value of the anti-colonial revolutions and uprisings for the worldwide proletarian movement. The advent of neo-colonialism (which he denounced in real time as 'financial and thermonuclear colonialism'), and the current rise of former ex-colonial countries, above all China, to the rank of major capitalist powers, in no way contradict this grand internationalist strategic vision. As Bordiga expected, the potential strength of the international proletariat has continued to increase, acquiring greatest specific weight precisely where the national-popular revolution went furthest. This has created *objectively* more favourable social-economic conditions for a new cycle of proletarian uprisings even more effectively internationalised than in 1917–27. The short twentieth century did not pass in vain.

---

174 Nucleo Comunista Internazionalista (ed.) 2012, p. 16.
175 Bordiga 1976c, p. 174; Bordiga 1979, pp. 240, 287.

11   Yesterday, Today and, above All, Tomorrow

At this point it will, I hope, be clearer why the 'unknown' Bordiga should, as
Goldner claimed, be considered 'a figure of the very first rank' of international
communism, 'one of the most brilliant and forgotten Marxists of the 20th century'.[176]
Without denying his importance, some historians have argued that Bordiga
saw very well in the distance but not so well close up, that his weak point
was the present day, especially after the Second World War. What they have
in mind is not only a certain rigidity of tactics and even his conception of
tactics per se, which he thought could be predefined in abstraction from the
actual development of the revolutionary process – a process shown by history
to be rather hard to predict. According to this point of view, even at the highpoint of the battle to constitute the communist party in Italy, Bordiga had a
tendency to simplify the terms of the class struggle and to produce analyses
less adequate than those of the Bolsheviks with regard to the structure and
dynamic of social classes and real-life experiences, considerably underestimating the role of the masses in the revolutionary process.[177] That may well be
true. Nor, in my view, is it wrong to mention the sharp difference on this very
question between Bordiga's thinking and that of Pannekoek, Gorter and the
KAPD,[178] which may not tell in his favour. In any case, this anthology does not
seek the 'canonisation' of Bordiga; that would have seemed grotesque to him,
the great sarcastic deprecator of individual merits and supermen (his motto:
'Soften up, Superman!').[179] Our aim has been to present a major figure of international communism to a public that does not know him at all or has merely

---

176   See 'Preface to the Swedish Edition of *Communism is the Material Human Community:*
       Amadeo Bordiga Today', http://www.riff-raff.se/en/3-4/pre_bordiga.php. This text contains
       another acute observation: 'The relationship between Bordiga and Lenin is complex, and
       Bordiga certainly considered himself a Leninist, despite frank disagreements between
       them in 1921–1922. Bordiga may in fact have been a Leninist, but not all Leninists are Bor-
       diga'.
177   This is the criticism of Bordiga contained in the previously mentioned works by De Clem-
       enti and Cortesi, as well as in De Felice 1971, pp. 129–233. Their views differ profoundly,
       however. Whereas De Clementi and Cortesi regard Bordiga's stance on the party – mass
       relationship as his weak point, to De Felice that was the very essence of Bordiga's thought;
       he adds that Antonio Gramsci was entirely right on the issue.
178   In making this reference, however, De Felice mentions Bordiga's political sympathy for
       Pannekoek. In 1920–21, in the introduction to a long article in his paper *Soviet*, the Dutch
       communist appeared as the uncle coming to the aid of his nephew (Bordiga), who had
       just been spanked by Daddy Lenin for his extremism (De Felice 1971, pp. 215 ff.).
179   *Il programma comunista* 1953/8.

glimpsed his name in some negative footnote. Here he appears not as Bordiga the Individual, though he was endowed with exceptional qualities, but as the expression of a collective organism (the intransigent and then abstentionist Left in the PSI, PCd'I, Communist International, groups of CP Internationalists and *Programma comunista*), a collective effort and gigantic collective struggle, which still today has not untied the intricate knot of the overthrow of the international capitalist order and the establishment of socialism.

Bordiga's huge workshop is a veritable goldmine, and I am sure that anyone who decides to enter it will not be disappointed. This applies to scholars of the workers' movement, and *a fortiori* to those who, tired or sick of the present state of things, aspire to a completely different world free of the domination of commodities, exchange value, capital and their devastating wars on workers and nature. The Neapolitan communist militant Amadeo Bordiga, I can guarantee, will greet you with his cordial style, his original language, his entertaining digressions and his wide culture. And he will guide you through a series of instructive, energising and often highly topical excursions into the near and distant past, into the present that he largely foresaw, and into the future that he sketched with science and passion.

Have a good read!

PART 1

The Italian Left in the Great Revolutionary Struggle (1912–26)

∴

Against the War

1 Against the War as Long as It Lasts[1]

There are some comrades whose opinion of the war may be summarised as follows: the war should not be happening, but now that we are engaged in it how can we be against?

Obviously those who say this consider it desirable – even in the interests of the proletariat – that the war should end well and be crowned with success and glory for the Italian armies. In my view, this is an outright concession to the nationalist idea; it stems from the false concept of the 'interests of the proletariat' that many hold, which has led so many comrades into the most aberrant debasements of socialism.

When socialism affirms the solidarity of exploited workers, transforming the interest of each into the collective class interest, it also subordinates the good of some individuals to the collective good; this brings about feelings of renunciation and self-sacrifice among the proletarians who are most conscious of the future of their class. In the same way, the present interest of the workers is transformed into the future good of the whole proletariat, and the socialist masses become capable of collectively foregoing today's small conquests because they have in view the great conquest ahead.

It follows logically that socialism should oppose all movements that may detract from the emancipation of the proletariat by stifling consciousness in its ranks, even if in some way they represent an improvement of present conditions.

The war now runs counter to and holds back the great revolutionary conquest of the working classes, stifling their consciousness of socialism in two crucial ways.

First, the war enshrines the principles of violence and collective arrogance as wellsprings of progress and civilisation, idealising brute force, seeking to destroy our vision of a society based on harmony and fraternity, and hindering the logical evolution of social relations in a way that will abolish the principle of might is right. (It should be remembered that, unlike enervated bourgeois pacifists, we do not deny that in some historical circumstances violence may be an unavoidable factor.)

---

1 *L'Avanguardia*, Yr. 6, No. 254, 25 August 1912 – Bordiga denounces here the war Italy waged on the Ottoman Empire in September 1911 for the conquest of Libya.

Second, the war deludes the masses into thinking that their well-being stems from the well-being of the *nation*, from its strength and dignity, and that to this end they should forego social dissent. By sowing an artificial patriotic idealism in the masses, the war assures the bourgeoisie of its class domination. For it induces workers to give up struggling against the insatiable exploitation that bleeds them dry within their *homeland*, while sending them off to be killed by *foreigners*.

Let us then outline the true dimensions of the problem: war and national exaltation; glorification of collective crime; a dulling of class struggle; a move away from demands for workers' rights and social transformation. Let us follow this through logically. If the war is victorious and triumphant for the nation, the proletariat will suffer as a result – not directly, but because it will put off indefinitely the hour of its revolt.

This is why, being against war in theory, we oppose it in practice, with no qualms that it might undermine the national government by breaking the unanimity of the nation.

All the other arguments against the Tripoli campaign are of secondary importance. When we say that the war is harsh and difficult, that the diplomatic situation is unclear, that the colonisation of Tripoli is a myth, and that the consequence of all this will be to damage and ruin Italian political and economic life, we should not lead our listeners to think that we would have been less opposed to the war if Turkey had succumbed in ten days and Tripolitania had been a Garden of Eden. Had that proved true, it would be bad news indeed for the future prospects of the proletariat in Italy!

Those objections of ours to the *wisdom* of the war are important only because they point to one thing. In some cases, the bourgeoisie has an interest in inflicting serious damage on the nation, by plunging it into a pointless war, provided that it gains in recompense a revitalisation of patriotism and an ensuing attenuation of the class struggle. This goes to show the bad faith of the main advocates of the war, and it provides us with the other side of the critique of the nationalist idea. This may be summarised as follows.

The interests of the nation are not those of the working class. Nor are they those of the bourgeois class, which does not hesitate to damage the fatherland so long as it can wave its flag before the eyes of the proletariat. So, there is *no common interest between the rulers and the ruled*; the concept of the nation and all that patriotic idealism are pure sophistry; the reality of history consists in the social struggle of classes.

All over the world the proletariat struggles in good faith, in broad daylight, against exploitation by capital. But the bourgeoisie that seeks to tame it in the name of the fatherland acts like one who, sword cast aside, approaches the enemy with a smile, only to plant a dagger treacherously in his heart.

Religion is a weapon of social domination, as is patriotism, and we are the heretics of the patriotic religion.

Might we quote Gustave Hervé,[2] now that the Right calls Filippo Turati[3] a Herveist?

2 From the Old to the New Anti-militarism[4]

After more than half a year of war, and of furious debate about the war, is it possible to draw some conclusions about the new light shed by the tragic events on the delicate and extremely serious question of the relations between socialism and war?

Today, discussion of this question is neither academic nor premature. Indeed, it is made necessary and timely by the conditions in which the socialist parties of the neutral states that may still enter the war find themselves. Tomorrow, when peace will have been made, in the light of history and of authentic retrospective chronicle, without the blinding of the passions that divide belligerents and neutrals in this hour of crisis, the matter will be examined more thoroughly and the debate completed, with socialists from all over the world taking part to draw – undoubtedly – conclusions that will be decisive for the future. But the feverish investigation and the at times chaotic and tumultuous debate have already been imposed on us today. The Italian socialist proletariat, faced with the outbreak of a war, would find itself in a very different condition from socialists in other countries, rocked by the storm of war in just a few days. The long period in which we have stood by as spectators of the action – and of the passion – of our brothers beyond the Alps charges us with a far more serious historical responsibility.

Of all the observations and inductions we have been exposed to these past six months, one thing in particular stands out: the theory and the propaganda of anti-militarism prior to this war were developed mainly in light of the proletarian interest and necessity of preventing and deprecating war in every way

---

2 Gustave Hervé (1871–1944) was first a fervent anti-militarist and then an equally fervent ultranationalist, founding the Parti socialiste national in 1919.

3 Filippo Turati (1857–1932) was one of the founders in 1892 of the Partito dei lavoratori italiani, which in 1895 became the Partito socialista italiano (to which Bordiga belonged until January 1921). As political leader of the PSI's reformist wing, he was a firm (and able) opponent of the Party's affiliation to the Third International. In 1922, after the split with the Maximalists, he founded together with Treves and Matteotti the Partito socialista unitario.

4 *Avanti!*, 19 February 1915 – Bordiga speaks out against the outbreak of WWI in July 1914.

possible and of combating the ill-fated consequences of militarism in peace-time (mad military spending, armed repression of workers' movements, the pernicious influence of military life on the young, and so forth). But, in all this, far too little attention was paid to the problem of what the socialists should have done, not to ward off the war but – rather – to defend the conquests of the proletariat and to save socialism from ruin, once war actually broke out.

The error consisted in viewing the problem of anti-militarism (reduction of armaments, a people's army, arbitration, and so forth) from a reformist perspective when, on the contrary, the task of socialism is not to restore bourgeois society to health but, rather, to precipitate its demolition *ab imis fundamentis*, undermining the foundations of its economic organisation. Anti-militarism is not, therefore, an end in itself, but is one of the facets of the anti-capitalistic action of socialism. Indeed, the *Communist Manifesto* tells us that only the socialisation of the means of production and of exchange will make conflicts between nations impossible.[5]

But, little by little, some people had come to believe that war, even in a bourgeois regime, was impossible. The outbreak of the current terrible war has demolished this mistaken conviction – and, at the same time, has sealed the Marxist condemnation of capitalism, whose civilisation, based on the exploitation of wage labour, is bending its historical parabola towards the abyss of the barbarities of war.

Socialism had to be ready to expect from this solemn theoretical confirmation something better than the effective disintegration of the International. But modern socialism has yet to achieve its completion in the crucible of history, has yet to pass through the fire of its own internal conflicts and errors, to free itself from all the dross that pollutes and encumbers it ...

Classical anti-militarism made little – too little – provision for the situation in which socialists and workers find themselves in the course of those few hours in which war passes from threat to reality.

Socialists had had the experience of partial crises, of limited or colonial wars – the Boer War, the Russo-Japanese War, the war in Libya ... But conflict between the world's most powerful states, between bordering countries ready to deploy the most devastating methods of attack, in the agonising period in which the coded telegrams exchanged by governments decide the fate of millions of men – in this unprecedented crisis, all opinions, tendencies, forecasts

---

5 Bordiga refers to the following passage: 'In proportion as the antagonism between classes within the nation vanishes, the hostility of one nation to another will come to an end'. Marx and Engels 1985, p. 102.

and intentions are overwhelmed. What happened is all too well known. Apart from not being able to ward off the war – and this failure was absolutely *not* the failure of socialism! – socialists in the leading states, with very few exceptions, expressed their full solidarity with their respective governments, giving them a great contribution of moral and material energies, to the greater joy of the conservative classes.

Overturning all their previous values and conceptions, the socialists who had converted to the war justified their conduct not only with the prejudicial question of a patriotism that prevented them from doing anything damaging to their country, engaged to the hilt in the terrible war – whatever the fault or responsibility of the government may have been – but, what is more, went on to proclaim a dualism between the 'historical missions' of the two sides in the war, which forced socialism to side openly with one or the other.

This complete distortion of the facts took place, in parallel, on either side of the charred frontiers. There is no point in repeating our confutation of these systems of inexactness, falsehood and prejudice, which, unfortunately, veiled the real vision of the cataclysm, misleading the masses and turning them away from their opposition and antagonism to the ruling classes.

There is practically no question that – contrary to public opinion – the various governments counted on the socialists' adhesion, and without this certainty would have been far more cautious in their warmongering. The German, Austrian, French, Belgian … socialists, for their part, were convinced that abandoning the socialist policy of intransigent opposition to the institutions was small fry compared to the danger of weakening the national cause, once war had been declared.

And so the effectiveness of socialist anti-militarism stopped on the threshold of the wide-open doors of the temple of Janus.

The great revision of socialism now in the offing will have to rectify this fundamental error. The socialists of Italy would do well to force themselves to draw some conclusions, right now, before the Italian state enters the war. Against the illusion that socialism will withdraw into the shadows and into the orbit of the nation, we pit our conviction that, on the contrary, socialism will turn to new and closer forms of union and of international action, while an increased disbelief in the possibility of a gradual civil improvement of the current regime will increasingly drive the proletariat towards the revolutionary tactic and tendency. In all the countries at war a profound change in the opinion of the socialists has already begun. They are beginning to think that they have sacrificed too much on the altar of the 'homeland'. A tendency to peace and to the reconstruction of international proletarian relations is beginning to take shape.

In this historic moment it would be deplorable if the Italian Socialist Party, in case of war, should allow itself to become a prisoner of the situation, should allow its hands to be tied in any form whatsoever of solidarity with the bourgeoisie, sacrificing the logical coherence of its political attitude.

Bourgeois pacifism, a sterile and in no way revolutionary movement, can halt before the war it has uselessly opposed and recall only the necessity of saving one's country. But socialism – anti-militarist because anti-bourgeois – must not allow the outbreak of war to make it desist from its action. It must not allow itself to be bound by patriotic scruples. Let other forces, other social factors, other parties, concern themselves about the salvation of the 'nation', if they happen to know the content of that so abstract a term. The Socialist Party does not and cannot have any other mission than that of saving socialism – and all the more so today, when many begin to regret having forgotten it. Italian socialism, despite this sad war to the death between old and new adversaries, must, and will – war or no war – pass through the fire and the ruins holding its banner high, sure that tomorrow workers of the other countries will be by its side, wakened from this blood-drenched dream of destruction and slaughter.

3   We Take Our Stand[6]

The decision for war has been taken. As we had anticipated, we socialists have received a hypocritical appeal for national solidarity in the name of the endangered 'homeland'.

We are proud to be the kind of socialists that in their staunch internationalism have no room for the superstition of the 'homeland'. Therefore, even if we believed that the appeal made to us by our enemies of yesterday were sincere and honest; even if we held the national government to be innocent of the war; even if we admitted the good faith and disinterestedness of all the supporters of this war – despite all this, we would remain, in the name of our principles and of our faith, tenacious champions of class strife, which, pitting the servants against the oppression of their masters, is the only true path towards a better future.

But the appeal for national concord makes us even more indignant about the entire system of falsehood, cowardice, and bullying we see being employed in order to create artificial popular enthusiasm for the cause of the war.

---

6   'Il Socialista' di Napoli, No. 35, 22 May 1915.

The demonstrations of proletarian will organised by our party have been violently crushed, while interventionist din has been given free rein. The bourgeoisie had all the major newspapers inflate the student hubbub while covering up and slandering the workers' protests, and even had the gall to intercept the news of socialist rallies at the one newspaper we [socialists] have. And, with all this, are we supposed to accept the invitation to join in and sing the hymn to the war of liberation and democracy?

Are we supposed to show we believe the official lies that base their justification for entering the war on rhetorical phrases, while history shows us once again that the politics of the bourgeois states and of the Italian state in particular is a tissue of hypocrisy and of cynicism?

Salandra's[7] declarations moved us no more than the Kaiser's declarations moved us at the time.

Indeed, the Kaiser's had the merit of greater sincerity.

Italy enters the fray in defence of its violated rights?

In that case you should have jumped in in August, when you wanted to go to war on the Austro-German side. The Austrian ultimatum to Serbia damaged Italian interests? But only after ten long months did you denounce the thirty-year alliance that, before the tribunal of history, made you accomplices of the German empires.

Why didn't you protest against Austria's annexation of Bosnia-Herzegovina? Perhaps because you were engaged in your own brigandage in Libya? Instead, you waited for a disheartened and enfeebled enemy that allowed you to trumpet your rhetoric. Across the eastern border the lands were Italian neither in language nor race, but the monarchy and the Italian state, weighing the pros and the cons, gave vent to their greed for territorial expansion all the same, just as they are doing for Vlora [in Albania] and the Dodecanese islands [in Greece], which lie within the province of non-belligerent nations.

It is not the principle of nationality that you have to invoke, but the right of the stronger.

It is not Garibaldi that you have to bring back to life, but Ninco Nanco.[8]

But drain your Walpurgis Night of lies to the dregs! We shall never be your accomplices!

---

7   Antonio Salandra, conservative Italian prime minister from March 1914 to June 1916.
8   Giuseppe Nicola Summa, known as Ninco Nanco (1833–64), was an Italian brigand.

4   The 'Fait Accompli'[9]

It was inevitable. In this tragic turn of history, which from neutrality has brought us to war, the semi-conscious have already tailored their alibi, to give a shared sheen of honesty to their defection. After having fully done their duty to avoid the war, it is now the socialists' duty to 'accept the fait accompli', and to accept the invitation to participate in the national cooperation of all parties for the victory of Italian arms!

Fully done their duty?

Let us begin by saying that those – and we sincerely hope there will be few of them – who now so hastily pass to the other side, without even waiting for the real war to begin, are those lukewarm neutralists who did *not* do their own duty and have always harboured a secret, but transparent, nostalgia for the convenient anti-socialist ideologies of the warmongers.

And never mind, for now, names and facts. Let us discuss, rather, this dubious and hypocritical thesis of the fait accompli, which, if it were to be accepted, would dishonour the Socialist Party and oblige us to recognise as right and deserved all of Mussolini and company's statements about our irresponsibility and our cowardice.

After having witnessed – to the satisfaction of the bourgeois world – the astonishing subjugation of the socialists of the principal states of Europe to the cause of the war, the Italian Socialist Party proclaimed that the International was not yet dead, and sided against Italy's entering the war in support of either one of the groups of belligerents.

It was said that we were propagandising cowardice, inactivity, absenteeism from the decisive historical tragedy; we were denounced as accomplices of the Catholics, of the pro-Austrian sympathisers, and, recently, of Giolitti[10] and of von Bülow.[11] We replied to our detractors, who are more or less in the pay of the Consulates of the Entente,[12] that the war had not destroyed socialism but had confirmed the need for it to continue its historical action of class struggle, rather than erasing its distinctive features in patriotic solidarity with the state and the bourgeoisie.

We said that our campaign for neutrality stemmed from reasons of principle and of class interest, which sharply distinguished it from bourgeois neutrality and its fishy backstage intrigues.

---

9   *Avanti!*, 23 Maggio 1915. This article was written on the day before Italy entered the WWI.
10   Giovanni Giolitti, an Italian Liberal, was Prime Minister five times between 1892 and 1921.
11   Karl von Bülow was a German Field Marshal during World War I.
12   A reference to the Entente Cordiale between Britain and France reached in 1904, forming the basis of Anglo-French cooperation in World War I.

Many of us – it is useful to acknowledge it – were perhaps wrong in giving priority to contingent and national considerations that militated against the arguments for intervention, and that by pure chance could have been shared by our adversaries. But we all proclaimed that our Party, through its anti-war propaganda, and by defending its class independence against any form of seduction and attack, was aiming at the high historic task of redeeming the dignity of socialism and of preparing the ground for the new proletarian International, a task far greater – and far more real – than those that could have been accomplished in the shadow of the national banner and in league with the bleak Pharisees of mercantile patriotism.

Is this limpid and sure line of action broken today *in limine belli*, on the threshold of the bourgeois war? No. As for national reasons – the bourgeois reasons for neutrality that for us were subordinate [to our own reasons] – they have in fact come to nothing, since the die is cast and no interest remains for the Italian state save victory against the enemy, with which it is already engaged. Today, those socialists who admit that the duty to defend one's country is indisputable have fallen into a trap that is clear as day. Today, is not Italy – despite its taking the initiative in a not unavoidable war – in a condition of national defence? Without doubt, since its leaders have thrown it into the fire from which they now invite us to rescue it. But we clamorously separated our responsibilities from this mad militaristic policy. It would be illogical and stupid to make ourselves prisoners of the arbitrary act our eternal adversaries have perpetrated, availing themselves of privileges that we unceasingly combated and despising the opinion of the working classes that we represent.

Surrendering, then, to the crime committed, becoming accomplices in its perpetration, even though we spoke out against its cold premeditation, would be absurd. It would lead us to confess that, after a Platonic propaganda of peace, we will agree to all the bourgeois wars: that when the bourgeoisie cries war we will ape the shameless capers of those great patriots who had first opposed the war for the most unmentionable of reasons, only to be all for it once it had been declared.

Even the socialists of other countries, for so long the butt of our reproof and our censure, *separated their responsibilities* and did their duty ... up to the moment of war. If we do no better than they did, after having had ample time to study the causes of their errors, we will cover ourselves with ridicule and shame.

We were not able to avoid this war. So now we have to go along with it, arm in arm with its authors! So say those who see in the war a coincidence of interests between all social classes.

We admit that such a coincidence has been forced upon us, in the sense that everyone wants to avoid the worst, to avoid defeat. But, under the big banner of party truce, is there an equitable distribution of the sacrifices and of the possible advantages?

Never again. The bourgeois class struggle against the proletariat not only is not suspended but is intensified to the extreme, since economic exploitation continues and culminates in the sacrifice of blood asked of the workers in the name of the fatherland – to which the capitalists sacrifice not a penny of the fruit of their speculations.

We hear demands for an end to civil strife, demands of the workers that they desist from their sacred defence against a system of oppression that its beneficiaries have no intention of softening.

Can those who admit that the workers have every right to protest against poverty and hunger dare to smother their indignation when the outrage of war threatens their very lives? We were unable to prevent this outrage, just as, for now, the immaturity of the proletarian forces keeps us from preventing capitalist exploitation.

But this does not make us desist from our unshakable aversion to today's world and to the sad reality that permits economic servitude and the infamy of military servitude to the detriment of the vast majority of men.

The losers are those who today see nothing other than the common denominator of patriotism, and therefore silence their own opposition. It would have been better for them if they had crossed over in time to sincerely professed interventionism. Yielding today, under the impetus of the high tide of war, they manifest the uncertainty and emptiness of their thinking and the elasticity of their conscience.

Today *neutralism*, this infelicitous word that brought us so much slander, is dead. For this very reason, now is the time to demonstrate the injustice of the defamation to which we were subjected. It is today that, magnificently alone against the entire bourgeoisie of every party, we can and must show that anti-militarism and internationalism are not empty concepts, are not a cover for the pusillanimous *panciafichista*.[13]

Now is the time to take a stand against the moral pressure of all sentimentalisms and attractions, against the material pressure of reactionary persecutions. Today we need to prove that our aspiration to the International was right, des-

---

13   *Panciafichista*: a 'neutralist'; specifically in the First World War. Literally, someone who wants to 'save his belly (*pancia*) for the figs (*fichi*)', that is, not expose himself to risks.

pite its alleged defeat, and that our neutralism was not devoid of historical sense, as the warmongers blathered. An interruption of socialist activity at the outbreak of the war would also belittle its precedents, putting it in the most equivocal and dishonouring light.

Once again, you trembling servants of the fait accompli – you who want to make us lick the hand that has felled us but not broken us down! – the two opposite ways are drawn, sharp and clear.

Either inside or outside the national preconception and its patriotic scruples. Either towards a nationalistic pseudo-socialism or towards a new International.

Today, with the war a 'fait accompli', only one position is possible for those who, yesterday, did not harbour a despicable duplicity in their opposition to it: against the war, for anti-militarist and international socialism!

5   Nothing to Correct[14]

Now and then the anti-socialist press suspends its inspired invective against us and plays another tune: the socialists are supposedly changing their position and 'correcting' their aim. Clearly, the second system is the more dangerous for us: the former approach involves calumnies that do us honour; the latter heaps praises that should make us blush. If anyone has the confidence and the right to see their enemies in the penitential dress of Mary Magdalene, then it is our Party. If anything interests the enemies of socialism, it is not the killing of socialism – a task for which they now see they are unequal – but its suicide or at least its self-emasculation.

For this reason they beat the drum for all turncoats, blow up and glorify all deviations, and make implausible efforts to highlight (through their indecent but powerful global organisation of deception) not the true manifestations of socialist proletarian organisation but the gestures of a Hervé, Lerda, Plekhanov or Russell that represent nothing but themselves.[15]

---

14   *Avanti!*, 23 May 1917.
15   Bordiga is here referring to figures who initially opposed the war but later went on to support it. Gustave Hervé, Georgii Plekhanov and Bertrand Russell probably require no further introduction. Giovanni Lerda (1853–1928), a PSI member and freemason, spoke out against the Libyan war in 1911, but then advocated Italian intervention in the First World War. In 1922 he became one of the founder-members of the Partito socialista unitario, along with Turati, Treves and Matteotti.

Of course, we could just smile at the ridiculous system of waiting and occasionally saying that our conversion is nigh, we could just let them blether on and fantasise in their successive delusions, except that this time the enemy's chatter has some pretext in signs within our own Party. By a strange irony, these have appeared just when the masses are beginning to trust us again and to recognise the correctness of our positions and our activity.

Let us quote without further ado from the manifesto 'To the Socialists of the World', issued on 12 April by the SP leadership and parliamentary group and by the Confederation of Labour.

> Under the veil of an apparent formal contradiction, this is the meaning of the intervention by the United States of America, which is consistent with the aims of Wilson's First Message that went unheeded and was reaffirmed in the War Message. Though determined by the defence needs of the great Republic and its dominant bourgeois interests, it essentially comes down to an intervention to restrict the war and to impose a more secure peace sooner rather than later. Instead of two conflicting imperialist groups, the British-Russian and the German, we now have an alliance of states dominated by the Russian-American spirit of renewal and democracy, against a weakened and drained autocracy that a decisive collision inside the country would suffice to shatter into pieces.

To clarify the content of this 'aim correction' that the bourgeois press reports, we might quote some lines from articles by Treves[16] and speeches by Turati, but let us base ourselves rather on collective statements by the party leaders, to express our radical and open disagreement with them that we know is shared by a large number of comrades.

We do not know what our American comrades opposed to US intervention, or our Russian comrades opposed to continuation of the alliance, will make of these statements, which are questionable even in factual terms; perhaps they will think that, in respect of the war, the Italian socialists fight against the intervention of their own country and justify that ... of others. In any case, the assertions contained in them have given rise to certain deductions on the part of *Il Giornale d'Italia* and other papers. How can they be thought wrong when their reasoning has all the rigour of a syllogism?

---

16   Claudio Treves (1869–1933) was, together with Turati, one of the most prominent figures in the reformist wing of the PSI, and like him was firmly opposed to its affiliation to the Third International.

Wilson's peace message is on a par with the Zimmerwald principles (first premise). *Wilson's intervention has the same aims as his peace message* (second premise). *The Zimmerwaldians too should therefore 'intervene' like Wilson, and side with the war of the Entente* (conclusion).

Yes, the manifesto of our leadership bodies does declare the bankruptcy of the war, but then it enters into contingent considerations that lead to the opposite conclusion. This is the result of the *union sacrée in the Party*, which gives us statements that comrades from opposing positions and tendencies each invest with their own thinking. It is easy to see how advantageous this is for the achievement of clarity and the preparation of the proletariat for events.

It is at least curious that, after the Party's bold campaign on neutrality or intervention, and the sharp debate between the internationalist thesis that saw the war as the result of bourgeois inter-imperialist rivalry and the social-patriotic thesis that it originated in a clash between bourgeois democracy and autocratic militarism – *and after things have gone as they have* – we can still give our opponents a pretext to say that we are beginning to accept that they are right!

The contradiction between the manifesto's concepts and the proper socialist approach seems to us so evident that – partly for space and other obvious reasons – we shall condense in a few summary arguments our understanding of the historical value of the recent American and Russian events, while recalling things that have been said more than once before in these columns.

The militarism that has manifested itself in this war is a *thoroughly modern product* of the bourgeois capitalist regime; it is compatible with the most progressive democracies and the most developed industrial economic framework, while conflicting with the economic, social and political institutions prior to the capitalist stage. For the militarism of other historical epochs – e.g., the barbarian invasions, the feudal wars or the autocratic monarchies – had quite different characteristics.

We must look at the bourgeois historical process to trace the 'conditions' for militarism as it manifests itself in this war. Technologically, it requires awesome development of the industrial means of production and complete mastery of the processes and cycles of the transformation of raw materials; economically, the state has to have great financial power and a vast network of tax revenues at its disposal; administratively, bureaucratic organisation is indispensable to recruit and mobilise the armed forces, to impose discipline in supply and consumption, and to raise the state machine to a maximum of activity; and politically, a regime of democracy or *illusory mass liberty* (in the historical sense of the term) is necessary if the masses are to accept the enormous burden of the war and to believe that the collective interests of the *nation* require it.

The last of these points finds support in the fact that military conscription and permanent armies were introduced on a stable basis after the democratic upheavals – in France by the Convention of 1793 – while the intensified arming of all European countries went together with suitable democratic reforms to make the new burdens more acceptable to the masses. On the other hand, if we compare the rising military budgets with the indices of capitalist industrial and commercial growth, we find a number of general analogies. Militarism, then, is not a surplus left over from older times but the product of new times; it is the child of capitalism and of its characteristic political form, democracy.

For these reasons we reject the thesis of a duel between democracy and militarism, and we have no preference for one or other group of belligerent countries.

The states in question are not at war under the banner of their respective social and philosophical ideologies, as the Italian socialists grasped very clearly in the case of the Libyan war.

In each state there are classes and tendencies that correspond to different degrees of historical development, but the war between the states is due to the cessation of internal dissent – the only ground on which a social upheaval can unfold.

The warring states are for us *the same kind of entities*. If we can be certain of one thing, it is that the most modern, industrial, bourgeois and democratic states are fighting the war best.

Thus, we do not relate Germany's military efficiency to the survival of medieval or feudal institutions, but rather to everything it has that is the most modern, bourgeois and 'democratic'. Have events given the lie to this thesis? Quite the contrary.

The country that proved the least suited to war, the one that snapped first, was Russia. It lacked, or was deficient in, all the aspects we have emphasised: industrial technology, capitalist economics, modern bureaucracy, political democracy. And the state that calculated its self-interest most coldly – that of its capitalist class – seeing it first in neutrality and then in intervention, was precisely the developed democratic republic of the stars and stripes.

We recognise that these points deserve to be treated at greater length. But it does not seem possible that socialists, or anyway those who have not surrendered to the lures of warmongering, should rest their critique of the situation on any other foundation and take seriously the high-sounding phrases cynical declarations of the capitalist regime. It does not seem possible that they should interpret the Russian Revolution in accordance with falsifications peddled by the press of our opponents, or value so highly Wilson's statements resting on a hollow humanitarian-Mazzinian ideology, instead of opening up with the scalpel of Marxist criticism the ultra-important phenomena that mark the present history of the capitalist colossus across the Atlantic and the awesome social relations in the new Russia, where the third estate will represent a very different part than in the France of 1789.

We well know that comrades who are overly concerned about the impression our attitudes make on the opposing stalls (the ones occupied by the hired claque) cannot bear it when they are accused of being *schematic, dogmatic, blinkered* and so forth. And we accept that our ideological concepts should be continually exposed to critical examination, in relation to events as they succeed one another. It seems to us that today such examination bolsters more than ever our fundamental conviction, which is not and does not wish to be a blind faith in fixed formulas. But revisions and corrections become pernicious and deplorable when they do no more than substitute for the powerful critical spirit and analysis of the truth that is the essence of Marxist socialism, replacing it with the little more than schoolboy idiocies that form the bien-pensant creed and the backbone of a 'common sense' cobbled together from thousands of prejudices.

If that happens, the socialist proletariat, having torn off the age-old blindfolds that prevented it from seeing reality, will allow itself to be fitted with tinted spectacles by means of which those yoked by lucre to the wagon of the existing order perceive and judge the world. The proletariat would then be eating straw instead of hay, like the proverbial ox with the green-tinted spectacles.

One thing that is incumbent on us in the period ahead is a greater firmness in our proposals and activity. The blathering of the hostile press about a supposed mending of our ways is a very bad sign in this respect. Let us hope that the future conduct of our movement will be such as to thwart these murky manoeuvres. But before we get too indignant about the enemy's tendentious (but understandable) exploitation of certain statements for their own ends, let us think of demanding a more certain and more socialist direction from our leaders.

It's high time.

CHAPTER 2

On Elections

1   Against Abstentionism[1]

In the coming election battle, our party – which will fight it alone against all, in the name of its full programme – shall not fail to guard and defend itself against a danger that is no less serious than all the others: the danger of abstentionism. Although the anarchist and syndicalist movements are not exactly flourishing here nowadays, the socialists – and especially the revolutionary socialists – should not remain indifferent to the attempted sabotage of the Party by the anti-electionists, or to their campaign of denigration against the sincerely revolutionary direction taken by socialism in Italy after the recent events. The whole campaign waged by revolutionaries against the reformist degeneration of the party and of its parliamentary activity had to remain, and has remained, quite immune from indulgence of any new leanings toward anarchist or syndicalist abstentionism. It is precisely the revolutionaries who must refute facile abstentionist arguments based on the errors and weaknesses of a section of the party that went seriously astray, and that has today been almost completely eliminated from it.

The revolutionaries have reaffirmed the political value of the revolutionary class struggle, in accordance with Marxist conceptions, as against all the discreditable forms of apoliticism and neutralism that have erased the Party's subversive profile. More than ever, revolutionaries must uphold the need for a class-political party, the need to 'colour' politically all working-class action and to guide it towards its communist goals. This approach is opposed to the opportunist neutralism of labour organisations, itself supported by a petty, vulgar reformism that completely overlooks any organic, unadulterated tendency with other than immediate limited aims. Syndicalism and reformism have now come together in the concept of apolitical trade-unionism, which is to say they have shown us that the proletariat will never be able to carry out the revolution with the strength of its economic organisations alone. The social

---

1   The following article appeared in *Avanti* on 13 July 1913, well before the First World War. It is useful evidence that neither historically nor doctrinally was there anything in common between the method of anarchism and that of the revolutionary left socialists, despite erroneous claims to the contrary after the war, when the Italian Communist Left proposed that the new Communist International should tactically withdraw from participation in parliament. [Note by Amadeo Bordiga].

revolution is a political phenomenon, prepared on the terrain of politics. And in the conception of the party's general political action, the electoral struggle enters as one of many spheres of socialist activity. All the other forms should not be ruled out. But in our view, it is necessary for the party to require all its militants to make a formal positive statement of their opinion and their decision.

One can have the most refined discussions regarding the influence of the parliamentary environment and everyday 'corruption' on socialist deputies. We do not dispute that there is such influence. But we do presume that, if all voters were true 'socialists' from our own intransigent point of view, the mistakes made by their representatives should have no effect on them. But if the voters are mustered up by other parties, lured with promises of a whole series of splendid reforms and immediate advantages, it is no wonder that the elected representative becomes a renegade.

This very accusation of ours against reformism is what the abstentionists want to use as an argument against participation in elections.

Now, to give the proletarian class politics of the Socialist Party a profoundly different character from bourgeois politicking presents grave difficulties that we do not hide from ourselves. But true revolutionaries must strive to work in that direction and not abandon the struggle. Abstentionism is no remedy – in fact, it renounces the sole method that can give the proletariat a consciousness capable of defending it from the opportunist politicking of the non-socialist parties. Electoral neutralism becomes a neutralism of conscience and opinion with regard to the great social problems, which, though built around an economic framework (as we Marxists maintain), always assume a political character.

It is not our ambition to develop such a complex issue in a few lines. We would only sound an alarm against the propagandists of anti-electoralism, who will come and sabotage our propaganda work in the election committees. We aim to test out the political consciousness of the people of Italy in a great anti-bourgeois contest. Our party is the only one that will come out in struggle against the clerical-monarchic-democratic dictatorship. We await the election period not because we are parliamentary fetishists, but in order to stir layers of proletarian consciousness lulled by one school of neutralism or another. We feel we are performing deeply subversive work, and we intend to deal a blow to any form of class collaboration.

The syndicalists (who are concocting some bloc to reward De Ambris[2] with a medal) and the anarchists (who, seeing eye to eye with bourgeois 'intellectu-

---

2   Alceste De Ambris (1874–1934): a prominent Italian syndicalist.

als', swim in a sickly-sweet democratic sea made up of culture, schooling and popular education) will claim to monopolise revolution and accuse us of shady dealing because we employ the weapon of the ballot.

We should be prepared to reply, so as not to be deprived of the vote of a few true revolutionaries – about which we care rather more than about a hundred dubious non-socialist votes. These champions of abstentionism wait with bated breath for Giolitti[3] to open the election campaign, so they can come and launch their shabby speechifying laced with assorted banalities, most of which they direct against us (whom they call their 'cousins'). But the Socialist Party no longer has any relatives, on either the left or the right! In the end, these anti-parliamentary gentlemen attach more importance than we do to the action of parliament. We basically care more about the street and the election halls than about the chamber at Montecitorio. They, on the other hand, are feverish canvassers for the candidate *Nobody*. And this Mr *Nobody* is but the representative of the most shapeless 'bloc' of them all: anarchists, syndicalists, Mazzini followers and Catholic intransigents.

He is the candidate of the vast party of indifference – all those people with whom we want nothing to do. And we await the true revolutionaries at the test of the ballot box. As tomorrow we shall await them at the test of the barricades!

2   The Electionist Illusion[4]

For many years – in fact, ever since the socialist party constituted itself as an independent party, separating from all the other democratic fractions with which it had been mixed – in its political activity it has followed the theoretical concept that the conquest of public powers by the proletariat must be achieved by virtue of electoral action.

A rather childish calculation that, nonetheless, has attracted many people, led many to believe that the day in which true universal suffrage is obtained – the day everyone has the right to vote – the majority of the legislative assemblies would inevitably be composed of socialist representatives.

Once these representatives – or, if you prefer, 'socialist deputies' – are in the majority, with a fine law they will not hesitate to sweep the bourgeois powers away and, with all the due legal formalities, will take power in the name of the proletariat. Under the effect of this enchanting mirage any electoral success,

---

3 Giovanni Giolitti (1842–1928), a historical leader of Italian liberalism, was prime minister of Italy five times between 1892 and 1921.

4 *Il Soviet*, Nos. 8 and 9, February 1919.

especially the winning of a new seat in parliament, was, in good faith, considered and duly exalted as a new step forward towards the goal, as a new stone laid in the magnificent edifice of the conquest of public powers by the proletariat.

The figures of the electoral struggles easily permitted many to ply the thankless trade of soothsayer and to set the exact date of the term of the promissory note to be paid to the proletariat by the bourgeoisie. Indeed, many entertained the strange illusion of feeling closer to the great event of the proletariat's taking its place in the limelight of history as the true owner of the world just because one more Cabrini, Bissolati, Turati or Ciccotti[5] had won a seat in the chamber of deputies.

Poor proletarian revolution in nightcap and slippers with a touch of rheumatism and a few missing teeth!

So much for theory. Practice was a bottomless pit of incredible disappointments.

The bourgeois regime – despite its being disembowelled and stuffed by this perilous revolutionary pulp, which was ready to explode and capable of shattering the old crust – did not suffer. Indeed, it grew stronger. In the parliamentary bourgeois environment our fiery revolutionaries cooled off and grew tame; in a little while one of them became a reformist, another a reactionary, yet another a government minister, and so on and so forth.

The poor proletariat, or at least the most conscious part of it, quite rightly grew convinced that, when with great difficulty it managed to send the fatal figure to a legislative assembly – one half plus one of its members! – it would be badly disappointed in the end. These formidable revolutionaries at best would be capable of giving them a perfectly bourgeois republic, American-style or perhaps the Ebert[6] model, which bases its precarious force of resistance on assassination.

And it could not be otherwise.

It is absolutely paradoxical to believe that the current political forms, which were created by the bourgeoisie for their own class domination, can themselves become the organs of an absolutely opposite function.

---

5 Members of parliament representing the reformist right-wing of the Italian Socialist Party.
6 Friedrich Ebert (1871–1925), leader of the German Social Democrats (SPD). He supported Germany's entering the First World War. As head of government in 1918–19 he used the army and the elite *Freikorps* to suppress a Spartacist uprising, and to assassinate Rosa Luxemburg and Karl Liebknecht in February 1919. Five days after the assassination, he was elected as first president of the German Republic.

Indeed the bourgeoisie, when it overthrew the old regime, had to create new state forms. So will the proletariat – and in spades!

The social transformation produced by the proletariat's conquest of power is far deeper. By abolishing private property it automatically destroys the bourgeois class, whose very essence is private ownership of the means of production.

To regulate, organise and discipline the new social relations no longer founded on the right to private property but on the association of workers, new institutions will necessarily have to arise, suitable for these functions that are so profoundly different from those that form the foundations of the bourgeois state.

If political immaturity – the legacy of the democratic ideas that penetrated the thinking of some socialists – and if, above all, the lack of the reality of power, have allowed erroneous conceptions to take shape and gain ground, we now have the great experience of the facts, which ought to serve as a lesson for everyone.

In Russia the dictatorship of the proletariat asserted itself and conquered, overthrowing all bourgeois organs and preventing the formation of new organs created by the old bourgeois mechanism of electoral action. The Bolsheviks in Russia at first combated the constituent assembly – the result of suffrage – with propaganda, and then suppressed it by force. In Germany the Spartacist League[7] has struggled against the constituent assembly promoted by the social-bourgeois leaders Ebert and Scheidemann. Today the Italian maximalists must rise up against the proposals for a constituent assembly formulated by the Confederation of Labour and supported by some socialist deputies. The question is by no means theoretical: when the reality of power is lacking, theory is the guide of action.

The election campaign is in the offing.

The socialist party has to decide whether one must participate in it and with what programme.

The proletariat must not be deceived and must not allow itself to be hoodwinked in the electoral struggle. It must be convinced that winning seats in parliament is of no revolutionary efficacy. It must know what the way to be followed is, and how it can make its effort useful. If it does agree to have socialist deputies, then the limits of their action and of their power within the party itself will have to be established once and for all.

The only organs the party has are the assemblies that deliberate, and the leadership that acts and accounts for its actions every year.

---

7   A left-wing Marxist revolutionary movement organised in Germany during World War I.

The parliamentary group as such, that is, as a group, does not exist for the party, since the role of deputy does not exist in the party. It is a purely bourgeois role, obtained with the votes of non-party members. Its function is extraneous to the party, and it is destined to disappear as soon as the party succeeds in implementing its maximum programme of the conquest of power.

The party leadership, drawing its energies from the party's confidence in it, must face up to its responsibilities by carrying out the deliberations of the party itself, faithfully interpreting its spirit, and in some cases consulting it by referendum.

It is not admissible that the leadership, for deliberations that commit the party to a line of action, should turn to the parliamentary group for advice. In so doing it would implicitly recognise a power in the group that it does not have, a function that is totally non-existent.

It is absolutely essential that these relations be disciplined now, especially after the latest order of the day presented to the group itself by Turati, an order of the day that is totally contrary to the directives clearly manifested by a vast majority of the party.

If this delimitation of relations should give rise to new split-ups, so much the better.

3   The Electoral Trap[8]

In two previous issues we have examined the theoretical reasons why we believe that participation in the future election campaign would be extremely harmful to the Italian Socialist Party, whose aim is the proletariat's taking of power.

To avoid the usual accusations of our not being realistic, we now wish to state our practical reasons for abstention in the current situation, in which quite other forms of action are possible for the attaining of socialist ends.

We are convinced that the electoral system of representation is a device concocted to codify the social domination of a class, the capitalist bourgeoisie, and to function exclusively in its interest.

This system – even when it is provided with all the so-called democratic guarantees of universality, proportionality, secrecy, and freedom of suffrage – inevitable acts to ensure the wealth-holding class the majority of mandates. An electoral mandate authorises the member of parliament to resolve not only

---

8   *Il Soviet*, No. 11, 2 March 1919.

single questions that are current and universally felt, which can thus be decided even by an illiterate, as is the case in a referendum, but all the country's political, economic, and cultural questions, which today's complicated social life can present him with during his mandate. This means that the deputy must have – and ordinarily does have – a culture superior to that which the socioeconomic conditions make it possible for the proletariat to acquire. So here we have the first of a series of class privileges. The parliamentary system of representation puts political power into the hands of an intellectual élite, which is an integral part of the bourgeois class, sharing and therefore fighting for its interests.

It will be said that also a proletarian can gain the culture needed to hold a parliamentary mandate. This is true, and has also been the case, because intelligence and the will to knowledge are not natural endowments of the rich, and at times can overcome the enormous difficulties that today's economic order sets in the way of the spiritual elevation of the poor. But the exceptions do not affect the general process, by which the affluent class is able to acquire higher culture, and the proletarian class is not. As soon as possible, the proletarian has to utilise his labour-power in order to live; the rich man's son can easily spend 15 years in school, since daddy's wallet takes care of his support, housing, clothing, books, fees, and small pleasures. So, while in theory anyone can become a representative of the people in Parliament, in practice, by the necessity of things, in Parliament we find almost exclusively lawyers, professors, journalists, and professionals – people with higher education, because their families had the means to get them that education. Hence in the parliamentary system the exercise of political power is reserved – by their very culture – exclusively for members of the affluent class.

Other conditions contribute to ensure the bourgeoisie a parliamentary monopoly. First of all, there is the economic pressure directly exerted on the electors. When an elector is confronted with the possibility of getting a loan, or a deferment of payment, or a favourable contract, or of avoiding a ruinous dismissal or other form of economic loss if he gives his vote and his support to a given candidate, he is effectively compelled to do so even if he does not share the candidate's political principles, or even know what they are. And it is only the candidates of the affluent bourgeoisie who can give him those things. Indeed, not infrequently these candidates buy votes outright, cash on the barrelhead. And, apart from all this, the candidates of the affluent classes have at their disposal means of electoral propaganda (works of charity, largess, high-class hospitality for group leaders, trips, banquets, posters, and so forth) and therefore probabilities of success that proletarian candidates, or representatives of the far from affluent proletariat, do not.

Add, then, the enormous influence on elections of the press. Newspapers, often the main element of culture for much of the population and, for the proletariat, almost the only one, shape the currents of opinion, attribute ideas and qualities to their candidates that they do not have, distort the programmes of their opponents, or ignore them, or slander them. They insinuate and bend towards their goal – namely, the victory of their candidates – uneducated minds, which is to say the vast majority of the proletariat that reads, or listens to what others have read. And since newspapers today, especially major newspapers, would be in the red if they were not supported by the rich, in an election they become the most effective instruments of victory for the people who pay them – capitalists, the rich, banking groups, industrial groups, suppliers, large landowners, and so forth. In this way too the privilege of wealth asserts itself in the electoral system. Where there is no economic equality there can be no civil and political equality; as long as there is a proletariat that is economically dependent on the capitalist class, the capitalist will be the boss politically as well.

And so far we have supposed that the ruling bourgeoisie loyally observes the electoral laws that it has itself prepared. But everyone knows that this loyalty is to be found only when in a certain place and in a certain situation there appears to be no danger for the ruling class. As soon as the danger appears, goodbye democratic scruples! Money and power – whoever has them will play every trick in the book to falsify the will of the electoral body, if it is slow in knuckling under to the ruling gangs. These gangs use the political power they currently possess to force the will of the masses in every way possible. The travesty is endless: they have the electoral rolls manipulated by state and municipal authorities under the thumb of the ruling class; they strike off their presumed opponents with quibbles, while enrolling their own followers even if unqualified; they have the absent and the dead vote for their delegations; protected by the authorities, they threaten and they bludgeon their opponents; they institute farcical proceedings and then drop them after the election, but in the meantime they have served their purpose of keeping 'dangerous elements' out of circulation; they find jobs and give licences to carry arms and sell state-monopoly goods to the delinquents in their own party while denying them to honest men in the other; and the list goes on and on.

But there is more! Apart from these little acts of low electoral policing, usually left to the local authorities, there are the big actions implemented by the Government. The Government sets the election date as it wishes. It will call for no election if the general state of the spirits is not clearly favourable to the class its members come from, and to which they are bound by a thousand ideal and material ties. It calls for an election as soon as some new circumstance has produced a change for the better in public opinion. It calls for no election as long as the war lasts. It calls for an election, as the English did, when the soldiers who have suffered the horrors of war have not yet come home and thus have to vote under the supervision of their officers, or, as in Germany, when the soldiers yearn for peace and voting for the Government seems to ensure it. In a word, the Government chooses the opportune moment, which gives it a great probability of victory – which means, as things stand now, of victory for the wealthy classes that *alone* hold power.

Elections, as long as wealth and power are in the hands of the bourgeoisie, can do nothing other than confirm this privilege. If they are truly to express the will of the majority – that is, of the proletarians – wealth and power will already have to be in proletarian hands. In a word, the proletariat will have to have already expropriated the bourgeoisie and taken possession of the government. In saying this we do not want to deny that for the proletariat, even in a bourgeois regime, it is possible to win some partial electoral battles. But partial and local successes, often at the cost of more or less clandestine transactions with this or that bourgeois element, which is tantamount to renouncing the fruit of victory in advance, do not destroy the perpetuation of capitalist rule in the state. In Russia and in Germany, the day after the disastrous failure of bourgeois policy, that is, after the defeat and the revolution, elections gave the majority back to the bourgeoisie. In Russia the proletariat perceived the error in time and did away with the elections and the elected; in Germany it allowed itself to be beguiled once again by the democratic fumes of electionism – an error that led to the inexorable re-consolidation of bourgeois class rule.

For all these reasons we believe that, at this point, socialist parties like our own that have set out in the direction of intransigent, revolutionary and maximalist class struggle must cease and desist from valorising with their participation the bourgeois trap of elections and of parliamentarianism. The Bolsheviks in Russia and the Spartacist League in Germany have done so, and now so must we.

Yes, the party's programme also takes into consideration the conquest of power through the participation in elections. But this programme dates from 1892, when it was still possible to believe that the electoral predominance of the bourgeoisie stemmed not from an innate defect in the system but from deficiencies of the electoral law in force. Since then, in Italy and even more so elsewhere, all the electoral reforms invoked by democracy have been implemented: universal suffrage, women's right to vote, proportional representation, and so forth. But the final result is no different. In Italy as in England, in Kerensky's Russia, in Germany, in Bavaria, in Austria, the election results have systematically been in favour of the bourgeoisie, because the electoral system in itself can give no other result. The case of countries such as Russia, Germany and Austria have been especially instructive. The elections were held in a revolutionary period, when the political power of the bourgeoisie had already been greatly shaken, and yet the bourgeois and lumpen-bourgeois parties once again won majorities thanks to their economic superiority. We believe that, at this point, this suffices to persuade the proletariat that it is not by the ballot that it will achieve its emancipation.

We insist, therefore, on the need to convoke our national congress as soon as possible. Despite the overwhelming victory of the extremists, the last congress left too many things unclear and, due to various circumstances, did not delineate a precise programme of action. We have to resolve once and for all and unambiguously, with no twists and turns, all the serious questions that the accelerated life of the past few years has posed for socialist action: the question of adhesion to the concept of 'homeland' and of so-called defensive war; the question of the theoretical legitimacy and actual possibility of the revolutionary conquest of power; the question of the proletarian dictatorship; the question of elections. It is high time that we put an end to the shame and the damage produced by the attitude of men who say they represent the party, and meanwhile take direct action to sabotage that which is the indisputable and crystal-clear will of the party's vast majority.

4   Revolutionary Preparation or Electoral Preparation[9]

We believe we have entered the revolutionary historical period in which the proletariat will succeed in overthrowing bourgeois power, since this result has already been achieved in many countries of Europe. In this period the communists in the other countries must bring all their forces together in order to achieve this goal.

The communist parties must therefore devote themselves to revolutionary preparation, training the proletariat not only for the conquest but also for the exercise of their political dictatorship and identifying within the working class the organisms capable of taking power and of governing society.

This preparation must be carried out in the programmatic field, shaping an awareness in the masses of the complex historical development through which the capitalist era will yield to the era of communism; and in the tactical field,

---

9   *Avanti!*, 21 August 1919.

with the formation of provisional soviets ready to take over local and central power, along with the organisation of all the means of struggle that are indispensable for overthrowing the bourgeoisie.

In the period devoted to this preparation, all the efforts of the communist party are dedicated to creating the environment of the dictatorship of the proletariat. The party must support with the propaganda not only of words but above all of facts the cardinal principle of this dictatorship, that is, of the governing of society by the proletariat class, with the bourgeois minority deprived of all political rights and actions.

If, at the same time, electoral action is adopted to send the representatives of the proletariat and of the party to the elective organs of the bourgeois system, based on that representative democracy which is the historical and political antithesis of the proletarian dictatorship, all effectiveness of the revolutionary preparation would be destroyed.

Even if in the electoral rallies and from the halls of parliament the maximalist programme is aired, the speeches of the candidates and the deputies rest on a de facto contradiction: insisting that the proletariat must govern society politically without the bourgeoisie is in blatant contradiction with the fact that proletarian and bourgeois representatives are permitted to continue to meet one another with equal rights within the legislative organs of the state.

In practice, all of our moral, intellectual, material and financial energies would be dissipated in the vortex of the electoral contest, and the party's people, propagandists, organisers, press, and all its resources would be diverted from the task of revolutionary preparation, to which, unfortunately, they are even now unequal.

Once we have established the theoretical and practical incompatibility between the two preparations, we think there can be no hesitation about the choice, and that electoral intervention can be logically admissible only for those who entertain not even the slightest hope of the possibility of revolution.

The incompatibility of the two forms of activity is not a momentary one, such that a succession of both forms of action would be admissible. Each form presupposes a long period of preparation, and absorbs all the activity of the movement for a very long time.

The concern expressed by some comrades that the current electoral abstention will not lead to the attainment of our revolutionary ends is completely unfounded. Even if remaining without parliamentary representatives, instead of being an advantage – as we firmly believe, based on vast experience – should prove to be a danger, such a danger would not be even remotely comparable to the danger of compromising or even just delaying the proletariat's preparation for the revolutionary conquest of its dictatorship.

Therefore, unless it can be proven that electoral action – not only with its historical approach in theory but also with its well-known practical degenerations – is not fatal to revolutionary training, we must without regrets throw the electionist method on the junk heap and, without looking back, concentrate all our forces on the attainment of the supreme maximal objectives of socialism.[10]

---

10   The PSI successfully participated in 1919 legislative elections held on November 16, securing 1,834,000 votes, 32.8% of the poll. However, this was to result in a Pyrrhic victory.

On Soviets

1   The System of Communist Representation[1]

In launching our communist programme, which contained the outlines of a response to many vital problems concerning the revolutionary movement of the proletariat, we expected all of its points to spark considerable debate.

Instead, the debate has been heated only with regard to the incompatibility of electoral participation, which is soberly affirmed in the programme. Indeed, although the electionist maximalists proclaim that for them electoral action is quite secondary, they are in fact so mesmerised by it that they have launched an avalanche of articles against the few anti-electionist lines contained in our programme. On our side, apart from the ample treatment given in these columns to the reasons for our abstentionism, we have only now begun to use *Avanti!* as a platform to reply to this deluge of electoralist objections.

Hence we are delighted to see that the Turin newspaper *L'Ordine Nuovo* is demanding clarification of the point in the communist programme that states: 'Elections to local councils of the workers will be held *independently of the sectors in which they work, on the basis of their city and province'.*

The writer, comrade Andrea Viglongo, asks whether this is a way of denying that the power of the soviets must come from the masses consulted and voting *at the very place where they work*: in the factories, workshops, mines, and villages.

What the drafters of the programme had in mind was as follows. The *soviet* system is a system of *political* representation of the working class, whose fundamental characteristic is denial of the right to vote to anyone who is not a member of the proletariat.

It has been thought that soviets and trade unions[2] were the same thing. Nothing could be further from the truth. It may have been the case that in various countries, in early stages of the revolution, soviet-type bodies were set up with representation from such organisations, but this was no more than a temporary expedient.

---

1   *Il Soviet*, No. 38, 13 September 1919.
2   Bordiga writes 'economic trade unions', to make the sharpest possible distinction between the economic nature of the trade union and the political nature of the soviet.

While the trade union is designed to defend the sectoral interests of the workers insofar as they belong to a given trade or industry, in the soviet the proletarians are members of a social class that has conquered and exercises political and social power insofar as their interests are shared by all workers of all trades. In the central soviet we have a political representation of the working class, with deputies representing local constituencies.

National representatives of the various sectors have no place in this scheme at all. This in itself gives the lie to trade-unionist interpretations and to the reformist parody of hypothetical constituent assemblies of trades masquerading as soviet-type institutions.

But, in the local soviets of the cities or rural villages, how is the mechanism of representation to be constituted?

If we refer to the Russian system, as stated in Articles 11, 12, 13 and 14 of the Constitution of the Soviet Republic, we may conclude that what is essential is that in the cities there be one delegate for every thousand inhabitants, and in the countryside one for every hundred inhabitants, and that elections be held (Article 66) according to the established customs of the local soviets.

So we are not told that the number of delegates to be elected depends on the number of factories or workplaces, and we do not know whether the elections work by grouping the electors who have a representative, or by some other criterion.

But if we refer to the programmes of communists in other countries, it would seem safe to conclude that the nature of the electoral units, while giving rise to extremely important considerations, is not the basic problem of the soviet order.

The mechanism of the soviets undoubtedly has a dual nature: political and revolutionary on the one hand, economic and constructive on the other.

The first aspect is dominant in the early stages, but as the expropriation of the bourgeoisie proceeds it gradually becomes less important than the second.

The school of necessity will gradually refine the bodies that are technically competent to fulfil this second function: forms of representation of trade-union sectors and production units will emerge and connect with one another, especially in matters of technique and work discipline.

But the fundamental political function of the network of workers' councils is based on the historical concept of dictatorship: proletarian interests must be allowed free play, since they concern *the whole class over and above sectional interests and the entire historical development of the movement for its emancipation.*

The conditions needed to accomplish all of this are, substantially, the exclusion of the bourgeoisie from any participation in political activity, and the appropriate distribution of electors into local constituencies sending delegates to the Congress of Soviets, which appoints the Central Executive Committee and implements the subsequent socialisation of the various sectors of the economy

Seen in relation to this historical definition of the communist representative system, it seems to us that *L'Ordine Nuovo* slightly exaggerates the *formal* definition of this mechanism of representation.

What groups do the voting and where is not a substantial problem: there can be a variety of solutions at the national and regional levels.

Only up to a certain point can the factory internal commissions be seen as precursors of soviets; more precisely, we consider them precursors of the factory councils, which have technical and disciplinary duties during and after the socialisation of the factory itself. The civic political soviet, then, can be elected wherever it is most opportune, and probably in assemblies not very different from the present electoral polls.

The electoral rolls themselves will have to be different. Viglongo poses the question of whether all the workers in the factory will have the right to vote, or only those who are unionised. We invite him to reflect on the fact that some workers, even if unionised, can be struck off the electoral roll of the civic political soviet if it is discovered that, in addition to working in a factory, they live on the proceeds from a small pecuniary or landed capital. This is a not uncommon occurrence among us: the Russian Constitution itself clearly makes provision for it in the first sub-section of Article 65. The legitimately unemployed and incapacitated must also have a vote.

What characterises the communist system, then, is the definition of the right to be an elector, which depends not on membership in a particular trade but on whether or not the individual, in the totality of his or her social relations, is a proletarian engaged in the rapid achievement of communism, or a non-proletarian engaged in preserving the economic relations of private property.

This extremely simple condition guarantees the political functionality of the soviet system of representation. In parallel, new and flexible technical-economic bodies will emerge, which, however, are subordinate to the guidelines established and the measures taken by this system, because until classes are totally abolished only the political system of representation will embody the collective interests of the proletariat, acting as the prime accelerator of the revolutionary process.

On another occasion we shall tackle the question of whether it is possible and appropriate to set up political soviets even before the revolutionary battle for the conquest of power takes place.

2   Is This the Time to Form 'Soviets'?[3]

Two of the articles in our last issue, one devoted to an analysis of the communist system of representation and the other to an exposition of the current tasks
facing our party, concluded by asking whether it is possible and appropriate to
set up workers' and peasants' councils today, while the power of the bourgeoisie
is still intact.

Comrade Ettore Croce, in a discussion of our abstentionist thesis in an article in *Avanti!*, asks us to have a new weapon at the ready before getting rid of
the old weapon of parliamentary action, and looks forward to the formation of
soviets.

In our last issue we clarified the distinction between the technical-economic
and political tasks of the soviet representative bodies, and we showed that
the real organs of the proletarian dictatorship are the local and central political soviets, in which workers are not sub-divided according to their particular
trade.

The supreme authority of these organs is the Central Executive Committee,
which nominates the People's Commissars; parallel to them an entire network
of economic organs arises, based on factory councils and industrial trade unions, which culminate in the Central Council of the Economy.

In Russia, we repeat, while in the CEC and Soviet of Soviets representation is not based on trades but only on local districts, this is not the case
in the Council of the Economy, the organ that is responsible for the technical implementation of the socialisation measures decreed by the political
assembly. In this Council, trade federations and local economic councils play a
role.

The 16 August issue of *L'Ordine Nuovo* contained an interesting article on the
soviet-type system of socialisation.

This article explained how in a first stage, dubbed anarcho-syndicalist, the
factory councils would take over the management of production, but that subsequently, in later stages involving centralisation, they would lose importance.
In the end they would be nothing more than clubs and mutual benefit and
instruction societies for the workers in a particular factory.

If we shift our attention to the German communist movement, we see in the
programme of the Spartacus League that the Workers' and Soldiers' Councils
(WSCs), the bodies that are to take the place of the bourgeois parliaments and
municipal councils, are quite different from factory councils, which (Article 7

---

3   *Il Soviet*, No. 39, 21 September 1919.

of Section III) *regulate working conditions and control production in agreement with the workers' councils, and eventually take over the management of the whole enterprise.*

In Russia only one-third of factory management was constituted by representatives from the factory council, with one-third by representatives from the Supreme Council of the Economy, and one-third by representatives from the Central Federation of Industry (interests of the workforce – general interests of society – interests of the particular industrial sector).

Getting back to Germany, elections to the WSCs follow this mechanism: one council member for every thousand electors. Only the large factories with over a thousand workers constitute a single electoral unit; in the case of small factories and of the unemployed, voting takes place in accordance with methods established by the electoral commission in agreement with various craft and industrial unions.

It seems to us that we have marshalled enough evidence here to be able to declare ourselves supporters of a system of representation that is clearly divided into two divisions: economic and political.

As far as economic functions are concerned, each factory will have its own factory council elected by the workers; this will have a part to play in the socialisation and subsequent management of the plant in accordance with suitable criteria.

As far as the political function is concerned – that is, the formation of local and central organs of authority – elections to proletarian councils will be held on the basis of electoral rolls in which (with the rigorous exclusion of all members of the bourgeoisie, that is, of people who in any way whatsoever live off the work of others) all proletarians are included on an equal footing, irrespective of their trade, and even if they are (legitimately) unemployed or incapacitated.

Bearing all this in mind, is it possible, or desirable, to set up soviets today?

If we are speaking of factory councils, they are already spreading in the form of internal commissions, as in the English 'shop stewards' system. As these are organs that represent the interests of the workforce, they should be set up even while the factory is still in the hands of private capital. Indeed, it would certainly be to our advantage to urge the formation of these factory councils, although we should entertain no illusions as to their innate revolutionary capacity.

This brings us to the most important problem, that of political soviets.

The political soviet represents the collective interests of the working class, insofar as this class does not share power with the bourgeoisie but has succeeded in overthrowing it and excluding it from power.

Hence the full significance and strength of the soviet lies not in this or that structure, but in the fact that it is the organ of a class that is taking the management of society into its own hands. Every member of the soviet is a proletarian conscious that he [or she] is exercising dictatorship in the name of his [or her] own class.

If the bourgeois class is still in power, even if it were possible to convene proletarian voters to elect their own delegates (for there is no question of using the trade unions or existing internal commissions for the purpose), one would simply be giving a formal imitation of a future activity, an imitation devoid of its fundamental revolutionary character.

Those who can represent the proletariat *today*, before it takes power *tomorrow*, are workers who are conscious of this historical eventuality; in other words, the workers who are *members of the communist party*.

In its struggle against bourgeois power, the proletariat is represented by its *class party*, even if this consists of no more than an audacious minority.

The soviets of tomorrow must arise from the local branches of the communist party. These soviets will call on elements who, as soon as the revolution is victorious, will be proposed to the proletarian electoral masses as candidates to form the councils of local worker delegates.

But if it is to fulfil these functions, the communist party *must abandon its participation in elections to organs of bourgeois democracy*. The reasons supporting this statement are obvious.

The party must be composed exclusively of those individuals who can cope with the responsibilities and dangers of the struggle during the period of insurrection and social reorganisation. The conclusion – we shall abandon our participation in elections only when we have already formed soviets – is wrong. A more thorough examination of the question leads, on the contrary, to the following conclusion: for as long as bourgeois power exists, the organ of revolution is the class party; after the smashing of bourgeois power, it is the network of workers' councils.

The class party cannot fulfil this role, nor be in a position to lead the assault against bourgeois power in order to replace parliamentary democracy by the soviet system, unless it renounces the practice of dispatching its own representatives to bourgeois organs.

This renunciation, which is negative only in a formal sense, is the prime condition to be satisfied if the forces of the communist proletariat are to be mobilised.

Unwillingness to make it is tantamount to admitting the uselessness of preparing ourselves to take advantage of the first suitable occasion to declare class war.

3   Take the Factories or Take Power?[4]

The workers' unrest of the last few days in Liguria has featured a phenomenon
that has been occurring quite frequently for some time now, and that deserves
to be considered symptomatic of a particular state of mind among the working
masses.[5]

Instead of stopping work, the workers have so to speak taken over their
factories and attempted to run them on their own account, or rather, without
the presence of the top management. This means, first of all, that they realise
a strike is not such a suitable weapon, especially in certain circumstances.

The economic strike, being directly harmful to the workers themselves, has
its defensive uses because a work stoppage harms the industrialist by reducing
the labour product accruing to him.

This is the normal state of affairs in the capitalist economy, when price-
cutting competition forces continuous growth of production itself. Today, especially in engineering, the industrial sharks are emerging from a period when
they made huge profits with minimal effort. During the war, the state provided
them with raw materials and coal, while also being their only assured pur-
chaser; the state itself, with its militarisation of the factories, ensured strict
discipline of the working masses. What conditions could be more favourable
for a healthy balance-sheet? Now, however, these people are no longer prepared to face all the difficulties bound up with the shortages of coal and raw
materials, market instability, and restlessness among the working masses. In
particular, they are not prepared to put up with the modest profits they usually
made before the war, or perhaps with even less.

So they are not worried by strikes – in fact, they rather welcome them, while
protesting verbally against the workers' excessive, insatiable demands.

The workers have understood this, and when they occupy the factories and
continue to work, instead of going on strike, their action signifies that they do
not simply want not to work, but not to work as the bosses tell them. They no
longer want to work for the bosses and to be exploited by them; they want to
work for themselves, or in the interests of the workforce alone. This state of
mind, which is becoming ever more clearly focused, should be taken fully into
account; but we would not want it to be led astray by wrong assessments.

---

4   *Il Soviet*, Yr. 3/7, 22 February 1920. Unsigned article, attributed to Bordiga.
5   Reports of the first factory occupations and the first experiments in self-management by
    factory councils (Campi di Sestri Ponente engineering plants, Mazzonis cotton mills at Pont
    Canavese and Torre Pellice, and the Ansaldo plants at Viareggio) had appeared in *Avanti!* 43
    and 44, on 19 and 20 February 1920.

It has been said that where there have been factory councils, they have taken over the workshop management and kept the work going there. We would not want the working masses to believe that they can take over the factories and eliminate the capitalists simply by developing factory councils. That would be the most harmful of illusions. The working class will conquer the factories – it would be too slight and uncommunist for each workshop to do it – only after the working class as a whole has taken political power. Without that, the Guardia Regia, the carabinieri, and so on – the mechanism of force and oppression at the disposal of the bourgeoisie, its apparatus of political power – will take care of dispelling all illusions.

All these constant vain efforts that are daily exhausting the workers must be channelled and fused together, organised into one big comprehensive effort that strikes directly at the heart of the bourgeois enemy.

Only a communist party can and must exercise this function; it must focus all its activities on making the working masses more and more conscious of the necessity of this great political action. For this is the only more or less direct path to the takeover of the factories; any other course will be so much effort in vain.

On Strategy and Tactics

1   Theses of the Abstentionist Communist Fraction of the Italian
Socialist Party – May 1920[1]

I.

1. Communism is the doctrine of the social and historical conditions of the
emancipation of the proletariat.

The elaboration of this doctrine began in the period of the first proletarian
uprisings against the consequences of the bourgeois system of production and
took shape in the Marxist critique of the capitalist economy, in the method of
historical materialism, in the theory of class struggle, in the conception of the
developments that the historical process of the proletarian revolution and the
fall of the capitalist regime will present.

2. It is on the basis of this doctrine – which found its first and fundamental
systematic expression in the *Communist Manifesto* of 1848 – that the communist party is constituted.

3. In the present historical period the situation created by bourgeois relations of production, based on the private ownership of the means of production and exchange, on the private appropriation of the products of collective
labour, and on free competition in the private trade of the products themselves,
is becoming more and more intolerable for the proletariat.

4. The political institutions characteristic of capitalism – namely, a state
based on democratic and parliamentary representation – correspond to these
economic relations. In a society divided into classes, the state is the organisation of the power of the economically privileged class. Although the bourgeoisie represents a minority within society, the democratic state represents
the system of armed force organised for the purpose of preserving the capitalist relations of production.

5. The struggle of the proletariat against capitalist exploitation takes on
a succession of forms, ranging from the violent destruction of machines to
craft unions for the improvement of working conditions, to factory councils,
to attempts to take possession of enterprises.

---

1   *Il Soviet*, Nos. 16 and 17, June 1920. These theses were approved by the national Conference of
the Abstentionist Communist Fraction held in Florence, 8–9 May 1920.

In all these particular actions the proletariat moves in the direction of the decisive revolutionary struggle against the power of the bourgeois state that prevents the present relations of production from being shattered.

6. This revolutionary struggle is the conflict between the whole proletarian class and the whole bourgeois class. Its instrument is the political class party, the communist party, which achieves the conscious organisation of the proletarian vanguard, aware of the necessity of unifying its action – in space, by transcending the interests of particular groups, sectors, or nationalities, and in time, by subordinating the partial gains and conquests that do not modify the essence of the bourgeois structure to the final outcome of the struggle.

It is therefore only by organising itself into a political party that the proletariat constitutes itself as a class struggling for emancipation.

7. The aim of the action of the communist party is the violent overthrow of bourgeois rule, the conquest of political power by the proletariat, and its organisation into a ruling class.

8. While parliamentary democracy in which citizens of every class are represented is the form assumed by the organisation of the bourgeoisie as a ruling class, the organisation of the proletariat as a ruling class will be achieved in the dictatorship of the proletariat; that is, in a type of state in which deputies (the system of workers' councils) will be elected by members of the working class alone (industrial proletariat and poor peasants), with the bourgeoisie denied the right to vote.

9. After the old bureaucratic, police, and military machine has been destroyed, the proletarian state will unify the armed forces of the working class into an organisation whose task will consist in repressing all counter-revolutionary attempts by the defeated class, and taking measures to transform the bourgeois relations of production and property.

10. The process of transition from a capitalist to a communist economy will be extremely complex and its phases will differ according to the differing conditions of economic development. The endpoint of this process will be the total achievement of the ownership and management of the means of production by the whole unified collectivity, the central and rational distribution of productive forces among the different branches of production, and the central administration of the allocation of products by the collectivity.

11. When capitalist economic relationships have been entirely eliminated, the abolition of classes will be an accomplished fact and the state, as a political apparatus of power, will be progressively replaced by the rational, collective administration of economic and social activity.

12. The process of transforming the relations of production will be accompanied by a wide range of social measures stemming from the principle that the

collectivity takes care of the physical and intellectual existence of all its members. In this way all the degenerative defects that the proletariat has inherited from the capitalist world will be progressively eliminated and, in the words of the *Manifesto*, in place of the old bourgeois society with its classes and class antagonisms we shall have an association in which the free development of each is the condition for the free development of all.

13. The conditions for the victory of proletarian power in the struggle to achieve communism consist less in the rational use of skills in technical tasks than in the fact that political responsibilities and the control of the state apparatus are entrusted to people who will put the general interest and the final triumph of communism before the limited interests of particular groups.

Precisely because the communist party is the organisation of those proletarians who have achieved this class consciousness, the aim of the party will be, by its propaganda, to win elective posts for its members within the social organisation. The dictatorship of the proletariat will therefore be the dictatorship of the communist party, which will be a government party in a sense totally opposed to that of the old oligarchies, since communists will take responsibilities that demand the maximum of sacrifice and renunciation, and will take upon their shoulders the heaviest burden of the revolutionary task incumbent on the proletariat in the difficult labour that will give birth to a new world.

II.

1. The communist critique that is incessantly being developed on the basis of its fundamental methods and the propagation of the conclusions that it draws are designed to extirpate the influence that the ideological systems of other classes and other parties hold over the proletariat.

2. First of all, communism sweeps away the idealist conceptions that take the facts of the world of thought as the base rather than the result of the real relations of human life and of their development. All religious and philosophical formulations of this type must be seen as the ideological baggage of classes whose rule preceded the bourgeois epoch and rested on an ecclesiastical, aristocratic, or dynastic organisation, justifiable only on the basis of claimed superhuman authority.

One symptom of the decadence of the modern bourgeoisie is the fact that those old ideologies that it had itself destroyed reappear in its midst under new forms.

A communism founded on idealist bases would be an unacceptable absurdity.

3. Even more characteristically, communism represents the critical demolition of the conceptions of liberalism and bourgeois democracy. The juridical

assertion of the freedom of thought and the political equality of citizens, along with the conception that institutions founded on the rights of the majority and on the mechanism of universal electoral representation are a sufficient base for a gradual and indefinite progress of human society, constitute the ideologies that correspond to the regime of private economy and free competition, and to the interests of the capitalist class.

4. One of the illusions of bourgeois democracy is the belief that the living conditions of the masses can be improved by increasing the education and training provided by the ruling classes and their institutions. In fact, the intellectual elevation of the great masses demands a high standard of material living that is incompatible with the bourgeois regime. What is more, the bourgeoisie, through its schools, attempts to propagate precisely those ideologies that prevent the masses from seeing the present institutions as the obstacle to their emancipation.

5. Another fundamental tenet of bourgeois democracy is the principle of nationality. Class necessities of the bourgeoisie, in consolidating its power, lead to the formation of national states, whose national and patriotic ideologies – corresponding to certain interests in the early period of capitalism that were common to people of the same race, language and customs – it exploits to delay and mitigate the conflict between the capitalist state and the proletarian masses.

National irredentism stems, accordingly, from essentially bourgeois interests.

The bourgeoisie itself does not hesitate to trample on the principle of nationality when the development of capitalism drives it to the often violent conquest of foreign markets, objects of contention between the great states. Communism overcomes this principle when it brings to light the similar conditions of disinherited workers, whatever their nationalities, in relation to their employers, and posits international union as the type of political organisation the proletariat will create when it, in its turn, comes to power.

In the light of the communist critique the cause of the recent world war is shown to be capitalist imperialism. In this light the various interpretations that see it, from the viewpoint of one or another bourgeois state, as a claiming of the right of certain peoples' nationality, as a conflict between states democratically more advanced and states organised in pre-bourgeois fashion, or as bourgeois self-defence against enemy aggression, have no validity.

6. Communism also opposes the views of bourgeois pacifism and Wilsonian illusions on the possibility of a world association of states, based on disarmament and arbitration, conditioned by the utopia of a subdivision of states based on nationality. For communists, war will be made impossible and national

questions will be solved only when the capitalist regime has been replaced by the International Communist Republic.

7. A third aspect: communism presents itself as the overcoming of the systems of utopian socialism that sought to eliminate the defects of social organisation by instituting complete plans for a new organisation of society, but whose possibility of realisation – left to the initiatives of potentates or to the missions of philanthropists – was totally unrelated to the real development of history.

8. The proletariat's elaboration of its own theoretical interpretation of society and history to guide its action against the social relations of the capitalist world gives rise to a multitude of schools or currents, influenced to a greater or lesser degree by the very immaturity of the conditions of struggle and by the full range of bourgeois prejudices. While this results in errors and setbacks of proletarian action, it is on the basis of this experience that the communist movement comes to express its doctrine and its tactics with ever greater clarity, sharply differentiating itself from all the other currents active within the proletariat and openly combating them.

9. The formation of producers' cooperatives, in which the capital belongs to the workers who work there, cannot be a path towards the suppression of the capitalist system, since the acquisition of raw materials and the distribution of products follow the laws of private economy, and credit – and thus the control of private capital – ends up dominating the collective capital itself.

10. Communists cannot consider trade unions to be sufficient for the struggle for the proletarian revolution or as fundamental organs of the communist economy.

Organisation in trade unions serves to neutralise competition between workers of the same trade and keeps wages from falling to rock-bottom levels, but, just as it cannot eliminate capitalist profit, neither can it bring together workers of all trades to combat the privilege of bourgeois power. Indeed, simply transferring the ownership of enterprises from private owners to workers' unions cannot realise the economic postulates of communism, which demand that property be transferred to the entire proletarian collectivity, since this is the only way to eliminate the characteristics of the private economy in the appropriation and distribution of products.

Communists consider the trade union as the field of a first proletarian experience, which permits the workers to go further, towards the concept and the praxis of the political struggle whose organ is the class party.

11. In general, it is an error to believe that the revolution is a question of the form of organisation of the proletarians according to the groups they form based on their position and their interests in the framework of the capitalist system of production.

This means that modification of the structure of economic organisation cannot give the proletariat the means it needs for its emancipation.

Company unions or factory councils emerge as organs to defend the interests of the proletarians of various enterprises when it begins to appear possible to limit capitalist authority in their management. The acquisition by these organs of a more or less ample right of control over production is, however, not incompatible with the capitalist system, and could therefore be a conservative resource.

As we said in the case of the unions, even the transfer of factory management to factory councils would not herald the advent of the communist system. According to the sound communist conception, workers' control of production will be achieved only after the overthrow of bourgeois power, and will take the form of control by the entire unified proletariat over the management of each enterprise in a workers' council state. Communist management of production will mean that every branch and unit of production will be directed by rational collective organs that will represent the interests of all workers united in the work of building communism.

12. The organs of bourgeois power cannot modify capitalist relations of production.

This is why the transfer of private enterprises to the state or to local administrations does not correspond in the least to the communist conception. Such transfers always entail payment of the capital value of the enterprise to the former owners, who thus fully retain their right to exploit. The enterprises themselves continue to function as private enterprises within the framework of the capitalist economy. For the bourgeois state, they often become convenient means of class preservation and defence.

13. The notion that capitalist exploitation of the proletariat can be gradually diminished and then eliminated by the legislative and reformist action of the current political institutions, sparked by representatives of the proletarian party in these institutions or even by mass struggles, leads only to complicity in the bourgeoisie's defence of its own privileges. On occasion the bourgeoisie pretends to give up just a few of these privileges, in an attempt to placate the impatience of the masses and to deflect their revolutionary attacks on the foundations of the capitalist regime.

14. The conquest of political power by the proletariat, also considered as the fundamental purpose of its action, cannot be achieved by winning a majority in the bourgeois elective organs.

The bourgeoisie, through the executive organs of the state, which are its direct agents, easily ensures its constituents – or those who, seeking election individually or collectively, play its game or come under its influence – a majority in the elective organs. Furthermore, participation in these institutions entails a commitment to respect the juridical and political cornerstones of the bourgeois constitution. The purely formal value of this commitment is nevertheless sufficient to free the bourgeoisie from even the minimal embarrassment of an accusation of formal illegality when, logically enough, it defends its domination by force of arms rather than relinquishing its power and allowing its bureaucratic and military machine to be shattered.

15. Recognising the necessity of insurrectionary struggle for the taking of power while, at the same time, proposing that the proletariat exercise its power by granting the bourgeoisie representation in the new political organisations (constituent assemblies or their combination with the system of workers' councils) is an unacceptable programme that clashes with the central communist concept of the dictatorship of the proletariat. The process of expropriating the bourgeoisie would be immediately compromised if it is left with footholds to influence representation in the expropriating proletarian state. This would permit the bourgeoisie to use the influence it will inevitably retain by 'virtue' of its experience and its intellectual and technical training to counterattack and re-establish its power in a counter-revolution. Any democratic preconception about the equal treatment the proletariat ought to grant the bourgeois regarding freedom of association, of propaganda, of the press, would come to the same sad end.

16. The programme of an organisation of political representation based on delegates from the various trades and professions of all the social classes is not even a formal step towards the system of workers' councils, because the councils entail the exclusion of the bourgeoisie from the right to vote and their central organ is not chosen on the basis of trades but of local constituencies. The form of representation in question is, rather, a stage even lower than the current parliamentary democracy.

17. There is a profound difference between communist concepts and anarchism, which tends toward the immediate installation of a society without a state or a political system. For the economy of the future, anarchism advocates the autonomous functioning of units of production, rejecting any central organisation and regulation of human activities in production and distribution. Such a conception is close to that of the bourgeois private economy, and is alien to the essential content of communism. Furthermore, the immediate elimination of the state as an instrument of political power is equivalent to non-resistance to the counter-revolution, or else it presupposes the immediate abolition of classes – so-called revolutionary expropriation – simultaneously with the insurrection against bourgeois power.

There is not the slightest possibility of this, given the complexity of the proletarian task in replacing the present economy with a communist economy, and given the necessity that this process be directed by a central organ that coordinates in itself the general interest of the proletariat and subordinates to this interest all local and particular interests, which are the principal conservative force within capitalism.

III.

1. The communist conception and economic determinism turn communists not into passive spectators of historical destiny but, on the contrary, into tireless fighters. Struggle and action, however, are ineffective if they are detached from the lessons of doctrine and of communist critical experience.

2. The revolutionary work of communists is based on the organisation into a party of the proletarians who combine consciousness of communist principles with the decision to devote their every effort to the cause of the revolution.

The party, organised internationally, functions on the basis of disciplined respect for the decisions of the majorities, and for the decisions of the central organs these majorities have chosen to lead the movement.

3. Propaganda and proselytism are fundamental activities of the party, based, for the admission of new members, on maximum guarantees. The communist movement – while basing the success of its action on the propagation of its principles and of its ends and struggling in the interest of the immense majority of society – does not make majority consensus a precondition for its action. The criterion for the advisability of taking revolutionary action is the objective evaluation of its own forces and those of its adversaries in their complex coefficients: here, number is not the only coefficient, or the most important one either.

4. The communist party, internally, conducts intense work of study and criticism, strictly connected with the need for action and for historical experience, doing its utmost to organise this work on an international basis. Externally, in all circumstances and with all possible means, it works to propagate the lessons of its critical experience and to refute its rival schools and parties. Above all, the party conducts its activity of propaganda and proselytism among the proletarian masses, especially at the moment in which they rise up against the conditions capitalism has imposed on them, and within the organisations they have formed to defend their immediate interests.

5. Hence communists enter into proletarian cooperatives, trade unions and factory councils, forming groups of communist workers within them. The objective is to win a majority and positions of leadership, in order that the mass of proletarians mobilised by these associations subordinate their action to the highest political and revolutionary ends of the struggle for communism.

6. By contrast, the communist party remains aloof from all institutions and associations in which proletarians and bourgeois participate on an equal footing or, worse still, in which management and patronage are in the hands of the bourgeoisie (reciprocal aid associations, charities, cultural schools, popular universities, Masonic lodges, and the like), and seeks to estrange the proletarians from them by combating their action and influence.

7. Participation in elections to the representative organs of bourgeois democracy and in parliamentary activity – despite the constant danger of deviation – could have been used for propaganda and for educating the movement in the period in which, with the possibility of overthrowing bourgeois rule not yet in the offing, the party's task was limited to criticising and to opposition. In the current period, which opened with the end of the world war, the first communist revolutions, and the rise of the Third International, for communists the direct objective of the political action of the proletariat of all countries is the revolutionary conquest of power, to which all forces and all the work of preparation must be devoted.

In this period we communists accept no participation in those organs that are in fact a powerful tool in defence of the bourgeoisie operating in the very ranks of the proletariat: in antithesis to the structure and to the functions of these organs we communists support the system of workers' councils and proletarian dictatorship.

Due to the great practical importance of electoral action, it is not possible to reconcile this action with the statement that elections are not the means of achieving the party's principal objective, namely, the conquest of power; neither can electoral action be prevented from absorbing all the activity of the movement, diverting it from revolutionary preparation.

8. The electoral conquest of local municipalities and administrations, while presenting to a greater degree the same disadvantages as parliamentarianism, cannot be accepted as a means of action against bourgeois power. This is because these organs have no real power but are subjected to the power of the state machine, and because this method – even though it can create some embarrassment for the ruling bourgeoisie by asserting the principle of local autonomy, which is antithetic to the communist principle of centralised action – would give the bourgeoisie a foothold in its war against proletarian power.

9. In the revolutionary period all efforts of the communists focus on making the action of the masses as intense and effective as possible. The communists combine propaganda and preparation with large and frequent proletarian demonstrations especially in the cities, and seek to utilise economic movements to organise political demonstrations in which the proletariat asserts and consolidates its will to overthrow the power of the bourgeoisie.

10. The communist party brings its propaganda into the ranks of the bourgeois army. Communist anti-militarism is not based on a sterile humanitarianism, but is aimed at convincing proletarians that the bourgeoisie arms them to defend its own interests and to exploit their strength against the cause of the proletariat.

11. The communist party trains itself to act as the general staff of the proletariat in the revolutionary war. Therefore it prepares and organises its own network of intelligence and communication. Above all, it supports and organises the arming of the proletariat.

12. The communist party makes no agreements or alliances with other political movements that share with it some contingent objective but that diverge from it in their programme of further action. It also rejects the principle of allying itself with all those proletarian currents that accept insurrectionary action against the bourgeoisie (the so-called 'united front') but disagree with the communist programme in the carrying out of further action.

Communists have no reason to consider the growth of forces seeking to overthrow bourgeois power as a favourable condition when the forces working for the constitution of proletarian power on the basis of communist directives remain insufficient, since only communist leadership can assure their endurance and their success.

13. The soviets – councils of workers, peasants and soldiers – constitute the organs of proletarian power and can exercise their true function only when the bourgeoisie has been overthrown.

Soviets are not in themselves organs of revolutionary struggle; they become revolutionary when the communist party wins a majority within them.

Workers' councils can also arise before the revolution, in a period of acute crisis in which the power of the bourgeois state is seriously threatened.

The decision to form soviets may be a necessity for the party in a revolutionary situation, but it is not a means of provoking such a situation.

If the power of the bourgeoisie is consolidated, the survival of the councils can present the revolutionary struggle with the grave danger of a reconciliation and combination of proletarian organs with the institutions of bourgeois democracy.

14. What distinguishes communists is not their proposing that all the proletarian forces immediately enter the arena for a general insurrection in every situation and in every episode of the class struggle. On the contrary, what distinguishes them is their conviction that the insurrectional phase is the inevitable outcome of the struggle, and their preparing the proletariat to face it in conditions that are favourable to the success and further development of the revolution.

On the basis of situations that the party can better assess than the rest of the proletariat, the party can, therefore, be faced with the need for action to hasten, or to delay, the decisive collision.

In any case it is the party's specific task to fight against those who, desiring to hasten revolutionary action at all costs, could drive the proletariat into disaster, and against the opportunists who take advantage of circumstances unfavourable to decisive action to put definitive halts to the revolutionary uprising, diverting the action of the masses towards other objectives. The communist party must decisively lead the action of the masses in the direction of effective preparation for the inevitable and final armed struggle against the defenders of the bourgeois order.

2   The Tactics of the Communist International in the Draft Theses Presented by the Communist Party of Italy at the Fourth World Congress: Moscow, November 1922[2]

Conditions for the realisation of the revolutionary goals of the Communist International are objective to the extent that they derive from the situation of the capitalist regime and in particular the critical phase it is going through. They are subjective as concerns the capacity of the working class to struggle for the overthrow of bourgeois power and organise its own dictatorship through the unity of its actions; that is, by successfully subordinating all the partial interests of limited groups to the general interest of the proletariat as a whole and the final goal of the revolution.

The subjective conditions are of two kinds, namely:

a)   the existence of communist parties armed with a clear programmatic vision and a well-defined organisation that ensures its unity of action;

b)   a degree of influence of the communist party on the mass of workers and their economic organisations that gives it an advantage over the other political tendencies of the proletariat.

The problem of tactics consists in seeking the means that would best permit the communist parties to realise simultaneously these subjective revolutionary conditions, basing themselves on the objective conditions and their process of development.

_____

2   *Stato Operaio*, 6 March 1924.

2.1   Formation of Communist Parties and of the Communist International

The failure of the Second International and the Russian revolution gave rise to a reconstitution of the revolutionary ideology of the proletariat and to its political reorganisation within the ranks of the Communist International.

In order to fulfil its task of unifying and directing the struggle of the proletariat of all nations toward the final goal of the world revolution, the Communist International must above all ensure its own unity of programme and organisation. All sections and all militants of the Communist International must be united by their adherence in principle to the common programme of the Communist International.

By eliminating every vestige of the federalism of the old International, the international organisation must ensure maximum centralisation and discipline. This process is still unfolding, hindered by the difficulties resulting from the different conditions that exist in each country and the persistence of the traditions of opportunism. A favourable outcome will not be ensured by mechanical expedients but by the realisation of an effective unity of method that highlights traits common to the actions of proletarian vanguards in the different countries.

One cannot allow any political group to be integrated into the international revolutionary discipline and organisation by virtue of its simple adherence to certain texts and its promise to uphold a series of commitments. On the contrary, one must take into account the real process that unfolds within organised groups (parties and tendencies) acting in the proletarian political arena, the formation of their ideology and their active experience, in order to judge whether, and to what degree, they can be part of the Communist International.

Disciplinary crises within the Communist International derive from the two faces that traditional opportunism assumes today. At times it enthusiastically accepts the formulations of the tactical experience of the Communist International without understanding their solid connection with revolutionary goals, seeing their external forms of application as a return to the old opportunist methods destitute of all finalistic and revolutionary consciousness and will. At other times opportunism rejects these tactical formulations while criticising them superficially as a renunciation of or retreat from the objectives of the revolutionary programme. Both cases stem from a lack of understanding of the relations between the employment of communist means and ends.

In order to eliminate the dangers of opportunism and disciplinary crises, the Communist International must base its organisational centralisation on the clarity and precision of its tactical resolutions and on the exact definition of the methods to be applied.

A political organisation – that is, an organisation founded upon the voluntary adherence of all of its members – only responds to the demands of centralised action when its members know and accept the overall methods that the
centre can order them to apply in various situations.

The prestige and authority of the centre, which is not based upon material
sanctions but can only avail itself of psychological factors, demands absolute
clarity, firmness and continuity in its programmatic declarations and methods
of struggle. This is the only guarantee of being able to constitute a centre of
action that can truly unite the international proletariat.

A solid organisation can only arise from the stability of its organisational
norms; by assuring that these norms will be applied with impartiality, this stability reduces the risk of revolts and desertions to a minimum. No less than its
ideology and tactical norms, its organisational statutes must give an impression
of unity and continuity.

The preceding remarks, based on a wealth of experience, demonstrate that
in passing from the phase of constructing an International of communist
parties to that of the actions of the International Communist Party it is necessary to eliminate organisational norms that are abnormal. We refer to abnor-
malities such as: the fusion of individual sections of the International with
other political organisms; the constitution of certain sections not on the basis
of personal adherence but on the basis of the adherence of workers' organisations; the existence of fractions or groups organised as tendencies within
the communist organisation; the systematic penetration and *noyautage*[3] by the
sections of the International of other organisms whose nature and discipline
is political (this applies in particular to military organisations).

To the extent that the International employs such expedients, manifestations of federalism and breaches of discipline will be inevitable. If the process
of progressive elimination of such anomalies should stop or be reversed, or if
they become systematic, the International would be faced with the extremely
grave danger of a relapse into opportunism.

2.2   *Winning over the Masses*

Gaining ever-increasing influence over the masses is a fundamental task of
communist parties. In order to do so they must have recourse to all the tactical
means that the objective situation allows and that will ensure an ever-widening
extension of the forms of its ideological and organisational influence within the
proletariat.

---

3   Infiltration.

The masses cannot be won over simply by propaganda of the party ideology and proselytism; the party must participate in every action to which the proletariat is driven by its economic condition. It must be made clear to the workers that these actions by themselves cannot ensure the victory of their interests; they can only provide experience, such as a given result in the organisational area, and a will to struggle within the context of the general revolutionary struggle. These results will be achieved not by denying such actions but by stimulating them, by inciting the workers to undertake them and by presenting them with immediate demands that serve to bring about an ever-broader union of workers participating in the struggle.

For Marxist revolutionary parties the struggle for the concrete economic demands of groups of proletarians in trade unions or similar groups was a fundamental necessity even in normal conditions of capitalist development. Also social and political demands in general must be of service to revolutionary work. But such demands must not present an occasion for compromise with the bourgeoisie in which the proletariat pays for bourgeois concessions by giving up the independence of its class organisations, the propagandising of its programme, and its revolutionary methods.

By means of actions on behalf of partial demands, the communist party establishes contact with the mass that allows it to gain new recruits: by adding to its propaganda the lessons of its experience, the party gains sympathy and popularity and creates a larger organising network around itself linked, on the one hand, to the deepest layers of the masses and, on the other, to the central leadership of the party itself. In this way the unitary discipline of the working class develops. This is obtained by means of systematic *noyautage* of trade-unions, co-operatives, and all forms of organisation whose aim is the defence of the interests of the working class. Analogous organisational networks must be developed as soon as possible in every area of party activity: armed struggle and military action, education and culture, work with youth and women, penetration of the army, and so on. The objective of such work is to gain for the communist party an influence over a large part of the working class that is not only ideological but also organisational. Consequently, in their work in the trade unions the communists aim to broaden the base of the unions to the widest possible extent, as they do with all analogous organisations, combating any division and fighting for organisational unification where a division exists, as long as they are guaranteed at least some possibility of circulating their propaganda and promoting communist *noyautage*. In special cases, such activity can also be undertaken illegally and clandestinely.

Communist parties, while attempting to win over the majority of organised workers in order to gain control of trade-union federations, an indispensable lever for manoeuvring within revolutionary struggles, are nevertheless willing to discipline themselves to accept the decisions of the union leadership and do not demand that, in their statutes or in other special accords, these trade-union (or similar) organisations officially commit themselves to being controlled by the party.

2.3   The United Front

The capitalist offensive and its particular current characteristics present the communist parties with special tactical possibilities for developing their influence over the masses. It is this situation that has given rise to the tactics of the united front.

The capitalist offensive has a dual aim: on the one hand, to destroy the proletarian organisations capable of leading a revolutionary offensive; on the other, to intensify the economic exploitation of the workers in an attempt to reconstitute the bourgeois economy. Hence this offensive collides head-on with the interests also of those proletarians who have not yet attained revolutionary consciousness and entered the revolutionary organisation, and assails the very organisations that have no revolutionary programme and are directed by opportunist elements. The bureaucracy that manages these organisms understands that accepting the struggle, even defensively, is equivalent to posing a revolutionary problem, provoking the workers to draw up in a battle-front against the bourgeois class and its institutions. Hence it sabotages even simple defensive resistance, and in so doing renounces the illusory programme of gradual improvement of the living conditions of the proletariat.

This situation allows the communist parties to bring into the struggle also that part of the workers who have not developed a political consciousness. Communist parties can thus invite these strata of workers to join in unitary actions for such concrete and immediate demands as the defence of interests threatened by the capitalist offensive.

To this end, communists propose an action common to all the proletarian forces within organisations of the most divergent tendencies.

These tactics must never enter into contradiction with the fundamental task of the communist party: developing within the working mass the consciousness that only the communist programme and the organisational framework around the communist party will lead it to its emancipation.

The perspective of the united front is double. The call for a united front will serve as a campaign against the programmes and influence of other proletarian organisations, if they refuse the invitation to action launched by the communists; in that case, the communist party's advantage is evident. If, by contrast, the call effectively leads to an action in which all proletarian organisations as well as the entire proletariat participate, the communist party will make every effort to take control of the movement when general conditions allow it to lead the movement to a revolutionary outcome. If that should prove to be impossible, the communist party must make use of every available means – whether, given the vicissitudes of the struggle, it be a partial success or, if it is unavoidable, a failure – to convince the masses that it is the communist party that is best prepared to lead the proletarian cause to victory. If the communist party has previously waged a campaign on the basis of precise propositions that would guarantee the success of the struggle, it will be able, by means of its forces struggling in the front ranks of the common action, to create a conviction in the masses that victory will only be possible when non-communist organisations no longer hold a preponderant influence over them.

The tactics of the united front are thus a means of gaining overwhelming ideological and organising influence for the party.

The masses' instinctive tendency towards unity must be utilised when it can be useful for the favourable employment of united front tactics; it must be combated when it would lead to the opposite result.

The grave tactical problem of the united front thus presents limits beyond which our action would fail to achieve its ends. These limits must be defined in relation to the content of the demands and the means of struggle proposed, and to the organisational bases to be proposed or accepted as the platform of the proletarian forces.

The demands the communist party presents for the united front must not be in contradiction with the programmes of the various organisations with which it proposes to form a coalition, and must be attainable by methods of struggle that none of these organisms can in principle reject.

Only in this way will it be possible to wage a campaign against the organisations that refuse to adhere to the proposal for a united front: and, in the opposite case, only in this way will it be possible to utilise the development of the action to the advantage of communist influence.

All demands that can be pursued by means of direct action by the party can be presented: the defence of wages and of labour agreements in industry and agriculture; the struggle against dismissals and unemployment; and an effective defence of the right of association and agitation.

All the means of struggle that the communist party does not reject for its own independent actions can be proposed, hence all forms of propaganda, agitation and struggle in which the proletarian class sharply and openly takes its stand against capital.

Finally, the bases of the coalition must be such that, since the entirety of the communist proposals are known to the masses, even if other proletarian organisations, without having accepted them, nevertheless engage in a proletarian general action (using the same means of struggle advocated by the communist party – a general strike, and so on – but with other objectives), the communist party, while not refusing to participate in the common action, can nonetheless lay the responsibility for the leadership of the struggle on the other organisations in the event of a proletarian defeat.

Hence the communist party will refuse to be a part of organisms common to various political forces that act with continuity and with collective responsibility at the head of the general movement of the proletariat. The communist party will also avoid appearing to be in agreement with common declarations with political parties when these declarations even partially contradict its programme and are presented to the proletariat as the result of negotiations to find a common line of action.

When it is not a question of a brief public polemic by means of which the party invites the other organisations to act while predicting with certainty that they will refuse, but when, on the contrary, it is possible that a common action will result, the central leadership of the coalition will have to consist of an alliance of proletarian organisms of a trade-union (or union-related) character. In this way, the leadership will be perceived by the masses as susceptible to the influence of the various parties acting within the worker organisations.

Only in this way will it be possible to ensure the useful employment of the tactics of the united front even in an action that, due to the influence of the opportunists, leads to an incomplete victory or a defeat for the working class.

2.4   The Workers' Government

Immediate demands that concern the proletariat can also be connected with the politics of the state.

These demands must be formulated by the communist party and proposed as objectives for an action of the entire proletariat, performed by means of external pressure on the government in which all means of agitation are employed.

When the proletariat sees for itself that its demands can be met only if the government in place is changed, the communist party must make this fact the basis of its propaganda for the overthrow of bourgeois power and the proletarian dictatorship; the party must act analogously when the workers realise that their economic demands find no place in the context of the capitalist economy.

When the governmental regime finds itself in a critical situation as a result of the power relations between social forces, its overthrow must be presented not as a simple propaganda formula, but as a concrete demand accessible to the mass. This demand (power to the soviets, to the committees of control, to the committees of the trade-union alliance) can be presented to workers of all parties (or without parties) represented in such organisations. All the workers will be inclined to accept it, even against the will of their leaders. This demand is an integral part of the political task of the communist party, since its realisation entails the revolutionary struggle and the suppression of bourgeois democracy, and proposing it aligns the entire proletarian mass along this trajectory. But it cannot be excluded that an extra-parliamentary watchword of this kind be given in parliament itself or in the course of an election campaign.

To speak of a workers' government as a coalition government of workers' parties without indicating the form of representative institution on which such a government will be based does not express a demand that the workers can understand, but only a propagandistic formula that brings confusion into the ideological preparation and politics of the revolution. Parties are organisations constituted to take power, and the parties that form the workers' government cannot be the same parties that support the preservation of bourgeois parliamentary institutions.

To speak of a workers' government by declaring, or not excluding, that it can arise from a parliamentary coalition with communist-party participation is to deny in practise the communist political programme. It is to deny the necessity of preparing the masses to struggle for their dictatorship.

The world political situation gives no sign of the formation of governments of transition between the bourgeois parliamentary regime and the dictatorship of the proletariat, but rather of bourgeois coalition governments that will energetically lead the counter-revolutionary struggle for the defence of the system. If transition governments should arise it is a necessity of principle that the communist party leave the responsibility to lead them to the social-democratic parties, as long as such governments are based on bourgeois institutions. Only in this way can the communist party dedicate itself to the preparation of the revolutionary conquest of power and to the inheritance of the transitional government.

2.5   Winning over the Organised Masses

The existence of strong and flourishing union and union-related organisations is a condition that favours the work of winning over the masses. The deepening chaos of the capitalist economy has created an objectively revolutionary situation. But at the moment when, after the apparent prosperity of the immediate postwar period, the crisis appeared in all its gravity, the capacity for struggle of the proletariat showed itself to be insufficient. This is why we are now witnessing a veritable haemorrhage from trade unions and all analogous organisations in many countries, with the likelihood that many others will soon follow suit.

As a result, revolutionary preparation of the proletariat has become more difficult, despite the spread of misery and discontent.

We are confronted with the problem of how, under the leadership of the communist parties, to recruit the masses of unemployed workers and proletarians reduced to a state of chaos by the paralysis of the productive machine. It is possible that before too long this problem will appear even graver than that of winning over workers who follow other proletarian parties through the intermediary of the economic organisations these parties head – a problem to which the tactics of the united front offers a satisfactory solution. One can even expect that as the economic decline is accompanied by an intensification of the unitary counter-revolutionary activity of all bourgeois forces, non-communist proletarian economic organisations will be abandoned by their members all the more rapidly. The terms of the problem of how to win over the masses will be modified.

Since revolutionary work must always be based upon real concrete situations, a new form of organisation of proletarian interests will have to be created. The task in the current phase is that of enveloping the strata of non-organised proletarians with forms of adequate representation and aligning them around the committees and organs of the united front of organisations. The communist party will have to be the centre of the struggle and of the counterattack against the reactionary centralisation of capitalism that is crushing a scattered, dispersed working class, definitively abandoned by the opportunist bureaucracy.

3   Theses on the Tactics of the Communist Party of Italy (Rome Theses – 1922)[4]

VII. 'Direct' tactical action of the communist party

40. We have considered the case in which the attention of the masses is drawn to the demands the parties of the bourgeois left and of social democracy formulate as strongholds to be conquered and defended. In this case, the communist party presents them in its turn, with greater clarity and energy, while at

---

4   *Rassegna Comunista*, Vol. II, No. 17, 30 January 1922. Drafted by Amadeo Bordiga and Umberto Terracini. This excerpt is the last section of the Theses.

the same time openly criticising the insufficiency of the means that the other parties have proposed to realise them. But there are other cases where the immediate and pressing needs of the working class, whether for further gains or simple self-defence, have been met with indifference from the left or social-democratic parties. If the communist party does not dispose of sufficient forces for a direct appeal to the masses because of social-democratic influences over them, it will take up these demands and call for their realisation by a united front of the proletariat on economic issues. In this way it avoids having to make an offer of alliance with the social democrats, and can even accuse them of betraying the contingent and immediate interests of the workers. This unitary action would find the communist militants in the trade unions at their posts but would leave the party the possibility of intervening when the struggle took another course, which would inevitably be opposed by the social democrats, and at times by the syndicalists and anarchists. Moreover, a refusal by the other proletarian parties to create an economic united front for those demands will be used by the communist party to demolish their influence, not only with criticism and propaganda that demonstrate their rank complicity with the bourgeoisie but, above all, with front-line participation in those partial actions of the proletariat that will inevitably arise on the basis of those cornerstones on which the party had proposed the economic united front of all the local organisations and trades. This will serve as concrete proof that the social-democratic leadership, in opposing the spread of such movements, is only preparing their defeat. Naturally, the communist party will not limit itself to placing the blame for erroneous tactics on the other parties. With all the wisdom and discipline required, it will keep a steady watch for the right moment at which to crush the resistance of the counter-revolutionaries, when in the course of the struggle a situation arises in which nothing can prevent the masses from responding to the party's call to action. Such an initiative can only be taken by the party centre; in no case can it be taken by local communist party organisations or communist-controlled trade unions.

41. More specifically, the term 'direct tactics' refers to actions of the party when the situation prompts it to take the independent initiative of attacking bourgeois power to topple or seriously weaken it. To undertake such an action, the party must have at its disposal an internal organisation solid enough to warrant the absolute certainty that orders from the centre will be executed with the utmost discipline. It must also be able to count upon the discipline of the trade-union forces it controls, in order to be sure that a large part of the masses will follow it. Furthermore, the party needs military formations of a certain efficiency and, to enable it to maintain control over the direction of the movement in the likely event of its being outlawed by emergency measures,

it requires an underground apparatus and especially a network of communications and liaison that the bourgeois government is not able to control. In offensive actions, it is the fate of very lengthy preparatory work that is at stake. Before taking such a momentous decision, it is therefore essential that the party study the situation very thoroughly. This study must not only ensure the discipline of the forces the party directly manages and controls; it must not only serve to prevent the bonds uniting the party to the most vital fraction of the proletariat from being broken in the course of the struggle. The party will also have to be assured that its influence over the masses and the participation of the proletariat will increase in the course of action, since the development of such an action will awaken and put into play naturally widespread tendencies within the deep strata of the mass.

42. It will not always be possible to proclaim openly that the general movement unleashed by the party has as its aim the overthrow of bourgeois power. Except in the case of an exceptionally rapid development of the revolutionary situation, the party could engage in action on the basis of watchwords that are not those of the revolutionary seizure of power but can in part be realised only by means of this supreme victory, even though the masses consider them to be nothing but needs that are immediate and vital, and in part limited, since they can be realised by a government that is not yet that of the proletarian dictatorship. This party tactic would give it the possibility of stopping the action at a certain point where the organisation and combativeness of the masses would remain intact, if it appears impossible to continue the struggle to the end without compromising the possibility of taking it up again effectively when new situations present themselves.

43. There is another possibility that must not be ruled out. The communist party could deem it opportune to give the watchword for action knowing that it is not yet a question of taking power, but only of continuing a battle in which the prestige and the organisation of the enemy will be shaken, which would materially and morally reinforce the proletariat. In this case, the party would call the masses to the struggle either for objectives that can truly be attained or for more limited objectives than those it would propose in the event of success. In the party's plan of action, these objectives would be ordered successively in such a way that each success would constitute a platform from which it could strengthen itself for the struggles ahead. In this way the party could avoid as much as possible the desperate tactic of throwing oneself into a struggle whose only possible outcomes are either the triumph of the revolution or, in the contrary case, the certainty of defeat and the dispersal of the proletarian forces for an unforeseeable time. Partial objectives are therefore indispensable for maintaining secure control over the action, and their formu-

lation is not in contradiction with the criticism of their economic and social content since the masses could see them not as the occasion for struggles that are a means and a step towards the final victory, but as finalities of intrinsic value that can be dwelled upon once they have been conquered. To be sure, determining these objectives and fixing the limits of action is always a tremendously delicate problem; it is from experience and in the selection of its leaders that the party is strengthened for this supreme responsibility.

44. The party must be careful not to create and spread the illusion that, when the proletariat lacks combativeness, the example of a daring group of militants who throw themselves into the struggle and attempt feats of arms against the bourgeois institutions can suffice to reawaken the masses. It is in the development of the real economic situation that the reasons must be sought that will bring the proletariat out of its depression; the tactics of the party can and must contribute to this process, but with an operation that is far deeper and more sustained than the spectacular gesture of a vanguard hurled to the assault.

45. Nonetheless, the party will use its forces and discipline for actions conducted by armed groups, workers' organisations, and crowds, when it has full control over them in terms of planning and execution. Such actions, of demonstrative and defensive value, will be designed to offer the masses concrete proof that with organisation and preparation it is possible to counter some of the resistance and renewed offensives of the ruling class, whether they take the form of terrorist actions by reactionary groups, or police prohibition of certain forms of proletarian organisation and activity. The goal will not be to provoke a general action, but to give the depressed and demoralised mass the highest degree of combativeness through a series of actions that combine to reawaken in it a feeling and a need for struggle.

46. The party will do everything possible to prevent these local actions from leading to infractions of the internal discipline of trade-union organisations by local organs and their militants that support the communist party. Communists must not provoke ruptures with the national central bodies of the unions directed by other parties, since the support of these local organisations and their militants is essential for the conquest of the central union bodies by our party. However, the communist party and its militants will follow the masses attentively, giving them all their support when they respond spontaneously to bourgeois provocations also by breaking with the discipline of the inaction and passivity imposed by the leaders of reformist and opportunist unions.

47. At the moment when state power is being shaken and is about to fall, the communist party, in the heat of deploying its forces and stirring up the masses around its banner of maximum conquests, will miss no opportunity of influencing these moments of instability by utilising all the forces that may

momentarily be marching with it, though its action must remain independent. When it is absolutely certain of taking control of the movement as soon as the traditional state organisation has collapsed, it can have recourse to transitory agreements with other movements fighting in its camp, without – and this is essential – expressing this in mass propaganda or slogans. In all these cases, *success* will be the only measure of the appropriateness of these contacts and the appraisal that must be made. The tactics of the communist party are never dictated by theoretical preconceptions or ethical and aesthetic concerns, but only by the need to conform to the methods and reality of the historical process, in accordance with the dialectical synthesis of doctrine and action that is the heritage of a movement destined to be the protagonist of the greatest social transformation in history, the commander of the greatest revolutionary war.

On Fascism, against Fascism

1   Report to the Fourth Congress of the C.I. (1922)[1]

Chair: The congress is now in session. I give the floor to Comrade Bordiga for the report on Fascism.

Bordiga (Italy): Dear comrades, I regret that unusual circumstances affecting communication between our delegation and our party prevent me from having access to all the source material on this question.[2]

There is a written report from Comrade Togliatti, but I do not have it here; in fact, I have not had a chance to read it.

With regard to the precise statistical data, I must refer comrades who wish detailed information to this report, which will surely arrive soon and will be translated and distributed here.

I have just received new information from a representative of our party's centre who arrived in Moscow yesterday evening and informed us regarding the most recent Fascist attacks on Italian comrades. I will take up this news in the last part of my report.

Given what Comrade Radek said here yesterday in his talk regarding the Communist Party's response to Fascism, I must also take up another side of the question.

Our Comrade Radek criticised the stance of our party toward the question of the Fascists, now the dominant political issue in Italy. He criticised our position – our so-called position – as being that we want to have a small party and judge all issues solely from the point of view of the Party's organization and its immediate role, without addressing the great political questions.

Since time is short, I will try to be brief. In discussing the Italian question and our relationship to the Socialist Party, we will also have to take up the question of the new situation in Italy created by Fascism. Let me go directly to my report, beginning with the origins of the Fascist movement.

---

1   The following text was first published in *Towards the United Front: Proceedings of the Fourth Congress of the Communist International, 1922*, edited and translated by John Riddell (Leiden: Brill, 2011), pp. 403–23. The notes are taken from Riddell's edition.

2   The 'unusual circumstances' flowed from Mussolini's assumption of power on 31 October 1922.

What you might call the immediate and outward origin reaches back to the years 1914 and 1915, the period leading up to Italy's entry into the World War. It began with groups supporting this intervention, which included representatives of different political currents.

There was a right-wing current including Salandra, representing owners of heavy industry, who had an interest in war. In fact, before they came out for war on the Entente side, they actually had favoured war against the Entente.

In addition, there were currents of the left bourgeoisie: the Italian radicals, left-wing democrats and republicans whose tradition demanded liberation of Trieste and the Trentino.[3] And, thirdly, the intervention movement also embraced some elements of the proletarian movement: revolutionary syndicalists and anarchists. And this grouping also included an individual of particular importance, Mussolini, the leader of the Socialist Party's left wing and the director of *Avanti!*

By and large, the middle group did not take part in the Fascist movement and was reabsorbed into traditional bourgeois politics. What remained in the Fascist movement were the far-right groups plus those from the far Left: ex-anarchists, ex-syndicalists, and ex-revolutionary syndicalists. In May 1915, the country was dragged into the War against the will of the majority of the population and even of parliament, which found no way to resist this sudden political coup. This was a big victory for these political groups. But, when the War ended, their influence dwindled – in fact, they were aware of this even during the war. They had imagined the War as a very simple undertaking. As people saw that the war was dragging on, these groups completely lost their popularity, which, to be frank, was never that great. When the War ended, these groups' influence became minimal. During and after the period of demobilisation, toward the end of 1918, during 1919, and the first half of 1920, amid the generalised discontent generated by the results of the War, this political tendency was completely ineffective. Nonetheless, there is a political and organisational connection between the movement that then seemed almost extinguished and the powerful movement now deployed before our eyes. The *fasci di combattimento* [fighting bands] never went out of existence. Mussolini remained leader of the Fascist movement, whose paper is *Il Popolo d'Italia* [*The Italian People*]. In the elections at the end of October 1919, the Fascists were utterly defeated in Milan, where their daily paper and leadership was located. Their vote total was extremely small, yet they continued their work.

---

3   Trieste and the Trentino were territories with a substantial Italian population that had been retained by Austria-Hungary after the process of Italian unification of 1859–70; both were awarded to Italy in 1919.

Thanks to the revolutionary enthusiasm that had taken hold of the masses, the revolutionary-socialist current of the proletariat became much stronger after the War. There is no need for me to go into the causes for that here. Nonetheless, this current did not know how to utilise this favourable situation.

In the final analysis, this tendency withered away completely because all the favourable objective and psychological conditions for strengthening a revolutionary organisation were not matched by the existence of a party capable of utilising this situation to build a stable organisation. I do not claim, as Comrade Zinoviev has done, that the Socialist Party could have made the revolution in those days. But, at the very least, it could have succeeded in endowing the revolutionary forces of the working masses with a solid organisation. It was not capable of carrying out this task.

We therefore had to witness the decline of the popularity previously enjoyed by the socialist current in Italy, with its consistent anti-war stance. And, in this crisis of Italian social life, to the degree that the socialist movement made one mistake after another, the opposite movement, Fascism, began to gain strength. In particular, Fascism succeeded very well in taking advantage of the crisis that now gripped the economy and whose effects were increasingly felt by the proletariat's trade-union organisations.

At the most critical moment, the Fascist movement gained strength from D'Annunzio's expedition to Fiume, which endowed it with a certain moral authority Although D'Annunzio's movement was distinct from Fascism, that event led to the rise of its organisation and armed strength. We have referred to the conduct of the proletarian-socialist movement, whose mistakes were repeatedly criticised by the International. These mistakes led to a complete reversal in the attitude of the bourgeoisie and other classes. The proletariat was divided and demoralised. As the working class saw victory slip through its hands, its mood shifted radically. It can be said that, in 1919 and 1920, the Italian bourgeoisie had somewhat come to terms with the fact that it would have to witness the victory of the revolution. The middle class and petty bourgeoisie were inclined to play a passive role, following in the wake not of the big bourgeoisie but of the proletariat, which was on the edge of victory. But, now, the mood changed fundamentally. Rather than witnessing a proletarian victory, we see instead how the bourgeoisie is gathering its forces for defence. As the middle class saw that the Socialist Party was not able to organize itself to get the upper hand, they gave expression to their dissatisfaction.

They gradually lost the confidence they had placed in the proletariat's determination and turned toward the opposite side. At this moment, the bourgeoisie launched the capitalist offensive, capitalising above all on the mood of the middle class. Thanks to its very heterogeneous composition, Fascism was able to solve this problem; indeed, it was even able to rein in somewhat the offensive of the bourgeoisie and capitalism. Italy is a classic example of the capitalist offensive. As Comrade Radek explained here yesterday, this offensive is a complex phenomenon, which must be examined not only in terms of wage reductions or extension of the hours of work, but also in the general arena of the bourgeoisie's political and military campaign against the working class.

In Italy, during the period of Fascism's development, we have experienced every form of the capitalist offensive. From its very beginnings, after a critical discussion of the situation, our Communist party indicated to the Italian proletariat its tasks in unified self-defence against the bourgeois offensive. It drew up a coherent plan for the proletariat's mobilisation against this offensive.

In order to examine the capitalist offensive as a whole, we must analyse the situation in general terms, particularly with reference to industry, on the one hand, and agriculture on the other. In industry the capitalist offensive took advantage above all of the economic conditions. The crisis had begun, and unemployment was spreading. A portion of the workers had to be laid off, and it was simple for the employers to throw out of the factories the workers who led the trade unions, the extremists.

The industrial crisis enabled the employers to reduce wages and to place in question the disciplinary and moral concessions they had previously been forced to grant the workers of their factories.

At the outset of this crisis, the employers formed a class alliance, the General League of Industry, which organised this struggle and directed the campaign in each separate branch of industry. In the major cities, the struggle against the working class did not begin with the immediate use of force. In general, the urban workers were in large groups; they could readily gather in large numbers and offer a serious defence. The proletariat was, above all, driven into trade-union struggles, which, under the conditions of acute economic crisis, had unfavourable outcomes. Unemployment was growing steadily. The only way to successfully withstand the economic struggles unfolding across industry would have been to transfer activity from the trade-union domain to that of revolution, through the dictatorship of a genuinely Communist political party. But the Italian Socialist Party was not such an organisation.

During the decisive confrontation, it was not able to shift the activity of the Italian proletariat into a revolutionary framework. The period in which Italian trade unions had won major successes in improving working conditions now gave way to one of defensive strikes by the working class. The trade unions suffered one defeat after another.

In Italy, the revolutionary movement of agricultural classes, especially rural wage workers and also layers that are not fully proletarianised, has great importance. The ruling classes had to utilise a weapon of struggle to counter the influence that red organisations had won in the countryside.

In a large part of Italy, namely the plain of the Po, which is economically the most important, the situation looked surprisingly like a local dictatorship of the proletariat or at least of the rural workers. The Socialist Party had won control of many municipalities at the end of 1920 and instituted a municipal tax policy directed against the agricultural and middle bourgeoisie. We had flourishing trade-union organisations there, plus significant cooperatives and many branches of the Socialist Party. And, even where the movement was led by the reformists, the rural working class took a revolutionary stand. The employers were forced to pay taxes to the organisation, a certain sum that would provide a sort of guarantee that the employer would respect the contract imposed on him by trade-union struggle.

The situation was such that the agricultural bourgeoisie could no longer live in the countryside and was forced to retreat to the cities. The Italian Socialists committed certain errors, especially with regard to the acquisition of land and the tendency of poor tenants after the War to purchase land in order to become smallholders.

The reformist organisations forced these tenants to remain, as it were, slaves of the movement of rural workers. That enabled the Fascist movement to gain solid support here.

In agriculture, there was no crisis of vast unemployment, which would have enabled the landowners to wage a victorious counteroffensive on the level of trade-union struggles.

It was in this situation that the expansion of Fascism began, based on use of physical violence and armed force. Its base was the rural landowning class, and it also utilised the dissatisfaction aroused among the middle layer of agricultural classes by the organisational errors of the Socialist Party and the reformist leaders. Fascism based itself on the overall situation: the steadily growing discontent of all petty-bourgeois layers, the small merchants, the small landholders, the discharged soldiers, and the former officers, who, after the role they had played in the War, were disappointed by their current status.

All these elements were utilised, organised, and formed up into contingents. And then this movement tackled the task of destroying the power of red organisations in the Italian countryside.

The method utilised by Fascism is quite distinctive. Fascism assembled all the discharged soldiers who could not find their place in society after the War and put their military experience to work.

Its first step was to form its military detachments, not in the big industrial cities but in the localities that can be viewed as centres of Italian agricultural districts, like Bologna and Florence. They found support here from the municipal authorities, of which more later. The Fascists had weapons and transport, enjoyed immunity from the law, and made use of these favourable conditions even in districts where they were numerically still smaller than their opponents. To begin with, they organised 'punitive expeditions'. Here is how this was done.

They overran a specific small territory, destroyed the headquarters of proletarian organisations, forcibly compelled the municipal councils to resign, if necessary wounding or killing the leaders of their opponents, or at least forcing them to leave the region. The workers of this locality were not in a position to mount resistance against these contingents, armed and supported by the police and pulled together from all parts of the country. The local Fascist group, which previously had not dared challenge the strength of the proletarian forces in that area, could now win the upper hand. Peasants and workers were now terrorised and knew that if they dared mount any kind of campaign against this group, the Fascists would repeat their expedition with much stronger forces, against which no resistance was possible.

In this way, Fascism won a dominant position in Italian politics, marching across the land, one district after another, according to a plan that can very easily be traced on a map.

Its starting point was Bologna. A socialist city administration was installed there in September and October 1920, accompanied by a big mobilisation of red forces. There were incidents: [city council] sessions were disrupted by provocations from outside. Shots were fired at the benches of the bourgeois minority, perhaps by *agents provocateurs*. This occurrence led to the first big Fascist attack. Reaction was now unleashed, carrying out destruction, arson, and acts of violence against leaders of the proletariat. Aided by the government, the Fascists took control of the city. These events on the historic day of 21 November 1920 launched the terror, and the Bologna municipal council was never able to return to office.

Spreading out from Bologna, Fascism followed a path that we cannot describe here in all its details. We will say only that it expanded in two geographical directions: firstly to the industrial triangle of the Northwest: Milan, Turin, and Genoa; secondly to Tuscany and the centre of Italy, in order to surround and threaten the capital. It was clear, from the outset, that the same factors that had blocked the emergence of a large socialist movement in southern Italy also prevented the growth of a Fascist movement there. So little is the Fascist movement an expression of the backward sector of the bourgeoisie that it appeared initially not in Southern Italy but precisely in the area where the proletarian movement was most developed and the class struggle was most evident.

Given these facts, how should the Fascist movement be understood? Is it a purely agrarian movement? That was not at all what we meant when we explained that the movement grew up primarily in rural areas. Fascism cannot be described as an independent movement of any specific sector of the bourgeoisie. It is not an organisation of agrarian interests opposed to those of industrial capitalism. Let us note that, even in districts where Fascist actions took place only in the countryside, it built its political/military organisations in the big cities.

By participating in the elections of 1921, the Fascists obtained a parliamentary caucus. But, at the same time, independently from Fascism, an agrarian party was formed. In the course of further events, we saw that the industrial employers supported Fascism. A decisive step in this new situation was the recent declaration of the General League of Industry, which proposed that Mussolini be asked to form a new cabinet.

But even more significant in this regard is the phenomenon of the Fascist trade-union movement.

As I said, the Fascists knew how to profit from the fact that the socialists never had an agrarian policy, and that certain forces in the countryside, who were not clearly part of the proletariat, had interests counterposed to those of the Socialists.

The Fascist movement had to employ every instrument of brutal and savage violence. Yet it was able to combine this with the use of the most cynical demagogy.

Fascism attempted to build class organisations of the peasants and even the rural wage workers. In a certain sense, it even opposed the landowners.

There were examples of trade-union struggles under Fascist leadership that were quite similar in their methods to those of the earlier red organisations.

This movement, which uses compulsion and terror to create Fascist trade unions, is not in any way a form of struggle against the employers. On the other hand, it would also be wrong to conclude that Fascism is a movement of the agricultural employers as such. In reality, Fascism is a large and unified movement of the ruling class, capable of turning to its advantage and making use of every means and all particular and local interests of different groups of agricultural and industrial employers.

The proletariat did not succeed in unifying in a united organisation for a common struggle to take power, subordinating to this goal the immediate interests of small groups. It was not able to resolve this problem at the proper time. The Italian bourgeoisie seized on this fact and set out to do this in its own right. And this is an enormous problem. The ruling class built an organization to defend the power that it holds, pursuing a unified plan for an antiproletarian, capitalist offensive

Fascism created a trade-union movement. What was its purpose? To conduct a class struggle? Never! The Fascist trade-union movement was built with the slogan that all economic interests have the right to an association, be they workers, peasants, merchants, capitalists, great landowners, and so on. They can all organise around the same principle. The actions of all professional organisations must be subordinated to national interests, national production, national prestige, and so on.

This is class collaboration, not class struggle. All interests are welded together in a so-called national interest. We know well what such national unity means: the absolute and counter-revolutionary preservation of the bourgeois state and its institutions. In our opinion, the creation of Fascism can be put down to three main factors: the state, the big bourgeoisie, and the middle classes.

The first of these factors is the state, which played an important role in Italy in the creation of Fascism. Reports of the Italian bourgeois government's crises, occurring in quick succession, give rise to the belief that the Italian bourgeoisie posses a state apparatus that is so precarious that a single blow would suffice to overthrow it. That is entirely wrong. The bourgeoisie was able to build up the Fascist organisation precisely to the degree that the state apparatus stabilised.

During the period immediately following the War, the state apparatus experienced a crisis. Its obvious cause was demobilisation: all the forces that had been engaged in the War were suddenly thrown onto the labour market.

At this critical moment, the machinery of state, which, up until then, had been busy delivering all the means of struggle against the external foe, had to change into an apparatus to defend its power against internal revolution. For the bourgeoisie, this posed an immense problem, which could not be resolved either technically or militarily through an open struggle against the proletariat.

It had to be dealt with politically.

This was the period of the first left-wing governments after the War, when the political current led by Nitti and Giolitti was in power. It was precisely this policy that made it possible for Fascism to secure its subsequent victory. First there had to be concessions to the proletariat, and then, at the moment when the state apparatus had to be consolidated, Fascism appeared on the scene.

When the Fascists criticise these governments for cowardice against the revolutionaries, this is pure demagogy. In reality, the Fascists owe their victory to the concessions and democratic policy of the first postwar governments.

Nitti and Giolitti made concessions to the working class. Certain of the Socialist Party's demands were met: demobilisation, a liberal internal régime, and amnesty for deserters. These various concessions were made in order to win time to restore the state on a solid foundation. It was Nitti who created the 'Guardia Regia', that is, the Royal Guard, which was not exactly a police agency but, rather, had an entirely new military character. One of the reform Socialists' major errors was in not seeing the fundamental nature of this challenge, which could even have been countered on constitutional grounds by protesting the fact that the state was creating a second army. The Socialists did not grasp the importance of this question, viewing Nitti as someone that one could work with in a left government. This is yet more evidence of how incompetent this party is to develop any understanding of the course of Italian politics.

Giolitti completed Nitti's work. His war minister, Bonomi, supported Fascism's first stirrings. He placed himself at the disposal of the movement then taking shape and of the demobilised officers, who, even after their return to civilian life, continued to draw the greater part of their wage. He placed the entire state apparatus at the disposal of the Fascists, providing them with all the means needed to create an army.

When the factory occupations occurred, this government understood very well that, with the armed proletariat taking charge of the factories, and the revolutionary upsurge of the rural proletariat headed toward taking the land, it would be an enormous error to launch into battle before the counter-revolutionary forces had been organised.

The government prepared the organisation of the reactionary forces that would one day smash the proletarian movement. In this, it drew support from the manoeuvres of the treacherous leaders of the General Confederation of Labour, who were then members of the Socialist Party. By conceding the law on workers' control, which was never implemented or even voted on, the government succeeded at this critical moment in rescuing the bourgeois state.

The proletariat had taken control of the factories and the land. But the Socialist Party showed, once again, that it was incapable of resolving the problem of unity in action of the industrial and agricultural working class. This error enabled the bourgeoisie to soon achieve unity on a counter-revolutionary basis, a unity that put it in a position to triumph over the workers both of the factories and in the countryside.

As we see, the state played a most important role in the Fascist movement's development. After the governments of Nitti, Giolitti, and Bonomi came the

Facta government. This government provided a cover giving Fascism full free-dom of action in its territorial offensive. During the August 1922 strike, major battles took place between the workers and the Fascists, who were openly sup-ported by the government.[4] Let us take the example of Bari.

Although the Fascists mustered up all their forces, they were unable, during an entire week of fighting, to defeat the workers of Bari, who retreated to their homes in the old city and defended themselves arms in hand. The Fascists had to retreat, leaving a great many of their forces on the field of battle.

And how did the Facta government respond? During the night, it had the old city occupied by thousands of soldiers, hundreds of state police, and soldiers of the Royal Guard, who advanced to the attack. A torpedo boat stationed in the port aimed its fire on the houses. Machine guns, armoured cars, and artil-lery were brought up. The workers, surprised while they slept, were defeated, and their headquarters was taken.[5] That happened throughout the entire coun-try. Wherever it was evident that the workers had forced Fascists to retreat, the government intervened, shooting workers who resisted, and arresting and sen-tencing workers whose only crime was self-defence, while Fascists who had demonstrably committed despicable crimes were systematically set free by the authorities.

So much for the first factor, the state.

The second factor in Fascism is, as I have said, the big bourgeoisie. The big capitalists of industry, the banks, commerce, and the big landowners, have a natural interest in the founding of an organisation of struggle that defends their offensive against working people.

But the third factor also plays a very important role in constituting Fascist power. In order to create an illegal reactionary organisation beside the state, forces must be recruited that are different from those that the high ruling class can find in its own social milieu. This is achieved by turning to the layers of the middle class that we have mentioned and advocating their interests, in order to ensnare them. That is what Fascism set out to do, and it must be admitted that

---

4 An ad hoc Labour Alliance [Alleanza del lavoro], composed of the trade-union federations, called a general strike on 1 August 1922 for 'the defence of political and trade-union freedoms'. Only two days were allowed for preparations, and the action was hampered by sectarian-ism among left parties. The strike failed and gave way to a sweeping Fascist offensive against labour organisations, backed by the army and police. However, in Parma and Bari, where united fronts had been achieved locally, workers won striking victories over Fascist attack-ers. [It must be said that the PCd'I devoted much effort to the success of the general strike, whose low turnout Bordiga blamed on the reformist leadership (editor's note)].

5 The workers' successful defence of the old city in Bari, and also their simultaneous and decis-ive victory in Parma, flowed from the achievement of fighting unity of anti-Fascist forces, including the Arditi del Popolo [People's Commandos] – a unity rare at that time.

they succeeded. It recruited forces from the layers that are closest to the proletariat among those discontented because of the War, among petty bourgeois,
middle-level bourgeois, merchants and traders, and, above all, among intellectual bourgeois youth. In joining up with Fascism, they find again the energy to
lift themselves morally and cloak themselves in the toga of combating the proletarian movement, achieving an exalted patriotism in the interests of Italian
imperialism. These layers provided Fascism with a significant number of supporters and enabled it to organise militarily.

Those are the three factors that enabled our opponents to confront us with
a movement that knows no equal in brutality and savagery, and yet is a solid
movement with a leader of great political dexterity. The Socialist Party was
never able to grasp the meaning of the enemy organisation springing up in the
form of Fascism. *Avanti!* had no understanding of what the bourgeoisie was
preparing as it seized on the disastrous errors of the proletarian leaders.

It did not want to mention Mussolini, fearing that emphasising his role
would serve as an advertisement.

We therefore see that Fascism does not represent any new political doctrine.
But it has a powerful political and military organisation and an influential press,
which is managed with much journalistic skill and eclecticism.

But it has no ideas and no programme. And, now that it has taken the helm
of state, it faces concrete problems and has to address the organisation of Italy's
economy. Once it passes over from its negative to its positive efforts, it will show
signs of weakness, despite its organisational talent.

We have examined the historical factors and the social reality out of which
the Fascist movement took shape. We must now address the ideology that it
adopted, along with the programme it used to win the various forces that are
following it.

Our analysis leads to the conclusion that Fascism has added nothing to
the traditional ideology and programme of bourgeois politics. All things considered, its superiority and its specificity consist of its organisation, discipline,
and hierarchy. Aside from this exceptional and militaristic exterior, it possesses
nothing but a reality full of difficulties that it is unable to overcome.

The economic crisis will constantly renew the causes of revolution, while
Fascism will be unable to re-organise the social apparatus of the bourgeoisie.

Fascism does not know how to go beyond the economic anarchy of the capitalist system. It has a different historical task, which lies in combating political
anarchy and the organisational anarchy of political groupings of the bourgeois
class.

Different layers of the Italian ruling class have traditionally formed political and parliamentary groupings that, although not based on firmly organized

parties, struggle against each other and compete to advance their particular and local interests. This leads to manoeuvres of every kind in the parliamentary corridors. The bourgeoisie's counter-revolutionary offensive requires that the forces of the ruling class unite in social and governmental politics.

Fascism meets this requirement. By placing itself above all the traditional bourgeois parties, it gradually deprives them of content. Through its activity, it replaces them. And, thanks to the blunders of the proletarian movement, it has succeeded in harnessing to its plan the political power and human material of the middle classes. But it is incapable of developing an ideology and a specific programme of administrative reform of society and state that is any better than that of traditional bourgeois politics, which is bankrupt a thousand times over.

The critical side of the Fascists' supposed doctrine is of no great merit. It portrays itself as anti-socialist and also anti-democratic. As for anti-socialism, Fascism is clearly a movement of anti-proletarian forces and must take a stand against all socialist or semi-socialist economic forms. However, it does not succeed in offering anything new in order to shore up the system of private ownership, other than clichés about the failure of communism in Russia. It says that democracy must give way to a Fascist state because of its failure to combat the revolutionary and anti-social forces. But that is no more than an empty phrase.

Fascism is not a current of the bourgeois Right, based on the aristocracy, the clergy, and the high civilian and military officials, seeking to replace the democracy of a bourgeoisie government and constitutional monarchy with monarchical despotism. Fascism incorporates the counter-revolutionary struggle of all the allied bourgeois forces, and, for this reason, it is by no means necessarily compelled to destroy the democratic institutions. From our Marxist point of view, this situation is by no means paradoxical, because we know that the democratic system is only a collection of deceptive guarantees, behind which the ruling class conducts its battle against the proletariat.

Fascism expresses simultaneously reactionary violence and the demagogic adroitness that the bourgeois Left has always been able to use in deceiving the proletariat and guaranteeing the supremacy of big capitalist interests over the political needs of the middle classes. When the Fascists go beyond their so-called criticism of liberal democracy and reveal their positive, ideological notions, preaching an excessive patriotism and drivel about the people's historical mission, they are fashioning a mythology whose lack of serious foundations will be evident as soon as it is subjected to true social criticism, which exposes the land of illusory victories that bears the name Italy. As regards influencing the masses, we see here an imitation of the classical stance of bourgeois democracy. When it is asserted that all interests must be subordinated to the superior interest of the nation, that means that class collaboration is upheld in principle, while, in practice, the conservative bourgeois institutions are supported against the proletariat's efforts to free itself.

That is the role that liberal bourgeois democracy has always played. What is new in Fascism is the organisation of a bourgeois ruling party. Political events on the floor of Italy's parliament have awakened the belief that the bourgeois state apparatus has entered a crisis so profound that one blow from outside would be sufficient to break it. In reality, the crisis is merely one of the bourgeois methods of government, which arose because of the impotence of the traditional groupings and leaders of Italian politics, who were not able to conduct the struggle against revolutionary forces at a time of acute crisis.

Fascism created an organism that was capable of taking over the role of heading up this country's machinery of state. But, when the Fascists move from engagement in their struggle against proletarians to elaborating a positive and specific programme for the organization of society and administration of the state, basically they have merely repeated the banal themes of democracy and Social Democracy. They have not created their own consistent system of proposals and projects.

Thus, for example, they have always maintained that the Fascist programme will lead to a decrease in the bureaucratic state apparatus, beginning at the top with a reduction in the number of ministries and then carrying forward in all domains of administration. Now, it is true that Mussolini did decline the prime minister's personal railway car. But he otherwise increased the number of ministers and governmental undersecretaries, in order to find posts for his praetorian guard.

As for the question of monarchy or republic, Fascism made various republican or enigmatic gestures, only to opt for pure loyal monarchism. Similarly, after a great outcry about parliamentary corruption, Fascism has taken over entirely the practices of parliament.

Fascism showed so little tendency to adopt the features of unalloyed reaction that it allowed broad scope for trade unionism.[6] At its Rome Congress of 1921, where Fascism made almost comical efforts to specify its doctrine, an attempt was made to portray Fascist trade unionism as the primacy of the intellectual categories of labour. But this supposed theoretical conception has long since been refuted by ugly reality. The Fascist trade-union organisations are based on naked force plus the monopoly over job opportunities that the

---

6 Both the German and Russian texts for the preceding words translate as 'broad scope for syndicalism'. This is an apparent mistranslation of Bordiga's remarks, which were delivered in French, and would have used the word 'syndicalisme' – 'trade unionism'.

employers are offering in order to break the red organisations. However, it has not succeeded in extending its reach to the categories of work demanding greater technical specialisation, which give the worker an advantage. It achieved success only among the agricultural workers and some of the less qualified categories of urban workers, such as the longshoremen, for example.

It did not succeed among the more advanced and intelligent sector of the proletariat.

It did not even give an impulse to the trade-union movement among office workers and tradesmen. Fascist trade unionism has no serious theoretical foundation. The Fascists' ideology and programme contain a tangled jumble of bourgeois and petty-bourgeois ideas and demands. Its systematic employment of violence against the proletariat by no means prevents it from scooping up opportunism from Social-Democratic sources.

One indication of that is the stance of the Italian reformists. For a time, their policies were guided by anti-Fascist principles and the illusion that they could build a bourgeois-proletarian coalition government against the Fascists. Now they are joining up with the victorious Fascists. This rapprochement is not at all paradoxical. It was encouraged by many circumstances and was predictable, based on many indications. Consider, for example, the D'Annunzio movement, which was linked to Fascism, and nonetheless made the attempt to win the support of proletarian organisations on the basis of a programme derived from the Fiume constitution that was supposedly based on proletarian or even socialist principles. I should mention a few other things that I consider quite important to the Fascist phenomenon, but I lack the time. The other Italian comrades will be able to expand on my remarks when they take the floor. I have also left out everything relating to the feelings and sufferings experienced by Italian workers and Communists, because that did not appear to me to be essential to the question.

I must now take up the most recent events in Italy, regarding which the Congress expects a precise report.

1.1   *The Most Recent Events*

Our delegation left Italy before the most recent events and was at first rather poorly informed about them. Yesterday evening, a delegate of our Central Committee arrived and gave us a report. I can assure you that this is an accurate report on the facts we have received regarding the recent events in Italy, which I will now present to you.

As I said earlier, the Facta government afforded the Fascists the broadest freedom of action to carry out their policies. Here is an example. The fact that each successive government has included strong representation from the

Italian Catholic peasant People's Party did not prevent the Fascists from pursuing their struggle against the organisations, leaders, and institutions of this
party. The existing government was a total sham, whose only activity consisted of promoting the territorial and geographical drive of the Fascists toward
power.

In reality, the government was preparing the ground for a Fascist putsch.

Meanwhile, a new governmental crisis broke out. Demands were raised that
Facta resign. The most recent elections had produced a parliament in which the
party representation was such as to prevent the bourgeois parties from constituting a stable majority in their traditional ways. It was customary to say that
Italy was ruled by a 'huge liberal party'. But that was not a party at all, in the
usual meaning of the word. Such a party never existed and was not formed as
an organisation. It was just a mishmash of personal cliques of this or that politi-
cian of the North or South, plus cliques of industrial or rural bourgeois, run by
professional politicians. These politicians, taken together, formed in fact the
core of every parliamentary coalition.

Now, the moment had come when Fascism had to change this situation,
if it was to avoid a severe internal crisis. An organisational question was also
involved. The needs of the Fascist movement had to be met, and the organisation's costs paid. These material resources had been supplied on a massive
scale by the ruling classes and, it seems, by governments abroad. France had
given money to the Mussolini group. A secret session of the French cabinet
debated a budget that included significant funds passed on to Mussolini in
1915. The Socialist Party came upon documents of this type, but it did not pursue the matter, thinking that Mussolini was washed up. On the other hand, the
Italian government always made things easier for the Fascists, as for example in
enabling large groups of Fascists to use the railways without paying. Nonetheless the enormous expenses of the Fascist movement would have caused great
difficulties, had they not made a direct bid for power. They could not wait for
new elections, even though they could be sure of success.

The Fascists already have a strong political organisation with three hundred
thousand members; they claim it is even larger. They could have won by 'democratic' means. But they were in a rush to bring things to a head. On 24 October,
there was a meeting of the Fascist National Council in Naples. This event, trum-
peted by the whole bourgeois press, is now claimed to have been a manoeuvre
aimed at distracting attention from a coup d'état.

At a certain moment, the congress participants were told to stop deliberations; there was something more important to do. Everyone was told to go back
to their district, and a Fascist mobilisation began. That was 26 October.

In the capital, there was still complete calm.

Facta had stated that he would not resign until he had convened parliament one more time, in order to observe the usual procedure. Nonetheless, despite this statement, he presented the king with his resignation.

Negotiations began regarding formation of a new government. The Fascists marched on Rome, the focus of their activity. They were especially active in central Italy and Tuscany. Nothing was done to stop them. Salandra was asked to form a new government, but he declined because of the attitude of the Fascists. It is very probable that the Fascists, if not appeased by Mussolini's appointment, would have risen up like brigands, even against the will of their leaders, plundering and destroying everything in the cities and countryside.

Public opinion was somewhat aroused. The Facta government stated that they would declare a state of siege. This was done, and a major clash was expected between the government's forces and those of the Fascists. Public opinion waited through a long day for this to happen; our comrades were highly sceptical regarding this possibility.

The Fascists did not encounter serious resistance anywhere during their advance. And, nonetheless, there were some circles in the army disposed to counter the Fascists. The soldiers were ready to take on the Fascists, while most of the officers supported them.

The king refused to sign the declaration of a state of siege. That meant accepting the Fascists' conditions, which had been printed in the *Popolo d'Italia*, namely: 'Mussolini should be asked to form a new ministry, and this will provide a legal solution. Otherwise, we are marching on Rome and will take control of it.'

Some hours after the state of siege had been lifted, it was learned that Mussolini was headed for Rome. Measures had been taken for military defence; troops had been assembled; the city was surrounded by cavalry. But the agreement had already been finalised, and, on 31 October, the Fascists triumphantly entered Rome.

Mussolini formed a new government, whose composition is well known. The Fascist Party, which has only thirty-five seats in parliament, has the absolute majority in this government. Mussolini is not only the head of the council of ministers but also holds the portfolios for internal and external affairs.

Members of the Fascist Party divided up the other important portfolios and made themselves at home in most of the other ministries.

Since there had not yet been a full break with the traditional parties, the government included two representatives of the socially inclined democrats – that is, left-bourgeois forces; as well as right-wing liberals and a supporter of Giolitti. The monarchist forces were represented by General Diaz in the Ministry of War and Admiral Thaon di Revel in the Ministry of the Navy.

The People's Party, which is very strong in parliament, concluded a skil-full compromise with Mussolini. On the pretext that the Party's leading body could not meet in Rome, responsibility for accepting Mussolini's proposals was thrust onto a semi-official gathering of parliamentary deputies. Nonetheless, they succeeded in persuading Mussolini to grant some concessions, and the newspapers of the People's Party were able to state that the new government did not propose any major changes in the electoral system or parliament.

The compromise embraced even the Social Democrats. For a time, it seemed that the reform Socialist Baldesi would take part in the government. Mussolini was sufficiently adroit to relay the offer to Baldesi through one of his lieuten-ants. When Baldesi declared he would be glad to accept this post, Mussolini stated that the offer had been a personal initiative by one of his associates, for which Mussolini took no responsibility. And thus it was that Baldesi did not get to join the cabinet.

Mussolini did not accept a representative of the reformist General Confed-eration of Labour on the grounds of opposition by right-wing forces within his cabinet. But Mussolini is of the opinion that this organisation should be rep-resented after all in his 'broad national coalition', now that it is independent of any revolutionary political party.

We see in these events a compromise between the traditional political cliques and the different layers of the ruling class – the great landowners and the financial and industrial capitalists, who lean to support of the new gov-ernment created by a movement that has secured the support of the petty bourgeoisie. In our view, Fascism is a method to secure the power of the ruling classes by utilising every means available to them, including even making use of the lessons of the first proletarian revolution, the Russian Revolution. When faced by an economic crisis, it is not enough for the state merely to maintain its power. It needs a unified party, a unified counter-revolutionary organisation.

Through its contact with the entire bourgeoisie, the Fascist Party represents, in a certain sense, what the Communist Party is in Russia, thanks to its relation-ship to the proletariat, that is, a well-organised and disciplined body that leads and supervises the state apparatus as a whole. The Fascist Party in Italy has placed its political commissars in almost every significant post in the branches of the state apparatus. It is the leading body of the bourgeois state in the period of imperialist decline. In my view, that is an adequate historical explanation of Fascism and of the recent developments in Italy.

The first actions of the new government show that it does not intend to alter Italy's traditional institutions.

When I predict that Fascism will be liberal and democratic, I do not, of course, mean that conditions will be favourable for the proletarian and socialist movement. Democratic governments have never given the proletariat anything other than declarations and promises. For example, Mussolini's government guarantees that it will respect freedom of the press. But it did not refrain from adding that the press must be worthy of that freedom. What does that tell us? It means that the government will pretend to respect freedom of the press, while permitting its Fascist military organisations to strike out against Communist newspapers whenever they choose, as has already happened in the past. We must also note that the Fascist government is making certain concessions to the bourgeois liberals. Little confidence should be placed in the Mussolini government's assurances that it plans to convert its military organisation into sport clubs, or something of the like. However, we do know that dozens of Fascists were taken into police custody because they had resisted Mussolini's order to demobilise.

What is the impact of these events on the proletariat? It found itself in a situation where it could play no significant role in the struggle and had to behave almost passively.

As for the Communist Party, it always understood that a victory of Fascism would be a defeat for the revolutionary movement. We had no doubt about the fact that we are not at present in a position to take the offensive against Fascist reaction, and had to assume a defensive posture. The question is therefore chiefly whether the Communist Party's policies succeeded, in this framework, in protecting the Italian proletariat to the greatest extent possible.

If, instead of a compromise between the bourgeoisie and Fascism there had been an outbreak of a military conflict, the proletariat could perhaps have played a certain role in establishing a united front for a general strike, and achieving some success. But, in the given situation, the proletariat did not take part in the actions. Although the unfolding events had enormous significance, we must also bear in mind that the change on the political stage was less abrupt than it appeared, since conditions had become more and more acute before Fascism launched its final attack. The only example of a struggle against the government and Fascism was in Cremona, where six persons were killed. The proletariat fought only in Rome. The revolutionary worker contingents had a clash with the Fascist bands. There were some wounded.

The next day, the Royal Guard occupied the workers' district, robbing them of all means of defending themselves, and the approaching Fascists shot the workers down in cold blood. That is the bloodiest episode that took place during these struggles in Italy.

When the Communist Party proposed a general strike, the General Confederation of Labour disarmed the Communists, calling on the proletariat to ignore the dangerous directives of the revolutionary groups. A report was spread about that the Communist Party had dissolved; this was at a time when our newspapers were unable to publish.

In Rome, the bloodiest episode for our party was the seizure of the editorial offices of *Comunista*. The print shop was occupied on 31 October, just at the moment the newspaper was to appear, while one hundred thousand Fascists held the city under occupation. All the editors managed to slip out through side doors, except for the editor-in-chief, Comrade Togliatti. He was in his office, and the Fascists came in and seized hold of him. Our comrade's conduct was frankly heroic. He boldly declared that he was editor-in-chief of *Comunista*. He was quickly put up against the wall, in order to be shot, while Fascists drove back the crowd. Our comrade escaped only thanks to the fact that the Fascists got news that the other editors had fled over the roof and rushed up to capture them. All this did not prevent our comrade from speaking a few days later at a rally in Turin on the occasion of the anniversary of the Russian Revolution. (*Applause*)

But what I have just reported is an isolated event. Our party organisation is in rather good shape. The fact that *Comunista* is not appearing results not from a governmental decision but because the print shop does not want to publish it. The difficulties in publishing were economic, not technical. In Turin, the *Ordine nuovo* building was occupied, and the weapons stored there were seized. But we are printing the newspaper at another location. Also, in Trieste, the police seized our paper's print shop, but this paper too is coming out underground. Our party is still able to function legally, and our situation is not that bad. But we do not know how things will develop, and I must therefore be cautious in speaking of our party's future situation and activity.

The comrade who has just arrived is a leading worker in one of our important local party organisations. His has an interesting point of view, also shared by many other militants, namely, that we will now be able to work better than was the case before. I do not say that this opinion is a well-established fact.

But the comrade with this viewpoint is a militant who works directly with the masses, and his opinion has great weight. As I said, our opponents' press has spread the false report that our party has dissolved. We have published a denial and established the truth. Our central political publications, our underground military centre, our trade-union centre are working actively and their relationships to other regions have been restored in almost every case. The comrades who stayed in Italy never lost their head for a moment, and they are doing all that is required. *Avanti!* was destroyed by the Fascists, and a few days will be needed to enable this paper to appear once more. The Socialist Party's central headquarters in Rome was destroyed and all its private files burned, right down to the last piece of paper.

Concerning the position of the Maximalist Party [SP] regarding the polemic between the Communist Party and the General Confederation of Labour, we have not seen a declaration of any kind.

As for the reformists, it is clear from the tone of their newspapers, which are still appearing, that they will unite with the new government.

With reference to the trade unions, Comrade Repossi of our trade-union committee believes that it will be possible to continue our work.

That completes the information that we have received, which dates from 6 November.

I have spoken at length. I will not take up the question of our party's position during the course of Fascism's development, and instead reserve that for other points on the congress agenda. We only want to address here the prospects for the future. We have said that Fascism will have to cope with the dissatisfaction created by the government's policies.

Nonetheless, we know very well that when a military organisation exists alongside the state, it is easier to cope with dissatisfaction and unfavourable economic conditions.

Under the dictatorship of the proletariat, that was true in a much deeper sense, because historical development is on our side. The Fascists are excellently organised and firm in their views. Given this, it can be foreseen that the Fascist government will be far from unstable. You have seen that I have in no way exaggerated the conditions under which our party has struggled. We cannot make that into a matter of sympathy.

Perhaps the Communist Party of Italy has made mistakes. It can be criticised. But I believe that, at the present moment, the comrades' conduct demonstrates that we have accomplished a great task, the formation of a revolutionary party of the proletariat, which will provide the basis for an uprising of the Italian working class.

The Italian Communists have the right to ask for your respect. Their conduct has not always met with approval. Yet they believe they cannot be reproached for anything with regard to the revolution and the Communist International.

2   Report on Fascism to the Fifth Congress of the Communist
       International[7]

It is well known that I gave a report on the question of Fascism to the Fourth
Congress, at a decisive turning-point in the history of Fascism in Italy. Then I
left Italy with our delegation on the eve of the Fascist conquest of power.

Today I have to speak a second time on the subject, and again at a decisive moment for the development of Fascism, brought about, as you know, by
the Matteotti affair.[8] As chance would have it, this event too occurred just after
the Italian delegation set off, this time for the Fifth Congress. Both my reports,
therefore, have been at moments that shed further light on the extremely
important social and political phenomenon of Fascism.

Of course I shall not repeat everything I said in my first report about the historical development of Fascism, because I have too many other points to deal
with here. I shall therefore just recall very briefly the fundamental ideas in the
critique of Fascism that I developed before. I shall do this in outline only, since
I can stand fully by what I said at the Fourth Congress. [...]

In this connection [the communist opposition to Fascism], we should note the
characteristic fact that the CP had immediately proposed an Italy-wide general
strike in protest at the murder of Matteotti. Spontaneous strikes had already
broken out in a number of cities – which shows that it was a very serious and
down-to-earth proposal.

The other parties, with the approval of the maximalists, proposed a ten-
minute work stoppage as a protest action in honour of Matteotti. But to the dis-

---

7 *Protokoll v Kongress der Kommunistischen Internationale*, 23rd session, 2 July 1924.
8 Giacomo Matteotti (1885–1924), parliamentary deputy and secretary of the Partito socialista
   unitario, was active in denouncing Fascist illegalities and acts of violence. He was assassinated in Rome by a Fascist squad on 10 June 1924, and his body was not found until two months
   later in the countryside near Rome. The murder caused major, though only momentary, difficulties for the nascent Fascist regime. Under the leadership of Gramsci, who had become
   Party secretary after Bordiga and other exponents of the Left were removed on the authority
   of the Comintern executive committee, the PCd'I followed Turati's PSU in giving up parliamentary work (in August 1924), in the illusory belief that it could build a broad anti-Fascist
   front together with the Liberal and Popular parties and force Mussolini to resign (the so-called
   Aventino line). The pressure exerted by Bordiga and his close comrades – who described this
   tactic as 'senseless' and criticised the opening of a credit line for the bourgeois left – and the
   complete inertia of the 'democratic opposition' to Fascism eventually compelled the PCd'I
   to return to parliament in mid-November 1924, thereby breaking the fictitious unity with the
   other parties. Not by chance the Left deputy Luigi Repossi was chosen to make the speech
   announcing this return.

grace of the reformists, the maximalists, the CGIL and other opposition groups, the Confederation of Industry and the Fascist unions immediately accepted the proposal and officially joined forces with the opposition! So, of course, the protest lost all significance as a class action. Today it is as clear as daylight that only the communists proposed something that would have allowed the proletariat to intervene decisively in the course of events.

What prospects does the current situation offer to the Mussolini government? Before the latest events, we were bound to state that, although there was no lack of impressive pointers to a rising discontent with Fascism, its organisation at the level of the military and the state was too strong to glimpse a force capable of working practically to overthrow Fascism in the near future. Discontent was growing, but we were still a long way from the crisis point.

The recent events are a convincing example of how small causes produce big effects. The Matteotti assassination has speeded up developments in an extraordinary fashion, even though, of course, the premises for them were already latent in the social conditions. The pace of the Fascist crisis has sharply accelerated; the Fascist government has suffered a searing moral, psychological and, in a way, political defeat. This has not yet had repercussions in the field of political, military and administrative organisation, but it is clear that such a moral and political defeat is the first step towards a later unravelling of the crisis and of the struggle for power. The government has had to make significant concessions, handing over the interior portfolio, for example, to the ex-nationalist leader, now Fascist, Federzoni; it has been forced into other concessions too, although it still retains power in its hands. In his speeches to the Senate, Mussolini has openly said that he will keep his post and wield all the instruments of power still at his disposal against anyone who attacks him.

According to the latest news, the wave of public indignation has still not abated. But the objective situation has become more stable. The National Militia, which was mobilised two days after the assassination of Matteotti, has been demobilised again, and its members are returning to their usual occupations. This means that the government thinks the immediate danger has receded. But it is clear that important events will occur much sooner than we foresaw before the Matteotti affair.

Clearly the position of Fascism will be much more difficult in future, and the practical possibilities for anti-Fascist action are today different from those that existed before the intervening events.

How should we conduct ourselves in the new situation that has unexpectedly opened up? I shall now outline my own view.

The CP should emphasise the *independent* role that the situation in Italy assigns to it, and issue the following watchword: eliminate the existing anti-Fascist opposition groups and replace them with the open and direct activity of the communist movement. Today we are facing events that propel the CP to the forefront of public interest. For a while after the Fascists seized power, our comrades were arrested *en masse*. It was said then that the communist and Bolshevik forces had been annihilated, scattered to the wind, that the revolutionary movement had been liquidated. But for some time now, since the elections and other developments, the party has been giving signs of life that are too strong for such an assertion to be maintained. Mussolini is forced to mention the communists in all his speeches. And in the polemic surrounding the Matteotti affair, the Fascist press has to defend itself daily and take up position against the communists.

This attracts everyone's attention to our party and its special independent task in comparison with other opposition groups closely related to one another. Our party, with the special position it has assumed, draws a clear dividing-line between itself and those other groups. Moreover, because of earlier class-struggle experiences in Italy during and after the war, and because of the cruel disappointments it suffered, the Italian proletariat has a solidly rooted awareness of the need to eliminate entirely all social-democratic currents, from the bourgeois left to the proletarian right. All these currents have had the practical possibility to act and to make themselves known. Experience has shown that all are inadequate and incapable. The vanguard of the revolutionary proletariat, the Communist Party, is the only one that has never given in.

But to conduct an independent policy in Italy, it is absolutely necessary that the party have no defeatism in its ranks. Italian proletarians, who have trust in the party and its forces, must not be told that actions hitherto attempted by the communists represent lack of success or failure on their part!

If we demonstrate with facts that the party knows how to organise the struggle and to implement its autonomous tactics, if we demonstrate with facts that the party lives on as the only opposition party, if we know how to issue slogans that indicate a feasible path of attack, we shall succeed in our task of eliminating the opposition groups, and above all the socialists and maximalists. In my view, this is how we should take advantage of the present situation.

Work in this direction should not be limited to polemics; we need to engage in practical work to win over the masses. The aim of this work is to tie together and unify the masses for revolutionary action, to build the united front of the urban and rural proletariat under the leadership of the Communist Party. Only this tying together of the masses will achieve the condition that enables us to launch the direct struggle against Fascism. It is a great job of work, which can and must be done while maintaining the party's independence.

There is a possibility that, following the Matteotti affair, Fascism will unleash a 'second wave of terror', a new offensive against the opposition. But that too will be no more than an episode in the development of the situation. Perhaps we shall see the opposition retreat, and public expressions of discontent lose momentum because of this new terror. With time, however, the opposition and the discontent will begin to grow again. Fascism cannot retain power in the long run by means of ceaseless pressure. Perhaps there is also the other possibility: to tie together all the working masses on the initiative of the CP and to issue a slogan for the reconstitution of red trade unions. Perhaps it will be possible to begin this work tomorrow.

The opportunists do not dare to carry out this work. There are towns in Italy where the workers could be invited with every chance of success to rejoin the red unions. But since that would also be the signal for struggle, since it would be necessary at the same time to be ready to fight the Fascists, the opportunist parties are in no hurry to reconstitute the mass organisations of the proletariat. If the CP is the first to seize the favourable moment to launch this slogan, the possibility will arise that the reorganisation of the Italian workers' movement will take place with the CP at its centre.

Even before the situation created by the Matteotti affair, our independent stance was the best manoeuvre we could execute. At elections, for example, even non-communist elements voted for the communist lists because they saw in communism, as they said, the clearest and most radical anti-Fascism, the sharpest rejection of what they detested. Our independent position, therefore, is a means to exercise political influence over strata not directly linked to us. It was precisely because we stood with an unequivocal programme that the CP won a great success at the elections, despite the government offensive in advance against our lists and our electoral work. We stood officially with the watchword 'Unity of the Proletariat', but the masses gave us their vote because we were communists, because we came out openly against Fascism, because our opponents defined us as irreconcilable. This attitude assured us of noteworthy successes.

The same is true of the Matteotti affair. All eyes turned to the Communist Party, which speaks a language thoroughly different from that of any other opposition party. It follows that only a completely independent stance towards Fascism and the Opposition will allow us to exploit all the ongoing developments to bring down the gigantic power of Fascism.

The same work should be carried out to win over the peasant masses. We should develop a form of peasant organisation that allows us to work not only among agricultural wage-earners (who are basically aligned with industrial wage-earners) but also among tenant-farmers, smallholders, etc., within the organisations that defend their interests. The economic situation is such that no pressure, however great, can impede the development of such organisations. We must try to place this question before the peasant smallholders, and present a clear programme to combat their oppression and exploitation. We must break completely with the Socialist Party's ambiguous position in this area. We must use existing currents in the formation of peasant organizations, and encourage them to defend the economic interests of the rural population. For if these organisations turn themselves into electoral apparatuses, they will fall into the hands of bourgeois agitators, politicians and small-town lawyers. If, on the other hand, we manage to call into being an organisation to defend the economic interests of the peasantry (not a trade union, because the idea of a trade union of smallholders runs into serious theoretical objections), then we will have an association in which we can carry out group work, which we can imbue with our influence, and in which we find a point of support for the bloc of the urban and rural proletariat under the sole leadership of the Communist Party.

The point is not at all to present a terrorist programme. Myths have been created about us. It has been said that we want to be a minority party, a little elite, or things like that. We have never supported that idea. If there has ever been a movement whose criticisms and tactics have tirelessly sought to destroy the illusions about terrorist minorities once spread by ultra-anarchists and syndicalists, then our party has been that movement. We have always opposed such a tendency, and it is really to turn things upside down to present us as terrorists or champions of heroic, armed minority actions, and so on!

We do think it necessary, however, to take a clear position of principle on the question of disarming the white guards and arming the proletariat – a question with which our party is currently grappling.

Of course, struggle is possible only with the participation of the masses. The great mass of the proletariat well knows that an offensive by a heroic vanguard cannot solve the issue; that is a naïve conception that any Marxist party must reject. But if we launch the mass slogan of disarming the white guards and arming the proletariat, we must present the working masses themselves as vehicles of the action. We must reject the illusion that a 'transitional government' could be so naïve as to permit, by legislation, parliamentary manoeuvres or more or less skilful expedients, an outflanking of the positions of the bourgeoisie: that is, the legal dispossession of its whole technical and military machine and the peaceful distribution of weapons to the proletariat; and that, this being done, it will be possible calmly to give the signal for struggle. It is not so easy to make a revolution!

We are absolutely convinced that it is impossible to undertake the struggle with a few hundred or a few thousand armed communists. The CP of Italy will be the last to surrender to such illusions. We are firmly convinced of the strict necessity of drawing the broad masses into the struggle. But arming is a problem that can be solved only with revolutionary means. We can exploit the slowdown in the development of Fascism to create proletarian revolutionary formations. But we must get rid of the illusion that some kind of manoeuvre will one day enable us to seize the technical apparatus and the weapons of the bourgeoisie: that is, to tie the hands of our adversaries before we pass onto the attack against them.

To combat this illusion – which prompts the proletariat to indolence in respect of the revolution – is not terrorism. On the contrary, it is a genuinely Marxist and revolutionary attitude. We do not at all say that we are the communist 'elect', that we want to disturb the social equilibrium through the actions of a small minority. On the contrary, we want to win the leadership of the proletarian masses; we seek the unity of action of the proletariat. But we also want to use the experiences of the Italian proletariat, which teach that struggles under the leadership of an unconsolidated party – even one of mass proportions – or an improvised coalition of parties will necessarily end in defeat. We want joint struggle by the working masses of town and country, but we want that struggle to be led by a general staff with a clear political line, that is, by the Communist Party.

This is the problem facing us.

The situation will develop with greater or lesser complexity, but the basis already exists to launch slogans and agitate for the CP to assume the initiative and leadership of the revolution, and to state openly that it is necessary to advance on the ruins of the existing anti-Fascist opposition groups. The proletariat must be alerted that, at the moment when a proletarian seizure of power in Italy again appears to the capitalist class as an acute danger, all the bourgeois and social-democratic forces will rally to Fascism. Such are the struggle perspectives for which we must prepare.

In conclusion, I want to add a few words on Fascism as an international phenomenon, basing myself on the experiences we have had in Italy.

We are of the view that Fascism is tending in a way to spread outside Italy. Similar movements in other countries, such as Bulgaria, Hungary and perhaps also Germany, have probably had the backing of Italian Fascism. But while it is certain that the proletariat everywhere in the world must understand and use the lessons that Fascism has given in Italy, in case similar movements take shape in other countries as means of struggle against the workers, it should not be forgotten that only certain prerequisites enabled the Fascist movement in Italy to acquire such huge forces. The first ones I will mention are national and religious unity.

Now, I believe that both these prerequisites are necessary for the middle layers to be mobilised by Fascism; national unity and religious unity are required as the basis for a mobilisation of the emotions. In Germany, the presence of two major religious denominations and of different nationalities with some separatist tendencies evidently runs counter to the formation of a large Fascist party. In Italy, Fascism has found especially favourable ground: Italy was one of the victorious states in the war; chauvinism and patriotism reached fever pitch there, while the material benefits of victory fell short. The defeat of the proletariat ties in closely with this. The middle layers waited a while, so that they could feel sure that the proletariat did or did not have the strength to prevail. When the impotence of the revolutionary parties of the proletariat finally became apparent, the middle layers thought they could act independently and take the reins of government themselves. Meanwhile, the big bourgeoisie found a way to yoke such forces to the waggon of its own interests.

Given these facts, I do not think we should expect anything as forthright as Italian Fascism to emerge in other countries, that is, a movement uniting the upper strata of the exploiters with a broad mass mobilisation of the middle layers and petty bourgeoisie in the interests of those strata. Fascism in other countries is different from Italian Fascism. Elsewhere it is limited to a petty-bourgeois movement with some armed formations, but it is a movement that does not succeed in identifying completely with large industry, nor *a fortiori* with the state apparatus. The state apparatus may enter into coalition with the parties of large industry, the big banks and big landed property, while remaining more or less independent in relation to the middle layers and the petty bourgeoisie. Clearly this Fascism too is an enemy to the proletariat, but it is a much less dangerous enemy than Italian Fascism. In my view, the question of relations with such a movement has been fully resolved: it is madness to think of any links whatever with it. It is precisely that kind of movement that provides the basis for a counter-revolutionary political mobilisation of the semi-proletarian masses, as well as presenting grave dangers that it will carry the proletariat itself onto that ground.

In general, we can expect abroad a copy of Italian Fascism intertwined with manifestations of the 'democratic pacifist wave'. But Fascism will assume different forms from those in Italy. Political reaction and the capitalist offensive of various strata in struggle with the proletariat will not submit there to such a unitary leadership.

There has been much talk of Italian anti-Fascist organisations abroad. These organisations have been created by Italian bourgeois émigrés. Another question on the agenda is the judgement that international public opinion has of Italian Fascism, and the propaganda campaign waged against it by civilised countries. Some even think that the moral indignation of the bourgeoisie of other countries might be a means to do away with the Fascist movement

Communists and revolutionaries cannot yield to this illusion about the democratic or moral sensibilities of the bourgeoisie in other countries. Even where left and pacifist tendencies still manifest themselves today, Fascism will be used tomorrow without scruple as a method of class struggle. We know that international capital cannot but rejoice at the exploits of Fascism in Italy, at the terror it exercises there against workers and peasants.

For the struggle against Fascism we can count on the proletarian revolutionary International alone. It is a question of class struggle. We cannot turn to the democratic parties of other countries, to associations of idiots and hypocrites such as the Ligue des Droits de l'Homme, because we do not wish to foster the illusion that what they have in mind is something essentially different from Fascism, or that the bourgeoisie of other countries is not capable of preparing the same persecutions for its own working class and committing the same atrocities as Fascism in Italy.

Therefore, to achieve an uprising against Italian Fascism and an international campaign against the terror in our country, we count solely on the revolutionary forces in Italy and abroad. It is the workers of the world who must boycott the Italian Fascists. Our persecuted comrades who have fled abroad will make a not insignificant contribution to this battle and to the creation of an international anti-Fascist sentiment among the proletariat.

The reaction and terror in Italy should arouse a class hatred, a proletarian counteroffensive, which will help to group together revolutionary forces internationally and lead to worldwide struggle against international Fascism and all other forms of bourgeois oppression.

CHAPTER 6

The Lyons Theses

1   Draft Theses for the Third Congress of the Communist Party of Italy
Presented by the Left (Lyons, 1926)[1]

1.1   *General Questions*

1.1.1   Principles of Communism

The doctrinal cornerstones of the communist party are those of Marxism,
which the fight against opportunist deviations have reinstated and established
as the foundations of the Third International. These cornerstones include: dialectical materialism as the systematic conception of the world and human
history; the basic economic doctrines of Marx's *Capital* as the method for interpreting the modern capitalist economy; and the programmatic formulations of
the *Communist Manifesto* as the historical and political framework of the emancipation of the world working class. The grandiose experience of the victorious
Russian revolution and the work of its leader, Lenin, master of international
communism, constitute the confirmation, restoration and consistent development of this system of principles and methods. Anyone who rejects even a
single part of it is not a communist and cannot be a militant in the International.

In consequence, the communist party rejects and condemns the doctrines
of the ruling class, ranging from the spiritualistic and religious, which are idealist in philosophy and reactionary in politics, to the positivist, free-thinking and
Voltairean, which are politically Masonic, anti-clerical, and democratic.

It likewise condemns other political schools that have a certain following
in the working class: social-democratic reformism, which envisions a peaceful evolution, without armed struggle, from capitalist power to workers' power,
and advocates class collaboration; syndicalism, which belittles political action
by the working class and the necessity of the party as the supreme revolutionary organ; anarchism, which denies the historical necessity of the state and
of the proletarian dictatorship as the means for transforming the social order
and abolishing the division of society into classes. The communist party also
combats the many manifestations of spurious revolutionism, now commonly

---

1   *In difesa della continuità del programma comunista* 1970, pp. 92–123. The Lyons Congress,
which was held clandestinely in the French city of Lyons, marked the victory of Antonio
Gramsci's political line.

referred to as 'centrism', which attempt to ensure the survival of these erroneous tendencies by combining them with apparently communist theses.

1.1.2   Nature of the Party

The historical process by which the proletariat emancipates itself and establishes a new social order stems from the fact of class struggle. Every class struggle is a political struggle; that is, it tends to transform itself into a struggle for the conquest of political power and the leadership of a new state organism. *Consequently, the organ that leads the class struggle to its final victory is the political class party, the only possible instrument first of revolutionary insurrection, and then of government.* These elementary and brilliant formulations from Marx, which Lenin brought into maximum relief, lead to a definition of the party as an organisation of all those who adhere to the system of opinions that summarises the historical task of the revolutionary class and who are determined to work for its victory. In the party, the working class becomes conscious of the path it must take and gains the will to do so; *historically, then, the party represents the class in all the successive phases of the struggle, even though it may only contain a more or less small fraction of the class at any given time.* This is the meaning of the definition Lenin gave for the party at the Second World Congress.

This conception, shared by Marx and Lenin, is opposed to the typically opportunist conception of the labourist or workerist party, to which all individuals with the status of proletarians belong by right. Even though such a party would be numerically stronger, the direct counter-revolutionary influence of the ruling class may and even must prevail in certain situations, since the ruling class would be represented in it by the dictatorship of organisers and leaders who, individually, may come from the proletariat as well as from other classes. Marx and Lenin not only fought against this fatal theoretical error but did not hesitate to shatter false proletarian unity in practise, to ensure the continuity of the political function of the party in preparation for the proletariat's subsequent tasks, also at moments when the social activity of the proletariat was eclipsed, and also by means of small political groups of adherents to the revolutionary programme. This is the only possible way to achieve the future concentration of the largest possible number of workers under the leadership and the banner of a communist party capable of battle and of victory.

An *immediate* organisation of all those who, economically speaking, are workers, cannot fulfil political and therefore revolutionary tasks, because individual professional or local groups are driven only by the satisfaction of partial needs determined by the direct consequences of capitalist exploitation. The synthesis of these individual impulses in a common vision and action that enable individuals and groups to go beyond any particularism by accepting difficulties and sacrifices for the general, final triumph of the cause of the working class can only be achieved through the intervention of a political party, defined by the *political* convictions of its members, at the head of the working class. For Marx and Lenin, the definition of the party as the party of the working class does not have vulgarly statistical or constitutional value but, on the contrary, is inexorably connected with the historical objectives of the proletariat.

Any conception of the problems of internal organisation that stems from the workerist vision of the party reveals a serious theoretical deviation, since it replaces the revolutionary with a democratic perspective and gives more importance to utopian organisational schemes than to the dialectical reality of the conflict between two opposed classes. It contains the danger of a relapse into opportunism. The dangers of degeneration of the revolutionary movement cannot be eliminated by any organisational formula because there is no such formula that can ensure the necessary continuity in the political orientation of leaders and simple militants. Neither is the formula that only a genuine worker can be a communist able to avert degeneration, since it is contradicted by the vast majority of the examples of individuals and parties with which we are well acquainted. The guarantee against degeneration must be sought elsewhere, if we are not to contradict the fundamental postulate of Marxism: *The revolution is not a question of the form of organisation*. This postulate is a summa of the great victory of scientific socialism over the first raving of utopianism.

We can only resolve the current contingent questions of internal organisation of the International and the party on the basis of this conception of the nature of the class party.

1.1.3   Party Action and Tactics

The way the party brings its influence to bear on other groups, organisations and institutions of the society in which it operates constitutes its tactics. The general elements of this question must be established in connection with our principles as a whole. Only then will it be possible to specify concrete procedures responding to various kinds of practical problems and to successive phases of historical development.

By assigning the revolutionary party its place and role in the palingenesis of society, Marxist doctrine provides the most brilliant of solutions to the problems of freedom and determinism in human activity. As long as it is posed in terms of the abstract 'individual', this problem will continue to supply material for the metaphysical pedantry of the philosophers of the decadent ruling class for years to come. Marxism, by contrast, poses the question in the light of an objective, scientific conception of society and history. Just as the idea that the individual, and one individual, can act on the outside world, deforming and shaping it at will thanks to a power of initiative conferred upon him by some sort of divine virtue, is the antipode to our conception, we likewise condemn the voluntarist conception of the party according to which a small group of individuals, having made a profession of faith, can propagate it and impose it on the world by a gigantic effort of will, activity, and heroism. Then again, it would be an aberrant and foolish conception of Marxism to believe that history and the revolution obey fixed laws, and that we have nothing more to do than discover these laws through objective research and attempt to make predictions about the future, without attempting to do anything in terms of action: this fatalistic conception is tantamount to denying the necessity and function of the party. The powerful originality of Marxist determinism places it not mid-way between these two conceptions, but above both of them. Because it is dialectical and historical, it refuses all apriorism and makes no claim to apply to all problems a self-same abstract solution that is good for all times and all human groups. If the present development of the sciences does not allow a complete account of the causes that lead the individual to act, beginning with physical and biological data and culminating in a science of psychological activities, the problem can in fact be solved in the field of sociology by applying, as Marx did, the investigative methods of modern positive and experimental science, whose heritage socialism claims in its entirety and which are distinct from the so-called materialist and positivist philosophy that the bourgeoisie adopted during its historical ascension. By giving rational consideration to the reciprocal influences individuals exert on one another through a critical study of economy and history, once we have cleared the ground of all traditional ideology we can, in a certain sense, eliminate the indeterminacy of the processes operating in each individual. From this point of departure, Marxism has established a system of notions that is not an immutable and fixed gospel, but a living instrument for the study and discovery of the laws of the historical process. This system is based upon economic determinism, discovered by Marx, which sees in the study of economic relations and the development of the technical means of production the objective platform upon which to build a solid understanding of the laws of social life and, to a certain extent, to forecast its further evolution. With this in mind, it should be noted that the final solution is not an immanent formula by which, once we have found this universal key, it is possible to say that, letting economic phenomena take their course, a predictable and preordained series of political facts will follow.

To be sure, our critique completely and definitively dismisses the action of individuals even when they appear as the principal actors in historical events, along with the intentions and perspectives from which they imagine such action results. But this is by no means to say that a collective organism like the class party cannot and must not have initiative and will of its own. The solution to which Marxism leads has been formulated repeatedly in our fundamental texts.

Humanity and its most powerful aggregations – classes, parties, states – have up to now been as if playthings in the hands of economic laws the essentials of which they do not know. Lacking theoretical knowledge of the economic process, these aggregations have been incapable of mastering and directing it. But for the class that has appeared in the modern historical epoch, the proletariat, and for the political organisations – party and state – that must arise from it, the problem is now different. This is the first class that is not driven to base its rise to power on the consolidation of social privileges and a division of society into classes, in order to subjugate and exploit a new one. And, at the same time, it is the first class that – in Marxist communism – has shaped a doctrine of economic, historical and social development.

This is therefore the first time that a class struggles for the general abolition of classes, the general abolition of private property of the means of production, and not simply for the transformation of the social forms of this property.

The programme of the proletariat is both its emancipation from the yoke of the modern ruling, privileged class, and the emancipation of the entire human collectivity from the tyranny of economic laws that, once they have been understood, can finally be mastered in a rational and scientific economy that will be subject to the direct intervention of man. For this reason and with this in mind, Engels wrote that the proletarian revolution marks the passage from the world of necessity to the world of freedom.

It is not our intention to revive the illusory myth of individualism, which seeks to liberate the human ego from external influences when, in fact, this mesh of influences tends to grow ever more complex and the life of the individual ever more indistinguishably a part of collective life. On the contrary, the problem is posed in other terms: freedom and will are attributed to a class destined to become the unitary human aggregation, which is finally left to cope only with the adverse forces of the outside physical world.

If it is true that proletarian humanity alone (still far in the future) will be free and capable of a will that is not sentimental illusion but the capacity to organise and master the economy in the broadest sense of the word – if it is true that today the proletarian class (though less than the other classes) is still *determined* in the limits of its action by external influences – it is also true that the *political party* is the organ that expresses the full extent of its will and initiative in the entire field of its action. But here by 'political party' we clearly refer to the party of the proletarian class, the communist party, the party that is connected by an unbroken thread to the ultimate goals of the future process. This volitional faculty of the party, along with its consciousness and theoretical preparation, are collective functions par excellence. From the Marxist point of view, the task assigned by the party to its own leaders makes them the instruments and operators through which it can best manifest its capacities to understand and explain facts, to plan and lead actions – capacities never detached from their origin in the existence and characteristics of the collective organ. Hence the Marxist conception of the party and of its action shuns both fatalism – passive expectancy of phenomena, in the belief that no direct influence is possible – and voluntarism in the individual sense, by which the qualities of theoretical preparation, willpower, spirit of sacrifice – a special type of moral figure and a requisite of 'purity' – are demanded of every single party militant. The voluntarist error would reduce the party to an elite that is distinct from and superior to the rest of the social elements making up the working class; the fatalistic and passivist error, while not necessarily denying the function and usefulness of the party altogether, would equate it directly with the proletarian class understood exclusively in the economic, statistical sense. We insist on the conclusions given in the previous thesis on the nature of the party, which condemn both the workerist conception and the conception of an intellectual and moral elite: these two conceptions, both equally alien to Marxism, are destined to meet on the path of opportunism.

By defining the general question of tactics in conformity with the nature of the party, the Marxist solution is distinguished both from the abstract pedantry of doctrinaires who turn their backs on the reality of the class struggle and neglect concrete activity, and from sentimental aestheticism, which seeks to create new situations and new historical movements through the brash or heroic deeds of tiny minorities. At the same time, it distinguishes itself from opportunism, which forgets the connection with principles – that is, with the general objectives of the movement – and, seeking only immediate and apparent success, is content to clamour for limited and isolated demands, never wondering whether they contradict the necessities of preparing the working class for its supreme conquests. The error of anarchist politics stems from doctrinal sterility, incapable of understanding the dialectical stages of real historical evolution, combined with the voluntarist illusion that imagines it can speed up social processes by virtue of the example and sacrifice of one or more individuals. In its turn, the error of social-democratic politics stems, in theoretical terms, on the one hand from the false and fatalistic interpretation of Marxism which holds that the revolution will mature slowly and on its own without a proletarian insurrection. On the other, it stems from the voluntarist pragmatism that, unable to do without the immediate effects of its initiative and its daily interventions, is content to struggle for objectives that *appear* to be in the interest of groups of the proletariat when, in reality, achieving them plays into the hands of the conservative interests of the ruling class instead of serving to prepare the victory of the proletariat: reforms, concessions, partial economic and political advantages obtained from the capitalist class and from the bourgeois state.

The artificial introduction into the class movement of the theoretical postulates of 'modern' voluntarist and pragmatist philosophy based on idealism (Bergson, Gentile, Croce) cannot pass for a reaction to reformism on the pretext that reformism shows a certain superficial sympathy for bourgeois positivism, but only prepares the opportunist affirmation of new reformist phases.

The party's activity cannot and must not be limited to maintaining the purity of theoretical principles and organisational structures, nor to achieving immediate success or numerical popularity at any price. At all times and in all situations it must develop simultaneously in these three directions:

a) defend and clarify the fundamental elements of the programme in relation to new facts as they arise, developing the theoretical consciousness of the working class movement;

b) ensure the continuity and effectiveness of the party organisation and defend it against outside influences opposed to the revolutionary interest of the proletariat;

c) participate actively in all working class struggles including those that arise out of partial and limited interests, to encourage their development but constantly emphasising their links with final revolutionary goals and presenting the conquests of class struggle as stepping-stones on the way to the indispensable struggles to come, denouncing the dangers of taking partial gains for points of arrival to the detriment both of the proletariat's class activity and combativeness and of the autonomy and independence of its ideology and its organisations, first and foremost of which is the party.

The supreme goal of the party's complex activities is to achieve the *subjective* conditions of the proletariat's preparation, enabling it to take advantage of the objective revolutionary possibilities presented by history as soon as they appear, in order to avoid defeat and be victorious.

All this is the point of departure for resolving the problems posed by relations between the party and the proletarian masses, between the party and other political parties, and between the proletariat and other social classes. The following tactic is erroneous: a real communist party must be a mass party *in any and all situations*; that is, it must have such a numerically vast organisation and such a great political influence on the proletariat that it can overcome any challenge by other (self-styled) workers' parties. This formulation is a caricature of Lenin's thesis, which in 1921 established an absolutely correct practical and contingent watchword: for the conquest of power it is not sufficient to have formed 'real' communist parties and launch an insurrectionary offensive; it is also necessary to have numerically strong parties that have acquired a predominant influence over the proletariat.

This means that in the phase preceding the conquest of power the party must have the masses behind it – above all, it must win over the masses. In this formula it is only the expression *majority* of the masses that is dangerous in a certain sense, because it exposes and has exposed 'literal' Leninists to the danger of social-democratic theoretical and tactical interpretations. Instead of specifying whether this majority is to be sought in parties, trade unions or other organisations, the formula – while expressing a perfectly correct idea, necessary to avoid launching 'desperate' actions with insufficient forces in unfavourable situations – opens the way to procrastination in periods when action is possible and necessary, when it is necessary to have a truly 'Leninist' determination and initiative. But the formula that the party must have the masses behind it on the eve of the struggle for power has assumed a typically opportunist tone in the grotesque interpretation of modern-day pseudo-Leninists who spout that the party must be a mass party 'in any and all situations'. There are objective situations in which power relations are unfavourable to the revolution, even if perhaps closer to it in time than others: Marxism teaches that the velocity of historical evolution is extremely variable. In such situations, attempting to be a mass party at any price, to be a majority party, attempting with all one's strength to have a predominant political influence, can only lead to the renunciation of communist principles and methods in favour of social-democratic petty-bourgeois politics.

It is profoundly true that in certain past, present and future situations the proletariat, for the most part, has taken, takes and will necessarily take a non-revolutionary position – a position of inertia or collaboration with the enemy, depending on circumstances. But in spite of this, the proletariat everywhere and always remains the potentially revolutionary class and the repository of insurrectional possibilities, since within this class the communist party, while never renouncing a single possibility of coherent intervention, avoids the paths that would most easily win it immediate popularity but would divert the party from its task and deprive the proletariat of the indispensable foothold for its recovery. It is in this dialectical and Marxist arena, and never from an aesthetic and sentimental point of view, that we reject the ghastly opportunist formula that a communist party is free to adopt any and all means and any and all methods. It is said that, precisely because the party is truly communist – that is, sound in its principles and in its organisation – it can indulge in acrobatic political manoeuvres of all sorts. But what is forgotten here is that, for us, the party is both a factor and a product of historical development, and confronted with the forces of this development the proletariat behaves like an even more malleable material. The proletariat will not be influenced by the tortuous justifications party leaders may give for certain 'manoeuvres' but, rather, by actual results that the party must be able to foresee, learning from the experience of its past errors. It is not theoretical credos and organisational sanctions that will enable the party to safeguard itself against degenerations, but only its capacity to act in the field of tactics with precise and respected norms of action, assiduously avoiding false tracks.

Another error in the general question of tactics that stems directly from the classical opportunist position dismantled by Marx and Lenin is the following: the communist party, while a factor in the total and final proletarian revolution, when class and party struggles arise that are not yet those of its specific terrain, must choose between the two conflicting forces the one that represents the development of the situation more favourable to the general historical evolution, and must more or less openly support and ally itself with it – this, because it is convinced that the conditions of the proletarian revolution will mature only through an evolution of political and social forms.

The very premise of this position is without foundation: in the first place because the typical scheme of a social and political evolution that best prepares the final advent of communism, laid out in the most minute detail, is a 'Marxism' only of the opportunists – indeed, it is the basis of the defamation of the Russian revolution and of the present communist movement by Kautsky and his ilk. It cannot even be established that in general the most favourable conditions for fruitful work by the communist party arise in, for example, the most democratic of bourgeois regimes. While it is true that the reactionary, 'rightist' measures of bourgeois governments have often halted the advance of the proletariat, it is just as true, and much more frequently the case, that the liberal, *leftist* politics of bourgeois governments have stifled the class struggle and diverted the working class from decisive actions. A more precise evaluation, truly consonant with Marxism's breaking of the democratic, evolutionist, and progressive spell, only shows that the bourgeoisie attempts, often successfully, to alternate methods and government parties according to its counter-revolutionary interests; while all our experience shows us how the triumph of opportunism has always stemmed from proletariat enthusiasm for the vicissitudes of bourgeois politics.

In the second place, even if it were true that certain changes of government within the framework of the present regime do facilitate the further development of the proletariat's action, experience shows unequivocally that this is subject to an explicit condition: the existence of a party that has forewarned the masses against the disillusionment that will inevitably follow that which was presented as an immediate success. And we refer here not only to the mere existence of this party but to its capacity to act, even before the outbreak of the struggle, with an autonomy that is obvious to the proletariat, which will only follow it as long as its attitude is correct, and not on the basis of schemes it would be convenient to adopt officially. Faced with struggles that cannot lead to a victory of the proletariat, the party will not make itself the manager of transformations and achievements that do not directly interest the class it represents, and will not renounce either its specific character or its autonomous action to transform itself into a kind of insurance company for all the so-called 'new' political movements or for all the political systems and governments threatened by a supposedly 'worse' government.

Against the requirements of this line of action we often find misleading invocations of Marx's formula that 'communists support every movement directed against the existing social conditions', or of Lenin's argument against 'the infantile disorder of communism'.[2] The way these are being used inside our movement is not essentially different from the constant attempts of Bernstein revisionists and Nenni[3] centrists to hold Marxists up to ridicule in the name of Marx and Lenin.

Two observations need to be made. First of all, these positions taken by Marx and Lenin have a contingent historical value, since they refer to a not yet bourgeois Germany in the case of Marx, and to tsarist Russia for the Bolshevik case illustrated by Lenin in his book. But the solution to the problem of tactics under the classic conditions of a proletariat fighting against a fully developed capitalist bourgeoisie must not be based on this criterion alone. Secondly, when Marx speaks of support and Lenin of 'compromises' (as a great Marxist dialectician and champion of real and non-formal intransigence aimed and directed at an immutable goal, Lenin liked to 'flirt' with such terms) they are referring to support for and compromises with movements still constrained to advance by means of insurrection against the forms of the past, even if this is in contradiction with the ideologies and possible designs of their leaders. In such cases the communist party intervenes on the terrain of civil war, as demonstrated by Lenin's positions on the peasant and nationality questions, in the Kornilov episode and in a hundred others. Finally, even beyond these two essential observations, the meaning of Lenin's critique of 'the infantile disorder', the meaning of

---

2   See Lenin 1965.

3   A well-known leader of the Italian socialist movement, Pietro Nenni (1891–1980) was fiercely opposed to revolutionary communism.

all Marxist texts on the flexibility of revolutionary politics, is by no means in contradiction with the fact that they have voluntarily raised a barrier against opportunism, defined by Engels and later by Lenin as 'absence of principles' or forgetfulness of the final objective.

It would be against Marx and Lenin to construct communist tactics with a formalist rather than a dialectical method. It would be a huge mistake to say that means must correspond to ends not in virtue of their historical and dialectical succession in the process of development, but according to a similarity and an analogy of the aspects that means and ends can assume from an immediate and, we could almost say, ethical, psychological, and aesthetic standpoint. In matters of tactics we must not make the mistake the anarchists and reformists do in matters of principles, when they find it absurd that the abolition of classes and of state power must be prepared by way of the predominance of the proletarian class and its dictatorship, and that the abolition of all social violence is realised by employing both offensive and defensive violence, overthrowing existing power while preserving the power of the proletariat. All of the following claims are no less mistaken: a revolutionary party must be in favour of revolutionary struggle at every moment without taking into account the strengths of friends and foes; communists must always champion unlimited strikes; communists must shun such means as dissimulation, trickery, espionage, and so forth, because they are not noble or nice. The critique by Marxism and by Lenin of the pseudo-revolutionary superficialism that plagues the path of the proletariat exemplifies the effort to eliminate these foolish and sentimental criteria from the solution of the problem of tactics. This critique has become an integral part of the experience of the communist movement.

One example of the tactical errors this critique insists we must avoid is this: just because we communists split politically with the opportunists, we must also support the split with the unions headed by the yellows.[4] It is nothing but polemical trickery that has misrepresented the Italian Left as basing its conclusions on arguments such as: it is undignified to meet personally with the heads of the opportunist parties or others of their ilk.

---

4   The 'yellows' refers to the Amsterdam International Federation of Trade Unions, also known as the Amsterdam Bureau or the 'yellow' Amsterdam International. This colour, which was deliberately chosen at the beginning of the twentieth century by some French company unions in opposition to the 'red' unions associated with socialism, came to be used as a term of scorn by 'red' socialists and communists throughout the world. Founded in 1901, reconstituted in 1919 on the political principles of the League of Nations and the International Labour Organization, it was branded by the Communist International as an 'agent of the bourgeoisie', class collaborationist and an impediment to revolution. To counteract its influence, the International formed the Red International of Labour Unions (commonly known as the Profintern) in 1921.

But the critique of 'infantilism' does not mean that indeterminacy, chaos and arbitrariness must reign supreme in matters of tactics, or that 'all means' are appropriate for achieving our ends. It is claimed that the link between means and ends is guaranteed by the revolutionary character of the party and by the contributions made to its decisions by remarkable men or groups with a brilliant tradition behind them. This is a playing with words that is alien to Marxism, because it disregards the dialectical interplay of causes and effects and the fact that the party's means of action have repercussions on the party itself. Moreover, it forgets that Marxism denies any value to the 'intentions' that dictate the initiatives of individuals or groups, whether or not we be 'suspicious' of such intentions, which, as bloody experiences have taught us, must never be ignored.

In his book on 'infantilism', Lenin says that tactical means must be chosen in advance in accordance with the final revolutionary goal and on the basis of a clear vision of the historical struggle of the proletariat and its outcome. He shows that it would be absurd to reject one or another tactical means on the pretext that is 'ugly' or merits the name 'compromise': what must be established is whether such a means is or is not in conformity with the end. This question is still open, and it will always be a daunting task facing the collective activity of the party and the International. We can say that Marx and Lenin have left us a solid heritage of theoretical principles, without by any means saying that all theoretical research on matters of communism has drawn to a close. But the same cannot be said with regard to tactics, even after the Russian revolution and the experience of the first years of the new International, which was prematurely deprived of Lenin's presence. The problem of tactics is far too complex for the simplistic and sentimental answers of 'infantile' communists and must continue to be an object of study for the entire international communist movement, in the light of all its earliest and most recent experience. We do not contradict Marx or Lenin when we say that to solve it we must follow rules of action – not as vital and fundamental as principles, but compulsory both for militants and for the leading bodies of the movement – that consider the various ways in which situations may develop, in order to plan the party's line of action as precisely as possible, whatever the possible scenario.

Examination and understanding of various situations are necessary in making tactical decisions: not, however, to encourage arbitrary 'improvisations' and 'surprises' but, on the contrary, to indicate to the movement that the time has come for an action that has been foreseen to the greatest possible extent. Denying the possibility of foreseeing the broad outlines of a tactic – not of foreseeing the situations, which is possible with even less certainty, but of foreseeing what we ought to do as objective situations evolve – means denying the task of the party, and denying the only guarantee we can give that, in all eventualities, the members will respond to the orders of the party, and the masses to the central leadership. In this sense the party is not like an army or any other state mechanism, for in these organs hierarchical authority prevails and voluntary adhesion counts for nothing. At the same time, however, the party member always has the possibility of not executing orders without risk of incurring material sanctions: he can leave the party. The best tactic is the one that does not result in any unexpected repercussions, either in the party or among the masses, even when, at a given turn in the situation, the central leadership does not have time to consult either the former or, naturally, the latter.

The art of foreseeing how the party members will react to orders, and what orders will elicit the correct reaction, is the art of revolutionary tactics, which can only be relied upon if they collectively apply the experiences of the past, expressed by the party leaders in clear rules of action. In this way the party members are assured that their leaders will not betray their mandate, and commit themselves in substance, not just in appearance, to a fruitful and resolute execution of the orders of the movement. We can say without hesitation that, since the party itself is perfectible but not perfect, much has to be sacrificed for clarity's sake to the persuasive capacity of the tactical rules, even if this does entail a certain schematisation: when the tactical schemes we have prepared collapse under the weight of circumstances, the matter will not be remedied by relapsing into opportunism and eclecticism but only by renewed efforts to bring tactics back into line with the duties of the party. It is not – only – the good party that makes good tactics, but good tactics that make the good party, and good tactics can only be those that, in their broad outlines, we have all understood and chosen.

We deny any eventuality of the party's collective effort to define its own tactical rules being stifled by demands for unconditional obedience to one man, one committee, or one particular party of the International, and to its traditional apparatus of leadership.

The party's action takes the form of *strategy* at the culminating moments of the struggle for power, during which this action assumes an essentially military character. In the preceding phases, however, party action is not reduced to mere ideology, propaganda and organisation, but, as we have seen, consists in participating in the various struggles in which the proletariat is engaged. The system of tactical rules must therefore be built with the precise aim of establishing the conditions in which the party's intervention and its activity in such movements, its *agitation* in the life of proletarian struggles, is coordinated with the final and revolutionary goal and, simultaneously, guarantees the useful progress of ideological, organisational and tactical preparation.

In the following sections we will examine a series of problems, showing how our elaboration of the norms of communist action relates to the present stage of development of the revolutionary movement.

1.2   *International Questions*

1.2.1   Constitution of the Third International

From the standpoint of restoring revolutionary doctrine, the constitution of the Communist International has provided a complete and definitive solution to the crisis of the Second International, caused by the world war. But if the formation of the Comintern constitutes an immense historical conquest in terms of organisation and tactics, it cannot be said that it has provided an equally complete solution to the crisis of the proletarian movement.

The Russian revolution, the first glorious victory of the world proletariat, was a fundamental factor in the formation of the new Internationalism. However, due to the social conditions in Russia the Russian revolution did not provide a general historical model of tactics applicable to revolutions in other countries. In the passage from autocratic feudal power to the dictatorship of the proletariat, there was no period of real political rule by a bourgeoisie organised in a stable state apparatus of its own.

This is why the historical confirmation of the Marxist programme by the Russian revolution has been of the greatest significance, and also why this revolution has made such a powerful contribution to the defeat of social-democratic revisionism on the terrain of principles. But in terms of organisation, the fight against the Second International, an integral part of the fight against world capitalism, has not had the same decisive success, and the many errors that have been committed have prevented communist parties from having all the effectiveness objective conditions allowed.

With regard to tactics, many problems have not been resolved satisfactorily enough, and remain unresolved today. On this chessboard, the players are the bourgeoisie, the modern bourgeois parliamentary state with a historically stable apparatus, and the proletariat. The communist parties have not always obtained what they could have in the proletarian offensive against capitalism and in the liquidation of the social-democratic parties, political organs of the bourgeois counter-revolution.

1.2.2   The World Economic and Political Situation (1926)

The international situation today appears less favourable to the proletariat than in the first few years after the war. There has been partial economic stabilisation of capitalism, which is to be understood as a lull in the disturbances suffered by certain parts of the economic structure, and not as a state of affairs excluding an imminent return of new disturbances.

The crisis of capitalism remains open, and its definitive aggravation is inevitable. In the political sphere, there has been a weakening of the revolutionary workers' movement in almost all the most advanced countries – counterbalanced, fortunately, by the consolidation of Soviet Russia, and by the struggle of the colonial peoples against the capitalist powers.

This situation presents two dangers. First, if the erroneous method of situationism is followed, a tendency to pose problems of proletarian action from a Menshevik point of view threatens to arise, even in outline. And second, if genuine proletarian action loses momentum, the conditions that Lenin had advocated for a correct application of communist tactics in the national and peasant questions may fail to materialise in the Comintern's general policy.

The postwar proletarian offensive was followed by an offensive of the capitalist class against proletarian positions, to which the Comintern responded with the 'united front' watchword. The next problem to appear was the advent of democratic-pacifist situations in various countries, which comrade Trotsky correctly denounced as a danger of degeneration for our movement. It is necessary to avoid any interpretation that presents as vital for the proletariat the outcome of the conflict between two factions of the bourgeoisie, the right and the left, identified too closely with distinct social groups.

The correct interpretation is that the ruling class has several methods of governing and defending itself, which can essentially be reduced to two: the reactionary, Fascist method, and the liberal-democratic method.

Lenin's theses have shown, on the basis of economic analysis, that the most modern strata of the bourgeoisie tend not only to unify the productive mechanism but also to defend it politically in the most forceful way possible.

Hence as a general rule we do not claim that the road to communism must pass through a stage of left-wing bourgeois government. In the particular cases in which this occurs, the party – in its pursuit of proletarian victory – must take a firm stand against all illusions regarding the advent of the left-wing government, whose political forms it must oppose no less than it opposed its reactionary counterpart.

1.2.3   The International's Working Methods

One of the most important tasks of the Communist International has been to dissipate the distrust of the proletariat toward the political action stemming from the parliamentary degenerations of opportunism.

Marxism does not take politics to mean an art or technique of parliamentary or diplomatic intrigue common to all parties, which each uses for its own ends. Proletarian politics is opposed to the method of bourgeois politics. It anticipates higher forms of relations, culminating in the art of revolutionary insurrection. This opposition, which we will not delve into here, is a vital condition for the connection between the revolutionary proletariat and its communist general staff, or for the useful selection of this staff's personnel.

The working methods of the International fly in the face of this revolutionary necessity. In the relations between the organs of the communist movement a two-faced politics often prevails, a subordination of theoretical motivations to fortuitous motives, a system of agreements and pacts between persons that, in its failure to establish a reliable connection between the parties and the masses, has led to bitter disappointments.

Improvisation, surprise, and *coups de théâtre* enter all too often into the great and fundamental decisions of the International, disorientating comrades and proletarians.

We find all this, for example, in most of the internal party questions, which are resolved by international bodies and congresses by means of a series of laborious arrangements that various groups of leaders are forced to accept, but that play no useful role in real party development.

1.2.4   Organisational Questions

The urgent need for a vast concentration of revolutionary forces was a prime factor in the decision to found the Comintern, because at that time a much more rapid development of the objective situation was predicted than actually took place. It is now clear, however, that organisational criteria should have been established with greater rigour. The formation of parties and the winning over of the masses have been more hindered than helped by all of the following: concessions to syndicalist and anarchist groups; petty deals with the centrists permitted by the 21 conditions; organic fusions with parties and parts of parties achieved through political *noyautage*; tolerance of two different communist organisations in certain countries based on the formula of 'sympathising parties'. The watchword given after the Fifth Congress – organise the party on the basis of factory cells – does not achieve its objective of rectifying the defects universally recognised in the sections of the International.

In its generalisation, and above all in the interpretation of the Italian central leadership, this watchword lends itself to serious errors and to deviation, both from the Marxist postulate that the revolution is not a question of forms of organisation and from the Leninist thesis that an organic solution can never be valid for all times and all places.

Organisation on the basis of factory cells is less suitable than territorial organisation for the parties now operating in bourgeois countries with stable parliamentary regimes. Moreover, it is a theoretical error to claim that the territorially-based party is a social-democratic party, while the party based on cells is a true communist party. In practise, this second type of organisation hinders the party's work in unifying proletarian groups from different trades and industries – work that is all the more vital given the more unfavourable situation and more restricted possibilities for the proletariat to organise. Many practical problems arise from the organisation of the party exclusively on a cell basis. In tsarist Russia, the question was posed in other terms: relations between the industrial capitalists and the state were different, and the imminence of the struggle for power rendered the corporatist danger less acute.

The factory cell system does not increase the influence of workers in the party, since all the top positions in the apparatus of its functionaries are held by a network of non-workers or of former workers. Given the defects of the International's working methods, the 'Bolshevisation' slogan, from an organisational standpoint, is indicative of a pedestrian and inadequate application of the Russian experience. In many countries an apparatus whose selection and functioning are based on criteria that are largely artificial already tends to cause a – perhaps involuntary – paralysis of spontaneous initiatives and proletarian and class energies.

Keeping the organisation of the party on a territorial basis does not mean renouncing party organs in the workshops: these organs must be communist groups connected to the party and directed by it within the framework of its trade-union activity. This system establishes a much better contact with the masses while keeping the fundamental organisation of the party less visible.

1.2.5   Discipline and Fractions
Another aspect of Bolshevisation is that it considers complete disciplinary centralisation and the strict prohibition of fractionism to be a sure guarantee of the party's effectiveness.

The highest authority called upon to decide all controversial questions is the international central organ, in which the Russian Communist Party is acquiring a political, if not hierarchical hegemony.

In fact there is no such guarantee, and the entire approach to the problem is inadequate. In point of fact a flood of fractionism in the International has not been avoided, and disguised and hypocritical forms have been encouraged. From a historical standpoint, the overcoming of fractions in the Russian party was neither an expedient nor a miracle cure applied by means of statutes, but the result and expression of a felicitous approach to the problems of doctrine and political action.

Disciplinary sanctions are one of the elements that guarantee against degenerations, but on the condition that their application be limited to exceptional cases and not become the norm and virtually the ideal of the party's functioning.

The solution does not reside in the constant, hollow invocation of the authoritarianism of the hierarchy, whose credentials are inadequate, either because – however spectacular – Russian historical experience is incomplete, or because within the old guard itself, the guardian of Bolshevik tradition, dissension does in fact arise, and the given solution cannot be considered to be the best a priori. But, at the same time, the solution does not reside in a systematic application of the principles of formal democracy either, which Marxism regards only as an occasionally convenient organisational practise.

The communist parties must create an organic centralism which, through maximum consultation of the rank and file, ensures the spontaneous elimination of any grouping that tends to differentiate itself. This cannot be achieved through formal and mechanical hierarchical prescriptions, but, as Lenin said, only through correct revolutionary politics.

Prevention of fractionism, not the suppression of fractions, is a fundamental aspect of the party's development.

It is absurd, sterile and extremely dangerous to claim that the party and the International are mysteriously ensured against any lapse into opportunism or any tendency to deviate. Since these effects can in fact arise from changes in the general situation or from the weight of residual social-democratic traditions, in order to solve our problems we must admit that any difference of opinion not reducible to cases of individual consciousness or defeatism may turn out to be useful in preserving the party and the proletariat in general from serious dangers.

If these dangers worsen, the differentiation will inevitably, but usefully, assume the form of fractions. This could lead to splits, not for the infantile reason that the leaders were not energetic enough at repression, but only in the unspeakable hypothesis of the party's failure and its submission to counter-revolutionary influences.

We find an example of incorrect method in the artificial solutions adopted for the situation of the German party after the opportunist crisis of 1923 – solutions that not only failed to eliminate the fractionism, but that hindered the spontaneous determination in the ranks of the particularly advanced German proletariat to launch a correct class and revolutionary reaction against the degeneration of the party.

The danger of bourgeois influence on the class party is not manifested his-torically by the organisation of fractions, but rather by a shrewd penetration that waves the flag of unitary demagoguery and operates as a dictatorship from above, immobilising the initiatives of the proletarian vanguard.

This defeatist factor can be identified and eliminated not by raising the ques-tion of discipline against fractional attempts. Rather, the party and the prolet-ariat must be alerted to this danger at the moment in which it manifests itself not only as a revision of doctrine, but as a positive proposal in favour of a major political manoeuvre with anti-class consequences.

One of the negative aspects of so-called Bolshevisation is the replacement of full and conscious political elaboration within the party – which corresponds to real progress toward a more compact centralism – by the noisy, superficial agitation of mechanical formulas of unity for unity's sake and discipline for discipline's sake.

The results of this method are harmful for the party and the proletariat, and delay the formation of the 'true' communist party. The method is applied in many sections of the International, and is in and of itself a serious symptom of latent opportunism. In the present situation in the Comintern the formation of an international left opposition is not in the offing, but if the unfavourable factors we have indicated continue to develop the formation of such an oppos-ition will be, at the same time, a revolutionary necessity and a spontaneous reflex of the situation.

1.2.6   Tactical Questions up to the Fifth Congress
In the solution to the problems of tactics in the international situations referred to above, the errors that were made are analogous to those made in the organ-isational sphere. In both cases, the errors stem from the claim that everything can be deduced from problems faced in the past by the Russian Communist Party.

The tactics of the united front are not to be understood as a political coali-tion with other so-called workers' parties, but as a utilisation of the immedi-ate demands raised in specific situations in order to increase the communist party's influence over the masses without compromising its autonomous pos-ition.

The basis of the united front must therefore be formed by those prolet-arian organisations to which workers belong as a result of their social position, independently of their political convictions or their membership in an organ-ised party. There are two reasons for this: first, so that the communists not be prevented from criticising the other parties or from progressively recruiting new elements previously dependent on these parties into the communist party organisations and into its very ranks; second, to ensure the masses' understanding of the party's direct orders to mobilise them on its programme and under its exclusive leadership.

Experience has shown again and again that the only way of ensuring a revolutionary application of the united front is to reject the method of permanent or transitory political coalitions, committees of struggle that include representatives of various political parties, and negotiations, proposals or open letters to other parties by the communist party.

Practical experience has shown how fruitless this method is, and any initially positive effect has been discredited by the abuse that followed.

The political united front, based on a central demand relating to the problem of the state, becomes the tactic of the workers' government. This is not simply a wrong tactic, but is blatantly in contradiction with the principles of communism. If the party issues a call for the proletariat to seize power through the representative organs of the bourgeois state apparatus, or even fails to condemn such a possibility explicitly, it abandons and renounces the communist programme, not only with regard to proletarian ideology, with all the inevitable negative repercussions, but in the ideological formulation the party itself has enunciated and endorsed. The revision of this tactic at the Fifth Congress, after the defeat in Germany, was not satisfactory, and further developments in tactical experience justify the requests that the very expression 'workers' government' be abandoned.

With regard to the central problem of the state the party's only watchword is the dictatorship of the proletariat, since there is no other 'workers' government'.

The expression 'workers' government' leads only to opportunism; that is, to supporting or even participating in self-styled 'pro-worker' governments of the bourgeois class.

This is by no means in contradiction with the watchword 'all power to the soviets' or to soviet-type organisations (representative bodies elected exclusively by workers), even when opportunist parties dominate them. These parties oppose the taking of power by proletarian organisations, since precisely this is the dictatorship of the proletariat (the exclusion of non-workers from elected organs and from power) that only the communist party can lead.

It is not necessary (and we shall not do so) to formulate the watchword 'proletarian dictatorship' with its only synonym: 'government of the communist party'.

1.2.7   Questions of the 'New Tactics'
The united front and the workers' government were justified on these grounds:
For our victory it is not sufficient to have communist parties, we must win over
the masses. To win over the masses we must crush the influence of the social-
democrats on the terrain of demands that all the workers can understand.

Today a further step is taken and a dangerous question is posed: For our victory must we first convince the bourgeoisie to govern in a more tolerant and
flexible manner, or must we obtain governments of middle classes between
the bourgeoisie and the proletariat, so that we, too, can participate? The second
position, admitting the possibility of a government originating from the middle
classes, falls head over heels into the revisionism of Marx's doctrine and is equivalent to the counter-revolutionary platform of reformism.

The first position would only define the most favourable objective conditions for propaganda, agitation and organisation. It is no less dangerous than
the other, as we have already shown from the standpoint of the analysis of situations.

Everything points to the fact that liberalism and bourgeois democracy, in
antithesis to or in synthesis with the 'Fascist' method, will evolve toward an
exclusion of the communist party from their juridical guarantees (for the little
they are worth): since communism denies such guarantees in its programme,
it excludes itself from them. This, moreover, is not contrary to the principles
of bourgeois democracy, and in any case has de facto precedents in the operation of all the so-called 'left governments' and, for example, in the programme
of the Italian Aventine Secession.[5] The 'freedom' given the proletariat will substantially be greater freedom for counter-revolutionary agents to stir it up and
organise it. The only freedom for the proletariat is in its dictatorship.

But even within the limits of a left government's capacity to produce useful
conditions, we have already shown that these conditions can be utilised only
if the party has clearly and continuously maintained an autonomous position.
There is no need to attribute diabolical abilities to the bourgeoisie. But there is
one certainty, a certainty without which one can no longer call oneself a communist: the final struggle will pit the united front of bourgeois forces, be they
personified by Hindenburg, MacDonald, Mussolini or Noske, against the conquests of the proletariat.

To prepare the proletariat to distinguish the elements in this front that
will be its even involuntary supporters will be a coefficient of defeat, even

---

5   The withdrawal of the Italian Socialist Party from the Chamber of Deputies in 1924–25, fol-
    lowing the murder of Giacomo Matteotti. Bordiga regards the new centrist PCd'I leadership's
    decision to join the PSI in the Aventine secession as simply "absurd": see pp. 219–220.

if any intrinsic weakness of the bourgeois front itself will be an evident co-efficient of victory.

In Germany, after Hindenburg's election, there were electoral alliances with social democrats and other 'republican' (that is, bourgeois) parties and a par-liamentary alliance in the Prussian Landstag to avoid the formation of a right-wing government. In France there was support for the Cartel des Gauches in the local government elections (the Clichy tactic). Such tactical methods must be declared unacceptable. Also as a strict consequence of the Theses of the Second Congress [of the Communist International] on revolutionary parlia-mentarism, the communist party must take rigorously independent positions on all electoral and parliamentary questions.

Such examples of recent tactics present a very clear, if not complete, his-torical affinity with the traditional methods of electoral blocs and collabor-ationism adopted in the Second International, which went so far as to claim justification on the basis of a Marxist interpretation.

These methods represent a real danger for the principles and organisations of the International; what is more, they have not been authorised by any res-olution of international congresses, much less by the theses on tactics of the Fifth Congress.

1.2.8   The Trade-Union Question

Over the course of time the Communist International has modified its concep-tion of relations between political and economic organisations on the world scale. This is an important example of the method that, instead of deriving con-tingent actions from principles, improvises new and different theories to justify actions prompted by apparent ease of execution and a promise of immediate success.

At first it was in favour of admitting trade unions into the International, then it formed a Red International of Labour Unions of its own. Its position was this: the party must fight for that trade-union unity which constitutes the area of broadest contact with the masses and therefore not create its own uni-ons through scissions from unions led by the yellows; however, at the interna-tional level the Bureau of the Amsterdam International was to be considered and treated not as an organisation of the proletarian masses but as a counter-revolutionary political organ of the League of Nations.

At a certain point, for reasons that are certainly important, but still limited (its plan to utilise the left-wing of the English union movement), the Inter-national even considered the possibility of dissolving the Red International of Labour Unions and joining forces organically with the Amsterdam Bur-eau.

No consideration on the changing situation can justify such serious zigzags, because the question of relations between international political and trade-union organisations is a question of principle, reducible to the question of relations between party and class for the revolutionary mobilisation.

What is more, the internal statutory guarantees were not observed, and the international organs involved were confronted with a *fait accompli*.

Retaining the slogan 'Moscow against Amsterdam' did not and does not exclude the struggle for trade-union unity in every country, because the liquidation of separatist tendencies in the unions (Germany and Italy) was possible only by demolishing the separatist argument that the International was preventing the proletariat from breaking free of the influence of the Amsterdam International.

Then again, the apparently enthusiastic adherence of our party in France to the proposal of world trade-union unity does not prevent it from manifesting an absolute incapacity to deal with its national trade-union problem without resorting to splits.

However, we must not exclude the usefulness of a united front tactic on a world scale, even with the trade unions affiliated to Amsterdam.

The Left of the Italian party has always fought for proletarian unity in the trade unions, which sharply distinguishes it from the syndicalist and voluntarist pseudo-lefts combated by Lenin. Furthermore, in Italy the Left represents the exact Leninist conception of the problem of relations between trade unions and factory councils. On the basis of the Russian experience and the theses of the Second Congress on that subject, it rejects the serious deviation of principle that denies any revolutionary significance to voluntary membership in trade unions and replaces it with the utopian and reactionary concept of an institutional apparatus corresponding organically to the entire extent of the capitalist system of production, an error that translates in practise into an over-estimation of factory councils and a de facto boycott of trade unions.

1.2.9   The Agrarian Question

The agrarian question was fundamentally defined by Lenin's theses at the Second Congress of the International. Lenin's fundamental line consists first of all in the historical rectification of the problem of agricultural production in the Marxist system. The preconditions for the socialisation of enterprises were lacking in the agricultural economy at a time when they had already matured in the industrial economy.

Not only does this not delay the proletarian revolution (which is the only basis on which these preconditions will be realised) but this situation makes the general problems of the poor peasants impossible to solve within the framework of industrial economy and bourgeois power. This permits the proletariat to make the emancipation of the poor peasant from a system of exploitation by landed proprietors and the bourgeoisie an integral part of its own struggle, even if this emancipation does not coincide with a general transformation of the rural productive economy.

In the case of domains that are juridically large landed estates but, technically, are composed of very small productive units, the shattering of the legal superstructure appears as a division of land among the peasants, while in fact it is only the end of the common exploitation of these small enterprises, which were already separate. This requires a revolutionary destruction of the property relations that only the industrial proletariat can accomplish, since this proletariat, unlike the peasant, is not only a victim of the system of bourgeois relations of production but is the historical product of their maturity to give way to a system of new and different relations. The proletariat will therefore find valuable support in the revolt of the poor peasant, but in Lenin's tactical conclusions the essential points are, first, the fundamental difference he establishes between the proletariat's relations with the peasant class and its relations with reactionary middle strata of the urban economy, represented in particular by the social-democratic parties; and second, the concept of the intangible pre-eminence and hegemony of the working class in making the revolution.

At the moment of the conquest of power the peasant presents himself as a revolutionary factor. But if, during the revolution, his ideology changes with respect to the old forms of authority and legality, it changes very little with respect to the relations of production, which continue to be the traditional relations of isolated family production in competition with others. The peasant therefore continues to be a serious danger for the construction of the socialist economy, since only a major development of agricultural productive forces and technology can interest him.

According to Lenin, for tactical and organisational purposes the agricultural proletarian who owns no land (day-labourers) must be given the same consideration as the rest of the proletariat and incorporated into the same framework, while the alliance with the poor peasant, who cultivates his plot himself (a plot that may be insufficient to support him), becomes pure and simple neutralisation in the case of the middle peasant, who is both the victim of certain capitalist relations and an exploiter of labour-power. Finally, in the rich peasant, the direct enemy of the revolution, the character of exploiter of labour-power clearly prevails.

In applying its agrarian tactics the International must avoid the errors that have already manifested themselves (in the French party, for example) in the belief that the peasants can make an original revolution on a par with that of the workers, or that the revolutionary mobilisation of the workers can be sparked by an insurrection originating in the countryside, when the exact relationship is just the reverse.

The peasant who has been won over to the communist programme and is therefore eligible to become a political militant must become a member of the communist party. This is the only way to combat the formation of exclusively peasant parties that inevitably fall under the influence of the counterrevolution.

The Krestintern (Peasants' International) must comprise peasant organisations from all countries, which, as in the case of proletarian trade-unions, are characterised by their accepting as members all individuals who have the same immediate economic interests. Also the tactics of political negotiation, the united front, or the formation of fractions within the peasant parties – even in order to break them up – must be rejected.

This tactical rule is not in contradiction with the relations that were established between the Bolsheviks and the Socialist Revolutionaries during the civil war, when the new proletarian and peasant representative institutions had already been formed.

1.2.10   The National Question

Lenin also gave a fundamental clarification of the theory of popular movements in the colonial countries and in certain exceptionally backward countries. Even before economic factors and the crucial factors of the expansion of capitalism give rise to the relations of modern class struggle there, demands are made that can only be met by insurrectional struggle and the defeat of world imperialism.

When these two conditions are fully realised, the struggle can be sparked in the epoch of the struggle for proletarian revolution in the metropolises, even though it locally assumes the form of a conflict between races and nationalities, not classes.

In any event, the fundamental concepts of the Leninist formulation are that the world struggle must be led by the organs of the revolutionary proletariat, and that the class struggle in colonial areas, as well as the formation and independent development of local communist parties, must be encouraged, and never held back or stifled.

It is dangerous to extend these considerations to countries where the capitalist regime and the bourgeois state apparatus have long been established. In such cases the national question and patriotic ideology play a directly counterrevolutionary role by turning the proletariat away from its class struggle. We saw an example of such a deviation in Radek's concessions to German nationalists fighting against the inter-allied occupation.

Another example: in Czechoslovakia the task of the International is to erase every reflection of national dualism in the proletarian organisation, since the two races are at the same historical level and their common economic milieu is fully evolved.

To raise the struggle of national minorities *in and of itself* to the level of a principle is therefore a deformation of the communist conception, since determining whether such a struggle offers revolutionary possibilities or whether it will develop in a reactionary direction depends on completely different criteria.

1.2.11   Russian Questions (1926)

Lenin's 1921 speech on the tax in kind and Trotsky's report to the Fourth World Congress make it very clear that the new economic policy of the Russian state is an important matter for the Communist International. Given the premises of the Russian economy and the fact that the bourgeoisie remains in power in the other countries, for Marxists there was no other way to pose the question of the prospects for the development of the world revolution and the construction of the socialist economy.

The serious political difficulties confronting the Russian state in the internal relations of social forces, in production technology, and in foreign relations, have given rise to a series of divergences within the Russian Communist Party. It is deplorable that the international communist movement has not taken a more grounded and authoritative position on this matter.

In the first discussion with Trotsky, his observations on internal party life and on its new course were undoubtedly correct, just as his observations on the development of the state's economic policy were, on the whole, unmistakably revolutionary and proletarian. In the second discussion, his considerations on the errors of the International were equally justified, and he showed clearly that the best Bolshevik tradition did not militate in favour of the way the Comintern was being led.

Within the party this debate had a deformed and artificial echo due to the party's well-known method of highlighting absolutely unfounded anti-fractionist and, even worse, anti-Bonapartist intimidation. As for the most recent discussion, it deals with international questions. The fact that the majority of the Russian Communist Party has already pronounced itself on the issue cannot serve as an argument to prevent the International from debating it and giving its opinion; the question still stands even if the defeated opposition ceases to pose it.

As in other cases, questions of procedure and discipline are being used to smother questions of substance. What is at issue here is not a defence of the violated rights of a minority, with the leaders, if not the rank and file, sharing responsibility for numerous errors committed in the international domain, but questions that are vital for the world communist movement.

The Russian question must be placed before the International for a full study. The elements of the question are as follows: according to Lenin, in the present Russian economy there is a mixture of pre-bourgeois and bourgeois elements, state capitalism and socialism. State-controlled large-scale industry is socialist to the extent that it obeys the productive imperatives of the state, which is a politically proletarian state. The distribution of its products is nonetheless accomplished in a capitalist manner; that is, through the mechanism of the competitive free market.

In principle it cannot be excluded that this system not only keep (as it in fact does) the workers in a less than flourishing economic condition that they accept out of the revolutionary consciousness they have acquired, but that it evolve in the direction of an increased extraction of surplus value through the price paid by the workers for foodstuffs and the price paid by the state and the conditions it obtains in its purchases, in concessions, in trade, and in all its relations with foreign capitalism. This is the way to pose the question of whether the socialist elements of the Russian economy are progressing or retreating, a question that also includes the technical performance and sound organisation of state industry.

The construction of full socialism, extended to both production and distribution, industry and agriculture, is impossible in a single country. A progressive development of the socialist elements in the Russian economy, assuming the failure of counter-revolutionary plans based on internal factors (rich peasants, new bourgeoisie and petty-bourgeoisie) and external factors (imperialist powers), is nonetheless still possible. Whether these plans take the form of internal or external aggression or of a progressive sabotage and deflection of Russian social life and the life of the Russian state, which will lead them on a slow involution ending in a complete loss of their proletarian features – if these plans are to be thwarted, the close collaboration and contribution of all the parties of the International will be absolutely essential.

Above all it is necessary to ensure proletarian Russia and the Russian Communist Party the active and energetic support of the proletarian vanguard, particularly in the imperialist countries. Not only must any aggression be thwarted and pressure brought to bear on the bourgeois states as regards their relations with Russia, but it is necessary above all that the Russian party be assisted by its sister parties in resolving its problems. It is true that these parties have no direct experience in the problems of government, but in spite of this they will contribute to the solution of such problems by adding a revolutionary class coefficient deriving directly from the real class struggle as it unfolds in their respective countries

As we have shown, the present relations within the Communist International are not equal to these tasks. Changes are urgently needed, above all to counter the organisational, tactical and political excesses of so-called 'Bolshevisation'.

1.3   *Italian Questions*

1.3.1   The Italian Situation (1926)

Evaluations of the Italian situation that accord a decisive value to the insufficient development of industrial capitalism are erroneous.

Its limited quantitative expansion and relatively late historical emergence were counterbalanced by a series of other circumstances that enabled the bourgeoisie to entrench itself politically during the period of the Risorgimento, developing a rich and complex tradition of government.

It is not possible to identify, systematically, the political antitheses that historically characterise the parties in conflict – right and left, clericalism and Freemasonry, democracy and Fascism – with the social differences between landed proprietors and capitalists and between big and petty bourgeoisie.

The Fascist movement must be understood as an attempt to unify the conflicting interests of various bourgeois groups politically for counter-revolutionary purposes. Wanted and nurtured by all the upper classes together – landed aristocrats, industrialists, merchants, bankers – and supported, above all, by the traditional state apparatus, the crown, the Church, and Freemasonry, Fascism has pursued its goal by mobilising rootless social elements from the intermediate classes which, in a close alliance with all the bourgeois elements, it has succeeded in directing against the proletariat.

What has come about in Italy must not be explained as the coming to power of a new social stratum, or as the formation of a new state apparatus with an original programme and ideology, or as the defeat of a part of the bourgeoisie whose interests were better served by the adoption of liberal and parliamentary methods. The liberals and democrats, Giolitti and Nitti, are protagonists of a phase of the counter-revolutionary struggle dialectically connected with the Fascist phase and decisive for the defeat of the proletariat. Their policy of concessions, implemented with the complicity of reformists and maximalists, effectively permitted the bourgeoisie to deflect the proletariat's pressure and hold out in the period that followed the war and the demobilisation when the ruling class and all its organs were not prepared to resist frontally.

Directly aided and abetted in this period by the governments, bureaucracy, police, magistracy, army, and the rest, Fascism then completely replaced the bourgeoisie's old political personnel. But this must not mislead us, or much less serve as a basis for the rehabilitation of parties and groups that have in fact been ousted because the anti-proletarian function they had fulfilled for an entire period was completed, and not because they offered better conditions to the working class.

1.3.2   Political Orientation of the Communist Left

As the above situations were unfolding, the group that formed the communist party acted in accordance with the following criteria: rupture of the illusory dualisms presented by the bourgeois and parliamentary political scene and formulation of the revolutionary class dualism; destruction within the proletariat of the illusion that the middle classes are capable of producing a political general staff, taking power, and clearing the way for proletarian victories; confidence of the working class in its own historical task, gained through preparation based on original and autonomous tactical, political, and critical positions solidly connected throughout successive situations.

The traditions of this political current are already recognisable in the left wing of the socialist party before the war. While a majority capable of fighting against both the reformist and syndicalist errors (which had characterised the left until then) had formed following the congresses of Reggio Emilia (1912) and Ancona (1914), an extreme left aspiring to increasingly radical and class positions had also differentiated itself within the majority. This made it possible to tackle a series of class problems: electoral tactics, relations with trade unions, the colonial war, Freemasonry.

During the world war, while virtually the entire party opposed the policy of a *union sacré*, its extreme left, distinct from the rest, upheld Leninist directives at successive meetings and congresses (Bologna, May 1915; Rome, February 1917; Florence, November 1917; Rome, 1918): rejection of national defence and defeatism; exploitation of military defeat to pose the question of power; incessant struggle against opportunist trade-union and parliamentary leaders while demanding their expulsion from the party.

Immediately after the war this extreme left began to publish its own newspaper, *Il Soviet*. This was the first journal to expound and defend the directives of the Russian revolution, refuting anti-Marxist, opportunist, syndicalist and anarchist interpretations, correctly posing the essential problems of the proletarian dictatorship and of the party's task, and from the very beginning defending the necessity of a split within the socialist party.

This same group advocated electoral abstentionism, but its conclusions were rejected by the Second Congress of the International. The Left's abstentionism, however, did not derive from anarcho-syndicalist anti-Marxist theoretical errors, as its severe polemics against the anarchist press attest. The abstentionist tactic was designed above all for the political environment of fully developed parliamentary democracies, which make it particularly difficult to win the masses over to a proper consciousness of the watchword 'dictatorship'; a difficulty that, we believe, continues to be underestimated by the International.

Moreover, abstentionism was proposed for the general situation of the imminence of great struggles putting the great masses of the proletariat into motion (this, unfortunately, is not the case today), not as a tactic valid for all times and all places.

With the 1919 elections, Nitti's bourgeois government opened an immense safety valve for the release of revolutionary pressure, diverting the impetus of the proletariat and the attention of the party by exploiting its traditions of unbridled electoralism. At that moment, the abstentionism of *Il Soviet* was the only proper reaction to the real causes of the proletarian disaster that ensued.

At the Bologna Congress in October of 1919, the abstentionist minority was alone in correctly posing the problem of the split with the reformists. It tried in vain to come to an agreement on this point with a part of the maximalists, even offering to renounce abstentionism as a precondition. After the failure of this attempt and up to the Second World Congress, the abstentionist fraction was alone in working on a national scale for the formation of the communist party.

It was therefore this group that represented spontaneous adherence, based on its own experiences and the traditions of the left of the Italian proletariat, to the directives that had triumphed in the victory of Lenin and of Bolshevism in Russia.

1.3.3   The Left's Work in the Party Leadership

Once the communist party had been founded at Leghorn in January 1921, the abstentionists did everything within their power to forge solid links with other party groups. While for some of these groups the need for the split with the opportunists was based only on questions of international relations, for the group of the left the theses of the International coincided completely with the lessons of previous political experiences; and this was true for many other elements besides the abstentionists, who for discipline's sake had meanwhile expressly renounced their position on electionism.

The work of the party leadership was based on the interpretation of the Italian situation and of the tasks of the proletariat outlined above. With hindsight, it is clear that the delay in forming the revolutionary party, for which all the other groups bore responsibility, made a further retreat of the proletariat inevitable, and ineluctably determined it.

To put the proletariat in the best possible position for the struggles to come, the leadership based its action on the need to make a maximum effort to utilise the traditional apparatus of red organisations, while striving to convince the proletariat that it should not count on the maximalists and reformists, who went so far as to accept the pacification pact with Fascism.[6]

From its very inception the party declared itself in favour of trade-union unity and then made its central proposal of a united front, culminating in the formation of the 'Labour Alliance'. Whatever one may think of the political united front, the fact is that it was not feasible in the Italian situation in 1921–22 and that the communist party was never invited to a meeting to found an alliance of parties. The party did not intervene at the meeting called by the railway workers to form the trade-union alliance, not wanting to lend itself to manoeuvres that would have compromised both the alliance itself and the party's responsibilities, affirming, instead, both its paternity of the initiative, and that the communists would accept the discipline of the new organ. Subsequently, the communist party willingly agreed to meet with other parties but the contacts came to nothing, demonstrating the impossibility of an understanding, be it political or practical, and the defeatism of all the other groups. Also in the context of the retreat, the leadership was able to defend the workers' confidence in their own class and to raise the political consciousness of the vanguard by promptly cutting off the traditional manoeuvring of pseudo-revolutionary small groups and parties towards the proletariat. In spite of the party's efforts, it was only later, in August 1922, that a general action was possible. But the defeat of the proletariat was inevitable, and from then on Fascism, openly supported in its violent struggle by the forces of the state, governed by *liberal democracy*, was master of the country, its façade of legality coming later, with the March on Rome.

At this point, despite the shrinking of the field of proletarian action, the party's influence still exceeded that of the maximalists and reformists. Its advance had already been marked by the results of the 1921 elections and the great debates that followed within the Federation of Labour.

---

6   The Italian Socialist Party signed a 'pacification pact' with the National Fascist Party on 3 August 1921.

1.3.4   Relations between the Italian Left and the Communist
           International
The Rome Congress (March 1922) demonstrated the theoretical divergence
between the Italian Left and the majority of the International. This divergence
had been expressed earlier, very badly, by our delegations at the Third Congress
and at the Enlarged ECCI[7] of February 1922, where, especially on the first occasion, real errors in the 'infantile' sense were committed. The Rome Theses were
the correct theoretical and political liquidation of any danger of left opportunism in the Italian party.

In the party's practise the only divergence with the International had concerned the tactics to be followed in dealing with the maximalists, but this
divergence seemed to have been overcome by the unitary results of the Socialist Congress in October 1921.

The Rome Theses were adopted as the party's contribution to the decisions
of the International and not as an immediate line of action. The party leadership confirmed this at the Enlarged ECCI of 1922 and, in compliance with the
discipline of the International and by its decision, there was no theoretical discussion of the Theses.

However, in August 1922 the International did not interpret the reports of
the situation in the way indicated by the party leadership, but held that the
Italian situation was unstable due to the weakening of the state's resistance. It
therefore hoped to strengthen the party through a fusion with the maximalists,
considering the decisive factor to be not what the party had learned from the
vast manoeuvre of the August strike but, rather, the split between the maximalists and the unitarists.

From this time on the two political lines diverged definitively. At the Fourth
World Congress (December 1922) the old party leadership opposed the thesis
that prevailed. When its delegates returned to Italy, they unanimously dis-
claimed all responsibility, transferring it to the Fusion Commission,[8] while, of
course, retaining their administrative functions. Then came the arrests in February 1923, and the major offensive against the party. Finally, at the Enlarged
ECCI of June 1923 the old executive was deposed and replaced by a totally dif-

---

7   Executive Committee of the Communist International.
8   The reference is to the Interparty Commission for the fusion of the Communist Party of
    Italy (PCd'I) and the Italian Socialist Party (PSI) into the Unified Communist Party of Italy,
    deliberated by the Fourth Congress of the Communist International in December 1922. The
    commission (which Bordiga refused to join) met in early 1923 but failed to achieve the fusion,
    due to strong internal resistance in the two parties and Fascist repression of the PCd'I and the
    'Terzinternazionalisti' of the PSI (Terzini).

ferent one. At this point the resignations of some members of the leadership was a foregone conclusion. In May 1924, a consultative conference of the party once again gave the Left an overwhelming majority over the Centre and the Right, and this is how things stood at the Fifth World Congress in 1924.

1.3.5   The 'Ordinovist' Tradition of the Present Leadership

The *Ordine Nuovo*[9] group was formed in Turin by a few intellectuals who made contact with the proletarian masses in industry at a time when the abstention-ist fraction already had a large following in Turin itself. The group's ideology was dominated by bourgeois, idealist, and Crocean[10] philosophical concep-tions, which, naturally, were and are very much in flux. This group was very late in interpreting communist directives, and always with errors that reflec-ted its origins. When it finally understood the Russian revolution it was too late to apply its lessons usefully to the Italian proletarian struggle. In November 1917 comrade Gramsci published an article in *Avanti!* declaring that the Rus-sian revolution had refuted Marx's historical materialism and his theories in *Capital*, giving them an essentially idealist explanation. The extreme left of the party, which included the Youth Federation, immediately attacked this article.

As the articles in *L'Ordine Nuovo* show, the group evolved further towards a non-Marxist-Leninist theory of the workers' movement. In this theory the problems of the function of trade unions and of the party, questions of armed struggle, the conquest of power and the building of socialism are posed incor-rectly. Instead, it developed the conception that the systematic organisation of the working class was not 'voluntary' but 'necessary', with strict adherence to the mechanism of capitalist industrial production.

This system begins with the floor delegates, passes through the factory coun-cils, and culminates at the same time in the proletarian International, in the Communist International, in the system of the Soviets and of the Workers' State. According to the Ordinovist group, this system is supposed to exist even before the fall of capitalist power.

What is more, the functions of this system, even in bourgeois society itself, are functions that serve to build the new economy through the workers' demands and their exercise of control over production.

Later this current apparently abandoned all the non-Marxist positions of its ideology, its utopianism, its syndicalism à la Proudhon, its economic gradu-alism prior to the conquest of power (in other words, its reformism), only to

---

9   *L'Ordine Nuovo* was a weekly newspaper established in 1919 in Turin by a group within the Italian Socialist party that included Antonio Gramsci, Angelo Tasca and Palmiro Togliatti.
10   The reference is to the Italian idealist philosopher Benedetto Croce.

replace them little by little with the very different theories of Leninism. But the external and fictitious quality of this replacement could have been avoided only if the Ordinovist group had not detached itself from and aligned itself against the group whose traditions, as we have shown, converge spontaneously with Bolshevism and seriously represent a contribution stemming from the proletarian experience of class, and not from academic exercises on bourgeois texts studied in libraries. This certainly does not mean that also the 'Ordinovists' could not have learned and improved in a close collaboration with our group that, however, soon broke down. All this lends an ironic tinge to the claim of their leaders that they had Bolshevised precisely those who had set them on the path of Bolshevism – not mechanically, bureaucratically, and with chit-chat, but in the serious, Marxist sense.

Shortly before the 1920 World Congress the 'Ordinovists' were against splitting the old party, and posed all the trade-union questions incorrectly. The International's representative in Italy had to polemicise with them on the factory council question and on the premature formation of soviets.

In April 1920 the Turin section approved the 'Ordine Nuovo' theses drawn up by comrade Gramsci, which were adopted by the committee composed of Ordinovists and abstentionists. Apart from the electionist dissension, these theses, cited in the resolution of the Second Congress, in reality expressed the common thinking of the nascent communist fraction: their content did not consist in the particular constructions of Ordinovism, but in the points that had been accepted with absolute clarity long before by the left wing of the party.

The Ordinovists adhered to the Left's position on the International for a while, but in reality their thinking differed from the thinking expressed in the Rome Theses, even if they found it opportune to vote for them.

The true precursor of the Ordinovists' adherence to the tactics and general line of the International was comrade Tasca, architect of the opposition to the Left at the Rome Congress.

Given, on the one hand, the characteristics of the Ordinovist group, its particularism and concretism inherited from bourgeois idealistic ideology, and on the other, the latitude allowed by the methods of the present leadership of the International for superficial and incomplete recruitment, we must conclude that, despite resounding declarations of orthodoxy, the theoretical adherence of the Ordinovists to Leninism – and this is of decisive importance for imminent and very real political developments – is worth little more than their one-time adherence to the Rome Theses.

1.3.6   The Political Work of the Current Party Centre[11]

From 1923 to the present, the work of the party Centre, which, it must be acknowledged, has been carried out in a difficult situation, has given rise to errors that, in substance, are related to the errors we indicated with regard to the international question, but which in part have become more serious due to the original deviations of the Ordinovist construction.

Participation in the 1924 elections was an excellent political act, but the same cannot be said of the proposal for common action made to the socialist parties, under the banner of 'proletarian unity'. The excessive tolerance of certain electoral manoeuvres by the Terzini[12] was just as deplorable, but the most serious problems were posed by the crisis that followed the murder of Matteotti.

The Centre's policy was based on the absurd idea that the weakening of Fascism would have set first the middle classes and then the proletariat in motion. This indicates, on the one hand, a lack of confidence in the class capacity of the proletariat, even though it had remained vigilant under the crushing apparatus of Fascism and, on the other, an overestimation of the initiative of the middle classes. In point of fact, apart from the clarity of the Marxist theoretical positions on the subject, the central lesson of the Italian experience is that the intermediate strata are easily influenced and passively follow the strongest side: the proletariat in 1919–20, Fascism in 1921–22–23, and, after a period of frenzied agitation in 1924–25, Fascism once again.

The Centre was wrong to abandon parliament and participate in the first meetings of the Aventine; it should have remained in parliament, declared a political attack on the government, and immediately taken a position against the constitutional and moral foundations of the Aventine, which played a decisive role in tipping the scales of the crisis in favour of Fascism. The possibility of the communists' abandoning parliament was not to be excluded, but with their own physiognomy and only when the situation would have allowed them to call the masses to direct action. This was one of those moments in which the developments of further situations are decided; the error was therefore fundamental and a decisive test of the capacities of the leading group. It resulted in the working class's being dramatically unable to take advantage first of the weakening of Fascism, and then of the resounding collapse of the Aventine.

The return to Parliament in November of 1924 and the Repossi declaration were beneficial, as the wave of approval from the proletariat showed, but they

---

11   From here to the end of this text 'la Centrale' is translated as 'the Centre' and refers to the central leadership of the party, now composed of the Ordinovist group headed by Antonio Gramsci.

12   The internationalist fraction of the Italian Socialist Party (Terzinternazionalisti).

came too late. The Centre vacillated for a long time and only reached a decision when pressured by the party and the Left. The party's preparation was based on colourless instructions and a fantastically erroneous assessment of the immediate prospects (Gramsci's report to the Central Committee, August 1924). Bad as it was, the preparation of the masses, oriented not toward the defeat of the Aventine but toward its victory, was made even worse by the party's proposal to the oppositions to form an Anti-Parliament. To begin with, this tactic was alien to the decisions of the International, which had never contemplated proposals to openly bourgeois parties; worse still, it flew in the face of communist principles and policies, along with the Marxist conception of history. Independently of any explanation the Centre might have attempted to give of the goals and intentions that inspired the proposal (an explanation that in any case would have had extremely limited repercussions), it is certain that this proposal gave the masses the illusion of an Anti-State opposed to and actively fighting the traditional state apparatus, while in the historical perspective of our programme the only basis for an Anti-State is the representative body of the only productive class, the Soviet.

The call for an Anti-Parliament, based on workers' and peasants' committees, was tantamount to handing over the proletariat's general staff to representatives of capitalist social groups – to Amendola, Agnelli, Albertini, and the like.

Apart from the certainty that such a state of affairs – which can only be called a betrayal – will never actually come about, the very fact of presenting this as a communist perspective and proposal is a violation of our principles and a weakening of the preparation of the proletariat.

The details of the Centre's work are open to other criticisms. We have seen a veritable parade of slogans that correspond to nothing that could be attained, nor even to any appreciable agitation outside the party apparatus. The central watchword on workers' and peasants' committees, which was given only contradictory and twisted explanations, has been neither understood nor followed.

1.3.7   The Party's Trade-Union Activity

Another serious error was committed in the metalworkers strike in March 1925. The Centre failed to understand that the proletariat's disappointment after the collapse of the Aventine would spark a general impulse to class actions in the form of a strike wave. If it had understood this, just as we convinced the FIOM[13]

---

13   The metalworkers union of the CGL (the left-wing labour confederation). Founded in 1901, the FIOM is the oldest Italian industrial union.

to intervene in the strike called by the Fascists, it could have convinced the metalworkers to go much further and call a national strike, by forming an agitation committee within the union based on local organisations throughout the country that were more than ready to strike.

The Centre's trade-union orientation has clearly failed to correspond to the watchword of trade-union unity in the Confederation, which should have been maintained despite its organisational disintegration. The party's union directives have reflected Ordinovist errors with regard to action inside the factories: not only did it create or propose multiple contradictory bodies, but it often launched slogans that downgraded the trade union and the understanding that it is a necessary organ of proletarian struggle.

This resulted in the disgraceful agreement at FIAT in Turin, as well as the unclear directives on factory elections, in which the criterion of choice between the tactics of the class candidates and those of the party candidates was not posed correctly, that is, on the trade-union terrain.

1.3.8   Party Activity in Agrarian and National Questions
In the agrarian question, the call for peasants' defence associations was justified, but it has been too closely identified with work conducted exclusively from above, by a party bureau.

In spite of the difficult situation, in this context we must denounce the danger of a bureaucratic conception of our tasks, which is also present in other party activities.

Correct relations between peasants' associations and workers' unions must be clearly established, in the sense that agricultural wage labourers must form a federation belonging to the Confederation of Labour, while between the Confederation and the defence associations a close alliance must be built centrally and locally.

In the agrarian question a regionalist or 'southernist' conception must be avoided (there has already been evidence of such tendencies). This also applies to positions of regional autonomy defended by some new parties, which must openly be combated as reactionary, instead of holding fallacious negotiations with them.

The tactic of seeking an alliance with the left of the Popular Party (Miglioli) and with the peasant party has yielded unfavourable results.

Once again concessions have been made to politicians foreign to all class tradition without obtaining the desired mass movement, and often disorienting parts of the party organisation. It is equally wrong to overestimate peasant manoeuvres aimed at a hypothetical political campaign against the influence of the Vatican, a problem that certainly exists, but that in this way is resolved inadequately.

1.3.9   The Centre's Organisational Work
The work of reorganising the party after the Fascist storm undoubtedly yielded many good results. However, it retained an excessively technical character
rather than assuring centralisation through the implementation of clear, uniform statuary norms applicable to all comrades or local committees, and it
relied entirely on the intervention of the central apparatus. Greater steps could
have been taken to allow the rank-and-file organisations to elect their own
committees once again, particularly in the more favourable periods of the situation.

Given the increase and subsequent decrease in party membership, and given
the ease with which elements who were recruited with no less ease during the
Matteotti crisis are now departing, it is obvious that such facts depend on the
development of the situation, not on the hypothetical benefits of a change in
general orientation.

The results and benefits of the one-month recruitment campaign have been
exaggerated. As for the cell organisation, the Centre obviously had to act on the
general directives of the Comintern, of which we have already spoken. But this
was done without uniformity, haphazardly and with many contradictions, and
only repeated pressure from the rank and file brought about a certain systematisation.

It would be desirable to replace the system of interregional secretaries with a
team of inspectors, establishing a direct political, if not technical, link between
the Centre and the party's traditional rank-and-file organisms, the provincial federations. The inspectors' principal task should be to intervene actively
wherever the basic party organisation has to be rebuilt, following and assisting
it until it becomes capable of functioning normally.

1.3.10   The Centre and the Question of Fractionism
The campaign culminating in the preparation for our Third Congress was deliberately initiated after the Fifth World Congress, not in the form of an involvement of the whole party in propagandising and elaborating the International's
directives in order to create a more advanced, real and useful collective consciousness, but in the form of agitation aimed – as expeditiously and effort-
lessly as possible – at inducing comrades to renounce the positions of the Left.
There was no thought as to whether this method was useful or harmful to the
party and its effectiveness against external enemies, and no effort was spared
to achieve this internal objective.

Elsewhere we have given a historical and theoretical critique of the illusory
method of suppressing factions from above. In the Italian case, the Fifth Congress had accepted the Left's request that pressures from above be stopped,

while the Left committed itself to refrain from active opposition and to participate in all party activity, excluding political leadership. The Centre broke this agreement through a campaign conducted not on ideological or tactical positions, but based on unilateral accusations of indiscipline levelled against isolated comrades at federal congresses.

The formation of a 'Committee of Entente' when the Congress was announced was a spontaneous action designed to avoid individual and group reactions tending toward party disintegration, and to channel the action of all comrades of the Left along a common, responsible line within the strict limits of discipline, and with the respect of the rights of all comrades guaranteed by general party consultation. The Centre seized upon this fact and used it in its agitational plan, presenting comrades of the Left as fractionists and scissionists and prohibiting them from defending themselves until votes against them had been obtained from the Federal Committees through pressures applied from above.

The agitational scheme proceeded with a fractionist revision of the party apparatus and local cadres, with the way texts for discussion were presented, with the refusal to allow the Left's representatives to participate in federal congresses, culminating in unheard-of voting methods: anyone who was absent was automatically considered to have voted for the theses of the Centre.

Whatever the result of these actions may be in terms of the simple numerical majority, they have damaged, not advanced, the party's ideological consciousness and its prestige among the masses. The worst consequences have only been avoided through the moderation of the comrades of the Left, who have accepted such punishment not because they considered it justified in the least, but only out of devotion to the party.

1.3.11   Outline of the Party's Work Programme
The preceding points contain the premises from which, in the opinion of the Left, the party's general and particular tasks should arise. But it is first of all evident that such a problem can only be solved on the basis of international decisions. The Left can therefore only indicate an outline of an action programme to present to the International in order to accomplish the tasks of its Italian section.

The party must prepare the proletariat to resume its class activity and the fight against Fascism, drawing on the severe experiences it has had in recent years. At the same time it must destroy all the proletariat's illusions about changes in bourgeois policy and the possibility of receiving any help from the urban middle classes, utilising the experiences of the liberal-democratic period to avoid any repetition of any pacifist illusions.

The party will not make proposals for common action to parties of the anti-Fascist opposition, and by no means will pursue a policy aimed at detaching any alleged left wing from that opposition or influencing such parties to move left.

In order to mobilise the masses around its programme, the party will adopt a tactic of united front from below, and attentively follow developments in the economic situation to formulate immediate demands. The party will abstain from making a central political demand out of the accession of a government that will offer guarantees of freedom. It will not present 'freedom for all' as the goal of class conquest, but will make it clear that freedom for the workers means crushing the freedom of the exploiters and the bourgeois.

Faced today with the serious problem of a decimation of class unions and other immediate organs of the proletariat, the party must above all call for the defence of the traditional red unions and the need for their resurgence. Work in factories will avoid creating organs that could diminish the effectiveness of watchwords for the rebuilding of the unions. Considering the present situation, the party will work toward union activity within the framework of 'factory union sections' that, because they represent a strong union tradition, are the appropriate organs to lead the workers' struggles, which can best be waged today precisely in the factories. We will attempt to have the illegal internal commission elected by the workers of the factory union section, with the intent of having it elected, as soon as possible, by the mass of the factory workers.

As for organisation in the countryside, our remarks on the agrarian situation remain valid.

Utilising all the possibilities for the organisation of proletarian groups to the maximum, the party will have to make use of the watchword calling for workers' and peasants' committees, according to the following criteria:

a)   the watchword to form Workers' and Peasants' Committees will not be given intermittently and casually, but will be imposed with a vigorous campaign at a turning point of the situation that makes it clear to the masses that a new approach is necessary, and that the call is not simply for proletarian *organisation* but also for proletarian *action*;

b)   the nucleus of these Committees will have to be constituted by representatives of organisations such as trade unions and analogous bodies traditionally known to the masses even if they have been mutilated by the [capitalist] reaction, but not by meetings of political delegates;

c)   we will later be able to give the watchword for Committee elections, but it must be clear from the outset that these are not Soviets – organs of the proletarian government – but only the expression of a local and national alliance of all the exploited for common defence.

Regarding relations with the Fascist unions, which today no longer appear even formally as voluntary mass associations but are true official organs of the alliance between capitalists and Fascism, the call to penetrate them in order to destroy them from within must in general be rejected. The watchword for the rebuilding of the red unions must be accompanied by a denunciation of the Fascist unions.

The organisational measures to be adopted within the party have been indicated in part. In relation to the present situation, these measures must satisfy certain needs that must be dealt with elsewhere (in clandestinity). It is nonetheless urgent that they be formalised systematically in clear statutory norms binding on everyone, in order to avoid confusion between a healthy centralism and blind obeisance to arbitrary, heterogeneous directives that imperil the real solidity of the party.

1.3.12   Prospects of the Party's Internal Situation

The political and organisational situation within our party cannot be definitively resolved within a national framework, because the solution depends on the development of the internal situation and policy of the entire International. It will be a grave error and a shameful betrayal if the national and international leadership continues to subject the Left to the senseless method of pressure from above and to the reduction of the complex problem of the party's ideology and politics to cases of personal conduct.

Given that the Left is standing firm on its positions, all the comrades who do not intend to renounce these positions must be allowed to fulfil their loyal commitment to execute the decisions of party organs in an atmosphere free from bargaining and reciprocal accusations, renouncing all active opposition, but not being required to participate in the party Centre. It is clear that this proposal reflects a situation that is not abstractly perfect, but it would be dangerous to create the illusion in the party that the difficulties of the internal situation can be eliminated through simple and mechanical organisational measures and personal positions. Whoever spreads this illusion will be responsible for a grave attack on the party.

Only by freeing the problem from this petty approach and placing it before the party and the International in all its hugeness will it truly be possible to achieve the goal of not poisoning the party atmosphere and moving on to overcome all the difficulties the party is called on to combat today.

Against Stalin and 'Socialism in One Country'

1   The Trotsky Question[1]

The 'Trotsky question' was put on the agenda of a session of the Central Committee of the CP of Italy, on 6 February 1925, after the Russian Central Committee returned its verdict. Previously, a series of articles to which Bordiga refers here had been published to discredit Trotsky, in Italy and in other countries. Whereas the Left demanded the opening of a real discussion in the party on this question, the CC eagerly expressed its solidarity with the decisions of the Russian party leadership. The motion adopted included, among other things, this warning: 'Finally it is obvious that one must consider as counter-revolutionary any attitude which would tend to spread in the party a general mistrust towards the leading organisations of the International and the Russian party, either by seeking to distort the Trotsky question for this purpose or by seeking to reopen questions settled definitively by the 5th Congress.'

Some days later, Bordiga responded by sending this article to the party daily, L'Unità. Indeed, it was not published until July – after several months of internal manoeuvring and bureaucratic measures to liquidate the influence of the Left – and then only together with a rebuttal by the leadership. Bordiga himself was removed from the leadership of the Neapolitan Federation of the party, on the pretext that he was under too heavy police surveillance ...

The discussion that recently concluded with the measures adopted by the EC and the Control Commission of the Communist Party of Russia against Comrade Trotsky[2] was based exclusively on Trotsky's preface to the third volume of his book *Writings from 1917* (published in Russian a few months ago), dated 15 September 1924.

The discussion on the economic policy and internal life of the party in Russia, which had previously put Trotsky in opposition to the CC, was completed

---

2   The Plenum of the Central Committee of the Russian CP, at the end of January 1925, accepted Trotsky's resignation as 'war commissar', defined the 'present Trotskyism' as a 'falsification of communism', and accused Trotsky of continuing to uphold an 'anti-Bolshevik platform'.

by the decisions of 13th Congress of the party and 5th Congress of the International; Trotsky did not reopen it. In the present polemic, other texts are referred to, such as his speech to the Congress of Veterinary Surgeons and the brochure *On Lenin*; but the first dates from 28 July and had not raised any polemic at the time, when the delegations of the vth Congress were still present in Moscow; the second, written well before, had been widely quoted in the communist press of all countries without raising the least objection from any party organs.

The text of the preface around which the discussion is raging is not known to the Italian comrades. The international communist press did not receive it, and consequently, not having this text or any other by Trotsky to support his theses, it published only articles against the preface. The article by the editorial board of *Pravda*, which opened the polemic against Trotsky at the end of October, was published in an appendix by *L'Unità*. As for the preface itself, a summary appeared in Italian in *Critica Fascista*, Nos. 2 and 3, on 15 January and 1 February of this year, and the opening section was reproduced by *Avanti!* on 30 January. The entire preface was published in French in *Cahiers du bolchévisme*, the review of the French Communist Party, Nos. 5 and 6, on 19 and 26 December 1924.

The preface to *1917* deals with the lessons of the Russian October from the point of view of the revolutionary party's historical task in the final struggle for power. Recent events in international politics have posed the following problem: now that the objective historical conditions for the conquest of power by the proletariat have been realised – instability of the bourgeois state apparatus, mass enthusiasm for struggle, turning of broad proletarian layers to the Communist party – how can we ensure that this answers the necessities of the battle, as the Russian party responded in October 1917 under Lenin's leadership?

Trotsky presents the question in the following manner: experience teaches us that at the moment of the supreme struggle two currents tend to form in the Communist party; one understands the possibility of armed insurrection or the need not to delay it; the other, on the pretext that the situation is not ripe and the relationship of forces unfavourable, proposes at the last moment to call off the action and to assume in practice a non-revolutionary, Menshevik position.

In 1923, the second of these tendencies was on top in Bulgaria at the time of Tsankov's *coup d'état*, and again in Germany in October, where it caused the struggle that could have brought us success to be abandoned. In 1917, this tendency appeared within the Bolshevik party itself, and if it was beaten it was thanks to Lenin, whose formidable energy forced the waverers to recognise that the situation was revolutionary and to obey the supreme order to begin the insurrection. We should study the conduct in 1917 of the right opposition to Lenin in the Bolshevik party and compare it with that of the adversaries of struggle who appeared in our ranks in Germany in 1923 and similar cases. The language and positions of those who advocated calling off the struggle were so similar in the two cases that they raise the question of the measures to be taken in the International to make the truly Leninist method prevail at decisive moments, so that the historical possibilities for revolution are not missed.

In our view, the most important conclusion from Trotsky's effective analysis of the preparation and conduct of the October struggle in Russia is that the hesitations of the right do not arise solely from a wrong evaluation of the forces in play or a wrong choice of the moment for action, but from an actual failure to understand the principle of the revolutionary process in history; that is, the right thinks it can use another route than the dictatorship of the proletariat for the construction of socialism, which is the vital content of revolutionary Marxism that Lenin's gigantic work called upon and made a historical reality.

In fact, the group of leading comrades of the Bolshevik party who were opposed to Lenin did not only argue that it was still necessary to wait. They countered Lenin's watchwords – socialist dictatorship of the proletariat, all power to the Soviets, dissolution of the Constituent Assembly – with other formulas such as a combination of soviets and democratic parliament, a government of 'all the soviet parties' (that is, a coalition of communists and social democrats), and they espoused these not as transitory tactical expedients but as the permanent forms of the Russian revolution. Thus two principles were in opposition to each other: on the one hand, Lenin's conception of a soviet dictatorship led by the communist party, i.e. the proletarian revolution in all its powerful originality, and in historical dialectical opposition to the bourgeois democratic revolution of Kerensky; on the other hand, a push to the left, to deepen and defend the people's anti-tsarist revolution against foreign powers, which would have meant the success of the bourgeoisie and petty bourgeoisie.

Trotsky, a magnificent synthesiser of revolutionary experiences and truths and without equal among those still alive, shrewdly remarks that in revolutionary periods the reformists leave the terrain of purely formal socialism, i.e. the perspective of victory for the proletarian class by legal bourgeois-democratic means, and take the pure and simple ground of bourgeois democracy in becoming defenders and direct agents of capitalism. In parallel to this, a right wing of the revolutionary party will take its place in the vacuum left by the reformists, limiting itself in practice to calls for a 'true proletarian democracy' or something similar, even though the time has come to proclaim the bankruptcy of all democracies and to go over to armed struggle.

This evaluation of the attitude of those Bolsheviks who did not side with Lenin is undoubtedly very serious, but it follows from Trotsky's account and from his (unchallenged) quotations from the rightists' actual statements and Lenin's response to them. It is necessary to raise this problem because we do not have Lenin with us any longer, and because without him we lost our October revolution in Berlin; that is a fact of such international historical significance that it overrides any concern for the tranquillity of internal life. Trotsky's approach to this problem is the same as that of the Italian delegation to the 5th Congress: one cannot liquidate the German error by blaming it on the rightists who then led the German party; it shows us that we need to revise the international tactics of the International and to re-examine its mode of internal organisation, its style of work and its way of preparing for the tasks of the revolution.

The divergences in the Bolshevik Party on the eve of the revolution may be understood as a sequel to Lenin's vigorous earlier interventions to rectify the line and to eliminate hesitations. In his letter from Switzerland, Lenin had already begun this work. And from the moment of his arrival he placed himself resolutely against 'defencism', that is, against the attitude supported by *Pravda*, among others, which urged the workers to continue the war against Germany to save the revolution. Lenin established that we would only have a revolution to defend when the party of the proletariat, not the opportunist agents of the bourgeoisie, was in power.

It is well known that until then the watchword of the Bolshevik party had been 'democratic dictatorship of the proletariat and peasantry'. Trotsky does not claim in his text that this formula was wrong, that it failed historically, and that Lenin replaced it with one equivalent to the 'permanent revolution' for which Trotsky and his friends had argued in other times. Quite to the contrary, Trotsky asserts the correctness of this formula that Lenin's revolutionary genius conceived and applied, as a *tactical* agitational slogan to be used before the fall of tsarism. And this is what actually occurred, since after tsarism we did not have a pure bourgeois parliamentary democracy, but a duality of a weak bourgeois parliamentary state and nascent soviet organs of power of the proletariat and the peasantry.

But no sooner had history confirmed the accuracy of the Leninist-Bolshevik conception of the revolution than Lenin – in the party's political orientation, if not its external series of formulations at the level of propaganda – moved to a more advanced position. This was to prepare the second, authentic revolution, the march towards the soviet socialist dictatorship of the proletariat through armed insurrection, while, of course, guiding the peasant masses in their struggle for emancipation from the feudal agrarian regime.

Trotsky insists that those who (like so many of our Italian maximalists) constantly invoke Lenin's theory and practice of 'compromise' and flexible manoeuvre fail to understand his true strategic genius. Lenin manoeuvred, but the manoeuvre never lost sight of the supreme objective. For others the operation too often becomes the end in itself and paralyses the possibility of revolutionary action, whereas for Lenin we see this suppleness giving way to the most implacable rigidity in his will for revolution and for the destruction of its enemies and saboteurs.

Lenin himself, in passages quoted by Trotsky, condemns this incapacity to adapt to new revolutionary situations, and the taking of a polemical formulation essential to the Bolsheviks at a previous time as the last word in their later policy. This is the great question of communist tactics and their dangers that we have been discussing for years, apart from the conclusions we may reach to obviate this harmful evasion of the real revolutionary content of Lenin's teachings.

Trotsky explains why for Lenin it was always clear that, having passed through the transitional phase of the democratic dictatorship, that is, through a petty-bourgeois phase, the Russian revolution would arrive at the phase of full communist dictatorship, even before the advent of socialism in the West. When the rightists argued for a workers' coalition government and deplored insurrectionary struggle, they showed that they had adopted the Menshevik position according to which, even after liberation from tsarism, Russia had to await the victory of the socialist revolution in other countries before going beyond the forms of bourgeois democracy. In his preface Trotsky vigorously attacks this truly characteristic error of anti-Leninism.

These questions were heatedly discussed at the party conference in April 1917. From that moment on Lenin never ceased to reaffirm the perspective of the seizure of power. He charged into the breach against parliamentary illusions, later calling 'shameful' the party's decision to participate in the 'pre parliament' – the provisional democratic assembly convened while waiting for elections to the Constituent Assembly. After July, while following the evolving orientation of the masses with the greatest attention, and while understanding the need for a self-imposed waiting period after the 'test' and recognised failure of the insurrection in the same month, he warned his comrades against the trap of soviet legalism.

In other words, he said that one should not tie one's hands by postponing the fight until the Constituent Assembly or even the second Congress of Soviets, where opportunists might still be taking the decisions after the hour had sounded for the armed overthrow of the democratic government. At one point, we know, he stated that he would lead the party to power even without the soviets – which caused some rightists to accuse him of 'Blanquism'.

And Trotsky (upon whom the imbecilic champions of democracy would like to base themselves against the Bolsheviks' position in support of dictatorship) once again warns European comrades not to make a fetish of the majority, even within the soviets: our Great Elector is the rifle in the hands of the insurgent worker, who dreams not of depositing a paper ballot but of striking at the enemy.

This is not opposed to the Leninist conception that we need to have the masses on our side and that it is impossible for a resolute handful to substitute themselves for revolutionary mass action. But when a party or a military leadership has the masses with it – and this is the point at issue here – it must not put distractions or hesitations between them and the struggle. We can wait for the masses, and that is our duty, but the party cannot make the masses wait, on pain of causing defeat. This is one way of formulating the problem that weighs on us, with the world bourgeoisie still untoppled in the midst of its crisis.

On 10 October 1917, the Central Committee of the Bolshevik Party decided on the insurrection. Lenin had won.

But the decision was not unanimous. The next day, the dissidents sent a letter to the principal party organisations on 'the current situation'; it denounced the decisions of the majority, declaring insurrection impossible and defeat certain. On 18 October they wrote another letter taking issue with the party's decision. But on 25 October the insurrection was victorious and the soviet government was installed in Petrograd. On 4 November, following the victory, Lenin's opponents resigned from the Central Committee to have the freedom to appeal to the membership in support of their positions: the party should not, as Lenin maintained, form a government alone but make use of the newly conquered power to constitute a government of all the soviet parties, that is, together with the Right Mensheviks and Social Revolutionaries represented in the soviets. It was also necessary, they argued, to convene the Constituent Assembly and allow it to function. These theses were also defended in the Central Committee, until Lenin's line prevailed and the Constituent Assembly was dispersed by the red guards.

The history of these dissensions was quite short. The comrades in question 'recognised their error'. That was as it should be, and the point is not to sit in judgement on those comrades. But their recognition of their error, faced with the victory and consolidation of the revolution, was unavoidable – unless they were to pass directly into the camp of the counter-revolution. There remains the problem that poses itself in all its gravity on the basis of a simple observation: if Lenin had been in a minority in the Central Committee, if the insurrection had failed because of a preventive mistrust on the part of a section of the leadership, those leaders would have used exactly the same language that the comrades heading the German party leadership used in the crisis of October 1923. What Lenin managed to avert in Russia, the International could not avert in Germany. In these conditions, if the International really wants to live in the tradition of Lenin, it must make certain that it does not find itself in this situ ation again. History is not lavish with revolutionary opportunities, and to allow them to pass by has painful after-effects that we all know about and all suffer from.

Comrades should consider that this is not all there is to the debate, if we are referring to the motives for the public motion censuring Trotsky, and to the arguments in the polemic repeated and summarised by the author of the articles signed A.P. Concerning comrade Trotsky, the problems raised come down to what I have set forth; but it is true that the other side has responded by putting comrade Trotsky's lifelong political activity on trial. There has been talk of a 'Trotskyism' that has been continually opposed to Leninism from 1903 to the present day, having always existed in the form of a rightist struggle against the positions of the Bolshevik party. Such talk has sharpened and worsened the dispute, but above all it has diverted the debate by avoiding the vital problem posed by Trotsky in the passages we have outlined.

I will say just a few words on the charges concocted against Trotsky by a camp alien to the one on which his preface dwells.

There was a Trotskyism between 1903 and 1917; it was an attitude of integral centrism between the Mensheviks and Bolsheviks, rather confused and theoretically uncertain, oscillating in practice from right to left, and Lenin duly fought against it without too much consideration, as was his wont in dealing with opponents. In none of his writings from 1917 onwards, that is, after he joined the Bolshevik Party, did Trotsky reassert or defend his positions of that epoch. He recognised them as erroneous: in his latest letter to the Central Committee he says that he 'regards Trotskyism as a tendency that disappeared a long time ago'. He is accused of having spoken only of 'organisational errors'.

Trotsky's break with his anti-Leninist past should not, however, be sought in a legal act of abjuration, but in his activity and writings from 1917 on. In his preface, Trotsky is at pains to demonstrate his complete agreement with Lenin before and during October; but he refers explicitly to the period following the February revolution, noting that even before he returned to Russia, in articles he wrote in America, he expressed opinions comparable to those of Lenin in his letters from Switzerland. He never dreamed of hiding that it was he who, faced with the lessons of history, had moved onto Lenin's terrain, having wrongly fought against him in the past. Trotsky discusses with the rights and from the position of a Bolshevik Party member – one who reproaches the right wing of his party with having an attitude that repeats the errors of the

Mensheviks in the period of the revolution. The fact that, in the period leading up to the revolution and the supreme struggle, he was unscathed by such errors and fought at Lenin's side as part of his school, only increased the responsibility of Lenin's lieutenants to support the action effectively and not to lapse into rightist errors.

It is thus to stand the debate completely on its head, on the basis of one-sided information, to suggest that Trotsky's argument in the foreword to *1917* was that the proletarian revolution was impossible in Russia before it took place in other countries. On the contrary, his critique of that very position stated that it was at the root of the rightist errors.

If we conceded that there is a new Trotskyism, which is not the case, no link could attach it to the old. In any event the new Trotskyism would be on the left, whereas the old one was on the right. And between the two stretched the period of Trotsky's magnificent communist activity against the opportunist social democrats, which everyone else close to Lenin recognised without hesitation as rigorously Bolshevik. Where is Lenin's polemic against opportunism better supported than in the writings of Trotsky? It is enough to mention only one of them: *Terrorism and Communism*. In all the congresses of the Russian party, of the Soviets, of the International, Trotsky has given reports and speeches that set out the fundamental policy of communism in recent years. They have never been opposed to Lenin's positions on the key questions – absolutely never if we are speaking of the congresses of the International, for which Trotsky always drafted the official manifestoes, and where at every step he shared with Lenin the polemics and the work to consolidate the new International by eliminating opportunist residues.

During this period, no other interpreters of Lenin have attained the solidity of Trotsky's conception of the essential themes of revolutionary theory and politics. And he is on a par with the master in the sculptural precision and effectiveness of his presentation of these themes in debate and propaganda. I have no wish to speak here of Trotsky's role as leader in the revolutionary struggle and in the political and military defence of the revolution. I neither need nor intend to offer an apologia. But I do believe that this past must at least be invoked, to underline the injustice of exhuming Lenin's old judgement on his penchant for the 'left revolutionary phrase'. Such an insinuation is best reserved for those who have shown they can only see revolutions from afar, even including many of the West's ultra-Bolsheviks.

It is said that Trotsky represented the petty-bourgeois elements during the previous discussion in the party. We cannot deal with all the contents of this discussion, but a few things should not be forgotten. First, with regard to the economic policy of the republic, the majority of the party and the Central

Committee took over the proposals of Trotsky and the opposition. Second, the opposition had a heterogeneous composition, and just as one cannot attribute to Trotsky the views of Radek on the German question, so it is inaccurate to suggest that he shares those of Krassin and others in favour of more wide-ranging concessions to foreign capital. Third, on the question of internal party organisation, Trotsky did not support a systematic policy of dividing up and decentralising, but rather a Marxist conception of discipline, neither mechanical nor stifling. The need to examine this important matter more clearly becomes more urgent with each passing day, but it would require separate treatment. However, the insinuation that Trotsky became the spokesperson of petty-bourgeois tendencies is undermined by the other accusation that he underestimated the role of the peasantry compared with the industrial proletariat in the revolution – another uncalled-for plank of the polemic against him. The truth is that Lenin's agrarian theses found a disciple and faithful partisan in Trotsky (on this subject Lenin was not at all defensive but admitted he had purloined the programme of the Socialist-Revolutionaries). All these attempts to lend anti-Bolshevik features to Trotsky do not persuade us in the slightest.

After the revolution, Trotsky was opposed to Lenin on the Brest-Litovsk treaty and the question of state-organised trade unionism. These are undoubtedly important matters, but they are not sufficient to qualify other leaders who had the same positions as Trotsky at the time as anti-Leninists. It is not on partial errors of this kind that one can build a whole edifice in which Trotsky appears as our Antichrist, with flurries of quotations and anecdotes where the chronology as well as the logic is upside down.

It is also said that Trotsky has differences with the International over analysis of the world situation, that he considers this with pessimism, and that the facts have contradicted his forecast of a peaceful democratic period. It is a fact, however, that he was entrusted with the task of writing the Manifesto of the 5th Congress on precisely this subject, and that this was adopted with unimportant modifications. Trotsky speaks of the peaceful period as a 'danger', arguing that communists must react by underlining, during these democratic periods, the inevitability of civil war and the alternative between two opposite dictatorships. As for pessimism, it is precisely Trotsky who denounces and fights the pessimism in others, affirming, as Lenin said of October, that an unfavourable period ensues if one lets slip the opportune moment for insurrectionary struggle; the situation in Germany has confirmed this analysis only too well.

Trotsky's analysis of the world situation does not simply see the installation of left bourgeois governments everywhere; it is on the contrary a profound analysis of the forces at play in the capitalist world, which no declaration of the

International currently calls into question, and which is based on the fundamental thesis of the insurmountability of the present capitalist crisis.

Anti-Bolshevik elements have supported Trotsky, they say. Obviously, they must be delighted with the official assertion that one of our main leaders has rejected our fundamental political positions, that he is against the dictatorship and for a return to petty-bourgeois forms, etc. But already some bourgeois sheets have recognised that there is nothing to hope for there, that Trotsky more than any other is against democracy and for implacable violence of the revolution against its enemies.

If bourgeois and social-traitors really hope that Trotsky is revising Leninism or Communism in their direction, they have a hard time ahead of them. Only Trotsky's silence and inaction might give some life to this legend, to these speculations on the part of our enemies. For example, the foreword in question was undoubtedly published by a Fascist journal, but the editors were forced to state at the end that no one, for heaven's sake, could imagine that their views were remotely similar to those of Trotsky. And *Avanti!* simply makes everyone laugh when it praises Trotsky while publishing the very passage in which he mentions the Italian case to demonstrate the complete inadequacy of other parties for the revolution, referring precisely to the socialist party!

The German rightists accused of Trotskyism deny this on the grounds that they support the exact opposite of what Trotsky wrote: they maintain that revolution was an impossibility in Germany in October 1923. Besides, any dubious solidarity from opposing shores can never count as an argument in establishing our own orientation. This is what this experience has taught us.

Trotsky must be judged on what he says and what he writes. Communists should not attack people at a personal level; if Trotsky were one day to betray, it would be necessary to demolish him without showing any consideration. But we should not believe charges of treachery against him because his contradictors make them intemperately or have a privileged position in the debate. All the accusations about Trotsky's past collapse when we think that they have been provoked by his foreword to *1917* – which does not refer to such questions at all – and that such an assault was not previously thought necessary.

The polemic against Trotsky has left the workers with a feeling of sorrow and produced a smile of triumph on the lips of our enemies. Well, we want friends and enemies alike to know that the proletarian party will know how to live and conquer even without and against Trotsky. But as long as the conclusions are those to which the debate is leading today, Trotsky is not the man to be abandoned to the enemy.

In his declarations he has not disowned one line of what he wrote, and that is not contrary to Bolshevik discipline. But he also stated that he never wished to form a faction on a political and personal basis, and that he was more than ever loyal to the party. Nothing else could be expected of a man who is among those most worthy to stand at the head of the revolutionary party.

But beyond the sensational question of his personality, the problems he raised remain: they should not be avoided but squarely faced.

8 February 1925

2   **Bordiga at the Sixth Enlarged ECCI (Fifth Session, Moscow, 23 February 1926, Unabridged)[3]**

Comrades, we have before us the draft theses and the report of the Executive Committee, but I think it is absolutely impossible to limit our discussion to them.

In previous years, in various sessions of the CI,[4] I had occasion to back theses and declarations that were, at the time, excellent, satisfactory; but, in the course of the International's activity, the facts have not always fulfilled the hopes these declarations had raised in us. Hence it is necessary to discuss and examine the International's development critically in light of the events that have taken place since the last congress, along with the prospects of the CI and the task it must set itself.

I have to say that the situation in which the International finds itself cannot be considered satisfactory. In a certain sense we are faced with a crisis. This crisis did not begin today, but has existed for a long time. It is not only we and some groups of comrades of the extreme left who say this. The facts show that everyone recognises the existence of this crisis. Very often – especially at the critical moments of our general activity – watchwords are given in which it is effectively admitted that a radical change in our methods of work is necessary. It is true that, at present, it is said that no revision is needed, that nothing needs to be changed. But there is an evident contradiction in this. And, to show that the existence of deviations and of a crisis in the International is recognised by everyone present here and not only by the discontented ultra-lefts, I want now to take a bird's-eye view of our International, retracing its history and its different stages.

---

3   *Protokoll, Erweiterte Executive der Kommunistischen Internationale*, Moskau, 17 Februar bis 15 März 1926, Hamburg-Berlin: Verlag Carl Hoym Nachf., 1926, pp. 122–44. The italics in the text correspond to the italics in the German Protocol, along with a few added by the translator [note by G. Donis].
4   Communist International.

The foundation of the Communist International after the disaster of the Second International was based on the watchword: the proletariat must form communist parties. At that time everyone agreed that the objective powers relations were favourable to the final revolutionary struggle, but that we lacked the organ for this struggle. It was said: the objective revolutionary premises are there and, if we had communist parties truly capable of revolutionary activity, all the necessary conditions for a complete victory would be present.

At the Third Congress – based on the experience of many events but, in particular, on the experience of the March Action in Germany in 1921[5] – the International was forced to admit that the formation of communist parties alone was not sufficient. Fairly strong sections of the CI had been formed in nearly all the most important countries, but the problem of revolutionary action had not been solved. The German party had believed it was possible to go into battle and open an offensive against the enemy, but it was defeated. The Third Congress, faced with this problem, had to admit that the presence of communist parties is not sufficient when the objective conditions for the struggle are lacking. The most important thing had been forgotten: one must be sure of the overwhelming support of the great masses before launching an attack. In a situation that is in general revolutionary, not even the strongest communist party is capable of creating the conditions and factors necessary for an insurrection by a pure act of will if it has not been able to mobilise the support of the great masses.

This, then, was a stage in which the International realised that many things had to be changed. It is always claimed that the speeches of the Third Congress already contained the idea of the united front tactics, which were then formulated explicitly in the sessions of the subsequent Enlarged ECCI based on the political situation illustrated by Lenin at the Third Congress. This is not completely true, because in the meantime the situation had changed. In the period in which the objective situation was favourable we failed to utilise the good method of the offensive against capitalism in the proper way. After the Third Congress it was no longer simply a question of launching a second offensive, when we had succeeded in winning over the masses. The bourgeoisie had beaten us to it. It was the bourgeoisie that launched the offensive against the workers' organisations and communist parties in the most important countries, and our tactics of winning over the masses for the offensive we had dis-

---

5   The 'März Aktion' was an essentially spontaneous revolt in the mining and industrial districts of central Germany involving hundreds of thousands of workers. The reasons for its defeat and the behaviour of the communists were the subject of a heated and lacerating debate in the VKPD (Unified Communist Party of Germany) and in the International.

cussed at the Third Congress was transformed into defensive tactics against the action unleashed by the capitalist bourgeoisie. We worked out these tactics, together with the programme to be implemented, by studying the characteristics of the enemy offensive and by realising that concentration of the proletariat which alone can permit us to win over the masses through our parties, and launch our counteroffensive in a not-distant future. This was the basis of the tactics of united front.

It goes without saying that I have no objections to the theses of the Third Congress on the necessity of the solidarity of the masses: if I bring this question up, it is only to show that, once again, the International was forced to admit it was not yet sufficiently mature to lead the struggle of the world proletariat.

The application of the tactics of the united front led to right-wing errors, which became increasingly clear after the Third Congress and especially after the Fourth. These tactics, which can be applied only when we are on the defensive, that is, when the crisis of capitalist decomposition has grown less acute – these tactics that we employed seriously degenerated. In our opinion, they had been adopted without making their real meaning sufficiently clear. Preservation of the specific character of the communist party had not been ensured. I do not intend to repeat here the criticism we levelled against the tactics of the united front as they were applied by the majority of the Communist International. We had no objections as long as it was a question of basing our action on the proletariat's immediate economic demands, even the most elementary demands, raised by the enemy offensive. But when, under the pretext that the united front was only a bridge on our way towards the proletarian dictatorship, the International based it on new principles, directly regarding the central power of the State and the Workers' Government, we opposed it, and we said: here we are overstepping the bounds of good revolutionary tactics.

We communists know very well that the historical development of the working class must lead to the dictatorship of the proletariat; but this demands action that influences the great masses, and to reach the masses pure and simple ideological propaganda is not sufficient. Our success in shaping the revolutionary consciousness of the masses will be proportional to the strength of our conception and of our behaviour in every phase of the unfolding of events. Hence this behaviour cannot be in contradiction with our position on the final struggle, which is the specific goal for which our party was created. Agitation based on a slogan like that of the 'Workers' Government' can do nothing but breed confusion in the consciousness of the masses, and even of the party and its general staff.

We criticised all this from the very beginning, and here I limit myself to recalling the judgement we expressed in its broad outlines. When we were confronted with the errors these tactics had led to, and above all after the defeat in Germany in October of 1923,[6] the International recognised the fact that it had been wrong. The German defeat was not just a mishap, it was the result of an error that cost us the hope of conquering another great country, after the first in which the proletarian revolution had triumphed – and this, from the standpoint of the world revolution, would have been of enormous importance.

Unfortunately, all the International had to say was: we do not need a radical revision of the decisions of the Fourth Congress, we only need to remove certain comrades who misapplied the united front tactics; *we need to find the people responsible.* It found them in the right wing of the German party, and did not want to admit that it was the entire International that was at fault. In any event, the theses were revised and the conception of workers' government was *formulated* in a completely different way.

Why do we disagree with the theses of the Fifth Congress? Because, in our opinion, the revisions were not adequate; the individual formulas should have been made clearer. But, if we were opposed to the decisions of the Fifth Congress it is above all because they did not eliminate the serious errors and because, in our opinion, it was wrong to limit the question to *proceedings against individuals* when what was needed was *a change in the International itself.* But this sound and courageous path was not taken. We have repeatedly criticised the fact that among us, in the environment in which we work, *a parliamentary and diplomatic spirit* is fostered. The theses are far *to the left,* the speeches are far *to the left,* even those *against whom* they are directed *approve* them, because they think it will give them immunity. But we looked beyond the words, we foresaw what was going to occur after the Fifth Congress, and we could not be satisfied with it.

On more than one occasion the CI has been forced to recognise the need for a radical change of line. The first time, because the question of winning over the masses had not been understood. The second time, it was the question of the united front tactics, and at the Third Congress the line followed until then was completely revised. But there is more. At the Fifth Congress and at the Enlarged ECCI meeting of March 1925 it was clear all over again that everything was going badly. It was said: six years have gone by since the

---

6 In October 1923, after a decision by the Executive Committee of the International, the KPD (German Communist Party) formed coalition governments with the left-wing social democrats in Saxony and Thuringia, intending to make these two regions the base for an insurrection throughout Germany. The plan failed completely, and the defeat marked the end of the revolution in Germany.

founding of the International but none of its parties have succeeded in making the revolution. It is true that the situation has become more unfavourable: we are now confronted with a certain stabilisation of capitalism. In spite of this, we are told that, in the International's activity, many things need to be changed. We have not yet understood what is to be done, and the slogan 'Bolshevisation' is launched! Incredible but true: eight years have gone by since the victory of the Russian Bolsheviks, and now we are supposed to notice that the other parties are not Bolshevik! That a radical change is needed to raise them to the height of the Bolshevik parties! Had nobody noticed this before?

We hear the objection: Why didn't you protest against the Bolshevisation slogan immediately, at the Fifth Congress? Our reply: Because it was impossible to object to the statement that the other parties needed to attain the revolutionary capability that made the victory of the Bolsheviks possible. But now we are no longer speaking of a simple watchword, a simple slogan. Now we are faced with facts and experiences. Now it is necessary to take stock of Bolshevisation and see what it really means.

I maintain that its balance sheet is negative, from several points of view. The problem it was designed to solve has not been solved, no progress has been made with the application of its methods to all the parties.

I have to deal with the problem from different points of view and, first of all, from the viewpoint of history.

There is only one party that has achieved revolutionary victory: the Russian Bolshevik Party. For us it is of the greatest importance to follow the same path the Russian party pursued to achieve its victory. This is quite true: but it is not enough. It is undeniable that the historical path pursued by the Russian party cannot show all the aspects of the historical development awaiting the other parties. The Russian party waged its struggle in a country in which the bourgeois liberal revolution had not yet taken place. The Russian party – it is a fact – fought in particular conditions, that is, in a country in which the feudal autocracy had not yet been overthrown by the capitalist bourgeoisie. The period between the fall of the feudal aristocracy and the conquest of power by the proletariat was too short to allow this development to be compared with that which the proletarian revolution will have to achieve in the other countries. There was not enough time for a bourgeois state apparatus to arise on the ruins of the tsarist and feudal state apparatus. Hence the experience in Russia cannot help us with the fundamentally important question of how the proletariat is to overthrow the modern parliamentary, liberal, capitalist state, which has been in existence for many many years and is fully capable of defending itself.

In light of these differences, the fact that the Russian revolution confirmed our doctrine, our programme, our conception of the role of the working class in the historical process, is all the more important from a theoretical viewpoint, since the Russian revolution, even in these particular conditions, led to the conquest of power and to the dictatorship of the proletariat realised by the communist party. In this the theory of revolutionary Marxism found its greatest historical confirmation.

From an ideological point of view, this is of decisive importance; but, as regards tactics, it is not sufficient. We have to know how to attack and conquer the modern bourgeois state, a state that in armed struggle defends itself even more effectively than the tsarist autocracy did and, what is more, defends itself also with the help of the ideological mobilisation and defeatist education inflicted on the proletariat by the bourgeoisie. This problem is not present in the history of the Russian Communist Party, and if Bolshevisation is interpreted to mean that one can ask the revolution of the Russian party for the solution to all the strategic problems of revolutionary struggle, then this conception of Bolshevisation is inadequate. The International must construct a broader conception for itself; for problems of strategy it must find solutions outside the scope of the Russian experience. This experience must be utilised fully, nothing in it is to be rejected, it must always be held before our eyes; but we also need supplementary elements, drawn from the experience of the working class in the West. This is what must be said, from the historical and tactical viewpoint, about Bolshevisation. The experience of tactics in Russia has not shown us how we have to proceed in the struggle against bourgeois democracy: it gives us no idea of the difficulties and tasks the development of the proletarian struggle in our countries will bring to light.

Another side of the problem of Bolshevisation is the question of party reorganisation. In 1925, all of a sudden, we were told that the entire organisation of the sections of the International was wrong, that the ABC of organisation had not yet been applied. All the problems had already been posed but what was essential had not yet been done – that is, the problem of our internal organisation had not been solved. This, then, was tantamount to admitting that the CI had marched off in a direction that was completely wrong! Now I know very well that no one wants to limit the slogan of Bolshevisation to a problem of organisation. But this problem has an organisational side, and here it was emphasised that this side is the most important. The parties are not organised as the Russian Bolshevik Party was and is, because their organisation is not based on the principle of the workplace, because they conserve a type of territorial organisation, which – allegedly – is absolutely incompatible with the tasks of a revolutionary party, and which – allegedly – is typical of social-democratic

parliamentary parties. If one thinks it is necessary to transform our party organisations in this way,[7] and if this transformation is presented not as a practical
measure suitable for certain countries in certain conditions but, rather, as a fundamental measure for the entire International, as the correction of a basic error,
as the necessary premise for our parties to become truly communist parties –
if this is the case, then we have to disagree. After all, it is very strange that
nobody noticed any of this before. We are told that the transition to factory
cells[8] was already contained in the theses of the Third Congress. But, then, it is
very strange that the CI waited from 1921 until 1925 to implement it.

The thesis that a communist party must be unconditionally constructed on
a factory-cell basis is a theoretical error. Marx and Lenin, on the strength of a
well-known and precisely formulated principle, state that the revolution is not
a question of the form of organisation. To solve the problem of the revolution
finding an organisational formula is not sufficient. The problems that face us are
problems of *force*, not of *form*. Marxists have always fought the syndicalist and
semi-utopian schools that said: group the class in a certain organisation, trade
union, co-operative et cetera, and you'll have your revolution. Today one says,
or at least one conducts a campaign to this effect: if the organisation is built on
a factory-cell basis, all the problems of the revolution will be solved! Adding: the
Russian party was able to make the revolution because it was built on this base.

It will most certainly be said that I am exaggerating; but there are quite a few
comrades who can confirm the fact that the campaign was conducted on the
basis of theses like this. What concerns us is the impression these slogans have
on the working class and on the members of our party. As regards the work
of the cell, many comrades now have the impression that this is the infallible
prescription for true communism and for the revolution. I contest the thesis
that the communist party must necessarily be organised on a factory-cell basis.
In the theses on organisation Lenin brought before the Third Congress, it is
repeatedly emphasised that in questions of organisation there can be no solution that on principle is equally valid for all countries at all times. We do not
contest the fact that factory cells as the basis of party organisation were very
effective in the Russian situation. I do not want to dwell too long on this question: in the comprehensive debate preceding the Italian Congress, we already
said that in Russia there were a number of historical causes that militated in
favour of organisation on this basis.

---

7   That is, on a factory-cell basis, as prescribed by Bolshevisation.
8   'Cellule d'azienda': literally, 'enterprise cells', translated throughout as 'factory cells'. We note
    that 'factory' here also includes small factories and workshops, with a sufficient number of
    workers to form a cell.

Why do we believe the factory cell has disadvantages in other countries it does not have in the Russian situation? First of all, because the workers organised in the cell are never in a position to discuss all the political questions. In fact, the report of the ECCI in this Plenum notes that there is nearly no country in which the factory cells have been able to *discuss political problems*. The claim, then, is that the reorganisation of the parties went too far and too fast – merely a practical, a secondary error. But the fact that the party was stripped of its fundamental organisation, an organisation capable of discussing political problems, is most certainly not a mere trifle – and a year after its formation the new organisation still does not perform this *vital* function. A result like this cannot be the result of individual errors – no, it is the result of a wrong approach to the entire problem. And this is not a trifle. It is a very important question. In our opinion, it is not fortuitous that factory cells do not discuss political problems, because in a capitalist country the workers grouped in the small and restricted circle of their factories have no possibility of confronting general problems or of connecting their immediate demands with the ultimate goal of communism. Yes, in an assembly of workers of the same professional sector concerned with the same minor immediate problems, these immediate demands can be discussed; but in this assembly there is no basis for a discussion of the general problems, the problems that concern the entire working class. In short: it is impossible to carry on that political work based on *class* for which a communist party *exists*.

It will be said that what we ask for is what all the right-wing elements ask for – that we want territorial organisations where the intellectuals dominate the entire discussion in the assemblies with their long speeches. But there will always be this danger of demagogy and deception on the part of the leaders, it has existed as long as a proletarian party has; yet neither Marx nor Lenin, who thoroughly investigated this problem, ever thought to solve it by boycotting the intellectuals or non-proletarians. On the contrary, they repeatedly emphasised the historically necessary role in the revolution of deserters from the ruling class. We all know that, in general, opportunism and betrayal slip into the party through the action of certain leaders; but the struggle against this danger must be waged in a different way. Even if the working class could do without the ex-bourgeois intellectuals, it could nonetheless not do without leaders, agitators, journalists et cetera, and it would have no choice but to look for them in the ranks of the workers. But the danger of the corruption and demagogy of these workers who have become leaders is no different from the danger of the corruption and demagogy of the intellectuals. In fact, there have been cases in which ex-workers have played the dirtiest role in the workers' movement, and we all know it. What is more, has the role of the intellectuals been eliminated by the organisation in factory cells as it is practised today? Not at all. In fact the party apparatus is composed of intellectuals, together with former workers. The role of these social elements has not changed; on the contrary, it has become even more dangerous. If we admit that these elements can be corrupted by their position as functionaries, this difficulty subsists, because we have given them a position of far greater responsibility than in the past: in fact, in the small factory-cell meetings the workers have practically no freedom of movement, they do not have a sufficient base to influence the party with their class instinct.

Hence the danger of which we must beware lies not in the decreased influence of the intellectuals but, on the contrary, in the fact that the workers are only concerned about the immediate needs of their factory and fail to see the big picture of the general revolutionary development of their class. This means that the new form of organisation is less suitable for the proletarian class struggle in the most serious and broadest sense of the word.

In Russia, the big general problems of revolutionary development, the problem of the state, of the conquest of power, were on the agenda at every moment, because the feudal and tsarist state apparatus had been irremediably condemned and because every single group of workers, by its position in social life and by administrative pressure, was itself faced with these problems at every moment. Opportunist deviations were not a big problem in Russia because there were no bases for corruption of the proletarian movement by the capitalist state, ever so skilful in wielding the arm of democratic concessions and collaborationist illusions.

Furthermore, there is a practical difference.

Naturally we must give to the organisation of our party the form that lends itself best to resisting reprisals. We must protect ourselves against attempts by the police to break up our party. In Russia, organisation in factory cells was the form best suited to this purpose, because in the streets, in the cities, in public life, the workers' movement had been put out of action by extremely severe police measures. Hence it was materially impossible to organise outside the factory. Only in the factory could the workers meet to discuss their problems, without police surveillance. What is more, it was only in the factory that the problems of class were posed in terms of the antagonism between capital and labour. The small economic questions regarding the factory – the problem of fines raised by Lenin, for example – from the historical point of view were progressive demands, compared to the liberal demands the workers and the bourgeoisie made together against the autocracy; but, in relation to the taking of power in the struggle against the bourgeois democracy as a new form of state, the proletarians' immediate demands are of secondary importance. Since this question of the taking of power could be posed only after the fall of tsarism, it was necessary to shift the centre of the struggle to the factory, since the factory was the only environment in which the autonomous proletarian party could express itself.

If it is true that the bourgeoisie and the capitalists were allies of the tsar, it was also true that they were the very ones who had to overthrow him, the ones who represented the condition for the fall of autocratic power. Hence in Russia there was never a complete solidarity between the industrialists and the state, as is the case in the modern capitalist countries where the solidarity between the state apparatus and the entrepreneurs is absolute: it is *their* state, *their* political apparatus. And it is the state apparatus that historically proves to be the instrument of capitalism, creating the suitable organs and putting them at the entrepreneur's disposal. If a worker attempts to organise the other workers in the factory, the entrepreneur has recourse to the police, to espionage, et cetera. Hence in the modern capitalist states party work in the factories is much more dangerous. It is easy for the bourgeoisie to discover party work in the factories. This is why we propose to shift the fundamental organisation of the party not to the factories, but outside. I want to mention here just one little fact. Right now, in Italy, they are recruiting new police officers. The admission requirements are very strict. But for those who have a profession and can do factory work admission is facilitated. This shows that the police are looking for people capable of working in the various industries whom they can use to discover revolutionary work in the factories.

Furthermore, we have learned that an anti-Bolshevik international association has decided to adopt cell-based organisation to counteract the communist movement.

Another argument. It has been said here that another danger has raised its head, the danger of a workers' aristocracy. It is clear that this danger is typical of periods in which we are threatened by opportunism and by the role it aims to play in the corruption of the workers' movement. But the simplest way for the influence of a workers' aristocracy to infiltrate our ranks is unquestionably that of factory-cell based organisation, because in the factory the influence of the worker who occupies a higher position in the technical hierarchy of labour inevitably predominates.

For all these reasons, and without making it a question of principle, we ask that the base-organisation of the party, for political and technical reasons, continue to be territorial organisation.

Does this mean we want to neglect party work in the factories? Do we deny the fact that communist work in the factories is an important base for connecting with the masses? Absolutely not. The party must have an organisation of its own in the factory, but this organisation must not constitute the *base* of the party. In the factories there have to be party organisations that *are subject to the political leadership of the party*. It is impossible to connect with the working class without an organisation in the factory; but this organisation must be the communist fraction. To strengthen my thesis, I shall say the following. In Italy, in the days before Fascism, we created a network of fractions of this kind, and we considered this activity to be the most important thing for us. In practise, it is the communist fractions in the factories and the unions that have always fulfilled the specific task of bringing us close to the masses. The bond with the party provides the fractions and the unions with the political elements – the elements of class in the broadest sense of the word – that receive their impulse not from the narrow circle of the profession and of the factory alone. Hence we are in favour of a network of communist organisations in the factories; but, in our opinion, the political work must be performed in territorial organisations.

I cannot dwell here on the judgements passed on our treatment of this question during the debate in Italy. At the congress and in our theses we dealt exhaustively with the theoretical question of the nature of the party. It has been alleged that our viewpoint is not a *class* viewpoint; that we insisted that the party allow heterogeneous elements – the intellectuals, for example – to play a greater role in party activity. It is not true. We do not combat party organisation based exclusively on factory cells because it would lead to a party exclusively composed of workers. What frightens us is the danger of labourism and workerism, which is the greatest anti-Marxist danger. The party is proletarian because it treads the historical path of the revolution, of the struggle for the ultimate ends to which only the working class aspires. This is what makes a party a proletarian party, not the automatic criterion of its social composition.

The character of the party is not compromised by the active participation of all those who participate in its work, who accept its doctrine and want to fight for the ends of the class.

Everything that can be said on this terrain in favour of factory cells is vulgar demagogy, which does rest on the slogan of Bolshevisation, but leads us directly to the repudiation of the Marxist and Leninist struggle against the banal mechanical and defeatist conceptions of opportunism and of Menshivism.

2.1   [*Against Ideological Terrorism within the Party*]

This brings me to another aspect of Bolshevisation: I refer to the internal regime in force in the party and in the Communist International.

A new discovery has been made here: what all our sections lack is Bolshevik *iron discipline*, as exemplified by the Russian party. *Fractions* are absolutely forbidden, and all militants, regardless of their opinion, are required to participate in the common work. It is my opinion that, in this field too, the question of Bolshevisation has been posed *demagogically*.

When the problem is posed in the form: Can x or y be allowed to form a fraction?, every communist will answer No. But the problem cannot be posed in this form. The facts already show that the methods employed have been beneficial neither for the party nor for the International. From the Marxist perspective, this question of internal discipline and of fractions has to be posed in a way that is very different and far more complex. We are asked: What do you want? Perhaps that the party resemble a *parliament* in which everyone has the *democratic right* to struggle for *power* and to win over the *majority*? But posing the question in this way is wrong. Posed in this way, only one answer is possible: *Naturally, we are against such a ridiculous a system*, it is a fact that we must have an absolutely homogeneous party, without *differences of opinion* and *different groupings* within it. But this is not a dogma, it is not an a priori principle; it is an end that can and must be fought for in the course of the development that leads to the formation of a true communist party, *on the condition that all the ideological, tactical and organisational questions be posed and resolved correctly*.

Within the working class, the actions and initiatives of class struggle are determined by the economic relations in which the various groups live. It is the task of the communist party to bring together and unify everything these actions have in common from the viewpoint of the revolutionary objectives of the proletariat all over the world. The party's internal unity, the end of dissension, the disappearance of fractional struggle will show that it is on the best track to fulfilling its task in the right way. But when dissension arises, this means that the party's policy has fallen into error, that it does not possess the capacity to combat and defeat those *deviationist* tendencies of the workers' movement that often arise when the general situation takes crucial turns. When *cases of indiscipline* occur, they are a symptom of the fact that the party does not yet possess this capacity. Discipline is therefore *an end*, not *a beginning*; it is not a platform that can be considered *unshakable*. This, moreover, brings us back to the voluntary nature of the adherence to our party organisation. It is not in some sort of *penal code* that the party can find a remedy for its frequent cases of indiscipline.

Now, in recent years *a regime of terror* has been instituted in our parties, a sort of *sport* that consists in intervening, punishing, repressing, destroying – and all this with a particular gusto, as if it were the ideal of party life. The heroes of these brilliant operations even seem to consider them proof of revolutionary capability and energy. I do not agree. I believe that the good, the real revolutionaries are, for the most part, the comrades who are the butts of these exceptional measures, and who *endure them patiently to keep from turning the party upside down*. I think that this waste of energy, this sport, this struggle within the party, has nothing to do with the revolutionary work we have to accomplish. The day will come for us to strike and to destroy capitalism: it is here that our party will give proof of its *revolutionary energy*. We do not want *anarchy* in our party, but neither do we want a regime of *permanent reprisal*, which is the very negation of its unity and solidarity.

Today the official viewpoint is as follows: the current Centre[9] is eternal, it can do whatever it likes because, when it takes measures against whoever resists it, when it foils plots and routs oppositions, it is always right. But merit does not lie in *crushing revolts*, what counts is that there *be no revolts*. Party unity is recognised by the results obtained, not by *a regime of threats and terror*. It is clear that sanctions are necessary in our statutes; but they are to be applied only in exceptional cases, and must not be elevated to the status of *normal and permanent* procedures within the party. When there are elements that obviously stray from the common path, it is clear that measures must be taken. But when in a society recourse to the penal code becomes the rule, it is clear that this society is far from perfect. Sanctions must be applied to exceptional cases and not become *the rule, a sort of sport, the ideal of the party leaders*. This is why we have to *change* if we want to build a solid bloc in the true sense of the word.

The theses presented here take some steps in this direction. The International proposes to allow *a little more freedom*. Perhaps it is a little late. Perhaps it thinks it can allow a little more freedom to the 'vanquished' who no longer pose any threat.

But let us leave the theses and consider the facts. It has always been said that our parties must be built on the principle of democratic centralism. It might be a good idea to look for an expression other than *democracy*; in any event, this was Lenin's formula. How is democratic centralism to be realised? By means of the eligibility of the comrades, the consultation of the mass of the party for the solution of certain problems. Naturally, for a revolutionary party, there can be exceptions to this rule. It is opportune for the party regime that, at times, the Centre should say: Comrades, under normal conditions the party ought to consult you; but since this is a dangerous moment in the struggle against the enemy, since there is not a moment to lose, we are acting without consulting

---

9   'La Centrale', translated as the Centre, refers to the central leadership of the Communist International in the first part of this text; in the second part, it refers to the leadership of specific national parties.

you. But what is *dangerous* is *creating the appearance of a consultation* when, in fact, the decision comes from above. What is *dangerous* is exploiting the circumstance that the Centre holds the entire party apparatus and press in the palm of its hand. In Italy we said that we recognise *the dictatorship*, but we hate these *methods à la Giolitti*.[10] Is bourgeois *democracy* not in fact a *means of deception*? Is this the *democracy* you propose to *grant us* and to realise in the party? In that case, *a dictatorship that has the courage not to put on a hypocritical mask* would be preferable. Either the party assumes a true democratic form, that is, a democracy that permits the Centre to utilise the apparatus correctly, or moods of dissatisfaction and malaise will inevitably spread, especially among the workers.

We need a healthier internal regime. It is absolutely necessary to give the party the possibility of forming an opinion and of expressing and defending it openly. At the Italian party congress I said that the error was the failure, within the party, to draw a clear distinction between agitation and propaganda. Agitation is carried on among a great mass of persons to clarify a certain number of very simple ideas, while propaganda regards a relatively narrow stratum of comrades who are exposed to a great number of complex ideas. The error consisted in limiting ourselves to agitation within the party; in considering the mass of party members as, in principle, handicapped; in treating them as elements that can be set in motion, not as an effective factor of the common work. Agitation based on formulas learned by rote is conceivable up to a certain point, when it is a question of obtaining maximum effects with a minimum waste of energy, when the objective is to mobilise great masses where the factor of will and consciousness play no more than a secondary role. But, in the party, things are completely different. We ask that, within the party, these methods of agitation come to an end. The party must embrace that part of the working class which possesses and is pervaded by class consciousness – unless you champion that theory of the elites which was used in the past as an accusation (a groundless accusation) against us. It is necessary that the mass of party members develop a collective political consciousness, that they make a thorough study of the problems facing the communist party. In this respect, a change in the internal regime of the party is urgently needed.

Now, the question of fractions. In my opinion, the question of fractions is not to be posed from a moral viewpoint, from the viewpoint of the penal code.

---

10   Giovanni Giolitti (1842–1928), historical leader of Italian liberalism, five-time prime minister of Italy between 1892 and 1921, was a master of unscrupulous parliamentarian manoeuvring.

Is there a single example in history of a comrade's organising a fraction *for his own amusement*? No, not even one. Is there a single example in history in which opportunism infiltrated the party by way of a fraction – that is, in which the organisation of fractions served as a base for the mobilisation of the working class and the revolutionary party was saved thanks to the intervention of the killers of fractions? No, experience shows that opportunism always slips into our ranks behind the mask of unity. It is in its interest to influence the largest possible mass, hence it is behind the screen of unity that it makes its insidious proposals. In general, the history of fractions shows that they do not do honour to the parties in which they are formed but to the comrades who create them. The history of fractions is the history of Lenin. It is the history not of attacks on the existence of revolutionary parties, but of their crystallisation and of their defence against opportunist influences.

Before saying that the attempt to organise a fraction is a direct or indirect bourgeois manoeuvre to infiltrate the party one must have proof. I do not believe that, in general, such a manoeuvre takes the form of a fraction. At the Italian party congress we posed the question in relation to our party's Left. We all know the history of opportunism. When does a group become the representative of bourgeois influences within a proletarian party? Generally, such groups have found fertile soil among the trade-union functionaries or the party representatives in parliament, or among comrades who, in the questions of party strategy and tactics, advocated class collaboration, the alliance with other social and political line-ups. Before speaking of fractions that have to be crushed, one needs at least to give proof that they have links with the bourgeoisie or with bourgeois circles, or that they are based on personal relations with members of such circles. If this proves impossible, then one needs to seek *the historical causes that gave rise to the fraction*, instead of condemning it a priori.

The genesis of a fraction is an indication that something is wrong in the party. To find a remedy one must go back to the historical causes that produced it, that gave birth to the fraction or to the tendency to form it. And these causes *reside in ideological and political errors of the party itself*. Fractions are not *the sickness*, they are *a symptom*; to combat the sick organism it is pointless to combat the symptom, you have to try to establish the causes of the illness. Moreover, in most cases we are dealing with groups of comrades who had absolutely no intention of creating any sort of separate organisation, with groups seeking to assert themselves through the normal, regular and collective work of the party. The method of *fraction-hunting*, of *scandal-mongering campaigns*, of *police surveillance* and of *distrust of the comrades* – a method emblematic of the *fractionalism at its worst* rampant at the *upper levels of the party itself* – has done nothing but make the conditions of our movement worse, driving any objective criticism down the road to fractionalism.

These methods will never lead to party unity, but only to a regime that renders it *inept and impotent. A radical transformation* of working methods is absolutely necessary. Without it, the consequences *will be grave in the extreme*.

Take the example of the French party. How did this party proceed against fractions? Very badly indeed! – for example in the matter of the emerging syndicalist fraction. Comrades expelled from the party have returned to their old loves, and publish a newspaper in which they express their ideas. It is clear that they are wrong. But it is pointless to look for the causes of this grave ideological deviation in the caprices of these naughty boys, Rosmer and Monatte.[11] Look for them, rather, in the errors of the French party and of the entire International.

Joining battle in the ideological arena against the syndicalist errors, we managed to wrest broad swathes of workers from the influence of syndicalist and anarchist elements. And now these conceptions reappear. Why? Also because the party's internal regime, its exaggerated Machiavellism, made a bad impression on the working class and made the resurgence of these theories possible, along with the preconception that a political party is in itself something dirty and that economic struggle alone can save the proletarian class. These fundamental errors threaten to reappear in the proletariat because the International and the communist parties have failed to show with deeds, and with simple theoretical statements, the essential difference between revolutionary, Leninist politics and the politics of the old social-democratic parties, whose degeneration before the war had given rise to syndicalism as a reaction.

If the old theories of economic action and the opposition to all political activity had some success with the French proletariat, it is due to the fact that a whole series of errors were allowed to be committed in the political line of the communist party.

Semard:[12]

You say that fractions have their causes in the errors of the party leadership. But the right-wing fraction in France was formed at the very moment in which the Centre recognised and corrected its errors.

---

11   Alfred Rosmer (1877–1928) and Pierre Monatte (1881–1960), activists in the trade-union movement and leading figures of the Communist Party of France, were expelled from the party in 1924 for their opposition to 'Bolshevisation'.

12   Pierre Semard (1887–1942), trade-union activist and general secretary of the Communist Party of France from 1924 to 1929, was a fervent supporter of the united front with the socialist parties.

Bordiga:
Comrade Semard, if you want to present yourself to the good Lord with the sole merit of having recognised your errors, you will have done too little for the salvation of your soul.

I believe, comrades, that, with our strategy and our proletarian tactics, it is necessary to show the errors these anarcho-syndicalist elements commit. The working class has gained the impression that the communist party is no better than the others, and therefore harbours a certain distrust of our party. This distrust stems from the methods and manoeuvres that are employed in our ranks. One would say that, not only towards the external world but also in the party's internal political life, we act as if good 'politics' were an art, a technique common to all parties. As if we worked with a Machiavellian handbook on political skill in our pockets. But it is the task of the party of the working class to introduce a new form of politics, which has nothing in common with the base and insidious methods of bourgeois parliamentarianism. If we do not show this to the proletariat, we shall never succeed in gaining a useful and vigorous influence over them, and the anarcho-syndicalists will win out.

As for the right-wing fraction in France, I do not hesitate to say that I see it in general as a healthy phenomenon and not as proof of the infiltration of petty-bourgeois elements. The theory and the tactics it supports are wrong, but it is in part a very useful reaction to the political errors and bad regime of the party Centre. But the responsibility for these errors does not fall on the French party leadership alone. It is the general line of the International that provokes the forming of fractions. To be sure, on the question of the united front I totally disagree with the position of the French Right, but I think it is perfectly true that the resolutions of the Fifth Congress are not at all clear, that they are absolutely unsatisfactory. On the one hand, in many cases these resolutions approve the united front from above; on the other, they say that social democracy is the left wing of the bourgeoisie and its leaders must be unmasked. This is an untenable position. The French workers are tired of the tactics of the united front as they have been applied in France. Naturally, several heads of the French opposition are on the wrong track and in blatant contradiction with the true revolutionary road when they draw their conclusions in favour of a 'loyal' united front and a coalition with the social democrats.

It is obvious that, if we boil the problem of the right wings down to the question of whether it is permissible to collaborate with a journal outside the party's control, there is only one possible answer. But this is not the way out of the problem. We need to attempt to correct the errors and to carry out a conscientious examination of the political line of the French party and, on many issues, of the International as well. The problem will not be solved by subjecting the opposition – Loriot et cetera – to the rules of a mini-catechism on personal behaviour. To correct the errors it is not enough to cut off heads; it is also necessary to discover the underlying errors that cause and favour the formation of fractions.

They tell us: to find the errors in our Bolshevisation machine we have the International; it is the majority of the International that has to intervene when a party Centre falls into grave errors; this is the guarantee against deviations in the national sections. But, in practise, this system has failed. Germany is an example of this kind of intervention by the International. The KPD Centre had become omnipotent and rendered any opposition within the party impossible: and yet there was someone above it that, at a certain point, condemned all the crimes and errors committed by this Centre: the Moscow Executive Committee with its Open Letter. Is this a good method? No, absolutely not. What are the consequences of such an action? We ourselves in Italy had a good example, during the party congress debate. A good comrade, literally orthodox, was sent as a delegate to the German party congress. He sees that everything is going just fine, that the overwhelming majority approves the theses of the International, and that the new Centre is elected by this majority, opposed by a negligible minority. The Italian delegate returns and presents a report that is highly favourable to the German party. He writes an article depicting it, to the eyes of his left-wing Italian comrades, as a model Bolshevik party. As a result, it is quite possible that a number of comrades in our opposition became champions of Bolshevisation. However, two weeks later, the Executive Committee's Open Letter arrives ... It declares that the internal life of the German party is awful, there is a dictatorship, all the tactics are totally wrong, grave errors have been committed, deviations have come to light, the ideology is not Leninist. One forgets that, at the Fifth Congress, the German left was proclaimed to be the most completely Bolshevik Centre, and now all this is ruthlessly turned upside-down, with the same methods applied to the German left as had previously been applied to the right. At the Fifth Congress the slogan was: 'It's all Brandler's fault!'; and now: 'It's all Ruth Fischer's fault!'[13] As I see it, this is not the way to win the working class over to our side. It is wrong to say that a couple of comrades are at fault for the errors committed. After all, the International was

---

13   Heinrich Brandler (1881–1967), head of the German Communist Party from 1921 until January of 1924, was in favour of coalitions with the social-democratic parties; the ECCI held him responsible for the failed insurrection in the autumn of 1923. In the same party, Ruth Fischer (1895–1961), along with Ernst Thälmann and Arkadi Maslow, supported the policy of the 'united front from below'.

there, on the spot, observing the course of events, and it could not – it must not – ignore the capacities of the leaders and their political actions. Now it will be said that I defend the German left just as, at the Fifth Congress, it was said that I defended the right. But, politically, I don't side with either one; I just think that, in both cases, the International must take the responsibility for the errors committed; the International that had sided fully with these groups, that had presented them as the best leadership, that had entrusted the party to them.

Hence the intervention of the ECCI against the leadership of the national sections has been inappropriate in a number of ways. The question is: How does the International work? What are its relations with the national sections? How are its central organs elected?

I already criticised our methods of work at the last Congress. Our higher organs and our congresses lack collective collaboration. The supreme organ seems like something extraneous to the sections: it discusses with each section and one-by-one selects a fraction to which it gives its support. In each case, this national Centre is backed by all the remaining national sections, in the hope of *receiving better treatment when their turn comes*. At times it is purely personal groups of leaders who engage in this 'horse-trading'.

We are told: it is the Russian party that provides us with international leadership because it is the party that made the revolution, because it is the party that plays host to the International; hence it is right that decisive importance be given to the resolutions inspired by the Russian party. But here we pose the problem: How does the Russian party deal with international issues? This is a question we all have the right to ask.

After the latest events, after the latest debate, this fulcrum of the entire system is no longer sufficient. In the latest debate within the Russian party we saw comrades who could claim the same knowledge of Leninism, who had the same indisputable right to speak in the name of the Bolshevik revolutionary tradition, arguing with one another, using quotes from Lenin *against* one another to support their own interpretations of the Russian experience. Without entering into the merits of the debate, I want to establish this incontrovertible fact.

Who, in this situation, will decide in the last instance on international problems? The answer cannot be *the Bolshevik old guard*, because in practise this answer leaves the questions unresolved. This is the first fulcrum of the system that eludes our objective investigation. But, then, the solution must be completely different. We can compare our international organisation to a pyramid. This pyramid must have a *vertex*, and straight lines that tend towards this vertex. This is how the unity and the necessary centralisation is produced. But today, as a result of our tactics, this pyramid *rests dangerously* on its vertex. Hence it needs to be *turned upside-down*: what is now the bottom must become the top, the pyramid must be put *on its base* so that it be balanced. Our final conclusion on the subject of Bolshevisation is therefore that it is not a question of making simple, secondary modifications, but that the entire system must be modified from top to bottom.

Having taken stock of the past action of the International, I now go on to its current situation and future tasks. We are all in agreement on what has been said about the stabilisation of capitalism, so it is not necessary to go back to the subject. Its decomposition is now in a less acute phase. Within the framework of the general crisis of capitalism, the conjuncture has undergone some oscillations. We always have the perspective of the final collapse of capitalism before us, but – in my opinion – in posing the question of perspective an error of evaluation is committed. There are different ways of tackling the problem of perspective. Comrade Zinoviev reminded us here of some very useful things when he spoke of Lenin's double perspective.

If we were a scientific society for the study of social events, we could reach more or less optimistic conclusions without delving more deeply into actual facts. But a purely scientific perspective is not sufficient for a revolutionary party that itself participates in all the events – that is itself one of their factors and that cannot express its function metaphysically: on one hand in the exact knowledge of its function, on the other in will and action. Therefore our party must always remain directly connected with its ultimate ends. Even when scientific judgements force us to draw pessimistic conclusions it is necessary for us to have the revolutionary perspective always before our eyes. The fact that Marx expected the revolution in 1848, 1859 and 1870, and that Lenin, after 1901, prophesied it for 1907, that is, ten years before its triumph – this is not a banal question of scientific error. On the contrary, it shows the sharpness of revolutionary vision of these great leaders. This is not the infantile exaggeration that always hears revolution knocking on the door – no, it is the true revolutionary capacity that remains intact despite all the difficulties of historical development. The question of perspective is of enormous interest for our parties, we need to delve into it to the very bottom. Now, I consider it insufficient that one say: the conjuncture has taken an unfavourable turn, we no longer have the situation of 1920, and this explains and justifies the internal crisis in a number of sections of the International. No, this can help us to explain the causes of certain errors but does not justify them. From a political viewpoint, this is not sufficient. We cannot and must not resign ourselves to considering the current defective regime of our parties to be unmodifiable because the external conjuncture is unfavourable. Put this way, the question is badly put. It is clear that, if our party is *a factor* of the events, at the same time it is also their *product*, even if we succeed in creating a truly revolutionary world party. Now, in what sense are events reflected in our party? In the sense that our membership and our influence on the masses increase when the crisis of capitalism generates a situation favourable to us. If, *vice versa*, at a certain moment the conjuncture *becomes unfavourable*, it is possible that the number of our supporters may fall; but we must not allow *our ideology to suffer* on this account. Not only our *tradition* and our *organisation*, but also our *political line* must remain intact.

If we believe that we have to exploit the progressive crisis of capitalism to prepare our parties for their revolutionary task we create a completely erroneous scheme of perspectives for ourselves. This would mean that we deem a period of long and progressive crisis necessary for our party's consolidation, which means, in turn, that the economic situation ought to do us the favour of remaining revolutionary, allowing us to go into action. If, then, after a period of uncertain conjuncture the crisis suddenly worsens, we will not be able to exploit it, because – due to this wrong way of seeing things – our parties will inevitably find themselves bewildered and powerless. This shows that we are incapable of learning from our experience of the opportunism in the Second International. It cannot be denied that, before the world war, there was a period in which capitalism flourished and that it enjoyed a favourable conjuncture. But, if this in a certain sense accounts for the opportunist decomposition of the Second International, it does not justify the opportunism. We fought against this idea and we refused to believe that opportunism was a necessary fact, historically imposed by events. We maintained the thesis that our movement had to resist it, and the Marxist Left combated opportunism even before 1914, calling for the formation of sound and revolutionary proletarian parties.

The question, then, needs to be posed differently. Even if the conjuncture and the prospects are unfavourable or relatively unfavourable, we must not accept *opportunist deviations* with resignation and justify them with the pretext that their causes are to be sought in *the objective situation*. And if, in spite of it all, an internal crisis should arise, its causes and the means to remedy it must be sought elsewhere – that is, in the work and political line of the party, which to date have not been as they should have. This refers also to the leadership question, which comrade Trotsky raised in the preface to his book *1917*, in his analysis of the causes of our defeats. I fully agree with his conclusions. Trotsky does not speak of leaders in the sense that we need men delegated by heaven to this purpose. No, his formulation of the problem is very different. Also the leaders are a product of the party's activity, of its methods of work and of the confidence the party has won for itself. If the party, in spite of the variable and often unfavourable situation, *follows the revolutionary line* and combats opportunist deviations, then the *selection of its leaders* and the formation of its *general staff* will come about favourably. And if in the period of the final struggle we will most certainly not succeed in having another Lenin, we will succeed in having a *solid and courageous* leadership – something that today, in the current state of our organisations, *is but a pipe dream.*

2.2   [*Against the United Front with the Bourgeois Left*]

There is another scheme of perspectives that must be combated, which we must deal with in the passage from a purely economic analysis to the analysis of social and political forces. Many are of the opinion that a government of the petty-bourgeois left presents a favourable situation for our struggle. First of all, this erroneous scheme is in contradiction with the first scheme, because, generally, in a period of economic crisis the bourgeoisie chooses a government of right-wing parties in order to launch a reactionary offensive, which means that for us the objective conditions become unfavourable once again. To reach a Marxist solution of the problem these commonplaces must be abandoned.

In general, it is not true that a government of the bourgeois left is favourable to us; it may very well be unfavourable. Historical examples show us how foolish it is to imagine that our task will be facilitated by a government of the so-called middle classes, with a liberal programme that permits us to organise the struggle against a weakened state apparatus.

Here too we are confronted with the influence of an incorrect interpretation of the Russian experience. In the revolution of February 1917, after the fall of the previous state apparatus a government based on liberal bourgeois and petty-bourgeois parties was formed. But this did not give rise to a solid state apparatus capable of replacing the tsarist autocracy with the economic rule of capital and modern parliamentary representation. Before such an apparatus could be organised the proletariat led by the communist party managed to attack the government successfully and take power. Now, one might well think that in other countries things will take the same course, that one fine day the government will pass from the hands of the bourgeois parties to those of the intermediate parties, that in this way the state apparatus will weaken and that, in consequence, it will be easy for the proletariat to overthrow it. But this simplified perspective is completely false. What is the situation in the other countries? Is it possible to compare a change of government in which a government of the left takes the place of a government of the right (for example the coalition of the lefts in France instead of the national bloc) with a historic change of the foundations of the state? It is in fact possible that the proletariat exploit this period to strengthen its positions. But, if we have to do with the pure and simple passage from a government of the right to a government of the left, then the situation, favourable to communism, of a general decomposition of the state apparatus is not present. Do we have concrete historical examples of the process by which a government of the left paved the way for the proletarian revolution? No, we do not.

In 1919, in Germany, the bourgeois left formed a government. Indeed, there was a period in which social democracy was in power. Despite Germany's military defeat, despite an extremely grave crisis, the state apparatus did not undergo that substantial transformation which would have facilitated a proletarian victory. Not only did the communist revolution fail, but the social democrats proved to be its executioners.

If with our tactics we contribute to the rise to power of a government of the left, does this mean we will have a situation favourable to us? No, absolutely not. It is a Menshevik conception to imagine that the middle classes can create a state apparatus different from that of the bourgeoisie, and that this period can be seen as a phase of transition toward the conquest of power by the proletariat.

Certain bourgeois parties have programmes and make demands that aim to win over the middle classes. In general, this represents not the transfer of power from one social group to another, but only a new method employed by the bourgeoisie in their struggle against us; when a change of this sort takes place we cannot say that it is the most favourable moment for us to intervene. Yes, we can take advantage of it; but only on the condition that the positions we took previously were absolutely clear and did not call for a left-wing government.

For example: in Italy, is Fascism to be seen as a victory of the bourgeois right-wings over the bourgeois left? No! Fascism is something more: it is the synthesis of two means of defence of the bourgeois class. The latest measures taken by the Fascist government have shown that the petty-bourgeois and semi-bourgeois social composition of Fascism makes it no less a direct agent of capitalism. As a mass organisation (the Fascist organisation has a million members) it seeks to realise the mobilisation of great masses with the help of social-democratic methods, while at the same time reacting ferociously against all adversaries that dare attack the state apparatus.

On this terrain, Fascism has suffered some defeats. This confirms our view of the struggle between classes. But what comes fully to light is the absolute impotence of the middle classes. In the past few years they have accomplished three complete evolutions: in 1919–20 they flocked en masse to our revolutionary meetings and rallies; in 1921–22 they supplied the Fascists with cadres of 'black shirts'; in 1924, after the murder of Matteotti, they went over to the opposition; and today they are coming back to Fascism. They always try to pick the winning side.

There is another fact to be considered. In the programmes of nearly all the left-wing parties and governments we find the principle that, while all must be given the fundamental liberal 'guarantees', an exception must be made for those parties that seek to overthrow the institutions of the state – that is, for the communists.

The false perspective of the advantages that a left-wing government can give us corresponds to the supposition that the middle classes are capable of their own solution to the problem of power. In my opinion, the so-called new tactics that have been employed in Germany and France, and on the basis of which in Italy the communist party proposed the Anti-Parliament to the Aventine anti-Fascist opposition, rest on a serious error. I cannot understand how a party so steeped in revolutionary traditions as our German party can take seriously the social-democratic reproach that, by presenting its own candidate, its plays into Hindenburg's hands. In general, the bourgeoisie's plan for the counter-revolutionary mobilisation of the masses consists in substituting a political and historical dualism for the class conflict between bourgeoisie and proletariat. For its part, the communist party insists on this very dualism of classes not because it is the only dualism possible in the social perspective and on the terrain of changes of parliamentary power, but because it is the only dualism that is historically capable of leading to the revolutionary overturning of the state's class apparatus and to the formation of a new state. Now, we can bring this dualism to the consciousness of the great masses not with ideological declarations and abstract propaganda but with the language of our actions and the clarity of our political conception. When in Italy our party proposed an Anti-Parliament with communist participation to the bourgeois anti-Fascists, even if our press insisted that we absolutely could not trust these parties, even if the real objective was to unmask them, we effectively encouraged the great masses to expect the Aventine parties to bring about the fall of Fascism. We encouraged them to believe that a revolutionary struggle and the formation of an Anti-State was possible not on the basis of class, but on the basis of the collaboration with petty-bourgeois elements and even with capitalist groups. With this manoeuvre, we failed to bring the great masses into a class front. The 'new tactics' in their entirety not only are not based on the resolutions of the Fifth Congress but, in my opinion, are in contradiction with the principles and the programme of communism.

2.3   [*The Impending Degeneration*]

What are our tasks for the future? This assembly could not seriously consider the problem without tackling the fundamental problem of the *historical relations between Soviet Russia and the capitalist world* to its full extent and seriousness. Along with the problems of the proletariat's revolutionary strategy and the international movement of peasants and colonial and oppressed peoples, the state policy of the communist party in Russia is for us the most important question today. This means finding a good solution for the problem of the *class relations in Russia itself*, taking the necessary measures in relation to the influence of the *peasants* and of the budding *petty-bourgeois classes*, and struggling against external pressure, which today is purely economic and diplomatic, and which tomorrow may be military. Since there have not yet been revolutionary uprisings in other countries, it is necessary *to connect Russian policy in its entirety with the revolutionary politics of the proletariat in the closest way possible*. I do not intend to delve more deeply into this question here, but I insist that while the fulcrum of this struggle is, indisputably, *the Russian working class and its communist party*, it is also true that *the proletariat of the capitalist states* is of fundamental importance. The problem of Russian politics cannot be solved *within the closed perimeter of the Russian movement*: also the direct collaboration of the entire Communist International is absolutely necessary.

Without this effective collaboration *dangers will arise not only for the revolutionary strategy in Russia but also for our politics in the capitalist states*. Tendencies towards *a weakening of the role of the communist parties* could arise. On this terrain we are already being attacked, naturally not from within our own ranks but by the social democrats and the opportunists in general, in relation to our manoeuvres in favour of international trade-union unity and our attitude to the Second International. All of us here agree that the communist parties must unconditionally *maintain their revolutionary independence*; but they must be warned against the possibility of a tendency to *replace the communist parties with organs less clear and explicit in nature*, not based on class struggle and seeking to weaken and neutralise them politically. In the current situation, defence of the characteristics of our international and communist party organisation *against any liquidating tendency* is, unquestionably, our common task.

After our criticism of its general line, can we consider the International, as it is today, sufficiently prepared for this double task of strategy in Russia and strategy in the other countries? Can *we* demand an immediate discussion of all the Russian questions in this assembly? *Unfortunately, the answer to these questions is No!*

A serious revision of our *internal regime* is absolutely necessary. Furthermore, it is necessary to put the problems of *tactics throughout the world* and the *politics of the Russian state* on the agenda of our parties. But this calls for a new course and completely different methods.

In the report and in the theses proposed *we find no guarantee* of anything of the sort. It is not *official optimism* that we need. We have to understand that it is not with the *petty* methods we see all too often *employed* here that we can prepare ourselves for the important tasks now facing the general staff of the world revolution.

3   Letter to Karl Korsch[14]

Naples, 28 October 1926

Dear Comrade Korsch,

The problems we face today are so important that we should really be discussing them face to face in detail. This unfortunately is not a possibility at the moment. Also I will not be covering all the points in your platform in this letter, some of which could give rise to useful discussions between us.

For example, I do not think 'the way you express yourself' about Russia is correct. We cannot say that 'the Russian revolution was a bourgeois revolution'. The 1917 revolution was a proletarian revolution, even if generalising about the 'tactical' lessons that can be derived from it is a mistake. The problem now is what will become of the proletarian dictatorship in one country if revolutions do not follow elsewhere. There may be a counter-revolution, there may be an external intervention, or there may be a degenerative process whose symptoms and reflexes within the communist party will have to be uncovered and defined.

We cannot simply say that Russia is a country where capitalism is expanding. The matter is much more complex: it is a question of new, historically unprecedented forms of class struggle; it has to be shown how the Stalinists' entire conception of relations with the middle classes is a renunciation of the communist programme. You would appear to rule out the possibility that the Russian Communist Party will engage in any politics that does not equate to a justification of Stalin, or to support for the inadmissible politics of 'giving up power'. Rather, it needs to be said that a correct class politics would have been possible in Russia if the whole of the 'Leninist old guard' had not made a series of serious mistakes in international policy.

And then I have the impression – I restrict myself to vague impressions – that in your tactical formulations, even when they are acceptable, you attach

---

14   Montaldi 1975, pp. 47–52.

too much value to influences arising from the objective circumstances, which today may appear to have swung to the left. You are aware that we, the Italian lefts, are accused of refusing to analyse objective situations: this is not true. But we do aim to construct a *left line*, actually general and not occasional; a line applicable across different periods and situations, confronting them all from a revolutionary point of view, but certainly not ignoring their distinctive objective features.

I pass straight on to the subject of your *tactics*. To express myself trenchantly, rather than in official formulas, I would say that they still seem to me, as regards the international party relations, too elastic and too ... bolshevik. Your whole argument justifying your attitude to the Fischer group – that is, that you counted on pushing it to the left or, if it refused, on devaluing it in the eyes of the workers – is unconvincing, and it seems to me that good results have not in fact come out of it. In general, I think the priority today is not so much in the realm of organisation and manoeuvre as in the elaboration of an international political ideology of the left, based on the instructive experiences undergone by the Comintern. To be very backward in this respect will make any international initiative very difficult.

I am also enclosing a few notes on our position concerning some questions of the Russian Left. It is interesting that we see things differently: you who used to be very distrustful of Trotsky have immediately subscribed to the programme of unconditional solidarity with the Russian opposition, betting on Trotsky rather than Zinoviev (a preference I share).

Now that the Russian opposition has had to 'submit', you say we should make a declaration attacking it for having lowered the flag. I would not agree to do this, first of all because we do not think we should 'merge' under the international banner raised by the Russian opposition.

Zinoviev and Trotsky are eminently realistic men; they understand that they will have to take a lot of punches without passing openly onto the offensive. We have not yet reached the point at which things in Russia are clear once and for all, either internally or externally.

1.   We share the Russian Left's positions on the Russian Communist Party line on state policy. We do not agree with the direction taken by the Central Committee majority; it will lead to the degeneration of the Russian party and the proletarian dictatorship, and away from the programme of revolutionary Marxism and Leninism. In the past we did not contest the Russian Communist Party's state policy as long as it remained on a ground corresponding to the two documents: Lenin's speech on the Tax in Kind and Trotsky's report to the 4th World Congress. We agree with Lenin's theses at the 2nd Congress.

2. The Russian Left's positions on Comintern tactics and politics, leaving aside the past responsibility of many of its members, are inadequate. They are far removed from what we have been saying since the formation of the Communist International on the relationship between parties and masses, tactics and situation, communist parties and other parties ostensibly representing the workers, or on the assessment of bourgeois political alternatives. They are closer to our views, but not completely, on the question of the International's working methods and the interpretation and functioning of international discipline and factionalism. Trotsky's positions on the German question in 1923 are satisfactory, as is his appraisal of the present world situation. The same cannot be said of Zinoviev's amendments on the Red Trade Union International, or on various incidental points, which do not inspire confidence in tactics that avoid past errors.

3. Given the politics of pressure and provocation from the leaders of the International and its sections, any organisation of national and international groups opposed to the rightist deviation runs the risks of a split. We should not be seeking a split in the parties and the International. Before that is possible, we need to allow the experience of artificial and mechanical discipline, with its resulting absurd practices, to run its course, never renouncing, however, our political and ideological positions or expressing solidarity with the prevailing line. Groups that fully subscribe to a traditional left ideology could not solidarise unconditionally with the Russian opposition, but neither can they condemn its recent submission; this did not involve a reconciliation but signified that the only alternative to the conditions it accepted would have been a split. The objective situation, both in Russia and elsewhere, is such that to be hounded out of the Comintern would mean that it had even less chance of modifying the course of the working-class struggle than it would have if it remained inside.

4. Solidarity or joint political declarations with elements like Fischer and co. would be inadmissible. In the German and other parties, they have recently had leadership responsibilities on a rightist or centrist line, and their passing into opposition has coincided with their inability to keep leadership positions in agreement with the international centre, and with criticisms made by the International of their work. To solidarise with them would be incompatible with the task of defending the new method and course of international communist work, which must take over from parliamentary-bureaucratic manoeuvring.

5. All means that do not exclude the right to stay alive in the party must be used to denounce the prevailing trend; this is leading to opportunism

and it conflicts with loyalty to the programmatic principles of the International. Other groups apart from ours have the right to uphold these principles, so long as they set themselves the task of seeking out the original defects – not theoretical, but tactical, organisational and disciplinary – that have rendered the Third International still more susceptible to degenerative dangers. [...]

I will try and send you items on Italian matters. We have not accepted the declaration of war, which consists in the suspension of some leading supporters of the left; the matter has not led to measures of a fractionist character. The batteries of discipline have so far fired into the wadding. It is not a very satisfactory line and we are not happy about it, but it is the least bad option possible. I will send you a copy of our appeal to the International.

In conclusion, I do not agree with you that we should issue an international declaration; nor do I think this is a practical possibility. What I do think would be useful is declarations in various countries with a parallel ideological and political content regarding the Russian and Comintern questions, without going to the extreme of presenting a factionalist 'conspiracy', but with each fraction freely elaborating its own ideas and experiences.

As regards this internal question, I maintain that more often than not it is a good idea tactically to let matters take their course, which is certainly unhealthy and opportunistic in 'foreign' matters. I believe this to be the case especially with regard to the special mechanism of internal power and mechanical discipline, which I persist in thinking is destined to break down of its own accord.

I am aware this is inadequate and not very clear. I hope you will excuse me and in any case I extend to you my cordial greetings.

Amadeo Bordiga

PART 2

The Struggle for the Rebirth of
Revolutionary Communism (1945–65)

∵

SECTION 1

Russia, Revolution and Counter-revolution in Marxist Theory

∵

Lessons of Counter-revolutions

1   Summary[1]

For Marxism there are no 'surprises of history'

1. Neither the advent of forms of dictatorship of capital, nor the dissolution of
the international communist movement, nor the complete degeneration of the
Russian revolution are 'surprises of history', requiring a modification of Marxism's classical theoretical line to explain them.

Proppers-up and patchers-up of Marxism

2. The head-on deniers of Marxism as a theory of history are to be preferred to
its proppers-up and patchers-up (who are even worse if their language is not
collaborationist but extremist), for whom critical variants and complements
are needed to correct its failures and its powerlessness. We are clearly in a
period of social and political counter-revolution, but at the same time of full
critical confirmation and victory.

Russian counter-revolution and proletarian strategy

3. An analysis of the counter-revolution in Russia and its reduction to formulas
is not a central problem for the strategy of the proletarian movement in the
renewal that awaits it, since the counter-revolution in Russia was by no means
the first one, and Marxism has known and studied an entire series. Moreover,
opportunism and the betrayal of the revolutionary strategy have a course different from that of the involution of the Russian economic forms.

---

1   The text is part of Bordiga's report to the party's general meeting in Naples on 1 September
     1951, first published in *Bollettino interno del Partito comunista internazionalista*, 10 September
     1951, and republished as a booklet, *Lezioni delle controrivoluzioni*, by Edizioni 'Il Programma
     Comunista' in May 1981. The excerpts translated here are pp. 9–12 and 29–41 of the book-
     let.

Counter-revolution

4. Not only the study of past bourgeois counter-revolutions but also that of feudal counter-revolutions at the expense of the insurgent bourgeoisie lead to different historical types: military and social total defeat (German peasant war of 1525); military total defeat but social victory (defeat of France in 1815 by the European coalition); military victory but re-absorption and degeneration of the social bases (destruction of Italian capitalism despite the Communes' victory over the feudal Empire at the Battle of Legnano).[2]

The Russian economy 'tends' toward and 'aims' at capitalism

5. To classify the type of Russian counter-revolution, in which, of course, no invasion and military defeat by capitalist powers was involved, it is necessary to examine the economic fabric and its evolution, which, in a double sense, 'tends' toward and 'aims' at capitalism.[3]

Feudalism – capitalism – socialism

6. To do so, it is necessary to re-establish Marxist elementary concepts: *a*) the definition of *feudalism* as an economy of small producers with non-mercantile exchange; *b*) the definition of *capitalism* as a mass-production economy with totally mercantile exchange; *c*) the definition of *socialism* as a mass-production economy with non-mercantile distribution: an economy with rationing but that is already non-monetary at its lower stage, while at its higher stage it is unlimited.

The aim of the proletarian struggle

7. Class struggle at the capitalist stage: a struggle not for the simple reduction of the *quantum* of surplus value, but for the conquest and the social control of the *entire* product, of which the individual worker was violently expropriated. The working class struggles to conquer everything that today constitutes the wealth and the value of the means of production and of the total mass of commodities. It struggles to conquer: constant capital, which is the heritage of the

---

2 At Legnano (near Milan) on 29 May 1176 the troops of the League of the Lombard Communes defeated the King of Germany and Holy Roman Emperor, Frederick Barbarossa.

3 In Italian 'tende' signifies both 'tend toward' and 'aim at'. Bordiga in fact says 'in a double sense'. The two distinct senses become clear in point 59 below.

labour of past generations that has been usurped by the bourgeoisie; variable capital, which is the labour of the present generations, most of it exploited by the bourgeoisie; the surplus value that must be reserved for future generations to conserve and extend the means of production, today monopolised by the bourgeoisie, while all three factors are continually squandered by the anarchy of capitalism.

State capitalism

8. State capitalism not only is not a form that is new and of transition to socialism but, indeed, is pure capitalism. It appeared, with all its forms of monopoly, in the period of the bourgeois victory over the feudal powers, while the state-capital relation forms the basis of the bourgeois economy in all its phases.

One and only one type of capitalism

9. The Marxist vision of history would fail if, instead of recognising one and only one type of capitalist production (as of every other previous type of production) that runs from one revolution to the next, it were to admit a succession of different types.

Double revolutions

10. Like the German revolution of 1848, the Russian revolution was supposed to be the integral whole of two revolutions: anti-feudal and anti-bourgeois. The German revolution in its political and armed struggle failed to achieve either goal, but socially the anti-feudal goal of a transition to capitalist forms prevailed. The Russian revolution was politically and militarily victorious on both fronts and therefore more advanced. But economically and socially it did not advance at all, falling back on the goal of a capitalist industrialisation of the territory it controlled.

The post-revolutionary course of the Russian economy

11. After the great political victory few sectors of socialist economy took hold, and Lenin, with the NEP [New Economic Policy], was forced to sacrifice them, for the sake of international revolution. With Stalinism it was the international revolution that was sacrificed, intensifying the transition to large-scale industrialism, in Russia and also in Asia. Proletarian elements on one side,

feudal elements on the other, both tending towards capitalism. This is what results from an analysis of the Soviet economy based on the criteria premised here.

The third world war and its Marxist evaluation

12. The prospect of a third world war is not a central problem of the new revolutionary movement. Since the two anti-Fascist 'crusadisms' are converging – the West in a democratic sense, the East in a counterfeit proletarian sense (with small forces [*nuclei*] of the revolutionary proletariat the sworn enemy of both) – the situation during the war will be counter-revolutionary, just as it will be for a certain period in the alternative case of an agreement between Russia and the Atlantic powers on economic and territorial bases. The method of the colonial infeudation of the defeated country will ensure a counter-revolutionary balance in the postwar period to the extent that the imperialism better equipped and of greater historical continuity prevails. Therefore, just as the worst possible outcome of the first world war was the English victory, and of the second the Anglo-American victory, so, of the third, the worst would be an American victory.

[…]

2   Distinctions between Feudalism, Capitalism and Socialism

45. After our discussion of the precise terms of the passage from pre-capitalism to capitalism, we must now specify the characteristics that distinguish the capitalist economy from post-capitalism. For at least a century, for us post-capitalism has not been 'a pig in a poke' but, rather, something very precisely defined. According to the general rule, we can see around us actual examples of a post-capitalist economy, just as there was large-scale manufacturing centuries before the bourgeois revolution.

We quote here a passage from another text.[4]

As we've said on other occasions, there is even more: there are true communist types even under capitalist power. Firefighting is one example:

---

4   The text is a letter from Alfa (Bordiga) to Onorio (Onorato Damen) of 31 July 1951. Damen was an exponent of the Italian communist Left who broke with Bordiga in 1952; on the reasons for this break see Damen 2011.

when something burns nobody pays to put out the fire; if nothing burns the firefighters are fed all the same. I say all this to combat the thesis, whoever be its author, that schematises as successive stages: private capitalism, state capitalism – as the first form of lower socialism – higher socialism and communism.

State capitalism is not semi-socialism, it is full-fledged capitalism. The Marxist theory of concentration tells us that it is in fact the outlet of capitalism. What is more, it is the condemnation of the liberalist theory of a permanent regime of production in which the marvellous play of competition never fails to put a brand new slice of capital within everybody's reach.

To distinguish between capitalism and socialism the title to the possession of the instruments of production is not sufficient; it is necessary to consider the entire economic phenomenon, that is, who has the product at his disposal and who consumes it.

Pre-capitalism. Economy of individual producers: the product is the independent worker's, each consumes what he has produced. But, at the same time, subtractions of surplus production and therefore of surplus labour are perpetrated at the expense of the multitude of individual workers (at times united by force into masses but without the modern division of labour) by privileged castes, orders and powers.

Capitalism. Associated labour (in Marx: *social* labour), division of labour, with the product at the disposal of the capitalist and not of the worker who receives money and buys on the market what he needs to keep up his strength. The entire mass of products passes through the monetary form in its voyage from production to consumption.

Lower socialism. The worker receives from the unitary economic and social organisation a fixed quantity of products that are necessary for his life, and can have no more. Money comes to an end, replaced by consumer goods that cannot be accumulated, neither can their destination be changed. The voucher? Yes, lower socialism is the labour-time voucher for everyone, without the use of money and without markets.

Higher socialism or communism. In all sectors one tends-aims to abolish the voucher and everyone takes what they need. Some will go to the cinema a hundred days in a row? They can do it even today. They'll call the firemen after setting fire to their own house? They do it today, but back then there was no fire insurance. In any event, both then and now mental hospital services are in keeping with the pure communist economy: they are free and unlimited.

Recapitulating:

Pre-capitalism. Economy of individual producers without money or with the complementary employment of money.

Capitalism. Economy with the totalitarian employment of money. Social production.

Lower socialism. Economy without money and with vouchers. Social production.

Higher socialism or communism. Economy without money or vouchers, social production.

State capitalism – it would be idiocy to call it state socialism – is completely *within* capitalism.

3   The Counter-revolution in Russia

Counter-revolution and Russian social events

46. We returned to all these basic notions to explain the course of the current counter-revolutionary process of which the social events in Russian are a part. Such events cannot be examined unless they are seen as parts of a whole. If analysed separately, they lead the incautious to adulterate the Marxist doctrine, that is, to admit new analyses and new perspectives due to the intervention of a third class, of a third factor.[5] In this way they fall into the trap of the Stalinian trick that posits permanent functions for a state that is no longer an instrument of class but a generator of class, and abandon the notion of the emptying of the state.

The Marxist method of work always hammers home points already known

47. Our method of work always leads us to hammer home points already known and to extend our investigation to ever broader and more diversified sectors within the perimeter fixed by these points, but never to proceed to innovations or inventions.

Competition and monopoly are complementary notions

48. Competition and monopoly are not rival but, rather, complementary notions also in the market and in exchange, with the former developing into the

---

5   Namely, the bureaucracy: see below, points 54, 57 and 59.

latter. It is on the monopoly front that the bourgeois class asserts itself: the monopoly of the means of production and of products.

The historical development of the trade-union movement and the bourgeois reaction

49. The workers, to react to the social condition imposed on them by capitalism and which is fostered by their lack of unity, go on to institute a monopoly of their labour-power by means of trade unions. Consequently, capitalism must reveal its nature, found trusts, and assign its State not only police but also economic functions. Prior to the unions there were mutual aid societies that collected contributions from the workers, but did not yet demand higher wages from the capitalists.

Nothing could have been more conservative. Yet in the traditional mutual aid associations and even in the charitable congregations the socialist party made useful inroads.

Economy and politics after the revolution in Russia

50. The formulation contained in our draft manifesto[6] regarding the Russian economy that 'tends towards and aims at capitalism' ['*tende al capitalismo*'] needed to be clarified. What took place in Russia? What took place was precisely the reversal of the first communist characteristics of the economy, the overturning of internal and international policy, with the latter not ineluctably having to proceed from the former.

The Russian post-revolutionary economic crisis

51. In 1921, when Russia was completely isolated due to the failure of revolutionary victories in other countries to materialise, the level of its productive forces dropped to a limit below the minimum. It was no longer possible to supply the city with products from the countryside and vice versa, as had first occurred under war communism, with the proletarian state being short of the products of the city and of the countryside alike. It was necessary to legalise free commerce, which until then had been reserved for black marketeers or 'speculators'.

---

6 'Appello per la riorganizzazione internazionale del movimento', written in 1949, published in this booklet, *Lezioni delle controrivoluzioni*, pp. 43–54.

The NEP

52. Lenin and the Bolshevik party instituted the NEP in an economic ensemble that included forms of nomadic, patriarchal, feudal and bourgeois production, along with small units of socialist economy. Asked whether the NEP was capitalism, Lenin's answer was a categorical 'yes'.

And it could not have been otherwise, since from the moment in which wages are paid in money and with this money you buy food, you have capitalism. This does not change the nature of the state, which, because it can do so, remains proletarian. Thus its nature results not from the structure of the economy but, rather, from the position of class and of force in the development of the revolutionary struggle of the international proletariat.

Lenin's anti-NEP measures in the political sphere

53. Lenin, who in the economic sphere went so far as to consider permitting foreign private capital to enter Russia with the concession of entire territories, signalled the need to beef up state power to cope with the social reactions caused by the measures implemented by the NEP, and to play for time hoping for help from proletarian revolutions in the West.

In Russia, reversal in the political sphere the cause of retreats in the economic sphere

54. This is how the problem had to be posed. Trotskyism proclaims the intervention of a third factor, namely, the bureaucracy. For us the current situation in Russia presents nothing original, since capitalism is not distinguished by ownership of property but, rather, by the impossibility (realised through the force of the state) for the working class to take possession of the products, and by the payment of wages in money. The economic developments that have led to the current situation in which private individuals lend to the state, the state is itself an entrepreneur, the public debt swells, private possession of residences is permitted, houses are assigned to specialised workers – these developments are not due to the social manoeuvre of the NEP but to the reversal that has taken place in the political sphere and in the international position of the Russian state. The NEP left the state to the proletarian class that in fact already possessed it: retreats in the economic sphere by no means *necessarily* implied errors of revolutionary tactics and strategies at first, followed by the overturning of the position of the state.

German and Russian double revolution

55. Socialism could not be built in Russia alone, where in fact in February and October of 1917 the bourgeois and the proletarian revolutions joined forces — Also in Germany in 1848 a double, bourgeois and proletarian, revolution was attempted, unsuccessfully: the bourgeois revolution was victorious in the economic and social sphere, after the bourgeois-proletarian alliance had been defeated in the political sphere. – In Russia after the double, political and social, victory of 1917 came the proletarian social defeat, dateable to 1928. What remained was the capitalist social victory.

The enterprise is the essential factor of the current world capitalist phase

56. We do not have at our disposal documentary material for a detailed examination of the Russian economy, but the indications we do have permit us to make a reliable assessment. We see the essential factor of the current world capitalist phase to be the *enterprise* – the construction enterprise is an emblematic example – that works without a stable location, or installation, or equipment of its own, with minimum capital but for maximum profit, and can do so because it puts the state at its service, and the state provides it with capital and covers its losses.

The bureaucracy has a mediating function

57. The functionary is not a central figure but is simply a mediator. Lined up against the corps of state functionaries is the corps of counter-officials of the enterprises, swarming with consultants of all sorts intent on bending the state to the interests of their enterprises. In its outer forms and with very different names, we find an analogous mechanism in the USSR. The fact that the Moscow enterprises were able to give the city its Underground *as a gift* says it all about the sky-high profits they reap in all their other activities.

State capitalism

58. And this capitalism in Russia presents us with absolutely nothing that is unprecedented. The fact of state management directly connects it with a hundred other cases in the course of history. Take the example of the Italian Communes where, moreover, we find the first form of state investment for industrial production (private enterprise did not have sufficient capital for the building of ships, so the Communes provided it). Remember, it was states and kings

that equipped the first fleets and founded the imperial *companies*, seeds of the capitalist explosion! And now we have the recent example of the British nationalisations.

The Russian economy 'tends' toward and 'aims' at capitalism

59. The Russian economy's *tending* toward capitalism thus has a double sense. The first socialist and communist forms following the October Revolution degenerated, regressed, and were re-absorbed. The proletarian economy degenerated for a number of years, then degenerated definitively and disappeared, giving rise to mercantile and capitalist forms.

But, in the meantime, the entire vast sphere of the pre-capitalist, Asiatic, feudal Russian economy was powerfully *tending* toward [*aiming* at] capitalism, and this *tendency* is *positive* [is an *aim*] and, in its turn, is a premise of the world socialist revolution. Lenin and Trotsky themselves saw this necessity and were the pioneers of electrification, the only means of bringing production into line with the West, better to defeat imperialism. Stalin reversed the revolutionary international plan but gave a huge boost to industrialisation in the cities and the countryside. It must be said that this was an irresistible fact of the Russian social situation after the fall of the crumbling tsarist and boyar structure. Lenin glimpsed the possibility for his party to be the carrier of the proletarian political revolution throughout the world and, in the meantime, also of the capitalist social revolution in Russia: only with victories on both fronts could Russia become economically socialist. Stalin *says* that his party implements economic socialism in only one country (Russia); in fact, his state – and party – has been reduced to being the carrier of the only capitalist social revolution in Russia and Asia. Nevertheless, over the heads of individual men these historical forces work for the world socialist revolution.

Our evaluation of the Chinese revolution is no different. In China too, workers and peasants have struggled for a bourgeois revolution, in various phases, and they can go no farther. The alliance of the four classes – workers, peasants, intellectuals and industrialists – reproduces the alliances (fully in line with Marxism in doctrine and in tactics) in France 1789 and Germany 1848. Nevertheless the destruction of the age-old oriental feudal structure will be an accelerator of the world proletarian revolution, on the condition that it spreads to the European and American metropolises.

Current Marxism habitually focuses on the question of *who* is the personal profiteer and the consumer of capitalist exploitation, forgetting that Marx insisted again and again on the soul of capital and the depersonalisation of the capitalist, for whom the accumulation of surplus value counts more than his individual wallet and, indeed, the life of his very children. In light of this, it is not sufficient to describe the beneficiaries of the *fruit* of Russian capitalism (as we said, what counts is not the fruit but the entire plant) as 'crypto-entrepreneurs' and 'crypto-profiteers'. For us they are not functionaries of the Soviet bureaucracy but, rather, a separate stratum.

A bureaucrat in Russia is the simple mechanic in a factory, as he is in England today: all 'civil servants'.

Note that, curtain or no curtain, this mechanism or, more precisely, this network for the channelling of wealth *communicates* with the network of world capital. The foreign trade of the Soviet state is itself nothing other than a huge pair of scales that never weighs equivalents but continually cheats the masses of Soviet workers. Then there is the enormous *impasse* of the monetary manoeuvres that rebound between the legal and illegal markets of Asia and Africa. There are 'rents and loans' still waiting to be settled: after all, the rent and loan of millions of proletarian Russian corpses to defeat Germany was considered – by the Americans – a far better deal, economically speaking, than the production of the correspondent quantity of atomic bombs.

In Russia, today's co-existence and emulation, yesterday's blatant alliance with its pact to dismantle the communist parties of the West, and the full participation in the blocs of anti-Fascist liberation are, on the one hand, the confirmation of a political overturning to the point of counter-revolution; on the other, they are economic-market lots and premiums cashed by world capital at the expense of the supreme effort and the very life of the Russian worker. Hence, as party, power and state, the degeneration is no longer in progress but is an accomplished historical fact; and Trotsky's widow saw it very well for herself.[7] The historical function is in parallel on the economical and the political planes: the establishment of capitalism in all the Russias.

---

7 Natalia Sedova, Trotsky's widow, dissociated herself after World War II from the official position of the Trotskyite movement on the nature of the Russian state, seen as a workers' state that has degenerated due to its fundamentally counter-revolutionary political leadership but that still has a socialist economic base thanks to its nationalisation of the means of production.

4   The Lesson of Counter-revolution

Spartacus, the Christians, and the fall of slave society

60. The defeat of Spartacus at the foot of Vesuvius spelled, all at once, the political and social defeat of the slaves, with the social regime of slavery remaining
in power. But the victory of Diocletian's subsequent repression of the Christians, who were genuine political and class conspirators, led not to a consolidation of the slave regime but, with the triumph of the new religion, the social
fall of that regime and, subsequently, the advent of medieval feudalism.

Understanding the counter-revolution to prepare the revolution

61. When we are asked why Engels, after the defeat of the revolution of 1848,
decided to write *The Peasant War in Germany* and studied the peasant defeat
of 1525, we realise that it is necessary to understand the counter-revolution in
order to prepare the revolution of tomorrow.

This is what we need to do today – not to isolate a sector or a problem but to
fit it into the context of the whole.

Thus the bourgeoisie of the nineteenth century extolled its many and unfor-
gotten past defeats, in the act of building its definitive victory. Thus also the
proletariat that – as Marx says in *The Class Struggles in France, 1848 to 1850* –
not victory but a series of defeats 'qualify' for its world triumph, thanks to its
class party will be victorious by presenting itself anew as it was at the beginning of its struggle and in the programmatic, lapidary formulas, unsurpassed
because unsurpassable, of the *Communist Manifesto*.

Meanwhile it is right to profess and to defend the Marxist doctrine of history as an alternation of social classes, each made up of an ensemble of men
whose position is parallel to the forces and systems of production, since it can
be demonstrated that every social class in its entire historical course had a
continuous task and programme ever since its first achievements and battles.
Thus Christ's vindication of the enslaved multitudes links up with the fall of
the Roman Empire and of classical society; thus the first demands for civil
and peasant liberty link up with the storming of the Bastille and Bourgeois
Revolution throughout the world – and the banner waved is always the same.
And thus the modern proletariat, the first to free itself from the fideistic and
idealist formulations of its own aspirations, has all the more reason to be seen
as a genuine historical force in the Marxist sense. This proletariat cannot fail
to be victorious, since it is clear that, just arisen from the new order of productive forces, it mapped out its historical objective and the road, however

hard, that takes it there. A road that requires struggle against the manias of neo-Marxisms and of the 'new analyses'.

There are no 'new classes', just as there are no 'new types' of capitalism

62. The fact that we have been defeated, that therefore we are in a counter-revolutionary period, tells us why there are few of us and also why confusions arise among us. This, however, does not induce us to adulterate the theory of revolutionary Marxism by admitting that a *third* protagonist has come on the scene of society – a new class. We have no need to discover new types, new stages, no need to invent powers new to state capitalism that – as we said – presents us with nothing original, and was itself the first form through which the capitalist class asserted itself for the very first time, in the epoch of the Communes, in the year 1100.

Schema of Marxist centralism

63. In support of the exposition we have developed and to repeat the timely warning of the left regarding the degeneration of proletarian politics we attach a schema, representing the relations between the working class, the economic associations, the class political party, and the central party organs. The explanations added show that the two formulations, labourist and Stalinist, concordant in the formula of the mass party, stem from the same base in that economic determinants are replaced by determinants of the will of individuals, but both ultimately lead to the same result, namely, the imposition on the individual of decisions made by the top party leadership.

One and only one perspective of the international proletarian revolution

64. A point that has given rise to some doubt and hesitation: What is our *perspective*? As always, it is *one and only one*: the international proletarian revolution, when the conditions for it will have been realised. But today almost all these conditions are remote possibilities. As regards the current prospects, as we see it three hypotheses present themselves: the peaceful takeover of Russia by America, or a war between the USSR and the USA with the victory of the one or of the other.

First, Second, Third World War

65. Already in the case of the first imperialist war the victory of the strongest capitalist sector – England, which for two hundred years had not been defeated

and has never been invaded – inevitably created the least favourable conditions for the revolutionary attack of the international proletariat. A military defeat of that sector could have given rise to a less unfavourable course.

The same must be said for the second imperialist war, which ended with the victory of the London-New York axis. And for the third? We do not hesitate to affirm that a victory of the United States would represent the most sinister of eventualities. It is true that we lack class forces with which to intervene in these formidable events, and it is also true that we must maintain our autonomy with respect to these two equally anti-revolutionary powers, and fight the two 'crusadisms' to the end. But, finally, it is true that we cannot deviate from the only evaluation that is in keeping with the Marxist doctrine: the fall of the centre of capitalism entails the fall of the entire system, while the world bourgeois system can survive the fall of the weakest sector, given the modern method of military and state destruction of the defeated country and its reduction to passive colonialism. And it is precisely on this political line that capitalism can be prevented from absorbing the reactions to the policy of Stalinism that manifest themselves within the proletariat, so that these energies can be organised in the new organism that will be founded on the principles of revolutionary Marxism, once again becoming the active force of history.

Schema of Marxist centralism

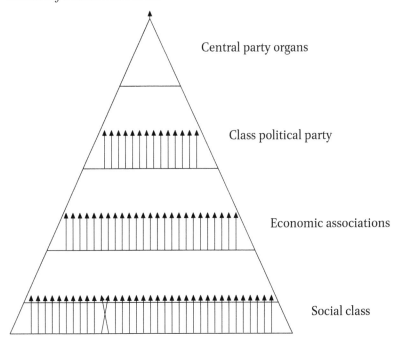

Central party organs

Class political party

Economic associations

Social class

1. The individuals that compose the class are driven to act in discordant directions. Some of them, if consulted and free to decide, would act in the interest of the opposing, ruling class.

2. The trade-union organisations tend to act in a direction contrary to the interest of the capitalists, but in an immediate sense and without the capacity to converge on one and only one action and one and only one aim.

3. The militants in the political party, as a result of their work within the class and within the associations, are prepared to direct their action according to one and only one revolutionary line.

4. The organs of party leadership, stemming from the base, act in the revolutionary direction, consistent with party theory, organisation, and tactical methods.

The position of the Left consists in the simultaneous struggle against the two deviations:

1. The base suffices to decide the action of the centre, *if it is democratically consulted* (workerism, labourism, social-democratism).

2. The supreme centre (political committee or party head) suffices to decide the action of the party and of the masses (Stalinism, Cominformism),[8] with the right to discover 'new forms' and 'new courses'.

Both deviations lead to the same result: the base is no longer the proletarian class but, rather, the people or the nation. Marx and Lenin are perfectly right: the result is a line of action that moves in the direction of the interests of the bourgeois ruling class.

---

8   Cominform (Communist Information Bureau) was founded in 1947 on the initiative of Stalin's Russia to ensure the exchange of information between the stalinist parties of the various European countries, though its true purpose was to provide the countries of Moscow's sphere of influence with a unitary structure capable of confronting US policy based on the Marshall Plan. It was dissolved in 1956.

CHAPTER 9

From 7 November 1917 to 7 November 1957: Forty Years of Organically Analysing Russian Events within the Dramatic Context of the Social and Historical Course of the World

1   Russia versus Europe in the Nineteenth Century[1]

1. A first battle over Russia's 'role' in European politics, waged by Marxist social-ists, dispelled the fallacy that the conclusions of historical materialism could not be applied to Russia. Just as, with regard to France, Germany and America, Marxist internationalism drew the social implications for world society of early capitalism in England, our school never doubted that that key to history would open the doors that had seemed to close for ever on bourgeois society and the routed Napoleonic bayonets, delaying everything for a century.

2. Marxism expected and advocated that in all European countries the great bourgeois revolution would follow in the tracks of France and England, and its outbreak in 1848 shook the whole of Central Europe. The overthrow of the feudal mode of production in Russia was especially predicted, awaited and demanded because Russia under the tsars assumed for Marx the function of an anti-liberal and anti-capitalist bastion of European reaction. During the period of European wars leading to bourgeois national settlements, which came to an end in 1871, each new war was presented as a useful development, in the sense that it might lead to defeat and disaster for St. Petersburg. For this reason, Marx was said to be a pan-Germanic, anti-Russian agent! In his eyes, as long as the resistance of tsarism remained intact, it was a barrier not only to the wave of bourgeois revolution but to the subsequent wave of European working-class revolution. The First (Working Men's) International fully supported the liber-ation movements of nations oppressed by the Tsar, the classic example being Poland.

3. In 1871, the historical doctrine of the Marxist school ended the period of socialist support for the wars that reconfigured Europe into modern states and for the struggles of the liberal revolution and national revival movements. The

---

1   *Il Programma Comunista*, Yr. 6, No. 21, 8–25 November 1957.

Russian obstacle still stood intact on the horizon, barring the way to working-class revolution against 'the confederate national armies', and sending its Cossacks out to defend not only holy empires but also capitalist parliamentary democracies, in the closed cycle of development in the West

4. Marxism soon concerned itself with the 'social affairs of Russia', studying its economic structure and the development of its class conflicts. The fact remains, however, that in studying the cycle of social revolutions it took account primarily of international relationships of forces, as Marx himself did in his massive construction on the stages of the march of the revolution and on the conditions regarding the maturity of the social structure. The problem then arose as to whether the progression could be shortened in Russia, which was still waiting to take the steps that Europe had taken at the beginning of the century and in 1848. Marx gave an answer in 1882 in his foreword to Vera Zasulich's translation of the *Communist Manifesto*, and in 1887 in a letter to a Russian journal. Is it possible, he was asked, for Russia to leap over the capitalist mode? His first response was partly positive: 'If the Russian Revolution becomes the signal for a workers' revolution in the West, so that the two supplement each other.' But his second response already said that the opportunity had been lost; he referred to the bourgeois land reform and abolition of serfdom in 1861, which had finally put an end to the primitive communism of the rural village, and for which Bakunin later became an apologist. For their part, Marx and Engels had fiercely distanced themselves from it: 'If Russia continues to pursue the path she has followed since 1861, she will lose the finest chance ever offered by history to a nation, in order to undergo all the fatal vicissitudes of the capitalist regime. [...] She will experience its pitiless laws like other profane peoples.' *Voilà tout*, Marx concluded. And it was all: the proletarian revolution having failed and been betrayed in Europe, today's Russia has fallen into capitalist barbarism. Engels's writings on the Russian communist *mir* showed that by 1875, and even more by 1894, the game seemed to have been won for the capitalist mode of production, which under the tsarist regime was dominant in the cities and to some extent in the countryside.

5. Capitalist industry in Russia, arising not so much through primary accumulation as through direct state investment, led to the growth of an urban proletariat and a Marxist workers' party. This was faced with the problem of the dual revolution, the same one that the early Marxists had confronted in Germany before 1848. The theoretical line of the party, represented in the first period by Plekhanov and then Lenin and the Bolsheviks, was perfectly consistent with European and international Marxism, especially in respect of the agrarian question that was so important in Russia. What contribution to the

dual revolution would be made by the rural classes – the serfs and the legally emancipated but poverty-stricken peasantry, whose conditions were worse than under pure feudalism? Everywhere the serfs and small peasants had supported the bourgeois revolutions, rising up against the privileges of the landed nobility. In Russia, characteristically, the feudal mode was not centrifugal as in Europe and Germany; the state power and the national army itself had been centralised for centuries; it was a progressive situation, historically speaking, until the nineteenth century. This was true not only politically for the history of the army, monarchy and state – which had been imported from abroad – but also for the social structure. The state, the crown and the (no less centralised) religious entities possessed more land than the feudal nobility; hence the emergence of a 'state feudalism', which withstood collision with the democratic French armies, and against which Marx for many years even invoked a clash with European, Turkish and German armies.

In essence, the road from state feudalism to state capitalism in Russia proved less protracted than the road from molecular feudalism to unitary capitalist states or from early autonomous capitalism to concentrated imperialist capitalism in Europe.

2   The Twilight of Late Feudalism

6. These centuries-old forms explain why a powerful bourgeois class on a par with those of the West never took shape in Russia; and why the interconnection of the two revolutions expected by Marxists proved even more difficult than in Germany. When Engels tackled the deficiency of the German revolutionary tradition, which, unlike in England, exhausted itself in the Reformation, he referred to the peasantry and the historic war of 1525 in which it was crushed by the cowardly action of urban bourgeois, Reformation clergy and gentry elements.[2] For Russia, the first contest between the Marxists and all other parties, both in doctrine and in actual struggle, was on the question of whether the bourgeois class, as absent from politics as the gentry or a rebellious clergy, could be replaced by the peasant class.

The historical formula opposed to ours was that the Russian revolution would be neither bourgeois nor working-class but a peasant revolution. We defined the peasant revolution as only a 'double' of the urban bourgeois revo-

---

2   Engels 1978, pp. 397–482.

lution. Throughout the long span of polemics and class wars, Marxism has for a hundred years or more rejected the monstrous perspective of a 'peasant socialism'; what happened in Russia was not a revolt by the lowest workers on the land seeking to become property-owners in utopian-egalitarian forms and eventually controlling the state as well as the urban classes (an impotent bourgeoisie and a new proletariat, which supposedly lacked the tremendous energy of a section of the European proletariat). The bourgeoisie is born national and does not transmit its energy across frontiers. The proletariat is born international and, as a class, is present in all 'foreign' revolutions. The peasantry is most accurately described as subnational.

This was the basis on which Lenin constructed the Marxist theory of the Russian revolution, in which the indigenous bourgeois class and peasantry were eliminated, and the working class selected, as the leading protagonist.

The development of this position is documented in our 'Russia e rivoluzione nella teoria marxista', published in issues of *Il Programma Comunista* from 21/1954 to 8/1955.

7. The two big questions were the land and politics. On the first, the revolutionary populist-socialists were for redistribution; the Mensheviks for municipal ownership; and the Bolsheviks for nationalisation. All these solutions, Lenin pointed out, were postulates of a bourgeois-democratic, not a socialist, revolution; but the third was the most robust and created the best conditions for proletarian communism. Again we shall do no more than quote from what he said in 'Two Tactics of Social Democracy': 'The concept of nationalisation of the land, in terms of economic reality, is a category of *commodity* and *capitalist* society.' In Russia today, only the minority *sovkhoz* sector of the land is at this level; the rest is even more backward.

On the question of power, the Mensheviks wanted to leave it for the bourgeoisie and then move into opposition (in 1917 they collaborated in a government with the bourgeoisie); the Populists were for a puppet 'peasant government' and they too ended up collaborating with Kerensky; the Bolsheviks were for the seizure of power and a democratic dictatorship of the proletariat and peasantry. Again in 'Two Tactics', Lenin explains as follows why he uses the adjective 'democratic' and the noun 'peasantry':

> Such a victory will by no means as yet transform our bourgeois revolution into a socialist revolution. [...] The [transformations] that have become a necessity for Russia, do not in themselves imply the undermining of capitalism, the undermining of bourgeois rule; on the contrary, they will, for the first time, really clear the ground for a wide and rapid, European, and not Asiatic, development of capitalism. [...] Such a victory will enable us

to rouse Europe, and the socialist proletariat of Europe, after throwing off the yoke of the bourgeoisie, will in its turn help us to accomplish the socialist revolution.[3]

So, what was to be done with the peasant 'allies'? Lenin was clear about this too. Marx had said that the peasants are 'the natural allies of the bourgeoisie'. Lenin wrote: '[In the] genuine and decisive struggle for socialism, [...] the peasantry as a landowning class will play the same treacherous, vacillating part as is now being played by the bourgeoisie in the struggle for democracy.'
At the end of the analysis I mentioned just now (No. 8/1955), we showed how Lenin followed through on his formula: seizure of dictatorial power in the bourgeois revolution, against the bourgeoisie itself and with the support of the peasants alone. The purpose was twofold: to arrive at the European proletarian revolution, without which there could be no victory of socialism in Russia; and to avoid a tsarist restoration, which would have been the restoration of the white guard of Europe.

3   The Indelible Russian Epic of the World Proletarian Revolution

8. In 1914 came the war that Marx had predicted between Germany and the united races of Slavs and Latins, and after the overthrow of the Tsar, as he had foreseen, came the Russian Revolution.
Russia was then allied with the democratic powers: France, Britain and Italy. Capitalists and democrats, together with the treacherous socialists who had embraced the cause of the war with Germany, now judged the Tsar, either as a coward or as tomorrow's secret ally of the Germans who had to be eliminated. The first Russian revolution of February 1917 was hailed by all the demopatriots and sociopatriots, who attributed it not to the weariness of the masses and the troops, but to skilful footwork on the part of Allied embassies. Although the majority of right-wing Russian socialists had not rallied to the war, they suddenly set their sights on a provisional government, which, in agreement with foreign powers, would continue the war. This was the basis on which a deal was sketched out with the bourgeois parties.

---

3 The quotation does not correspond *ad litteram* to what Lenin writes in 'Two Tactics of Social Democracy in the Democratic Revolution', but it is a faithful condensation of his thinking there.

The Bolshevik Party, at first hesitantly and then with vigour after Lenin and other leaders returned and Trotsky became a full member, called for the overthrow of the provisional government and its Menshevik and Populist supporters.

In our essay 'Struttura economica e sociale della Russia d'oggi', especially the first part,[4] we documented the historical sequence of events that led to the second revolution in October 1917 (whose 40th anniversary we are celebrating today). We also situated the struggle for power in 1917 in relation to the theoretical questions that had emerged previously in the life of the party.

9. The seizure of power by the Communist Party was expressed as a defeat of *all* the other parties, whether bourgeois or ostensibly working-class or peasant, that advocated continuation of the war alongside the Allies. The ensuing victory over these parties in the All-Russian Soviet rounded off their defeat and that of their allies outside the Soviet, taking the battle to the streets, dispersing the Constituent Assembly (which the provisional government had convoked), and finally breaking with the last ally of the Bolsheviks (the Left Socialist-Revolutionaries), who were strong in the countryside and supported the 'holy war' against the Germans.

This huge development did not proceed without grave struggles inside the Party, and its historical conclusion did not come until four terrible years later with the end of the struggle against the counter-revolutionary armies. These had their origins in the forces of the monarchy and feudal nobility (supported by Germany in 1918, both before and after the peace of Brest-Litovsk), and in those carefully mobilised by the democratic powers, including the Polish army.

Meanwhile, in European countries, there were no more than a few unsuccessful attempts to seize power by the working class, in a rush of enthusiastic solidarity with the Bolshevik revolution. The defeat of the German communists in January 1919, following the military defeat of Germany and the fall of the Imperial regime, was in practice decisive.

Lenin's historical line of march, which up to then had achieved formidable results – especially with the crucial acceptance of peace in March 1918 that an insane global democracy called betrayal – suffered a first major break. The subsequent years confirmed that the Russian economy, in a frightening state of collapse, would not be assisted by a victorious European proletariat. The power in Russia was solidly defended and saved, but it was not possible to reconfigure the Russian economic and social question along the lines that all Marxists

---

4   Bordiga 1976a, pp. 67–271. But see also 'Le grandi questioni storiche della rivoluzione in Russia', in the same volume, pp. 11–48.

had foreseen, that is, through the dictatorship of the international communist party over the productive forces – which were anyway overloaded, after the war in Europe.

10. Lenin had always ruled out – and, together with the genuine Bolshevik Marxists, continued to rule out until the end of his life – the possibility that, without repercussions of the Russian Revolution in Europe, the Russian economy could be transformed and acquire socialist characteristics while the European economy remained capitalist. Nevertheless, he always stuck to his position that the party of the proletariat, supported by the peasantry, should take power in Russia and hold it by dictatorial means.

Two historical questions arise here. First, can a revolution be defined as socialist if, as Lenin foresaw, it creates a power which, while awaiting fresh international victories, administers social forms of private economy when those victories have not come? The second question concerns the length of time for which such a situation is admissible, and whether there were alternatives apart from open political counter-revolution and the unconcealed return to power of a national bourgeoisie.

For us, October was socialist, and there were two not one alternatives to an armed counter-revolutionary victory (which did not happen): either degeneration inside the apparatus of power (state and party), such that it adapted to the administration of capitalist forms and declared it was abandoning the wait for world revolution (the alternative that actually occurred); or a long period during which the Marxist party remained in power, directly committing itself to support the revolutionary proletarian struggle in all other countries and bravely declaring, like Lenin, that social forms inside the country remained largely capitalist (and precapitalist).[5]

We shall prioritise the first of these questions; the second is linked to the social structure of Russia today, which is falsely claimed to be socialist.

11. The October Revolution should not be considered primarily in relation to immediate or very rapid changes in production forms and economic structure, but rather as a phase in the international political struggle of the proletariat. For it displays a number of powerful characteristics that go completely outside the confines of a national, purely anti-feudal revolution, and are not limited to the fact that the proletarian party stood at its head.[6]

a)   Lenin had established that the European and world war would have an imperialist character 'for Russia too' and that, as in the Russo-Japanese

---

5   See Lenin 1985, pp. 348–9.
6   Bordiga 1976a, pp. 13–36, 217–33, 294–319.

war that sparked the struggles of 1905, the proletarian party should therefore adopt an openly defeatist position. He did not argue this on the
grounds that the Russian state was undemocratic, but did so for the same
reasons that he said that socialist parties in other countries had the same
duty. There was not enough of a capitalist and industrial base in Russia to
provide the foundations for socialism, but there was enough to give the
war an imperialist character. The betrayers of revolutionary socialism –
who had espoused the cause of the imperialist bourgeois brigands, on the
pretext of defending the 'absolute value' of democracy against dangers
from Germany or Russia respectively – disowned the Bolsheviks for having left the war and the wartime alliances, and sought to stab October and
finish it off. Despite them, October prevailed over war and world imperialism; and it was a proletarian communist conquest alone.

b)   In triumphing over those people, October laid claim to the forgotten cards
       of revolution and restored Marxism from the theoretical collapse they
       had been plotting. It reconnected *any nation's* path to victory over the
       bourgeoisie with the use of revolutionary violence and terror, with the
       shredding of democratic 'guarantees', and with unlimited application of
       the *essential category of Marxism*: working-class dictatorship exercised by
       the communist party. It branded forever as dolts those who saw one man
       behind the dictatorship, and those who, trembling like democratic harlots
       before the spectre of such tyranny, saw in it an amorphous, unorganised
       class not built into the kind of political party that we find in our texts
       going back a century.

c)   At a time when the working class was artificially represented on the polit-
       ical (or worse: parliamentary) stage by different parties, the lessons of
       October, still intact, showed that the way ahead does not lie in the com-
       mon management of power by all and sundry, but in the elimination
       by force of that collection of capitalist servants until the single party
       achieves total power.

The greatness of the points outlined in the above three paragraphs lies in the
fact that, whereas Russia's special historical condition, with its despotic medieval survivals, might explain why it was an *exception* vis-à-vis the developed
bourgeois countries, it was precisely the *Russian road* that hammered home,
to the world's stunned terror or enthusiasm, the only worldwide path traced
by the universal theory of Marxism. At no point did Lenin – or with him the
admirable Bolshevik party – ever distance himself from that theory, in thought
or in deed.

It is ignoble that the names of Lenin and the Bolsheviks are exploited by
those who, in a wretched theatrical show, disgracefully pretend to celebrate

their glory. They apologise that Russia 'had to' follow the paths it did because of special circumstances and local conditions; and they promise or concede, as if it was their mission or in their power, that other countries will be brought to socialism by various other *national* roads, which their treachery or infamy will pave with all the materials that the pigsty of opportunism manages mixes together: liberty, democracy, pacifism, coexistence and emulation.

For Lenin, socialism needed the oxygen of revolution in the West. For those who line up in front of his inane mausoleum on 7 November, the oxygen is that the capitalism with which they seek to coexist and coalesce should make merry in the rest of the world.

4   The Ominous Parabola of the Suppressed Revolution

12. As to the other question concerning the economic structure of Russia after the October victory, the key points were already made by Lenin and have been dealt with more extensively elsewhere,[7] not by means of quotations taken out of context that can be inserted into short generic texts, but with the kind of illustration that relates all his formulations to the sequential historical conditions and relationship of forces of the time.

One of what we call the 'dual revolutions' brings three of the historical modes of production to bear on the theatre of operations, as it did for Germany before 1848. In Marx's classical view, it was a question of the medieval aristocratic-military Empire, the capitalist bourgeoisie and the proletariat, that is to say, of serfdom, wage labour and socialism. Industrial development in Germany was then limited, quantitatively if not qualitatively, but if Marx introduced the third of these figures it was because the technological-economic conditions existed for it in full in England, while the political conditions seemed to be present in France. The socialist perspective was certainly a presence in Europe, and the idea that German absolutism would soon collapse to the benefit of the bourgeoisie, and that the young proletariat would then pass onto the attack against the bourgeoisie, was bound up with the possibility of a workers' victory in France. Here, with the fall of the bourgeois monarchy of 1831, the proletariat of Paris and the provinces gave battle, which it fought selflessly but lost.

Great revolutionary visions are fertile even when history postpones their implementation. France provided the *politics*, with the attempts to found a workers' dictatorship in Paris in 1831 and 1848 and the actual creation of one

---

7   See Bordiga 1976a, esp. Part Two.

in 1871, although in the end the Communards gloriously succumbed arms in hand. Britain provided the *economics*. And Germany provided the *theory*, which prompted Leon Trotsky to claim the classical term 'permanent revolution' for Russia. But in Marx and Trotsky the revolution remained in an international setting, not in a wretched national framework. The Stalinists condemned permanent revolution in their campaign of ideological terror, but it is they who mimicked it in an empty parody soiled with patriotism.

Lenin's eyes in 1917, and all ours behind him, saw revolutionary Russia (industrially backward, like Germany in 1848) offer the flame of political victory and rekindle to the maximum the great theory that had grown up in Europe and the world. The productive forces, the economic potential, would have been attained by defeated Germany. The rest of tormented Central Europe would follow. A second wave would then hit the 'victors': France, Italy (where we hoped in vain to bring it forward in 1919), Britain, America and Japan.

But in the Russia/Central Europe core, the development of the productive forces in the direction of a socialist world would not encounter obstacles; all that was needed was the dictatorship of the communist parties.

13. What is interesting in this rough outline of our research is the other alternative: that Russia would remain alone, clutching its sudden political victory. The situation had a huge advantage in comparison with 1848, when all the belligerent countries had been in capitalist hands, and Germany had been more backward still.

Let us take a hard look at Lenin's internal perspective of awaiting revolution in the West. In *industry*, control of production and, later, its management by the state, meant destruction of the private bourgeoisie and therefore political victory, but it also involved economic administration in the capitalist market mode, developing only the 'bases' for socialism.[8] In *agriculture*, the destruction of any form of feudal servitude, together with cooperative management of large estates, tolerated the least possible degree of small-scale production for the market – the dominant form in 1917, inevitably encouraged by the economic and political destruction of the feudal mode. Landless labourers, the only 'poor peasants' truly dear to Lenin, were statistically less numerous, having been converted into landowners by the expropriation of rich farmers.

In the great debate of 1926, the question of tempos came to the fore.[9] Stalin said: if full socialism is impossible here, we should let go of power. Trotsky shouted that he believed in the world revolution, but that they would have to

---

8   Ibid.
9   See 'La Russia nella Grande Rivoluzione e nella società contemporanea' (1956), reprinted in Bordiga 1976a, pp. 691–742.

stay in power awaiting it for another 50 years. In reply, it was pointed out that Lenin had spoken of Russia being isolated for 20 years. We have documented elsewhere[10] that Lenin meant 20 years of 'good relations with the peasantry', after which, even in an economically non-socialist Russia, class struggle would flare up between workers and peasants over the elimination of small-scale rural production and private agrarian capital that were progressively eroding the revolution.

But in the hypothesis of a European workers' revolution, small-scale land ownership – which lives on ineradicably in today's kolkhozes – would have been rapidly squeezed out, without any postponement.

14. Marxist economic science has shown that Stalinism fell even further behind what Lenin saw as a distant prospect. Not 20 but 40 years have now passed, and relations with kolkhoz farmers are pretty 'good'; but they are pretty 'bad' with workers in state-run industry, who work as wage-earners in market conditions until now worse than those in undisguised forms of capitalism. The kolkhoznik is treated well as a co-operator within the kolkhoz (a private capitalist rather than state-owned form), and even better as a small-scale manager of land and spare capital.[11]

There is no need here to recall the bourgeois features of the Soviet economy, ranging from trade through inheritance to savings. Just as the economy is not directed to the abolition of exchange through money equivalents or to non-pecuniary remuneration of labour, so its relations between worker and peasant run opposite to the communist abolition of the difference between agricultural and industrial labour, manual and mental labour.

Forty years since 1917, and 30 since Trotsky set 50 years as the maximum tolerable period of rule (which will take us to around 1975), the proletarian revolution has not happened in the West. The murderers of Leon, and of Bolshevism, have largely built up industrial capitalism, that is to say, the basis for socialism, but their success has been more limited in the countryside; and they are another 20 years behind on Lenin's prediction in ending the henhouse form of kolkhozism, a degeneration of classical free-market capitalism, which they would now like to inject into industry and people's lives in covert agreement with capitalists abroad. Production crises will hit both these areas of emulation even before 1975, sweeping away the illusory Arcadia of populist capitalism, and the haystacks, chicken coops, micro-garages and beggarly installations of the crude, modern *domestic kolkhoz ideal*.[12]

---

10   Ibid., pp. 698–9.

11   Ibid., pp. 478–525.

12   On the 'revenge of rural egotism' in the shape of the kolkhoz, see ibid., pp. 491–501.

15. In a recent study of the global dynamic of trade, some bourgeois US economists calculate that the present race to capture markets, based on the sinister
America-to-the-rescue puritanism of the postwar period, will reach crisis point
in 1977. Twenty years still separate us, then, from the new flame of permanent
revolution envisaged in an international framework – which tallies with the
conclusions of the debate way back in 1926, and with our own research in the
last few years.

If there is not to be another setback for the proletariat, the renewal of theory
must not take place, as in Lenin's huge effort in 1914, after a third world war has
already lined up the workers beneath all their wretched flags; it must happen
long before that, with the organisation of a world party that does not hesitate
to propose its own dictatorship. Such corrosive hesitation is to be found in the
weakness of those who regret the imbecilic venture in petty personal dictatorship, often lined up with those who explain Russia in terms of palace coups
organised by creepy little men, demagogues or time-serving generals.

During the 20 years in question, a major crisis of world industrial production and the trade cycle, comparable to the American crisis of 1932 but not
sparing Russian capitalism either, may underpin the return of determined but
visible proletarian minorities to Marxist positions, miles away from the apology
of anti-Russian pseudo-revolutions of the Hungarian type (in which peasants,
students and workers fought arm in arm in the Stalinist manner).

Is it possible to hazard a guess at the shape of the future international
revolution? Its central area will be Germany (including the East), Poland and
Czechoslovakia, the part of Europe where, following the ruin of the Second
World War, a powerful revival of the productive forces is taking place. The proletarian insurrection, which will follow the ferocious expropriation of all the
owners of 'populised' capital, will probably have its epicentre between Berlin
and the Rhine, and soon draw in northern Italy and north-eastern France.

Such a perspective is incomprehensible to dimwits who do not wish to grant
an hour's reprieve to any of the existing capitalisms, on the grounds that all
are the same and should be lined up and shot, even if they dispose of breech-
loading syringes instead of atomic missiles.

As proof that Stalin and his successors have industrialised Russia in a revolutionary manner, while castrating the world proletariat in a counter-revolutionary manner, Russia will be the reserve of productive forces for the new
revolution, and only later a reserve of revolutionary armies.

With the third wave, a communist continental Europe will exist politically
and socially – or the last Marxist will have disappeared.

English capitalism has already burned up its reserves of Labourist *embour-
geoisement* of the workers with which Marx and Engels already reproached

it. When the time comes, even United States capitalism – which is ten times more vampiric and oppressive – will lose its reserves in the ultimate showdown. Today's lurid *emulation* will be replaced with the social antagonism of *mors tua vita mea*.

16. This is why we have not commemorated the 40 years that have passed, but the 20 that remain to pass – and their eventual winding-up.

The Critique of Triumphant Capitalism

∴

CHAPTER 10

Property and Financial Capital

1   Monopoly Necessarily Derives from Allegedly Free Competition[1]

The basic position of the bourgeois economy is that selection of the socially most useful enterprises is ensured by the phenomena of the free market and by an equilibrium of prices based on the availability and the need of products.

Marxism demonstrated that, even supposing for a single moment the existence of an economy of free competition, production, and exchange, which is in fact a bourgeois fiction and a petty-bourgeois illusion, the laws of accumulation and of circulation that act within it lead to terrible crises of overproduction, destruction of products and labour-power, the closing of factories, unemployment, and general misery. It is the successive waves of such crises that heighten the antagonism between the rich and powerful capitalist class and the misery of the employed and unemployed masses, which are driven to organise themselves in classes and to revolt against the system that oppresses them.

The bourgeoisie, the ruling class, at first found a sufficient base for its unity in the political and administrative state, its 'committee of interests' despite the fiction of elective institutions, in which it governed by means of those parties which, as revolutionary oppositions, had led the anti-feudal revolution. The force of this power was immediately directed against the first manifestations of pressure coming from the working class.

The organisation of workers in economic trade unions remained within the limits of the struggle to lower the rate of surplus value; its further organisation in a political party expresses its capacity, as a class, to set as its objective the overthrow of the power of the bourgeoisie and the abolition of capitalism, with a radical reduction of the quantity of labour, and an increase of consumption and of general welfare.

For its part the antagonist, the bourgeois class, compelled to accelerate the accumulation of capital, took steps to cope with the enormous dissipation of productive forces, the consequences of the periodical crises, and the effects of the workers' organisation. At a certain point it developed forms (already present in the course of primitive accumulation) of understandings, agree-

---

1   *Prometeo*, second series, February 1951; republished in *Proprietà e capitale*, Florence: Iskra, 1980 (writings 1948–52), pp. 120–3. The title and section titles are the editor's.

ments, associations and alliances between entrepreneurs. These forms were limited at first to market relations, both in the sale of products and in the purchasing of labour-power, with commitments to respect given indices, thereby avoiding competition. Later they were extended to the entire productive mechanism: monopolies, trusts, cartels, associations of enterprises that make similar products (horizontal) or provide for the successive transformations that lead to given products (vertical).

For this phase of capitalism, as a confirmation of the rightness of Marxism, which 'had proved that free competition gives rise to the concentration of production, which, in turn, [...] leads to monopoly', we have Lenin's classic description: Imperialism.[2]

2   Capitalism Becomes Increasingly Parasitical

The entrepreneur needs, in addition to a factory and to machines, a liquid monetary capital, which he advances to purchase raw materials and pay wages, and then takes back when he sells his products. As with the factory and the machines, he is *not necessarily* the official owner of this capital either. Without losing ownership of the enterprise, which is protected by law, the entrepreneur or his company has this capital provided by banks, which charge an annual rate of interest.

Having reached his ideal form, the bourgeois presents himself to us as free of and without immovable or movable property, without money, and above all without scruples. He no longer invests and risks anything *of his own*, but the total product remains legally in his hands, and therefore also the profit. It is the bourgeois who has stripped *himself* of his property, obtaining many advantages; now it is his strategic position that he must be stripped of. This is a social, historical and juridical position that falls only with the political revolution, premise of the economic revolution.

The bourgeois class, through the apparent separation of industrial from financial capital, actually tightens the connection between them. The supremacy of financial operations leads to a situation in which big trusts and cartels control small enterprises and the small associations of enterprises and subsequently swallow them up, nationally and internationally.

The financial oligarchy that concentrates immense amounts of capital in very few hands and exports it from one country to another, investing it in one

---

2 Lenin 1971a, Chapter I, p. 180.

country after another, is an integral part of the entrepreneurial class itself, the centre of whose activity is shifting incessantly from productive techniques to business manoeuvres.

Moreover, with the system of joint-stock companies, the capital of the industrial enterprise composed of buildings, equipment and ready money is officially owned by the stockholders, who take the place of the hypothetical landlord, lessor of machinery, and credit institution. The rents and leasing fees and interest on the loans take the form of an always modest return or 'dividend' distributed to the stockholders by the 'management', which is to say, by the enterprise. The enterprise is a distinct organisation, which enters share capital on the *debit side* of its balance-sheet, and with various manoeuvres loots its creditors; this is in fact its central form of accumulation. The banking manoeuvre, with share capital in its turn, performs this service of plundering people with small amounts of money for industrial and business groups.

The production of super-profits swells more and more as we move away from the figure of the captain of industry, who was a source of socially useful innovation thanks to his technical skill. Capitalism increasingly becomes *parasitical*; that is, instead of earning and accumulating little while producing much and having much be consumed, it earns and accumulates enormously while producing little and satisfying social consumption badly.

CHAPTER 11

Welfare Economics

The word 'welfare' signifies well-being, prosperity, a high standard of living.[1] It is fashionable in America, having become a sort of watchword for the defenders of the current course of things: euphoria, ever greater spending, ever greater production, and the claim to demonstrate that average well-being is constantly rising.

This trend tells us many interesting things. Let us listen to what J.J. Spengler of Duke University has to tell us in his very recent article, *Welfare Economics and the Problem of Overpopulation*.[2]

The doctrine in question sharply contrasts with Marxist doctrine, and yet its approach is of the greatest interest to us because it demonstrates that our rival theoretician must now accept open combat and can no longer shut himself up in the muddle of subjectivism or of wavering and deliberately incomprehensible mercantilism.

Mathematically and historically speaking, with this extremely modern doctrine the defence of capitalism enters a space that is better illuminated.

First of all, by giving maximum importance to the famous index of 'individual income' in relation to 'national income' – and the relation that connects them is precisely the knotty problem of demographic growth – the economists of capitalism enter the arena of *production*, and acknowledge the fact that mercantile tricks will not allow them to escape the relation between productive force and the social number of consumers. We shall see that for these theoreticians prices are no longer uncontrollable 'natural' facts that are superior to the social will; they now contend that if the capitalist economy wants to resist, it will have to shape the 'price structure' according to given plans. Let us say immediately that they are referring to the level of prices in various sectors of consumption, and we shall see them immediately opt for a high price of foodstuffs and a low price of manufactured goods! We knew it all along!

These theoreticians no longer seek Fisher's *equations of exchange* but, rather, formulate – after their fashion – a *production function*. Spengler adopts the pro-

---

1 *il programma comunista*, Yr. 3, No. 19, 15–29 October 1954; republished in *Economia marxista ed economia controrivoluzionaria*, Milan: Iskra, 1976 (writings 1954–57), pp. 127–34 and 153–6. The text consists of excerpts from '*La struttura tipo della società capitalistica nello sviluppo storico del mondo contemporaneo*'.

2 See Spengler 1954, pp. 128–38.

duction function of Douglas Cobb [...] while at the same time opposing it to that of Marx. Naturally in the production function in his article classes play a very minor role, unlike the major role they play in the quantities we use. But the reasons for this are quite clear.

Historically, it is interesting how this author, without polemising with Marx, whom he neither names nor quotes, goes farther *back* than Marx, and declaredly connects this brand new school of 'welfare' with – of all people! – Malthus, and with his well-known works of the 1820s, *Principles of Political Economy* and *An Essay on the Principle of Population*.

For Spengler, Malthus glimpsed the solution that made it possible to adapt foodstuffs to population; or even to improve the first index with respect to the second. Malthus drafted two models: the first, for the phase in which a society is able to increase production in proportion to the number of its members; the second, in which it is actually able to improve the ratio. Thus, in both cases, Malthus supersedes his famous formula (considered more literary than scientific) that population increases in geometric proportion, while food production only in arithmetic proportion.

1   Good for You, Malthus!

Behold old Malthus elevated to the rank of benefactor of human well-being! His real theory was not that births had to be reduced by 'moral restraint', that is, by chastity dictated by reasoning and asceticism, and it didn't say population had to be compressed at all costs either! For him population could even remain constant or grow slowly, and there could still be sufficient products. What he proposed was perfectly clear: make access to food products difficult and keep the working class in hardship; make luxury objects cheaper and more accessible.

No doubt about it, such things are better said by the unbridled admirer a full century later. For us, this parallel is precious: it confirms our thesis that at a given historical watershed theories of class are defined and counterposed, and that social science advances by great centennial explosions and not by the tiresome trickling of half-baked scholars and slipshod compilations that, as Marx said, usurp the name of scientific research.

Malthus, like Ricardo, and like Marx, wrote at a decisive turning point of history: capitalism is taking clear shape against the old feudal economic systems; proletarian socialism is already drafting its theoretical critique of the transition from feudalism to capitalism and of the development of the new bourgeois society.

Here is how Spengler reports the doctrine of the rediscovered Master:

> While Malthus seems to have been aware of the import of price-structure changes, he did not clearly specify their origin, probably because he had model (2) equilibrium in mind [average standard of living rising despite the increase of population], and because he did not attach much importance to the possible effect of such changes under model (1) conditions [average standard of living constant with increase of population]. Apparently he was aware that a substitution effect would be set up against (in favour of) more children by a change in the price-structure embracing a relative increase (decrease) in the prices of elements entering into the cost of reproducing and rearing children and a relative decrease (increase) in other prices. For he [Malthus] described it as 'desirable' that the 'habitual food' of the common people 'be dear' and that the prices of conveniences, decencies, and luxuries be sufficiently low to extend their custom through the population. Presumably, having in mind model (2) conditions, he was supposing that the introduction of this kind of price structure would check natality, stimulate consumption, generate wants, cushion per capita income against population pressure, and retard the transformation of model (2) into model (1) conditions.[3]

2   Our Response

Before any other development and to demonstrate that Malthus is properly presented and rightly followed by modern American super-capitalism, allow us to report a few words written by Marx, many generations before these Spenglers and their 'cynical optimism'.

The passages, truly classic and decisive, are from his *Theories of Surplus Value*.

> Malthus's theory of value gives rise to the whole doctrine of the necessity for continually rising unproductive consumption which this exponent of over-population (because of shortage of food) preaches so energetically. [...]
>
> Malthus correctly draws the conclusions from his basic theory of value. But this theory, for its part, suits his purpose remarkably well – an apolo-

---

3   Spengler 1954, pp. 133–4.

gia for the existing state of affairs in England, for landlordism, 'State and Church', pensioners, tax-gatherers, tenths, national debt, stock-jobbers, beadles, parsons and menial servants ('national expenditure') assailed by the Ricardians as so many useless and superannuated drawbacks of bourgeois production and as nuisances. For all that, Ricardo championed bourgeois production insofar as it [signified] the most unrestricted development of the social productive forces, unconcerned for the fate of those who participate in production, be they capitalists or workers. He insisted upon the *historical* justification and necessity of this stage of development. His very lack of a historical sense of the past meant that he regarded everything from the historical standpoint of his time. Malthus also wishes to see the freest possible development of capitalist production, however only insofar as the condition of this development is the poverty of its main basis, the working class, but at the same time he wants it to adapt itself to the 'consumption needs' of the aristocracy and its branches in State and Church, to serve as the material basis for the antiquated claims of the representatives of interests inherited from feudalism and the absolute monarchy. Malthus wants bourgeois production as long as it is not revolutionary, constitutes no historical factor of development but merely creates a broader and more comfortable material basis of the 'old' society.

On the one hand, therefore, [there is] the working class, which, according to the population principle, is always redundant in relation to the means of life available to it, over-population arising from under-production; then [there is] the capitalist class, which, as a result of this population principle, is always able to sell the workers' own product back to them at such prices that they can only obtain enough to keep body and soul together; then [there is] an enormous section of society consisting of parasites and gluttonous drones, some of them masters and some servants, who appropriate, partly under the title of rent and partly under political titles, a considerable mass of wealth gratis from the capitalists, whose commodities they pay for above their value with money extracted from these same capitalists; the capitalist class, driven into production by the urge for accumulation, the economically unproductive sectors representing prodigality, the mere urge for consumption. This is moreover [advanced as] the only way to avoid over-production, which exists alongside over-population in relation to production. The best remedy for both [is declared to be] over-consumption by the classes standing outside production. The disproportion between the labouring population and production is eliminated by part of the product being devoured by non-producers and idlers. The disproportion arising from over-production by the capitalists [is eliminated] by means of over-consumption by revelling wealth.[4]

3   Spengler Is Not Alone

It is not only Spengler who follows in the Malthus's footsteps. The nostalgic feudal English bishop and the modern 'spokesmen' of big capital share the same historical law: in order to have more product and fewer consumers, consumption by the working masses, especially of basic necessities, must be kept down, but at the same time the full product must be kept up. So, Malthus sees the parasites of the pre-bourgeois retinue as the solution to the problem of how to consume the extra product; the ultra-modern solution is the 'price structure', equivalent to 'consumption structure'. The structure championed at both ends of this long span of time is the same: few foodstuffs, many 'differentiated' – luxury – consumer products.

The ultra-moderns replace the parasitical band of nobles and their mobs with the same indistinct mass of national consumers, forcing them to consume like imbeciles: little food, lots of supplies for fictitious needs.

They are convinced that a mass that is over-stimulated and *addicted* but undernourished will reproduce less and their famous 'per capita' product will remain high.

We have responded to this for over a hundred years, ever since we adopted the classical word *proletariat* – which comes from *'prole'*, meaning *children*. The overworked and exploited mass has *too many* children, and the law goes not towards balance but towards imbalance and revolution.

The two laws are diametrically opposed. Every modern thinker of the ruling class is tormented by the demographic problem. It is not only Spengler who sees salvation in hunger. Doctor Darwin Jr foresees five billion people a century from now – and terrifying figures *after that*, portending the destruction of the species. A certain Professor Hill raises his sword against the application of scientific progress to save human lives. The population of India increases by five million every year. He proposes we not use penicillin and DDT there, as a demographic inhibitor, mindful of the frightful historic epidemics and famines in that country.

---

4 Marx, *Theories of Surplus Value*, Chapter XIX, Sections 11 and 12 (translation modified); available at http://www.marxists.org/archive/marx/works/1863/theories-surplus-value/ch19.htm.

The demographic 'optimists' like our English friend[5] Calver and our German friend Fuchs think, by contrast, that the demographic increase will lead to *improved* living conditions, and uphold the hypocritical formula of 'freedom from need' and of the struggle against poverty. Fuchs sees not five but eight billion a century from now, and insists that, up to ten billion, we'll manage to eat.

But Mr Cyril Burt, another British friend, is so kind as to give us a 'theory of the stupid'. He notes that the well-to-do classes are reproducing less and less while the poor are reproducing more and more – and the same thing is happening with advanced white versus savage peoples. As he sees it, then, the course is heading towards an increase, by heredity, in the mass of the uncultured (for him 'worker' equals 'stupid'), and in the mass of non-white peoples who will overwhelm us Europeans. He claims that his years of study have demonstrated an increase in social stupidity over the past 40 years. What else can we say! He's right!

But all these 'friends' of ours are stuck in a blind alley because they want to discover the meaning of this course while assuming aprioristically that everything must remain as it is today: division of society into classes, and mercantilism.

We say that as soon as class division is socially overcome – as soon as the mercantile link between production and consumption is abolished – the problem will solve itself, with reduced production, ultra-reduced social working time, and population increase reduced and, in some cases, reversed.

A consumer structure not for the 'stupid'. Yes, my friends, you're right, it's the stupid who reproduce, and today they make you sweat blood to keep your figure for 'per capita' [income] from decreasing.

The true defence of the species is also against the inflation of the species. But it has only one name: communism. Not the mad accumulation of capital.

[...]

4   Economic History

Marx's classic chapters on primitive accumulation show the ways in which emerging capitalism satisfied its hunger for labour-power. One of the first ways was by increasing the length of the working day to its maximum physical limit.

---

5   'Friend' (here and below) has been added by the translator to render the extremely sarcastic tone of this part of the text [note by G. Donis].

Then, the bringing of women and children into the field of work – something practically unknown in the artisan ages, and made possible by the simplicity of the work to be done in collective-labour farms and then in factories. And, finally, the emptying of the countryside and urbanism.

Just think of the enormous social differences of production between the countryside and the city! For agriculture, from time immemorial the active population tended to coincide with the total population, or very nearly so. Not only did men and women alike work the land, but also children and the elderly were systematically utilised for suitable, also semi-domestic functions. It is true, however, that this totalitarian utilisation of the labour force was limited by the hours dictated by the seasons, and by the almost total lack of artificial lighting. Hence the day's working hours varied greatly, but the total number of annual working hours had a limit that was invariable.

Despite all these conditions, the technical productivity of labour could vary very little: the very surface over which farm labour has to spread made it impossible to concentrate the number of workers and the successive operations in tighter and tighter spaces.

Hence in the countryside, despite the presence of capitalist enterprise with wage-earning employees, the characteristic phenomena of capitalism could not enjoy the same murderous pace they had in the city. What is more, cooperative labour and the technical division of labour, which [in the cities] had quickly multiplied the possibilities of manufacturing a hundred times over, had far less influence on work in the countryside.

Manufacturing, then, had ineluctably drawn labour-power away from agriculture, in such a way that all these unfavourable elements ended up by compensating for the little that the applied sciences had contributed in terms of increasing the production intensity of agricultural victuals per acre of cultivated land.

Here we find the root of the classical concerns that, as the general population increases, the volume of food production cannot keep pace – when, on the other side of the fence, nothing prohibits the unlimited exaltation of the production of manufactured goods and of non-agrarian products and services. For this over-production the labour-power made available is sufficient. Indeed, from capital's standpoint, to swallow it all it would be good if the population were to rise even more.

Hence the direction of development is towards an ever greater accumulation of capital – especially industrial capital. With this development the number of proletarians increases, both in an absolute sense and relative to the total population, forming Marx's great reserve industrial army, made up of persons without property, of men now stripped of any individual reserve, *separated from their working conditions.* This is an 'army' that suffers the consequences of the alternating waves of advance and of crisis that has characterised the general march of accumulation throughout history.

As for the phenomenon of the concentration of enterprises, if capital increases, the number of capitalists decreases, and further along in the process this number diminishes both in relation to the population and in an absolute sense. Therefore it is not a sacrifice of the personal standard of living of the members of the privileged class that threatens the progress of the trend towards accumulation. No, since they are so few, the social plague is not in their personal consumption. Not even when they were many was this the case, because then they were engaged in earnest to 'rolling forward the wheel of history'.

5   Parasitism and Illness[6]

Today's decrepit Western capitalism has therefore this possibility: to render parasitical the consumption of the general producer himself, through the pandered 'price structure' and the structure of the 'consumer sector'.

The accumulation of greater capital with the necessary mobilisation of ever greater labour-power, becoming an end in itself, means that every increase of labour productivity, however much it has surpassed every old and new forecast, is an effective incentive to *produce even more.*

As long as the economy remains within entrepreneurial and mercantile limits, the solution is not made visible. But we *know* what it is: instead of consuming more in artificial needs, which not only pass from necessity to usefulness, but from usefulness to uselessness, and from there to harmfulness, which is worse than privation, *stop saving – stop accumulating –* and reduce the labour supplied, in the only way possible – namely, by reducing the length of the working day.

As we have said in all our propaganda for a century and more, this is the only concrete significance that can be attached to the liberation not of the person but, indeed, of the human species from the pitiless necessity determined by the forces of the natural environment in which human beings live.

Not being able to stop the infernal pace of accumulation, this humanity, parasite of itself, burns and destroys surplus profits and surplus values in a

---

6   Bordiga contrasts *malessere* (illness, discomfort, malaise – literally 'ill-being') with *benessere* (well-being, prosperity, or 'wellness'), also the Italian translation of the English word 'welfare'.

circle of madness, and makes its conditions of existence ever more straitened and senseless.

The accumulation that made humanity skilful and powerful now makes it tortured and stupid, until the day when the relation – the historical function it has had – will be dialectically overturned.

This passage from 'progressivism' – if for a moment the word has serious meaning – to parasitism is not only of the bourgeois mode of production.

At the birth of feudalism each class had a useful function of its own. The nomad could not have become a farmer, and the now settled nomad of the classical age would have been overwhelmed and scattered, if the arm-wielding class had not taken up the task of circumscribing a territory in which to work and sow, and of defending it until the harvest and beyond.

But by Malthus's day this function had changed its historical role, and the descendants of the ancient condottiere did not defend but attacked and op- pressed the poor people working the land.

It is not fortuitous that an analogous cycle of capitalism has led to the present situation of the monstrous volume of a production nine tenths of which is useless for the healthy life of the human species, and has given rise to a doctrinal superstructure reminiscent of Malthus's position, crying out – at the cost of raising the hounds of hell! – for consumers who will swallow incess- antly whatever accumulation spews out.

The school of *wellness* – with its claim that the individual absorption of con- sumption can rise beyond all limits, swelling the few hours left after necessary labour and repose with no-less-necessary steps and rites and morbid follies – actually expresses the *illness* of a society in ruin. Seeking to write the laws of its survival it does nothing but confirm the course – uneven perhaps, but inexor- able – of its horrible agony.

CHAPTER 12

The Law of Hunger

Marx develops a number of hypotheses on the taking into cultivation of lands whose fertility is progressively better, progressively worse, and criss-crosses between the best and the worst lands already tilled.[1] He shows that however the series is chosen it always leads to the formation of differential rents, with an increase of the total rent. In this way he refutes West, Malthus and Ricardo,[2] who claim that there is always a progression from the best to the worse soil, or, in other words, that *agricultural fertility constantly declines*. In the capitalist mode of production things proceed towards a rise of the real price of wheat, even when there is a substantial increase of the overall cultivated area and improved production per unit of cultivated land.

Hence it is strictly a notion of *capitalist* society that there is no use investing capital to increase the fertility of the soil (better seen in the study of the second form) because, while the product does increase, the profit on the successive advances of capital decreases, and this *horrifies* capital.

The point Marx wants to make here is this: in the sphere of agriculture, the market value of the entire product is always greater than its production price. While it is well known that in the sphere of industry, in spite of overprofits and underprofits, and even business losses, which intersect in time and in space, the total social product has, in theory, a market price equal to the production price, that is, to the value calculable on the basis of labour-time.

In fact, in Marx's famous Table,[3] in all four cases the market price is the same: 60 shillings, and so the entire product is sold for 600. But the production price differs: 1 quarter of A at 60; 2 quarters of B at 30, makes 60; 3 quarters of C at 20, makes 60 again; 4 quarters of D at 15, makes 60 again. This makes for a total of 240 shillings for ten quarters, and therefore 24 shillings per quarter is the average production price.

---

1   *Il programma comunista*, Yr. 3, No. 6, 19 March–2 April 1954; republished in *Mai la merce sfamerà l'uomo*, Milan: Iskra, 1979 (writings 1953–54), pp. 181–6.
2   See Marx 1991, pp. 798 ff.
3   See Marx 1991, p. 791. In this Table Marx assumes four pieces of land for the production of wheat, of equal size but whose soil differs in fertility (A, B, C, D, in progression, from the worst to the best soil), with the same sum of capital invested in each. In all four cases the market price of a quarter of wheat (8 bushels) is the same: 60 shillings. The Table illustrates the first of the forms of differential rent examined by Marx.

Therefore the market price represents 250 percent of the production price of the grain.

If the same criterion were to be applied to our Table of today's values[4] and with smaller differences of fertility (from 5 to 7.75 [quintals per hectare], while in fact there are cases of production of over 40 quintals [1 quintal = 100 kg.] per hectare [2,471 acres]: nevertheless to be treated under the second form, namely, increased capital)[5] we would have 5 quintals at a production price of 8,000 lire; 6.5 at 6,200; 7 at 5,700; 7.75 at 5,100. The total is 160,000 lire for 26.25 quintals and the average production price is 6,100 lire per quintal versus the market price of 8,000, which is thus 131 percent more expensive.

But what is fundamental here is Marx's illustration of this inexorable law: *capitalism = high cost of bread*. This law does not derive from the fact that capitalists are individual persons or companies or collectivities or states. No! It derives from the mercantile nature of exchange, from the infamous *law of value*, which, say the Stalinists – from the Pontiff to the stooge – rules the capitalist and the socialist economy alike!

Let us ponder, then, over Marx's words.

1   The Mercantile Cancer

This is determination by a *market value [rather than by the production price]* brought about by competition on the basis of the capitalist mode of production; *it is competition* that produces a *false social value*.[6]

What does Marx mean here by *social value*? He means the opposite of the mercantile value that arises from the exchange between two economic individuals: an elementary fact on which the bourgeois economy would like to construct the entire economic mechanism. The social value of a product is the entire sum of labour that it costs society, divided by the entire product obtained, calculated in the average time of social labour. This value includes accumulated labour, act-

---

4   On page 176 of this text Bordiga presents and discusses a Table structured like Marx's but with the figures updated to 1953.

5   Bordiga refers here to Marx's second form of differential rent, in which 'sums of capital are invested successively in time on the same piece of land with varying productivity, or invested alongside one another on different pieces of land' (see Marx 1991, Chapter 40, p. 812). In this second form the sums of capital invested are increased.

6   Ibid., p. 799. In the entire series of quotes, the italics in brackets are Bordiga's.

ive labour, and also an amount of surplus labour for general services: as long as none of the terms takes on the form of a commodity or of capital:

> This results [*the result of false social value*] from the *law of market value* to which agricultural products are subjected. The determination of the market value of products [*as long as this law is in force*], i.e. also products of the soil, is a *social act*, even if performed by society unconsciously and unintentionally, and it is based necessarily on the exchange-value of the product and not on the soil and the differences in its fertility.[7]

Pay hazardous homage to the law of mercantile value, of the balance between equivalent exchange values and equal use values, and you will be able to do nothing to stop every quarter of grain from being sold for 60 shillings, without wondering whether it is one of those produced at 60, or at 30, or at 20, or at 15 shillings per quarter, and without anything's making it possible for them all to be sold at 24. Note well that Marx, here, launches his attack not against the 10 shillings of normal surplus value that go to capital, but against the overprofits-rents that are 36 shillings on average. All together, all the free and voluntary demands *chosen* by the millions of acts of the market upon which (also in Russia) they want to base the bourgeois economy leads to no other regulation than that of a society which, also as a whole, is irresponsible and powerless.

And now once again (have you made a necklace with these pearls?) we come to the explanation and definition of communist society:

> If we imagine that the capitalist form of society has been *abolished* and that society has been organised as *a conscious and systematic association* [*just five words, to be cut with scalpels in the dura mater*], the 10 quarters represent a quantity of *autonomous labour-time* equal to that contained in 240 shillings. *Society* would therefore not purchase this product at two and a half times *the actual labour-time contained in it*; the basis for a class of landowners would thereby disappear.[8]

So, is this entire critique valid only where one accepts the Ricardian theory of abolishing landed privilege, giving it to the state?

---

7   Ibid., p. 799.
8   Ibid., p. 799. Translation modified, following Bordiga.

Correct as it is to say that – keeping to the present mode of production, but assuming that differential rent accrued to the state – the prices of agricultural products would remain the same [*Ricardo*], if other factors did so too, it is still wrong to say that the value of these products would remain the same if capitalist production were replaced by association [= *communism*].[9]

With this second position, Ricardo maintains that normal capitalist profit is not a parasitical form, but is in keeping with the just value, as labour, of every commodity, when rent has disappeared. Marx answers him, and all the defenders of capitalism, directly:

The fact that commodities of the same kind have an identical *market price* [*in other words, always the law of value*] is the way in which the social character of value is realised on the basis of the capitalist mode of production, and in general of production *depending on commodity exchange between individuals*.

2 Not Building Socialism but Destroying Mercantilism

Thus also in capitalist times a social and not an individual value of commodities is realised. But as long as the way of fixing this quantity of value results from personal economic acts, one of them being the act of paying a wage in money for labour-time, the social value obtained *is false*. Due precisely to its fundamental equality on the entire market, this value does not express the average social effort, which can only be calculated with the real facts of production and in a production that is *not for the market*. Only this *non-market* production will *not be unconscious and unintentional*.

Where society, considered as a consumer, pays too much for agricultural products, this is a minus for the realisation of its labour-time in agricultural production, but it forms a plus for one portion of society, the landowners.

The evil, Marx says in this passage, is not that the landowners eat up this differential conquest, their hands on their bellies; the evil is in the fact that, by

---

9 Ibid. This and the following two quotes are on p. 800.

determining all values according to the market and with the law of the market, it is not possible to overcome the unconsciousness, anarchy and powerlessness of the social organisation. And as long as the mercantile criterion is the yardstick of all economic acts, it will not be possible to pass from capitalism to communist 'association'.

The importance of Marx's theory of rent (certain points in his analysis are quite difficult) resides in its containing the essential critique of capitalism in its entirety. To bring market prices back to the values *in production* it does not suffice to eliminate those who benefit from the gap between them. On the contrary, this ever more monstrous squandering will arise *as long as* the productive acts and the subsequent calculation of these acts is based on the facts of the sphere of the circulation of commodities, with the application of the *law of value*.

The thousand parasitical forms of commercial and industrial monopolies, cartels, trusts, state enterprises and state capitalists, do not need a new theory under the asinine pretext that Marx dictated a theory of capitalism that was based on competition.

Since Marx in fact scoffed at competition or, more precisely, since he demonstrated that it is a phenomenon not essential to capitalism, the theory of monopoly and of imperialism has already been fully written, down to the last sentence and the last formula: in the doctrine of agrarian rent.

Do you want new patents for this? Do you want to fill in the gaps left by Marx? To liquidate you there is no need to be flowery: scram, you loafers!

CHAPTER 13

Murder of the Dead

In Italy we have long experience of 'catastrophes that strike the country' and we also have a certain expertise in 'staging' them.[1] Earthquakes, volcanic eruptions, floods, cloudbursts, epidemics ... The effects, of course, are felt above all in areas of high population density and among the poor, and if cataclysms often far more terrifying than ours strike all corners of the earth, not always do these unfavourable social conditions coincide with geographical and geological ones. But every people and every country has its own delights: typhoons, drought, tidal waves, famine, heat waves and frosts, all unknown to us in the 'garden of Europe'. Just open a newspaper and you'll be sure to find news of such catastrophes, from the Philippines to the Andes, from the polar ice caps to the African desert.

Our capitalism – which, as has been said a hundred times, is quantitatively small fry, but in a 'qualitative' sense has long been in the vanguard of bourgeois civilisation, whose greatest precursors flowered amidst Renaissance splendour – has masterfully developed its *disaster economy*.

We wouldn't dream of shedding a tear if monsoons raze entire cities on the coasts of the Indian Ocean, or if the sea whipped to a frenzy by underwater earthquakes buries them in a *raz de marée*, but for the Po delta we've managed to collect alms from all over the world!

Our monarchs were glorious in their rushing off not to where one danced (Pordenone) but to where one died of cholera (Naples), or to the ruins of Reggio and Messina razed to the ground by the earthquakes of 1908. Now our little squirt of a President[2] has been taken off to Sardinia and – if the Stalinists tell us no lies – has been shown the teams of 'Potemkin workers' in action – now here, and now they've already dashed off to the other side of the stage, like the warriors in *Aida*.[3] It was too late to pull the flood victims out of the raging Po, but never too late – once the motion-picture cameras and microphones had been

---

1 *Battaglia Comunista*, No. 24, 1951; republished in *Drammi gialli e sinistri della moderna decadenza sociale*, Milan: Iskra, 1978 (writings 1951–66), pp. 33–46.
2 Luigi Einaudi, President of Italy 1948–55. He was, in fact, short.
3 Potemkin had constructed prefabricated villages to show Catherine II on her tour of the Russian countryside. They gave the impression of rural prosperity but, after each visit, were hastily dismantled and then re-assembled elsewhere on the tour.

properly set up – for a worldwide broadcast of MPs (male and female) and ministers paddling about in their knee-high rubber boots, begging for alms in grand style.

Here we have the inspired formula: *the state intervenes!* And we've been applying it for a good 90 years. In Italy the professional disaster victim has replaced the grace of God and the hand of Providence with *government aid*, convinced that the national budget is vaster by far than the mercy of the Lord. A good Italian happily forks out ten thousand lire today so that months and months later he can 'guzzle a thousand lire of the government's'. And on one of these periodic occasions, now fashionably called emergencies, but which crop up in all seasons, the instant the central government unfurls its unfailing *measures* and *provisions*, a band of no less professional 'disaster victimisers' roll up their sleeves and plunge into the procuring of concessions and the orgy of contracts.

With authority, the Minister of Finance of the day (today Vanoni) suspends all other functions of the state and declares he will not dispense a single dime for all the other 'special laws', because every red cent is needed for the current disaster.

There could be no better proof of the uselessness of the state. If the hand of God existed it would give the disaster victims of all types a really big hand by earthquaking and bankrupting this charlatan dilettante state.

But if the foolishness of the petty and middle bourgeoisie shines brightest when it seeks a remedy for the terror that chills it in the warm hope of the subsidy and indemnity lavished upon it by the *government*, the reaction of the 'fearless leaders' of the working masses is no less senseless when they scream that the workers have *lost everything* in the disaster. Everything – but unfortunately not their chains!

In these supreme circumstances that shatter the well-being the proletariat enjoys thanks to *normal* capitalist exploitation, these leaders who pretend to be 'Marxists' have an economic formula even more foolish than that of state intervention. The formula is well-known: *make the rich pay!*

Vanoni, then, is vilified because he was unable to discover and tax *high incomes.*[4]

But just a crumb of Marxism suffices to show how high incomes flourish wherever there is 'high' destruction, fertile soil indeed for big business. 'The

---

4 In 1951 Ezio Vanoni, Minister of Finance, introduced income tax to Italy, with the lowest rates in the world at that time (or of all time), along with a stratospheric rate of tax evasion.

bourgeoisie must pay for the war!' cried those false shepherds in 1919, instead of inviting the proletariat to overthrow it. The Italian bourgeoisie is still here, and enthusiastically invests its income in paying for wars and other plagues, for which it is repaid fourfold.

1   Yesterday

When a catastrophe destroys houses, crops and factories, throwing the active population out of work, it undoubtedly destroys *wealth*. But this cannot be remedied by a transfusion of wealth from elsewhere, as with the miserable operation of rummaging around for old jumble, when the advertising, collection and transport cost far more than what the stuff is actually worth.

The wealth that disappeared was an accumulation of past, age-old labour. To eliminate the effect of the catastrophe an enormous mass of present, living labour is needed. If, then, we define wealth not abstractly but concretely and socially, we can see it as the right of certain individuals forming the ruling class to *subtract* living contemporary labour. In the new mobilisation of labour new incomes and new privileged wealth will be formed. But the capitalist economy offers no means of 'shifting' wealth accumulated elsewhere to plug the yawning chasm in the wealth of Sardinia or the Veneto, any more than the banks of the Tiber can be 'shifted' to rebuild the ones swallowed up by the Po.

This is why it is a stupid idea to tax the owners of the fields, houses and factories left intact in order to rebuild the ones that were destroyed.

The centre of capitalism is not the ownership of such properties but is a type of economy that permits withdrawal and profit on what human labour creates in never-ending cycles, subordinating the employment of this labour to this subtraction.

Thus the idea of solving the war-time building crisis with an income freeze on the owners of undamaged houses produced housing conditions worse than the conditions caused by the bombing. But the demagogues shout their facile arguments, 'accessible to the working masses,' in defence of the freeze.

The basis of Marxist economic analysis is the distinction between dead and living labour. We define capitalism not as the ownership of heaps of past, crystallised labour, but as the right to extract from living and active labour. This is why the present economy can lead neither to a good solution that realises the rational conservation of what past labour has transmitted to us with a minimum expenditure of present labour, nor to better bases for the performance of future labour. What interests the bourgeois economy is the frenzy of the contemporary work pace, which furthers the destruction of still useful masses of past labour, and posterity be damned.

Marx explains that the ancient economies, based more on use values than exchange values, had less need to extort *surplus labour*, and recalls the sole exception: in the extraction of gold and silver (it is not fortuitous that money was the mother of capitalism) the worker was forced to work himself to death, as in Diodorus Siculus.

The *hunger for surplus labour* not only leads to extortion from the living of so much labour-power that it shortens their existence but also turns the destruction of dead labour into a good deal, replacing still useful products with other living labour. Like Maramaldo,[5] capitalism, oppressor of the living, is the murderer also of the dead:

> But as soon as peoples whose production still moves within the lower forms of slave-labour, the *corvée*, etc. are drawn into a world market dominated by the capitalist mode of production, whereby the sale of their products for export develops into their principal interest, the civilised horrors of over-work are grafted onto the barbaric horrors of slavery, serfdom etc.[6]

The original title of the paragraph quoted is 'Der Heisshunger nach Mehrarbeit', literally: 'The voracious appetite for surplus labour'.

The hunger for surplus labour of infantile capitalism, as described by the power of our doctrine, already contains the entire analysis of the modern phase of a capitalism grown out of all proportion in its ravenous hunger for catastrophe and ruin.

Far from being a discovery of ours (to hell with the balladeers, especially when even their do–re–mi is out of tune and they think they are creators!) the distinction between dead and living labour lies in the fundamental distinction between constant and variable capital. All objects produced by labour that are not for immediate consumption but are employed in a further work process (today they are known as producer goods) form constant capital.

---

5   The Italian condottiere Fabrizio Maramaldo, a ruthless mercenary and ravager, has a bad
    name in Italian history and popular memory for the way he murdered Franceso Ferrucci, cap-
    tain of the Florentine army and his old enemy, grievously wounded and a prisoner, in 1530,
    violating all principles of chivalrous action in wartime.
6   Marx 1976, Chapter 10, Section 2, p. 345.

Therefore, whenever products enter as means of production into new labour processes, they lose their character of being products and function only as objective factors contributing to living labour.[7]

This is true for principal and accessory raw materials, machines and any other equipment that progressively wears out: the loss due to wear that has to be compensated requires the capitalist to invest another share of constant capital. This is what is known in current economics as depreciation. Depreciate rapidly is the supreme ideal of this grave-digging economy.

We recalled, a propos 'the devil in the flesh', how in Marx capital has the demoniacal function of incorporating *living labour* into *dead labour*, which has become a thing.[8] Great! The banks of the Po are not immortal, and today one can merrily 'incorporate living labour into them'! Projects and specifications were drawn up in just a few days! Bravo! You have the devil in your flesh!

'Commendatore, the projects department of our Enterprise has done its duty in preparing technical and economic studies: here they are, all nice and ready'. And in the cost analysis the stones of Monselice are worth more than Carrara marble!'[9]

The property therefore which labour-power in action, living labour possesses of *preserving value, at the same time that it adds to it, is a gift of nature* which costs the worker nothing, but is very advantageous to the capitalist since it *preserves the existing value of his capital.*[10]

Marx calls this capital that is simply 'preserved', thanks to the work of living labour, the constant part of capital or *constant capital*. But:

that part of capital which is turned [*vulgo*: invested] into labour-power [wages] does undergo an alteration of value in the process of production ... and produces an excess, a *surplus-value.*[11]

We therefore call it the variable part, or simply *variable capital.*

7   Ibid., p. 289.
8   *Dottrina del diavolo in corpo* is the title of an article (*Battaglia Comunista*, No. 21, 1951) on the role of state investments in capitalism. The article is available in internet in English: see *Doctrine of the Devil in the Flesh*, Historical Archives of 'Italian' Communist Left.
9   The nearest stone quarries to the Po are in Monselice; Carrara is the main centre of marble production in Italy.
10   Marx 1976, p. 315. Bordiga's italics.
11   Ibid., p. 317. Bordiga's italics.

The key is right here. Bourgeois economics relates profit to constant capital, which stays right here and doesn't move. Indeed, it would go to the devil if the worker's labour did not 'preserve' it. Marxist economics, on the contrary, relates it *to variable capital alone* and demonstrates how the active labour of the proletariat: a) preserves constant capital (dead labour); b) exalts variable capital (living labour). This exaltation, surplus value, is snapped up by the entrepreneur.

Marx explains that this process of establishing the rate without taking *constant* capital into account is equivalent to making it *equal to zero*: a current operation in the mathematical analysis of all questions that involve variable quantities.

Set constant capital at *zero* and the tower of capitalist profit remains standing. Saying this is the same as saying that the enterprise's profit remains if the capitalist is liberated from the inconvenience of preserving constant capital.

This hypothesis is nothing but the present-day reality of *state capitalism.*

Transferring capital to the state means making constant capital equal to zero. Nothing changes in the relation between entrepreneur and worker, since this relation depends solely on the magnitudes *variable capital and surplus-value.*

Is the *analysis* of state capitalism *anything new?* In all modesty, we've been serving it on a silver platter ever since 1867 and even earlier, boiled right down to its bones: $cc = o$.

After this cold little formula, we shall not leave Marx without quoting these scorching words: 'Capital is dead labour, which, vampire like, lives only by sucking living labour, and lives the more, the more labour it sucks'.[12]

It is in the interest of modern capital, whose need for consumers is driven by its relentlessly inflating need to produce, to drive the products of *dead* labour into disuse as soon as possible, to then replace them with living labour, the only type from which it 'sucks' profit. This is why it delights in war, and why it is so well trained for the practice of disasters. Car production in America is tremendous, but almost every family already has a car: at this rate demand will soon be exhausted. The solution: cars *not made to last.* To this end, first of all *make them badly*, with plenty of botched parts. Yes, drivers will break their necks more often but, never mind: you lose a customer but sell a new car! Then, there's the question of *fashion.* With waves of cretinising advertising/propaganda everyone will just have to have the latest model, like the women who wouldn't be caught dead wearing 'last year's' dress – perfectly

---

12   Ibid., p. 342.

good, but 'out of style'. The fools fall for it, and no one cares that a Ford built in 1920 lasts longer than a brand new 1951 model. And, finally, when a car is dumped it is not even used for scrap, but is thrown into a car *cemetery*. If anyone should dare to revive it, saying – You threw it away as something of no value, what's the harm in my fixing it up and driving it around? – he'll be rewarded for his efforts with a shot across the bows and a spell in the pokey.

To exploit living labour, capital must annihilate dead labour that is still useful. Loving to suck warm young blood, it kills corpses.

So while maintenance of the banks of the Po for ten kilometres requires human labour costing, let's say, one million a year, it suits capitalism better to rebuild them completely, spending one billion. Otherwise it would have to wait a thousand years. Does this mean that the *black government*[13] sabotaged the banks of the Po? Certainly not. It means that no one put pressure on it to allocate one miserable million a year – money that was gobbled up in the billions that funded other 'grandiose projects', of 'new construction'. Now that the devil has swept away the embankments, they find someone who, with the best of intentions in the *sacrosanct* national interest, re-opens the *projects department* and rebuilds them.

Who is to blame for this fondness for grandiose investments? The 'blacks' and the 'reddish'.[14] Both of them prattle that they want a *productivist* and *full-employment* policy. Today, productivism – Don Benito's pet – consists in setting up 'timely' cycles of living labour, with which big business and high-style speculation make billions. So let us *update* – at Pantalone's expense – the out-of-date machines of the 'high' industrialists, and let us also update the banks of the rivers after we let them burst. The history of these past few years of the management of public works and of the protection of industry is replete with these masterpieces, ranging from the provision of raw materials sold below cost to make-work projects designed to 'combat unemployment' based on the premise 'constant capital equals zero'. To put it simply, we spend everything in wages, and since the only equipment the enterprise has are shovels, it convinces the *commendatore* how useful a *movement of earth* would be: first move it from here to there, and then, right away, move it back again.

---

13   A reference to the right-wing Christian-Democratic governments of the time.
14   For Bordiga, the 'blacks' were the Christian-Democrats ('reminiscent' of the Fascists), while the Italian Communist Party (PCI) that he referred to as 'Stalinians' and 'false communists' were not 'red' but 'reddish'.

If the commendatore should hesitate, no problem, the enterprise already has the trade union in its pocket: a demonstration of hired hands, shouldering shovels, under the windows of the ministry, and that's that. The 'balladeer' arrives and goes beyond Marx: shovels, the only constant capital, have given birth to surplus value.

2   Today

The proportions of the disaster along the Po have, unquestionably, been gigantic, and the estimated cost of the damage is still rising. We admit that the cultivated area of Italy has lost one hundred thousand hectares or one thousand square kilometres, about one three-hundredth of the total, or three out of a thousand. One hundred thousand inhabitants have had to leave the area, which is not the most densely populated in Italy, or, in round figures, one five-hundredth of the total population, or two out of a thousand.

If the bourgeois economy were not insane, one could do a simple little calculation. The *national wealth* has suffered a serious blow. Still, the area has been only partially destroyed. When the floodwaters recede, the agricultural land will be left substantially intact and the decomposition of vegetable substances, with the contribution of the mire, will partially compensate for the lost fertility. If the damage is one third of total capital, it amounts to one thousandth of the *national capital*. But the national capital has an average 'income' of five percent or fifty out of a thousand. If for one year every Italian saved just one fiftieth of his consumption, the gap would be filled.

But bourgeois society is anything but a co-operative, even if the 'high' freebooters of indigenous capital evade Vanoni's taxes by demonstrating that they have distributed 'shares' of their enterprises among all their employees.

All the *productivist* operations of the Italian and the international economy are more or less as destructive as the Po delta disaster: the water comes in one side and goes out the other.

In the field of capitalism such a problem is insurmountable. If the problem is a one-year plan to supply Eisenhower with arms for his hundred divisions, a solution will be found. We're talking, here, about short-cycle operations and capitalism is delighted if an order for ten thousand guns is to be filled in a hundred days rather than a thousand. That's what the steel pool is all about!

But a pool of hydrological and seismological organisations – no, that's out of the question, unless, of course, the 'high' science of the bourgeois epoch, after its serial bombardments, also manages to provoke serial floods and earthquakes!

Here we are confronted with a slow and non-accelerable age-old transmission, from generation to generation, of the results of labour that is 'dead' but tutelary of the living, of their lives and of their lesser sacrifice.

If, for example, the water in the Po delta recedes in a few months and the breach at Occhiobello is closed before the spring, then only one annual harvest cycle will be lost: no productive 'investment' can replace it, but the loss is reduced.

If, by contrast, one believes that all the banks of the Po and of the other rivers could break down frequently, due to the lack of maintenance during thirty years of crisis along with the disastrous deforestation in the mountains, then the remedy will be even slower in coming. No capital will be invested for the greater glory of our great-grandchildren.

Our daddies wrote in vain: There are only a few specimens of virgin forest left, growing without the intervention of human labour. The forestry system becomes, then, almost *aphrodisiac*, despite the *minimum* capital involved in managing it. Nevertheless, *high growing* trees, the most important for the public economy, always demand an extremely long wait before they yield products of value. Even though forestry science has shown that the best year to fell timber is not that of the tree's maximum longevity but, rather, the year in which its *current* growth is equal to its *average* growth, for an oak forest for example you always have to reckon with 80, 100, *and even 150 years of waiting*. Minimum capital; 150 years of waiting until it yields! Di Vittorio and Pastore[15] would throw *this* book out the window, if they ever opened it!

Just like in the operetta: *steal, steal, Capital* (love) *cannot wait ...!*

Worse things have happened. Relatively little has been said about the disaster in Sardinia, Calabria, and Sicily. Here the geographical fact is radically different.

In the Po valley the very slack gradient made the waters stagnate, bogged down in the clayey and impermeable soils below. In the South and the Islands the same causes of heavy rains and deforestation in the mountains combined with the extremely steep slope down to the sea to create a disaster: in just a few hours the mountain streams stripped sand and gravel from the bedrock, destroying fields and houses, even if the victims were few.

Not only is the plundering of the magnificent forests of Aspromonte and the Sila by the allied *liberators* irreparable, but here the renewal of the land

---

15   The 'communist' and 'catholic' union leaders of the period, respectively.

swamped by the flood is not only practically *impossible* but is *anti-economical* for the 'investors', and for the 'rescue workers' too – who, if possible, are even greedier!

Not only the few patches of arable land but also the thin non-rocky strata that gave them minimal support have been washed away – soil that time and again over a span of many long decades had been carried up the slope by the grindingly poor farmers. Every plantation, every grove of trees, was washed down with the soil; uprooted orange and lemon trees, the basis of a profitable cultivation and industry, floated out to sea.

It takes about two years to replant a vineyard that has been destroyed but a citrus orchard takes seven to ten years before it yields a full harvest, and its replanting and management require a great deal of capital. Of course in the 'good treatises' we shall never read about the cost of the unthinkable labour of carrying the dissolved soil hundreds of metres back up the slope; in any case, the rainwater would wash it back down again before the plant roots could fix it to the subsoil.

Not even the houses can be rebuilt where they were before – for technical, not economic reasons. Five or six unfortunate villages on the Ionian coast in the province of Reggio Calabria will be rebuilt not on their ancient sites in the hills but along the shore.

In the Middle Ages, after devastations had blotted out even the traces of the magnificent coastal cities of Magna Graecia, the apex of culture and art in the ancient world, the poor agrarian population found refuge from the raids of the Saracen pirates in villages built on the mountain tops, less accessible and easier to defend.

Later, the new 'Piedmontese' government built roads and railways along the coast and, when malaria did not prohibit it, where the mountains ran down close to the sea every village had its own 'marina' near the railway station.[16] As a result, it became *profitable* to carry the timber away.

Tomorrow only the 'marinas' will remain, where a few houses will be laboriously rebuilt. Why in the world would the peasants climb back up the slope, where nothing can take root and they can't even rebuild their houses on the bare and friable rock? And the workers by the sea, what will they do? Today they can no longer emigrate; like the Calabrians of the unhealthy lowlands and the Lucanians of the 'cursèd claylands', made sterile by the greedy fel-

---

16   'Marina' here refers to a small group of houses around the railway station, on the coastal plain not far from the sea, since, obviously, the railway could not reach the city 'on the hill'.

ling of the woodlands that once covered the mountains, and of the trees scattered over the pastures in the hills.

Rest assured that in such conditions no capital and no government will intervene, to the total disgrace of the obscenely hypocritical exaltation of national and international 'solidarity'.

It is not a moral or sentimental fact that is the basis of all this. No, it is the contradiction between the convulsive dynamic of the super-capitalism we have today and the healthy need to organise the sojourn of the human groups on this earth, to hand on useful conditions of life in the course of time.

The 'Nobel Prize winning' Bertrand Russell, who pontificates placidly in the world press, denounces humanity for excessively plundering natural resources, whose complete exhaustion can already be calculated. He recognises the fact that the policies of the great powers are absurd and mad, denounces the aberrations of the individualist economy, and tells the joke about the Irishman who says: Why should I care about future generations? What have they ever done for me?

Russell counts among the aberrations, along with those of mystical fatalism, that of the communist who says: Let's get rid of capitalism and the problem will be solved. After such a display of physical-biological-social science, he is still not able to see the enormous waste of both natural and social resources, essentially connected with a certain type of production, as an equally *physical* fact, and thinks that everything could be resolved with a moral telling-off or a Fabian appeal to high and to low human wisdom.

His retreat is pitiful: Science grows impotent before the problems of the soul!

Those who truly cross the street to humanity, taking decisive steps forward in the organisation of human life, are – truly – not the bullies and oppressors who still dared to boast of their will to power. No, there the oppression was all in the swarms of washed-out benefactors, in the pitchers of Marshall Plans and chains of brotherhood, as if of dovecotes of peace.

Passing from cosmology to economics, Russell criticises the liberal illusions on the cure-all of competition, and has to admit: 'Marx predicted that free competition between capitalists would end up in monopoly, and was proved right when Rockefeller established a virtually monopolistic regime for oil'.

Starting from the explosion of the sun that one day will instantaneously transform us into gas (proving his Irishman right!), Russell concludes miserably, sweetness and light: 'The nations that desire prosperity must seek collaboration rather than competition'.

Is it not true, Mr Nobel Prize – you who have written treatises of logic and scientific method – that Marx calculated the advent of monopoly a good fifty years in advance?

If that was good dialectics, then the opposite of competition is monopoly, not collaboration.

Take careful note that Marx also predicted that the capitalist economy – class monopoly – would dissolve not into *collaboration*, which you, like all the Trumans and Stalins of goodwill, so assiduously adulate, but into *class war*.

Just as Rockefeller came, *Baffone*[17] has to come! But not from the Kremlin. Stalin, *in barba a Marx*,[18] is about to shave 'American-style'.

---

17   'Big Moustache': namely, Stalin.
18   In defiance of Marx: literally 'in beard to Marx'.

CHAPTER 14

Inflation of the State

1   Yesterday[1]

The settlement of the question of the state in Marx-Engels-Lenin[2] was such a clear and solid conquest in the theoretical and political field that after World War I it seemed that the revolutionary communist movement would be limiting its work to questions of organisation and tactics, and never again take up questions of programme. But this great conquest is gravely compromised when someone who advocates a programmatic entente with the bourgeois parties on the question of the national 'constitution' and, internationally, a historical and social collaboration between 'proletarian' and capitalist states, dares to call himself a representative of Marxist and Leninist parties.

Our basic texts give its just deserts most especially to the vision of the state proper to theocratic and authoritarian conceptions, as well as to the democratic-bourgeois immanentist perspective.

Both systems make the goal of the entire course of thought and of history the building of the perfect and eternal state.

In the Old Testament as it is still dogmatically accepted by the leading churches in most of the advanced world, the Eternal Father Himself took the trouble of dictating to Moses a full-fledged Constitution for the chosen people, down to the smallest detail. In the organic unity of this system, church, justice, state and army form a single whole. Even the statistics and the administrative division of the territory is geographically prescribed, along with the rules for putting to the sword the former occupants if they showed no intention of clearing out. Then Christianity arrived to extend the borders of the chosen people to all of humanity, and to distinguish the City of God from the City of Caesar and the priestly from the military hierarchy, while taking the greatest pains not to repudiate the rules of authority-domination-extermination of the first and greatest of the prophets.

The new systems of modern bourgeois critical thought shook the foundations of dogma and authority based on revelation, but among so many myths

---

1   *Battaglia Comunista*, No. 38, 1949.
2   In this text, as in the 'America' series in the next chapter, Bordiga frequently strings words together without commas. I have used hyphens to reproduce this stylistic singularity [note by G. Donis].

the myth of the state remained intact – indeed, grew even more obsessive. From Luther to Hegel to Hobbes to Robespierre, behold the descriptions of the new Leviathan, which Marx-Engels-Lenin will later deride-strip down-demolish: 'reality of the moral idea' – 'image and reality of reason' – 'actualisation of the Idea'. Lenin blasted such phrases as equivalents of the 'Kingdom of God on earth' in his repeated violent attacks on the despicable 'superstition of the state'.

'The state is a product of society at a particular stage of development' (Engels).[3] The state appears when society divides into economically antagonistic classes, when class struggle appears. 'The state is nothing but a machine for the oppression of one class by another' (Engels).[4]

In all capitalist countries, in every part of the world and in every period of their histories, since there can be no capitalism without class struggle this machine is present, and it has the same function of exercising the 'dictatorship of the bourgeoisie' (Lenin), be it in a monarchy or in the most democratic of republics (Marx).

Let us say once again that in this construction of ours the capitalist bourgeois state is not the *last* state machine in history (as the anarchists apparently believe). The working class cannot 'utilise' this machine (as all the reformists and opportunists claim) but must 'smash' it, and must build a new state in the revolutionary dictatorship of the proletariat.

This workers' state, dialectically opposed to the capitalist state, in the course of the construction of a communist economy will progressively dissolve, deflate, and wither away, until it disappears.

We return, now, to the historical process of development of the current, concrete capitalist state to see its historical course, awaiting its foundering foretold in Marx's vision, to be followed by the foundering of the *state* tout court.

The capitalist state, under our very eyes – the eyes of a generation harrowed by three bourgeois 'peaces' spanning two imperialist universal wars – is swelling to terrifying proportions, taking on the proportions of Moloch, devourer of sacrificial victims, of Leviathan with its belly swollen with treasures, grinding up billions of living beings. If it were actually possible, as in the exercises of philosophical speculation, to personalise the Individual, Society, Humanity, the entire horizon of the dreams of these innocent beings would be covered by the Stalinist nightmare.

---

3 Engels, *The Origin of the Family, Private Property and the State*, Chapter IX, available at http:// www.marxists.org/archive/marx/works/download/Engels_The_Origin_of_the_Family_Priva te_Property_and_the_Stat.pdf.

4 See Marx and Lenin 1968, p. 22. The quote is from Engels's Introduction to *The Civil War in France*.

For this terrible Monster, we (who for our revolutionary state foresee a gradual dissolution, an *Auflösung*) await from storm to storm the *Sprengung* calculated by Marx, the terrible but dazzling Explosion.

What we demand, then, is not that the Monster become refined, grow thinner, and come back to its human 'line'. No, under the pressure of its inexorable internal laws and of their class hatred, we demand its horrible *inflation*.

In the ultra-modern world the inflation of the state takes two directions, one social and one geographical (territorial). The second direction is fundamental. State and territory are born together. Engels, in *The Origin of the Family, Private Property and the State*, in fact says: First of all, the state distinguishes itself from the ancient organisation of the *gens*, of the tribe or of the clan, by its division of the population according to the territory.

This is true of the ancient state, the feudal state, the modern state. Moses dictatorially gave each of the 12 tribes a precisely delimited province of the promised land of Israel, while Popes and Emperors invested medieval Lords with Lands and Vassals. And the modern-civil-democratic states of today sort masses of population out among its territories like herds of work animals and handle crowds of prisoners of war like stocks of commodities, along with political internees, people displaced by invasions, stateless refugees, and proletarian emigrants. Today, the Peplum of Liberty to which they burn incense is woven with barbed wire.

As for territorial extension, the ancient world presents us with small state units reduced to cities and large Empires resulting from military conquests, while in the Middle Ages we find small autonomous Communes and large state complexes. By contrast, the capitalist world gives us a definite unbroken concentration of state units on immense extensions, and the ever more total domination of the large over the small.

This process runs parallel to the increased interference of the state machine in all phases of life of the populations it dominates, spreading its influence from the political, police and juridical spheres ever more explicitly and stiflingly to the social, economical and physical domains.

In *The State and Revolution* Lenin gives us a decisive analysis of this internal process with reference to all the countries of Europe and America, and above all to the most parliamentarian and republican among them:

Imperialism – the era of bank capital, the era of gigantic capitalist monopolies, of the development of monopoly capitalism into state-monopoly capitalism – has clearly shown an extraordinary strengthening of the 'state machine' and an unprecedented growth in all its bureaucratic and military apparatus in connection with the intensification of repressive measures against the proletariat both in the monarchical and in the freest, republican countries.[5]

Words written in 1917.

There is no better way of evidencing the substantial falsehood of the juridical and political construction characteristic of the dominant bourgeoisie than by recalling how it presents the two world wars as struggles for the demands of autonomy and freedom of individuals, ethnic groups and nations, of small states in their unlimited sovereignty. If the truth be told, these wars were nothing other than gigantic and blood-drenched stages in the concentration of state power and of capitalist domination.

In the theory of bourgeois law, just as each individual is guaranteed a series of illusory prerogatives in the face of public power, in matters of thinking, speaking, writing, associating, voting, in any direction whatsoever – but not when it comes to eating! Shall the hungry be allowed to sit at the table where the disinterested body of Solons sit! – likewise each individual state is sovereign and can administer as it wishes within its own borders, whether they wend their way for ten or for ten thousand kilometres.

But already in the rosy and pearly picture of the late nineteenth century a distinction between Great and Small Powers was made. Apart from America that 'had no foreign policy' in Europe we had six of them: England, splendidly alone, Russia and France in the Double Alliance, and Germany, Austria-Hungary and Italy in the Triple. In the East the force of a Japan that aspired to control Asia was growing, just as the falsely Malthusian North America had already extended it hegemony over Central and South America. One after the other, history had already reduced Sweden, Spain, Portugal, Holland, Turkey ... to the ranks of former powers.

If you listen to the gossip, the war broke out not because the strongest capitalist states were hungry for vaster empires and markets, but because a small free state, Serbia, had been offended by the arrogance of the despotic empire of Vienna.

The defeat of the Germans eliminated two world powers, and the Russian Revolution knocked out a third in settling the peace. The usual lying liberals shouted to the four winds about the self-determination of the small nationalities and the liberation of oppressed peoples. The five great military states that won the war promised the birth of new small powers in old Europe – more or

---

5   Lenin 1971b, Chapter II, Section 2, p. 286.

less historical nations, whose power was more apparent than real – but without giving up a square kilometre of their own imperial dominion over peoples of a great variety of languages and colours. Poland, Czechoslovakia, Croatia and Slovenia (united with Serbia), Albania, Finland, Estonia, Latvia, Lithuania were constituted as 'sovereign' states.

In fact, given the motives and characteristics of the modern organisation of production this entire pleiad of mini-states, together with the traditional ones, served as nothing more than constellations of satellites for the hegemonies straining to assert themselves. France and England made great efforts in this field, dividing central and eastern Europe into spheres of influence but united in their attacks on the proletarian Russia of that time; even Italy tried its hand at this game, with a certain success, while the United States in the West and Japan in the East continued to widen the visible and invisible limits of their domination.

2 Today

The eve of the second world war presented us with the further monopolistic evolution of big capitalism coupled with the evolution of military technique that increasingly required formidable masses of economic means. Hence it was already clear that any state of no more than a few million people could exercise no economic-diplomatic-military autonomy and had to take its place in the orbit of and under subjection to a larger state. Meanwhile Germany rose once again, and following the general historical law – not making it up, as the fools were led to believe – re-assimilated the left-over pieces of the dissolved Austro-Hungarian Empire (which, let us say parenthetically, had the worst literature but the best, most serious, and most honest contemporary administration). Russia, developing a historical cycle of the greatest interest based, at first, on the right of nations to self-determination, at the height of the struggle between the old and the new regime settled, in its turn, into a powerful unitary state.

Thus it was clear that in the new diplomatic and military game only the Big State Beasts would count. They alone could count on substantial forces, particularly in the sea and the air war – a war that was long, cumbersome, expensive to prepare, involving not only immense amounts of capital but long geographical distances between their bases and their political borders. This was a major problem for densely populated countries – that is, countries with large populations and quite possibly considerable wealth, but territories which are relatively small. Even the 'great powers' of yesterday, Germany-

England-France-Italy-Japan, had to take some tremendous military beatings, with various political outcomes.

Also this [second world] war of even more ferocious domination and concentration of destructive power was presented as a war fought in defence of the 'small fry' of history – in defence of their liberty and sovereignty violated by bullies. The first thing was to keep Hitler from overpowering free Poland, where the democratic glue that stuck its three historic pieces together was not yet dry. It was immediately broken in two and divided between the two colossuses on either side. Since one colossus has disappeared, Poland is once again a single piece at the service of a single master. The worst possible fate for a romantic, generous, civil and free Nation with a capital N is this fate of Poland's today, the 'division in one'.

The true survivors of the war are the states that came in first in the frantic rush after Territorial Inflation. The rush started early on – not that anyone ever refrained from their daily hymn to freedom, or from speaking of 'Greats'. There were Three, Four, Two or Five 'Greats'? It makes little difference. There were at least eight at the start of the war.

The true 'Greats' are the states that add a vast constellation of 'Satellites' to the vastness of their own territory and to their already large population (a good reason to keep a close eye on China, where a great state of the modern capitalist variety has arisen despite the profoundly hybrid nature of its society). These 'Satellites' are left to fiddle with the fiction of Sovereignty, while their personal leaders are ever more drunk-corrupt-paid off at the teahouses and cocaine dens that are passed off as the great Congresses and Councils of international politics.

With Italy now a satellite of the worst sort, Great Britain and France will have to decide whether or not they accept the position of First Lord and First Lady in the American Constellation. What's more there is also the Russian Constellation, wrestling with some undisciplined little planet that would like to leap out of its primitive sphere of attraction.

So, basically, the Great Monsters boil down to two. Will they head for unification by means of Peace or by means of War? In either case it will be terrible. But it will be equally terrible that, after each has devoured half the large and small zoological species of the political map of the world, they attack one another for the third time, each accusing the other of wanting to devour the sacred liberty of the last little mouse.

3   More on Inflation of the State[6]

Just to show that radical orthodox Marxists (Archeio-Marxists, as the Greek comrades put it), while they do not budge from the original doctrine in order to blow a storm or a gentle breeze, tickling from behind, fully grasp the meaning of the modern course of this die-hard capitalist regime, the argument of my article *Inflation of the State* would require a complete exposition based on a reordering of the facts.

We would need a treatise bristling with figures, documents and historico-geographical maps updated every few months, while the maps we used when we went to school were usually centuries old.

Hence we shall limit ourselves to a few examples relative to the recent and current States of Europe. The history of many of them tempts us not, let's say, to romanticise it as the bourgeoisie makes it fashionable to do today. No, our temptation is to 'Aesop' it, to 'La Fontaine' it in fables where big beasts and innocent little birds play out their admonitory dialogues. It would be a joking matter, if the tragedy did not reside in the fact that while *all* the turning points, transformations and upheavals are played out in the presence of the incessant publicity that justifies them based on the civilisation, redemption and elevation of peoples, the real superstructure of this rhetorical orgy shows us entire territories of hard-working and unknowing people devoured by skies of fire and flame, piles of dead rotting flesh, live flesh thrown into barbed-wire prisons and then sent off on tracks of martyrdom with whips and bayonets at their backs. Headed for new destinations, dictated by the victorious powers. There are strips of the weeping soil of Europe where dozens of times in just a few years war-invasion-canon-TNT-war police have ground up the wretched inhabitants for the express purpose of fabricating a *Homeland* for them – that monstrous supreme good which reigning Capital promises to and inflicts on the masses it holds as slaves.

Estonia. A small country on the Gulf of Finland of 46,000 sq kms, the size of Tuscany and Lombardy put together: a population of one million, that is, less than the Marches. Naturally (as for all the other countries we shall examine) the local petty-bourgeois and intellectuals explain that we have here an ethnographic *unit*, a distinct race of Ugro-Finnic origin, a definite language, with a literature, a history.

This was sufficient to give those one million peasants the right to a series of delightful adventures, after centuries ruled by the tsars. Independence in

---

January 1918, at the height of the European war, thanks to the great Russian Revolution. In August 1940, in the course of the Second War but before Russia intervened, annexation to Russia. In July 1941, when the Germans attacked Russia, it became part of a war governorate of Germany. With the end of the war, 'liberation' from the German occupation, and return to Russia. End of the beautiful tale.

Lithuania. 62,000 sq kms, as big as Piedmont-Lombardy-Liguria; population 3 million – less than Tuscany. With the interpolation of disputes and exchanges with Poland to take back its *historic* capital, Vilnius, the succession of events is analogous to Estonia.

Latvia. The same size as Lithuania or a little bigger, but with a population of only 2 million (Marches plus Umbria). Independent in November 1918 only by the will of the victorious allies, who (like the Germans before them) saw these little satellites, their vassals, as footholds against a still red Russia. Then the same game replayed in 1940. Russians-Germans-Russians. The curtain falls.

Finland. Bourgeois sentimentalism could give the little fable the pretty tints of legend. Independence was proclaimed on 6 December 1917, after the long oppression of the tsars and the useless revolts against them for centuries, for this population of 4 million, almost as large as the Veneto, on the huge territory that, with its Artic region, is larger than Italy's. The sympathies of bourgeois Europe seek to instil an intense anti-Bolshevism. In the general distraction, Stalin's Russia tries to swallow it up in 1939–40. In Germany and in America by turns, literary and 'Western civilisation' enthusiasms for this small democratic nation, which got off with a small – but heart-felt – amputation of 35,000 sq kms and half a million people. These people painfully begin their displacement to what remained of Finland. In December 1941, taking advantage of the German siege of Leningrad, the Finns re-annex the territories and migrate in the other direction. The new German defeat was followed by a new Russian attack, a new armistice, and a new amputation. In fact, with the Treaty of Paris of 1947 Finland was reduced by 45,000 sq kms.

(Another question concerns the reconquest of these unfortunate countries by powers of the West or of the East once the official military wars had ended, by political means – that is, by their own political parties, with this filthy game passed off as 'class struggle', albeit in the castrated version of 'structural social reform'. But right now we are dealing with statistics of square kilometres and animal-men, not of political philosophies.)

Czechoslovakia. Another bilingual daughter of the war 1914–18. When night fell on the Austrian empire it had a population of 15 million and a territory of 140,000 sq kms, larger than all northern Italy. A third of the population were neither Bohemians nor Slovaks. In 1938 Germany, without firing a shot, snatched 'back' the Sudetenland – the same size as Piedmont, a delicacy fit for a king. During the war the Germans gobbled up the rest, leaving a protected Slovakia of 38,000 sq kms and a population of 2.5 million (Lazio). When Germany was defeated the state of 1918 was resuscitated, with a few little pieces cut off (by the Russians: one of 7 and one of 11,000 sq kms, about the size of Umbria). The population is now 13.5 million. A Russian satellite. Between the wars, a typical Western satellite. A country for governments of Monsignor-cops and renegade revolutionaries.[7]

Hungary. Another epic story. United with Austria in 1914 as an independent state,[8] it was a little bigger than Italy in surface area, with a population of 21 million. In 1920 the Treaty of Trianon 'liberated' it, cutting off a series of slices: population, 9 million; 93,000 sq kms. Linked to Germany in '38, in '39 and in '41, it made off with pieces of its neighbours and traditional enemies and swelled to 15 million. The victory of 1946 reduced it to the *reasonable* dimensions of the Treaty of Trianon. A people bursting with indigestion after centuries of patriotic excess in the name of civil Europe-Faith-Freedom and the more the merrier. A people that saved Germans, Slavs and Latins from the Turks but that, ethnographically speaking, was more Mongolian than the Turks themselves and, like the Mongols, had poured into the fertile Danubian plains ...

Romania. Another country whose geographical history folds and unfolds. After making it through the two Balkan wars and the first European war unscathed and sailing before the wind of a Latin literary nobility, its population was composed of 19.5 million people of all races. In 1940 things took a political turn for the worse: the Russians made off with Bukovina and Bessarabia, the Hungarians with Transylvania, the Bulgarians with Dobrugia. In 1941 the Russians and the Germans quarrelled, the Germans occupied and Fascisticised the country, which was then allowed to re-annex everything, including 'Transnistria' nearly as far as Odessa. Then came 1944 and all the annexed territories were vomited up again. But in 1945 Transylvania was annexed *again*, at Hungary's expense. The population is now 16.5 million on 237,000 sq kms, nearly the size of the Italian peninsula. As for its series of monarchical and republican regimes, we'll spare you the gory details.

---

7   The reference is to Monsignor Josef Tiso, from 1939–45 prime minister of the pro-Nazi Slovak Independent Republic, and, among the various 'renegades', in particular to Klement Gottwald, one of the founders, in 1921, of the Czechoslovakian Communist Party, who later distinguished himself, until his death (in 1953), inside and outside Czechoslovakia, as a leading exponent of Stalinism.

8   In fact in 1914 Hungary was united with Austria in the Austro-Hungarian Empire by a so-called 'personal union', meaning that two sovereign states have the same person as head of state.

Albania. Happily born in 1914 with hymns to the democratic 'holy carbine',[9] as big as Piedmont but with only a million people, in April 1939 it had the great good fortune of uniting with the Italian crown, and in 1941, in wartime, to the detriment of Greeks and others, its population shot up temporarily to nearly two million. Albania's victory over the Axis gave it back its freedom and its old borders. Having socially achieved 'high' capitalism, it can now boast of being on the threshold of freak-show socialism.

Yugoslavia. Complicated business. Born after the [first world] war to stand guard over the Tsars, reuniting the 'southern Slavs', the Kingdom of sHS [Serbs, Croats and Slovenes] was composed of three peoples with accessories [Bosnia-Herzegovina and Macedonia]. As big as Italy without islands, it had a population of over 15 million. During the latest war it was really put through the mill, cut up in no less than eight pieces in 1941, after military-political business had taken its usual course: in a few days governments equally inflated with popular 'self-determination' allied themselves with one group and then with the other. The Germans soon arrived and tore the state to pieces. The pick of the crop was the State of Croatia, replete with Savoy king *designate*:[10] just a hundred thousand or so sq kms and 6.5 million people, a little more than Lombardy. On 29 November of 1945 the republic was pieced back together, same size as in 1918. Politically we need to wait a few more months to find out at which end it has its tail and at which end its horns.

Poland. *Dulcis in fundo*. Recomposed after an age-old parenthesis in November 1918 with three Prussian-Russian-Austrian pieces, it had a population of 34 million on 388,000 sq kms; fewer people than Italy, on a larger territory.

Here the orchestra that for the history of Hungary needed weeping gypsy violins can select, in the most classic of classical music, the funeral march.

It was November first of 1939 when the German blitzkrieg annexed the western part; Russia, 17 days later, after its pact with Germany, annexed the eastern part. Fortunately for the Polish ram the two ferocious carnivores got into a fight. With these zoological indications we refer to the organised state systems and to their praetorians: for the mass of the population 'fortune' is something else. The Poland of today, consecrated on 9 May 1945, is smaller: 24 million people and 310 sq kms. But this does not mean much. Russia, in the end, kept 80,000 sq kms and the 14 million people that lived there, but Poland took 103,000 sq kms back from Germany, along with its population of 5 million. Over two million

---

9   On 25 December 1914 Italian troops occupied Vlona, under the 'holy' democratic pretext of defending Albania against Greek expansion.

10   The Italian prince Tomislav II, Duke of Spoleto, was designated king of the independent state of Croatia, which was in fact a monarchy.

of the Germans were sent back to a defeated and occupied Germany, while the Poles who had remained on the other side of the borders with the USSR were 'invited' to migrate to the current Polish area. It seems like a bad dream in which crazed lines and colours dance on the pages of an Atlas.

Naturally we have made no mention of the professional neutrals – the Swiss, the Iberians, the Scandinavians – who also had their troubles, or will have them; or of the bigger states that scraped through the war as best they could; and, with the British Lion and the French Cockerel, we let the Italian Donkey go about its business.

Let us just take a little peek at the figures of the two monsters of 'Inflation of the State': Germany until yesterday, Russia today.

The statistics of the Germany of Versailles present 14 stages of expansion through annexation and conquest, until the ruin. The Hohenzollern Empire had a population of 65 million on 540,000 sq kms. Versailles left the figures pretty much intact. At the height of the victorious war, in August 1941, apart from the immense militarily occupied territories and the satellite states, the Reich had swollen to some 120 million subjects. After their defeat, the Germans were distributed as follows: American zone, 17 million; English, 22; French, 6; Russian, 17; Berlin, 3.

As for the Russian Bear, in 1939 the population was figured to be 173 million, in the Russian and Asiatic territories in which figures begin to have no meaning. After the annexations to the west the population is now some 195 million, after having made up for the frightful loss of 17 million on account of the war. The territories gained on the west are the ones taken away from Finland-Estonia-Lithuania-Poland-Slovakia-Hungary-Romania – all together, a territory around the size of Italy.

Dealing with other issues, we have not spoken of the types of central or federal order but, rather, have focused on units in terms of all-encompassing armed forces. Neither was this the place to speak of overseas empires, where – certain appearances notwithstanding – the fact of centralisation prevails. On the non-European continents, America in its entirety is tending to become a single state under the hegemony of Washington (see the aptitude of the minor states in the European wars). Japan has followed Germany in its course from Inflation to Deflation. The Chinese regimes respond, basically, to the need to replace the autonomous practice of a hundred provinces nominally united in the old Celestial Empire with a single Central State under the banner of Cap-ital. The supposed liberation of India is, in its turn, the end of the autonomy of hundreds of feudal principalities and sultanates to the advantage of two modern centres of bureaucracy and profiteering. And so it is for all the fool-ish figurants of colour at the General Assembly of the United Nations, a true market where peoples are bought and sold and their hides are tanned for the yellow leather bags of a few dozen capitalist pimps. Marx wrote that the worker is 'like someone who has brought his own hide to market and now has nothing to expect but – a tanning'.[11] The UN, not Ilse Koch,[12] has fulfilled his prophecy

---

11   Marx 1976, Chapter 6, p. 280.
12   Wife of the commandant of the Nazi concentration camps of Buchenwald and Majdanek. She was one of the first prominent Nazis to be tried by the US military.

The United States of America (1947–57)

1   America[1]

The daily readers of today's press see appalling numbers pass before their tired eyes. Not in the writings that popularise astronomy or corpuscular physics – no, it is the very writings that feed them their politics that more and more, for political motives, stuff them with economy, and serve up numbers.

Billions of dollars. A billion is a thousand millions, and is written with a *one* followed by nine *zeros*. Before long a dollar will correspond to a thousand of our lire and, less or more,[2] they'll end up by stopping the lira there (which means that the lira will buy two hundred times less than at the beginning of the century). Thus a billion dollars would be worth a thousand billion lire; a trillion (billion or milliard, it's the same thing) is written with a *one* followed by twelve *zeros*.

Let's look at the matter more palpably. Let's say that the average worker earns 1,600 lire a day. In three hundred working days that comes to 480,000 lire a year, more or less 500 dollars. Great optimism, no doubt about it.

With a *billiondollar*,[3] a trifle for today's victors, one can buy the labour of two million productive persons (our figures are arbitrarily rounded off, but arbitrary here, arbitrary there, things balance out in the end); the billiondollar acquires the labour for one year of a population of ten million souls (s.o.s. – Save Our Souls).

All that people talk about these days is the reconstruction of destroyed Europe and the money America has to lend it for this purpose. The billion-dollars whirl in the polemic. Truman, to aid Greece and Turkey, has Congress allocate just three tenths of a billiondollar for now, but they've already realised that the aid is not sufficient to destroy the guerrillas. In any event, to the few congressional objections raised Truman responded loud and clear that the war cost the United States 341 billiondollars, and for the guarantee of this 'invest-ment' – or, as the French say, *placement* – hesitating to spend those few bucks in

---

1   *Prometeo* No. 7, 1947.
2   Less or more: the normal Italian expression is *su per giù* – 'more or less' – but here Bordiga writes *giù per su*: more less than more.
3   A *miliardollaro* is Bordiga's purely invented word.

Greece and Turkey would be the height of penny-pinching. After all, it amounts to just one per thousand of the capital that was risked to save Liberty.

France, for now, has had just a quarter of a billiondollar, but it sufficed to get Thorez[4] and company out of the government. For Italy they're dangling one entire billiondollar, of which one or two tenths are allegedly already ready. But we'll come to that in a moment.

These are loans that, of course, will be paid back with interest, but then there is also pure charity, pure and simple donation, the latest and most refined form of capital 'investment'. Here too the UNRRA[5] directives, in accordance with the Truman Doctrine, are clear: country by country the allocations depend on the colour of the local government or on its subjection to American policy; in dubious cases the allocations are reduced to zero. It isn't war, but it's still playing on death.

But there's more. The – rather coarse – Truman Doctrine consists in managing the dollar in order to destroy Russian influence zone by zone, and the Doctrine is applied with the delicacy of a bison. Luckily in the 'land of the free' there is the democratic clash of opposite opinions, and in this case, against the Truman Doctrine, we have Henry A. Wallace,[6] a great friend of Russia, who adopts extremely refined diplomacy and pushes disinterestedness to the limits of the unlikely. Give-lend-advance dollars,[7] this is America's sacred duty, and we need above all to offer Russia a tidy sum, immediately. Naturally, the figures here go up. We must put at Europe's disposal 50 of our units, fifty billiondollars, and, Mr Wallace insists, we must not hesitate to give Russia from a fifth to a third of this, from 10 to 17 billiondollars.

The devastations of the war, by one calculation, amount to 150 billiondollars and Wallace supposes that in the local capitals they can come up with 50 more to invest, while it will be America that will lend the other 100 billiondollars to the rest of the world.

Getting back to the 50 that are up to us Europeans, according to our quick little calculation they would be just enough to buy the labour-power of 500 million inhabitants for one year – exactly the population of Europe.

---

4 Maurice Thorez was secretary general of the French Communist Party from 1930 until his death in 1964.

5 United Nations Relief and Rehabilitation Administration, later replaced by the Marshall Plan.

6 Roosevelt's Vice President from 1941–45 and Truman's Secretary of Commerce, he was fired in 1946.

7 In the text: 'Give lend advance dollars'. It is typical of Bordiga's style to omit the commas in such cases; in the translation the phrases are hyphenated.

The reconstruction can certainly not be done in one year, since all the products of the European workers, two thirds of which, in Wallace's theory, have become American property, cannot be used to rebuild destroyed plants and structures, since the workers themselves have to eat and consume.

With consumption reduced, as is the case almost everywhere in Europe, let us suppose that the workers absorb half of their product. In this case, if the entire 50 billiondollars could – but this is definitely impossible – be advanced and invested all at once, in two years Europe would have renovated its machinery and its plants, but two thirds of all the returns on capital that this would produce would be American, by right, 'forever'.

The figures are highly debatable, but it's clear that Mr Wallace, a true pacifist, is planning a first-rate investment.

Naturally he needs guarantees for the collection of his formidable interest due, even though, of course, he is still owed the sum advanced. What guarantees are needed? Truman – who, let's say, is not overly refined – sees them in the disarmament of others and the creditor's formidable armament, by its mass and quality capable of keeping the world in subjection and deterring the eventual whims of anyone who might be unhappy about paying his instalments.

Wallace, by contrast, explains to us and explains to the residents of the Kremlin – who, we suppose, will swallow it, which is not to say that they believe it – how this generous advance will be the foundation of peace. The guarantees will be purely legal. During the construction of the Super-State, which will have the same functions on a world scale as the state that is sovereign for the citizens and the private organisations in its own territory, the system of mortgages will be internationalised. Structures and plants in the debtor countries will guarantee with their value and with their activity the full settlement of the credit.

In this second – civil – version of American supremacy a new character comes on the scene: the international bailiff, executor of writs. We know very well how he acts in the national arena. He is far more powerful than the gendarme, even if he carries no arms other than an old leather briefcase full of papers and is physically unassuming and modestly dressed: in fact his salary is far lower than that of military men, sturdy lads dressed in spiffy uniforms. But his legal and civil power is so tremendous that often his victim, after playing all his cards in this tragic war of papers, at the sight of the bailiff coming – the bailiff! trembling and defenceless! – is so astonished that, far from attempting to offend or repel him, without ado blows his own brains out. The bailiff wins his battle without bloodying his hands, or staining his spotless police record, or compromising the confessor's absolution.

In this way the dollar, with its world organisation of advances for the poor, sets out to conquer Europe to the Urals and beyond, and plans the success of its mission without recourse to the trajectories of atomic torpedoes and of fighter planes overflying the Pole.

As far as Italy is concerned things have already begun to become magnificently clear. The process will be more difficult in those countries that for geographical reasons are in direct contact with Russian might and are garrisoned by the Soviet army. In the intermediate countries we witness original developments. For Hungary it seems it is Russia itself that is offering 200 million dollars (definitely not roubles) to avoid the competition. What's wrong here is that in the end they'd take those dollars from Wallace's billions, and the banker will take his cut twice over.

But for us everything will be OK soon. The inflation will be curbed when the billiondollar loan is established (verily, we are one tenth of the population of Europe and have been hit harder than most but, for now, of Wallace's 50 billiondollars we're getting just the fiftieth part; it's the fate of those who don't scare anyone). Soon the big deals in Italy will be quoted in dollars and not in lire – in fact, they already are. The lira will be *pegged*[8] to the dollar (what a nice term ... we can't resist the temptation of saying that it will be pegged more firmly than Vulcan's chains pegged Prometheus to his rock ...). The formula of Italian life will be simple: *nothing is lost, only honour.*

Naturally we shed no tears over the honour of the bourgeois homeland. The concept of honour is in force in societies divided in castes or in classes, it has meaning as long as men are divided between gentlemen and *mechanics*, it does not interest the revolutionary proletariat that has no honours to lose, but only the ... pegs that fix him to the *onorata società*[9] of capitalism.

So far the foreign-loan operation has not even been contested by today's opposition, yesterday's allies of the government.[10] This opposition – in reply to De Gasperi's programme – writes shamelessly: '*We need the dollars, what a great discovery!*' They agree to the dollars and to UNRRA, otherwise, after years and years of idiotic propaganda that presented the social structure of American capitalism as the epitome of civility, it would mean electoral bankruptcy.

---

8   The Italian word is 'anchored', but with 'pegged' Bordiga's metaphor does not change very much.

9   'Honourable society': a common name for the Mafia.

10   A reference to the Italian Communist Party (PCI) and the Italian Socialist Party (PSI), which had participated in a government of national unity with the Christian Democrats from 1945 to 1947.

These sycophants maintain that it would be possible to take the dollars and avoid the influences on our 'domestic policy'. But with the dissolution of the boundaries dividing the economies of the various countries from their commercial and monetary areas, the difference between foreign policy and domestic policy is history. The socialcommunists say that, for the dollars, our guarantees have to be our industries, not the state; economic, not political guarantees. Marxists such as these tell us it's possible to give an economic guarantee that won't be reflected in political influence ... But then those industries, in the programme of those gentlemen, and especially the large monopolistic industries (the only ones we have that are capable of guaranteeing a few dollars, and they're already up to their necks in American mortgages) – weren't they supposed to be nationalised, with state money (taken from the loan)? And wouldn't this be tantamount to *both the selling and the renting* of the state?

Whether they're in the same Ministry or not, they're all in agreement on the economic policy of loans. They were all in agreement on the internal loan, and we witnessed the nauseating spectacle of the advertising for loans in what claimed to be the newspapers 'of the working classes'. The loan to the state, the constitution of the ever more elephantine public debt, is one of the cornerstones of capitalist accumulation. Marx, in Chapter 31 of the first volume of *Capital*, 'The Genesis of the Industrial Capitalist', writes: 'The national debt, i.e. the alienation [by sale] of the state – whether that state is despotic, constitutional or republican – marked the capitalist era with its stamp. The only part of the so-called national wealth that actually enters into the collective possession of a modern nation is – the national debt. Hence, quite consistently with this, the modern doctrine that a nation becomes the richer the more deeply it is in debt. Public credit become the *credo* of capital. And with the rise of national debt-making, lack of faith in the national debt takes the place of the sin against the Holy Ghost, for which there is no forgiveness'.[11]

One of the essential theses of Marxism is that the greater the wealth concentrated in the hands of the national bourgeoisie, the greater the misery in the working masses. The *Cop-State*, a simple defender of bourgeois privilege, is today increasingly being transformed into the *Coffer-State*. The cash assets of this coffer serve to increment the accumulated wealth of the bourgeoisie, while its liabilities crush the shoulders of the proletariat. With national loans the economic servitude of the working class is reasserted. Then, if the workers

---

11   Marx 1976, p. 919.

actually accede to the state's senseless appeal and buy their exploiters' government bonds, their servitude is asserted for the third time over!

In Italy it is most certainly not De Gasperi who risks sinning against the Holy Ghost!

But his current adversaries in Parliament, partners until yesterday in the policy of loans, still partners today in the policy of the servitude of labour unions, continue to be his partners in the policy of the loan from America with which the Italian state alienates itself to foreign capital.

We have already said that for the proletariat to be sold to foreign capital or to indigenous capital is equally unfortunate.

In the case of the current Italian ruling political class it must be said, however, that through the disgraceful metamorphoses of its line-up, in selling the honour of *its* state it will manage to go down a few more rungs.

The alienation of one's own honour is not the worst deal one can make. Even here – and, again, we are at the heart of the mechanics of the bourgeois world, which we oppose and hate – there is a question of price. Honour can be sold below cost. And, in Italy today, this is where the political *gerarchi*[12] are headed, negotiating the conditions of its financial intervention with the foreign victor, concerned only with fighting among themselves, be they pro-American or pro-Russian, for their percentages of the commissions on the deal.

2   America Again![13]

The atmosphere of Europe, still turbid and oppressed by the haze of war, is full of the controversy over America, over the aid from America, over America's intentions.

The slaughters of the war have not thinned the crowd of stomachs in the most anciently and densely populated part of the planet: old Europe is hungry, it doesn't have enough to eat, it no longer produces enough food, and it no longer has the strength to go off and plunder the other continents of the world.

And here comes rich America, giving-lending-advancing dollars, and planning further advances. Is it advancing gold, currency, instruments of credit, and all the other ingenious and idiotic black arts of mercantilism? Substantially, it is advancing means of subsistence, in the broadest sense, since subsistence means more than simply what we eat.

---

12   A *gerarca* is a Fascist party official.
13   *Prometeo* No. 8, 1947.

This funding in foodstuffs represents the height of the 'generosity' of which capitalism is capable. It started with *cash and carry*: if you want to eat, pay your bill before being served. Next came the law of *rent and lend*, which means, with a sense of great trust, that you deliver the goods and put the buyer in debt.

In short, the American innkeeper gave us a meal ticket, but on credit. And then came UNRRA, where he gives the meal away without even making a note of the debt: the rich restaurateur feeds the hungry out of the love of God.

Whoever knows anything at all about the Marxist vision of the economy knows very well that, here, the degree of coercion has to be reversed. The three methods present successively greater degrees of the oppression and exploitation that the rich exercise over the poor.

In the devastation of its production system Europe is left, more and more, with only one of its production forces, namely, its working masses.

America did not suffer destruction; its industries, plants, machinery, and all of its constant capital are intact.

Constant capital represents the legacy that past generations, through centuries of accumulated labour, hand down to the successive generations. But the course of this succession is diverted by class privilege, since the billions of working days bequeathed by the dead do not belong to all of the living but only to a small minority.

This legal relation would be of little use to the satraps of capitalism if they had only constant capital at their disposal: let these 'captains of industry' contemplate their forests of motionless machines and smokeless chimneys all day long, it won't keep them from starving to death.

Constant capital, if profit is to be generated and the accumulation of wealth to continue, must be integrated with variable capital, that is, with human labour, insofar as the economic mechanism allows the monopolisers of the plants to advance the workers their means of subsistence while continuing to be the beneficiaries of the entire product of the combination between machinery and labour.

As long as in the classic capitalism of free enterprises all this takes place on many economic islands, the owner of constant capital not only does not need to advance the means of subsistence, but it is the workers who advance him a week or a fortnight of labour. If, without dying of starvation, they could advance a year of their labour, or however much is needed for the entire cycle of transformation of raw materials, bourgeois law and morality would gladly sanction this relationship.

In its evolution capitalism has made enterprises increasingly interdependent, with the fertilisation of fixed capital by variable capital planned by the bourgeoisie on a world scale.

The recent war[14] has, in a sense, distanced the two generators of capitalist profit,[15] and bringing them back together – the only condition that will make it possible to get the wheels of the exploitation machine back into full spin – will require indefinite waiting periods.

To keep the working masses of all branches of production from thinning and dispersing during these waits capitalism constructs an apparatus that advances the famished populations their means of subsistence.

This advance presented as a 'gift', precisely because the part that effectively produces profit is the variable capital, will be repaid at conditions ten times more usurious than was the case with cash payment or, successively, with the opening of a regular credit account in the name of vacillating European capital.

The literature of the budding bourgeois era was horrified by Shylock, who converted his instrument of credit into the right to cut himself a pound of his debtor's flesh. But today intelligent capitalism keeps the poor beggar on his feet with a tin of meat and vegetables. In this way the afflatus of Christian and enlightened mercantile civilisation – sailing the high seas, setting out from our shores to conquer the world – returns, refined, from the Far West.

After the other war that Germany lost, a visitor travelling through that country militarily prostrated by the battles fought on the territories of others was astonished by the unimpaired condition of the powerful modern plants that a highly accelerated industrialisation had built up in just a few decades. The forest of iron and reinforced concrete planted in the soil represents the constant capital in which the labour of generations is crystallised. It is a reserve like the coal of the vegetal forests buried in the geological millennia. If the proletarian Spartacus, instead of so brutally falling victim to the champions of a Germany perfectly democratic (much like the renegade Marxists of today), had been able to grasp Germany in the pincers of his red dictatorship, twinning his Russian sibling, perhaps imperialism would not have been able to drag the world into yet another bloodbath.

The current conquistadors of Germany, who were in fact the conquistadors of Europe, were very careful not to proclaim their V-day before they had traversed the entire territory of the vanquished, already torn to pieces by the bombings, both to see what was left of the production plants and to prevent revolutionary convulsions in the sacrificed masses.

---

14   In the text: 'The current war'.
15   Capital and labour.

But it was not only German constant capital that was ruined. Economic power relations – the foundation of political dominance – arise in the same way for the countries, such as England and Russia, that burned out their plants and machinery fighting the Germans. The masses in these countries will have to work like mad to refill the void produced in that which the bourgeoisie calls national wealth. In this grandiose investment of variable capital gigantic profits are reaped by reconstructive capital. But the cycle cannot get underway without advances, and for now we have a spectacle not of intense labour but of unemployment and of hunger. The country, with the force of its production system intact, that can advance the dollars and the tins becomes the master and exploiter of the enslaved European masses.

There is only one force – the force of a coherent revolutionary movement and party – that is capable of waging the campaign against America, the plutocratic monster that keeps under its classic iron heel our proletarian comrades, who also in America are victims of the tremendous crisis. The proteiform mobilisation of means of all kinds, which will spectacularly dominate the years we are about to live through, can be combated with some hope of success only by an international party that has not severed the connection between theory, organisation and tactics, climbing directly up towards the totalitarian revolution.

The liquidators of Internationals futilely turn to provincial committees to rekindle the flame of the workers' struggle against imperialism, whose world centre now operates outside Europe.

By what means shall you mount a resistance to this world superpower comparable to its inexorable resources? By no means! Because you spent all the years of the war grazing with the flocks of the bourgeois imbecility of Europe, calling on the industrial and military force of America for supreme salvation!

How wrong it was to have conceived of a proletarian struggle that admitted in a first phase the alliance with Nazism in order to take a few steps into eastern Europe and, in a second phase, the war against Nazism and the no less dishonouring alliance with the capitalist democracies under the illusion of taking other steps as far as Berlin.

A military conquest and the outbreak of a revolution are two very different things. A revolution must simultaneously attack all the structures of bourgeois power in each and every country.

Hence the international anti-American campaign now being organised with adroit – incurably *progressive* – moves by the Moscow ex-communists[16] is a lost cause.

---

16   For Bordiga, the Stalinists in Russia have betrayed communism and no longer deserve to be called communists.

In its cautious first steps it leaves the door wide open to the possibility, not excluded in principle, that the Marshall Plan be rejected not because it is the supreme expression of class oppression, compared to which Hitler's and Mussolini's fanfaronades were child's play, but only because the advances earmarked for Russia and its satellites are too low.

And in fact in Italy they are quick to declare, when the American delegates point out that it would be the end if the rosary of ships full of grain now spanning the Atlantic should be broken, that there is no question of *refusing* the aid.

But the one and only word of the proletarian battle against the reconstruction of Europe according to the Marshall Plan is, precisely, *refusal*.

When in the struggle for the remuneration of labour the worker has recourse to a strike – a method the repudiators of everything have for the time being not yet repudiated – he is responding to the low wages he receives precisely by refusing his wages altogether.

But the word from Belgrade is to sabotage the influence of America also with 'government' action, that is, from within the state. Are the historic cyclones of this latest war not sufficient proof of the fact that the state is a unitary power that cannot be cut up in slices! To say nothing of the fact that, to take government action, first you have to win elections!

Hence the amphibious positions and the tactics of gradual conversion will not be able to keep the adhesions to so-called communism – now coming from all the slime of the middle classes in the conviction that communism is heir to the Camorrist functions of protection previously exercised by Fascism – from vanishing at the first whiff of a few red cents, when we come to the decisive point.

3 Attack on Europe[17]

Wars of defence and of aggression: at the outbreak of the European conflict in 1914 there was heated debate over this distinction, with regard to the attitude of the socialists.

For right-thinking people the question is simple, as usual. Government, State, Homeland, Nation, Race, without splitting hairs – all are assimilated to a single subject with right, wrong, rights, and duties. It all boils down to the Human Person and the doctrine of his behaviour, be it based on Christian morality, natural law, an innate sense of justice and fairness, or – expressed more

---

17   *Prometeo*, No. 13, 1949.

philosophically – on the ethicality of the categorical imperative. So, just as the just man, foreign to evil, if attacked, defends himself against the aggressor – leaving aside for a moment that business about the other cheek – so the People, if attacked, have a right to defend themselves. War is barbarous but the defence of the homeland is sacred. Every citizen must democratically speak out for peace and against wars, but the instant his Country is attacked he must rush to its defence against the invader! This holds for the individual, it holds for the entire Nation made Person, so it also holds for political parties, in their turn moved and treated as personified subjects in their obligations; and it holds for classes.

The result of all this is the general betrayal of socialism, warmongering on all fronts, the triumph, in all languages, of militarism. And, no less obviously, we have yet to see a war that the State or the Government waging it has failed to describe as defensive.

The first thing the Marxist polemic did was, naturally, to clear the field of all those phantom persons with one head, several heads, or no head, or no head and with someone else's head on its shoulders, restoring to their proper place the character and the function of those organisms known as classes, parties, states. Such organisms have a historical dynamic of their own, and to investigate it good moral principles are of no use.

The Marxists responded to the bourgeois that the proletarians have no homeland, the proletarian party pursues its ends by breaking up domestic fronts, and wars can offer excellent occasions for this pursuit; that he does not see historical development in the greatness or in the salvation of nations; and that in his international congresses he has already been engaged in breaking up all the war fronts, beginning where best he could.

Those who distort and corrupt Marxism launched a long – and not only verbal – struggle, in which in various ways and in various languages they attempted to dismantle the theory that, as Marx taught, in a first phase the proletariat can establish itself as a national class only by imposing its dictatorship over the bourgeoisie. They shamelessly replaced this theory with one of their own, maintaining that the proletariat and its party assume a national character only when political democracy and liberalism have been realised.

The Marxists went to great lengths to illustrate the various problems of the consequences that wars – their course and their dissolution – have on the domestic and the international events of the socialist class struggle and of the behaviour of the socialist party in the countries at war, since the condition for any exploitation of new conditions or new fragilities of regimes is the revolutionary party's continuity, autonomy, proud class opposition, and theoretical and material disposition for social war on the home front.

Once any and all adhesion to the war of states or of governments had been rejected, any distinction between defensive and offensive wars broke down, along with any excuses that justified the passing of the socialists to the fronts of national unity on the basis of this non-existent distinction.

Then again, the vacuity of the scuffle stemmed from a difference over the significance of *aggression* and *invasion*. When two snotty kids have a fight they are quick to holler that it was the other one who started it, but when territorial integrity is involved it's quite another matter. Once upon a time wars did physical harm to soldiers sent into combat, but there was practically no risk of death for civilians far from the front. (This was largely the case in the First World War.) If, however, a territory was invaded by an enemy army, well, here we have the usual picture of the destruction of goods-hearths-homes-families, violence against women, children, the elderly and so forth – all propaganda material widely used to lure the socialist parties into the trap. Even the worker without property, it was said, ripe for the class struggle, has something to lose and sees a threat to his vital interests in a material and immediate sense if an enemy army invades the city or the countryside where he lives and works. Therefore he must hunt down and repel the invader. Literarily flawless! Look! The defence mounted in the castle of the Unnamed against the marauding Landsknechts![18] We hear the strains of the Marseillaise: *ils viennent jusque dans vos bras, égorger vos fils, vos compagnes* ...

In response to all these pleasantries Marxists have demonstrated a hundred times over that all these reasons for justifying war, used in the end to provide cannon fodder and dispel the movements and parties that cross the street to militarism, are unfounded and cancel each other out. This, of course, does not mean that Marxists fail to engage in critical and historical evaluation of the distinctions between wars in their repercussions on the developments of social struggles and revolutionary crises. But the point here is that *aggression* – a seriously overworked reason for justifying 'defensive' war – and the no less exploited one of *invasion* can conflict with one another. A state may be the aggressor in a war but, if it then suffers military defeats, can soon expose its territory to invasion, as in Togliatti's theory of pursuit of the aggressor.

No less contradictory are the other well-known reasons based on nationalist and irredentist claims, and the ones that many easily satisfied Marxists came up with to justify support for the colonial wars, designed to bring the 'benefits' of the modern capitalist economy to 'barbarian' countries. The Boer

---

18   The Unnamed is a character in Alessandro Manzoni's *The Betrothed*. The Landsknechts were mercenary Germany soldiers.

War of 1899–1902 was blatant aggression, the Boer colonists of Dutch descent defended their homeland-freedom-nation-violated territory, but the Labourites managed to justify the British undertaking as *progressive*. In May of 1915 Italy's war on Austria, its former ally, was blatant aggression, justified by the various social-traitors on the basis of the liberation of Trent and Trieste coupled with the 'war for democracy', without blushing at the fact that on the other side of the front Austria-Hungary was up against the armies of the Tsar.

A classical case is reported in the extremely interesting book by Bertram D. Wolfe *Three Make a Revolution*, a veritable mine of historical facts, with all due reservations regarding the author's [political] line. On 6 February 1904 the Japanese, Pearl Harbor style, attacked and liquidated the Russian fleet anchored at Port Arthur, Manchuria, with no declaration of war. Blatant aggression. After a long siege by land and by sea the citadel fell in January of 1905. Deep deep mourning for Russian patriotism. In the 4 January 1905 issue of *Vperiod* Lenin wrote: 'The proletariat has cause of rejoicing ... It is the autocratic regime and not the Russian people that has suffered ignoble defeat. The Russian people has gained from the defeat of autocracy. The capitulation of Port Arthur is the prologue to the capitulation of tsarism. The war is not ended yet by far, but every step towards its continuation immeasurably increases the unrest and discontent among the Russian people, brings nearer the hour of a new great war, the war of the people against the autocracy, the war of the proletariat for liberty'.[19] The entire question merits greater analysis if one wishes to clarify the complex problems regarding the historical relationships between absolutism, bourgeoisie, and proletariat, resolving by means of the Marxist dialectic the presumed contradiction Mr Wolfe sees between the different historical phases of Lenin's doctrine and work. For the moment, suffice it to note that this article by the isolated émigré lives on the very content of the gigantic Russian revolutionary battle of 1905, sparked by the national defeat of a few months earlier.

Then forty years go by, and on 2 September 1945 a Japan defeated by the Americans with the atomic bombs on Hiroshima and Nagasaki surrenders unconditionally. Even though Russia had not declared war on Japan until the very last days of the war, Marshal Stalin delivered a Victory Address in which he stated: 'The defeat of the Russian troops in 1904 during the Russo-Japanese War left bitter memories in the minds of our people. It lay like a black stain on our country. Our people believed in and waited for the day when Japan would be

---

19   See Lenin, *The Fall of Port Arthur*, available at http://marxism.halkcephesi.net/Lenin/FPA05.html.

defeated and the stain would be wiped out. We of the older generation waited for this day for forty years, and now this day has arrived'.[20]

The suggestive history of adhesions to wars thus provides decisive arguments in support of Lenin's revolutionary defeatism, and in support of the rule of tactics that in this field the proletarian parties cannot make the slightest concession without putting the working class at the mercy of the moves of the military states. These states, with a simple telegram, can make irreparable moves that will endanger the nation, its soil and its honour, and any sympathy for such arguments will be the ruin of the national and international class movement. When the Italian aggression of 1915 led to invasion after the rout at the Battle of Caporetto, the meritorious opposition of the Italian socialists wavered, in Turati's cry, 'The homeland is on Mount Grappa!' despite the fact that Treves, his intellectual brother, had dared to warn, 'Not another winter in the trenches!'

What is more, the bourgeois states and government parties coined the theory of *vital spaces*, of preventive invasion, of preventive war, justifying it on the basis of national well-being. All these reasons, while not without real historical foundations, must not persuade the revolutionaries, just as they must not be persuaded by the reasons of defence and liberty advanced by the most pure and innocent of capitalist governments (if such a thing existed!). The war of 1914 itself, clamorous Teutonic aggression, was an English preventive war. Every government sees its interests and its vital spaces where it wishes. For centuries the English have been playing the game of having its borders on the Rhine and the Po – a game, supposedly, that saved (their) Liberty time and again. But then they were mortally offended by Hitler's claim to have his vital borders on the far side of the Sudetenland and in Danzig ... a few kilometres outside, or even a few kilometres inside his own homeland, in light of that ineffable democratic masterpiece of the Treaty of Versailles, with its Polish corridor.

Wars can turn into revolutions (whatever the judgement of Marxists on a given war) on the condition that the core of the international revolutionary proletarian movement survive in every country, completely detached from the policy of the governments and from the movements of the military General Staffs, and that it pose no theoretical or tactical reservations of any kind between itself and the possibility of defeatism and of sabotage of the ruling class in war – of its political, state and military organisations.

---

20   See Stalin, 'Stalin's address to the people. September 2, 1945', available at http://www .marxists.org/reference/archive/stalin/works/1945/09/02.htm.

For that matter, on a previous occasion we made it clear that this proclaimed defeatism is no great scandal, given the fact that all our adversaries, be they self-styled revolutionaries or genuine bourgeois, have extolled and applied it in various cases and places. Except that in all these cases the dialectical content of the defeatism is not the revolutionary conquest of a new class regime but, rather, a simple changing of the political guard in the framework of the bourgeois order in force. Defeatists of this ilk risk many words and little skin, their sole incentive being that a given regime will fall only if defeated in war, and only if it falls will they then have a chance of personal success and positions of power. These men – and they are the same gentlemen we saw earlier, with their patriotic-national-free and democratic motives – are ready at the drop of a hat to see their country and its population in the material sense, given the modern techniques of war, crushed by destructive bombing and torn to pieces by all the irreparable manifestations of war itself and of military occupation.

Having said all this for the umpteenth time, let's see what sort of war a next – American – war might be like, since the Americans are already busy allocating immense resources to their military, holding meetings of their General Staff, and issuing preparation orders and strategic dictates to foreign and distant countries. It might turn out to be the noblest of wars from the standpoint of exalted literary arguments. Or it might turn out to be teeming with monsters worse than Cecco Beppes,[21] Big Wilhelms,[22] Benitos, Adolfs, Tojos, or a reborn Nicholas, his hands stained with blood. None of this would induce the revolutionary Marxists to attenuate the struggle against the bourgeoisie and against the state, everywhere.

This doesn't alter our right to analyse this war and to describe it as the most stunning feat of aggression-invasion-oppression-enslavement of all time. This, moreover, is not just a possible and hypothetical war since it is already underway, and is an enterprise connected to and, strictly speaking, a continuation of the interventions in the European wars of 1917 and 1942. What is more, since this war is, fundamentally, the coronation of the concentration of an immense military and destructive force in a supreme centre of domination and defence of the current class regime, that of capitalism, it is the construction of the best possible conditions for stifling the revolution of workers in every country of the world.

---

21   Franz Joseph I of Austria, in Italian Francesco Giuseppe. Cecco is short for Francesco and
      Beppe for Giuseppe.
22   Kaiser Wilhelm II of Germany.

This process could unfold even without a war in the full sense between the United States and Russia, if Russia's vassalage could be ensured not by a full and proper campaign of destruction and occupation but, rather, by the pressure of the predominant economic forces of the maximum capitalist organisation in the world – perhaps tomorrow the single Anglo-American State of which one already speaks. Yes, a compromise might be arranged, in which the Russian leadership sells the country out at a high price; it seems that Stalin has already set the figure at two billion dollars.

The fact remains that the high-handedness of our historical European aggressors who took such unimaginable pains to conquer a city or a province a cannon-shot away is laughable indeed compared to the impertinence of the public discussions – and we can easily imagine what the secret plans will be like – over whether the security of New York and San Francisco will be defended on the Rhine or on the Elbe, in the Alps or the Pyrenees. The vital space of the American conquistadors is a strip that goes right around the globe; it is the end of the story of a method that began with Aesop, when the wolf accused the lamb of muddying his water, even though the lamb was drinking downstream. White-black-yellow, not one of us can take a sip of water without muddying the cocktails served to the kings of the plutocratic Camorra in the nightclubs of the States.

When the American regiments disembarked in France the first time the military technicians laughed and the Anglo-French General Staffs begged them to give right back the few stretches of western front they'd been given, if they didn't want to see Wilhelm in Paris by nightfall. But the American 'boys', drunk then and now, could have very well responded that the shoe was already on the other foot, and today we are dazzled by the top guns of a militarism that outclasses anything our own pluri-millennial military history can offer. To make war, it is money, capital, production plants that count; military ability and courage are commodities on sale on the world market, teeming with super-foxes and super-fools.

The Americans have boasted ever since of that first victory, they turned up their noses for having to come out of their isolationism (in England's wake), they withdrew after having designed a Europe more absurd than Tamerlane or Omar Pascià would have ever done. Twenty years of peace were just what was needed for the preparation – and the consecration of super-statued Liberty – of a superfleet-superaviation-superarmy. At the service of superaggression.

In the meantime the colonies of the Far West brushed up on the alphabet and even studied history – without, of course, renouncing the ineffable convenience of being without a history. At the second landing in Normandy it may have been Clark himself or some other graduate who, coming across the grave of the French general who fought for American independence, came up with the truly sensational expression: 'Nous voici, Lafayette!' Which is to say: we have come to return the courtesy and liberate France.

And in fact just as in Moscow they teach in the history books that Vladimir Ulyanov known as Lenin asked and received from Tsar Nicholas permission to form a volunteer corps to rush to the defence of Manchuria against the Japanese, so they will be teaching in Washington how the Frenchman Lafayette, in the alliance of all the democratic world's forces captained by England, land of liberty, fought to liberate North America, until then a colony oppressed by the Germans, who ever since, in one war after another, have attempted to win it back. And in a future edition it may well be that the Yankee manuals will go so far as to speak of a struggle of colonial emancipation against the Moscow conquistador, whose avidly revengeful intentions have been evident ever since it sold Alaska for a few pounds of gold.

Not even the second time around were their military actions first rate, but when it boils down to bravura in war quantity turns into quality. Apropos of Clark, they say that the Americans themselves deny him the glory of the battle of Cassino. Perhaps they have discovered that there never was a battle at Cassino, and there never was a Gustav Line. There were, in fact, a few dozen (unscathed) German soldiers and several hundred thousand Italian civilians bloodily bombed for five months, until the Americans found a way to send a few units of Poles and of Italians into the fray and, between Sessa and Ausonia, some Moroccans as well, who occupied themselves with raping all the women between the ages of ten and seventy (and not only the women), *engaging* fewer *deutsche Grenadiere* than the number of Salvatore Giuliano's bandits engaged by the Italian police.

In the European theatre, then, one of the major decisions of the American top brass was the rearming of the Italians. Italy played a curious role in all this manoeuvring of giants, given the fact that in recent decades demographic power has no longer been the prime factor in military strength.

After having been on the threshold, in the First War, of at least one great attempt at revolutionary defeatist, in the second our country had a full-fledged experience of attempted bourgeois defeatism.

In short, no one plotted to undermine the Fascists' war as long as the Germans were winning so many battles. Many did have defeatist hopes, but for personal reasons. Mussolini stood between them and the delight of power. That's the whole story. They couldn't plot behind the back of Benito's and Hitler's army while hiding behind the back of the opposing army.

In the autumn of 1942 the news spread that the American landing forces – after reciprocal deceptions and long discussions with their Russian allies, who day after day were bleeding themselves dry on the second front – were on the coasts of Morocco, with a clear itinerary: the Mediterranean, the Italian peninsula.

They were the stages of one single invasion, starting at Versailles in 1917–18 and headed for Berlin. Just for Berlin? No, you fools, with your stale applause. Also headed for Moscow! For great specialists in sensitivity to the changing of history you are late today in crying imperial threat and aggression. Being late would be bad enough, but you're literally gasping for breath. You cannot put history into reverse and resuscitate the millions fallen at Stalingrad. No one will answer you.

That piece of news should have been sufficient to foretell the ordeal awaiting Italy. For reasons of class, for reasons of revolution, the Marxist draws even greater cataclysms to the area where he operates. But here it was a question of pure blindness. The Fascist radio that played its propaganda pop songs made more historical sense – sure, to bring grist to its own mill, but today just right for yesterday's allies of the American colossus, rejoicing at the failure of the classic Italian-German military countermove in a Tunisia originally promised to neutralised France. The countermove was well executed, technically, by the last Italian army since Scipio's day (we rejoice at the fact that there will no longer be Italian armies without other adjectives, and will rejoice all the more when there will be no armies with any adjective at all), but faced with the overwhelming power of the forces accumulated, nice and easy, on the other side of the Atlantic while European corpses were piling up at the Volga, it did not avoid the bloody farce of the shore-line.[23]

The Italian patriots, nationalists, and leaders of the Italian Popular Party were enjoying their rosy future.

But what was that popular song, Fascist but not so foolish? It remembered that Columbus was Italian and said in the refrain: 'Columbus, Columbus, Columbus, who made you do it?'

In keeping with an already widespread fashion, I greatly fear that Stalin will have to make the Moscow historians discover that Columbus was Russian.

---

23   'Bagnasciuga': a reference to Mussolini's famous 'bagnasciuga speech' of 24 June 1943, ten
      days before the American-led landing on Sicily, proclaiming that 'the landing would be
      blocked on the shore-line'.

4   The USA's European Policy[24]

4.1   *Yesterday*

Also in the war of 1914–18 the Americans intervened half way through, after two years as spectators. They abandoned the so-called Monroe Doctrine, which established their disinterestedness in European affairs and demanded that Europe renounce any claim to control over the new continent. Their coming out of isolationism recalled that of England, number one country of modern capitalism and, until that time, number one worldwide protector of the bourgeois regime. Hypocritically flaunting its model domestic organisation of liberty and democratic practise, not maintaining a standing army, endeavouring through imperial exploitation of the world to achieve class collaboration with its homeland proletariat through reformist conceptions, Great Britain kept under arms the world's largest fleet and had subdued the overseas empires of the Spanish, the Portuguese, the Dutch, plundering the planet. Alert to European conflicts, it intervened promptly to destroy the feared political and military hegemonies that threatened to compete in the exploitation of the world.

America's isolationism proved to be no less a tissue of hypocritical claims to be a model for the world. A capitalism, no less pitiless and cruel in its origin and its development than the English variety, claimed to educate humanity with pietistic doctrines and sham examples of prosperity, tolerance and generosity.

At the end of the war one of the most hateful exemplars of false moralists and anaemic preachers history has ever seen, the notorious Woodrow Wilson, bolstered by the economic and military aid given by his allies, made a show of wanting to reorganise old Europe according to new principles and imposed those masterpieces of the world bourgeois regime, the Treaty of Versailles and the League of Nations.

In the ranks of the socialist movement of the day naturally the opportunist currents went into ecstasy over this despicable version of capitalist oppression. Even in the ranks of the Italian party, highly resistant to the seductions of 'democratic war', there were some – after the American intervention, and even after the first Russian revolution of February 1917, which they saw as merely a bourgeois and patriotic democratic development – who spoke of reconsidering their positions, in the sense of throwing themselves into the ridiculous crusade against *Teutonic militarism*.

---

24   *Battaglia Comunista*, No. 4, 1949.

The revolutionary currents reacted. They had always seen the centres of greatest class potential in the imperialist capitalism and militarism of France first and then England, and saw the new centre of super-capitalism rising in America. The development of the Russian revolution was a far cry from what the social democrats and social patriots of all countries thought it was. The new movement of the left put Wilson in the front line of the direct adversaries of the proletarian and revolutionary cause, along with that Geneva of his[25] – which America, to perfect the Quakeristic hypocrisy of its method, failed to join.

4.2   Today

Also in the Second World War America intervened halfway through. This time, too, the central note of the propaganda was German provocation and defence of those attacked. We Marxists have never believed in the distinction between wars of defence and of aggression: we have a completely different judgement on the causes. The new war stemmed directly not only from the laws of the current social regime but from the world order and from the conditions imposed on Germany at Versailles, with the confirmation of the great colonial monopolies of the ultra-imperialist centres.

Contingently, just as England ended up intervening in the First War after having used that war to destroy the German threat, so the entire policy of the bourgeois American state between the two wars was a direct continuous preparation for an expansionist struggle at Europe's expense.

The seasoning of humanitarian and democratic falsehoods was employed on an even greater scale, in support of an economic-industrial-military development whose stages span twenty years of history.

The progressive *diminutio capitis*[26] of Great Britain – Hitler miscalculated the reaction to this, underestimating the determinations of class interests – was first sanctioned by the Washington Treaty of 1930, which modified the formula of one English fleet equal to the sum total of the two other strongest fleets in the world to one of parity between the English and the American fleets, with France and Japan kept behind. Hitler wasn't around yet, and Mussolini didn't scare anyone.

America's de facto economic, political and military interventionism all over the world – and what exact term can be substituted for aggression if not interventionism? – is even more openly declared in Mr Truman's message.

---

25   Bordiga often refers to the League of Nations simply as 'Geneva'.
26   In Roman Law, the loss of 'caput', that is, of the civil status of a Roman citizen.

The message is based on the usual philanthropic premises worthy of the sanctimonious and conformist picture of a presidential investiture based on Bibles and Gods Almighty, and on the usual extensions of the immortal principles of bourgeois democracy to economic demands, with the magnates of high capitalism promising bread for the hungry and even an abundant seasoning – *American prosperity, perhaps?* – for the already rancid dish of political and ideological freedom.

The highpoint of Truman's message is his direct desperate attack on communism – that is, on the demand for an anti-capitalist economy now pressing on the world, which is kept sharply distinct from an attack on Russia. Indeed, Russia is told that it has a chance of belonging to a world combination, despite its historical traditions as an imperialist power.

Truman wants to negotiate with Stalin, but he will not come to terms with communism. The situation could not be clearer. Among the other spokesmen old man Cachin responded that between the Russian regime and the capitalist regimes there can be collaboration.

Where *there cannot be* collaboration is between the great world centres of super-capitalism and the movement of the revolutionary proletariat. This movement is what the Trumans fear, more than war.

If for Truman public enemy number one is communism and if he urgently combats its 'philosophy' at a moment in which its class and revolutionary fronts are not in evidence, this, for us, is a comfort. The day may not be far off in which powerful strata of the world proletariat will understand that the number one enemy is Truman. Not Truman the person, the functionary unknown until Roosevelt's death, this face of a small-town priest with his hands on two Bibles and his honeyed smile – no, the enemy is the bestial force of the capitalist oppressor today concentrated in the formidable structure of economic *investments* and *armaments* organised across the Ocean.

But to understand this fully and to draw up for class war there is another thing the proletariat has to understand: that this relation of things and of powers has been constructed not in two years but in a hundred, and that just as in Lenin's day the proletariat drove the renegade leaders who praised Wilson's help in the war into the dungheap, it must do the same with those who in the Second War obscenely and traitorously defended the help of Roosevelt-Truman, and were at their service.

5   Korea and the World[27]

Four months were more than enough for the Marxist critique to trace the war
in Korea back to its real causes and fix it in its historical framework. It was not
a contingent or local episode, an accident, a disgraceful incident: it was one
among the many – and certainly one of the most virulent – manifestations
of an imperialist conflict that has neither parallels nor meridians but is being
played out in the theatre of the entire world, in the international time limits of
imperialism. Its protagonists were neither the Koreans of the North reclaiming
a broken national unity, nor the Koreans of the South, heralds of a violated right
and justice. No! they were the unwitting soldiers and the hired hands of the
two great world centres of capitalism, both driven by an ineluctable impetus
to the verge of war. The prize was not liberty, socialism, progress, and the thousand Ideologies in capital letters with which – like a thousand crosses – the
path of bourgeois society is strewn but, rather, the power relations and survival
conditions of the two maximum economic and political systems of capitalism,
America and Russia.

     And it made no sense to pose the question, so dear to the pettifoggers of
all wars, of who was attacked and who attacked, since the aggressor is always
imperialism. Just as it is true that the Russian pawn was the first to cross the
ridiculous and absurd parallel (it too the expression of a particular phase of
the power relations between the two imperialisms), so is it true that on a world
scale the most violent force of expansion and aggression, be it in the form
of arms or dollars or tins of meat, is the one that smoulders in the viscera of
the gigantic production machinery of the United States. But, quickening the
tempo, the entire red-hot explosive potential of a world war was condensed
in a very small place. More than in any previous episode of localised war, the
forms this conflict is destined, necessarily, to assume all over the world are projected as if onto a tragic screen: America's unabashed exploitation of machines
and weapons of war, of accumulated labour, of constant capital; and Russia's
equally unabashed use of human flesh, of living labour, of variable capital (we
take the liberty of expressing the external manifestations of the war in the
terms of Marxist economy). And, at the same time, we find the following par-
ticularity, valid above all for the Asian countries: the Russian drive – directed
far more to protecting itself against the pressing march of the dollar than to setting out on a march of its own – clings to a social underground in turmoil, to the
possibility of appealing to bourgeois stratifications fed up with the latest relics

---

27   *Prometeo*, No. 1, 1950.

of the past, to peasant classes with an illusory hunger for land, to exploited and deluded proletarian masses (with good reason Stalinism proclaimed the famous tactic of the 'bloc of four classes'); while all the American drive has to support it is the gigantic scaffolding of its production machinery expanded to the limits of the impossible. Once again, war roused to fever pitch the economic and political exploitation of the working masses, that work of pitiless destruction of goods and of labour-power which is the inevitable historical prerogative of capitalism.

It was not war in Korea but war in the world. And the 'peace'? The impending end of the conflict, with the traditional abandoning of the forces hurled into the massacre by their superpowerful master and their partial re-utilisation in later phases in renewed partisan experiments – which will be another way of continuing the real war beyond the fictions of an illusory peace – has already furnished a scenario for new conflicts. Indochina seems to be the next link in the chain. The millstone of imperialism takes no breaks.

    And, just as it takes no breaks in time, it is unbroken in space and in its morbid manifestations. Who can say that the war is more in the Far East or more in Europe, where, on both sides of the barricades, the sweat of the proletarians is exploited, yesterday in the reconstruction, today at the necessary historical epilogue of the reconstruction, in the preparation of new weapons of war? Where the State tightens the links of its machinery of repression, economic intervention, centralisation and, in short, of war – and does so not of its own volition but under the constant pressure of the international master, be it America or Russia? Where so-called 'mass' parties and organisations have – openly – no other content and reason to struggle apart from the mobilisation without call-up notice of proletarian cannon fodder for this or that imperialist master? Where instead of the ancient slogan 'butter or cannons' one openly cries out for 'bread and cannons' – that is, arms and, if possible, bread alone? Where, in short, everything is a marshalling for war and for defence of the international regime of exploitation of the proletariat, deploying government democratic parties and opposition democratic parties, entrepreneurial and trade-union associations, mass organisations linked to the 'black' parish or to the myriad 'red' sub-parishes?

    Korea is the whole world; Koreans are the proletarians of all countries, predestined victims of the third slaughter. The capitalism that divides them into opposing barricades unifies them involuntarily, by the very logic of its development, in a common destiny. For the Marxist critique, imperialism is the translation of the permanent crisis of a putrefying society into a spectacular and violent form. The terribleness, the gigantic pitilessness of its march, do not cloud the Marxist vision of the fact that the hack reporters, the theorists, the secular and religious priests of capitalist society all have the same interest in concealing behind the smokescreens of the press and the cannons the reality that imperialism, just as it brings the manifestations of violence, arrogance, and oppression of the bourgeois mode of production to the highest degree of exasperation and tension, also brings, and will continue to bring into broad daylight, its internal conflicts, the objective reasons for its undoing, and the impact capacities of the subjective forces that, born from its womb, will be called upon to destroy it. If it is true that the starting point of war is the defeat of the working class and that the enterprises of imperialism advance unhindered because of the decline of the international revolution, it is also true that the imperialist dynamic contains in itself the seeds of the revolutionary revival of the proletariat. Imperialism may or may not use the atomic bomb as a technical instrument of war. But what imperialism will not be able to avoid, however great its superpower today may seem and be, is the atom bomb of the international and internationalist revolution of the working class.

6   Democratic 'Points' and Imperial Programmes[28]

6.1   *Yesterday*

Three phases in America's behaviour with respect to the general wars originating in Europe: First phase, observation and speculation on the war – Second phase, intervention in the war – Third phase, liquidation of the war, direction of the peace.

Contained in all three phases: dirty capitalist wheeling-dealing, producing mountains of billions using human blood and hunger as raw materials. Form of the third phase: superemployment of all the ideological canons that can be mobilised, calling on heaven and earth, from the Bible to the Declaration of the Rights of Man, from Gospel precepts to democratic humanitarianism.

In the guise of apostle of this despicable hotchpotch, history does not fail to provide us with a president *pro tempore* of the star-spangled republic, have he the Quaker face of Wilson or the high-society barman face of Truman. In both cases the ideological cocktails smack of holy water, bootleg liquor, and *coco*:[29] the middle-culture crowd goes wild.

---

28   *Battaglia Comunista*, No. 2, 1950.
29   Liquorice water: a French 'cocktail'.

The phlebotomist Woodrow Wilson delivered Fourteen Points to suture the lacerated flesh of Europe in 1918. Has his text been forgotten? Christian charity and bourgeois liberty dance the most languid of waltzes. In the bass clef the inexorable and totalitarian step of imperialism resounds.

The first of the points was all the rage as a postulate of the Russian revolution of 1917. The Bolsheviks themselves paid it abstract homage, making the treaties public and putting an end to their *secret diplomacy*. You don't have to be a political scientist to feel, thirty years later, the enormity of the hypocrisy and charlatanism of that time, and of the disappointment today – the knock-knock-knock of all the micro-bourgeois skittles going down.

The requests of points 2, 3 and 5 mimic ancient pacifist and second-rate liberal demands, but it takes no effort to see them for what they are: conditions favourable to the expansion of the ultracapitalism of the United States, which at the time had practically no military fleet, colonial bases, or control over European, intercontinental, and interimperial economic and monetary relations.

Absolute freedom of navigation on all the seas in peace and in war (!) 'except as the seas may be closed' by 'international covenants' ... a point clearly of great interest to a country that, of the great straits and canals in the sea routes of the world, had only Panama to its name. All the European powers that attained world maritime hegemony by crushing the previous hegemony did so by raising – often with pirate fleets – that flag of free navigation, of the 'abolition of the private property of the sea', which Don Christopher delivered for the first time to the King of Castile. From the struggle against the monopoly of the three caravels we come to the struggle against the monopoly of the floating cities of the *Orient Line* or *Cunard*. The Germans, for that matter, had raised the same cry.

The third point is for the *removal of all economic barriers* and 'the establishment of an equality of trade conditions' – another obvious way of revising the quotas of large-scale oceanic and intercontinental traffic.

The fourth point – *sunt lachrimae rerum* – regards *safety* and the *reduction of armaments*. It's clear as day how (little) this tallies with the (albeit relative) power relations of the three branches of the American military between 1918 and 1942.

The fifth point on *colonies* declares that the interests of the indigenous peoples and the 'title' of the metropolitan government 'must have equal weight'. Having put all the positions acquired back into the pot, for the moment America will refuse with consummate Lutheran hypocrisy to participate in colonial mandates or 'protection'. For the lands of the white race (not for those of people of colour) the hour of Japan's permanent garrisoning has not yet come.

These points are followed by all the particular points on individual national problems and contain the scheme of the new 'peaceful' European Charter, whose stability and incombustibility have been tested by history. The crowning point is number 14, which calls for that League of Nations that the new Russia is warmly invited to join, but which, in the end, the White House Jesuitically will not. In Wilson's words, it was to be formed 'for the purpose of affording mutual guarantees of political independence and territorial integrity *to great and small states alike'*. In light of the sovereignty, the liberty, the very right to draw breath that has been left to the 'small states' in the past thirty years of world events, this statement deserves to be branded the greatest perjury in history.

Here too, it is easy to see the relation between this trend toward the fragmentation of old empires in Europe and abroad, between this alleged legal balance that was supposed to keep the new English and French hegemonies from rising on the ruins of the old Imperial hegemonies of Austria, Turkey, Germany and Russia, and the effort to create an unbalance of power to the advantage of American capitalism. Once it had obtained financial-commercial-industrial superiority, the Monster State of America only needed the time to build – in the shadow of its complaisant humanitarian theorems – the most tremendous military apparatus that has ever strolled through the planet.

This frightful and sinister construction, child of the great world capitalist accumulation, most certainly deserves the harshest possible criticism. But such criticism is totally inadmissible when it is made by those[30] who fail to realise that all this stems directly from Wilson's unctuous homilies. Today such people insist on seeing American policy in the period between the struggle against the Geneva League and the current struggle against the United Nations as a historical parenthesis worthy of support, presenting America as a force mobilised against oppression and barbarism, permitting it the maximum advance and consolidation of its military strongholds, and allowing it to transform [into voices of American propaganda] the stations that, yesterday, broadcast philanthropic theses and moral dictates. Today, America has its finger on the trigger of the atomic bomb.

6.2   Today

With a wide grin, as trivial as Woodrow's decorous grit was glum, Mr Harry, in his turn, in his 'mid-century message', rattles off five 'points' to run the world, outlining – like every captain of industry – his 'master plan' for the treatment of

---

30   A reference to Italian Stalinians.

all human beings from today until the year two thousand.[31] With good reason he takes credit for having liquidated the centuries of Fascism and the Thousand Year Reich.

Charity-goodness-philanthropy is, of course, this time too, the background of the perspective. Peace-liberty-justice is the usual mirage of tomorrow, but there's more to come! Universal prosperity and wealth for all! If Truman's Tables are applied to humankind, not only will the salvation of souls be ensured for all eternity, not only will the citizens of the American World have their papers in order with modern civilisation and the immortal principles of liberty and justice, but even the stomachs of the world will be redeemed from the painful cramps of 'need'! Hunger and misery will be a faded memory of centuries that did not know the radiant gift of the capitalist system ...

The first point, clear as day, is *world peace*. For the members of a generation that has been through the efforts to exorcise war three time already, only when we finally hear our leaders singing the praises of a world war will we be able to breathe a sigh of relief and be done with the ritual exorcisms.

The second point is the *United Nations* – for Wilson it was number fourteen. As with the old one, this new League has to 'provide the framework of international law and morality without which mankind cannot survive'. Another Presbyterian ring of good wishes!

The third point descends a little from the sidereal planes of the ethical, while still responding to the Christian 'give what is superfluous to the poor' ... It is the ERP,[32] described as 'an effort for world economic recovery'. If the United States were to discontinue it, it would be curtains for 'permanent peace' and play into the hands of the 'enemies of democracy'.

Therefore the International Trade Organisation is essential. But didn't they say in the 'old' points that the important thing was 'freedom of international trade'? Infernal bourgeois! Is it freedom or organisation that you want? We want organisation for all working people, and the gallows for everyone you have made free not to work.

So it was *freedom* that was needed to undo the ties that bound trade and commerce to the European centres; debts in dollars and the monopoly of gold did not yet suffice. But freedom, this superplucked dove, has by now done its duty. What is needed today is *organisation* – which means American worldwide control of the commerce and exchange of commodities and currencies, for a clear reason. This high functionary of the American regime is pretty blunt

---

31   The reference is to Truman's State of the Union message of 4 January 1950.
32   European Recovery Program, commonly known as the Marshall Plan.

and minces no words: prevent that kind of *anarchy* and *irresponsibility* that did so much to bring about the *world economic crisis of 1930!* If world crises in the past spelled sleepless nights for American presidents, there's no doubt that a big one today would be even more maddening than that of 1930, but the bugbear for Mr Truman is just one, it's the Wall Street *Black Friday* – this is what he wants to insure himself against, *by organising all of us.*

The fourth point regards the famous 'backward'[33] areas. There are parts of the world that do not enjoy 'the benefits of scientific and economic advances', with all their delights. In these areas misery 'prevails'. Naturally Mr Truman never stops to think about the fact that perchance misery prevails in those areas precisely because capitalist 'progress' has prevailed in the others, with its manufacturing, among other things, of submarines, airplanes, and atom bombs.

These deplorable backward areas will have to catch up, and they will be helped to do so in two ways: *technical assistance and capital investments.* This is the point. Man, after inventing shoes, went on to invent the automobile and the train – not to keep from wearing out the muscles of his legs and the soles of his feet, but because in autos-trains-shoes he can *invest* capital! Something that, under barbarian skies, he could not do in legs and in feet, at least since the day when the priest and the pastor decided it was a sin to hold slaves.

This point 'will require the movement of *large* amounts of capital from the Industrial Nations, and *particularly* from the United States, to *productive* uses in the underdeveloped areas of the world'.[34] The *particularly* is thrown in to give the point just a touch of decency: everyone knows how on the subject of foreign capital investment the other nations, however industrially advanced, are forced by the postwar economic and monetary situation to 'disinvest'. To understand this mysterious fact of long-distance investment it is essential not to fall under the spell of the enigmas of the bourgeois economy, which the proletarian Oedipus deciphered long ago.

The characteristic of Capital is that it does not need to *move*, except symbolically, in the form of radio telegrams and, at most, of a few little rectangles of printed paper. It stays home, and from there exploits and oppresses. Capital is not a supplementary element of production, it is an instrument that makes it possible to exploit production by lying in wait at crucial passages. During the barbarous Middle Ages the brigands lay in wait at the narrow pass to attack the stage coach, and they're still doing it today in certain *backward* areas: they have

---

33   Truman's word was 'underdeveloped'.
34   Bordiga's italics and capital letters.

to have the necessary technical *assistance*, in order to learn how to lie in wait without risk of death or prison and without physical discomfort in luxurious offices with plush armchairs and elegant white telephones.

The newspapers and the radio have reported recently that the Americans are irritated by the delay in the application of their plans for international *investment*. Here's the problem: Argentina has too much land, Italy too many workers, the United States too much capital. The solution: transport – we wouldn't dare say 'deport' – the Italian workers to the land of Argentina, and the United States provides the capital. The Italian works; the Argentinean receives a little ground rent; the American pockets the profit of the brilliant enterprise.

The land has obviously stayed where it was, the labour has been painfully *moved across* the Ocean, the capital has remained in the fist of the Yankee investor. But this Yankee – the bourgeois economist reminds us, triumphantly – with his dollars has had to buy and ship machinery, equipment, and so on and so forth, without which the Argentinean land would not have been made fertile by the Italian labour.

Harry took care of this too with his international *organisation*, and the Export-Import Bank, with a special fund, will cover the *risks* of American private *investors* abroad. In other words, if the deal is *productive* the dollars advanced will be returned in a few financial years, and the permanent claim to the Argentinean enterprise will remain; if it goes badly the American working masses will foot the bill and the capitalist loses nothing.

In the fifth point Truman throws his hat into the ring in the race with Moscow 'communism', certainly not – oh no! – in the preparation for war and the arms race – no! – but in the campaign for the *ideals* of democracy and peace. A noble campaign, a most worthy race, within the framework of that 'emulation' which, in the speeches of big and little Stalinist chiefs, is pitted against the class war between capitalism and communism.

Not only do all these chiefs tirelessly echo the American democratic and pacifistic ideals but – oh yes! – they publicly proclaim a parallel economic plan perfectly faithful – apart from the dollars – to Truman's third and fourth points. In the face of a suffering proletariat, of unemployment, of the disorganisation of the production system caused by the war, and more than the dirty subjection to speculative wheeling-dealing of governments, parties, and trade unions of all colours, the [Italian] Stalinians have no other economic recipe: *investments*! and, naturally: *productive*! *And with Di Vittorio*[35] *as president of the*

---

35   Giuseppe Di Vittorio was general secretary of the Italian left-wing trade union CGIL from 1945 to 1957.

Export-Import Bank of rags! He'll know how to find, with *plans* that will bowl the ERP over, the three trillion lice that are needed.

In drafting his world plan – which, unfortunately, is no joking matter – Truman said: this programme of investments has nothing to do with the old imperialism of the last century or with the new Muscovite imperialism!

As a matter of fact, the *old imperialism* had before it unpopulated and virgin lands just waiting to be discovered or, at worst, lands occupied by peoples that, 'thanks' to the 'scientific progress' already attained, could easily be exterminated or poisoned. Exploiting the colonised and colonists alike, the old imperialism managed to enhance the profits from capital in the motherland. Having reached the limits of the habitable world, fights broke out for the best areas.

The new imperialism has the same ends, but is confronted with countries swarming with hungry and unemployed people. Its modern plan tends to downplay its territorial possession and its armed guard over lands and seas, but with a worldwide monopoly of capital and of the monetary masses it wants to get to the same point: extremely high profits and a relatively high standard of consuming and living in the imperial country, in order to ensure the incessant reproduction of 'savings' to be invested.

One day we'll have to take a little look at the figures Truman sets as his goal for an American economy founded on the exploitation of the world – his fifty-year plan with its trillion dollars of capital annually (to write this figure in lire we need a two followed by sixteen zeros).

As for the *new Muscovite imperialism* its situation is tragic. It has huge masses of workers but the standard of living is nearly as low as that of the countries it wants to subjugate. If it invests outside its own area it will have to reduce its *average* standard of living at home, not raise it fivefold as Truman plans to do in the States. Otherwise, it will have to exchange the skin of a few tens of millions of militarised workers, as it did during the world war, for machines of war and peace, or for dollars, the world currency, boosting capitalism's potential on this earth. No war will break this circle, if not the war, within every nation, between proletarians and the delegates of *capital*, be it indigenous or foreign.

7   'Old' and 'New' Imperialism[36]

7.1   *Yesterday*
The essential characteristic of opportunism is the claim to recognise at every turn that *new* and unexpected forms of capitalism have appeared, and therefore everything must be changed both in one's own assessments of communist doctrine and in the methods of action of the proletariat.

If – claims the opportunist – Marx, Engels, Lenin had 'known' that things had to turn out this way – what better example than Truman's 'new' trillionaire imperialism! – they themselves would have eventually replaced class struggle with national policy and international *emulation*, the dictatorship of the proletariat with popular democracy, the destruction of the intermediate classes with the defence and alliance with small property-small business-small industry and the 'patriotic' capitalism of Mao Tse-tung.

You don't say?

It must be observed that in Great Britain the tendency of imperialism to split the workers, to strengthen opportunism among them, and to cause temporary decay in the working-class movement, revealed itself much earlier than the end of the nineteenth and the beginning of the twentieth centuries. Indeed, two important distinguishing features of imperialism were already observed in Great Britain in the middle of the nineteenth century – vast colonial possessions and a monopolist position in the world market. Marx and Engels traced this connection between opportunism in the working-class movement and the imperialist features of British capitalism systematically, over the course of several decades. For example, on October 7, 1858 (not *nine*teen but *eigh*teen fifty eight), Engels wrote to Marx: 'The English proletariat is actually becoming more and more bourgeois, so that this most bourgeois of all nations is apparently aiming ultimately at the possession of a bourgeois aristocracy and a bourgeois proletariat *alongside* the bourgeoisie. For a nation which exploits the whole world this is of course to a certain extent justifiable'. Almost a quarter of a century later, in a letter dated August 11, 1881, Engels speaks of the 'worst English trade unions which allow themselves to be led by men sold to, or at least paid by, the middle class'. In a letter to Kautsky of September 12, 1882, Engels wrote: 'You ask me what the English workers think about colonial policy. Well, exactly the same as they think about politics in general. There is no workers' party here, there are only Conservatives and Liberal-Radicals, and the workers gaily share the feast of England's monopoly of the world market and the colonies'. (Engels

---

expressed similar ideas in the press in his preface to the second edition of *The Condition of the Working Class in England*, which appeared in 1892.)

This clearly shows the causes and the effects. The causes are: 1) exploitation of the whole world by this country; 2) its monopolist position in the world market; 3) its colonial monopoly. The effects are: 1) a section of the British proletariat becomes bourgeois; 2) a section of the proletariat allows itself to be led by men bought by, or at least paid by, the bourgeoisie.

We can just imagine the expression of consummate vexation of the great politicians of today in the face of this mania for rehashing old quotes fished out of Marx's and Engels' writings, when today they have investigated-accomplished-navigated matters of far greater import in the waters of political 'life'.

But, in this case, we haven't even done any *fishing*. Our erudition is not worth much more than our attitude to modern politicking, and boils down to that of the priestling who, whenever queried, took out his breviary. For the occasion we took out a 'book-ling', Lenin's *Imperialism*, and all we did was copy it – from our question 'You don't say?' as far as the paragraph that so stupendously recapitulates the causes and effects of imperialism.[37]

We needed to do this, on the one hand, to refute Truman's claim that his plans for world control '*have nothing to do with the old imperialism*' and, on the other, – help us, oh dialectic! – the no less absurd claim of Stalin and company that their plan of demo-national-popular agitation '*has nothing to do with the old opportunism*'.

We are not the ones who built Lenin a Pharaonic tomb, neither are we the ones who asked Marx's heirs for his mortal remains, to keep Lenin company in the Kremlin. Neither Marx nor Lenin would ever have dreamed that, after a lifetime spent fighting for the abolition of the ownership of human labour, like Christ had fought to abolish the ownership of the body of living man, they would have ended up being subjected to the legal canons of the ownership of corpses. What's more, unlike Christ, Marx and Lenin didn't even have the privilege of taking their bodies away from their tombs, to avoid Pharisaic profanation.

But if we think of a Marx, Engels, Lenin alive today, we have no doubt that they would see the same characteristics in the current American policy as in the English policy of their day, and would reconfirm the method of revolutionary struggle of the workers' party against the indigenous bourgeoisie. They would conclude that, also today, the phenomena of worldwide capitalist planning – which must not be opposed, as the opportunist Kautsky did, with reactionary

---

37   See Lenin 1971a, Chapter VIII, pp. 246–7.

requests for freedom of trade and of competition, for peace and for democracy (Lenin, *Imperialism*, Chapter IX) – are living proof that *the shell of private economic and private property relations* is rotting away, but it can endure in this state of putrefaction *for a fairly long period* (which, in any event, will *come to a bad end* if one waits too long before *lancing the opportunist abscess*).

With these *exact*[38] words Lenin concluded his writing on 26 April 1917.[39] The October revolution lanced the abscess. The germs remained in the world, and took shape once again, weighing heavy on the lid of that monumental tomb.

7.2   *Today*

In his New Year's message the president of the United States attempted to formulate the characteristic perspective of the new form of imperialism in figures that claim to contain a fifty-year plan. Who isn't making plans today? The very supporters of classical economic liberalism, who trusted in a spontaneous play of forces and laws sufficient to keep things going just fine (you just had to leave people in peace to produce-trade-speculate), now captiously maintain that the very housewife buying food for dinner regulates her decisions according to an economic plan ...

Truman, at any rate, has been studying the recipe and the bill for a dinner he definitely won't be around to enjoy himself, *in the year two thousand*. Capitalism is vulgarly aping socialism more every day, and now we see it stealing the title of Bellamy's famous utopian novel![40]

Let's act like the astronomers who pretend to be in a machine that goes faster than light and, setting out from the year 2000, journey back to this poor old 1950. Truman assures us that, in the year 2000, the United States will have an annual national income of one trillion dollars, and that thanks to peace – he says sometimes – or thanks to the control of the world guaranteed by formidable armaments – he says other times – the income of each family will be three times what it is today.

Today the American Federation has a population of nearly 150 million; we have to think that, according to Truman, in half a century it will be at least 200 million. The country will still be sparsely populated: 26 people per square kilometre, while in Italy we are already in 150 today. The per capita income – that is, for each person – will be 5,000 dollars a year, or 96 dollars a week, equivalent to about 64,000 in today's lira – nearly 10,000 lire a day.

---

38   Cf. Lenin 1971a, Chapter X, p. 262. In this case I have translated from Bordiga's text, which is quite different from the standard English translation [note by G. Donis].

39   Lenin finished writing *Imperialism* in June 1916; 26 April 1917 is the date of the Preface.

40   The reference is to Edward Bellamy (1850–98) and his novel *Looking Backward*.

Since with such a standard of prosperity Mr Truman tells us that the current revenue will be tripled, this means that today every American has an income of 32 dollars a week, which is about 21,000 lire, just 3,000 a day. The average annual income is 1,670 dollars, or just over a million lire, and the national income is 250 billion dollars. This must be how things are. Statistics don't lie.

Such an income is about eight times what it is in Italy, which based on Pella's[41] latest figures is no more than 225 dollars a year, or 4 dollars 35 cents a week per capita; in lire: 150,000 and 2,900, just 400 little lire a day ...

The emblematic sense of the 'new imperialism' lies in the higher standard of living in the imperial country, produced in this way: superprofitable investment abroad of capital it draws from its reserve funds, plus a programme to improve the standard of living in the subject countries. The 'average' figures serve this purpose magnificently.

In fact Truman, two days later, unveiled a shorter-term economic plan – a mere five-year plan. Affirming that, after a short depression in 1948 and 1949, the American domestic economy is already strongly recovering, he thinks that *in five years* 300 billion dollars of the national income can go into savings, thanks precisely to the famous private investments abroad that the state will guarantee against the 'risks peculiar to them'. Hence 60 billion a year, a forty percent slice of the current revenue, which the Americans will not be consuming, in order to invest it – in any case, they'll still be consuming five times more than we will. Nevertheless in the next five years income will already be rising: the president is sure he can raise it by at least a thousand dollars a year per family, ensuring at the same time 64 million *jobs* of all kinds. Liberty-equality-fraternity – and jobs! *Voilà* the principles of the perfect modern democracy. So, this means that, if we call 'family' a group of people per job, family income will have to rise from 4,000 to 5,000 dollars a year, from 80 to 100 dollars a week. The employed head of a family will earn on average 10,000 lire a day.

What is happening in the world that surrounds Truman's America and that depends on its plans? Let us examine another statistic from a reliable source that compares the weekly earnings of workers in all countries of the world, expressed in American dollars. At the vertex we have the American Federation with 27.62, and at the base, China, with just 2.40. These figures represent the income of employed workers, and are therefore *lower* than the average income of all the heads of families that have a job. Thus it so happens that for Italy, a poor country, these statistics give 6.86 dollars, which is *higher* than the average per capita income, since there are many people without income, and

---

41   Giuseppe Pella was the Italian Minister of the Treasury at the time.

few with high incomes; vice versa, for America the figure is *lower* than the 32 dollars a week per capita we saw earlier.

This striking scale certainly does not force planner-capitalism to admit that to raise the standard of living in America and in a few other partners in privilege (on the current scale Canada, New Zealand ... precede Great Britain herself, their former mistress) it's necessary to lower the already low averages of the Oriental and Western European countries even more. In short, to get rich by starving the world. On the contrary! say the Americans. They say that by exporting not only capital but scientific high technology, maintained with costly institutes of American Capital, this production will lead to a boom in foreign *consumption* – namely, of those American exports that people of the civilised world will be able to pay for in Marshall Plan dollars. The purpose of the Plan is to raise per capita earnings in the 'assisted' countries – in southern Italy, a *backward* area, you're *assisted* if you dream the winning lottery numbers – to 350 dollars a year; that is, about 6 dollars and sixty cents a week per person, which means that in the not-very-rich countries an employed head of a family has to earn at least nine dollars a week. In Italy we're far from it – far from the 550 of the Truman Plan, our per capita income is only 225 dollars a year.

Not only does the supermodern world-plan not admit that it wants to starve the world but – we have to have the courage to say something more. To demonstrate that the capitalist system must fall, to demand its overthrow, to have the 'right' to denounce its infamy, the proof that – surviving – it will lower the worldwide average standard of living is not a necessary condition. Capitalism must yield to forms of higher economic return *not only* due to its infinite consequences of oppression, destruction and slaughter, its impossibility of reducing income inequality not only between metropolises and colonial and vassal states, between advanced industrial areas and backward agrarian areas or areas of primordial agriculture, but *above all* between social classes of the same country, including the one where the prince of imperial capitalism raises its slave-dealing banner.

Super-rich and prosperous America, looking down from its 1,670-dollar standard of living, promises 350 to countries that are descending step by step to the perhaps 50 of rural China. But the statistics of the States of the Federation are already passing judgement on their much vaunted and progressive prosperity. The average of the four least-industrialised falls to 150 dollars: in Tennessee, 137. They're worse off than we Italians! But some sergeant from Tennessee will be sent to colonise Calabria, some Calabrese will be sent to colonise Somalia ... An old story.

America! If the bourgeois figures allowed it, a statistical comparison between the standard of living of its various social classes would paint quite another picture. Sure, there will be a greater gap between the New York kings of capital and the workers (mostly Italians) of the construction-industry underground than between the first farmer and the last farmhand of Tennessee. With good reason Truman's programme includes price supports for agricultural products and measures to keep the Western farmers from starving – at the expense, of course, of the industrial workers.

Lenin, in *Imperialism*, identified one of the essential characteristics of imperialism as the exportation of capital; that is, foreign investment. He showed how in 1917 the most emblematic confirmation of this came from two countries, Germany and the United States, which his sham scholars had depicted as opposite poles of the world, swapping Marxism for miniscule bourgeois doctrines.

Revolutionary Marxists, from Karl Marx on, have pitted against the plans for the exportation of capitalism – capitalist technology and economy – from the most [to the least] advanced countries, the very force of domestic class struggle, the destruction of capitalism *in its own home.*

The statistical scale [of the weekly earnings of workers in all countries of the world] we have used here brings us to a stunning conclusion. If we cut the scale in half at the level of Czechoslovakia, all the countries above that level are with Truman, all the countries below it are with Stalin. With just two exceptions – great comfort for the career opportunities of the Nosakas and the Togliattis: Japan and Italy!

The iron curtain, seen from Moscow's side, is a golden curtain.

The average of the *superior* countries is about three times that of the inferior countries. Well, even if it were true that *a third* of the world's population is already on *Stalin's* side, Stalin has no more than *a ninth* of the economic forces. In an economy of armaments and of war, today, when it is not men who fight but machines and the men who do fight all tend to become professionals, the margins that can be salvaged for peacetime consumption are even more desperately low.

So, apart from betraying the revolutionary working-class line, the policy of a war on national fronts, of a war of poor countries against rich countries – and this, fundamentally, was the Hitler-Mussolini policy – is a policy of defeat. It is the best policy the Truman Plan could ever desire: it kills class war from both sides of the curtain, and ensures the final worldwide victory of 'western' arms.

It would be useless to calculate the *unintentional* consequences of a Stalin victory, just as it was useless to calculate those of a Hitler victory. The maximum throne of capitalism will not tremble on its base, opening a possible way to the revolutionary cataclysm, which, as Lenin saw, reduces imperialists and opportunists, losers and winners, to the selfsame rubble.

8   You Cannot Stop, Only the Proletarian Revolution Can Stop You,
     Destroying Your Power[42]

The mass of humanity has twice been hurled into the maw of a world war,
with the bestial triumph of the tale of the Wolf, the doctrine of the Ogre, the
humbug of the Aggressor, and the farce of the War Criminals. Both times, in
corroboration of this colossal deception, of this immense fraud, the world was
bombarded with the idiotic legend that its saviour was the free, civil, and peaceful republic of the stars and stripes.
     The legend has gained credit in the slimy layers of the middle class and the
petty bourgeoisie in ways that are plain for all to see, in the glaring hypocrisy-
cowardice-philistinism of deceived and deceivers, coarse seducers and child-
ishly prattling admirers. But this same legend has claimed, not without vast success, to be credited in the ranks of the proletariat and in the socialist position. In
the diagnosis and in the condemnation of capitalist society and the bourgeois
states, the prosperous and blessed Republic was an exception. Class struggle
and oppression on one hand, misery on the other, were phenomena limited
to this old Europe swollen with 'reactionary' dangers. Socialists of the current
stamp would also have willingly excepted that green and pleasant island on the
other side of the Channel, if that impossible man named Marx – so cantanker-
ous! – hadn't repaid its generous hospitality by singling it out as an example of
capitalism at its most ferocious. But America! America! They had no Middle
Ages there, in America they were born free and in freedom, they could not
slip back into the darkness of obscurantism, or fall into the trap of 'looming
reaction'. They had no need of an anti-feudal revolution, which was brilliantly
replaced by a simple hunting campaign for biped game, foreign to Genesis
and to Christ's redemption, to Reformation and to Philosophical Enlightenment.
     It's clear, then: dialectic and class antagonism, socialism, proletarian revolu-
tion, this whole European bag of tricks doesn't apply to the other World, the
one across the Atlantic. And if among our peoples and governments of the
old world there is always the danger that the medieval plague sprout anew
from the subsoil, giving rise to aggressors, militarists, tyrants, and international
war delinquents, in America the very earth is immune to such infections. It is
unthinkable that, there, oppression, outrage, and spirit of conquest can take
root. America is always on the right side, America is always on the side of right,
America is always right.

---

42   *Battaglia Comunista*, No. 1, 1951.

Every time the lamb is about to fall into the clutches of the Wolf it will need this mighty transatlantic sheepdog, with fangs more terrible than the wolf's, but vegetarian by tradition and disposition.

This is what the lackeys have been telling us for decades on end. Let's see how things stood, and how they stand now.

8.1   *Yesterday*

We shall not repeat the Marxist description of the rise of the capitalist economy in the case where its technical and mechanical premises find not the old framework of medieval society with its agrarian natural economy but, rather, the virgin and free land that greets the white colonist – apart, of course, from his hunt for the aboriginal occupiers, to disperse their race or enslave them. The starting point is different but the result is the same, be it in England, where they struggled inch by inch through centuries of history and where today there are three hundred people per square kilometre, or in the United States, where a population whose density is fifteen times less – twenty per square kilometre – has settled in a way that appears socially peaceful.

Two cases, identical programme: overthrow the capitalist system and capitalist power.

If it is true, then, that the analysis of the historical process can have different characteristics, with respect to the method and the ends of the socialist movement there is only one conclusion.

From Marx's main work we could cite numerous references to America, in its successive phases: initial slavery of a patriarchal type, brutal slavery leading to extermination in the South, economy of small farm-owners in the North, industrial economy in the East, its rapid evolution from capitalism of a colonial type to a capitalism of ever greater self-sufficiency. And today: hegemony.

Here is a striking reference to its low population density: 'A relatively thinly populated country, with well-developed means of communication, has a denser population than a more numerously populated country with badly developed means of communication. In this sense, the northern states of the USA, for instance, are more thickly populated than India'.[43] Today the density in India is nearly one hundred, which is five times that of the United States; but the USA has 27 kilometres of railway per 10,000 people while India has only 1.6 – fifteen times less. The indices that underlie the Marxist evaluation lead to good collimations: the capitalism born in Europe took root more quickly in colonial possessions that were sparsely populated or populated by unorganised and eas-

---

43   Marx 1976, p. 473.

ily exterminable peoples than in possessions with very ancient organisation and a civilisation of their own, that is, with their own mode of productive economy and social hierarchy. 150 million Americans count far more on the world political scene than 400 million Indians, however much the Indians' would-be representatives (who 'would-be' free from the yoke of 50 million Englishmen, that is, of fallen British imperial capitalism) try to pull off masterly double-crosses and pose as protagonists in mediations on a world scale.

The extensive use of black slaves for agricultural production in the southern states was conducted at first with a certain humaneness (apart from the methods used to capture them). As long as the number of slaves was not great, it was not easy to get new ones to replace those that died. Treating them well meant that they would *breed* and produce young labour-power; that is, the children of the adult slaves that had been bought, or captured in raids. The result was a patriarchal lifestyle, with the slave being part of the master's family. But when black flesh began to become plentiful, especially in certain states of the Union, and full-fledged [slave] markets were flourishing, it became economically advantageous to tear the greatest amount of labour in the shortest possible time out of the slave, who is now half-starved and with a life expectancy of less than thirty years: norms cynically enunciated by Yankee economists and pastors. This is basically no different from the incarceration of English children for fourteen hours a day in the cotton mills. Don't think that it's only Marx who is always harsh. Here, he quotes Shakespeare's *The Merchant of Venice*: 'My deeds upon my head! I crave the law,/ The penalty and forfeit of my bond'. 'Ay, his breast', – exclaims Shylock – 'So says the bond'. And in a note Marx says: 'The nature of capital *remains the same* in its developed as it is in its undeveloped forms. In the code of law which was imposed on the Territory of Mexico under the influence of the slave-owners, shortly before the outbreak of the American Civil War, it is asserted that the worker *"is his"* (*the capitalist's*) *"money"* since the capitalist has bought his labour-power'.[44]

It was in the Civil War between the North and the South for the abolition of slavery that the capitalist form of production fully asserted itself. In texts we have recalled on other occasions – the inaugural address of the First International is a prime example – it is clearly shown how the industrial slave-drivers were no better than slaveholders 'properly speaking'.

At the time of the first edition of *Capital*, just after that war, capitalism in America was already advancing with gigantic strides, but was still largely based on European, and especially English, investment. 'The same thing is going on

---

44   Marx 1976, pp. 399–400; Bordiga's italics.

today [that is, as went on when capitalist powers that were still rich but whose power was waning lent their capital to the newly emerging powers] between England and the United States. A great deal of capital, which appears today in the United States without any birth-certificate, was yesterday in England, the capitalised blood of children'.[45]

Nevertheless, despite the fact that the American War of Independence dates back to the late eighteenth century and, according to Marx, had sparked the bourgeois revolutions on the Continent of Europe, in 1867, after nearly a century of political autonomy, America was, in the Marxist sense, still a European economic colony. This is repeated in two explicit passages: for Marx a colonial economy is one in which the occupation of 'free' land is still possible on a large scale, with the mass absorption of labour-power that is not yet forced to submit to the slavery of the industrial wage. In a note to the fourth edition of *Capital* in 1889, Engels remarked that in the meantime the United States had become the second greatest industrial power in the world, but without having fully lost its colonial character. In 1912 Kautsky could already add that America had become the leading industrial country, and had lost its character as a Colony so completely that it was pursuing a policy of colonial expansion of its own.

The doctrine of president Monroe, 'Europe on its own, America on its own' (he's entitled to a Stalinian card in his memory), opened the fight to overcome the last vestiges of passive colonial relations. Once the zero point had been attained, it became a fight for active colonial relations, just as a thermometer, when heated up to zero, does not stop there.

Getting back to Marx's original edition, his profound analysis and implacable condemnation are never without an element of cutting derision. Capital seeks insatiable markets of labour; Malthus, the puritan, calls for depopulation through abstention from procreation as a remedy for poverty; a bourgeois economist is so enthusiastic about the effect of machines that he compares it to that of overpopulation. Even more ingenuously, [William] Petty writes that the machine 'replaces polygamy'. This point of view, laughs Marx, could be acceptable at most for a certain part of the United States, with an evident allusion to the Salt Lake Mormons.

But it is precisely the last page of the first volume that strikes American bourgeois society in all its infamy, with its peaks of hypocrisy and exploitation. It is here that Marx says, in lapidary reply to the imbecile boast of not having traditions of monarchy and nobility, that the effect of the Civil War – 'capitalist

---

45   Marx 1976, p. 400.

production advances with gigantic strides' – was, in classical terms, 'the creation of a finance aristocracy of the vilest type'.[46]

The most powerful statement of our Marxist anthology on America comes, however, from Engels' 18 March 1891 Introduction to *The Civil War in France* – the one that concludes with the words, 'Look at the Paris Commune. That was the Dictatorship of the Proletariat'.[47]

Engels, with great directness, reformulates the central theory of the state.

> Society had created its own organs to look after its common interests, originally through simple division of labour. But these organs, at whose head was the state power, had in the course of time, in pursuance of their own special interests, transformed themselves from the servants of society into the masters of society, as can be seen, for example, not only in the hereditary monarchy, but equally also in the democratic republic.

He then goes on to an example of the doctrine, and seems to be responding to this precise objection: this parasitical and oppressive function of the state can be explained only where the modern bourgeoisie did not inherit the bureaucratic-police-military mechanism of the old feudal regimes now overthrown. Engels therefore takes as his example a bourgeois state born 'without a history'.

> Nowhere do 'politicians' form a more separate, powerful section of the nation than in North America. There, each of the two great parties which alternately succeed each other in power is itself in turn controlled by people who make a business of politics, who speculate on seats in the legislative assemblies of the Union as well as of the separate states, or who make a living by carrying on agitation for their party and on its victory are rewarded with positions. It is well known that the Americans have been striving for thirty years to shake off this yoke, which has become intolerable, and that in spite of all they can do they continue to sink ever deeper in this swamp of corruption. It is precisely in America that we see best how there takes place this process of the state power making itself independent in relation to society, whose mere instrument it was originally intended to be. Here there exists no dynasty, no nobility, no standing army, beyond the few men keeping watch on the Indians [Engels could not have

---

46   Marx 1976, p. 940.
47   See Marx and Lenin 1968, pp. 20–1.

known that now it is his fellow-Germans of sixty years later ... who are the Indians], no bureaucracy with permanent posts or the right to pensions. And nevertheless we find here two great gangs of political speculators, who alternately take possession of the state power and exploit it by the most corrupt means and for the most corrupt ends – and the nation is powerless against these two great cartels of politicians, who are ostensibly its servants, but in reality exploit and plunder it.

Against all this, Engels says, the Commune applied two *infallible* means. But that is another question. The functionaries of the Paris Commune fell in a shower of glory serving the Revolution, while those of the Soviet state have applied two basic means: apology and alliance.

We resisted the temptation to open another parenthesis where Engels says that the politicians would do anything for a 'position'. But judge for yourselves the correctness of his description from this episode: the most elevated, learned, and philosophical thing that the employee Harry Truman managed to say in his election campaign is the following: If you don't elect me you'll have to find me another job ('job' means position, post, salary, and outermost circle of the universe, in the North-American language) or add me to the ranks of the unemployed!

This, then, is the true judgement that genuine Marxism passes on American capitalism, on American class power, which holds under Jack London's 'iron heel' workers and the children of workers of every race and every colour. Has such a judgement ever been proved false?

Lenin, in *Anti-Kautsky*, to the tendentious thesis that armed revolution is not necessarily inevitable in bourgeois nations that are *without* militarism and bureaucracy, forcefully responds that *today* (1918) in England and America both militarism and bureaucracy *exist*. His pamphlet *Imperialism* is, from beginning to end, a demonstration of the fact that American capitalism is in the front line on the way to monopoly, expansion, the struggle to divide up the entire world between industrial trusts and imperialist powers. This process had already fully established its premises at the beginning of the century – a far cry from the disinterested defence of freedom anywhere in the world that it may be attacked!

In the United States, the imperialist war waged against Spain in 1898 stirred up the opposition of the 'anti-imperialists', the last of the Mohicans of bourgeois democracy who declared this war to be 'criminal', regarded the annexation of foreign territories as a violation of the Constitution, declared that the treatment of Aguinaldo, leader of the Filipinos (the

Americans promised him the independence of his country, but later landed troops and annexed it) [pardon our interruption: Aguinaldo was the first of the partisans to be made a fool of] was 'Jingo treachery', and quoted the words of Lincoln: 'When the white man governs himself that is self-government; but when he governs himself and also governs others, it is no longer self-government; it is despotism'. But as long as all this criticism shrank from recognising the inseverable bond between imperialism and the trusts, and, therefore, between imperialism and the foundations of capitalism, while it shrank from joining the forces engendered by large-scale capitalism and its development – it remained a 'pious wish'.[48]

The Marxists knew all this perfectly well in 1915. Therefore they knew perfectly well what to think of the American intervention in the First World War and of Wilson's claim to organise international democracy and the peace, obviously a stage in an enormous march of expansion, conquest, and imperial aggression that has continued unabated for half a century now.

Let us listen to the words of a delegate to the Moscow Second World Congress in 1920: 'The ten million negroes that live in the United States are the butt of constant measures of repression and of unjustifiable cruelty. They are outside the common law of the white Americans, with whom they are not allowed to live or travel. You have heard about the lynching of negroes doused with petrol and burnt alive ... If they are hanged instead, their body parts are distributed as good-luck charms'. Another delegate follows, in the same session on 26 July:

It is not only the negroes who are slaves but also the foreign workers and the workers from the colonies ... the atrocities perpetrated against the colonised workers are not a whit less serious than the atrocities against the foreign workers. For example in 1912 in a miners' strike at Ludlow, the armed forces were employed to force the miners to leave their houses to live in tents. During a clash between the miners and the soldiers, another detachment burnt the tents – hundreds of women and children were killed. The fundamental task of the Communist International and the only means of ensuring the victory of the World Revolution is the destruction of American imperialism.

So, we didn't know enough about the 'particular' characteristics of American capitalism? Here is the concluding Manifesto of the Second Congress. Who-

---

48   Lenin 1971a, Chapter IX, p. 250.

ever signed this text, and then – for five minutes! – defended the America of the legend, is a jinx, unfaithful to communism.

> Monroe's programme, America for the Americans, has been replaced by the programme of imperialism: the whole world for the Americans! ... The United States has sought to chain the peoples of Europe and of other parts of the world to their triumphal wagon, subjecting them to the Washington government. In short, the League of Nations was not supposed to be anything other than a world monopoly under the aegis of Yankees & Co.

8.2   *Today*

With unimaginable impertinence our bourgeoisie, be it Vaticanesque or Freemason, parrots Turgot's[49] judgement: 'America is the hope of humanity'. Turgot – like the French bourgeoisie of thirty years ago, represented by the renegade, Millerand[50] – did so in the hope 'that his debts be remitted, he, who never remitted anybody's debts!'

President, secretary of state, government, congress, parties, and so-called 'public opinion' in America make up a complex whose [moral and intellectual] baseness has been well known for some time; but instead of denouncing this shameful reality everyone bows down and grovels. Even the Fascist writers, who so violently cursed the avaricious American *plutocracy* and went wild with joy the day Pearl Harbor was bombed, today presumptuously extol the sensitivity of the American people and public to the fate of liberty in the world and to the defence of the weak who are attacked – that conscience and moral courage which guide the decisions and the energy of Truman and his diplomats and generals! What low comedy!

The Italians, who watched the war go by a few feet away, huddled in caves like troglodytes – the Italians! helpless and partisans of no one, especially of no past or present Italian regime, could converse calmly with German soldiers and officers one day, and with their American counterparts the next. The Germans carried out their acts of war with cold technique, without bursts of enthusiasm or love of risk, but also without omissions or errors. Almost none of them posed the question of why they were carrying out their orders with such precision, but almost all of them had one firm conviction: I make war, I have no personal interest in it, I gain nothing from it. What they seemed to hold in contempt was not making war but making a profit on war.

---

49   Turgot (1727–81): French economist and statesman, an early advocate for economic liberalism.

50   Millerand (1859–1943): one of the first socialists to participate in a bourgeois government.

Then came the Americans, self-assured, convinced they were bringing *the hope of the world*. Why were they fighting the war? Good heavens, they themselves had ordered their government to do it, since they were convinced that this was in the interest of every [American] citizen. 'The President is my servant' or some such – this was what they all said! The President, the Secretaries, the functionaries, the generals, are my servants, they carry out the orders of the people and of me, the citizen, who votes and who 'pays them'. With my taxes I give them what is coming to them for their 'jobs'. So they all had an interest in the war, or dreamed that they did: in a country where everything is commerce and commercial advertising and everything is bought and sold, by instalments if necessary, war, too, is something you 'order' and you pay the commission: by instalments, when the costs are too high.

In any event, paying for this *last* war was definitely worthwhile. With the Germans out of the way – a mad people, a criminal people, a people that dares to fight a war even if convinced it will pay its money and make no profit whatsoever, a people that will immediately have to undergo cures and treatments to inoculate them with 'Made in America' civilisation and consciousness – yes, with these Germans out of the way we'll all be peaceful, free, and masters of our destiny. We'll elect a committee of our 'servants' who for a modest salary will administer, with our mandate, the government of the free and peaceful world.

We ourselves have not had the chance to hunker down in some mountain ravine in Korea to study the philosophy of war of the people passing by, headed to the South or to the North. Probably they too will say they believe they're fighting the last war. Or, at any rate, this is what the UN soldiers will say, since it's been explained to them that in the ranks of yesterday's allies the new Wolf, the new Aggressor, the new Criminal has raised its ugly head.

Truman speaks, announcing all those 'police actions', and says: the leaders of the Soviet Union have created this danger for the peace we so dearly wanted, they ordered the aggression in Korea.

The spokesmen of the Soviet government respond: we are the ones who lead the movement for peace, it's the leaders in Washington who want war and are getting ready to attack. Both sides make counter offers and take counter positions on a possibility of immediate entente and permanent co-existence.

If, to this dialogue, we could add another voice – the voice of the traditions of the communist movement – it would draw just a few simple conclusions.

Truman on one side and the heads of the USSR on the other have no possibility of provoking the war or preventing the war. We can also admit that Truman, Acheson, Eisenhower, MacArthur, personally do not want the war to break out today or do not find it opportune to press for it. But their intentions, one way or another, count for very little.

The oligarchy of high capitalism that they represent operates in the economy, in production, in industry, in finance, *with a practise that leads to war*, since operating differently would reduce its profits and damage its interests in various ways. But the individual members of this oligarchy could not operate in a radically different way even if they wanted to. Even if they sought to reconcile protecting their interests with postponing or averting war, the consequences would be no different.

Instead, then, of the great foolishness – just publicity to win a few new partisans (tomorrow who knows how many will be around) – of shouting at the government and business leaders: stop in time, live, produce, earn, but don't make war, remember that you were the salvation of the world until 1945 and be careful not to blow it up – no, instead of all this we have something else to tell them. We know your road better than you do, your road to the imperial oppression of the world. You, as a class, cannot stop, only the world revolution can stop you, destroying your power: it will not desist if you are in a state of peace and, if there will be a state of war, it will look for opportunities to hasten your fall, and your *peace* will not be missed.

For the proletarian world, there is no other way of salvation.

Appendix: With the Academic Seal of Approval the American Economy Becomes 'People's Capitalism'[51]

[Bordiga's note] to the reader: the following is our translation of an Associated Press release. The sentences in parentheses or in italics are our additions to the original text.[52]

The 'People's Capitalism' of America has come closer to the socialist goal of full wellbeing for everyone than any socialist system existing today (*true; not a single one exists*).

This was one of the conclusions reached by a commission of twelve outstanding Americans who met last November at Yale University. The conclusions were announced in a booklet published by Yale and by the Advertising Council (*Advertising Council, Inc. – in America when academicians have a get-together, one question is compulsory: who pays?*).

---

51   *il programma comunista*, Yr. 6, No. 16, 13–18 August 1957.
52   The original English text must exist, or have existed, but here it has been translated from Bordiga's Italian.

The commission was composed of businessmen (*good*), labour leaders (*better*), a newspaper publisher (*excellent*), and seven Yale professors (*magnificent*). Their task in the debate was to 'rethink' and 'clarify' the modern economy of the United States (*dumbbell committee members! you're off to a good start for your thousand dollars a day! You do not know – in America the awards for asininity know no limits – that the only position in defence of capitalism is this: the economy 'cannot be thought'. The 'classical' school of the bourgeois revolution dared to 'think it', and laid the foundations for the communist machine of Karl Marx. Then you went back to 'vulgar' economics and your university sciences, horrified by the theorems of the 'red terror doctor'. Then in the secrecy of your political committees you trembled, seeing that Marx had thought well, and that only revolutions can be 'thought' in advance. Now you have decided to 'rethink' economics, which we, outside all your Yales and Anonymous Academies, have been thinking for a century: be our guests! We won't let you off the hook!*).

They find that the national economy is 'dictated' by the people (*you see! you run smack into dictatorship, not into freedom: people's dictatorship emulates the popular democracy of that other Oriental scum of the lackeys of 'rethinking'!*), which casts its ballots with dollars in the market squares – 'thus deciding for itself what ought to be produced, instead of just taking what the government gives the people'. (*This first 'rethinking' is in inverted commas in the text – what a novelty! it's as old as the hills: the 'demand' of the paying customer who 'dictates' the production plan; and not state dictatorship: so say the old and the new 'libertarian mercantilists'; why drag in the perks of 'Advertising Council, Inc.'? Either commercial advertising or 'consumer dictatorship', my good sirs!*).

(*Let's let them speak for themselves for a while*). At the opening of the debate on 16–17 November, Dean Edmund W. [censored] (*Sinnott: do not sin*) of the Yale Graduate School, 'moderator' of the commission, said that the American economic system has changed ever since president McKinley's day. He said that, although it is a capitalist system (*oh, thank you Sinnott*), characterised by free enterprise, competition, and the profit motive, 'it differs [from capitalism] in two respects: a 'fair' participation in the property of all the people, and the great efficiency with which it satisfies the most various necessities and aspirations of the people themselves'.

He said that the term 'People's capitalism' is an 'appealing (*it's the Advertising Council that is paying!*) term that will help us in undertaking a fresh and unconventional vision of our system' (you too, dear Sinnott, pass with flying colours into the ranks of the anti-dogmatists!).

This terminology was adopted by the Advertising Council (*for the paying-dictating people?! just think!*).

(*Here comes the good part, we won't interrupt anymore*). The Commission said that the style of American capitalism cannot be fully duplicated, and that the leaders of the nation must not try to get other nations to adopt it precisely.

Nevertheless we must make every effort to present our system clearly, and in terms that show others how they can profit from some parts of it, for a use that will change from case to case.

The Soviets made a great mistake when they refused to let other peoples attain socialism (!) in their own way. We must be more flexible than the Russians in recognising that the peoples of other countries can attain 'people's capitalism' in their own ways.

(*Perfect emulation, then, from both sides, in making room for 'national ways' of attaining the popular socialism of the Russians and the popular capitalism of the Americans. A moving agreement, in passing back and forth the reciprocal 'discovery of errors', along with 'fresh and unconventional' modern visions ... We 'conventionalists' insist, again, that capitalism is the same everywhere, and that the way to socialism is the same everywhere. If proof of this is needed, it resides in the fact that the 'popular communism' launched from the East, and the 'popular capitalism' launched from the West, speak the same language. And give off the same stench.*)

On the 'Gigantic Movement of Emancipation' of the Coloured Peoples

∵

CHAPTER 16

The Factors of Race and Nation in Marxist Theory (1953)

1 Introduction: Impotence of the Banal 'Negativist' Position[1]

1.1 Races, Nations, or Classes?

1. The method of the Italian and International Communist Left has never had anything in common with the false dogmatic and sectarian extremism that claims with empty verbal and literary negations to overcome forces present in the real processes of history.

In a recent 'sul filo del tempo'[2] that introduces a series of essays on national-colonial and agrarian questions – and thus on the main contemporary social questions in which major forces not limited to industrial capital and proletarian labour are involved – we demonstrated with documentary quotations that perfectly orthodox and radical revolutionary Marxism recognises the current importance of these factors and the need to have a suitable class and party practice in regard to them. In these essays we do not quote Marx, Engels and Lenin alone, but also the fundamental documents, from 1920 to 1926, of the Left opposition in the International and in the Communist Party of Italy, which was an integral part of the International at that time.

The adversaries of the Left, ever since the 1920s on the path of opportunism and today abysmally fallen into the repudiation of classist Marxism and into counter-revolutionary politics, have vainly insinuated that the Left itself fell into the absolutist and metaphysical error which maintains that the communist party must not concern itself with anything other than that duel pitting the pure forces of modern capital against industrial workers which will give rise to the proletarian revolution. In short, we are falsely accused of denying and ignoring the influence of every other class and every other factor on the social struggle. In our recent exposition of the foundations of Marxist economic theory and of the Marxist revolutionary programme we have thoroughly demonstrated that this pure 'phase' does not exist in the real world. It does not exist

---

1 *il programma comunista*, Yr. 2, No. 16, 11–25 September 1953.
2 'On the Thread of Time' was the title of a series of articles Bordiga wrote in 1953 for the journal *il programma comunista*.

anywhere today, not even in the most highly industrialised of countries and in those where bourgeois rule is of the longest standing, such as England, France, the United States. What is more, it will never exist anywhere in the future; the expectation of such a phase is by no means a condition for the revolutionary victory of the proletariat.

Hence it is absolute nonsense to say that, since Marxism is the theory of the modern class struggle between capitalists and workers, and since communism is the movement that leads the proletarian struggle, we deny the historical effect of the social forces of other classes – for example, the peasants – and of racial and national trends and pressures, and consider such elements to be superfluous.

2. *Historical materialism, in presenting the course of prehistory in a new and original way, has not limited itself to considering, studying and evaluating the processes of formation of families, groups, tribes, races and peoples, right up to the formation of nations and political states. Most importantly, it has shown how these processes are connected with and conditioned by the development of the forces of production, and are thus the manifestation and confirmation of the theory of economic determinism.*

It is perfectly true that the family and the horde are forms we find also in the animal domain. It is often said that even the most highly evolved of animals, even if they begin to display collective organisation for the purpose of common defence and preservation and begin to gather and store food, still do not display productive activity, which, by contrast, distinguishes even the most ancient of men. But it would be better to say that what distinguishes the human species is not knowledge or thought or the particle of divine light but, rather, the capacity to produce not only objects to consume but also objects to dedicate to further production, such as the first rudimentary tools for hunting, fishing, gathering fruits, and then for agricultural and artisanal work. To characterise the human species, this first necessity of organising the production of tools joins up with the necessity of disciplining and regulating the reproductive process, thereby overcoming the chance nature of sexual relations and realising far more complex forms than those of the animal world. It is above all Engels' classic work that shows the inseparable connection, if not the identity, between the evolving of family institutions and the evolving of production institutions.

Therefore there was a time before social classes were present – indeed, our entire theoretical battle is designed to show that such classes are not eternal but, rather, had a beginning and will have an end. The Marxist vision of historical development gives the only possible explanation, on a scientific and materials basis, of the function of the clan, tribe and race, and of their ordering themselves in increasingly complex forms due to the characteristics of their physical environment, and to the increase of the productive forces and techniques at the disposal of the collectivity.

3. *The historical factor of nationalities, of their great struggles and the great struggles for them – which, throughout history, have been constant, if to a variable degree – has been decisive for the appearing of the bourgeois and capitalist form of society as it gradually spread over the earth. Marx, in his day, paid extremely close attention – not less than he paid to the processes of the social economy – to the struggles and wars for the creation of national states.*

Since the doctrine and the party of the proletariat had existed since 1848, Marx did not only give theoretical explanations of those struggles in accordance with economic determinism but was also concerned with establishing the limits and the conditions of time and place for the support of insurrections and wars of independence.

Once large units of peoples and of nations have taken shape and state forms and hierarchies have been superimposed on them and on their social dynamism, now articulated in castes and classes, the racial and national factor takes hold in various ways in the various epochs of history: slavery, seigniory, feudalism, capitalism. Its importance varies in the various forms. In the modern era, the transition began and spread from the feudal – based on personal dependence and limited and local exchange – to the bourgeois form of economic servitude and the formation of large national unitary markets, culminating in the world market. In this period of transition the building of nations according to race, language, traditions and culture was of fundamental importance in the dynamics of history. Lenin summed up this nationalist demand in the formula '*one nation, one state*' (he explained that it was necessary to fight for it but to say that the formula was bourgeois and not proletarian and socialist). What Lenin saw in eastern Europe for the period before 1917 was true for Marx for all of western Europe (except for England) from 1848 up to 1871, as is well known. And it is true today outside Europe in immense parts of the inhabited lands, however much the process has been stimulated and accelerated by the power of economic trade, and trade of all sorts, on a world scale. The problem of the position to be taken with regard to the irresistible trends toward national struggles for independence is therefore of great importance today.

1.2   Opportunism in the National Question

4. The dialectical crux of the matter does not consist in showing that an alliance in the anti-feudal revolutionary physical struggle between the bourgeois state and class and the workers' party entails a repudiation of the doctrine and the politics of class struggle. It consists, rather, in showing that also in the historical conditions and geographical areas in which that alliance is necessary and ineluctable, the theoretical, programmatic and political critique of the ends and ideologies for which the bourgeois and petty-bourgeois elements are fighting must be maintained and intensified.

Marx, while supporting with all his strength such causes as Polish and Irish independence, never stopped condemning the idealistic baggage of the bourgeois and petty-bourgeois champions of democratic justice and the freedom of peoples. Indeed, he razed this brand of idealism to the ground and crushed it beneath his derision. For us the national market and the centralised national capitalist state are a bridge for the inevitable passage to the international economy that will one day suppress both state and market. But for the gurus mocked by Marx – Mazzini, Garibaldi, Kossuth, Sobietsky, and others of that ilk – the democratic system of national states was a goal that, once attained, would bring all social struggle to an end, in a homogeneous national state in which the exploited workers no longer see their bosses as enemies and foreigners. At that historic moment there was to be a change of front, with the working class throwing itself into the civil war against the state that is its 'homeland'. This moment was approaching and its conditions were developing in the course of the process of the bourgeois national revolutions and wars for the systematisation of Europe (today also of Asia and Africa): this is the problem – in constant change and with wildly fluctuating lines – that must be deciphered.

5. The opportunism, betrayal, repudiation, and counter-revolutionary and pro-capitalist action characteristic of the current Stalinist false communists have a dual significance in this question (no less than in the strictly economic and social question of so-called 'domestic' politics). These 'communists' put national democratic demands and values back on their pedestals by means of openly declared and indecent political blocs, also in the highly advanced capitalist West where the plausibility of such alliances had been excluded since 1871. But, what is more, they diffuse in the masses a sacred respect for the national-patriotic-people's ideology identified with that of their bourgeois allies. Indeed, they court the champions of this policy, which Marx and Lenin ferociously scourged, continuing the extirpation of all sense of class consciousness in the workers who, unfortunately, follow them.

The Marxist method permits workers' parties to participate in revolutionary national alliances, as long as they are far from the borders of the twentieth century and of historical-geographical Europe, but it would be foolish to consider this fact an extenuating circumstance for the infamy of the parties that today claim to represent the workers, especially in Italy, under the false name of 'communist' and 'socialist'. When, in the war in the heart of the developed West (France, England, America, Italy, Germany, Austria), the Russian state and all the parties of the defunct Third International form alliances with all the bourgeois states in turn, since there are no more Napoleon the Thirds or Nicolas the Seconds, they tear to shreds, on the one hand, Marx's Address in the name of the First International on the 1871 Paris Commune, which put an end to and denounced forever any alliance with 'national governments' since 'the national governments are *one* as against the [insurgent] proletariat!';[3] and, on the other, Lenin's theses on the 1914 war and for the foundation of the Third International, which stated that, with the advent of the era of imperialist general wars, demands for democracy and independence no longer had anything to do with the policy of states, while condemning social-national traitors on both sides of the Rhine and of the Vistula.

The proposal to 'postpone' the end of the national question from 1871 and 1917 to 1939 and 1953, with no end in sight, represents the discrediting of the entire Marxist method of interpreting history, precisely in relation to those crucial moments in which its doctrinal power began to settle accounts with the defence of the past: the European 1848, the Russian 1905. What is more, such a proposal entails the repudiation of the entire classic economic and social analysis, when it attempts to assimilate the recent Fascist totalitarianisms into the surviving feudal forms of that time (Fascist but also non-Fascist, at the time of the division of Poland!).

But the sentence of total betrayal is in the second aspect: the total and complete obliteration of the criticism of the 'values' of bourgeois mentality, which exalt, as the final destination of the tremendous journey of humanity, a classless world of popular autonomies, of free nationalities, of independent and peaceful homelands. And in fact Marx and Lenin, when they were still obliged to come to terms with the advocates of this rotten baggage, raised to its greatest virulence the struggle to liberate the working class from the fetishes of homeland-nation-democracy brandished by the 'gurus' of bourgeois radicalism. At the historic turning-point they were able to break with them not only in theory but in practice: when power relations permitted, without pity they

---

3   Marx and Lenin 1968, p. 80.

slit the movement's throat. The gurus of today have inherited the function of priests of those fetishes and those myths. Here, it is not a question of a historical pact that they will break later than was expected – no, it is a question of total enslavement to the demands of the capitalist bourgeoisie for the optimum of the regime that grants it privilege and power.

The thesis is of interest because it tallies with our demonstration of the fact that Russia today is a state in which the capitalist revolution has been accomplished, and that on its social commodity the flags of nationality and homeland, and of extreme militarism, can proudly wave.

6. It would be an extremely grave error not to see, and to deny, the fact that in the world today ethnic and national factors still have an enormous effect and enormous influence. It is still of crucial importance to make an exact study of the limits in time and space in which movements of national independence, linked to a social revolution against precapitalist (Asiatic, slave, feudal) forms, can still be characterised as necessary conditions of the transition to socialism, with the founding of national states of a modern type (for example in India, China, Egypt, Persia, and so on).

Discriminating between these situations is hampered, on the one hand, by the factor of xenophobia determined by pitiless colonial capitalism and, on the other, by that of the current extreme diffusion of productive resources and commodities to distant markets all over the world. But on a world scale the burning question in 1920 also in the area of the former Russian empire – the question of giving political and military support to struggles for independence of the Oriental peoples – is by no means closed.

Saying, for example, that the relation between industrial capital and the working class presents itself in the same way, say, in Belgium and in Siam, and that the struggle is waged in either case with no regard for factors of race and nationality, is no sign of being extremist, but is a sure sign of not having understood anything about Marxism.

It is not by depriving Marxism of its depth, breadth, and hard and harsh complexity that one gains the right to give the lie to, and one day chop down, its despicable renegades.

CHAPTER 17

East

In the picture of the ongoing conflict the peoples of the East are most definitely in the foreground.[1]

They are grouped in a powerful bloc around Russia and rise up against the Western bloc, led by the great white colonial powers.

It is not only the opponents of these powers who exclaim that this has been the great Russian revolutionary perspective from the very beginning: the working class of the Western countries on the one hand and the oppressed peoples of colour on the other, in alliance with the Soviet state to overthrow capitalist imperialism. It is the American journalists themselves who, recalling the struggle as it was structured thirty years ago, pay homage to their enemy for the powerful historical continuity of its world strategy.

Those journalists recall how in September of 1920, between the Second and the Third Congress of the Third International, the Congress of the Peoples of the East was held in Baku, firmly based on the directives of revolutionary Marxism. Nearly two thousand delegates attended, from China to Egypt, from Persia to Libya.

Zinoviev, president of the Proletarian International, presided over the Congress. Although Zinoviev did not possess the *allure* of the warrior, at the end of his speech at the first session the men of colour responded to his worlds with tumultuous applause, brandishing swords and scimitars. 'Comrades! Brothers! The time has now come when you can set about organising a true people's *holy war* against the robbers and oppressors. The Communist International turns today to the peoples of the East and says to them: Brothers, we summon you to a *holy war*, in the first place against British imperialism!'[2]

But the war cry against Japan was no different, calling for a Korean national insurrection, while Zinoviev also proclaimed the Bolshevik hatred of France and of America, railing against 'the American sharks who drank the blood of the workers of the Philippines'.

Even though Zinoviev was executed fifteen years later, the challenge he launched is still our challenge today. Lenin, reading the account of that vibrant

---

1 *Prometeo*, No. 2, Series II, February 1951; republished in *I fattori di razza e nazione nella teoria marxista* 1976, Milan: Iskra (writings 1950–1953), pp. 137–147.

2 *Baku Congress of the Peoples of the East*, see First Session (Zinoviev), 1 September 1920 (Bordiga's italics), available at http://www.marxists.org/history/international/comintern/baku/index.htm.

appeal, immediately understood the need to heighten the imperial rivalry between Japan and the United States, to the point of offering the Americans a military base in Kamciatka from which to strike the Japanese. We have our doubts about this historical point, but Lenin's perspective was explicit (ever since the Theses on the Eastern Question of the Fourth Congress of the Communist International at the end of 1922). We quote Lenin's words: 'A new world war, this time *in the Pacific*, is inevitable unless international revolution forestalls it. [...] The new war threatening the world will involve not only Japan, America and Britain, but also the other capitalist powers such as France and Holland (*the Dutch Indies, too, was a theatre of the struggle in 1941, even though the metropolis was under German occupation*), and threatens *to be even more destructive* than the 1914–1918 war'.[3]

A Russia of today that openly attacked in the East the troops of the metropolises of the West, at the head of Chinese, Koreans, Indochinese, Filipinos, along with Arabs, Egyptians, Moroccans, would be, then, on the high road of revolution? On the road Lenin showed us, and foresaw?

For the filthy bourgeoisie of our countries the yellow peril and the red peril are the same, and no divinity but the dollar can save it. But, for the bourgeoisie, the spectre of the yellow peril is even more ancient. In the first years of the century Europe was polarising into the two enemy blocs that were preparing the first conflagration of imperial rivalries. The Russia of the Tsars squared off against Japan, the most developed of the Asian peoples thanks to its domination of those waters of the Yellow Sea and the Sea of Japan which, today, are stained anew with the blood of war, and European military prestige was dealt a stunning blow. The fact was that the Tokyo yellows had gone further in the direction of capitalism than the Moscow whites.

Kaiser Wilhelm, later described as the Ogre who provoked the first great war, at that time had a mania for painting. One of his pictures showed Germany, in the cuirass of Valkyrie, convoking the white peoples and pointing to the livid light of the Asian threat on the distant horizon. But the white powers paid no heed to the vatication of the daubing emperor, and Germany's only ally turned out to be Turkey, a Mongol people. The Russians, French, English and Italians jumped all over the Germans, and the great Entente took in other continents as well – not only America but even Japan and China.

The facile picture of a contest between human races coming from opposite continents to conquer world hegemony was, therefore, not complete. And in

---

3 Lenin, *Theses on the Eastern Question*, VII, (Bordiga's italics), available at http://ciml.250x
.com/archive/comintern/ci_forth_congress_eastern_question.html.

vain do the writers of today attempt to complete it, when they go so far as to see a risen Carthage taking its revenge on Rome, in a spreading to the Mediterranean world of colour of agitation stemming from Korea, Tibet, Indochina ...

In the second world war Germany, rearmed and, once again, accused of provocation, was opposed, in the name of liberty, by all the rulers and oppressors of the coloured races. This time its only ally was yellow Japan. As for the Russia of the Soviets, at the beginning it did not complain about the declaration of war contained in the 'Anti-Comintern Pact' that had united Germany and Japan. With the Japanese it only went to war pro forma, when they were already dead and buried. With Germany it came to an agreement, whose content was nothing other than the skin of an 'oppressed nationality', namely, Poland's. It takes considerable effort to see the events in the foreshortening of that vision which one bourgeois journalist attributed to Lenin: phase of revolutionary national wars of the nineteenth century – then phase of revolutionary class wars in Europe and victory in Russia – finally the third phase: at the same time national revolutions in the East and class revolutions in the imperialist countries.

It takes an even greater effort to fit the second period of the latest world war into the anti-Western and anti-metropolitan strategy. The holy wars Moscow was supposed to lead were silent, and it entered into *open alliance* – far more than just giving a few *bases* – with the revolution's number one enemy, Great Britain, and with number two as well, just about to ascend to the age-old throne: North America. To save these centres of imperialism and keep them from cutting off their own tentacles, which strangle the globe and its peoples of colour with their Suez and their Panama canals, it threw into the oven of war the cream of Soviet proletarian youth. And to arm them it contracted debt after debt with world capital, in the form of rent, of loans, or – even worse – of gifts.

Today, after the smashing of the German centre of power, which did not lord it over any non-European peoples but only attempted to overcome the united world control of the sea and the air, this control is now, uncontested, in the hands of the Anglo-Saxon metropolises. Today – not yesterday! – [Moscow] encourages the immense but semi-defenceless masses of the peoples of the East to attack these metropolises. It replays the card of holy war and invokes a host of scimitars against the pitiless threat of a rain of atomic bombs. It deceives fanatical but ignorant fighters about the sordid and traitorous retreat, unmasked by the English press, of motorised divisions and air-force wings in the face of a handful of men advancing on foot.[4]

---

4 A reference to the ongoing Korean War.

In all this there is something fundamental that is wrong.

A small man with a short blond moustache, with a calm voice and bright limpid eyes, reads his theses on the national and colonial questions from the platform in the Kremlin, raising them to a new level of clarity, winning, again, the admiration of the worldwide representatives of the proletariat and of Marxism. Yes, the Second International had understood absolutely nothing about all this. It had condemned imperialism but then had fallen into its coils, since it had not understood that it was necessary to mobilise every possible force against it: in the homeland, the defeatism of the social insurrection; in the colonies and in the semi-colonial countries, national revolt. It had fallen into the trap of the defence of the homeland, its traitorous leaders had been eating on imperialism's plate, inviting the workers of heavy industry to accept a few crumbs of the ferocious exploitation of millions of workers overseas.

Today we, Communist International, we, Russia of the Soviets, we, communist parties that in all the developed nations seek the conquest of power, in open war against the bourgeoisie and its social-democratic servants, stipulate an alliance in the countries of the East between the very young workers' movement, the emerging communist parties, and the revolutionary movements that seek to expel the imperialist oppressors. In the light of our doctrine, we have come to the decision to speak not of *bourgeois democratic* movements but, rather, of *revolutionary nationalist* movements, since we do not accept alliances with the bourgeois class but only with movements that stand on the ground of armed insurrection.

The word *bourgeois* was too strong, but the word *nationalist* was no less strong: old socialists like Serrati and Graziadei – the first ingenuous, the second subtle – expressed their perplexities.

Lenin continued his analysis calmly, without a hint of perplexity. The theses contain his unequivocal facts. What is needed first is 'a precise appraisal of the specific historical situation and, primarily, of economic conditions'.[5] Without this fundamental guide it would not be possible to understand the Marxist method, which does not admit ideological rules that hold good for all times. I, said Serrati, had to struggle for six years against the nationalist infatuation with Trieste that had to be liberated from the Germans, an infatuation that was said to be revolutionary. How can I applaud the Malayan national-revolutionary? But, thinking historically, a national struggle in Trieste in the situation of 1848 would have had the support of the proletariat because it was revolutionary, in

---

5   Lenin 1965, pp. 144–51, see Thesis 2.

the midst of a Europe still struggling to emerge from the anti-feudal revolution: this was the situation for the Leninist progressive national wars in Europe up to 1870. In 1914 the wars were imperialist and reactionary, even if their theatre was the same border, their banner the same ideology. For the Marxist what counts is the stage of social development.

In what historical and economic circumstances did Lenin speak at the Kremlin, and Zinoviev a few months later in Baku? The theses make them perfectly clear.

'The fundamental task [of the Communist Party is that] of combating bourgeois democracy and exposing its falseness and hypocrisy'.[6] This hypocrisy covers up the reality of the social oppression of capitalists over workers in the bourgeois world, and the reality of the oppression of the few large imperial states over the colonies and semi-colonies. To establish our strategy in the East, Lenin's theses reassert a series of cornerstones. '[We must] hasten the collapse of the petty-bourgeois nationalist illusions that nations can *live together in peace and equality under capitalism*'. 'This union [of the proletarians and the working masses of all nations] alone will guarantee victory over capitalism, without which the abolition of national oppression and inequality is impossible'. 'The world political situation has now [1920] *placed the dictatorship of the proletariat on the order of the day*. World political developments are of necessity concentrated on a single focus – the struggle of the world bourgeoisie against the Soviet Russian Republic, around which are inevitably grouped, on the one hand, the Soviet movements of the advanced workers in all countries, and, on the other, all the national liberation movements in the colonies and among the repressed nationalities'. In the task of the Communist International it must be taken into account that 'there is a tendency towards the creation of *a single world economy, regulated by the proletariat of all nations* as an integral whole and according to a common plan'.[7]

There are other fundamental points of the 'Eastern' tactic. They could not be more reassuring. 'The mounting exigency of the task of converting the dictatorship of the proletariat *from a national dictatorship* (i.e., existing in a single country and incapable of determining world politics) *into an international one* (i.e., a dictatorship of the proletariat involving at least several advanced countries, and capable of exercising a decisive influence upon world politics as a whole)'. And above all: '[P]roletarian internationalism demands, first, that the interests *of the proletarian struggle in any one country* should be subordinated

---

6   Ibid., Thesis 2.
7   Ibid., Theses 3, 4, 5, 8 (Bordiga's italics).

to *the interests of that struggle on a world-wide scale*, and, second, that a nation which is achieving victory over the bourgeois should be able and willing to make *the greatest national sacrifices for the overthrow of international capital*.[8]

With all this firmly established, and with a firm confidence in the anti-capitalist revolutionary struggle in all the bourgeois countries, even the most radical of the Left European Marxists cry out in approval of the conclusions of the theses, and of the iron dialectic of the orator.

On these bases, and in a manner far more genuine than that of the world press, we can reconstruct Lenin's historical picture.

The way of life of human associations down through the long millennia did not make the peoples of the various countries directly dependent: sometimes they never met or even knew of one another. But when the capitalist era began, the methods of production and of communication had already linked together all parts of the world. The political revolution against feudal powers leaped violently from one end of Europe to the other; there were no longer national histories but only one history, at least for the entire Atlantic part of the continent. The class of the proletarians appeared on the scene of history and fought together with the bourgeoisie in its revolutions, taking part in a united front for liberal and national conquests, and offering the new masters of society the irregular troops of the insurrections and the regular troops of the great wars for the creation of nations. This is a historical fact, and even in the Manifesto of 1848 it is still a rule of strategy for certain countries and peoples, such as the ones still oppressed by Austria and Russia.

There is no reason to cover up the fact that national action means a bloc of classes: in that phase, capitalists and workers against feudal lords.

For the entire field of Europe, Marxism closes this phase in 1870. In the Paris Commune the working class denounced the national bloc – as, for that matter, it had attempted to do in 1848; it struggled on its own, and took power – long enough to show that the form of its power is its dictatorship.

Since then, whoever *in the European arena* continues to call for national blocs of classes is a *traitor*: the Third International, the Russian revolution, Leninism, liquidated this party for ever – in theory, in organisation, in armed struggle.

In the East the regimes continue to be feudal. How will they develop? The colonial powers have brought the products of their industry, and in a few cases their industrial plants, to the coastal regions. Local crafts decay and the crafts-

---

8 Ibid., Thesis 10 (Bordiga's italics).

men move inland, turning to agricultural work. A wretched peasantry is subjected to the direct exploitation of indigenous lordlings and to the indirect
exploitation of world capitalism. Wherever a local industrial bourgeoisie arises,
it is bound to its foreign counterpart and depends on it. It is difficult for a
bloc against the foreigners to take shape. In only a few countries (Morocco, for
example) is it composed of the feudal lords themselves and the large landowners. Generally the pressure comes from the peasants, and from the few workers,
who are joined, as in Europe in the Romantic era, by the intellectuals, divided
between traditionalistic xenophobia and the attractions of white science and
technology. This shapeless mass rebels, and its rebellion creates serious problems for the European capitalist class, which now has two enemies: the people
of the colonies and the proletariat at home.

How can the Eastern system of social economy give rise to socialism? Will
it be necessary, as it was in Europe, to wait for a bourgeois revolution with its
national rebellions supported by the masses of workers and of the poor and –
only after that – for the establishment of local class struggle, the workers' movement, the struggle for power and for soviets? With a road this long the world
proletarian revolution would take countless centuries to be accomplished.

More or less clearly, the delegates from the East in 1922 said *no*, they did not
want to pass through capitalism with its infamies, no longer masked by popular and nationalist parades – no, they wanted to join up with the working-class
world revolution in the capitalist countries and lead their own countries to the
dictatorship of the masses of have-nots and the system of soviets.[9]

The Western Marxists accepted the plan. This means that whenever a
struggle breaks out in the East against the local agrarian or theocratic feudal
regime and, at the same time, against the colonial metropolises, the local and
international communists enter the struggle and support it. And not with the
intent of forming an autonomous and local bourgeois democratic regime but,
on the contrary, to spark the *permanent revolution*, which will not stop until it
obtains the dictatorship of the soviets. Marx and Engels, as Zinoviev recalled,
taken aback by Serrati's surprise, had always said so: they said so for the Germany of 1848!

So, now the series of three periods looks like this: support for national insurrections in the metropolises, up to 1870. Then, class insurrectional struggle in
the metropolises, 1871–1917, with just one victory, in Russia. Then, class struggle
in the metropolises and national-popular insurrections in the colonies with

---

9 In 1922, in addition to the Fourth Congress of the Communist International, also the First Congress of the Communist and Revolutionary Organisations of the Far East was held in Moscow.

revolutionary Russia at the centre, in a single world strategy that was to stop only with the overthrow of capitalist power EVERYWHERE, in Lenin's time.

In this perspective, the socio-economic problem was overcome by the guarantee contained in the 'unitary world economic plan'. The proletariat, coming to power in the West and master of the modern means of production, shares them with the economies of the backward countries with a 'plan' that, *like the one* already offered by the capitalism of today, is unitary, but *unlike that one* does not seek conquest, oppression, exploitation, and extermination.

The [Stalinist] perspective in the light of the third world war that is possible today IS NOT THIS ONE.

First of all, Moscow has jettisoned the concept of a world-wide interdependence of struggles – as doctrine, as strategy, as organisation. The Presidium of the Communist International, violating its statutory faculties, decided on 15 May 1943 to dissolve the organisation, claiming that decisions regarding the problems of a single country can no longer be made internationally, since the situation in 1920 no longer exists and each national party must be autonomous. In the statement of reasons for the decision, the separation of the Communist Party of the United States in November 1940 is approved! But this had taken place because of the division of Poland with Hitler! And then it states that the breaking of the world-wide bond is necessary because, while the parties in the Hitlerian countries have to wage a defeatist struggle, the parties in the opposing countries have to work for the national bloc – here are the exact words: '*support to the utmost the war effort of the governments*'.

Lenin's great way, his great perspective, was shattered! In the Western camp, and no longer *in a colony or semi-colony*, a bloc was to be formed not with nationalist groups risen up against a home or a foreign government but, rather, *with the constituted government* – bourgeois, capitalist, imperial, possessor of overseas colonies. The crystal clear formula of the alliance of the day – a league of all the enemies of the great capitalist powers of the West – was shattered and turned upside-down.

History is never simple or easy to decipher, and the forming of alliances – today when the orders have been changed once again, and they are to tear out the guts of the warmongering governments of America and Europe (like last time, with Hitler) – will prove to be more or less complicated, as it was on the eve of the other two wars.

Meanwhile the decision on the dual task of the parties in the various states still comes from that presidium of the Kremlin which dared to dissolve itself.

But the goal of the alliance of oppressed classes and oppressed peoples is no longer – as it was in Lenin's programme – *the fall of capitalism* in America and in England. We therefore lack any way to the *international dictatorship of the proletariat*, and any possibility of that *unitary world economic plan* which was the only way of resolving the problem of 'leaping over' the bourgeois regime in China, rather than creating it for the benefit of yesterday's Chiang Kai-sheks or tomorrow's Mao Tse-tungs (or today's Titos). Everything has been renounced, since the high road has been replaced by the winding path that permits 'peaceful co-existence' under the capitalist regime; because the *interest of the first proletarian nation* [Soviet Russia] is no longer subordinated to that of victory in the most advanced countries, and the 'national sacrifices' that Lenin required and promised are denied, to be replaced by an egotism of the nation and of the state.

On these conditions, just as the total support for the wartime governments of the anti-German alliance was base opportunism, perfectly analogous to that of the Second International which in 1914 advocated national blocs, so, after all of Lenin's guarantees had been denied and destroyed, the same base opportunism has characterised the national alliance in the countries of the East, with its 'bloc of four classes' that embraces local bourgeois leaders of industry and commerce and guarantees them a long future of capitalist economic practice. Military support for a Mao Tse-tung regime is no less reactionary than the support for the Roosevelt regime or – in Lenin's day – than the support in the first world war for the Kaiser's empire or the French republic.

The Marxist Left warned in time that the guideline of the historical perspective of the revolutionary class does not change, from the moment when new productive forces cause it to appear in society until the moment when it definitively disperses the ancient relations of production.

But the majority of the working class today seems to follow the school that pretends to modify the great perspectives, on the pretext that the study of new situations and experiences requires it. Late-nineteenth-century revisionism defended itself similarly, on the assumption that the peaceful forms of bourgeois development meant that the armed struggle and the dictatorship proclaimed by Marx could be jettisoned.

If there is one thing that the three decades after Lenin's has taught us, it is that the world-wide interdependence of constituted states and of social economies has not slackened. Otherwise, how could the Russian leaders – at Yalta, at Potsdam – have embraced and committed themselves to the ultramodern politics of war, which decreed that the losers be destroyed and annihilated under the true international dictatorship of the winning bloc, and which perpetrated the deception (even greater than that of Wilson's old 1918 League) of the United Nations, in whose Glass Palace – while the blood flows like wine

on the fields of Korea – champagne flows in the toasts proposed, with easy
smiles, by the adversaries of the new holy wars?

It makes no sense to propose to the working class a perspective that confines
it to the limited enclosure of national politics.

The theory that barters the world socialist plan for socialism in one country, that insists on the possible co-existence, before world capitalism has been
defeated, not only of hypothetical proletarian states with states of the bourgeoisie, but also of opposing centres of constituted military power – this theory is no different from that 'petty-bourgeois theory on the juridical equality
of nations in a capitalist regime' condemned in Lenin's 1920 theses, and no
different from the programmes of the 'League for Peace and Freedom' of the
Mazzinis and the Kossuths, condemned in his 1864 theses by Marx.

Since Capital today has not the slightest intention of renouncing its world
unitary plan for power but, on the contrary, is taking action to reinforce the
chains of the working class of all countries, be they 'prosperous' or poor, and to
intensify the subjection of the small states and the immense colonial masses,
every theory of *co-existence* and every great world-wide movement *for peace* is
tantamount to complicity with that plan for starvation and oppression.

Any attempt [by Moscow] to propose a holy war as a defence against attacks
on that impossible equilibrium, made after decades of renouncing the supreme
request to raze the imperialist centres to the ground, can lead to nothing other
than the immolation of the efforts of partisans and rebels to the ends of imperialisms, which will exploit them just as American imperialism did, after being
touted in 1943 as a champion of world freedom.

But, today, the majority of the world working class falls into the trap of the
campaign for Peace, and perhaps tomorrow will fall into the trap of a new and
futile partisan immolation. It is not returning to its revolutionary autonomous
perspective, as it was able to do after 1918.

Perhaps we have to wait for another Lenin. But wasn't Lenin – as the cold
Zinoviev let slip in a moment of lyricism – 'l'homme qui vient tous les cinq-
cent ans'?

Five hundred years – today, when big magazines glitter for equally big pub-
lics for such short cycles, like Ike's cycle from West Point linebacker to Washington commander-in-chief, or the cycles of the changing of the guard in the
alcoves of political chiefs?

The path of communism, which is not enclosed in the life cycle of men or
of generations, will not need this [will not need another Lenin, or another five
hundred years], *on the condition* that the politics of yesterday's anti-German
and anti-Fascist Western bloc, and the politics of the self-styled Eastern bloc
today – which no longer pursues the world socialist republic but, rather, a

national and popular democracy, falser than the one Washington proclaimed –
are branded with the same mark that Lenin, in 1914, burned into the flesh of
social-nationalism: Traitor! And, this time, branded by a reconstituted unit of
organisation and struggle of the exploited and the oppressed of all countries.
   Until then, there is no peace that is desirable, no war that is not infamous.

CHAPTER 18

The Multiple Revolutions

1. The position of the Communist Left is sharply distinguished not only from the eclecticism of the [communist] party with regard to tactics but, in particular, from the brute superficiality of those who reduce the entire struggle to the always and everywhere repeated dualism of two conventional classes, which are its only actors.[1] The strategy of the modern proletarian movement has precise and stable lines that are valid for every hypothetical future action, which are to be referred to distinct geographical 'areas' in which the inhabited world is divided, and to distinct cycles of time.

2. The first and classical area whose play of forces provided the basis for the irrevocable theory of the course of the socialist revolution is England. From 1688 the bourgeois revolution surprised the power of feudalism and rapidly eradicated its forms of production; from 1840 it is possible to deduce the Marxist conception of the play of three essential classes: bourgeois landed property – industrial, commercial, financial capital – and proletariat, in its struggle with the first two.

3. In the area of Western Europe (France, Germany, Italy, smaller countries) the bourgeois struggle against feudalism took place from 1789 to 1871. In the situations of this course the proletariat allied itself with the bourgeoisie when, by force of arms, it fought to overthrow feudal power – while the workers' parties had already rejected any ideological confusion with economic and political apologies for bourgeois society.

4. By 1866 the United States of America had placed itself in the condition of Western Europe after 1871, having liquidated spurious capitalist forms with its victory over the rural and slaveholding South. Since 1871, in the entire European-American area, radical Marxists have rejected any alliance or bloc with bourgeois parties, on any ground whatsoever.

5. The situation before 1871, described in point 3, continued in Russia and in other eastern European countries until 1917. These countries were confronted with the problem – posed in Germany in 1848 – of provoking two revolutions, and therefore struggling also for the goals of a capitalist revolution. The condition for a direct passage to the second – the proletarian – revolution was a

---

1   *Sul filo del tempo*, May 1953.

political revolution in the West, which failed to materialise despite the Russian proletariat's conquest of political power on its own: power it held for just a few years.

6. While in the European area of the East the capitalist mode of production and exchange has fully replaced the feudal mode, in the Asian area the revolution against feudalism and against even more ancient regimes is still going on, waged by a revolutionary bloc of bourgeois, petty-bourgeois and working classes.

7. The analysis we have developed amply illustrates how these attempts at double revolution have had various historical outcomes: partial victory and total victory, defeat on the insurrectional plane with victory on the socio-economic plane and vice versa. The lesson of the semi-revolutions and of the counter-revolutions is fundamental for the proletariat. The examples are legion, but two classic cases come to mind. First, Germany after 1848: double insurrectional defeat of bourgeoisie and proletariat, social victory of the capitalist form, and gradual consolidation of bourgeois power. Second, Russia after 1917: double insurrectional victory of bourgeoisie and proletariat (February and October), social defeat of the socialist form, social victory of the capitalist form.

8. Russia, or at least its European part, today has a fully capitalistic mechanism of production and exchange, whose social function is reflected politically in a party and a government that has adopted all the possible strategies for alliances with bourgeois parties and states of the area of the West. The Russian political system is a direct enemy of the proletariat and any alliance with it is inconceivable, even though its having led the capitalist form of production to victory in Russia is a revolutionary result.

9. For those countries of Asia where an agrarian local economy of a patriarchal and feudal type is still predominant, the – also political – struggle of the 'four classes' must be considered an element of victory in the communist international struggle when national and bourgeois powers arise as an immediate result, both because new areas are formed that are suitable for further socialist demands, and because of the blows struck by these insurrections and revolts against European-American imperialism.

'Racial' Pressure of the Peasantry, Classist Pressure of the Coloured Peoples

1   Rules of Marxist Work[1]

Since what concerns us is not aesthetic or literary production and criticism, our comrades and readers, rather than stopping to appreciate a passage, page or writing, must always focus on the connection between the various parts of the work done by our small movement, in redrawing all the lines of the Marxist edifice on a single plane.

Since we are also not concerned with writing our will, we do not pursue a systematic exposition of reality but, rather, are driven by the need to deal with the fractures and rifts that have debilitated the revolutionary movement at various points. But in all our work we remain focused on the link with the single structure from which all our individual works branch off.

After reading this article, we do not want you to call 'free elections' in your head, to convene a legislative body in your ventricle, and then cast your ballot. We want you, rather, to make every effort to 'fit' the facts we present you with into the ordered system of our shared positions. We ask you not to pass judgements, but to carry out your part of the work.

It is not persons or theoreticians or professors who speak here but, rather, past facts that confront and collide with present and future facts, experimentally weighing the results of analogous *comparisons* made over the past hundred years.

In a letter to one of those people who believe in the Cartesian mission of criticism (a respectable instrument that we admire in the hands of the bourgeoisie, with which it has forged almost five centuries of the history of human society; we had passed on to other tools), a comrade wrote: 'The current situation, characterised by the temporary absence of an independent proletarian movement, compels us – in the field of our practical activity – to lay claim to the integrity of our classic texts, to combat any adulteration, to wait until the inevitable upsetting of the situations poses anew the problem of the practical connection between programme and proletarian struggle, and *not to replace*

---

1   *il programma comunista*, Yr. 2, No. 14, 23 July–24 August 1953; republished in *I fattori di razza e nazione nella teoria marxista* 1976, Milan: Iskra (writings 1950–1953), pp. 161–174.

these struggles with our own intellects to solve problems that one-hundred-and-one times out of a hundred have been slipped into our ranks by the bourgeoisie'.

2   Two Points to Be Settled

It seems the time has come to turn our attention to two points of Marxism, which we have often taken up in the past and which, moreover, are inseparable: namely, the *agrarian* and the *national-colonial* questions. We shall do this in writings and in oral discussions in the coming months – naturally not without interruptions, parentheses and new beginnings: we are not a ministry that distributes portfolios on the clownish pretext of special competences.

Naturally, in this endeavour we promise to invent nothing but to rely strictly on the solid historical material at our disposal. Our task is not to invite democratic opinions on this material but, rather, to show that when all the facts in their materiality are nailed to their place, then Madam Opinion is left with as much *freedom* as the image that forms on the screen in honour of the laws of optic propagation and the sensitivity of light.

In the past few years we have concentrated on Marxist economic theory as scientific description and as a programme for socialist society, which are two dialectically inseparable aspects. This part of Marxist criticism 'supposes' a totally developed capitalist society – for two reasons. The first is that the enemy school maintains that all social difficulties and the reasons for imbalance would vanish if all society's economic relations were based on commerce and wages. The second is that in our endeavour to describe scientifically, in its characteristics opposed and antithetical to those of capitalism, communist society as the final destination of history's course and not as a cold static picture, we have to begin with a fully developed pre-communist society, and therefore with a supposed total capitalism. We showed that Marx chose England since it was a goldmine for the collection of facts; but he knew very well that it had never been purely capitalistic and left out of account its non-capitalistic features. (We showed on another occasion how Marx openly declared this, and emphasised all the social forms present in England – perhaps less than elsewhere – that were extraneous to the three sole forms upon which he based his demonstrative calculation of the inevitable crisis: industrial enterprise, landed property, wage labour.)

Nevertheless, in the historical – or, we might say, geographical, in the sense of social geography – part of his work, developed side-by-side with his 'backbone theory' of the pure capitalist economy, he brought all those 'non-pure' areas and phases onto the scene and examined them thoroughly. And he took fully into account the absolutely leading role often played by the classes deriving from pre-capitalism that still survive today – peasants, artisans, small merchants and so forth – as well as the historical development of those countries that had not yet entered the capitalist arena, and most especially countries inhabited by non-white peoples, still characterised not only by feudal but also by slave and barbarous forms.

3   The Historical and 'Philosophical' Part of Our Work

Marx dedicated a substantial part of his work to the study of the entities and laws that regulate the capitalist economy and to the specification of the communist demand (today, as in Lenin's day, most of Marx's correct theses have been forgotten or distorted, even though current historical facts have given them all great vigour). Accordingly, we ourselves have not neglected the 'geography of the areas of class struggle and revolution' and the way in which, in the advanced countries, the limits of these areas change as pure industrial forms come to prevail and capitalist production and the capitalist market spread to the backward countries.

The basis of Marxist doctrine is the collision between a complete capitalist form and a proletariat that covers the entire field of productive labour, while the goal of the [party] organisation is an internationally complete network for world-wide struggle: in the light of all this, it would be sheer nonsense to affirm that *mixed* situations must simply be ignored, and that the weight of the social forces and state authorities relative to them cannot be influential and even decisive for the task and the action of the modern working class.

In developing the economic and social theory of capitalism and of its transformation into communism, with many references to the history and geography of the *impure phases*, we have by no means neglected that which in current language is called the 'philosophical part' of Marxism. By this we refer to the theory of the historical dynamic, of the causes and laws of historical facts, resolving the well-known problems (the cause of many false formulations) regarding consciousness, will, action, showing that Marx's economic determinism, his historical and dialectical materialism, which many repudiate (and we are readier than ever to refute their arguments), can mean nothing other than denying the individual both action preceded by will and consciousness, and influence by means of that action on the events of the collectivity, as recorded by history. In this way, the nature and function of the class party is once again brought into focus, in a way that immutably and literally corresponds to the original statements of the method. It is only in the impersonal organ of the class party that one can speak of a praxis sustained by doctrinal knowledge and voluntary deliberation, both of them dictated not by unlimitedly free choices but, rather, by pre-established directions and by the occurrence of conditions that can be studied and discovered and tested, but never provoked with prescriptions, resources, stratagems or manoeuvres.

This leads us straight to the heart of the problem of tactics, that is, of the methods of action proper to the various phases and facts of development. On this question too, as on the earlier one (not that this means *de hoc satis*: there is much more to be said!), useful and sure material has been collected, going back at almost every step to the indispensable clarifications of the principles, due to the constant dangers of getting off the track.

One of the greatest dangers is the conclusion – so often falsely attributed to the communist 'left' by its adversaries, to free themselves from its rebukes that began in 1920 and were followed by resounding historical confirmation – that we must concern ourselves exclusively with a situation involving just two players: wage-earning proletarians against capitalist entrepreneurs; and that the proletarian party has nothing to see, do or make when third parties are on the scene. It is opportune, then, to examine thoroughly once again the questions of the peasantry and of nationalities, for the moment with a simple brief documentary synthesis, showing how the 'left' has always tackled the questions in earnest, and has most certainly never neglected them.

4   Yesterday

4.1   *Before Lenin*

Our first task is to show what Marx established with regard to these two major questions, the agrarian and the national.

We find fundamental elements of the agrarian question in the treatment of land rent in the Third Volume of *Capital*. In order to show how in the hypothetical pure capitalist society, until the power of capital frees itself from the landed proprietors by nationalising lands and buildings (which would not yet by any means be socialism), Marx utilised the method of economic determinism to give us the theory and the 'pictures' of the types of pre-capitalist society, dominated by a landed economy in not yet bourgeois forms. And just as he pitted his 'picture' of modern industrial production against those of the classical and vulgar economists, so he pitted his pictures and schemas of pre-industrial economies against those of the physiocratic and mercantilist economists.

Then, in Marx's and also Engels' studies on the class struggles in France and in German we find a host of historical applications, and there are all the elements of the doctrine that Lenin later utilised in his struggle against the crass revisionist socialism of the Second International conservative bonzes who had set themselves up as leaders of the urban proletariat.

As for the question of nationalities, Marx dedicated no less attention to it: in addition to the discussions in the historical parts of his economic works, he often tackled the question in the texts of the First International and in his incessant correspondence.

It is indisputable that Marx not only took an interest in, but, in fact, committed proletarian and communist support to Poland's struggle of national liberation against Russia and Ireland's (backward and agrarian) against England (modern and industrial); while no less fundamental was the interest Engels took in the wars for the creation of national states on the European continent, which preceded the war of 1870–71.

4.2 Dialectical Crossroads

The point of all this is the following: in geographical areas and in historical phases that have been precisely determined in the general theory of the historical course (and that don't just pop up like a jack-in-the-box), it often occurs that the pressure of a mass of small peasants against landed proprietors accelerates the bourgeois revolution and the liberation of modern productive forces from their traditional chains. This alone makes the successive struggle and demands of the workers possible; just as, on many other occasions, it has occurred that an analogous liberation of forces compressed for future developments can only be triggered by the success of a war of national independence or of an irredentist demand. Not only must such situations be recognised and declared in doctrine, but if there are already mature proletarian forces they must take a position in favour of such an uprising, which provides an outlet for new productive forces. Therefore – in those spaces and times from which, for instance, post-1871 bourgeois Europe is strictly excluded – support will materialise for those movements that are indisputably engaged in battle with the advanced bourgeois classes.

In those places and periods, the error and the defeatism do not lie in entering into alliance with – insurrectional – agrarian or national uprisings, but precisely in refusing to recognise the fact that the movement and its finality are democratic and capitalistic. Marx, around 1860, exhorted the workers to struggle for the Warsaw insurgents, but at the same time he ferociously hammered at the ideology of the liberal, patriotic, radical-democratic leaders of those movements. By contrast, the danger to be weighed is that, to cross that critical point, one barters a proletarian force already developed on the autonomous plane of class, allowing it to absorb the doctrine and the politics of national liberty as an end in itself, and admitting that such liberty is *sub specie aeternitatis* a legacy, a platform, which is *common* to the bourgeoisie and the proletariat. Lenin, when he said that it was inevitable to favour a bourgeois form, called it *bourgeois* in the most explicit way possible and did not describe it as proletarian, as the renegade communists still do today (just look at the bordello of the partisans' liberation movement). It is a question of having grasped the dialectic – which cannot be replaced by a negation of the facts – of the historical necessities of the chalices from which neither we nor the very gods can drink. But every pre-dialectical revolution unconsciously presupposes in its conscious and freely reasoning ego, put outside and against the world, an immaterial crumb of sanctity. It is not a question, then, of asking the workers and militants to wear chastity belts but, rather, of grasping the historical meaning of the event, which is twice *negated*: Forward! Warsaw workers side-by-side with the bourgeoisie to negate tsarist power, because you are offered no other way to negate bourgeois power. Try – even though it has proved difficult – to give the bourgeois a hand, but try, nonetheless, not to think with his brain. Determinism is the play of thousands of units and forces in the field of the world, not an adhesion obtained with glue between the action, will, consciousness, and thought of each individual.

4.3 Congress of the Communist International

We shall most certainly return to the Marxists texts, but let us now focus our attention on the approach to these two questions at the time of the constitution of the Moscow International, and especially at the 1920 World Congress in which, as is well-known, the author and supporter of the theses was Lenin himself. At this congress, which was prior to the constitution of the Communist Part of Italy, the Left current expressed its blunt disagreements on a number of questions. In particular, on the question of parliamentarianism, in opposition to Lenin himself; on the question of the Italian split, in agreement with Lenin; and on the question of the conditions of admission that were specifically directed against the French and German right-wing currents, also here with proposals that Lenin introduced and accepted (the famous 21st point).

The question of parliamentarianism led to that of tactics, and the disagreement on this issue was rendered sharper and more explicit in 1921, '22, '23, '24 and '26 by the Italian delegations of the left wing of the communist party itself, which up to 1924 represented its vast majority.

If, then, the Italian leftists had been in disagreement on any aspects of the agrarian and colonial questions, they would not have hesitated to express this openly. In fact, in the reports and the minutes, there is not the slightest trace of any such disagreements. There are, by contrast, openly taken positions on the clear Marxists theses on the subject, fully coinciding with the core of Lenin's doctrinal and historical reconstruction.

It was, in fact, right-wing members of the [Italian] party, in the persons of Serrati and Graziadei, who heatedly contested Lenin's theses. Indeed, nothing changed in the position of the Italian Left from 1920 to 1953 – as, it seems, some comrades have believed with regard to the Genoa conference [in April, 1953], which did examine the question of 'impure revolutions' in its historical aspects, but whose main theme was the discussion of a fully capitalist economy: specifically, the American economy.

Returning to 1920, it is clear why points that Western socialism had nearly forgotten were of vital interest to the Third International. The Second International, drowning in trade-union and electoral reformism, focused all its attention on the population of the towns and the metropolises, since that was where it recruited the bulk of its voters. But the formidable preparation of the Russia Marxist and Bolshevik party could not disregard the presence in Russia of forces numerically far greater than those of the industrial proletariat – forces that were already active in the open struggle against tsarist power: peasants oppressed by their servitude to big landowners and to the Church, and the peoples of the hundred different nationalities subjugated by the Great Russian State. These forces had to come together – as indeed they did in the Russian revolution. It was necessary to weigh them and utilise them, while maintaining the revolution firmly on a working-class and socialist footing.

If the revolution had been limited to a struggle for the liberation of small nationalities and oppressed races and for the emancipation of bonded peasants, not only would it have been centuries behind a socialist revolution, led by the Russian proletariat and the World International, but it would have also been historically behind a revolution leading to full capitalism and an accelerated industrialisation of the country not only for the cities but also for the countryside.

It was therefore impossible not to pose the question that – like it or not – is still vitally important for countries with huge populations (among other things) such as India and China, namely, the question of the behaviour of revolutionary Marxists in a social field occupied by feudalism, patriarchal seigniory, foreign capitalism, national bourgeoisie, poor peasantry, artisanship, and finally – in a minimal dose and with limited distribution – a wage-earning proletariat.

4.4   *What the Theses Said*

4.4.1   Agrarian Theses

A pamphlet on the agrarian question, later reprinted, explained the precise meaning of the agrarian theses to the Italian communists, to counteract the falsehood that the communists wanted to spark peasant revolutions and establish a society based on the defence of small farms. The distinction between property (legal criterion) and enterprise (technico-economic criterion) was sufficient to establish the fact that the communist line is always for the large, also agrarian, settlement, but the presence of vast tracts of land in the name of a single enterprise (large landed estate) prevents the conditions for it to materialise. There can be an immense property divided up in a thousand small settlements (leased or sharecropping), just as the opposite is possible if a large industrial settlement should rent many small neighbouring properties. The small agrarian enterprise is always socially passive and weak; it is the opposite pole of the socialist goal; it is the base of the most reactionary of ideologies. The theses of the Second Congress [of the Communist International] confirm this. We limit ourselves to a passage from Meyer's report: 'When is it permissible to divide up big landed property? A division can only come into question when it is leased to small peasants, that is to say when this big landed property is not farmed as a unit. In this case the division does not at all mean relinquishing large-scale operation. Further, this division is possible when the big property is scattered in small peasant settlements. [...] The most important thing in any case is that the landowners should not be left on their estates, that they must be driven out'.[2]

The report goes on to say that the Commission eliminated the section stating that it would be an error not to undertake the division of the land and replaced it with an amendment, stating that the principle of the large-scale enterprise must be maintained.

Graziadei's and Serrati's objections (Serrati was a good and resolute organiser of city workers, but absolutely did not understand the terms of this question) regarded above all the tactics to be used with respect to the small peasant owners. But what the theses say about the conflict of interests between these owners and the capitalist state in the field of taxes, mortgages, and usurious capital is exactly the same as what Marx said with regard to France. Graziadei, for his part, however well-versed he may have been in other matters, on the question of strikes and organisations in common confused farm labourers

---

2 *Minutes of the Second Congress of the Communist International*, Tenth Session, 4 August 1920, Meyer's Report, available at http://www.marxists.org/history/international/comintern/2nd -congress/ch10.htm.

(pure, extremely pure first-rate proletarians) with small landowners: Lenin, in fact, referred only to the group of semi-proletarians, that is, peasants whose patch of land is too small to support them, so that they and their families have to work as day-labourers on other people's lands. In his report, Meyer notes that their interests coincide with those of landless day-labourers, and they can most certainly strike for better wages.

4.4.2   National-Colonial Theses

We have discussed the national theses in our article *East* [above]. Lenin spoke briefly to justify the substitution of the term 'democratic-bourgeois' movements in the backward countries with the term 'nationalist-revolutionary'. The latter term made explicit reference to an armed indigenous insurrection against imperialist white occupiers, while the former might have led one to think of a law-abiding bloc with a local bourgeoisie aping Western parliamentarianism. But the entire discussion is concerned with a fact of undeniable historical importance, which is even more vital today: now, after the defeatism of the Stalinists, the uprisings in the colonies and semi-colonies create greater problems for Western imperialism than the proletarian uprisings in the metropolises; now, such tremendously static institutions as the landed and theocratic institutions of the East are frighteningly collapsing in a surge of civil wars.

[At the Second Congress] the Indian delegate Roy presented supplementary theses, accepted by Lenin. The sixth thesis, with which we conclude this part of our work, is Marxistically indisputable.

The foreign imperialism violently forced upon the peoples of the East has without doubt hindered their social and economic development and robbed them of the opportunity of reaching the same level of development as has been achieved in Europe and America. Thanks to the imperialist policies whose efforts are directed towards holding up industrial development in the colonies, the native proletariat has only come into existence fairly recently. The dispersed local cottage industries have given way to the centralised industries of the imperialist countries. As a result the vast majority of the population was forced to engage in agriculture and export raw materials abroad. On the other hand we can observe a rapidly growing concentration of the land in the hands of big landowners, capitalists and the state, which again contributes to the growth of the number of landless peasants [we quote this above all to show the close connection between the national-colonial and the agrarian questions]. The vast majority of the population of these colonies lives under conditions of oppression. As a result of these policies the underdeveloped spirit of outrage that lives in the masses of the people can only find an expression in the numerically small intellectual middle class [do not forget that it is an Indian who is speaking here, and he, like a Chinese, can give us more millennia of 'civilisation' and of 'culture' than we can give to America].[3] Foreign domination constantly obstructs the free development of social life; therefore the revolution's first step must be the removal of this foreign domination. The struggle to overthrow foreign domination in the colonies does not therefore mean underwriting the national aims of the national bourgeoisie but much rather smoothing the path to liberation for the proletariat of the colonies.[4]

The picture was already flaming in 1920. But today the situation in much of Asia and Africa is at the height of tension. No intellectual turning up of one's nose can make it possible to ignore forces in motion of such enormous power.

5   Today

5.1   *The Position of the Left*
Although the national question was not taken up as a separate issue at the Rome Congress of 1922, the agrarian question was in fact the subject of a specific series of theses, consistent with what we have said here.

In 1926 at the Lyons Congress, the last occasion on which the Left was strong (it still held a numerical majority in the Italian party, for the little that was worth), it proposed a complete system of theses, later presented at the Moscow Enlarged ECCI, as an organic manifestation of opposition to the downwards slide of the entire Comintern, which today, as we know, has fallen to the bottom of the abyss. There are sections on the agrarian and on the national questions.

The first chapter not only reaffirms the concepts we have referred to here but, to a great extent, accepts the possibility of utilising the small landowning peasants in the revolutionary struggle, even though we showed, as Lenin had, the many dangers involved.

The other chapter is also based on Lenin's *fundamental clarification*. We formulated it this way:

---

3 The two remarks in brackets are Bordiga's. Bordiga's text, rather than 'the numerically small intellectual middle class' of the English version, has 'cultured middle class'.

4 *Minutes of the Second Congress of the Communist International*, Fourth Session, 25 July 1920, available at http://www.marxists.org/history/international/comintern/2nd-congress/ch04 .htm#v1-p115.

> Even before [in the countries of colour] a mature basis has been provided for modern class struggle ... demands are made that can only be resolved by insurrectional struggle and the defeat of world imperialism. When these two conditions are fully realised, the struggle can be launched in the epoch of the struggle for proletarian revolution in the metropolises, even though in the colonies it will take shape as a conflict not of class but of race and nationality.

The line, then, is continuous, and there is no reason for anyone to be surprised.

Coming to our more recent work, in the *Tracciato di impostazione* published in the journal *Prometeo*,[5] while not expressly referring to the colonial issue, we said: 'The workers of all countries cannot fail to fight alongside the bourgeoisie to overthrow feudal institutions. [...] Also in the struggles the young capitalist regimes wage to repel reactionary resurgence, the proletariat cannot refuse to support the bourgeoisie'.

This, of course, applies to the France of 1793 or the Germany of 1848. But how can one reasonably refuse to apply it to the Chinese revolution of 1953, which, what's more, is fighting against capitalist imperialism at its most mature? Of course, we still have the problem of the right connection between a fierce struggle against this imperialism in the metropolis and in the colony. The Stalinists replaced Lenin's perspective on this matter with their shameful alliance with the French, English, and Americans, and their defeatism is the root of the ineffectiveness and isolation of the desperate struggles of the oppressed and exploited peoples of colour, and of their betrayal.

In the theses of the Left, or 'Platform', which was published in the first issues of *Prometeo* in 1947, we insisted on the condition, already present in Lenin's theses, of that unitary reconstitution of the party of the international revolution which is lacking today. What is more, we criticised – as we did throughout the polemic of 1920–1926 – the excessive transferral of tactics that were valid in Russia to the situation of the countries of advanced capitalism, as well as to non-European and colonial countries, noting that with the second world war the unitary character of the enemy force was greatly accentuated all over the world.

The problem is in fact historical, not tactical. In our 'Platform' we reaffirmed our position that support for struggles for democracy and independence was logical in Europe in the first half of the twentieth century, on insurrectionary

---

5 *Tracciato d'impostazione – I fondamenti del comunismo rivoluzionario* [Draft Outline – The foundations of revolutionary communism] was a presentation of the programmatic line of the journal *Prometeo*, published in No. 1, July 1946.

grounds. This fundamental Marxist position is still valid today in the East, as it was in Russia before 1917. But our struggle was, precisely, against the demand to apply the same ruinous tactical prescriptions – united front, penetration into the other parties, organisation in cells, functionaryism, and so forth – without distinction to the parties that work, say, in Asia, or in England or in America, promising fabulous results when, in fact, today it is no longer possible to conceal the total ruin of all revolutionary energy.

5.2   *Freedom neither of Theory nor of Tactics*

We need to come to an understanding on this fundamental concept of the Left. The substantial and organic unity of the party, diametrically opposed to the formal and hierarchical unity of the Stalinists, must be understood as being required for its doctrine, its programme, and its so-called 'tactics'. If we understand tactics as the means of action, they cannot but be established by the same research that, based on the facts of past history, has led us to establish our final and complete programmatic demands.

The means cannot vary and be distributed as one pleases, at later times or, even worse, by distinct groups, unless the evaluation of the programmatic objectives and of the way leading to them is different.

It is obvious that the means are not chosen for their intrinsic qualities – beautiful or ugly, sweet or bitter, soft or hard. But, with great approximation, also the prevision of the means to be chosen must be the common equipment of the party, and not depend 'on the situations that crop up'. This is the old struggle of the Left. This is also the organisational formula that requires the so-called base to carry out the movements indicated by the centre, since the centre is connected to a 'shortlist' of possible moves already foreseen in correspondence with no less foreseen eventualities. Only with this dialectical connection is it possible to overcome the point foolishly pursued with the applications of consultative internal democracy, which we have repeatedly shown to be senseless. Everyone demands such applications, but everyone is ready to make a spectacle, be it great or small, of strange and incredible *coups de forces* and *coups de théâtre* in the organisation.

Therefore no militant of the reconstituted communist party will be exempt, in matters of doctrine, from understanding the difference, in class structure and power relations, between a country such as China and the countries of Western capitalism – a difference that will mean struggles characterised by different processes and developments, within the framework of a modern world increasingly united by the facts of its economic base.

No militant will be exempt from understanding how the utilisation of anti-imperialist pressures present in the peoples of colour also influences the power relations between the imperial blocs in latent conflict, giving rise to very different assessments of the consequences of the one's prevailing over the other.

No militant will be exempt from understanding, in matters of tactics, that the exaltation of the anti-European and anti-American colonial uprisings becomes excessive, as is still the case in the Fourth International, if it is separated from the very first condition we have always insisted on: the condition of the unity of method of the world proletarian class and of its communist party. This unity of method has been ruined precisely by the freedom of tactics and by the mania for manoeuvres and expedients, for stratagems and brainstorms.

Then, the militant will be able to understand that, in addition to the two paradigmatic forces of the 'schema' that is theoretically useful for us to prove the collapse of capitalism with mathematical certainty, there are other immense forces on the scene: in the metropolitan countries, the non-proletarian lower classes; in all the rest of the planet, the 'backward' races and peoples – a term for which, at the Second Congress, no satisfactory definition was given.

This, then, is nothing more than a documentary introduction on the 'precedents', to be followed by a fuller discussion of the question in the future.

One must realise that in the modern countries there are still pockets of small peasants who, still excluded from the mercantilist circle, hand down ancient stigmas that the modern circle has blotted out in all city dwellers, be they billionaires or beggars. As Marx said, such peasants constitute a true race of barbarians in an advanced country – advanced in its horrible civilisation. Nevertheless also these barbarians could, against this civilisation, become one of the missiles of the revolution that shall submerge it.

One must realise that overseas, in the yellow, black and olive countries, there live immense collectivities of peoples that, awakened by the clamour of the capitalist mechanism, seem to be opening the cycle of their own struggle for freedom, independence, and patriotism, like the one that inebriated our grandparents. But these peoples come on the scene as a significant factor in the class conflict the present society carries in its womb. The longer it is suffocated, the more fiercely will it blaze in the future.

Appendix: 'Negro' Rage Shook the Rotten Pillars of Bourgeois and Democratic 'Civilisation' (1965)[6]

After the storm of the 'Negro riots'[7] in California, before international conformism buried the regrettable fact under a thick blanket of silence, while the
'enlightened' bourgeoisie was still anxiously trying to discover the 'mysterious'
causes that had jammed the 'peaceful and regular' functioning of the democratic mechanism, a few observers of the two sides of the Atlantic took comfort
in the fact that, after all, explosions of collective violence of people 'of colour'
are nothing new in America, and that, for example, a no less serious one took
place – without consequence – in Detroit in 1943.

But there *was* something profoundly new in this blazing episode of rage. For
those who followed it not with cold objectivity but with passion and hope, the
episode was not only vaguely popular, but *proletarian*. And this is what makes
us say: *The Negro revolt has been crushed. Long live the Negro revolt!*

What *is* new – for the history of the struggles of emancipation of the underpaid Negro worker, certainly not for the history of class struggle in general – is
the almost exact coincidence between the pompous and rhetorical presidential
proclamation of political and civil rights and the explosion of an anonymous,
collective, 'uncivilised' subversive fury on the part of the 'beneficiaries' of the
'magnanimous' gesture; between the umpteenth attempt to tempt the tormented slave with a miserable carrot, which cost nothing, and this slave's instinctive
refusal to let himself be blindfolded and to bend his back again.

Rough, rude, not educated by anyone – not by their leaders, most of whom
are more Gandhian than Gandhi; not by 'communism' USSR style, which, as
l'Unità[8] was quick to remind us, rejects and condemns violence – but trained
by the hard lesson of the facts of social life, the Negroes of California cried out
to the world. Without theoretical consciousness, without the need to express
it in articulate language, but making their statement with their bodies and
their actions, they cried out that there can be no civil and political equality
as long as there is economic inequality, and that the way to end this inequality is not with laws, decrees, lectures and sermons, but by overthrowing *by*

---

6   *il programma comunista*, Yr. 14, No. 15, 10 September 1965.
7   Bordiga uses the Italian word 'negro' (initially in quotes), which was the common (not dis-
    paraging) term at the time (1965). In Italy 'nero' came into use in the late 1960s, following the
    use in the US of 'black'. In this translation I used 'black' just a couple of times; I'm sure Bor-
    diga would have appreciated it. This article was published a month after the Watts riots in Los
    Angeles [note by G. Donis].
8   Newspaper of the Italian Communist Party.

force the bases of a society divided into classes. It is this brutal laceration of the tissue of legal fictions and democratic hypocrisies that disconcerted the bourgeoisie (and how could it do otherwise!). This is what aroused such great enthusiasm in us Marxists (and how could it do otherwise!). This is what must give food for thought to the listless proletarians, dozing in the false mollycoddling of the metropolises of a capitalism historically born with white skin.

When the Northerners, already well on their way to full capitalism, launched a crusade for emancipation from the slavery in the South, they did so not for humanitarian reasons or out of respect for the eternal principles of 1789 but, rather, because they needed to break the fetters of a pre-capitalist patriarchal economy and to 'free' its labour-power – 'free' this gigantic resource so that it could 'devote' itself to the avid monster of Capital. Even before the War of Secession, slaves were encouraged to flee the southern plantations by Northern capitalists enticed by the dream of infamously cheap new workers on the market who, in addition to this direct advantage, would also have allowed the capitalist to lower the wages of the workers already in his employ, or at least to keep them from rising. During and after that war the process was rapidly accelerated, and generalised.

All this was a historically necessary step to overcome the limits of an ultra-backward economy; and Marxism welcomed it, even though it knew that the Negro workers 'freed' in the South would find in the North a mechanism of exploitation already in place that, in some respects, was even more ferocious. In the words of Capital, the 'good Negro' would be free to put his hide to the labour market and have it tanned: free from the chains of Southern slavery but also from the protective shield of an economy and of a society based on personal and human relationships, rather than impersonal and inhuman ones – and therefore alone, naked, and *defenceless*.

And, indeed, the slave who escaped to the North discovered he was no less inferior than before: because he was paid less [than the other workers]; because he had no vocational skills; because he was isolated in new ghettoes as the soldier of a reserve army of labour, and as a potential threat to the connective tissue of the regime of private property and appropriation; because he was segregated and discriminated against as someone who had to feel he was not a man but a beast of burden and thus had to give himself to the first bidder, asking for neither more nor better.

Today, a century after his presumed 'emancipation', he is granted the 'fullness' of civil rights at the very moment in which his average income is inordinately lower than that of his white fellow citizen – half that of his non-dark-skinned brother, while his wife earns one third as much as the wife of a worker not 'of colour'; at the very moment in which the golden metropolis of big business closes him in frightful ghettoes of misery, disease, and vice, isolating him behind invisible walls of prejudices, customs, and police regula- tions; at the very moment in which the unemployment that bourgeois hypo- crisy calls 'technology' (by which it means 'fate', the 'price of progress', cer- tainly not a sin of contemporary society) takes the heaviest toll of its victims in the ranks of his fellow Negroes, because they are the manual labourers, and the lumpenproletariat doing the filthy and exhausting jobs; at the very moment in which, equal to his white fellow soldier in the face of death on the battlefield, he is made profoundly unequal to him in the face of the police- man, judge, tax collector, factory owner, trade-union bonze,[9] landlord of his hovel.

And it is also true – however absurd it may be for the Jesuit logician – that the fire of his revolt broke out in California, where the Negro worker earns more on average than in the East. But it is precisely in those lands of booming capitalism and fictitious proletarian 'affluence' that the disparity of treatment between people of different skin colours is greatest. It is precisely there that the ghetto is fast closing in on the black population, right across the street from the haughty ostentation of luxury, extravagance and *dolce vita* of the ruling class – which is white! It is against the hypocrisy of an egalitarianism Jesuitically written on paper, but denied in the facts of a society mined by deep furrows of class, that black rage vigorously exploded. It is not unlike the explosion of anger of the white proletarians, vortically drawn into and then piled up in the new indus- trial centres of advanced capitalism, packed into the bidonvilles, the 'Koreas',[10] the hovel neighbourhoods of ultra-Christian bourgeois society, in which they are 'free' to sell their labour-power to ... stave off starvation. In this very way the sacred rage of the oppressed classes will *always* explode, exploited and – what is more – derided!

'Premeditated revolt against respect for the law, the rights of one's neighbour, and the maintenance of order!' exclaimed Cardinal McIntyre of the Roman Catholic Church, as if the slave who had just had the shackles taken off his ankles had any reason to respect a law that bends him to the ground and keeps him on his knees, or had even known – he, a 'neighbour' of the whites – he

---

9   Bordiga frequently used the word *bonzo* – bonze, Buddhist monk – in the sense of a preacher of social peace and harmony, hence an adversary of class struggle.
10   'Korea' was the name given in the early 1960s to a Milan neighbourhood of immigrant workers from southern Italy, soon applied to other ghettoes of southern Italians in north- ern Italy.

had rights, or had been able to see in a society based on the lying trinomial 'liberty, equality, fraternity' anything other than disorder raised to the level of a principle.

'Rights are not won with violence', Johnson exclaimed. False! The Negroes recall, if just by hearsay, that the conquest of the rights denied the whites by the English metropolis cost them a long war; that the scrap of an 'emancipation' still impalpable and remote cost whites and Negroes temporarily united an even longer war; every day they see and hear the xenophobic rhetoric exalting the extermination of the redskins who opposed the march of the 'white fathers' towards new lands and 'rights', and the coarse brutality of a West 'redeemed' for the civilisation of the Bible and of Alcohol. What was all this, if not violence? Obscurely, they have understood that there is no problem in the history of America, or of any other country, that has not been resolved *by force*; that there is no right that is not the result of a conflict – often bloody, always violent – between the forces of the past and those of the future. One hundred years of peacefully waiting for the magnanimous concessions of the whites – what has it brought them, apart from the little that the occasional explosion of rage has been able to wrest – even just out of fear – from the miserly and cowardly hand of the master? And what was the response of governor Brown, defender of rights that the whites felt were threatened by the 'riots', if not the democratic violence of machine guns, clubs, tanks, and a state of siege?

And what is all this, if not the experience of the oppressed classes all over the world, whatever the colour of the skin, whatever the 'racial' origin? The Negro – be he proletarian or lumpenproletarian, it makes little difference – who in Los Angeles shouted 'Our war is here, not in Vietnam' formulated a concept no different from that of the men who 'stormed heaven' in the Communes of Paris and Petrograd, destroyers of the myths of order, of national interest, of civilising wars, and heralds of a civilisation that is human at last.

Let the [Italian] bourgeois take no comfort in the thought that, well, the episode was far away, it doesn't concern us – for us, there is no problem of 'race'. Today, ever more clearly, the *racial* question is a *social* question. Suppose that the unemployed and the underemployed of our [own] ragged South no longer find the valve of emigration. Suppose that they can no longer go to get themselves flayed outside our sacred borders. (And to get themselves killed in accidents due not to fate, or unforeseeable freaks of the atmosphere, or, who knows, the evil eye, but to Capital's thirst for profit, its longing to save on the costs of materials, housing, means of transport, safety devices, all for the sake of a higher margin of unpaid labour, and all set to profit from the reconstruction that follows the inevitable, by no means unforeseen, and always hypocritically lamented disasters.) Suppose that the bidonvilles of our industrial cities and of our moral capitals (!!) swarm, even more than today, with pariahs without jobs, without bread, and without reserve and, have no doubt, you will have an Italian 'racism', which is visible even now in the complaints of [our] Northerners about the 'barbarous' and 'uncivilised' *terrone*.[11]

It is the social structure in which we are condemned to live today that gives rise to these infamies; it is under its ruins that they will vanish. It is of this that the 'Negro riots' in California warn and remind the forgetful sleepers in the illusory sleep of affluence, drugged by the opium of democracy and reform – these 'Negroes', not far away, not exotic, but present in our midst. Immature and defeated, but heralds of victory!

---

11   *Terrone* (from *terra*, 'earth') is a disparaging term for southern Italians, comparable to 'nigger'.

SECTION 4

On the Revolutionary Prospects of Communism

∵

CHAPTER 20

The Revolutionary Programme of Communist Society

1   Marxist Texts and the Turin Report[1]

In the course of the discussions in Turin, and especially at the second session, dedicated to the reciprocal accusations of *revisionism* levelled by the Yugoslavian and Russian 'communists', as is customary we made substantial use of the basic texts of Marxism, with quotations that were not all included in the report published in the four issues [of *il programma comunista*].

In that discussion we were concerned with showing that our evaluations and formulations of the problems never deviated from the classical judgements of Marx's doctrine. This concern was all the more fitting in a debate in which the adversaries each claimed to follow fully the traditional line of principles, each accusing the other of having wrongfully deviated from it.

The polemic could take a different form and course if the two opposing groups would openly admit that they are moving further and further away from socialist theory as formulated by Marx and strenuously defended by Engels and then Lenin. For us, both groups are characterised by forms of opportunist degeneration that are even more extreme than that of the historically classical 'revisionists' of the late nineteenth century and during the first world war. It is true that these gentlemen have long claimed that, in the course of time, one has the right to modify the party's original principles, and we are absolutely sure that they will ultimately end up openly *confessing* the fact that they have literally turned them upside-down. But, then, the phase of struggle 'against all revisionism' that they have presented us with today is strange indeed – this flaunting of their conviction that today's revisionism ideologically and scientifically merits no less a condemnation than that of over half a century ago, while going so far in hurling insults at one another as to use the term 'revisionist' as the most defamatory insult of all!

Hence opposing all the claptrap these people spout with authentic quotations from the classic texts becomes decisive – by their own choice. The pos-

---

1   *Il programma comunista*, Yr. 7, Nos. 16 and 17, 1958, republished in *Proprietà e capitale*, Florence: Iskra, 1980 (writings 1948–52), Appendix (1958), pp. 161–202. Full title: The Revolutionary Programme of Communist Society Eliminates Every Form of Landed Property, of Production Plants, and of the Products of Labour.

ition is completely different from the one in which a revolutionary Marxist is confronted with another sector of contradictors and adversaries, who expressly wish to adopt the historical facts of the period from 1848 to the present to show that, in economics and in historical science, the facts themselves give the lie to the Marxist theory advocated by revolutionary communists.

It must be said that this latter group of enemies is more consistent not only in its intrinsic theoretical and scientific construction, but also if we compare its doctrine with its political activity designed to preserve those forms whose destruction and disappearance was the ultimate goal of Marx's formidable construction.

We shall address such adversaries in other stages of our work devoted to the integral defence of Marxism, which for us is to be formulated today exactly as it was formulated in the classic texts over a century ago. Indeed, we shall do so at an upcoming meeting of our movement.

Confronted with an enemy of this kind, we have to rebut a frontal, not a masked, attack. But when it comes to combating the supposed 'virgins' of Belgrade or of Moscow and other capitals, pure and untouched by revisionism, we are faced with enemies who treacherously cut the fetlocks of our horses and are always ready to stab us in the back.

2 Engels and the Agrarian Socialist Programmes

In September of 1894 the French Marxist workers' party (the party of Guesde and of Lafargue) adopted a programme of 'action in the countryside' at its congress in Nantes. In October in Frankfurt the Social Democratic Party of Germany took up the same question. Engels, at the end of his long life, closely followed the activities of the Second International, founded after Marx's death in 1889. He had to disagree sharply with the French party's resolution, while he was more satisfied with the German congress, which rejected a right-wing tendency analogous to the one that prevailed in Nantes.

Engels wrote an article of the greatest importance on this question, published in *Die Neue Zeit* in November of 1894.[2] The article was published in a not-very-accurate French translation in the Stalinist journal *Cahiers du Communisme* of November 1955. In their presentation of the text, the editors of the journal say that they found in the possession of a great-grandchild of Marx's

---

2 Bordiga refers to *The Peasant Question in France and Germany*. I quote from the translation available at http://www.marxists.org/archive/marx/works/1894/peasant-question/index .htm [note by G. Donis].

(Lafargue, as we know, was his son-in-law) a most notable collection of letters from Engels to Lafargue himself. Engels does not spare him his reprimand, and his formulations are of the greatest interest. What's strange is the Stalinists' gall in presenting historical material that condemns them so unequivocally!

You – the old Engels tells Lafargue with a certain bitterness, despite his serene tone – 'you, *intransigent revolutionaries* of yesteryear, now lean towards opportunism a little more than the Germans'.[3] In a successive letter Engels is careful to emphasise that he wrote the critical article in a friendly spirit, but does not hesitate to repeat: 'you've allowed yourselves to be drawn a little too far towards opportunism.'[4] These quotes are useful also for the dating of the terminology of our discussions, to which we have always given the greatest importance. Before Engels' death, the left Marxists [in France] (who in 1882 at the congress in Roanne split away from the 'possibilists', who favoured entering bourgeois ministries) had described themselves as 'intransigent revolutionaries'. In the first decade of the new century, the left fraction of the Italian Socialist Party, opposed to Turati's reformism and Bissolati's possibilism, described itself in the very same way. This was the fraction that, further reduced, was to give birth to the Communist Party of Italy.

The word 'opportunism', which many younger comrades believe was coined by Lenin in his overwhelming battle during the first world war, was in fact used by Engels and by Marx in their writings. We have often remarked that semantically it is not very well chosen, because it leads to the idea of a moral rather than a social-determinist judgement. Nevertheless, the word has gained the historical right to express for all of us the scum and the filth that sound Marxism is confronted with.

In that letter written to 'ménager' Lafargue a little (Lafargue, after all, was a revolutionary above suspicion), Engels gives the word 'opportunism' a definition that is as straight as a sword. The phrase 'drawn a little too far towards opportunism' is followed by this one: 'In Nantes, you were sacrificing the party's future to the success of a day'. The definition is lapidary: *opportunism is the method that sacrifices the party's future to the success of a day.* Shame on all those, then and since, who have practised it!

It is time to get down to the substance of the question and to Engels' text. He concluded that there was still time for the French to change course, and hoped that his article would contribute to their doing so. But *where* are the French (and the Italians) in 1958?

---

3   Engels to Lafargue, 22 August 1894.
4   Engels to Lafargue, 22 November 1894.

2.1   *Socialists and Peasants in the Late Nineteenth Century*

Engels' study begins with a picture of the general situation of the farm population of Europe at that time. The bourgeois parties had always believed that the socialist movement was active only in the sphere of urban industrial workers; hence they were greatly astonished to find the peasant question placed on the order of the day by all the socialist parties. Engels replies in the way we generally do in such cases, for example when in the heart of the twentieth century we show that the social questions of the countries of colour and not industrially developed cannot be forced into the rigid capitalist-proletariat dualism. But Marxism must always and everywhere have responses of doctrine and of action for the full multi-class and not bi-class picture of society.

Engels was able to make only two exceptions to the general rule of a large class of peasants who were neither wage-workers nor entrepreneurs: Great Britain proper and Prussia east of the Elbe. Only in those two regions had big, landed estates and large-scale agriculture totally displaced the self-supporting peasant. We note that also in these two exceptional cases the picture is composed of *three* classes (as is always the case in Marx when dealing with *model* bourgeois society): urban and rural wage-labour, industrial or agrarian capitalist entrepreneur, and landowners of a bourgeois, not a feudal, type.

For Engels and for all Marxists, in all other countries 'the peasant is a very essential factor of the population, production and political power'. Hence no one can say: for me the peasants don't exist, as in the palinode: for me the movements of colonial peoples don't exist.

But to say that the theory of the function of these social classes and the manner in which the Marxist party behaves toward them must be a copy of the theory and manner of the parties of petty-bourgeois democracy – this is another outrage against which Engels deploys one of his 'clarifications'. Indeed, we would say that it is just another formulation of the same outrage.

Since only a madman could contest the weight of the peasants in the demographic and economic statistics, Engels comes straight to the thorny point: what is their weight as a factor of the political struggle?

The conclusion is clear: most of the time the peasants have manifested nothing but their *apathy*, 'which has its roots in the *isolation* of rustic life'. But this apathy is not a fact without effects: 'it is the strongest pillar not only of the parliamentary corruption in Paris and Rome but also in Russian despotism'. It is not we who put Rome on this list but Engels himself, some 64 years ago.

Engels shows that since the rise of the working-class movement [in western Europe] the bourgeoisie has never ceased to 'render the socialist workers suspicious and odious' in the minds of the landowning peasants, depicting them as those who abolish property. And the big landowners have done the same, pretending to have a common bulwark to defend together with the small peasant.

Must the industrial proletariat accept as inevitable that in the struggle for political power the entire peasant class is and will be an active ally of the bourgeoisie the proletariat seeks to overthrow? Engels introduces the Marxist vision of the question, immediately affirming that such a standpoint is to be condemned, and is of just as little use to the cause of the revolution as the claim that the proletariat cannot take power until all the intermediate classes have disappeared.

In France – and here, Marx's classic works on the subject are unequalled – history has taught that the peasants with their weight have always tipped the scales away from the interests of the working class, from the First to the Second Empire and in the Paris revolutions of 1831, 1848–49 and 1871.

How, then, can these power relations be shifted? What is to be presented and promised to the small peasants? We are at the heart of the agrarian question. But the real purpose of Engels' treatise is to reject as anti-Marxist and counter-revolutionary any conservative protection of small landed property. What would old Frederick the Great have said if someone had proposed, as some do in Italy and France today, that the programme must become one of fighting for total ownership of the land worked throughout the rural population?

3   French Programmes

Back in 1892 at the Marseilles Congress the French workers' party drafted an agrarian programme (in Italy, it was the year of the separation from the anarchists and the constitution, in Genoa, of the Italian Socialist party).

Engels is less harsh in his condemnation of this programme than he is of the one drafted two years later in Nantes, since the latter programme, as we shall see, was guilty of misrepresenting theoretical principles in order to win the party's support for the immediate interests of the small peasants. In Marseilles the party limited itself to indicating the practical objectives of peasant agitation (in those days one followed the famous distinction between the *maximum and minimum* programme, which later led to the great historical crisis of the socialist parties). Engels notes that the programmes for small peasants, with special consideration for tenant farmers, were so limited in scope that other parties had already proposed them and many bourgeois governments had already carried them out. They consisted in little more than such things as co-operatives for the purchase of machinery and of manure, purchase of machinery by the community to be leased at cost price to the peasants, landlords prohibited from distraining crops, and revision of the general cadastre.

Engels thinks even less of the demands for wage-working farmers. Some are obvious since they are the same as those for industrial workers, such as minimum wages; others are somewhat better, such as the formation of common lands (of the public domain) for co-operative cultivation.

Despite the dim view taken by Engels, in the 1893 elections this programme won the party considerable success. On the eve of the following congress, party leaders wanted to ride the wave to make new conquests for the peasants. But *they felt they were treading on dangerous ground*, and so decided to preface their new proposals by a theoretical preamble to show that there was no contradiction between the socialist maximum programme and the protection of the small peasant, also in his right as a *propertied* peasant! It is here that Engels, listing the 'whereas' clauses of the preamble, focuses all his criticism. One seeks, he says, 'to prove that it is in keeping with the principles of socialism to protect small-peasant property from destruction by the capitalist mode of production, although one is perfectly aware that this destruction is *inevitable*'.

The first 'whereas' states that 'according to the terms of the general programme of the party producers can be free only in so far as they are in possession of the means of production'. The second states that whereas in the sphere of industry one can foresee the restitution of the means of production to the producers in a collective or social form, in the sphere of agriculture, at least in France, in most cases the means of production, namely, the land, is 'in the hands of the individual producers themselves as their individual possession'.

The third 'whereas' affirms that 'small-holding ownership is irretrievably doomed [is fatally destined to disappear]'[5] but 'socialism' must not 'hasten its doom, as its task does not consist in separating property from labour but, on the contrary, in uniting both of these factors of *all* production by placing them in the same hands.'

The fourth states that just as the industrial plants must be taken away from the private capitalists to be given to the workers, so the great domains must be given to the agricultural proletarians, and therefore it is the 'duty of socialism' to 'maintain the peasants themselves tilling their patches of land in possession of the same as against the fisk, the usurer, and the encroachments of the newly-arisen big landowners'.

---

5 'Fatally destined to disappear' is a more literal translation of the French text, and corresponds to Bordiga's Italian.

But it is the fifth 'whereas' that Engels considers the most scandalous: the first four thoroughly muddle the doctrine, but this one effectively annihilates the concept of class struggle: 'Whereas it is expedient to extend this protection also to the producers who as tenants or sharecroppers (me'tayers) cultivate the land owned by others and who, if they exploit day labourers, are to a certain extent compelled to do so because of the exploitation to which they themselves are subjected –'.

3.1   The Lamentable Conclusion

These wretched premises give rise to the practical programme 'to bring together all the elements of rural production, all occupations which by virtue of various rights and titles utilise the national soil, to wage an identical struggle against the common foe: the feudality of landownership'. Here, as Engels shows – despite his evident concern not to call old professed Marxists *jackasses* straight to their faces – the entire historical formulation crumbles to dust. In the France of 1894, this programme confuses the feudal lords, wiped out by the great revolution a century earlier, *not with the big capitalist tenants*, the industrialists of agriculture, whom (and remember what we are always rebuking today's Italian *comuntraditori*[6] for!) they actually invite to enter the 'great bloc'[7] since their activity adds value to the land (!), *but with the bourgeois agrarian landowners*, who do not run the agricultural enterprise personally but live off the rent paid by the small farm workers or the big tenants. This third Marxist class of capitalist society has nothing to do with ancient feudal nobility. The bourgeois landowner class bought its landed property with money, and can sell it too, since 'the bourgeois revolution turned the land into an article of commerce'; the feudal class had an inalienable right not only to the land but to the workers who populated it. Engels will remind these ill-advised disciples that the bloc against the feudal class was 'during a certain time and with definite aims', but it is clear that this historical bloc, whose time in France was long past, in Russia in 1894 was still current, and the 'bourgeois lords of the land' were part of it.

The same deadly error still darkens the horizon of the European proletariat – darkened by the triumph of Stalinist opportunism. The doctrinal arms to combat its ruinous effects are not to be sought in facts furnished by the course of time from 1894 to the present, but in the same valid arsenal utilised by Engels.

This decidedly 'bloc-based' agrarian policy kills the class struggle, and implemented by the party of the factory workers (!) does so all to the advantage of

---

6   A word coined by Bordiga, meaning 'betrayers of communism'.
7   'Great bloc' refers to the coalition of all the anti-feudal 'elements of rural production' proposed by the French socialists.

the industrial capitalists, and will guarantee the survival of the bourgeois form of society until these elephantine parties finally disintegrate.

But, before going on to the political aspects, we have one more, no less pessimistic, remark to make on questions of doctrine, which it would be wrong to omit today, when unlike 1894 opportunism is not merely a threat but has already violently drained the energy of the working class. Many, nearly all, the groups that are standing up against the big Stalinist and post-Stalinist parties and have left them – which would lead one to hope that the disintegration we invoked may begin – show that their ideas on the *contenu du socialisme* (since we are in France, we refer you to the group *Socialisme ou Barbarie*) are no less *a-Marxist* [bereft of Marxism] than those of the Nantes programme. We would call them *anti-Marxist* if we were not in the presence of the serene language of Frederick Engels, who evidently learned by experience, and by the effects of many hirsute rebuffs from Father Marx, that the Frenchman does not wish to be *choqué* (struck), or *froissé* (grazed) either. In the first case he shows the grit of a d'Artagnan, in the second that of a Talleyrand. Watch out! For you who remember a *calembour* at the Moscow Second Congress: *Frossard* (a world record holder of a-Marxism) *a été froissé*. And the man who dared make this little play on words was named Lenin!

3.2   Series of False Formulas

False formulations are extremely useful to clarify the true 'content' of the modern revolutionary programme. The ancient social ideologies had a *mystical* form. This, however, does not mean that they were not condensations of the human experience of a species of the same nature as the more developed ones attained in the capitalist age and in the struggle to overcome it. We could say that ancient mysticisms had the respectable form of a serious action of affirmative theses. Present-day mysticism, the rules of action of the subversive forces of contemporary society, is better ordered in a series of *negative* theses. The degree of consciousness of the future, which not the individual but only the revolutionary party can attain, is developed – at least until the classless society becomes a fact – most expressively by means of a series of rules such as: we do not say this – we do not do this.

We hope we have presented in a humble and accessible form an elevated and quite arduous conclusion. To this end – with Engels, master of such a method, as our guide – we shall make a closer examination of the mistaken formulas of the Nantes 'whereases'.

Engels begins by saying, with regard to the first, that it is not right to deduce from our general programme the formula 'producers can be free only in so far as they are in possession of the means of production'. In fact the French programme in question immediately adds that such possession is only possible 'either as individual possession, which form never and nowhere existed for the producers in general, and is daily being made more impossible by industrial progress; or as a common possession, a form the material and intellectual preconditions of which have been established by the development of capitalist society itself'. The only goal of socialism, Engels concludes, is the collective possession of the means of production 'fought for by all means at the disposal of the proletariat'. The point Engels makes here is that conquest or conservation of individual possession of the means of production on the part of the producer cannot be 'the sole principal goal' of the socialist programme. And this is so, he adds, 'not only in industry, where the ground has already been prepared, but in general, hence also in agriculture'.

This is the fundamental thesis of every classic Marxist writing. The proletarian party – unless it has declared itself to be openly revisionist – cannot for a single moment defend and protect that union of the worker with the means of his work which is realised on the basis of their individual possession. The text we are studying here repeats this in almost every sentence.

Engels also contests the concept expressed in the mistaken formula regarding the producer's 'freedom'. Such freedom is by no means ensured by those hybrid forms present in contemporary society in which the producer owns the land and also a part of his instruments of labour. In the present economy, Engels says, all this is highly precarious and not guaranteed for the small peasant. The bourgeois revolution did unquestionably give him advantages, releasing him from the bonds of feudalism – from the personal servitude of giving away part of his labour-time or part of his products. But, now that he has come into possession of his 'lopin' [patch] of land, he risks being separated from it in a hundred ways, which Engels lists together with the concrete part of the programme, but which are inseparable from the essence of capitalist society: taxes, mortgage debts, destruction of the rural domestic industry, distraints and expropriation. No measure of law (reform) can ensure the peasant against being compelled to sign his land and himself away 'voluntarily', *body and soul*, before he dies of hunger. Here, the critique becomes invective: 'Your attempt to protect the small peasant in his *property* does not protect his *liberty* but only the particular form of his servitude; it prolongs a situation in which he can neither live nor die!'

3.3   False Mirage of Freedom

We shall denounce the unsound formula of the first 'whereas', which from one error leads to a greater error, with less generosity than that of the great Engels. We ourselves are not faced with a Paul Lafargue in whom Marxism has dozed for a moment, and so needs to be reawakened, but with a dirty band of traitors and defeatists whose souls are already damned.

The first 'whereas' intends to answer this question: When will the producers be free? Its answer: When they will not be divided from their means of labour. In this way it comes to idealise an impossible and miserable society of small peasants and craftsmen that Engels cannot fail to denounce as reactionary, because such a society is far more backward than the society of proletarians and capitalists. But the entirely metaphysical and idealist error that has squandered every historico-dialectical and determinist vision is the error of presupposing the foolish proposition, which many supposed 'leftists' on both sides of the Atlantic profess today, that socialism is a striving for the individual liberation of the worker. This proposition inscribes certain economical theorems within the limits of a philosophy of Freedom.

We repudiate this starting point. It is stupidly bourgeois and leads to nothing other than that spectacle of degeneration which the Stalinians present us with all over the world. The formula would be no less distorted if it referred to the collective liberation of the producers. This, in fact, would involve establishing the limit of this collectivity, and it is here that all the 'immediatists' crumble to dust, as we shall see. This limit must be vast enough to contain manufacturing and agriculture and, in general, every human form of activity. When human activity, which means something far broader than production, a term bound up with mercantile society, will have no limits in its collective dynamic, or any temporal limit from generation to generation, it will be clear that the postulate of Freedom was a transient and fleeting bourgeois ideology, explosive in the past but today soporific and deceptive.

3.4 Property and Labour

The third infelicitous 'whereas' thinks it is saying something indisputable when it claims that the task of socialism is to unite and not to separate property and labour. Engels did not want to be ferocious, but he heatedly repeats that 'in this general form [this] *is by no means the task of socialism*. Its task is, rather, only to transfer the means of production to the producers *as their common possession*'. In light of this, Engels says, it is clear that 'the preamble thus imposes upon socialism the imperative duty to carry out something that it had declared to be impossible in the preceding paragraph. It charges it to "maintain" the smallholding ownership of the peasants although it itself states that this form of ownership is "irretrievably doomed" [fatally destined to disappear]'.

But we need to dig into this more deeply, keeping all the fabric woven by Marx and Engels and all our doctrine in mind. First of all, the question of this 'separation' is not metaphysical but historical. It is not a question of saying:

the bourgeoisie has separated property from labour, and we, to annoy it, will unite them again. This would be sheer nonsense. Marxism has never described the bourgeois revolution and the advent of bourgeois society as a process of separation between property and labour, but rather as a process of separation of the *people* who work from the conditions of their work. Property is a historico-juridical category; *this* separation is a relation between perfectly real and material elements – on the one hand the people who work, on the other the possibility of acceding to the land and of brandishing the tools of work. Feudal servitude and slavery had united the two elements in a very simple way, by closing both of them in a single concentration camp, from which the ruling class took the part of the products (another concrete physical element) that it wished. The bourgeois revolution kicked down the fences of that enclosure and told the workers 'you're free to go'; then it closed it back up again and created the *separation* we are discussing now. The bourgeois ruling class monopolised the conditions for tearing down the barbed wire and giving permission to produce, keeping the entire product for itself, while the servants who fled towards hunger and powerlessness are still courting the miracle of Freedom!

Socialism wants to abolish in each and every individual, group, class and state the possibility of hammering out circles of thorny iron. But brandishing senseless words about re-uniting property and labour will never do it! The only way is to put an end to bourgeois property and wage labour, the last and worst servitude. To put them to death!

Then, when the Nantes text says that labour and property are the two factors of production, whose division is the cause of the servitude and misery of the proletarians, it plunges into an even greater outrage. Property a factor of production! Here Marxism is forgotten – indeed, is totally repudiated! Also in its description of the capitalist mode of production the central thesis of Marxism is that there is *only one factor* of production, and it is human labour. Landed property, or tools and equipment, is not *another factor* of production. To call them factors would be to fall back into the *trinity formula* annihilated by Marx in the third volume of *Capital*. For it, wealth has three sources – land, capital and labour – and this crass doctrine justifies the three forms of recompense: rent, profit and wages. The socialist and communist party is the historical form in struggle against the rule of the capitalist class, whose doctrine insists that capital is no less a factor of production than labour. But to find the doctrine that holds the third term, *land*, to be a factor of production, we must go even further back, beyond Ricardo, to the physiocrats of the feudal era, whose theory (surprise surprise!) provided the historical justification for the rule of that abomination, feudality!

Uniting land to labour is a grave Marxist heresy – equally grave, be it individual or collective labour.

4   Industrial and Agrarian Enterprise

The fourth slippery 'whereas' that contains the trap of the defence of the small peasant parcel-enterprise sets out from a comparison between the big industries whose 'present idle ownership' must be expropriated (namely the urban bourgeois, who were nevertheless not 'idle' in the days of the *Maître de Forges*) and the 'great domains' that must be given to the agricultural proletarians in 'collective or social' form. Later on Engels formulates the comparison between the socialist and revolutionary expropriation of workshop proprietors and agrarian proprietors in completely different terms. The Nantes programme, apart from its failure to examine properly the essential distinction, barely touched upon, between 'collective' and 'social' management, also neglects the no less important distinction between great domain or big landed property and big agrarian enterprise. When the unitary management of production by means of wage-workers – even when part of the wages is given not in cash but in goods, a form Marx describes as a medieval remnant, and which Togliatti's Italian *Marxists* 'protect', better to bind the rural proletariat to the dirty form of partial participant – constitutes a single technical exercise, there is no reason not to treat this productive unit just as one treats the factory – to use Engels' example – of Mr Krupp. But the difficulty arises in the case of a big rural estate owned by a single person, even if it is broken up into a large number of small, technically autonomous family holdings of small tenants or small sharecroppers. In this case expropriation does not have the historical character of expropriation of big centralised industry. Rather, if feudal forms still survive, as was the case in Russia in 1917, it is reduced to a liberation of serfs that does not yet overcome the inferiority of parcel division. For Engels, in a well-established bourgeois regime like the one in France in the late nineteenth century the programmatic formula must not limit itself to the transformation of tenant farmers paying rent in money or in kind into 'free' worker-owners. On the contrary, the socialist parties must decisively support as the objective of the peasants, who can be accepted into the party and under the party's influence, the formation of co-operatives of agricultural production operated co-operatively – a form that is itself transitory, since it will have to tend gradually towards the institution of a 'great national producers' co-operative'. Engels uses this formula to stigmatise with adequate severity any inclusion, even in the immediate programme, of a dividing up of the big agrarian estate among the peasants, to reduce it to parcel or family enterprises.

On this point we need to add a further consideration, to be linked up with other Marxist texts, on the goal of the socialist programme. It will be possible to see the collective management of enterprises, already unified under bourgeois ownership, as a transitory expedient if the collectivity of the workers in the enterprise is seen as the object of this management. But this consideration must not make us think that socialism has been exhausted once it has replaced the entrepreneurial or capitalist property of the factory (which today is already collective in the joint-stock company) with a *collective property* of the workers. When the formulas are correct we do not find the word property but, rather, possession, or taking possession, of the means of production or, even more exactly, the management and direction of production, whose proper subject remains to be established. The expression 'social management' is better than 'co-operative management', while the notion of 'co-operative property' is completely bourgeois and non-socialist. The expression *national* management' serves to express the supposition that the appropriation of factories and of the soil can come about in one country and not in another, but it leads one to think of 'state management', which is nothing other than capitalist ownership of enterprises by the state.

Remaining in the sphere of agriculture, we want to make it clear that, in the communist programme, the land and the means of production must become part of the *society* that is organised on a new basis, which can no longer be called commodity production. Therefore the land and the rural installations become part of the integrated whole of all the workers, both industrial and agricultural, just as the industrial factories do. This and this alone is what Marx means when he speaks of abolishing the differences between city and countryside and overcoming the social division of labour as cornerstones of communist society. The old forms of agitation – 'the factories to the workers and the land to the peasants', to say nothing of the even more inane 'the ships to the sailors' – even if overused even recently, are nothing but a parody of the formidable potential of the Marxist revolutionary programme.

4.1   *The Extreme Aberration*

Before looking to other texts of Marx's for an inkling of the principles we have recalled, we shall conclude our ample paraphrase of Engels' study with his outburst of indignation – enormously important for our own time – with regard to the last of the five 'whereases', which states that it is the party's duty to help also the tenants and sharecroppers who exploit wage labourers!

We omit the part of Engels' text with his subtle destructive criticism of the detailed section of the Nantes programme, containing reformist measures that either were impossible to realise or would have brought the peasants right back to the point where their misery and their brutalisation in France and elsewhere all began, misapplying the lever that was supposed to improve their condition. We also omit the final part of his study dealing with the situation in Germany, where fortunately the party had not made analogous errors, in which he discusses the need to 'win over to our side' the propertyless peasants east of the Elbe, in semi-servitude to the Prussian Junkers, rather than the lumpen-peasantry of the west, devoid of revolutionary potential.

It is regrettable that we find no mention of Italy in Engels' writing. In Italy at that time the party, with high class spirit, led the often violent struggle of the farm labourers in Romagna and in Apulia against the fat bourgeois share-croppers, realising what Engels presents as the just desideratum – namely, that the wage-working peasants be in the socialist party, and the sharecroppers and tenants in a petty-bourgeois party (in Italy, the republican party). Alas, in Italy today it is the 'communists' who do what was so impudently programmed in France in 1894, to strangle the class struggle of wage-workers in the hire of the middle peasants and tenants, as we have seen.

Engels' words hold for the traitors of today:

Here, we are entering on ground that is passing strange. Socialism is particularly opposed to the exploitation of wage labour. And here it is declared to be the imperative duty of socialism to protect the French tenants when they 'exploit day labourers', as the text literally states! And that, because they are compelled to do so to a certain extent by '*the exploitation to which they themselves are subjected*'!

How easy and pleasant it is to keep on coasting once you are on the toboggan slide! [Oh Father Engels, you could not imagine the extremes this lust for demagogic success and betrayal was to reach!] When now the big and middle peasants of Germany come to ask the French Socialists to intercede with the German Party Executive to get the German Social-Democratic Party to protect them in the exploitation of their male and female farm servants, citing in support of the contention the 'exploitation to which they themselves are subjected' by usurers, tax collectors, grain speculators and cattle dealers, what will they answer? What guarantee have they that our agrarian big landlords will not send them Count Kanitz [a representative of the landed proprietors in the Reichstag] (as he also submitted a proposal like theirs, providing for a state monopoly of grain importation) and likewise ask for socialist protection of their exploitation of the rural workers, citing in support 'the exploitation to which they themselves are subjected' by stockjobbers, moneylenders, and grain speculators?[8]

Let us conclude with a final quote on the peasants and on party membership that is truly a rule we must never again forget:

> I flatly deny that the socialist workers' party of any country is charged with the task of taking into its fold, in addition to the rural proletarians and the small peasants, also the idle and big peasants and perhaps even the tenants of the big estates, the capitalist cattle breeders and other capitalist *exploiters of the national soil.*
>
> *We can use in our party individuals from every class of society, but have no use whatsoever for any groups representing capitalist, middle-bourgeois, or middle-peasant interests.*

This is how the party defends itself, its nature, its non-commercialisable doctrine, its revolutionary future! And this is why the political party alone is the form that saves the class struggle of the urban and rural proletariat of all countries from degeneration.

4.2   A Great Dictation of Marx's

Our French comrades brought us in Turin a text of Marx's, with a publisher's note reading as follows: 'This manuscript found after the death of Karl Marx in his files is probably an *addenda* to a work on the nationalisation of the soil that Marx had written at Applegarth's request. This work has not yet been found. The title of the extract is *The Nationalisation of the Land*'.[9]

This masterly discussion substantiates the modest lesson we ourselves teach: Marxism does not modify the forms of property but, rather, radically rejects the appropriation of land. Let us begin with a theoretically less demanding passage.

> At the International Congress of Brussels, in 1868, one of our friends [we were at the First International and the friend was not a Bakunian libertarian][10] said: 'Small private property in land is doomed by the verdict of

---

8   In this and the following passage, the italics and the remarks in brackets are Bordiga's.

9   Marx, *The Nationalisation of the Land*, a paper read at the Manchester Section of the International Working Men's Association, 1872. Available at http://www.marxists.org/archive/marx/works/1872/04/nationalisation-land.htm.

10   The remarks in brackets in Marx's text are Bordiga's. The friend Marx refers to is César

science, large land property by that of justice. There remains then but one alternative. The soil must become the property of rural association or the property of the whole nation. The future will decide that question.'

I [Marx] say on the contrary: the social movement will lead to this decision that the land can but be owned by the nation itself. To give up the soil to the hands of associated rural labourers *would be to surrender society to one exclusive class of producers.*[11]

The content of this brief remark is gigantic. First of all, it demonstrates that the Marxist line does not free itself of difficult questions by deferring them to the revelation and decision of future history. From its very beginnings Marxism has been perfectly able to formulate, sharply, the essential characteristics of the future society, and it does so explicitly.

Secondly: Marx speaks of the *nation*, and *national* property, only in the context of a Socratic dialogue with his interlocutor. In the positive thesis Marx speaks of transfer and not of property, and no longer of the nation but of *the entire society*.

Finally, this *proposition*, which is masterly in the highest sense of the word, can be formulated in the following manner. The socialist programme is not well expressed as abolition of the surrendering of one sector of the means of production to a class of private individuals, or to a minority of idle non-producers. The socialist programme demands that no branch of production be supported by only one class, *even of producers*, but only by *the whole of human society*. Therefore the land will go neither to *associations of peasants* nor to the peasant *class*, but to the *entire* society.

This is the pitiless condemnation of all the immediatist distortions that we have been tracking down relentlessly, also in self-styled revolutionaries of the left.

This Marxist theorem demolishes all forms of communalism, unionism [as ideology], and enterprisism because those *surannés* [outmoded] programmes, ruinously out-of-date, 'surrender' the indivisible energies of society as a whole to limited groups.

But, before all this, Marx's fundamental formulation annuls any possibility for Stalinists or post-Stalinists to describe – as they wish, and as the wind blows – as *socialist property* any agrarian forms in which the entire society, the

---

De Paepe, in his report on landed property at the meeting of the Brussels Congress of the International Working Men's Association, 11 September 1868.

11 In Marx's text all the italics are Bordiga's. Here, in the original text in *il programma comunista* the italicised words are in all caps.

material life of the entire society, is surrendered to a *particular class of producers* – in this case, the kolkhoz groups [collective farmers].

For that matter, not even the surrender of all industrial enterprises to the state, as in today's Russia, deserves the name of socialism. This state, which for the very same reason is 'surrendering' to 'exclusive classes of producers', by enterprise or by province, is no longer a historical representative of the full, *classless* society of tomorrow. This characteristic is attained and preserved only on the plane of political theory, thanks to the party form. All forms of immediatism brutally trample on it, but it alone can ward off the opportunist plague.

But let us return for a moment to Marx's paper, which shows us how any attribution of ownership – indeed, any material 'surrender' of the land, to 'exclusive classes', cuts off the high road to communism.

> The nationalisation of land will work a complete change in the relations between labour and capital, and finally do away with the capitalist form of production, whether industrial or rural. Then class distinctions and privileges will disappear together with the economic basis upon which they rest, and society will be transformed into an association of 'producers'. [Note that the inverted commas are Marx's, and 'an' association must be read as '*a single*' association].[12] To live on other people's labour will become a thing of the past. There will be no longer any government or state power, distinct from society itself!

Before going on once again to these essential, unchangeable and never-changed principles of Marxism, let us put on the record the fact that Marx never hesitates to describe, resolutely, how communist society will be, taking an unlimited responsibility for the entire revolutionary movement of a historical phase.

It is the pure metal of the original casting that shines forth from the gangue of the thousand successive encrustations, and will shine forth intact in the light of tomorrow.

4.3 *Marx and the Ownership of the Land*

In Marx's text he discusses two aspects of the communist programme. Historically and economically the large agrarian enterprise (he often uses the term large

---

12   In the second part of this sentence I follow Bordiga, along with his comments on Marx's text. However, Marx's actual text is different, and reads as follows: 'National centralisation of the means of production will become the national basis of a society composed of associations of free and equal producers, carrying on the social business on a common and rational plan' [note by G. Donis].

property) must be supported, against the small enterprise and the small property. What is more, the communist programme contains the disappearance – or as is customarily, and less accurately, said, the abolition – of any form of landed property, which means of any subject of property, be it single or collective.

Marx does not dwell upon the traditional philosophical and juridical justifications of 'private property in land'. They go back to the antiquated banality that *property* is an extension of the *person*. The falsehood of this musty syllogism begins in its tacit premise itself: my person, my physical body, belong to me, are my property. We deny this too, which at bottom is nothing but a preconceived idea stemming from extremely ancient forms of slavery, by which brute force preyed upon land and human bodies together. If I am not a slave I am the master of myself. It seems so clear, yet it's sheer nonsense. At that watershed of the social structure in which the hateful form of lordship over human beings came to an end, instead of making provision for the end of all further forms of property it was logical that the ideological superstructure – the illustrious Ultimate of all the real processes! – should take no more than the pygmy step of simply *changing* the master of the slave, something to which the poor human mind was habituated. First I went from being the slave of Tom to being the slave of Dick, and now I've become the slave of myself ... Perhaps a very bad bargain!

The vulgar anti-socialist way of reasoning is more foolish than the myth that there was a first man all alone, who thought he was the King of Creation. According to the Biblical account one had to admit that with the multiplication of humans the system of bonds between the unique first man and the others grows stronger, and the illusory autonomy of the 'I' progressively vanishes. For the Marxist, at every passage from simpler modes of production to newer, more intricate modes the network of multiple relations between the individual and all his fellow men increases, while the conditions commonly designated by the terms autonomy and freedom diminish. All individualism pales.

The modern and atheist bourgeois who defends property, in his class ideology (whose wrecks are reserved today only for the petty-bourgeois and for many self-styled Marxists) sees the course of history backwards, as the sequence of stages of a ridiculous freeing of the individual man from social bonds (correctly, also the bonds between man and external nature historically strengthen their network). The liberation of man from slavery, the liberation from servitude and from despotism, the liberation from exploitation!

In this construction – the opposite of our own – the individual is released, is freed, and constructs for himself the autonomy and the greatness of the Person! And many people take this sequence for *revolutionary*.

Individual, person and property fit well together. Given the false principle that my body is mine, and therefore so is my hand, therefore the tool with which

I increasingly lengthen them in my work is also *mine*. The land (and here the second premise is correct) is also an instrument of human labour. The products of my hand and of its various extensions are also mine: Property is therefore an imperishable attribute of the Person.

The contradictory nature of this construction is revealed by the fact that in the ideology of the defenders of property on agrarian soil who preceded the Enlightenment thinkers and the capitalists, the land is in and of itself a producer of wealth, before and without the labour that man performs upon it. How, then, does the right of human ownership over plots of land become a mysterious 'natural right'?

4.4   *How Marx Handles It*

Asked to state his position on the nationalisation of the land, Marx liquidates these impotent philosophemes in the fist sentences of his text.

> The property in the soil is the original source of all wealth, and has become the great problem upon the solution of which depends the future of the working class.
>
> I do not intend discussing here all the arguments put forward by the advocates of private property in land, by jurists, philosophers and political economists, but shall confine myself firstly to state that they have tried hard to disguise the *primitive fact* of conquest under the cloak of *'Natural Right'*. If conquest constituted a natural right on the part of the few, the many have only to gather sufficient strength in order to acquire the natural right of reconquering what has been taken from them.
>
> In the progress of history [Marx means after the first acts of violence had created property in land – land that had been born free, and later was in common] the conquerors found it convenient to give to their original titles, derived from brute force, a sort of social standing, through the instrumentality of laws imposed by themselves.
>
> At last come the philosopher and demonstrates that those laws imply and express the universal consent of mankind. If private property in land will be indeed founded upon such a universal consent, it will evidently become extinct from the moment the majority of a society dissents from warranting it.
>
> However, leaving aside the so-called 'rights' of property ...

It is our intention here to follow Marx's thought as far as the negation of *any form* of property, that is, of any form of *subject* (private individual, associated individuals, state, nation, and even *society*) and any form of *object* (land, which has been our starting point, the instruments of labour in general, and the products of labour).

As we have always maintained, all this is contained in the initial form of negation of private property, that is, in the consideration of this form as a transitory characteristic in the history of human society, and which in the present course of history is destined to disappear.

Also terminologically property is seen exclusively as *private*. For the land this is most evident, since the characteristic of this institution is the enclosure within a border that cannot be crossed without the proprietor's permission. Private property means that the non-proprietor is *deprived* [*privato*][13] of the power to enter. Whatever the subject of the 'right of property', be it a single or a multiple person, this character of 'privatism/privation' survives.

4.5   Against All Parcel Property

In the successive lines of his text Marx takes a position against agrarian production carried on in enterprises of limited surface-area.

Setting aside the philosophical question after a few sarcastic remarks, he says:

> I assert that the economical development of society, the increase and concentration of people, the very circumstances that compel the capitalist farmer to apply to agriculture collective and organised labour, and to have recourse to machinery and similar contrivances, will more and more render the nationalisation of land a '*Social Necessity*', against which no amount of talk about the rights of property can be of any avail. The imperative wants of society will and must be satisfied, changes dictated by social necessity will work their own way, and sooner or later adapt legislation to their interests.
>
> What we require is a daily increasing production and its exigencies cannot be met by allowing a few individuals to regulate it according to their whims and private interests, or to ignorantly exhaust the powers of the soil. All modern methods, such as irrigation, drainage, steam ploughing, chemical treatment and so forth, ought to be applied to agriculture at large. But the scientific knowledge we possess, and the technical means of agriculture we command, such as machinery, etc., can never be successfully applied but by cultivating the land on a large scale.

---

13   *Privato* signifies 'deprived of' or, more simply, 'without', and also 'private'.

If cultivation on a large scale proves (even under its present capitalist form, that degrades the cultivator himself to a mere beast of burden) so superior, from an economical point of view, to small and piecemeal husbandry, would it not give an increased impulse to production if applied on national dimensions?

The ever-growing wants of the people on the one side, the ever-increasing price of agricultural produce on the other, afford the irrefutable evidence that the nationalisation of land has become a social necessity.

Such a diminution of agricultural produce as springs from individual abuse, will, of course, become impossible whenever cultivation is carried on under the control and for the benefit of the nation.

It is evident that this writing is propaganda, addressed to a circle of not-yet-followers of Marxism. Nevertheless it will soon voice the radical theses we dealt with earlier in the section 'A great dictation of Marx's'. In the above passage Marx shows a preference for national management by the state, in so far as costs and profits are concerned. Later, he makes it clear that the bourgeois state will always be powerless to change the role it has imposed on agriculture.

But Marx is still dealing with contingent questions. It is interesting to see how he poses them with reference to 1868,[14] exactly as Engels will do in 1894, as we saw in the first part of this study. How, today, can one dare call himself a Marxist when he claims that first the tenant, then the sharecropper, and then even the farm labourer must become a proprietor, as today's Italian and European 'communists' do! For us this essential part of Marxism, just as it was valid for the period from 1868 (indeed, from long before) to 1894, is still absolutely valid for us today.

4.6   The French Agrarian Question

At this point Marx goes on to rebut the commonplace of 'wealthy' small French agriculture. His words need no comment. The reader must connect them not only with Engels' formulation but also with that of Lenin, whose strict orthodoxy as an agrarian Marxist we have dealt with thoroughly in our discussions of Russia.[15]

---

14   It is clear that Bordiga is referring to the 1868 International Congress in Brussels.
15   Bordiga's studies on Russia both before and after the revolution are collected in the book Bordiga 1976a.

France was frequently alluded to, but *with its peasant proprietorship* it is farther off the nationalisation of land than England with its landlordism. In France, it is true, the soil is accessible to all who can buy it, but this very facility has brought about a division into small plots cultivated by men with small means and mainly relying upon the land by exertions of themselves and their families. This form of landed property and the piecemeal cultivation it necessitates, while excluding all appliances of modern agricultural improvements, converts the tiller himself into the most decided enemy to social progress and, above all, the nationalisation of land. Enchained to the soil upon which he has to spend all his vital energies in order to get a relatively small return, having to give away the greater part of his produce to the state, in the form of taxes, to the law tribe in the form of judiciary costs, and to the usurer in the form of interest, utterly ignorant of the social movements outside his petty field of employment; still he clings with fanatic fondness to his bit of land and his merely nominal proprietorship in the same. In this way the French peasant has been thrown into a most fatal antagonism to the industrial working class.

Peasant proprietorship being then the greatest obstacle to the nationalisation of land, France, in its present state, is certainly not the place we must look to for a solution of this great problem.

To nationalise the land, in order to let it out in small plots to individuals *or working men's societies*, would, under a middle-class government, only engender a reckless competition among themselves and thus result in a progressive increase of 'Rent' which, in its turn, would afford new facilities to the appropriators of feeding upon the producers.

In the hypothesis advanced in this last sentence, Marx predicts that the state's letting out the land would create a class of entrepreneurial landlords who avail themselves of wage labour, exploiting it.

4.7   *Classes of Producers*

At this point of the manuscript Marx inserts the fundamental passage on the debate at the International Congress in 1868 that we quoted and commented on above. In this passage we gave immense importance to the thesis that the land is to be given to the 'nation' and *not to associated rural labourers*. This latter formula – we must not forget this – is anti-socialist because it would 'surrender society to *one exclusive class* of producers'. Socialism rules out not only the subjection of the *producer* to the *possessor* but also of *producers* to *producers*.

In light of the communist perspective, the Russian agrarian formula with its kolkhoz[16] is completely false. The members of the kolkhoz – the kolkhozniks – form a *class of producers* that have the subsistence of the entire 'nation' in their hands. From year to year their rights increase with respect to the 'state': for example each association of producers sets its own prices, since they are exempt from delivering their products at prices set by the state. We shall make a sharp distinction between the terms *state, nation* and *society*; for now we have the right to say that *competition* and *rent* reappear in the Russian economic structure.

In the sovkhoz, which will soon be legally liquidated, the workers on the land are reduced, like the industrial workers, to pure wage-labour, with no right to the rural products (until now), and do not form a class of producers that stand up to society – any more than the industrial proletarians do, vaunted as *masters* (though in Russia they blush to say the word!) of society itself, *hegemons* over the peasants (!).

The classical Russia debate about the land shifted between three solutions: division (Populists); municipalisation (Mensheviks); nationalisation (Bolsheviks). Lenin, in doctrine and in revolutionary policy, always championed nationalisation, just as Marx defended it in his 'Nationalisation of the Land' manuscript. Populist division, an ignoble peasant ideal, is on a par with the policy of today's communist parties, say, in Italy, who proudly use the adjective *popular* and are equally worthy of the description *populist*. Municipalisation was based on the programme to give the monopoly of the land not to society but to the peasant class alone. The Russian municipality referred to here was the rural village, populated exclusively by peasants, and which is palely related to the tradition of the primitive community, the *mir*.[17] The kolkhoz system is not Marxist let alone Leninist, since, in the ongoing 'reforms', it can best be described as a *provincialisation of the land* over which the cities and their workers are increasingly losing influence. This deformation, presented by the historical fact of 1958, had already been attacked by the party's doctrinal position in 1868, which insisted that the land must not be given to 'one exclusive class of producers' (the members of the kolkhoz) but to the entire collectivity of rural and urban workers.

---

16   The *kolkhoz* (collective farm) and the *sovkhoz* (state farm) are the two components of the socialised farm sector that began to emerge in Soviet agriculture after the October Revolution of 1917 as an antithesis to individual or family farming.

17   The *mir* was a pre-sixteenth-century self-governing peasant community, which antedated serfdom.

The nationalisation thesis must not be understood in the sense of Ricardo's position: the land to the state along with all the ground-rent, which would mean the land to the industrial capitalist class or to its potential representative, the industrial capitalist state (as in Russia). The Marxist nationalisation of the soil is the dialectical opposite of its parcelling and distribution to peasant associations or co-operatives. This dialectical opposition holds both for the structure of the communist society without either classes or state, and for the political and party and class struggle within capitalist society, where the demand for parcel division is far more indecent than it was when it was made under the regime of the tsar. The theses of the party's doctrine, when they are posited as immutable and inviolable both by the centre and by the base of the militants, contain the defence against the future threat of the opportunist disease, of which this is a fitting and typical example.

4.8   Nation and Society

The term *nation*, however, has an advantage with respect to the term *society*, in its use both in theory and in agitation. As extension in space, it is common knowledge that we consider socialist society to be international, and that internationalism is a concept inherent in class struggle. But Marx, each time he criticises the capitalist economic structure, tells us that he will speak of 'nation' without distinguishing it from a society composed of more than one nation when he is studying the dynamic of economic forces, but without ever closing the revolutionary transition to socialism within narrow national limits. Moreover, also when it is useful to speak of *nation* and not of *state*, we must not forget that, as long as there is a class state that expresses the rule of the capitalist class, the *nation* does not unite all the inhabitants of a territory in a homogenous whole, and will not yet do so even after the establishment of the revolutionary dictatorship of the proletariat in one or more countries.

The term 'nation', while limiting as to internationalist, class and revolutionary demands, is meaningful as opposed to the distribution of certain spheres of productive means (land, in the case considered here) to *parts* and to isolated classes of the national society, to local groups and enterprises, to trade-union and professional sectors.

But the other advantage we hinted at regards *limitation in time*. The word 'nation' derives from [the Latin] *nasci*, 'to be born', and embraces the succession of living (also past, and future) generations. For us, the real subject of social activity is broader, in time, than the *society* of the men living at a certain date. The idea of the 'race'[18] (by which we mean the 'family' of the entire human race,

---

18   The Italian word *stirpe* signifies 'race' as in the expression 'human race', or 'family' in the very broadest sense.

the *species*, as the word was used by Marx and Engels, and which is more power-ful than either *nation* or *society*) supersedes all bourgeois ideology of power and juridical-political sovereignty characteristic of the democrats.

The class concept suffices to belie any notion of the state's representing all living citizens, and we laugh at the pretence of drawing such a conclusion from the registration of all adults in the electoral rolls. We know perfectly well that the bourgeois state represents the interests and the power of a single class, even if the vote be plebiscitary.

But there is more. Even if a representative or structural network is closed within the limits of the single class of wage-labourers (it is worse if one refers to the generic Russian *people* without distinction), we will not be satisfied with a construction of sovereignty based on the mechanism (if such a thing exists) of consultation with all the individual elements of the base. And this applies both under bourgeois power, to lead the revolutionary struggle, and after it has been overturned.

On numerous occasions we have insisted that *the party alone*, though clearly a minority in the society and in the proletarian class, in its spatial and tem-poral unity of doctrine, organisation and combat strategy, is the form that can express the historical influences of successive generations in the transition to a new form of social production.

Therefore the proletarian revolutionary force is not expressed by *a consultat-ive democracy within the class*, be it struggling or victorious, but by the unbroken span of the historical line *of the party*.

Clearly, we admit not only that a minority of the living and present can lead the historical advance against the majority (also of the class) but, what is more, we think that *only such a minority* can tread the path that connects it with the struggle and the efforts of the militants of past generations and of generations to come, working to realise the programme of the new society as it has been clearly and precisely formulated by the historical doctrine.

This construction that makes us proclaim, in spite of every Philistine, this unequivocal demand – *dictatorship of the communist party!* – is incontestably contained in the system of Karl Marx.

5   Not Even Society is the Owner of the Earth

In Volume 3 of *Capital*, published by Engels after Marx's death, the title of Chapter 46 is 'Rent of Buildings. Rent of Mines. Price of Land'. The analysis is part of Marx's tremendously powerful doctrine of ground-rent, which Lenin, that great fighter, vindicated line by line throughout his life. Since our economic science maintains and demonstrates that the rent from landed property has the character of an aliquot part subtracted from the surplus value the working class produces and that becomes capitalist profit, it is clear that our adversary can raise the following objection. Deals are made and the proprietor collects capitalised rent also with the transfer of building sites, while they just lie there sleeping under the sun and not even one worker shows up to turn over a clod of earth. From what labour and relative surplus value does this proprietary gain come?

But our economic science is not impaired by this. We are not a university department but an army drawn up in battle order, and we defend the cause of those who are dead and worked, just as we do of those who have not yet worked and are not yet born.

We ask those who want to reason within the narrow-minded bureaucratic formulas of double-entry bookkeeping kindly to stand aside, together with those who mechanically reduced legal power to the names and numbers of the electoral rolls.

Marx answers our question by bringing the future generations onto the scene of the battle. This is a time-honoured element of our doctrine, and not a clever invention of ours to get the right thesis approved. Against the theory and the programme of the revolution, also the majority of the proletarian class present today *can* be wrong and stand with the enemy side.

The fact that it is only the title a number of people have to property in the earth that enables them to appropriate a part of society's surplus labour as tribute, and in an ever growing measure as production develops, is concealed by the fact that the capitalised rent, i.e. precisely this capitalised tribute, appears as the price of land, which can be bought and sold just like any other item of trade.[19]

Is that clear? If, in my appraisal, a plot of land that in the future presumably will bring its owner a return of five thousand lire a year can be sold for a hundred thousand, I have made an active force the surplus labour of workers who will work not for twenty years, but for an infinite number of future years.

In exactly the same way, it appears to the slaveowner who has bought a Negro slave that his property in the Negro is created not by the institution

---

19   Marx 1991, pp. 910–11. The passages that follow are all on p. 911. The remarks in brackets are Bordiga's.

of slavery as such [which past generations have handed down to him] but rather by the purchase and sale of this commodity.

And he will discount from his initial expense all the future years of the Negro and of his descendants!

> But the purchase does not produce the title; it simply transfers it. The title must be there before it can be bought, and neither one sale nor a series of such sales, their constant repetition, can create this title. [The allusion of Marx, the law graduate, is to the fiction of the bourgeois codes that 'proof of ownership' is obtained by piling up the heaps of transfer titles dating back a certain number of years, twenty or thirty for example.] It was entirely created by the *relations of production*. Once these have reached the point where they have to be sloughed off, then the material source, the economically and historically justified source of the title that arises from the process of life's social production, disappears, and with it all transactions based on it.

For example – we add this to make the concept clear to the reader – when slavery production ceases, because it is no longer profitable or because of the revolt of the slaves, all the slaves will become free men and every past contract of sale of slaves will be null and void! But here we invite the reader once again to note the passage – always as sudden as it is powerful – from Marx's brilliant and original interpretation of the history of human society to his no less rigorous characterisation of the society of tomorrow.

> From the standpoint of a higher socio-economic formation, the private property of particular individuals in the earth will appear just as absurd as the private property of one man in other men. Even an entire society, a nation, or all simultaneously existing societies taken together, are not the owners of the earth. They are simply its possessors, its beneficiaries, and have to bequeath it in an improved state to succeeding generations, as *boni patres familias*.[20]

5.1   *Utopia and Marxism*

Also in this decisive passage Marx's method is clear. Our prediction of the death – the disappearance – of property and of capital, which expresses a far

---

20   These lines are in all caps in Bordiga's original text.

higher purpose than their craven transferral from the individual to the social subject, is based on a complete scientific analysis of present-day society and of its past, as is the decision and the will that we attribute not to the individual subject, though he be of the downtrodden class, but only to the party collectivity, whose energy is measured not in *quantity* but in *quality*. We have a duty to study and to know in its structure and its real course the capitalism we want to shame and to kill. This is not a duty in the moral and personal sense; it is, rather, an impersonal function of the party, which goes over the heads of individual thinking men and the borders between successive generations.

In this point we find the reply to a possible objection to our understanding of Marxism, the only one that grasps its power and stature. The Marx that the revolutionary current has presented for decades on end when it gives pride of place to the maximum programme of the communist social structure is, precisely, the Marx who overcame, fought against, and left behind any form of utopianism.

The opposition between utopianism and scientific socialism does not reside in the fact that, with regard to the characteristics of the future society, the Marxist socialist declares that he stands at the window waiting for them to pass by, to describe what they look like! Although the utopian does see the effects of present-day society (in fact Marx praises respectfully some of the masters of utopian thought), his error lies in deducing the shape of future society not from a concatenation of real processes that link the course of the past to that of the future, not from natural and social reality, but from his own head, from human reason. The utopian believes that the goal of society's course must be contained in the victory of certain general principles that are innate in the human spirit. Be these principles infused by a creator god or discovered by introspective philosophical criticism, they are ideologisms with a thousand names: Justice, Equality, Liberty, and so on, which form the colours of the palette where the socialist idealist dips his brushes to paint the world of tomorrow *as it ought to be*.

This ingenuous but not always ignoble origin induces utopianism to seek its legitimisation by means of persuasion or, to use the term fashionable today, *emulation*, to present the blaze of history in a truly indecorous manner. Carried away by their good intentions, the utopians once thought they could triumph by winning the centres of already constituted power over to their rosy projects. They rejected out of hand any idea of participating in the process of struggle, social conflict, the overthrow of power, and the use not of persuasion but of force without reservations in the travail that will give birth to the new society.

Our formulation of the human problem is the opposite. Things do not go as they do because someone made a mistake, someone stepped out of line (we leave these exercises to the rascals – Marxist-Leninists!!! – who had a field day pursuing the Montesi and the Giuffrè affairs),²¹ but because a causal and determinate series of forces came into play in the development of the human species. The task now is, first, to understand how and why and with what general laws, and then to induce the future directions.

Thus Marxism is not at all reluctant to declare in its battle programmes what the characteristics of tomorrow's society will be and, specifically, in what way they will be opposed to the characteristics rigorously individuated in the latest social form, the capitalist and mercantile. Marxism is the way to declare them with a validity and certainty far greater than that attained by the pale – even if, for their day, sometimes bold – utopian descriptions.

Reluctance to commit to indicating the distinctive features of the communist social structure in advance is not Marxism, neither is it worthy of the powerful corpus of the classical writings of our school. Such reluctance is in point of fact a shirking and conservative *revisionism*, which flaunts as objectivity that which is nothing but cowardice and cynicism, showing on a white screen a mysterious drawing that is purportedly the secret of history. In its Philistine self-conceit this method is nothing but the *alibi* prepared for the professional political gangs, who have never experienced the height of the party form and have reduced it to a theatre stage for the contortions of a few activists. If these features were supposed to remain *secret*, one might as well have waited in the sacristies for the divine will to be revealed, or in the servants' rooms of the powerful for the lucky chance to lick the plates in the kitchen.

6   Property and Usufruct

We have an example of this strict opposition between Marxism and utopianism in the passage from Marx that describes the structure of the future society – a passage no less binding than the one in which he describes a society *that is not the owner of the earth*.

The cultivation of the land must not be managed in a way that is designed to satisfy the desires of the present generation alone. Marx repeatedly accuses capitalism of perpetrating this form of production, which exhausts the re-

---

21   The reference is to two cases (the presumed murder of an actress and a colossal bank fraud) that caused an outcry on account of the direct or indirect involvement of prominent members of the Italian Christian Democratic Party and of the Roman aristocracy and haute bourgeoisie. Bordiga's objection is to the press connected with the Italian Communist Party (PCI) that dedicated so much time, space and energy to the 'scandals', 'pursuing' them furiously.

sources of the soil and makes it impossible to solve the problem of feeding the world's people. Today, faced with our ever-growing population, the 'scientists' – with their well-known seriousness – are looking for *new ways* of appeasing the hunger of the planet's inhabitants.

Management of the land, the keystone of the entire social problem, must be directed towards the best future development of the earth's population. The *society* of living human beings can be seen to be above the limitations of states, of nations and, when it will be transformed into a 'higher organisation', of classes as well (we will not only be beyond the somewhat pedestrian opposition of 'idle classes' and 'productive classes' but also that between urban and rural, manual and intellectual productive classes, as Marx teaches). And yet this society that will present itself as an aggregation of several billion people will, in its temporal limit, represent an ever smaller portion of the 'human species', even as it grows larger due to the longer life expectancy of its members.

For the first time in history, this society will voluntarily and scientifically subordinate itself to the *species*; which is to say, will organise itself in forms that best respond to the ends of future humanity.

That in all this there is nothing fanciful – or, heaven forbid, science fictional! – or utopian either, goes back to the realistic and palpable criterion that Marx calls the difference between property and usufruct.

In the current theory of law property is 'perpetual', while usufruct is temporary, limited to a pre-established number of years, or to the lifetime of the usufructuary. In bourgeois theory property is 'ius utendi et abutendi', that is, *to use and to abuse*. Theoretically the owner can destroy his own good; for example, by irrigating his field with salt water, making it sterile, as the Romans did with the soil of Carthage after they had burned the city. Today's jurists split hairs over a social limit, but this is not science, it is only class fear. The usufructuary, by contrast, has a more limited right than the owner: *use*, yes, *abuse*, no. At the end of the term of usufruct, or at the death of the usufructuary if the term is his lifetime, the land returns to the owner. Positive law prescribes that it be returned with the same efficiency it had at the beginning of the term. Also the simple tenant who has rented the land cannot change the crop but must cultivate it as a *good head of the household*, that is, as the *good* owner does; thus the perpetuity of use or enjoyment consists in the hereditary passage to his children or heirs. In the Italian civil code we find the sacramental formula of 'boni patres familias' in articles 1001 and 1587.

Society, then, has only the use and not the ownership of the land.

Utopianism is metaphysical, Marxist socialism is dialectical. In the respective phases of his gigantic construction Marx successively vindicates: big property (also *capitalist* big property, even though its workers are beasts of burden) against small property, even if without wage-labourers (for the sake of decency, let us skip over small enterprises like those of the sharecropper in the France of 1894 and the Italy of 1958, which add reactionary parcel division to the use of the human beast of burden); state property, also capitalist state property, against big private property (nationalisation); state property after the victory of the proletarian dictatorship; and, finally, vindicates for the higher organisation of full communism the exclusively rational use of the land by society, and buries in Engels' old tools museum the grim term *property*.

6.1   Use Value and Exchange Value

The fundamental thesis of revolutionary Marxism easily extends the negation of individual and then social property from the land to the other instruments of production prepared by human labour, and to the products of labour in the case both of production goods and consumer goods.

Work on agrarian land requires capital goods. One fundamental good – the one from which the word 'capital' derives, as Marx often recalls – is the livestock for work and for breeding. In Italian we call it 'scorta viva' [literally 'live stock'], in French 'cheptel'. The term that indicates the dirty thing that is *capital* comes from the Latin *caput*, meaning 'head'. But let not the bourgeois delude themselves in thinking that this refers to the human head, so as to serve us up another natural right: Capital as an extension of the Person.

It refers to a head of cattle. The extension of the bourgeois head is not the *eternal principles* of human law, but only the horns.

It is clear that the toiler who works the land cannot eat up all his livestock (there are some historical examples) without destroying this special instrument of production, which is fit for reproduction if wisely bred.

Society is usufructuary and not proprietor of the animal species. In Engels' little study there is a charming passage on the ludicrous demand for free hunting and fishing for the French peasants. He was concerned about the danger of wiping out certain species of game, as in fact occurred.

It would not be short, but not difficult either, to extend our deduction to all enterprise capital in agriculture and in industry. But we shall attempt to proceed by large stages.

In his masterly chapters on the land, Marx shows that its *price* and *value*, the result of capitalised rent, *do not enter* into the capital for running the agricultural enterprise. This is because, if the land is spared the deprecated devastation of fertility, its price and value remain intact at the end of the annual cycle. He then makes the obvious comparison with the 'fixed part of constant industrial capital' that does not enter into the calculation of circulating capital apart from the smaller part of it that wears out during the cycle and must be replaced (depreciation). The land renews itself on its own; also the 'live stock' renews itself on its own (with some help from the breeder). In agriculture, a great deal of the *dead* stock must be replaced every year, at the expense of the total value of the products. In industry the extent of the renewal is less.

Leaving the quantitative examination to Marx, we wish to note that humanity does indeed have dead stock or *fixed capital* whose depreciation takes place over extremely long cycles. There are Roman bridges, for example, that are still serviceable after two thousand years. Capitalist criminality seeks short-cycle depreciations and attempts to replace all fixed capital rapidly – at the proletariat's expense. Why? Because fixed capital is under the mad dominion of ownership, while on circulating capital there is simply a usufruct. We refer again to the distinction between dead labour and living labour in our Pentecost and Piombino reports.[22]

Capitalism insists on madly dissipating the labour of the living, and makes the labour of the dead its inhuman property. In the communist economy we shall reverse the terms, and call *enlivening* that which its technicians term 'depreciation' of 'dead' capital (that is, the [cost of] replacement of fixed capital).

The antithesis between property and usufruct is directly related to the antithesis between fixed and circulating capital; and to the antithesis between dead and living labour.

We are on the side of the eternal life of the species; our enemies are on the sinister side of eternal death. Life will sweep them away, synthesising these opposites in the reality of communism.

But we shall give yet another formulation of that same antithesis: monetary exchange, and physical use. Mercantile exchange value versus use value.

The communist revolution is the killing of mercantilism.

6.2 *Objectified Labour and Living Labour*

Our readers and comrades who, in our method of working, actively contribute to the party's collective effort, should now refer to the second part of our articles on the Piombino meeting, in which we discuss Marx's text, the *Grundrisse*.[23]

---

22   The report of the 'Pentecost' meeting of the International Communist Party (in Paris on 8–9 June 1957) was published with the title 'I fondamenti del comunismo rivoluzionario nella dottrina e nella storia della lotta proletaria internazionale' in Nos. 13, 14, 15/1957 of *il programma comunista*; the report of the meeting at Piombino, in Tuscany, on 21–22 September 1957, was published with the title 'Traiettoria e catastrofe della forma capitalistica nella classica monolitica costruzione teorica del marxismo' in Nos. 19 and 20/1957 of *il programma comunista*.

23   See the text 'Who's Afraid of Automation?', chapter 21.

In Marx's magnificent construction, economic individualism is erased and *social man* appears, with boundaries that are those of the entire human society – indeed, of the human *species*.

Whether or not it be behind the capitalist as a *person*, industrial fixed capital, as opposed in its capitalist form to human labour, becomes the measure of the exchange value of products or commodities. *This* is the enemy Monster that hangs over the mass of producers, monopolising a product that concerns not only all present human beings but the entire course of the species down through the millennia. This product is the science and technology elaborated and deposited in the *social brain*. Today, with the degeneration of the capitalist form, this Monster is killing science itself, misgoverning it, criminally exploiting it fruits, squandering the heritage of future generations.

In those pages [of the *Grundrisse*] the current phenomenon of automation is theorised and predicted for the distant future. The history we take the liberty of calling *The Tale of Objectified Labour* has an epilogue, 'The Palingenesis of Objectified Labour'. In this Epilogue, the Monster becomes a beneficial force for all humanity, enabling it not to extort useless surplus labour but, rather, to reduce necessary labour to a minimum, 'all to the advantage of the artistic, scientific etc. education of individuals', who have now been raised to the condition of Social Individual.

Our aim here is to draw another, no less genuine, conclusion from genuine sources that are far more valid and clear today than in the epoch of their origin. When the proletarian revolution puts an end to the squandering of science, a work of the social brain; when labour time is reduced to a minimum and becomes human joy; when the Monster of fixed capital – *CAPITAL*, this transient historical product – is raised to a human form, which does not mean *conquered* for man and for society but *abolished* – *THEN* industry will behave *like the land*, once instruments such as the soil have been liberated from *any form of ownership*.

We would not call it a *conquest* if the means of production ceased to be monopolised by a 'band of idlers' – which is itself a vacuous platitude, since in its early days the bourgeoisie was a class of bold bearers of the social brain and of social practise at its most advanced. As for the means of production, in the society organised in a higher form – international communism – they will not be held as property and capital but as *usufruct*, saving the future of the species, at every step, against the physical necessity of nature, which will be its only adversary.

With the death of property and of capital, both in agriculture and in industry, another platitude that was a concession to the arduous task of traditional propaganda, namely 'personal ownership of consumer products', must be relegated to the shadows of the past. Indeed revolutionary palingenesis in its entirely crumbles to dust if every single object does not throw off its commodity character, and if labour does not cease to be the measure of 'exchange value' – another form that, together with the measure based on money, must die with the death of capitalism.

Marx writes in the *Grundrisse*: 'As soon as labour in the direct form has ceased to be the great well-spring of wealth, labour-time ceases and must cease to be its measure, and hence exchange value [must cease to be the measure] of use value'.[24] Pitying the smallness of Stalin, and of the Russians who follow him, for bringing the *law of value* into socialism (!), we were led to conclude: The thunderbolts of the Last Judgement hit their targets!

The poor wretch who gulps down his alcohol saying 'it's mine, I bought it with the money from my wages' (private or from the state) is, none the less – victim as he is of the *Capital* form – a faithless usufructuary of the health of the species. Along with foolish smoker of cigarettes! Such 'property' will be eliminated by the higher organisation of society.

The debasement of the wage slave worsens in unemployment crises. Engels wrote to Marx on 7 December 1857: 'Among the Philistines here the crisis leads to heavy drinking. No one can stand to stay home alone with his family and his worries, the clubs grow lively and the consumption of liquor greatly increases. The deeper someone's in trouble the more he tries to cheer himself up. The next morning he's the most striking example of a moral and physical hangover' – 1857, or 1958?!

Members of the future society will no longer consume as *human beasts*, in the name of the infamous *ownership* of the *exchanged* object. Use – consumption – will be based on the higher need of social man, perpetuator of the species, and no longer, as is the rule today, under the effect of drugs.

6.3   *The Death of Individualism*

It is not possible for the party of the proletarian class to steer itself in the right revolutionary direction without a *total* give-and-take between the material of agitation and the stable and non-evolving bases of theory.

The questions of contingent action and of the future programme are nothing but two dialectical sides of the same problem, as so many of Marx's writings, right up to his death, and Engels' writings, and Lenin's writings (the April Theses, the October Central Committee!) have attested.

---

24   Marx 1973, p. 705.

These men neither improvised nor revealed, but brandished the compass of our action, which is all too easily mislaid.

This compass signals the danger clearly, and our questions are well posed only when we stand firm against the wrong general course. The formulas and the terms can be falsified by traitors and by imbeciles, but their use is always a sure compass when it is continuous and consistent.

If we are in the sphere of philosophical and historical language, our enemy is individualism, personalism. If we are in the political sphere – democratic electoralism, of all sorts. If in the economic sphere – mercantilism.

Any accommodation with these insidious rhumbs for an apparent advantage means the *sacrifice of the party's future to the success of a day,* or of a year. It means unconditional surrender to the Monster of counter-revolution.

CHAPTER 21

Who's Afraid of Automation?

In recent years and above all due to the technical progress of industry in America, whose economy can more easily bear the weight of a rapid (and therefore costly) replacement of fixed equipment that is still productively valid, there has been a great deal of talk about automatism in production, now referred to as *automation*.[1] The replacement, at breakneck speed, of the work of man with the action of mechanical automatons devoid of life and thought, running on their own, self-regulating and self-managing, has, apparently, been one of the greatest novelties of these postwar years. The social problem has been posed – as if it were new and original – of the drastic reduction of industrial workers, and of the foreseeably high unemployment that would result, preventing great masses of people from earning money and, consequently, from spending it, also to buy the enormous mass of products churned out for the market by the inanimate installations of the practically deserted factories, their machines incessantly churning.

The economists of capitalism and the economists on the other side of the fence – the rival band of false Russian socialism – have been equally bewildered. At an equal distance from the revolutionary science of Marxism, neither band knew that the problem had been posed long before – posed and already masterfully solved, in a manner very different from the dull methods of the bourgeois 'intelligentsia'. In the jargon of this decadent society a problem is any sort of 'bother' that may crop up – a new 'mishap' added to the same old routine of daily life, to be dodged, done away with, and buried under a heap of clichés, so that after eliminating it without disturbing one's own nasty business, one can boast that it has been 'solved'.

This time the capitalists have dealt with the 'problem' better, proclaiming the sacramental 'decrease of the costs of production', which, they allege, is the salvation of scientific and machine society, and which – in their twisted formulas – would help raise the average standard of living, along with the illusion of placating all class conflict.

---

1 *il programma comunista*, Yr. 6, No. 20, 23 October–6 November 1957; republished in *Economia marxista ed economia controrivoluzionaria*, Milan: Iskra, 1976 (writings 1954–57), pp. 189–94, 199–208 and 213–14. The text consists of excerpts from 'Traiettoria e catastrofe della forma capitalistica nella classica monolitica costruzione teorica del marxismo'. The title is the editor's.

It will be easy to silence them and their clumsy emulative pursuit of the Soviet formula of 'full employment', and to show the absurdity of their doctrines on the democratisation of capital. For centuries an economic-juridical democracy has been a historical absurdity: the only form that could abstractly correspond to it is that of the productive micro-enterprise, with the means of production divided up among the workers. More gallows than the gallows!

But most embarrassed of all before the prospect of a totalitarianly automatic production are the countless half-pint Marxists that abound also among the sparsely serried ranks of Marxists not linked to Stalinism, or to post-Stalinism. How oh how – these poor fellows have said to themselves – shall we claim that all the value society adds in every cycle of its equipment derives from wage-labour, when it turns out that production will no longer require either work or effort, neither of the muscles nor even of the mind, since machines can now calculate and plan everything on their own? This will spell the end of the law of labour that generates value, the doctrine of surplus value, and our entire critical construction of the economy and of the capitalist form of production ...

Now, the fact is this. The *immediatists* inanely attribute the daily subtraction of surplus value from the individual workers, this bookkeeping antagonism closed in a pay packet, to the clash of two epochs, two forms of production, two worlds, which with the 'cash payment' have a connection that, while logical, is dialectically *mediated* by revolutionary transformations involving antitheses of far greater breadth, and immense spans of time, space and mode. As a result of their position, tailing after philosophies of exploitation and of the executor's independence of the executive, they condemn themselves to the failure to understand this fact: *we have been waiting for this* [advent of automation] *for a hundred years.*

Away with the laws of value, of equivalent exchange and of surplus value! With their fall into nothingness the very mode of bourgeois production falls with them. The laws are valid only as long as the bourgeois mode of production lives, and the day that science and technology break them – even though they have held a class monopoly for centuries – will be, precisely, the supreme example of the revolt of productive forces against forms whose time has come.

This doctrine of automatism in production boils down to our entire deduction of the necessity of communism – a deduction based on the phenomena of capitalism itself.

We shall base our deduction on Marx's original text,[2] but this deduction speaks for itself, and has done so for a long time.

---

2   Marx's original text: here, Bordiga refers to the Italian translation of the *Grundrisse* done, privately, by the Paris section of the International Communist Party, based on the German

1   The Labour Process and Machinism

We could draw our entire demonstration from the 'official' text of *Capital*, citing the chapters 'The Division of Labour and Manufacture' and 'Machinery
and Large-Scale Industry'[3] (the question we tackled at our meeting in Rome
on 5 July 1952), but the text we have now is particularly expressive, and pulls
no punches in showing the strict connection between the internal dynamic
present in capitalism and its revolutionary overthrow, stemming not from the
fact that it is 'too exploitative' but, rather, from the necessary violent generation of a form that denies it face-to-face and reverses all its characteristics.

To avoid misunderstandings in relation to the usual insane claim that Marxism is a doctrine 'in continual evolution', and that its texts of different years
contained constructions later forgotten (!) or replaced, let us make it clear
that in the thousand pages [of the *Grundrisse*] we have here, the exposition
follows the same line as that of *Capital* and all the same theories are formulated in the same substance and form, with exactly the same terminology and
with the same mathematical expressions; and with all the developments of
the second and third Volumes of *Capital* prepared by Engels. From the pages
of the chapter 'On Capital' (whose sections tackle exactly the same questions Marx will later discuss in *Capital*: 'The Production Process of Capital',
'The Circulation Process of Capital', 'Capital as Fructiferous', 'Transformation
of Surplus Value into Profit', and an Appendix on the history of economic
doctrines) it would be easy to cite many of them in which the same formula
for the three terms that form circulating capital (constant + variable + surplus value = total product) is expressed in narrative, arithmetic, and algebraic
form.

Therefore the passage on automatic production is 'valid' not only for Marxist thought of 1857, but also for Marx's thought until his death, and for Marxist
thought up to 1957 and beyond.

We begin on page 584 of the Moscow German edition: 'Once adopted into
the production process of capital, the means of labour passes through different metamorphoses, whose culmination is the *machine*, or rather, an *automatic
system of machinery*'.[4]

---

text published in Berlin in 1953 from the Moscow edition of 1939–41. The first published Italian
translation was in 1968–70.

3   Marx 1976, Chapters 14 and 15.

4   Marx 1973, p. 692. The five passages quoted in this section are on pages 692 and 693.

(We make the following pact with the reader: We shall make our comments, but the italics are always those of the original text and we prefer to capitalise the nouns frequently, German-style.)[5] The text continues:

> (System of machinery: the *automatic* one is merely its most complete, most adequate form, and alone transforms machinery into a system), set in motion by an automaton, a moving power that moves itself; this automaton consisting of numerous mechanical and intellectual organs, so that the workers themselves are cast merely as its conscious linkages. In the machine, and even more in machinery as an automatic system, the use value, i.e. the material quality of the means of labour, is transformed into an existence adequate to fixed capital and to capital as such; and the form in which it was adopted into the production process of capital, the direct means of labour, is superseded by a form posited by capital itself and corresponding to it.

Marx makes it clear that the *instrument of labour*, having become *fixed capital*, has completely lost the character it had in 'immediate' (or 'specialised') production, to which those we call 'immediatists' (and reactionaries) would like to return.

> In no way does the machine appear as the individual worker's means of labour. Its distinguishing characteristic is not in the least, as with the means of labour, to transmit the worker's activity to the object; this activity, rather, is posited in such a way that it merely transmits the machine's work, the machine's action, on to the raw material – supervises it and guards against interruptions.

We cannot fail to note the eloquence of this passage, while remarking for a moment just how pathetic are those who chitter-chatter that after the fact of modern automatism, all the Marxist positions must be 'revised'!

---

5 I have not followed Bordiga in his extremely profuse utilisation of capital letters 'German-style'. English is sparing in its use of capital letters, and throughout this book I have in fact used them sparingly. ('The State', for example, is practically never capitalised, while in the Italian 'lo Stato' is often capitalised.)

  The 'Paris translation' of the *Grundrisse* that Bordiga follows here is splendid: very clear, straightforward and readable – much more so than the standard English translation (which is almost certainly more precise), which I have nevertheless adopted, modifying it to follow Bordiga's in one case (indicated in the notes). Bordiga's glosses are bracketed and in italics. [Note by G. Donis.]

Not as with the instrument, which the worker animates and makes into his organ with his skill and strength, and whose handling therefore depends on his virtuosity. Rather, it is the machine which possesses skill and strength in place of the worker, it itself the virtuoso, with a soul of its own in the mechanical laws acting through it; and it consumes coal, oil etc. just as the worker consumes food, to keep up its perpetual motion. The worker's activity, reduced to a mere abstraction of activity, is determined and regulated on all sides by the movement of the machinery, and not the opposite.

And pay attention here:

The science which compels the inanimate limbs of the machinery, by their construction, to act purposefully, as an automaton, does not exist in the worker's consciousness, but rather acts upon him through the machine as an alien power, as the power of the machine itself.

Let those who today abase themselves in adoration of science in general reflect on these words written one century ago, when, that is, the 'ideas of the eighteenth century' of which Marx speaks in the Introduction [of the *Grundrisse*] had an immense power of suggestion over the world, and in any case constituted an undeniable historical stage that was still threatened by the return of restorations. Yes, let them reflect – those who invite the workers to follow them in their adoration and instil reverential fear in them, forgetting that science and technological superiority is first and foremost the monopoly of an exploiting minority. And, what is more, that as long as the relations of production remain mercantile, monetary, and based on wages the entire system of *automatic machinery* will be a monster that crushes under the weight of its oppression an enslaved and wretched humanity. This is the Monster that dominates the entire picture Marx drew of present society, Capital itself, depersonalised, and even 'declassed', as in our frequent replies to those who rave that in one third of the world the Enemy Class, the Bourgeoisie, has disappeared.

[...]

2   The Horror of Dead Labour

Marx's text will eventually be published in its entirety, but that is something we cannot do now. Hence we shall limit ourselves to excerpting a few passages, giving them an order that, while facilitating the dialectic, takes light and power away from this exceptional exposition. But, in our task as faithful popularising pupils, we see no other way of getting round the eternal obstacle: Marx is too difficult; the texts are incomprehensible; the author changes his position from page to page; the development bristles with puzzling contradictions (!!). In fact, in Marx, the play of the dialectic is so pressing and powerful that the *character* that, just for the sake of simplification, we have called objectified labour or fixed capital, appears in almost every period as the protagonist in the black mask and the white: the destroyer and the redeemer.

We – poor bouncers – will bring this character on stage first of all in the sinister guise it has in the period of capitalism, and under the capitalist regime. Afterwards we shall make it reappear accompanied by the now irrepressible blare of the Communist Revolution:

> The appropriation of living labour by objectified labour [...] which lies in the concept of capital [...].
>
> [In machinery,] objectified labour confronts living labour within the labour process itself as the power which rules it [...].
>
> The transformation of the means of labour into machinery, and of living labour into a mere living accessory of this machinery, as the means of its action, also posits the absorption of the labour process in its material character as a mere moment of the realisation process of capital.
>
> A power [*of fixed capital*] which, as the appropriation of living labour, is the form of capital.[6]

These propositions – we have rearranged them slightly – can be easily understood if the reader relates them to the historical transition Marx was thinking of at the time. In this case, the transition from craft work to the associated labour of mechanical industry. In the first proposition, what is the 'form of appropriation'? (We refer the readers to our series of articles *Proprietà e Capitale*.)[7] The artisan is the owner of his instrument of labour, which means that he also owns his workplace and the raw material he transforms (in the production cycle he has enough money to buy it). The consequence is that the specialised worker *possesses the manufactured product* – he sells it wherever he wants, and pockets the price of the commodity-product. This is a true labour process, that is, a process of *commodity production*.

---

6   See Marx 1973, p. 693.
7   Now collected in *Proprietà e capitale*, Florence: Iskra, 1980.

But, quite soon, in this form the productive forces can no longer develop; hence, the need for heavy machinery. Now the producer is owner neither of the machine, nor of the factory, nor of the raw material. He swaps his labour-power, his sole possession, for a wage that allows him to feed himself and to reproduce (proletarians). The consequence: Who appropriates the product? The worker perhaps? No, not even a crumb. It all goes – the easy propagandistic answer is obvious – to the capitalist, the owner, the bourgeois. Marx often made use of this easy answer. But here his construction rises to the heights in which any concession to idiotic success through minimum effort is spurned. The juridical formula is held in contempt. He who appropriates the capital produced by living labour (surplus value) is presented as neither a human person nor as a human class: he is the Monster, objectified labour, fixed capital – monopoly and fortress of the *form of capital in itself*. A Beast without soul and, even, without life, but that devours and kills living labour, the labour of the living, and the living themselves.

Why do we measure this Capital *par excellence* on the basis of the cyclical 'product' (the *turnover* of the accountants)? Because the *entire* product is *appropriated* by the man, corpse, beast, or Thing (Enterprise!) that has the monopoly ownership of fixed capital.

Here those who lack dialectical gumption will run the risk of suffocating in *immediatism*. Will the demand not be to transform the production process of capital into a labour process? It is in fact *direct labour* that controls and dominates the raw material, the tool, the manufacture, and the product (rather than being dominated by the machine, and ultimately by the harrowing *automaton*).

But falling back on this, even when monetary fictions replace the material disposition of what today is constant capital and product, means 'rolling back the wheel of history', condemning the 'free' worker to lose more hours of sacrifice for the same standard of living.

Now the historic and human problem is to reduce working hours – to reduce *necessary work*. In the artisan system there is no explicit overwork (and for this very reason its society was closed in a narrow limit) but necessary work is enormous, more than the entire working day in the industrial system of machines.

3   Dead Labour and Dead Science

The transition from the artisan to the industrial mode of production is a *fait accompli*. No one can contest it and turn the Luddite revolts against machinery into a programme for the development of science and technology. What, in Marxism, is the relation between theoretical and applied science and objectified labour, between science and capital?

Marx, here, has a formidable expression: the 'social brain'. Technology first, and then science, are passed down from generation to generation as an endowment of social man, of the species, which has worked and collaborated in their production with all its individuals. In our construction the prophet, the priest, the discoverer, the inventor are headed for liquidation, one and all. In these pages social man is also referred to as the social individual, which means not 'human person' as a cell of society but, by contrast, human society treated as a single organism that lives just one life. (In this form, the ingenuous and sublime myth of immortality enters the arena of science – a myth infantile human thought attributes to the individual, just as, today, the law and the economy seek to base themselves on the individual, and are headed for an analogous collapse.) This organism, whose life is history, has a brain of its own – an organ constructed by its age-old function, and which is not the inheritance of any skull or any cranium. For us, the knowledge of the species, science, far more than is the case with gold, are not private inheritances, and potentially belong entirely to social man.

Hence our text refers to the fate of human science under the miserable mercantile regime, which continues to suffocate it throughout the planet:

> The accumulation of knowledge and of skill, of the general productive forces of the social brain, is thus absorbed into capital, as opposed to labour, and hence appears as an attribute of capital, and more specifically of *fixed capital*, in so far as it enters into the production process as a means of production proper.[8]

Here Marx insists that fixed capital appears as the most adequate form of capital as such 'in so far as capital's relations with itself are concerned'. But 'as regards capital's external relations, it is *circulating capital* which appears as the adequate form of capital, and not fixed capital'.

Socially, politically, historically, as a ruling power, capital has the form of machinery, of fixed capital. Economically, as a measure in the process of production of capital by capital (*id est* by living labour) it has its principal (adequate) form in circulating capital, equivalent to the global social product of a

---

8 Marx 1973, p. 694. The other three passages quoted in this section are on pages 695, 699 and 704.

cycle. Having confirmed once again this dialectical position of Marx's words, let us return to the role of fixed capital.

In so far as the *means of labour*, as a physical thing, loses its direct form, [it] becomes *fixed capital*, and confronts the worker physically as *capital*. In machinery, knowledge appears as alien, external to him; and living labour [as] subsumed under self-activating objectified labour. The worker appears as superfluous to the extent that his action is not determined by [capital's] requirements.

Capitalism is still on the scene, but it has a partner in shame.

The entire production process appears as not subsumed under the direct skilfulness of the worker, but rather as the technological application of science. [It is,] hence, the tendency of capital to give production a scientific character; direct labour [is] reduced to a mere moment of this process. [...] [capital] presupposes a certain given historical development of the productive forces on one side – science too [is] among these productive forces – and, on the other, drives and forces them further onwards.

We conclude this section limited to the history of capitalism with a final description of the link between science and capital:

In machinery, the appropriation of living labour by capital achieves a direct reality [...]. It is, firstly, the analysis and application of mechanical and chemical laws, arising directly out of science, which enable the machine to perform the same labour as that previously performed by the worker. However, the development of machinery along this path occurs only when large industry has already reached a higher stage, and all the sciences have been pressed into the service of capital [...]. Invention then becomes a business, and the application of science to direct production becomes a prospect which determines and solicits it [*1857 or 1957?*] [...]. Thus, the specific mode of working here appears directly as becoming transferred from the worker to capital in the form of the machine, and his own labour capacity devalued thereby. Hence the struggle of the workers against machinery. What was the living worker's activity becomes the activity of the machine. Thus the appropriation of labour by capital confronts the worker in a coarsely sensuous form; capital absorbs labour into itself – 'as though its body were by love possessed'.

4   Palingenesis of Objectified Labour

We shall not select other images of the capitalist relation between dead labour
and living labour after this image of their monstrous copulation.

Marx introduces us for the first time to the revolutionary overturning of
this obscene function of the Monster-Automaton with a lapidary title, which
crushes forever the theoretic dementia of the Divine Stalin, namely: 'Contradiction between the foundation of bourgeois production (value as measure)
and its development'. Thus in post-bourgeois society it will not be a question of
'measuring value correctly according to labour-time' as the simpletons believe,
but rather of *doing away with value as measure* (*Wertmaß*). (You Soviet publishers of the year 1953! Are you so deaf to doctrine that you do not hear the
whistling bullets of the firing squads?)

Marx's text repeats it no less bluntly:

> The exchange of living labour for objectified labour – i.e. the positing
> of social labour in the form of the contradiction[9] of capital and wage
> labour – is the ultimate development of the *value-relation* and of produc-
> tion resting on value.[10]

In the development that we present not only is the measure of exchange
value based on working time valid only for an antagonistic economy based on
wage labour, but the not-distant demise of value as the measure of labour is
potentially prepared by the very appearance of the machine industry, especially when it rises to the level of an automatic system of machinery. And
now, are we supposed to be *afraid* of automation, as of a doctrinal battle lost?
If we were, we would truly be ignorant of the prime objectives of our class
war!

We can say that in the early days of capitalism 'real wealth' was measured by
the mass of direct labour, of average working time:

> But to the degree that large industry develops, the creation of real wealth
> comes to depend less on labour-time and on the amount of labour em-
> ployed than on the power of the [*mechanical*] agencies set in motion

---

9   In the text, Bordiga (as in the 'Paris translation' of the *Grundrisse*) uses the word *antag-
        onismo* (antagonism) here, and '*antagonistico*' in the following paragraphs, which I have
        translated as 'antagonistic' rather than 'contradictory' [note by G. Donis].
10   Marx 1973, p. 704. The three passages quoted in this section are on pages 704 and 705.

during labour-time, whose 'powerful effectiveness' is itself in turn out of all proportion to the direct labour-time spent on their production, but depends rather on a general state of science and on the progress of technology, or the application of this science to production.

This discourse, inherent in our texts for exactly one century [1857–1957], puts us in a position to say that, even though the antagonistic (class, wage, mercantile) character of the production process has not yet been overcome, the possibilities of its being overcome rose to the highest degree when *automation* was employed in industry on an immense scale; and, in virtue of the same deductions, when these powerful mechanical agencies were joined by *nuclear energy*, the latest of the lot, truly and hugely disproportionate to the strength of human muscles.

The time to kill the law of value and value as measure has truly come. And far more in America than in the Russia of the *switchmen* Stalin and Khrushchev, who shunt the express train of the Revolution onto a dead-end track.

We have known how this will come about for over a century. And today, in the offing, we see an even higher version, with the demise, simultaneously, of the law of labour-time as exchange value, class antagonism, the social division of labour, mercantile production, and necessary – forced – wage labour. The change of scene happens with a swiftness worthy of this Epilogue:

No longer does the worker insert a modified natural thing [*the instrument of labour*] as the middle link between the object [*the material he works on*] and himself; rather, he inserts the process of nature, transformed into an industrial process, as a means between himself and inorganic nature, mastering it. He steps to the side of the production process instead of being its chief actor.

The text presents a *triple step*, which is the negation of which Marx speaks at the end of Chapter 24 of *Capital*, Volume 1. Overcoming the odious wage parenthesis of capitalism the worker becomes 'free', which is to say 'master' of the labour and the production process. Once again he 'handles' his tool and engraves his capacity and intelligence in the 'manufacture'. But the hand and the worker are no longer of the *single individual* but, now, of the *species*, which with its hand-brain sets in motion on nature a 'mechanical' process created by the knowledge of natural laws. We hope that the glosses we 'insert' do not seem gratuitous variations but, rather, help the reader follow this arduous text.

5   The Transformation Has Exploded

> In this transformation, it is neither the direct human labour he himself
> performs, nor the time during which he works, but rather the appropri-
> ation of his own general productive power, his understanding of nature
> and his mastery over it by virtue of his presence as a social body – it is,
> in a word, the development of the social individual which appears as the
> great foundation-stone of production and of wealth.[11]

Marx speaks here in a general sense of wealth as a faculty of both bourgeois and
socialist society, even if he shows the opposing aspects of wealth before and
after the transformation. But his description of capitalist wealth is extremely
harsh: 'The *theft of alien labour-time, on which the present wealth is based*,
appears a miserable foundation in face of this new one, created by large-scale
industry itself'.

We decided, at our meeting,[12] to leave the term *wealth*, deriving from
wealthy, for the current form of theft of another's value and labour. Property
and wealth have meaning for the individual insofar as he can bar others from
appropriating his goods. Once the individual – today's deformed *homo eco-
nomicus* – has been elevated to the condition of social body, there are no more
measures of time and value, and therefore no thefts. No wealthy people and no
wealth, and the 'wealth' of society, of the species, of the immortal social body –
here sculpted for the first time with features that make Michelangelo's Eternal
Fathers pale – we shall not call wealth, but wisdom, efficiency, and power, not of
men but of reality and of nature. Marx's text continues, in that which – perhaps
carried away – we shall describe as the Last Judgement on mercantile society.
In the war of doctrine, even if not yet in that of arms, we have already relegated
it to its sinister past.

> As soon as labour in the direct form has ceased to be the great well-
> spring of wealth, labour-time ceases and must cease to be its measure,
> and hence exchange value [must cease to be the measure] of use value
> [*Stalin! Stalin!*]. The *surplus labour of the mass* has ceased to be the con-
> dition for the development of general wealth, just as the *non-labour of the
> few*, for the development of the general powers of the human head.

---

11   Marx 1973, p. 705. The five passages quoted in this section are on pages 705 and 706.
12   A reference to Bordiga's report on the capitalist economy in the West at the meeting of the
       International Communist Party in Piombino on 21–22 September 1957.

The thunderbolts of the Last Judgement hit their targets!

> With that, production based on exchange value breaks down, and the direct, material production process is stripped of the form of penury and antithesis.[13] [They are replaced by] the free development of individualities, and hence [we do not have] necessary labour-time reduced to form surplus labour, but rather the general reduction of the necessary labour of society to a minimum, which then corresponds to the artistic, scientific etc. development of the individuals in the time set free, and with the means created for all of them.

The text, here, outlines the contradiction to which capital is condemned. On the one hand, having posited labour-time as the measure of wealth and as its source (pure Ricardo), capital must increase total labour-time. Then, when necessary (paid) labour-time diminishes, it exalts superfluous labour-time, since for it this is a life-or-death condition (the process of the progressive production of other capital). On the other hand, capital arouses all the forces of science and of nature, as well as those of social organisation and circulation and, in spite of itself, lays the foundations to reduce the creation of wealth that is *independent* of the labour-time destined to it.

Once the class rule of capital, our leading player, has been broken, dead and objectified labour, the fixed capital we saw earlier, rises from its condition as the slave-driving instrument of living labour and is transformed into its opposite. Behold its triumph:

> Nature builds no machines, no locomotives, railways, electric telegraphs, self-acting mules etc. These are products of human industry; natural material transformed into organs of the human will over nature, and of human participation in nature. They are *organs of the human brain, created by the human hand*; the power of knowledge, objectified. The development of fixed capital indicates to what degree general social knowledge has become a *direct force of production*, and to what degree, hence, the conditions of the process of social life itself have come under the control of the general intellect and been transformed in accordance with it. [*allow us to add: Fixed capital no longer indicates the brutal subjugation of living labour, but indicates*] [t]o what degree the powers of social produc-

---

13   Bordiga: 'antagonism'. I have made major changes in the next sentence of the English
       translation, following Bordiga's 'Paris translation' [note by G. Donis].

tion have been produced, not only in the form of knowledge, but also as immediate organs of social practice, of the real life process.

Once again, we know that Marx is describing future society, and in a way that leaves not the slightest doubt about its specific differences from the society in which we live today, about its definitive characteristics, which in the revolutionary transformation will have to be swallowed up by nothingness.

[...]

6   The Putrefied Trinity Formula

At our Milan meeting in September of 1952 we examined in depth the chapters in which Marx dismantles the trinity theory of incomes and of their sources: part of income comes from labour, and is paid in wages; part is from nature, and is rent; part is from money, and is interest. The profit of capital is obliterated in this formula – the formula to which the entire New Science of the ultra-modern professors of *Phlogiston Economics*[14] boils down.

In these pages of Marx's we see blazing in opposition to the bourgeois concept of individual freedom the communist concept of time available for the species – for its material and mental development, and its harmony of delights.

Humanity, says Marx, will not be free of necessity, but necessity will not take the form of one part of humanity against the other part, but only that of an environmental nature increasingly controlled and subdued by a science finally free of phlogistons and trinities (*Capital*, Volume 3, Chapter 48: 'The Trinity Formula'):

> This realm of natural necessity expands with [the] development [*of man*], because his needs do too; but the productive forces [*the natural forces disciplined by the automatic mechanism described in the* Grundrisse] to satisfy these expand at the same time [*with a minimum of necessary labour and, at the apex, with only voluntary labour-pleasure*]. Freedom, in this sphere

---

14   Bordiga speaks of phlogiston in the previous section of this long text, only parts of which are published here, referring to 'Engels' magnificent passage in the Preface to Volume 2 of *Capital*, against Rodbertus' (see Marx 1978, pp. 97 ff.). Bordiga criticises those who 'attempt to bring dead theories back to life, as in the example of the chemistry of *phlogiston*, which was overturned by Lavoisier's discovery (on the nature of combustion as combination with oxygen, and not as loss of the mysterious *phlogiston*)'.

[*communism*], can consist only in this, that socialised man, the associated producers, govern the human metabolism with nature in a rational way, bringing it under their collective control instead of being dominated by it as a blind power; accomplishing it with the least expenditure of energy and in conditions most worthy and appropriate for their human nature.[15]

A monument and a jewel risen from the social brain, Karl Marx's theory of exchange value is complete throughout the decades of the writing of his great work. It proceeds without regrets, and without the criminal improvements and enrichments of the modern ravers closed in the depths of impotence to stare at the light that sparkled in a single flash.

Exchange value rules capitalist time, and in the course of this time value is measured by labour-time.

In socialism there are no longer measures of labour, or of value. There are no longer exchanges between men and men. Only one exchange remains: between human society and nature.

---

15   Marx 1991, p. 959.

CHAPTER 22

The Immediate Revolutionary Programme in the Capitalist West (1953)

[...] If in ten years [the United States] boasts a rise in wages of 280 percent, while the rise in the cost of living was 180 percent, it means that the worker with wages of 380 has to buy 280, that is, the improvement is reduced to 35 percent.[1] At the same time it is admitted that productivity has risen 250 percent! Thus the worker who gives three and a half times as much receives only one and a third: exploitation and surplus value have increased enormously.

It has been made fully clear that the law of increasing poverty does not mean a fall in nominal and real wages but, rather, an increased extortion of surplus value and an increased number of workers fallen into the deprivation of all reserves.

[...] The theory of recurrent and increasingly serious crises is founded on the theory of the rise in productivity and of the fall in the rate of profit. It is alleged that the crisis will be overcome only when those indices characteristic of the capitalist course disappear. In America things are completely different, as is shown also by comparison with our [Italian] industrialists, who for example in the iron and steel industry would like to go from 80 tons per worker per year to America's 200 tons. Who wouldn't like to get 4 percent on 200 instead of 5 on 80!

The intrinsic economic crisis we find in the abstract (as in Marx) in an America that has to eat everything it produces is written with formulas and is drawn with inexorable curves. A basket of products that oscillates around the average price of bread tells us that today the worker purchases a pound of bread with the remuneration of 6 minutes of his labour, when in 1914 it cost him 17 minutes. The working-class population has certainly increased more steeply than the total population percentage-wise. How will each American manage to gulp down three times as much bread as in 1914, and perhaps ten times as much as in 1848? To keep their stomachs from exploding, maybe they should switch to brioches! There will come a time when, on the one hand, they won't sell a pound more of bread and, on the other, the workers will be out of work

---

1 Extracts from Bordiga's reports at the party meetings held in Forlì on 28 December 1952 and in Genoa on 26 April 1953, published in the pamphlet *Sul Filo del Tempo*, Internationalist Communist Party, May 1953.

and won't be able to buy a pound either. This, *en bref*, is why Black Friday is still to come, and blacker than ever before.

One solution is to stuff with bread the peoples that until now have eaten millet, rice or bananas. (Who can say that the Mau Mau get it wrong?) To accomplish this one begins by cannonading whoever tries to stop the bread's being unloaded, and then whoever was selling millet, rice and bananas. Welcome to imperialism! If the Marxist theory of crises and catastrophe fits like a glove, so does the theory of imperialism and war. The facts of 1915 that form the basis of Lenin's *Imperialism* we find today in the American statistics with ten times the virulence.

Among other things, the statistics compare the standard of living in America with the other countries that are its retinue – first allies, then enemies. If a pound of flour is worth 4 of those 6 minutes of bread in America, it is worth 27 minutes in Russia, the American statistic tells us. The Russian statistic might say it's less, but there's no question that, in the Eastern zone, the laws of increasing productivity, of the composition of capital, and of the fall of the rate of profit still have a long way to go, to the great confusion of those who read revolutionary conditions and distances upside-down.

Once you [Russians] have positioned your first piece of artillery wherever you wish and launched your first V-2 rocket, maybe from the moon, there's no question that you'll have to strike the very centre of the American system, slamming the brakes on its madly rising consumption and production. These Americans need to be taught that while it's quite true that 'non de solo pane vivit homo', when this 'homo' earns his daily 'pane' in six minutes, if he works more than two hours a day he's not a man but a fool.

[...] The communist party defends the future situation of reduced labour-time on the basis of ends that are useful for life, and works to accomplish this future result, making use of all real developments. This conquest that seems miserably expressed in hours, reduced to a material computation, in fact represents an enormous victory – the greatest possible victory – over the necessity that drags and enslaves us all. Even then, when capitalism and classes have been eliminated, the human species will still be subject to the necessity of natural forces, and the philosophical absolute of freedom will still be a vain illusion.

Whoever, in the vortex of today's world, instead of finding the line of the current of this impersonal notion of future conditions in a work that has been going on for generations, wants to cram new prescriptions into his poor head and dictate new formulas, is – in our judgement – worse than the worst conformists and lackeys of the capitalist system, and worse than the priests of its eternity.

1   The Immediate Revolutionary Programme

[...] With the gigantic movement of renewal after World War I, powerful on a
world scale and in Italy constituted by the solid party of 1921, it was clear that
the urgent demand was to take political power and that the proletariat does not
take it by legal means but by armed force, that the best opportunity presents
itself after the military defeat of one's own country, and that the political form
following the victory is the dictatorship of the proletariat. The task after political victory is economic and social transformation, and its prime condition is
the proletarian dictatorship.

The *Communist Manifesto* made it clear that, since the path to full communism is long and hard, the successive social measures that are made possible or
'despotically' provoked differ according to the degree of development of the
productive forces of the country in which the proletariat has triumphed, and
to the speed with which this victory spreads to other countries. It indicated
the measures that were suitable at that time, in 1848, for the most advanced
European countries, and made it clear that what it indicated was not a programme for full socialism, but a group of measures which it described as transitory, immediate, variable, and essentially 'contradictory'.

Subsequently – and this was one of the elements that deceived the advocates
of a theory not stable but of continual re-elaboration from historical results –
many measures dictated at the time by the proletarian revolution (compulsory
education, a state bank, and the like) were implemented by the bourgeoisie
itself in various countries.

This, however, was no reason to believe that the precise laws and predictions
on the transition from the capitalist to the socialist mode of production, with all
its economic, social and political forms, had been modified in any way. It only
meant that the first post-revolutionary period became different and easier: the
economy of transition to socialism, preceding the successive period, the lower
level of socialism, and the last period – of higher socialism, or full communism.

Classical opportunism consisted in leading one to believe that all those
measures, from the lowest to the highest, could be applied by the democratic
bourgeois state under the pressure of the proletariat, or even by the proletariat
itself after its legal conquest of power. But in such a case those various 'measures', if compatible with the capitalist mode of production, would have been
adopted in the interest of capitalism's continuation and to postpone its fall. If
they were incompatible, they would have never been put into practise by the
state.

Today's opportunism, with its formula of popular and progressive democracy within the framework of a parliamentary constitution, has a different –

and worse – historical task. Not only does it seek to fool the proletariat into believing that some of the proletariat's own measures can be realised by an inter-class and inter-party state (like yesterday's social democrats, it is defeatist on the subject of proletarian dictatorship), but it goes so far as to lead the organised masses to fight for 'popular and progressive' social measures that are directly *opposed* to the measures that proletarian power *has always fought for* – ever since 1848 and the *Manifesto*!

Nothing can better show the ignominy of this involution than a list of measures that, when we posit the future taking of power in a country of the capitalist West, ought to be formulated, to replace (after a century!) those of the *Manifesto* – without excluding the most essential of the 1848 demands.

Here is a list of such demands:

a) 'Disinvestment of capital', namely, destination of a far smaller part of the product to instrumental rather than consumer goods.

b) 'Raising the costs of production' to be able to give higher pay for less labour-time, as long as wage-market-money continues to exist.

c) 'Drastic reduction of the working day', at least to half the current hours, absorbing unemployment and antisocial activities.

d) Once the volume of production has been reduced with a plan of 'under-production' that concentrates production in the most necessary areas, 'authoritarian control of consumption', combating the fashionable advertising of useless-damaging-luxury goods, and forcefully abolishing activities devoted to reactionary psychological propaganda.

e) Rapid 'breaking of the limits of enterprise', with the transferral of authority not of the personnel but of the materials of labour, moving towards a new plan of consumption.

f) 'Rapid abolition of social security of a mercantile type', to replace it with the social alimentation of non-workers, up to an initial minimum.

g) 'Stopping the construction' of houses and workplaces around the large, and also the small, cities, as a first step towards the population's uniform distribution in the countryside. Prohibition of useless traffic to reduce traffic jams, speed and volume.

h) 'Resolute struggle against professional specialisation' and the social division of labour, with the abolition of careers and titles.

i) Obvious immediate measures, closer to the political ones, to make schools, the press, all the means of the diffusion of information, and the network of shows and entertainment subject to the communist state.

There is nothing strange in the fact that the Stalinist parties of the West now ask for exactly the opposite, not only in their 'institutional' (politico-legal) but also in their 'structural' (socio-economic) demands. This makes it possible for them to act in parallel with the party that leads the Russian state and its allies, in which the task of social transformation is the transition from pre-capitalism to full capitalism, with all its baggage of ideological, political, social and economic demands, all aimed at the bourgeois zenith, and directed with horror only against the feudal and medieval nadir. But these dirty renegades of the West are even filthier, since the danger that is still real and physical for an Asia today in upheaval[2] is non-existent and a sham for those who look to the conceited capitalarchy on the other side of the Atlantic, and for the proletarians who are under its civil, liberal, and United National heel.

---

2   The danger of a return to pre-capitalism or feudalism.

SECTION 5

On the Party

∵

Considerations on the Party's Organic Activity When the General Situation Is Historically Unfavourable (1965)

1. The question of the party's internal organisation has always been an object of debate for traditional Marxists and for the present Communist Left, which arose as an opposition to the errors of the Moscow International.[1] Naturally this question is inseparable from our overall positions; it is not an isolated sector in a watertight compartment.

2. All the elements of the doctrine, of the party's general theory, are to be found in the classical texts and are taken up in detail in more recent documents, in Italian texts such as the Rome and the Lyons Theses, and in many others in which the Left foresaw the destruction of the Third International by phenomena no less serious than those that destroyed the Second. Today we have used some of this material in our work on organisation (in the limited sense of party organisation, not the broad sense of organisation of the proletariat in its various historical and social forms). Rather than summarise this work here, we refer the reader to the texts themselves and to the major study under way on the History of the Left.

3. Everything concerned with theory and the nature of the party and relations between the party and the proletarian class, which can be summarised in the obvious conclusion that only through the party and the party's action does the proletariat become a class for itself and for the revolution – all this belongs to pure theory, which all of us accept and which is therefore beyond discussion.

4. We normally refer to as tactics (always with the reservation that there are no autonomous chapters and sections) those questions that arise and develop historically in relations between the proletariat and other classes, between the proletarian party and other proletarian organisations, and between the proletarian party and bourgeois and non-proletarian parties.

5. The relationship between tactical solutions (which must never be in contradiction with doctrinal and theoretical positions) and the manifold developments of the objective situation, which, in a sense, lies outside the party, is

---

1 *il programma comunista*, Yr. 14, No. 2, 1965, 24 January; republished in *In difesa della continuità del programma comunista*, Milan: Edizioni il programma comunista, 1970, pp. 165–169.

certainly very variable. But as can be seen in the Rome Theses on tactics, which were draft theses for international tactics, the party must master and foresee this relationship.

In extremely simplified terms, there are periods when the objective situation is favourable, although the party as subject is in unfavourable conditions. The opposite may also be true. There are also rare but significant examples of a well-prepared party and a social situation that pushes the masses towards revolution and towards the party that foresaw it and described it in advance. As Lenin showed, the Bolsheviks in Russia fall into this category.

6. We might ask ourselves, without indulging in pedantry, 'what is the condition of present-day society?' The obvious answer is that it is the worst imaginable; a large part of the proletariat has not only been crushed by the bourgeoisie, but is controlled by parties that operate on its behalf, preventing any revolutionary proletarian class movement. Consequently it is not possible to predict how long it will be until this mortal paralysis is overcome and there are once again signs of what we have defined as a 'polarisation' or 'ionisation' of social molecules, the prelude to an explosion of powerful class antagonisms.

7. What are the consequences of this unfavourable period for the internal organic dynamics of the party? In all the texts mentioned above, we always stated that the party cannot fail to be affected by the real situation in which it finds itself. As a result, any large proletarian parties are now necessarily and avowedly opportunist.

One of the fundamental theses of the Left is that our party, however unfavourable the situation, must not cease its resistance, but must survive and transmit the 'flame' along the historical 'thread of time'. Clearly this would have to be a small party, not because we wanted or chose it that way, but because it is an unavoidable necessity. With regard to the party's structure, we have refuted a number of accusations, with arguments it is not necessary to repeat, dating from the degeneration of the Third International, and in a number of polemics. We definitely do not want the party to be a secret sect, or an elite that refuses any outside contact because of its mania for purity. We reject any formula for a workerist or labourist party that excludes non-proletarians – a formula that has characterised all opportunists in the course of history. As can be seen from polemics going back more that half a century, we do not wish to reduce the party to a sort of cultural, intellectual or scholastic organisation. Nor do we believe, as certain anarchists or Blanquists do, that the party can be thought of as a conspiratorial group that plots armed actions.

8. Given that the degeneration of society as a whole is characterised by the falsification and destruction of the theory and correct doctrine, the small party of today must essentially be devoted to restoring the doctrinal principles, even

though the favourable conditions under which Lenin accomplished this task after the disaster of the first world war are now lacking. However, we have no reason to raise a barrier between theory and practice on that account. Beyond a certain limit, this would be tantamount to destroying ourselves and our principled basis. We therefore undertake all the forms of activity characteristic of favourable periods to the extent that the real relations of forces permit.

9. This question should be developed in more detail, but we are now in a position to draw some conclusions for the organisational structure of the party in a difficult period. It would be a fatal error to divide the party into two groups, one devoting itself to study and the other to action. Such a distinction would be fatal for the entire party but also for the individual militant. Unitarianism and organic centralism mean that the party develops within itself organs specialised for various functions (such as propaganda, proselytism, organisation of the proletariat, trade-union work – and, tomorrow, armed organisation), but the number of comrades delegated to such functions means nothing in itself, because in principle no comrade should be alien to any of them.

It is a mere accident of history that, in the present phases, comrades working on the theory and history of the movement seem too many, while those prepared for action seem too few. It would be senseless to try to determine how many comrades should be occupied in one activity or another. We are all aware that when the situation becomes radical innumerable elements will flock to our side immediately and instinctively, without having had to obtain any academic diplomas along the way.

10. We are conscious of the fact that, ever since Marx's fight against Bakunin, Proudhon and Lassalle, and in all subsequent phases of opportunist infection, the danger of degeneration has always been tied to the influence of petty-bourgeois false allies on the proletariat.

Our infinite distrust of the contribution of these social strata must not and cannot prevent us, following the monumental lessons of history, from utilising some of their exceptional elements that the party will employ in restoring the theory, without which we would be dead and which must be disseminated in the future throughout the revolutionary masses.

11. The high-voltage discharges that have leapt from the poles of our dialectic have taught us that the comrade, the communist and revolutionary militant, is someone who has been able to forget, renounce, free his spirit and soul from the classification in which the civil state of this putrefying society has placed him. The comrade is someone who sees himself and integrates himself into the age-old perspective that unites our tribal ancestors fighting against wild animals with the members of the future community, living in the fraternity and joyful harmony of social humanity.

12. *Historical party and formal party.* Marx and Engels, who drew this distinction, had no need to be in a formal party, and they correctly concluded that their work placed them in the line of the historical party. This does not mean that any militant today has the right to choose to be in line with the 'historical party' while snubbing the formal party – and not because Marx and Engels were supermen of a distinct kind or race, but precisely because of the sound intelligence of their position, both dialectically and historically.

Marx says: The party *in its historical sense*, and the *formal* or *ephemeral party*. The first notion implies continuity, and has given rise to our distinctive thesis of the invariance of the doctrine since Marx formulated it, not as an invention of genius but as a discovery of a result of human evolution. But there is no metaphysical opposition between these two notions, and it would be foolish to express them in a formula such as: I turn my back on the formal and move towards the historical party.

When we deduce from our invariant doctrine that the revolutionary victory of the working class can only be achieved through the class party and *its* dictatorship and, guided by Marx's own words, we affirm that before the existence of the revolutionary and communist party the proletariat might be a class for bourgeois science, but certainly not for Marx or for us, we cannot but draw the following conclusion: to achieve victory it will be necessary to have a party worthy of being called both historical party and formal party. In other words, there will have to be a resolution in the reality of action of the apparent contradiction, which has dominated a long and difficult past, between the historical party, which regards *content* (the invariant historical programme), and the contingent party, which regards *form*, acting as the force and physical practice of a decisive part of the fighting proletariat.

This synthetic restatement of the doctrinal question must also be applied to past historical transformations.

13. With the founding of the First International in 1864 the collection of small groups and leagues that grew out of workers struggles was transformed for the first time into the International party stipulated by the doctrine. This is not the place to recapitulate the history of the crisis of that International, which Marx took the lead in defending against the infiltration of petty-bourgeois programmes, such as libertarianism.

The Second International was reconstituted in 1889, after Marx' death, but under Engels' control, although his instructions were not always heeded. For a time, the formal party tended to represent the continuity of the historical party, but the bond was broken in subsequent years by the International's federalist, non-centralist system, by the influence of parliamentary practice and the cult of democracy, and by the nationalist outlook of certain sections, which no longer saw themselves as armies at war with their own states, as the Communist Manifesto had indicated. An overt revisionism appeared, depreciating the historical objective and exalting the contingent, formal movement.

When the Third International arose after the disastrous failure of 1914, when almost all the sections fell into pure democratism and nationalism, we saw it in the years immediately following 1919 as a complete convergence of the historical party with the formal party once again. The new International was declaredly centralist and anti-democratic, but the historical process by which the federated sections of the failed International were integrated into the new organisations was particularly difficult, and was hastened by the immediate concern to extend the conquest of power in Russia to the other European countries.

The section that formed in Italy on the ruins of the old party of the Second International was especially quick to grasp the necessity of welding the historical movement to its momentary form not because of the merits of any individuals, but for historical reasons. It had waged determined struggles against the degenerate forms, resisting infiltration not only by currents infected with nationalism, parliamentarism and democratism, but also by currents (such as maximalism in Italy) that allowed themselves to be influenced by anarcho-syndicalist petty-bourgeois revolutionism. This Left current fought especially hard to make the conditions of admission rigorous (construction of the new formal structure). It applied them fully in Italy, and when they yielded dubious results in France and Germany, it was the first to point out the danger for the entire International.

The historical situation, in which a proletarian State had been built in just one country while in the others power had not yet been conquered, made difficult the clear *organic* solution of leaving the helm of the world organisation to the Russian section.

The Left was the first to realise that any signs of deviation in the internal economy and international relations of the Russian state would give rise to a discrepancy between the policy of the historical party, that is, of revolutionary communists all over the world, and the policy of a formal party defending the interests of the contingent Russian state.

14. Since then this abyss has been dug so deeply that the 'apparent' sections, dependent on the Russian leading party, pursue (in the ephemeral sense) a vulgar policy of collaboration with the bourgeoisie, which is no better than the traditional politics of the parties corrupted by the Second International.

This gives the groups that stem from the struggle of the Italian Left against the degeneration of Moscow the possibility – we will not say the right – of understanding better than anyone else the path on which the true, active, and therefore formal party can continue to adhere fully to the characteristics of the revolutionary historical party. This party has existed potentially since 1847, while in practice it asserted itself in great historical gashes through the revolution's tragic series of defeats.

To effect the transition from this undistorted tradition to an effort to create a new organisation of the international party without historical rupture, it is not possible to organise on the basis of a selection of especially qualified individuals versed in the historical doctrine. Organically, and in the most faithful way possible, we must follow the line between the action of the group in which the tradition manifested itself forty years ago and the current line.

The new movement cannot expect any supermen, nor will it have a Messiah, but must be founded on a reviving of what has been preserved over a long period of time. This process is not restricted to the teaching of theses or the search for documents, but also makes use of living instruments to form an old guard capable of transmitting its mandate, uncorrupted and powerful, to a young guard preparing itself for new revolutions that will perhaps require only ten years before they appear on the stage of history. The names of these militants, young and old, is of no consequence to the party and to the revolution.

Transmitting this tradition correctly from generation to generation (the names of the living and dead actors matters little) means not only transmitting critical texts and using the doctrine of the communist party in a manner faithful to the classics. It also means joining the class battle that the Marxist Left (we don't confine ourselves to Italy alone) waged in the fierce struggle that followed the events of 1919, and which was broken less by the power relations with the enemy class than by the bond that subordinated it to a centre degenerating from that of the historical world party to that of an ephemeral party infected with opportunism, on the way to its definitive historical breakdown.

Without abandoning the principle of centralised world discipline, the Left attempted to wage at least a defensive revolutionary battle to save the proletarian vanguard from collusion with intermediate strata and their defeat-prone parties and ideologies. When we were deprived of the historical possibility of saving, if not the revolution, at least the core of its historical party, we were forced to resume our work, in the present objective situation of total paralysis, with a proletariat deeply infected by petty-bourgeois democratism. But this nascent organisation, utilising all the doctrinal tradition and practice confirmed by the historical verification of our predictions, also applies this tradition to its daily activity, striving to re-establish contact on an ever-widening scale with the exploited masses. It purges its structure of one of the initial errors of the Moscow International by doing away with the thesis of democratic centralism and the use of voting mechanisms, just as it has eliminated any concession to democratic, pacifist, autonomist or libertarian positions from the mentality of every last member.

Annotated Bibliography of Bordiga's Writings

A complete Italian edition of Bordiga's work has yet to be published. Since 1996, however, Fondazione Bordiga (www.fondazionebordiga.org/chiSiamo.htm), has begun to publish his writings from the years 1911–26 (9 volumes). By 2019, the Fondazione has published eight volumes:

Bordiga, Amadeo. *Scritti 1911–1926*, edited by Luigi Gerosa.

Bordiga, Amadeo 1996. *Scritti 1911–1926. Dalla guerra di Libia al Congresso socialista di Ancona 1911–1914*, Vol. 1, Genoa. Graphos.

Bordiga, Amadeo 1998. *Scritti 1911–1926. La guerra, la rivoluzione russa e la nuova Internazionale 1914–1918*, Vol. 2, Genoa. Graphos.

Bordiga, Amadeo 2010. *Scritti 1911–1926. Lotte sociali e prospettive rivoluzionarie del dopoguerra 1918–1919*, Vol. 3, Formia: Fondazione Amadeo Bordiga.

Bordiga, Amadeo 2011. *Scritti 1911–1926. La frazione comunista del PSI e la Terza Internazionale 1920–1921*, Vol. 4, Formia: Fondazione Amadeo Bordiga.

Bordiga, Amadeo 2014. *Scritti 1911–1926. La fondazione del Partito Comunista d'Italia, Sezione della Terza Internazionale 1921*, Vol. 5, Formia: Fondazione Amadeo Bordiga.

Bordiga, Amadeo 2015. *Scritti 1911–1926. Di fronte al fascismo e alla socialdemocrazia. Il fronte unico proletario 1921–1922*, Vol. 6, Formia: Fondazione Amadeo Bordiga.

Bordiga, Amadeo 2017. *Scritti 1911–1926. Le 'Tesi di Roma' e i contrasti con l'Internazionale Comunista*, Vol. 7, Formia: Fondazione Amadeo Bordiga.

Bordiga, Amadeo 2019, *Scritti 1911–1926. La crisi della Internazionale Comunista e la nuova direzione del partito in Italia 1922–1924*, Vol. 8, Formia: Fondazione A. Bordiga.

We shall also refer to the following useful documentary research:

Gerosa, Luigi. 2006. *L'ingegnere 'fuori uso'. Vent'anni di battaglie urbanistiche di Amadeo Bordiga. Napoli 1946–1966*, Presentazione di Michele Fatica, Formia: Fondazione A. Bordiga.

Gerosa, Luigi. 2013. *Archivio della Fondazione Amadeo Bordiga. La biblioteca, la corrispondenza, le carte di argomento politico ed urbanistico di Amadeo Bordiga*, Formia: Fondazione A. Bordiga.

While Bordiga used to sign his works during the years 1911 to 1926, his postwar writings are anonymous except for the only interview he did:

Osser, Edek 1970. *Una intervista ad Amadeo Bordiga*, June, available at: http://www.fondazionebordiga.org/intervista.htm.

Bordiga's anonymity has gradually unravelled, so we can here refer without uncertainty to his most significant works from the years 1945 to 1966. They were mostly collected and published in volume after Bordiga's death by several 'Bordigist' organisations and tendencies, sometimes maintaining the anonymity, sometimes with Bordiga's name. Though Bordiga's name is not always mentioned, the attribution is certain, according to the most comprehensive bibliography of his works:

Peregalli, Arturo and Saggioro, Sandro (eds) 1995, *Amadeo Bordiga (1889–1970), Bibliografia*, Paderno Dugnano: Colibrì.

On Russia

Struttura economica e sociale della Russia d'oggi. 1976, Milan: Edizioni il programma comunista.

Dialogato con Stalin. 1975, Borbiago: Edizioni sociali.

Dialogato coi Morti. Il XX Congresso del Partito comunista russo. 1977, Rome: Sul Filo del Tempo.

Lezioni delle controrivoluzioni. 1981, Milan: Edizioni il programma comunista.

Russia e rivoluzione della teoria marxista. 1990, Milan: Edizioni il programma comunista.

On Late Capitalism

Bordiga, Amadeo 1976, *Economia marxista ed economia controrivoluzionaria*, Florence: Iskra (it includes a 1957 comment on Marx's *Grundisse*, the first ever in Italian).

Bordiga, Amadeo 1980, *Proprietà e capitale. Inquadramento nella dottrina marxista dei fenomeni del mondo sociale contemporaneo*, Florence: Iskra.

Bordiga, Amadeo 1982, *Imprese economiche di Pantalone. Intervento dello Stato nell'economia e nella società dal punto di vista del marxismo rivoluzionario*, Florence: Iskra.

America. 1992, Turin: Editing.

Vae Victis Germania! 1994, Turin: Editing.

On Democracy and State Repression

Lebbra dell'illegalismo bastardo, superstizione riformista e democrazia blindata. 1995, Turin: Editing (also includes Bordiga's 1923 'self-representation').

On the Agrarian Question and the Nature-Capital Relationship

Bordiga, Amadeo 1978, *Drammi gialli e sinistri della moderna decadenza sociale*, Milan: Iskra.

Bordiga, Amadeo 1979, *Mai la merce sfamerà l'uomo*, Florence: Iskra.

La questione agraria. 1992, Turin: Editing.

On the Fight against Colonialism

Bordiga, Amadeo 1976, *I fattori di razza e nazione nella teoria marxista*, Florence: Iskra.

La dottrina dei modi di produzione. Le lotte di classi e di stati nel mondo dei popoli non bianchi, storico campo vitale per la critica rivoluzionaria marxista. 1995, Turin: Editing.

On Communism

Bordiga, Amadeo 1972, *Testi sul comunismo*, Naples: La Vecchia Talpa (also includes a 1959 comment on *Oekonomisch-philosophische Manuskripte aus dem Jahre 1844*).

Dall'economia capitalistica al comunismo. 1995, Turin: Editing (also includes two works from the Twenties).

On the History of Italian Communist Left

Storia della Sinistra comunista 1912–1919. 1964, Milan: Edizioni il programma comunista.

La sinistra comunista in Italia sulla linea marxista di Lenin. 1964, Milan: Edizioni il programma comunista.

In difesa della continuità del programma comunista. 1970, Milan: Edizioni il programma comunista 1970 (also includes Rome Theses, the Theses on International's tactics and Lyons Theses).

Storia della sinistra comunista. Comunismo e fascismo. 1992, Turin: Editing.

On the 'Reconquest' of Revolutionary Marxism

Per l'organica sistemazione dei principi comunisti. 1973, Milan: Edizioni il programma comunista.

Tracciato di impostazione. I fondamenti del comunismo rivoluzionario. 1974, Milan: Edizioni il programma comunista.

Forza, violenza, dittatura di classe. 1975, Milan: Edizioni il programma comunista.

L'assalto del dubbio revisionista ai fondamenti della teoria rivoluzionaria marxista. 1992, Turin: Editing.

Il battilocchio nella storia. Contro la concezione della storia come opera della volontà di individui e di capi geniali o criminali. 1992, Turin: Editing.

The following websites provide the English version of several Bordiga's writings. Translations are not always of the highest quality as Bordiga's writing style is often challenging:

Historical Archives of 'Italian' Communist Left: http://www.quinterna.org/lingue/engli sh/historical_en/o_historical_archives.htm

International Communist Party – Publications in the English language: http://www .international-communist-party.org/EnglishPublications.htm

Amadeo Bordiga Archive 1889–1970: http://www.marxists.org/archive/bordiga/index .htm

Bordiga Archive: http://www.reocities.com/CapitolHill/lobby/3909/bordigao.html

Many of the writings published in the above-mentioned websites are anonymous.

Annotated Bibliography on Bordiga in Italian

Fatica, Michele 1971, *Origini del fascismo e del comunismo a Napoli (1911–1915)*, Florence: La Nuova Italia.

A fundamental study of the 'local' context of Bordiga's early formation and political activity: Naples at the beginning of the twentieth century, in its economic, social and political evolution. The author argues that the metropolis is of extreme interest 'because the first Italian international-communist vanguard was born there'; its theoretical contribution marked a qualitative leap with regard to the ideological heritage of the Italian Socialist Party, linking up the young Neapolitan proletariat to the wider national and international class. Particular attention is paid to the maturing of Bordiga's anti-militarism and to the opposition between the social patriotism of the Second International and Bordiga's new revolutionary proletarian internationalism. Some of Bordiga's youthful writings are contained in an appendix.

De Clementi, Andreina 1971, *Amadeo Bordiga*, Turin: Einaudi.

In Europe, the author argues, the Bordighian experience 'presents the greatest similarities with that of the Bolsheviks', even before Bordiga's involvement in the activity of the Communist International; it also captures best the differences between the revolution in Russia and the revolution in Western Europe. Bordiga's weak point was the gap between his rigorous theoretical-programmatic elaboration and the inadequacy of his instruments for analysing the social-economic reality and political developments of his time. In the struggle against Stalinism, however, 'the figure of Bordiga clearly stands out, rising even above that of Trotsky'.

De Felice, Franco 1971, *Serrati, Bordiga, Gramsci e il problema della rivoluzione in Italia*, Bari: De Donato.

In official PCI historiography, this is the most penetrating critique of Bordiga's conception of the revolutionary process. Bordiga, the author argues, attributed a 'secondary' role to mass initiative in relation to the party; he kept party and class exaggeratedly separate and paid little attention to actual processes or the 'concrete analysis of concrete situations', especially the experiences undergone by the masses. From this stems his 'incapacity to conduct politics', to intervene actively in given situations. On the other hand, Bordiga's practice demonstrates greater flexibility than is to be found in his writings.

Damen, Onorato 1971, *Bordiga fuori dal mito*, Milan: Editoriale Periodici Italiani.

The author, a valiant internationalist militant from the beginning, reproaches Bordiga for a 'mathematical vice' that led him to subordinate historical events to 'the calculus of probability'. In particular, he hesitated too long to break with the PSI after the First World War; he remained silent in the 1920s and 1930s in the face of such 'colossal events' as the insurrection of the Spanish proletariat, the outbreak of war and the end of the International; and he was late to recognise the existence of state capitalism in Russia after the Second World War. Damen is also sharply critical of the 'Programma comunista' experience in the 1950s and 1960s: 'a sect consisting of people who repeated standard, not always digested, formulas', in relation to which Bordiga played the role of 'theoretical leaderism'. According to Damen's point of view, Bordiga suffered from an 'inferiority complex' with regard to the Third International, remaining trapped beneath its rubble.

Montaldi, Danilo 1975, *Korsch e i comunisti italiani*, Rome: Savelli.

This short, intense essay takes its cue from the exchange of letters between Korsch and Bordiga in 1926, criticising the tendency of PCI historians to suggest grotesque or simplistic identifications such as a closeness between Bordiga and Stalin or between Gramsci and Korsch (in De Felice's case). The author defends Bordiga against the charge of sectarianism amid the events of 1925–26 and attributes to him a vision of the International that is 'anything but arid' or 'scholastic' – a defect that he locates, rather, in 'Kommunistische Politik'.

Livorsi, Franco 1976, *Amadeo Bordiga*, Rome: Editori Riuniti.

Livorsi is the first, and until now the only, researcher belonging to the PCI to have proposed 'studying Bordiga in the same way that – as far as I know – Bukharin, Rosa Luxemburg and Kautsky are now studied': that is, without being guided by an obligation to demonise him. He is also one of the very few scholars who have seriously taken account of Amadeo Bordiga's theoretical activity in the 1950s and 1960s. His argument is that there is a radical contradiction between, on the one hand, the force and validity of Bordiga's theoretical elaboration on central questions such as 'the alleged degeneration of the USSR and the Communist International' or 'the mechanism of the current social-economic crises in the capitalist West', and, on the other hand, the weakness and falseness of his proposed political solutions, which bear the marks of 'infantile extremist or even reactionary aspects', of hyper-sectarianism, rejection of alliance tactics, and at the least a schematic vision of democracy. Bordiga appears here, then, as a good diagnostician but a bad therapist, and in an assessment of his actions 'the pros and cons [...] are encapsulated in almost perfect symmetry'. Livorsi has also edited a collection of Bordiga's writings: *Scritti scelti*. Milan: Feltrinelli, 1975.

Grilli, Liliana 1982, *Amadeo Bordiga: capitalismo sovietico e comunismo*, Milan: La Pietra.

An excellent account of Bordiga's theoretical reflection after the Second World War on the social-economic structure of the USSR and the distinguishing features of socialist society in Marx's thought. The author stresses how Bordiga demystified the ostensibly socialist character of the USSR at the very height of the myth; he followed a materialist method that made no concessions to personalist interpretations of Stalinism, concentrating on the economic laws operating in the USSR and on the persistence there – at least beneath the mantle of statisation – of the categories of commodity, money, wage and enterprise that Marx used to describe the capitalist economy. Bordiga, she concludes, is 'the revolutionary communist theorist most contemporary to us today, indeed in advance of our times'.

Peregalli, Arturo and Saggioro, Sandro 1998, *Amadeo Bordiga (1889–1970). Bibliografia*, Paderno Dugnano: Colibrì.

A priceless, indispensable working tool, given that Bordiga's vast output up to 1926 included many anonymous texts and, after the Second World War, appeared only in an anonymous form that he elevated to a key principle in the life of a healthy communist organisation. The authors do not claim to have compiled a 'complete and exhaustive bibliography'; they explain the doubts and uncertainties they had to confront, but rightly point to the usefulness and value of the task and the special worth of Bordiga's production after the Second World War, which has been buried beneath 'a mountain of darkness and silence'. The work also lists books containing writings by Bordiga, as well as books, articles, studies and graduate and doctoral theses concerning his activity and thought.

Peregalli, Arturo and Saggioro, Sandro 1998, *Amadeo Bordiga. La sconfitta e gli anni oscuri (1926–1945)*, Paderno Dugnano: Colibrì.

This study starts with a reconstruction of the final, dual defeat that Bordiga suffered in 1926 in the space of a few weeks, from the Lyons Congress of the

Communist Party of Italy (at the hands of the centrist group around Gramsci) to the Sixth Enlarged Executive Committee in Moscow (at the hands of Stalin and the Comintern leadership). It then documents Bordiga's life and activity between prison and confinement, from the end of 1926 to March 1930, when he was expelled from the PCI; it considers his obstinate and hard-to-fathom refusal to maintain stable relations with other comrades of the Left in exile in France, Belgium and elsewhere. Peregalli and Saggioro also dwell on Bordiga's 'heterodox views' on the Second World War, when he said that, unless the revolution returned, the defeat of the strongest, democratic imperialisms would be preferable, since it would not allow a durable stabilisation of capitalism. In relation to these views, the leaders of the PCI – 'who from 1939 to 1941 [...] had openly acclaimed Hitler's victories' – launched a violent campaign against Bordiga. The text also contains some information about the lasting friendship between Bordiga and Gramsci, who, as chance would have it, happened to meet in Formia between 1934 and 1935.

Cortesi, Luigi (ed.) 1999, *Amadeo Bordiga nella storia del comunismo*, Naples: Edizioni Scientifiche Italiane.

This work is the result of a research meeting held in Bologna in June 1996 on the initiative of the 'Potlash Informal Group'; it brought together some of the most meticulous scholars of Bordiga's work (Cortesi, Fatica, Peregalli, Grilli, Gerosa) and set itself the aim of defining Bordiga's place within the history of the communist movement. For Luigi Cortesi, the editor, the Bordiga of the period after the First World War was a political leader of great stature, who was able to foresee the defeat of the newly ascendant Bolshevism, but who, like the rest of left-wing anti-Stalinism, was not capable of 'providing new strategic directions and gathering the necessary forces' for effective resistance to the rise of Stalinism. To this, Cortesi directly counterposes the 'oracular, sectarian' Bordiga of the final period of his life, although his merits are recognised, in different ways, in the contributions of Grilli and Di Matteo.

Gerosa, Luigi 2006, *L'ingegnere 'fuori uso'. Vent'anni di battaglie urbanistiche di Amadeo Bordiga. Napoli 1946–1966*, Presentazione di Michele Fatica, Formia: Fondazione Amadeo Bordiga.

Luigi Gerosa accurately reconstructs Bordiga's twenty years at the Naples engineering and architectural college, where 'with great civil courage and technical competence' he subjected 'the disastrous Neapolitan urbanistic policy [to] a radical exposure that was in many ways prescient and far more timely than the high-profile efforts of others in this regard'. His activity there cannot be separated from the political activity of the Neapolitan communist. The author even hypothesises that in Bordiga's work 'the critique of modern city planning and the observation of its real dynamic' played a role analogous to that of the critique of political economy in Marx's work.

Saggioro, Sandro 2010, *Né con Truman, né con Stalin. Storia del Partito Comunista Internazionalista (1942–1952)*, Paderno Dugnano: Colibrì.

The Internationalist Communist Party came into being in the course of the Second World War, in the (mistaken) perspective that what happened in and after 1917 might repeat itself. Bordiga believed otherwise, as the author documents, holding that revolution was not imminent and that it was not appropriate to build a party; he also thought the material produced in the early phases of the party's life was 'dreadfully confusionist'. Nevertheless, he let himself be increasingly drawn into the twists and turns of this organisation, which in 1952 split for reasons that remain unclear. The opposition between Bordiga/Maffi and Damen can only partly be summed up in the formulation: determinism/wait-and-see against voluntarism/activism, but the author does not give sufficient elements for an adequate reconstruction of the positions of the various groups and comrades.

Erba, Dino 2012, *Nascita e morte di un partito rivoluzionario. Il Partito Comunista Internazionalista 1943–1952*, Milan: All'Insegna del Gatto Rosso.

In the view of Alessandro Mantovani (which I share), the great merit of this book is to have demonstrated that 'the Internationalist Communist Party was originally by no means a purist sect isolated from the masses, but on the contrary a combat organisation rooted in the proletariat and the struggles of the period'. Evidence of this comes from extremely rich documentation. According to the author, the main reason for the demise of the organisation should be sought in the powerful cyclical economic upturn driven by the Marshall Plan and postwar reconstruction. But he also shows how both of the two tendencies in the party, led by Bordiga and Damen, 'had a rather nebulous conception of the period then under way' in Italy and the rest of Europe, as well as internationally (with the rise of national liberation movements, for example).

Basile, Corrado and Leni, Alessandro 2014, *Amadeo Bordiga politico. Dalle lotte proletarie del primo dopoguerra alla fine degli anni Sessanta*, Paderno Dugnano: Colibrì.

Bordigism, the authors argue, was nothing other than 'a left variant (certainly more coherent and worthy of respect) of the old socialist intransigentism', which they counterpose to Bolshevism because of the latter's ability to confront 'the complex problems of the class struggle'. They fault Bordiga with having foregrounded the struggle against social democracy, and thus with having persistently underestimated the Fascist danger and inadequately applied the united front tactic 'without a precise plan'. The authors' approach largely takes up again the criticisms that Angelo Tasca made of Bordiga.

Gerosa, Luigi 2013, *Archivio della Fondazione Amadeo Bordiga*, Formia: Fondazione Amadeo Bordiga.

This substantial volume minutely describes the library, correspondence and papers detailing arguments on political questions and urbanistic issues that belonged to Bordiga, and which are now at the disposal of the Amadeo Bordiga Foundation. (In her lifetime, his second wife Antonietta De Meo refused to hand them over to the Feltrinelli Foundation, which was seeking to acquire them.) Gerosa's introductory essay is most interesting, partly because it gives us an idea of the intense labours that went into the publication of *Programma comunista* in the 1950s and 1960s (the correspondence between Bordiga and the twenty or so steady contributors to the work of the journal amounts to 3,400 letters), but also because it critically re-examines some of Bordiga's postwar *idées fixes*, such as the anonymity and invariance of Marxist theory. The book also contains the bitter letter of 28 March 1966 to Bruno Maffi, in which Bordiga, noting 'my and your failure' to found an organisation capable of keeping on 'the right path' without his constant directives and rebukes, decides to end all 'direct and indirect communication' with Maffi and the other comrades.

Saggioro, Sandro 2014, *In attesa della grande crisi. Storia del Partito Comunista Internazionale 'il programma comunista' (dal 1952 al 1982)*, Paderno Dugnano: Colibrì.

'The aim here is to brush up all the terms of class struggle theory relating to determinant causes, agencies and relationships of force', wrote Bordiga in a letter of 13 June 1948 to a small group of comrades. This work of Saggioro's refers precisely to the 'tireless activity' in which Bordiga was taken up from the end of the war until the day in June 1966 when a stroke robbed him of his strength. It should be mentioned, however, that the contents of the book do not match the title, since very little is said about Bordiga's research activity and theoretical formation, or about the great importance that the certainty of a great crisis ahead in the mid-1970s had in the life of 'Programma comunista' and Bordiga's work of elaboration. In fact, a large part of the book is devoted to the continuous bitter and divisive disputes in the organisation that would eventually blow it apart in 1982. The text concludes with a documentary appendix containing *inter alia* Bordiga's correspondence with Bruno Rizzi, and his unfortunate piece of April 1968, one of his last, on the student movement.

Savant, Giovanna 2017, *Bordiga, Gramsci e la Grande Guerra (1914–1920)*, Naples: La Città del Sole.

Many years after the publication of De Felice's study, this work directly compares and contrasts Bordiga and Gramsci with each other in relation to the Great War. It does so without fully taking Gramsci's side, as De Felice did. The author conveys the lucidity with which Bordiga identified the nexus of militarism and democracy, 'completely absent from Gramsci's thought', and saw Wilson as the most dangerous adversary for socialists. But she finds fault with his absolute counterposition of democracy and socialism, and with his lack of interest in 'the fierce disputes within capitalist strata and the effects they may have on the development of the class struggle'. The contradictory picture of Bordiga that emerges from these pages is of an 'extraordinary political organiser, courageous agitator and caustic polemicist' (to quote Frosini's preface) but also of a man largely lacking confidence in relation to the working class.

References

Anderson, Perry 1976, 'The Antinomies of Antonio Gramsci', *New Left Review*, I/100.

Archivio della Fondazione Amadeo Bordiga. La biblioteca, la corrispondenza, le carte di argomento politico ed urbanistico di Amadeo Bordiga 2013, Formia: Fondazione A. Bordiga.

Arfé, Gaetano 1977, *Storia del socialismo italiano*, Milan: Mondadori.

Basile, Corrado and Alessandro Leni 2014, *Amadeo Bordiga politico*, Paderno Dugnano (Mi): Colibrì.

'Bilan' 1979, *Contre-révolution en Espagne 1936/1939*, 10/18, Paris: Union Générale d'Editions.

Bongiovanni, Bruno (ed.) 1975, *L'antistalinismo di sinistra e la natura sociale dell'Urss*, Milan: Feltrinelli.

Bordiga, Amadeo 1972 [1964], *Storia della sinistra comunista*, Vol. 1, Milan: Edizioni il programma comunista.

Bordiga, Amadeo 1972, *Testi sul comunismo*, [prefazione di J. Camatte] Naples: La Vecchia Talpa.

Bordiga, Amadeo 1973 [1960], *L'estremismo malattia infantile del comunismo, condanna dei futuri rinnegati*, Milan: Edizioni il programma comunista.

Bordiga, Amadeo 1975, *Dialogato con Stalin*, Borbiago: Edizioni sociali.

Bordiga, Amadeo 1976a, *Struttura economica e sociale della Russia di oggi*, Milan: Edizioni il programma comunista.

Bordiga, Amadeo 1976b, *Economia marxista ed economia controrivoluzionaria*, Milan: Iskra.

Bordiga, Amadeo 1976c, *I fattori di razza e nazione nella teoria marxista*, Milan: Iskra.

Bordiga, Amadeo 1977, *Dialogato coi Morti. Il xx Congresso del Partito comunista russo*, Rome: Il filo del tempo.

Bordiga, Amadeo 1978, *Drammi gialli e sinistri della moderna decadenza sociale*, Florence: Iskra.

Bordiga, Amadeo 1979, *Mai la merce sfamerà l'uomo (la questione agraria e la teoria della rendita fondiaria secondo Marx)*, Florence: Iskra.

Bordiga, Amadeo 1980, *Proprietà e capitale. Inquadramento nella dottrina marxista dei fenomeni del mondo sociale contemporaneo*, Florence: Iskra.

Bordiga, Amadeo 1982, *Imprese economiche di Pantalone. L'intervento dello stato nell'economia e nella società dal punto di vista del marxismo rivoluzionario*, Florence: Iskra.

Bordiga, Amadeo 1990, *Russia e rivoluzione nella teoria marxista*, Milan: Edizioni il programma comunista.

[Bordiga, Amadeo] 1992, *America*, Turin: Editing.

Bordiga, Amadeo 1996, *Scritti 1911–1926, Dalla guerra di Libia al Congresso socialista di Ancona 1911–1914*, Vol. 1, Genoa: Graphos.

Bordiga, Amadeo 1998, *Scritti 1911–1926. La guerra, la rivoluzione russa e la nuova Internazionale 1914–1918*, Vol. 2, Genoa: Graphos.

Bordiga, Amadeo 2010, *Scritti 1911–1926. Lotte sociali e prospettive rivoluzionarie del dopoguerra 1918–1919*, Vol. 3, Milan: Fondazione A. Bordiga.

Bordiga, Amadeo 2011, *Scritti 1911–1926. La Frazione comunista del PSI e la Terza Internazionale 1920–1921*, Vol. 4, Formia: Fondazione A. Bordiga.

Bordiga, Amadeo 2014, *Scritti 1911–1926. La fondazione del Partito Comunista d'Italia, Sezione della Terza Internazionale*, Vol. 5, Formia: Fondazione A. Bordiga.

Bordiga, Amadeo 2015, *Scritti 1911–1926. Di fronte al fascismo e alla socialdemocrazia. Il fronte unico proletario 1921–1922*, Vol. 6, Formia: Fondazione A. Bordiga.

Bordiga, Amadeo 2017, *Scritti 1911–1926. Le 'Tesi di Roma' e i contrasti con l'Internazionale Comunista*, Vol. 7, Formia: Fondazione A. Bordiga.

Bordiga, Amadeo 2019, *Scritti 1911–1926. La crisi della Internazionale Comunista e la nuova direzione del partito in Italia 1922–1924*, Vol. 8, Formia: Fondazione A. Bordiga.

Bourrinet, Philippe 2016, *The 'Bordigist' Current (1912–1952). Italy, France, Belgium, USA*, https://libcom.org/history/bordigist-current-1912-1952-italy-france-belgium-usa-philippe-bourrinet.

Broder, David 2013, 'Bordiga and the Fate of Bordigism', *Weekly Worker*, 19 December.

Broué, Pierre 2005, *The German Revolution, 1917–1923*, Leiden: Brill.

Buick, Adam 1987, 'Bordigism', in M. Rubel and J. Crump (eds), *Non-Market Socialism in the Nineteenth and Twentieth Centuries*, Basingstoke: Macmillan.

[Camatte, Jacques] 1972, *Bordiga e la passione del comunismo*, Introduction to Bordiga A., *Testi sul comunismo*, Naples: La vecchia talpa.

Camatte, Jacques 1978, *Verso la comunità umana*, Milan: Jaca Book.

Caprioglio, Sergio 1962, 'Un mancato incontro Gramsci-D'Annunzio nell'aprile del 1921', *Rivista storica del socialismo*, 5, Nos. 15–16: 263–74.

Carr, E.H. 1954, *The Interregnum 1923–1924*, London: Macmillan & Co.

Carr, E.H. 1978, *A History of Soviet Russia*, Vol. 3: *Socialism in One Country 1924–1926*, Part One, London: Macmillan.

Castronovo, Valerio 1975, 'La storia economica', in *Storia d'Italia. Dall'unità a oggi*, Vol. IV, Turin: Einaudi.

Chiaradia, J.E. 1972, *The Spectral Figure of Amadeo Bordiga: A Case Study in the Decline of Marxism in the West, 1912–1926*, PhD thesis, New York University.

Chiaradia, J.E. 2001, *Amadeo Bordiga and the Myth of Antonio Gramsci*, available at: https://libcom.org/library/amadeo-bordiga-myth-antonio-gramsci-john-chiaradia.

Ciferri, Elvio 2009, 'Bordiga Amadeo and the Italian Communist Party', in *International Encyclopedia of Revolution and Protest*, Vol. 2, Malden: Wiley-Blackwell.

Corrente comunista internazionale 1984, *La sinistra comunista italiana 1927–1952*, Naples.

Cortesi, Luigi 1975, 'Palmiro Togliatti, la "svolta di Salerno" e l'eredità gramsciana', *Belfagor*, 31 January: 1–44.

Cortesi, Luigi (ed.) 1999, *Amadeo Bordiga nella storia del comunismo*, Naples: Edizioni Scientifiche Italiane, Naples.

Damen, Onorato 2011, *Bordiga au-delà du 'mythe'. Validité et limites d'une expérience révolutionnaire*, Milan: Éditions Prometeo.

Dauvé, Gilles 2009, *Notes on Trotsky, Pannekoek, Bordiga*, www.libcom.org

De Benedetti, Augusto 1974, *La classe operaia a Napoli nel primo dopoguerra*, Naples: Guida.

De Clementi, Andreina 1971, *Amadeo Bordiga*, Turin: Einaudi.

De Felice, Franco 1971, *Serrati, Bordiga, Gramsci e il problema della rivoluzione in Italia 1919–1920*, Bari: De Donato.

De Felice, Renzo 1972, *Le interpretazioni del fascismo*, Bari: Laterza.

Degras, Jane (ed.) 1956, *The Communist International. Documents 1919–1943*, Vol. 1, Oxford: Oxford University Press.

Drake, Richard 2003, *Apostles and Agitators: Italy's Marxist Revolutionary Tradition*, Cambridge, MA: Harvard University Press.

Engels, Friedrich 1978, 'The Peasant War in Germany', in *Marx Engels Collected Works*, Vol. 10, London: Lawrence & Wishart.

Engels, Friedrich 1990, 'The Peasant Question in France and Germany', in *Marx Engels Collected Works*, Vol. 27, London: Lawrence and Wishart.

Erba, Dino 2008, *La leggenda nera degli Arditi del Popolo. Una messa a punto storiografica*, Milan: All'Insegna del Gatto Rosso.

Erba, Dino 2012, *Nascita e morte di un partito rivoluzionario. Il partito comunista internazionalista 1943–1952*, Milan: All'Insegna del Gatto Rosso.

Fatica, Michele 1971, *Origini del fascismo e del comunismo a Napoli (1911–1915)*, Florence: La Nuova Italia.

Frazione di Sinistra e Trotzkij: 1927–1936, 'Partito e classe' November 1978, Cividale: Nucleo comunista internazionalista.

Galli, Giorgio 1976, *Storia del Partito Comunista Italiano*, Milan: Edizioni Il Formichiere.

Gerosa, Luigi and Michele Fatica 2006, *L'ingegnere 'fuori uso'. Vent'anni di battaglie urbanistiche di Amadeo Bordiga – Napoli 1946–1966*, Formia: Fondazione Amadeo Bordiga.

Goldner, Loren 1995, 'Amadeo Bordiga, the Agrarian Question and the International Revolutionary Movement', *Critique: Journal of Socialist Theory*, 23, No. 1: 73–100.

Gramsci, Antonio 1971, *La costruzione del Partito comunista 1923–1926*, Turin: Einaudi.

Gramsci, Antonio 1972, *Scritti politici*, Rome: Editori Riuniti.

Gramsci, Antonio 1978, *Selections from Political Writings, 1921–1926*, London: Lawrence & Wishart.

Gramsci, Antonio 1979, *Pre-Prison Writings*, Cambridge: Cambridge University Press.

Grilli, Liliana 1982, *Amadeo Bordiga: capitalismo sovietico e comunismo*, Milan: La Pietra.

Hajek, Milos 1972, *Storia dell'Internazionale comunista (1921–1935). La politica del fronte unico*, Rome: Editori Riuniti.

Hajek, Milos 1980, 'La discussione sul fronte unico e la rivoluzione mancata in Germania', in *Storia del marxismo. Il marxismo nell'età della Terza Internazionale*, Vol. 3, I, Turin: Einaudi pp. 441–463.

Il corso del capitalismo mondiale nell'esperienza storica e nella dottrina di Marx 1750–1990 1991, Florence: Edizioni 'Il Partito Comunista'.

Il processo ai comunisti italiani 1924, Rome: Libreria editrice del PCI.

In difesa della continuità del programma comunista 1970, Florence: Edizioni il programma comunista.

Isaacs, Harold R. 1961, *The Tragedy of the Chinese Revolution*, Palo Alto, CA: Stanford Junior University.

La frazione comunista al convegno di Imola 1971, Rome: Editori Riuniti.

La guerra di Spagna 2000, Ariano Irpino: A. Schiavo Editore.

Lenin, V.I. 1965, *Collected Works*, Vol. 31, Moscow: Progress Publishers.

Lenin, V.I. 1966, 'Reply to P. Kievsky', in *Collected Works*, Vol. 23, Moscow: Progress Publishers.

Lenin, V.I. 1971a, *Imperialism, the Highest Stage of Capitalism*, in *Selected Works in One Volume*, New York: International Publishers.

Lenin, V.I. 1971b, *The State and Revolution*, in *Selected Works in One Volume*, New York: International Publishers.

Lenin, V.I. 1971c, *Lenin e l'Italia*, Moscow: Edizioni Progress.

Lenin, V.I. 1973, *Collected Works*, Vol. 33, Moscow: Progress Publishers.

Lenin, V.I. 1985, 'The Tax in Kind', in *Collected Works*, Vol. 32, Moscow: Progress Publishers.

Luxemburg, Rosa 1970, 'Mass Strike, the Party, and Trade Unions', in *Rosa Luxemburg Speaks*, edited by Mary Alice Waters, New York: Pathfinder Press.

Maione, Giuseppe 1975, *Il biennio rosso. Autonomia e spontaneità operaia nel 1919–1920*, Bologna: Il Mulino.

Manacorda, Gastone 1971, *Il movimento operaio italiano*, Rome: Ed. Riuniti.

Manifesti e altri documenti politici 1922, Rome: Libreria editrice del PCd'I.

Mantovani, Alessandro 2012a, *Note a margine di 'Nè con Truman né con Stalin'*, mimeo.

Mantovani, Alessandro 2012b, *Intorno alla storia del Partito comunista internazionalista di D. Erba. È tutta un'altra storia ... o forse no*, mimeo.

Mantovani, Alessandro 2016, *Insegna qualcosa la disgregazione del bordighismo? Commento a Benjamin Lalbat, 'Les bordiguistes sans Bordiga'*, mimeo.

Mantovani, Alessandro 2019, *Gli 'Arditi del popolo', il Partito comunista d'Italia e la questione della lotta armata (1921–1922)*. Prefazione di Marco Rossi, Milan: Pagine marxiste.

Martinelli, Renzo 1977, *Il Partito comunista d'Italia 1921–1926*, Rome: Editori Riuniti.

Marx, Karl 1973, *Grundrisse*, London: Penguin.

Marx, Karl 1976, *Capital*, Volume 1, London: Penguin.

Marx, Karl 1978, *Capital*, Volume 2, London: Penguin.

Marx, Karl 1991, *Capital*, Volume 3, London: Penguin.

Marx, Karl and Friedrich Engels 1972, *Scritti italiani*, edited by G. Bosio, Rome: Samonà e Savelli.

Marx, Karl and Friedrich Engels 1985, *The Communist Manifesto*, London: Penguin.

Marx, Karl and V.I. Lenin 1968, *The Civil War in France: The Paris Commune*, New York: International Publishers.

Mészáros, István 1995, *Beyond Capital*, London: Merlin Press.

Montaldi, Danilo 1975, *Korsch e i comunisti italiani*, Rome: Savelli.

Natoli, Claudio 1982, *La Terza Internazionale e il fascismo. 1919–1923. Proletariato di fabbrica e reazione industriale nel primo dopoguerra*, Rome: Editori Riuniti.

Negri, Antonio 1991, *Marx beyond Marx*, London: Pluto Press.

Nettlau, Max 1928, *Bakunin e L'Internazionale in Italia* (preface by E. Malatesta), Geneva: Edizione del Risveglio.

Nucleo comunista internazionalista (ed.) 2012, *Scritti sulla questione nazionale e coloniale nel secondo dopoguerra (raccolta di articoli tratti da 'il programma comunista')*, Stregna: Quikcopyservice.

Pannunzio, Guglielmo 1921, *Ciò che ho visto nella Russia bolscevica (giugno-settembre 1920)*, Turin: Libreria editrice dell'Alleanza Cooperativa Torinese.

Peregalli, Arturo and Sandro Saggioro 1998, *Amadeo Bordiga. La sconfitta e gli anni oscuri (1926–1945)*, Paderno Dugnano (Mi): Colibrì.

Perrone, Ottorino 1976, *La tattica del Comintern*, Borbiago: Edizioni sociali.

Popa, Adrian (ed.) 1972, *Processo al socialismo*, Rome: Edizioni del Borghese.

Prometeo, organo del Partito comunista internazionalista, 1943–1945 1995, Biella: Edizioni Elf.

Quaderni del Programma comunista 1980, *La crisi del 1926 nel partito e nell'Internazionale*, 4, April: 29–30.

Quaderni internazionalisti 1992, *Storia della sinistra. Comunismo e fascismo*, Turin: Editing.

Quaderni internazionalisti 1996, *La Sinistra e il Comitato d'intesa*, Turin: Editing.

Red Link 2006, *L'ONU e i 'signori della pace'*, Naples.

Riddell, John (ed.) 2012, *Toward the United Front: Proceedings of the Fourth Congress of the Communist International, 1922*, Chicago: Haymarket.

Riechers, Christian 1970, *Antonio Gramsci: Marxismus in Italien*, Frankfurt/Main: Europäische Verlaganstalt.

Rosmer, Alfred 2016, *Lenin's Moscow*, Chicago: Haymarket.

Rosdolsky, Roman 1977, *The Making of Marx's 'Capital'*, Vol. 2, London: Pluto Press.

Saggioro, Sandro 2010, *Né con Truman né con Stalin. Storia del Partito Comunista Internazionalista (1942–1952)*, Paderno Dugnano: Edizioni Colibrì.

Saggioro, Sandro 2014, *In attesa della grande crisi. Storia del Partito Comunista Internazionale 'il programma comunista' (dal 1952 al 1982)*, Paderno Dugnano: Edizioni Colibrì.

Salvadori, Massimo 1973, *Gramsci e il problema storico della democrazia*, Rome: Einaudi.

Širinja, Kirill 1970, 'Lenin e la formazione del PCI', *Critica marxista* 8, No. 6: 107–29.

Souzo [Leonetti, Alfonso], *Bordiguisme et Trotskysme*, 'La lutte de classe', 15 mars 1932, No. 36.

Spengler, J.J. 1954, 'Welfare Economics and the Problem of Overpopulation', *Scientia*, 89: 128–38.

Spriano, Paolo 1976, *Storia del Partito comunista italiano. Da Bordiga a Gramsci*, Vol. I, Turin: Einaudi.

Stalin, Joseph 1972, *Economic Problems of Socialism in the USSR*, Beijing: Foreign Languages Press.

Storia della sinistra comunista. Dal luglio 1921 al maggio 1922 1997, Vol. IV, Milan: Edizioni il programma comunista.

Tasca, Angelo 1972, *Nascita e avvento del fascismo*, Bari: Laterza.

Through Fascism, War and Revolution: Trotskyism and Left Communism in Italy, 'Revolutionary History', Spring 1995, Vol. 5, No. 4.

Togliatti, Palmiro 1953, *Conversando con Togliatti. Note biografiche a cura di M. e M. Ferrara*, Rome: Edizioni di cultura sociale.

Togliatti, Palmiro 1969a, *La formazione del gruppo dirigente del Partito comunista italiano nel 1923–1924*, Rome: Editori Riuniti.

Togliatti, Palmiro 1969b, *La politica di Salerno aprile–dicembre 1944*, Rome: Editori Riuniti.

Togliatti, Palmiro 1971, *Antonio Gramsci*, Rome: Editori Riuniti.

Trotsky, Leon 1970, *My Life*, New York: Pathfinder Press.

Trotsky, Leon 1971, *The Struggle Against Fascism in Germany*, New York: Pathfinder Press.

Trotsky, Leon 1973, *The First Five Years of the Communist International*, Vol. 1, London: New Park.

Trotsky, Leon 1975, 'Letter to the Italian Left Communists', in *Writings of Leon Trotsky 1929*, New York: Pathfinder Press.

Trotsky, Leon 1979, *Writings of Leon Trotsky: Supplement (1934–40)*, New York: Pathfinder Press.

Trotsky, Leon, Alfred Rosmer and Marguerite Rosmer 1982, *Correspondance 1929–1939*, Paris: Gallimard.

Trotsky, Leon, Vojislav Vujovic and Grigory Zinoviev 1977, *Scritti e discorsi sulla rivoluzione in Cina 1927*, Milan: Iskra.

Turati, Filippo 1982, *Scritti e discorsi* (1878–1932), Parma: Guanda.

[Turco, Paolo] 1981, 'Amadeo Bordiga a dieci anni dalla sua scomparsa', *Il lavoratore comunista*, January – February.

[Turco, Paolo] 1983, 'Programma comunista: necessità di un bilancio', *Il lavoratore comunista*, 13, January – March.

[Turco, Paolo] 1992, *The Proletarian Revolution and the 'Russian Question': Yesterday, Today and Tomorrow*, Rome: Internationalist Communist Organization.

Van der Linden, Marcel 2007, *Western Marxism and the Soviet Union: A Survey of Critical Theories and Debates Since 1917*, Leiden: Brill.

Index

Illustrations

∵

FIGURE 1   Ortensia De Meo, Bordiga's first wife, with their new born daughter
Alma, 1915
WITH KIND PERMISSION BY THE FONDAZIONE BORDIGA

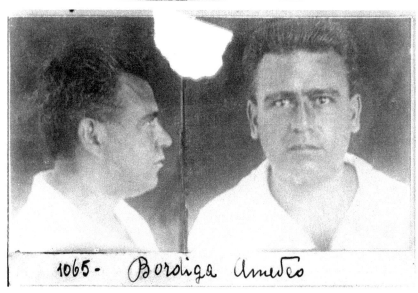

FIGURE 2   Bordiga's Mugshot taken by the Messina police, December 1929
WITH KIND PERMISSION BY THE FONDAZIONE BORDIGA

FIGURE 3   Bordiga with Antonietta De Meo (who will
             become his second wife) and his nephew,
             1949/1950
             WITH KIND PERMISSION BY THE
             FONDAZIONE BORDIGA

FIGURE 4   Bordiga with friends and Antonietta De
             Meo, in Formia, outside his home, early
             1950's
             WITH KIND PERMISSION BY THE
             FONDAZIONE BORDIGA

FIGURE 5   Bordiga with Ottorino Perrone, comrade of the
International Communist Party, early 1950's
WITH KIND PERMISSION BY THE FONDA-
ZIONE BORDIGA

FIGURE 6
Bordiga at Portovenere, the day before the Conference of
the International Communist Party, La Spezia 25–26 aprile
1959
WITH KIND PERMISSION BY THE FONDAZIONE BOR-
DIGA

FIGURE 7   March 1955, discussing with comrades
WITH KIND PERMISSION BY THE
FONDAZIONE BORDIGA

FIGURE 8   Bordiga with (what appears to be) his nephews Cesare and
Raffaele, probably in the mid-50s
WITH KIND PERMISSION BY THE FONDAZIONE BORDIGA

FIGURE 9   Bordiga with Antonietta De Meo, his son Oreste and Fortu-
            nato La Camera, comrade of the International Communist
            Party, Naples, June 1962
            WITH KIND PERMISSION BY THE FONDAZIONE BORDIGA

Caricatura di Bordiga
Ustica 1927

FIGURE 10
Caricature of Bordiga by Giuseppe Scalarini, one of the most famous Italian caricaturists; a socialist caricaturist, who was confined
to Ustica together with Bordiga
WITH KIND PERMISSION BY THE FONDAZIONE BORDIGA

Amadeo Bordiga and the Italian Communist Left Continuity with Marx

The Amadeo Bordiga Foundation was established in 1998 to promote the research activities and publications related to the activity and thought of Amadeo Bordiga, founder of the Communist Party of Italy in 1921 and its political leader.

Amadeo Bordiga, as a prominent figure in contemporary Marxism, was perhaps the only western communist to be on a par with Lenin at a theoretical level, and to perceive early on the counter-revolutionary nature of Stalinism as well as of the involutional processes in motion within communist movements worldwide.

The political defeat of the Communist Left and of internationalist positions would be accompanied by gloomy years for the communist project, along with the historical setback of the world proletarian movement. These were the years when the figure of Bordiga was removed both historiographically and theoretically, following his expulsion from the Communist Party of Italy in March 1930.

Hence, the twenty-year work undertaken by the Amadeo Bordiga Foundation – and in particular, by Luigi Gerosa – in attempting to recover the missing texts, often censored by 'official' communism, and to publish everything produced up until 1926.

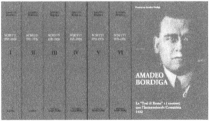

Fondazione Amadeo Bordiga
WWW.FONDAZIONEBORDIGA.ORG

In View of the Future Society

After the direct confrontation with Stalin during the Sixth Enlarged Executive Committee of the Communist International in 1926 – a confrontation which, in Cortesi's words, represented 'the highest page in the history of Italian Communism' – Amadeo Bordiga was ousted from the 'official' Communist Party. He devoted himself to an intense theoretical activity intended to unearth and preserve the categories, structure and method of Marxian analysis and of the critique of political economy as key to understanding both the historico-social reality and the politico-programmatic red thread. An approach to theoretical Marxism as 'science', representing the passing of the baton to future generations.

Bordiga's work, rigorously anonymous, appeared in the press of the Internationalist (then International) Communist Party until his death, exhibiting a theoretical coherence without the least crinkle.

If invariant is the form of capital, Bordiga's elaboration, already able to anticipate with analytical force some fundamental trends of world history, can still provide scholars and international movements with theoretical instruments and weapons with which to analyse contemporary crises. Theoretical and political, as well as socio-environmental crises: of urban and rural models, the depletion and illicit plunder of natural resources, the inequality and unsustainability of the dominant development model.

The present material is intended to serve as a catalyst for the production of research directed towards a critical analysis of the limits of the current mode of production as well as towards the remoulding of the relationship between humans and nature according to the *Bordighian* conception of society's higher economic formation and, ultimately, of a social plan of life for the *species*.

Editorial and Project Research Secretariat
c/o Maria Scattola, via F. De Sanctis 69 – 20141 Milano – Italy
Tel. +39 02 89531743 – mobile +39 335 6164060 | email: FAB.edizioni@gmail.com
Fondazione Amadeo Bordiga, via A. Bordiga 10/11 – 04023 Formia (LT) – Italy

Printed in the USA
CPSIA information can be obtained
at www.ICGtesting.com
LVHW022322071123
763356LV00039B/1185